CW00818726

LOCOMOTIVES of the GSR

Jeremy Clements (right) is a commercial model builder. He usually prefers his locomotives in Brunswick green, copper, and brass but has become intrigued in recent years by the Irish railway scene.

Michael McMahon has had a life-long interest in Irish railways, greatly encouraged by the late 'Mac' Arnold. He is a past operations officer and council member for the Railway Preservation Society of Ireland, and a past Chairman of the Modern Railway Society of Ireland.

First Edition
First impression

Designed by Colourpoint Books, Newtownards
Printed by GPS Colour Graphics Ltd

ISBN 978 1 904242 26 8

Colourpoint Books
Colourpoint House
Jubilee Business Park
21 Jubilee Road
NEWTOWNARDS
County Down
Northern Ireland
BT23 4YH
Tel: 028 9182 6339
Fax: 028 9182 1900
E-mail: info@colourpoint.co.uk
Web site: www.colourpoint.co.uk

Cover pictures

Front: GSR P1 class 2-6-2T No 850, built at Inchicore in 1928, is depicted at the Amiens Street station turntable when new.

A painting by Norman Whitla

Rear: J15b class 0-6-0 No 712 depicted at Inchicore shed.

A painting by Norman Whitla

End Papers

Front: K1a class 2-6-0 No 398 at Kildare in 1932. The train is a combination of the 3.50 pm ex-Limerick (via Nenagh) and the 4.00 pm ex-Clonmel.

Kelland Collection,
Courtesy Bournemouth Railway Club

Rear: D14 class 4-4-0 No 89 at Nenagh on 23 June 1939 with the 9.20 am Limerick to Dublin. The locomotive will work only as far as Ballybrophy.

CP Friel collection

LOCOMOTIVES of the GSR

Jeremy Clements
Michael McMahon

COLOURPOINT

GSR 4-6-0 Class 400 (B2) No 405, as rebuilt in two cylinder form in 1933.
IRRS collection

Contents

The GSR route network in 1925

Preface and Acknowledgements

The impetus for this work came from realisation that, despite the proliferation of excellent publications in recent years on the history and development of Irish railway companies, there had appeared no attempt comprehensively to review the motive power fleet of the Great Southern Railways.

The creation of the GSR brought together an extraordinarily diverse collection of locomotives, some of considerable age. The new company allocated 124 individual classifications to this fleet and then introduced ten more new classes between 1925 and 1939. There were sometimes considerable differences within classes whereas in a few cases, locomotives that were largely identical were allotted separate classifications on the basis of quite minor detail differences. The potential for confusion will be readily apparent to anyone exploring the GSR locomotive story for the first time.

It was a challenge to organise a review of this multitude of classes, and variations within classes, in such a way as to provide a survey of manageable size. Firm decisions had to be taken on what to include and what to omit. With the exception of the locomotives of the Great Southern & Western Railway, the motive power histories of the pre-grouping companies have been covered in detail in other publications. Hence, on the basis of space limitations several notable classes are accorded less attention than is their due. This is no more apparent than with the GSWR Class 101 which has been the subject of several specialised publications. Also, the fascinating and varied narrow gauge fleet inherited by the company has been extensively covered elsewhere.

The assembly of research material yielded a large collection of drawings and diagrams, many of which have not appeared in print before. It was tempting to include some but within the limitations of available space, only a few could have been admitted, and many require explanatory notes concerning variations and modifications to do them justice. If sufficient interest is aroused by the appearance of this work, then consideration will be given to the publication of a supplement aimed specifically at the needs of modellers.

More detailed attention has been devoted to the significant modifications carried out by the GSR to pre-grouping types, particularly regarding installation of superheaters and changes of boiler types, as this work was integral to the company's motive power strategy. Although outside the company's time frame, the full story of the 400 and 500 classes from their inception under GSWR auspices has been included as this is germane to their later history, quite apart from the attraction of exploring the diverse nature of the large Irish 4-6-0s. Although the first batch was ordered by the MGWR, the pre-Irish story of the Woolwich moguls is related because their introduction coincided with the creation of the GSR, and because their presence had a direct impact on the economics and later development of the 4-6-0s.

Regarding units introduced by the GSR, several were purchases from established manufacturers, modified for the Irish gauge but otherwise familiar to motive power students – Sentinel steam shunters and railcars, Clayton railcars, and petrol powered Drewry railcars. Others that are 'pure' GSR designs have been given more detailed coverage. In this category is 2-6-2T No 850 which was the GSR's solitary example of a modern tank locomotive and a developmental dead-end. Similar treatment is accorded the enigmatic 4-6-0s of Class 800. Partial references to the Drumm Battery electric project can be found in many places but the attention given in Chapter 12 attempts a fuller review of this unique exercise than has appeared previously.

The authors' objective of providing an overall survey and source of ready reference has been amplified by an attempt to explain the managerial and financial background against which motive power policy evolved. The GSR, as a common carrier and as the country's principal form of inland transport, bore a major responsibility for moving people and goods efficiently at the lowest operational cost. Proper investment in the locomotive fleet was critical to the future of the whole enterprise. The unique problems that management confronted, particularly in the opening and closing years, evokes sympathy. That they were able to maintain services in the face of such difficulties with aged and sometimes under-powered equipment engenders much respect.

The considerable age of some of the GSR stud underlines the fact that decisions taken years previously could have long-reaching effects for good or bad. The company was blessed with some ancient power units of such notable intrinsic worth that it is hard to imagine services being maintained in their absence. Equally, some ill-judged decisions over larger locomotives endowed the fledgling company with operational and financial headaches. Trying to understand why certain controversial decisions were taken and assessing the character of the individuals responsible has not been straightforward. Reliance on secondary printed sources emanating from a more polite and discreet age often revealed little more than a briefly factual account of an individual's career.

Accordingly the rationale for certain actions has been divined through interpolation and by assessment of contemporary conditions and events. Assertions made through such processes risk establishment of spurious authority that might mislead later historians. Wherever possible, speculative or assumed conclusions and views have been qualified as such.

While this work is focused on the 20-year period of the GSR, for reasons given above, there has been trespass into pre-1925 locomotive history to help explain the context of later events. With respect to photographs, some of those accompanying Chapters 1 to 3 were chosen from the pre-amalgamation period to help set the scene in the evolvement of motive power. The photographs in Chapters 4 to 12 were selected to provide the best possible coverage of variations within classes; in trying to be comprehensive it has been necessary to include some pictures of indifferent quality, and also a few that date from the CIÉ era.

Completion of the GSR steam story required commentaries and photographs in Chapters 13 and 14 that stretched well into CIÉ days, with particular emphasis on two important areas.

Firstly, the extraordinary problems encountered in the 1940s over procurement of adequate fuel stocks were to have lasting repercussions for the GSR's successor. The implications for public transportation and economic recovery were severe, and the unremitting nature of energy shortages must have created a climate of considerable desperation. The efforts to tackle these problems at operating level and the search for alternative means of persuading boilers to generate adequate amounts of steam dominated motive power policy throughout the 1940s. It is thus appropriate to provide a commentary on the events of that tumultuous decade.

Secondly, years of under-investment in equipment modernisation linked with the operational stresses during the 1940-1944 period meant that the GSR handed on to its successor a complex bundle of problems. Views differed about the solution. Ex-GSR management within Córas Iompair Éireann favoured a batch of new boilers to extend the life of already aged steam locomotives – a policy that was essentially a repetition of that of the 1920s and 1930s. The Milne Report of 1948 proposed a new family of modern, versatile steam locomotives with high route availability working to a radically revised timetable of lighter, more frequent trains. Both strategies, neither of which came to fruition, were seen as stop-gaps pending the availability of diesel motive power of adequate reliability to replace steam across-the-board. Diesel power was introduced prematurely and proved unreliable. GSR steam therefore had to soldier on increasingly against the odds; few among the travelling public would have acknowledged the excellent service the diminishing and increasingly run-down fleet gave in the 1950s and early 1960s.

--- o O o ---

The decision to write this book was aided by extensive private library facilities available to the authors. Nonetheless, it became apparent that despite the richness of this data source, it would be inadequate for the task and recourse was soon made to the library and archives of the Irish Railway Record Society. The contemporary material available through the good offices of the Society was invaluable in piecing together a complex jigsaw. Company files and back copies of magazines were a mine of information but the Fayle Bulletins held a particular fascination. Inevitably, writing about the Great Southern Railways over sixty years after the company's demise has meant use of the past tense; the Bulletins as a set of contemporary records written mainly in the present tense helped to bring the company and its locomotives to life. Indeed during the project, the authors concluded that even if this work never reached the publication stage, the research would have been worth the effort just for the pleasure of studying these records.

The passage of time has sadly depleted the ranks of eye-witnesses to the GSR's motive power affairs. The years also have the unfortunate effect of eroding or distorting personal memories. These factors complicate the verification of the dates, the sequence, and the full significance of key events in the lifetime of individual locomotives. Heavy reliance upon contemporary written records, such as Fayle, was thus essential in assembling and checking facts. However, the book would not have been possible without the scholarship and dedication of one man in particular.

The archives of the late RN (Bob) Clements, a vast collection of typed and handwritten notes collated in the days before word processors, provided a stunningly comprehensive record. In fact, the absence of modern technology in their preparation greatly aided the sifting of data, as manual corrections helped to prove the 'audit trail' of modifications and rebuildings, and to clarify often thorny questions, such as records of changes in locomotive weights. These notes were also invaluable in plugging gaps in official records as, for example, with the pre-1940 disposition of tenders

A great debt is thus owed to Bob Clements for his thoroughness and commitment over many years. Much of what he wrote might have been considered trivia at the time; today it is gold dust. One of the objectives in recording so much soon became apparent as the archives contain preliminary drafts of a book obviously intended to cover the ground which this work seeks to embrace. Bob Clements had the great advantage over the present authors of knowing the locomotives, the trains, the routes and above all, the men at first hand. It is to the lasting loss of all with an interest in the Irish railway scene that this project never developed beyond the early stages. What a book it would have made.

In the trawl for information at the Society's premises, the authors have relied heavily on the guidance and help of certain individuals and wish to thank most sincerely Brendan Pender, Tim Moriarty and Herbert Richards for their help, patience and forbearance. The authors solemnly promise not to be such a nuisance again, should another writing project emerge . . .

The chapter describing the trials and tribulations with locomotive fuel drew heavily upon a paper read to the IRRS in October 1947 by JH Dudley, Assistant Locomotive Running Superintendent, Córas Iompair Éireann. The commentary on the Drumm Battery Trains stemmed from a variety of sources but the authors are indebted to Gerry Beesley for his general advice and for the diary of milestone events in the lives of these interesting vehicles.

The authors also acknowledge with gratitude, the assistance provided by Ms Geraldine Finucane, Group Secretary, Córas Iompair Éireann and her colleagues in allowing access to the Board Minutes and other statutory records of the GSR.

Grateful thanks are extended to Charles Friel for his kindness in allowing a wide scale plunder of his vast photographic collection, and for his creative criticism of the work's structure and style. Sincere appreciation goes to Clifton Flewitt who also undertook the tedious task of proof-reading the manuscript and whose helpful comments greatly improved the final draft.

Late in the project, Bill Scott and Peter Rowledge generously volunteered details of their own researches which were of considerable value in double-checking the accuracy of numerous points of detail.

Mark Kennedy of the Ulster Folk and Transport Museum was most helpful too.

The project would not, of course, have got off the ground had it not been for the ready acceptance of the draft synopsis by the publisher, and for his forbearance concerning the many modifications that followed. The authors are thus extremely grateful for the help, advice and general support provided by Norman Johnston and his team at Colourpoint Books.

Others have provided much help in the project and if they are not mentioned by name, this does not detract from the authors' appreciation. Finally, the authors express thanks for the efforts of they who can only be named collectively as 'Anonymous' – the railwaymen and enthusiasts who recorded in writing what they witnessed during those days long ago.

AJ O'Toole collection

Vignette

. . . on Wednesday, Sept 15th, I made a journey to the historic old town of Athlone; my ticket costing 2/6d I had obtained well before-hand, so that I arrived at Kingsbridge some ten minutes before the advertised departure time, to find a train of 9 plus 2 already well filled; the station officials were, at the moment, waiting to see how many more of us would offer, in order that they might delete one of the coaches, which had been carefully locked. Insufficient patronage appearing, an Aspinall 4-4-0 very slowly shunted the superfluous vehicle to a siding, and replaced a bogie van and a six wheeler. Time was running exceedingly short, but I did not know what the staff were capable of, for Nos 343 and 345 having coupled on, we got away only four minutes late . . .

At Lucan, reached in 10 minutes, No 343 left us and we set off fairly on our trip, pausing only at Portarlington and Ballycumber; we were checked by signals outside Athlone, being ahead of schedule, and eventually arrived exactly on time.

The trip had been none too comfortable, for the niggardly behaviour of the Kingsbridge officials left at least a hundred of us no alternative to standing in the corridors. However, looking at such slight scenery as offers on the line, and enjoying the contributions of sundry persons of the class known as 'itinerant musicians', passed the time tolerably. The van at the head of the train was apparently the travelling ball-room of the affair, a piano accordion serving as orchestra; the refreshment car was well patronised, which explains much in the behaviour of some of my fellow travellers.

Athlone does not take long to see, and I returned to the station long before the 2½ hour stay was up; the small shed held Nos 531, 532, 590 and 623. In the main shed or near it were nos 589, 606, 609, 621, 635, 642, 659, 663, 665, 533 and 535. No 667 had been passed at Kildare on a goods train, with 713 light.

Saturday, Sept 18th, brought another half crown excursion, this time GNR to Armagh . . .

Verbatim extract from ***Fayle's Bulletins*** No 35.8 (1937)

Chapter 1
Twenty difficult years

GSWR 0-4-4T Class 47 No 83. A classic example of the styling of the Aspinall/ Ivatt era which remained little changed even after the 1925 amalgamation. *IRRS collection*

Few major business undertakings can have faced as much adversity as did the Great Southern Railways of Ireland. The circumstances of the company's creation, the conditions under which it had to operate during most of its existence, and the environmental factors that led to the company being wound up presented immense challenges.

The creative seeds were sown during the closing years of British rule in southern Ireland and in the necessity, as in Britain, for a major re-organisation of railway company ownership at the start of the 1920s. The demands of wartime conditions had stimulated the need for change, the first evidence of which was the assumption on 22 December 1916 of governmental control over all railway companies operating in the 32 counties of Ireland. This was exercised through the Irish Railways Executive Committee. This body and its successor, the Ministry of Transport, continued in control until 15 August 1921. Then, notionally at least, responsibility reverted to the respective directors and managements of the individual companies. However, this was a period of great unrest. The Treaty establishing the Irish Free State was signed with the British Government on 6 December 1921, and during the Civil War that followed, de facto control of the railway system in the 26 counties of the new country remained in governmental hands.

Some semblance of normality was not achieved until April 1923 by which time the Irish railway companies were in a strained financial condition. In the period 1916 to 1921, wages and other operating costs had risen by some 300 per cent while revenues had grown by about 100 per cent. Moreover, the backlog of maintenance and repairs occasioned by the pressures of operating under wartime conditions between 1914 and 1918 had been exacerbated by extensive malicious damage sustained during the Civil War. In March 1923, the Great Southern & Western Railway (GSWR) announced that it had suffered no fewer than 467 cases of material damage to permanent way and 291 cases of damage to bridges. Further, 103 signal boxes had been destroyed or damaged and 468 items of locomotives, carriages and wagons had been destroyed. The most serious single destructive act had been the severing of the Dublin-Cork main line at Mallow through the blowing up of the River Blackwater viaduct. This was one of the very few occasions in the railway history of these islands that a major trunk route was closed for a significant period through a malicious act. Overall, the damage sustained by the Dublin & South Eastern

The constituents of the GSR and their routes

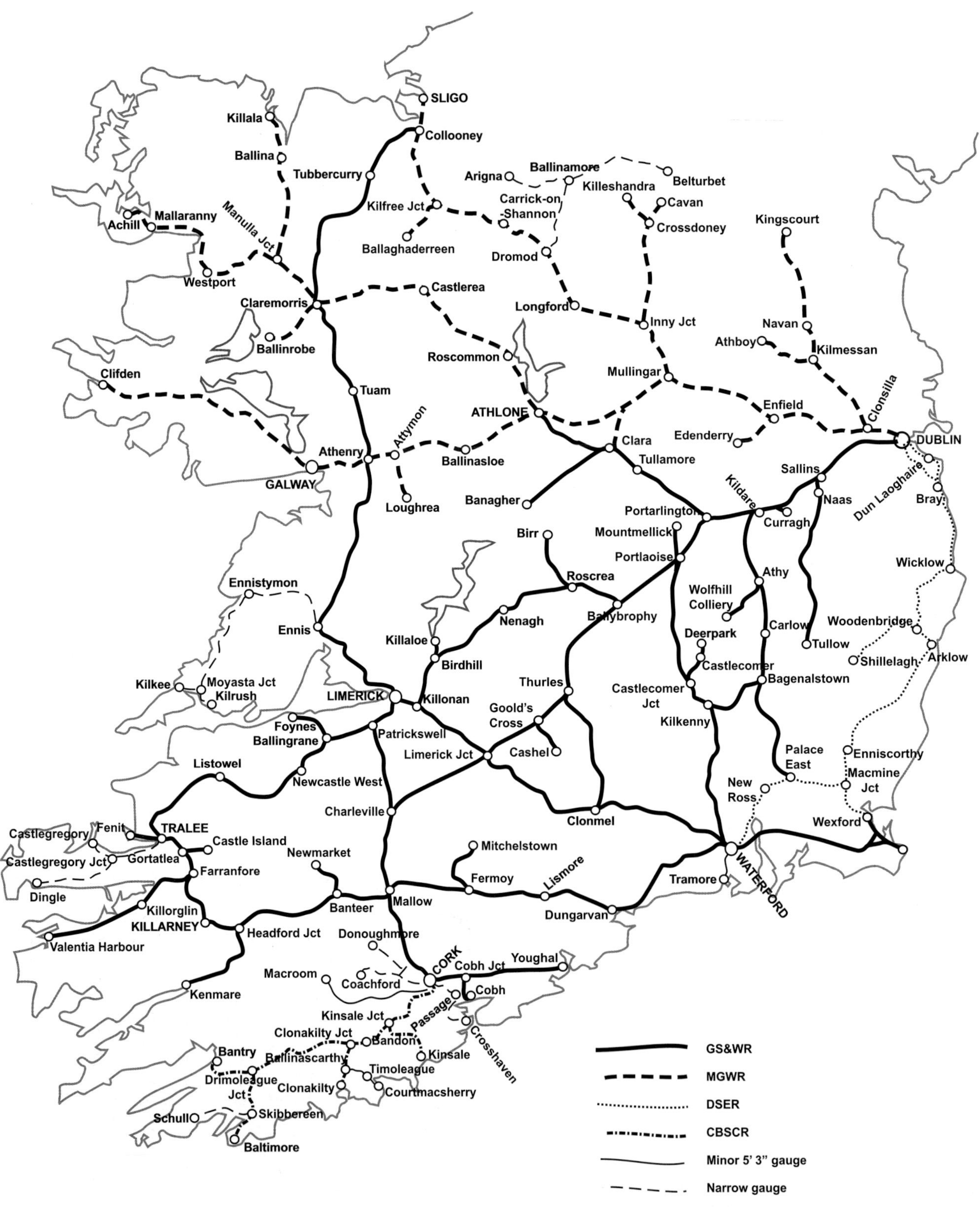

GSWR 4-4-0 Class 305 No 307, as built in 1903. By now GSWR design styling was more modern. This locomotive carried a tapered boiler from 1906 until 1937. Note the elaborate equipment for tablet exchanges.

IRRS collection

Ex-WLWR 2-4-2T No 14, as GSWR Class 266 No 267. One of a class of two (the other came to the GSR by way of the Cork & Macroom Direct Railway), and one of Robinson's earliest designs. It is interesting to detect the emergence of his classically stylish chimney profile.

IRRS collection

Railway through 31 major incidents and other smaller offensive acts was equally as severe.

With operating costs far out-stripping revenues combined with the burden of repairing civil war damage, the GSWR served notice of its intention to cease operations with effect from 8 January 1923. This prompted the provision of interim financial support by the new Irish Free State government pending formulation of a policy on the future of the railway system.

As early as April 1922 the government, in recognition of the importance of the railway network to the fledgling state, had established the Railways Commission to investigate and to advise on ownership of the system. A succinct report appeared late that year which recommended full state ownership with an 'independent' board. However, the government did not accept these recommendations, preferring to encourage a voluntary amalgamation programme with a deadline of 1 July 1923.

In the absence of any tangible response from the companies, a Bill was then introduced for outright nationalisation into Dail Éireann but lacking governmental support, this failed. The government then took the initiative by sponsoring the Railway Bill 1924 which proposed a merger of the Great Southern & Western Railway (GSWR), the Midland Great Western Railway (MGWR) and the Dublin & South Eastern Railway (DSER) into a new public company, the Great Southern Railway. On completion of this merger, it was intended that the new organisation should then absorb the remaining railway companies.

Consequent upon passage of the Bill, its actual implementation varied slightly from that intended. The Cork Bandon & South Coast Railway (CBSCR) had previously agreed in principle to merge with the GSWR and so joined the fold when the new company was established on 12 November 1924. The DSER, which was predominantly British owned, expressed a preference to merge with the Great Northern Railway (Ireland). This latter company had been excluded from the amalgamation process on grounds of its

Ex-WLWR 2-4-0 No 48, as GSWR Class 276 No 293. This engine was a survivor. It was one of a class of eight of which four were withdrawn between 1903 and 1913, being thought obsolete. The remaining four not only survived to join the GSR fleet but actually outlived the company. The last but one to be withdrawn, No 293 was 60 years old when taken out of service in 1954. *IRRS collection*

cross-border operations following the partition of Ireland. Additionally, the DSER camp objected to the compensation terms and reference was made to the Transport Tribunal which had been set up to adjudicate in such matters. The objections being over-ruled, the DSER duly joined with the new company on 1 January 1925. At that date the new company's title was slightly altered, becoming the Great Southern Railways (GSR).

During 1925, the amalgamation process was completed with the absorption of various minor railway companies. Of these, only the following railway companies actually owned locomotives that were added to GSR stock:

5' 3" Gauge: Cork & Macroom Direct; Timoleague & Courtmacsherry Light; Waterford & Tramore.

3' 0" Gauge: Cavan & Leitrim; Cork Blackrock & Passage; Cork & Muskerry Light; Schull & Skibbereen Light; Tralee & Dingle Light; West Clare.

Some companies were excluded from the amalgamation process. Because of their cross-border operations, the GNR(I) as previously mentioned, the Sligo, Leitrim and Northern Counties Railway and the Dundalk, Newry & Greenore Railway came into this category together with two 3' 0" gauge operations – the County Donegal Railways and the Londonderry & Lough Swilly Railway. Additionally, three other entities that operated exclusively in the newly created Irish Free State were omitted, apparently on pragmatic grounds. The Listowel & Ballybunion monorail system was on its last legs and indeed closed in 1924. The 3'6" gauge Dublin & Lucan Electric Railway Company went bankrupt and closed at the end of January 1925. This concern was re-constructed, re-gauged and absorbed into the empire of the Dublin United Tramway Company (DUTC) three years later. It seems to have been anticipated that the DUTC would also take over the run-down Dublin & Blessington Tramway but this concern remained independent and closed at the end of 1932.

The constituents' territories

Of the four major broad gauge companies that comprised the newly created GSR, the largest in terms of route mileage and size of locomotive fleet was the Great Southern & Western. This company had an aggregate mileage of 1150 miles and, as will be seen from the route map, it operated a number of secondary mainlines plus several branch services. Its most important route was that between Dublin and Cork, a distance of 165½ miles. Irish broad gauge railways did not traverse particularly mountainous terrain but the Dublin-Cork main line presents particular operating challenges, as departure from either city meant a substantial climb from a cold start. For northbound trains, the gradient began at the platform end in Cork and entailed 15 miles of continuous climbing, including 2 miles at 1 in 60. A further challenge was presented by the important station of Mallow, 144½ miles from Dublin where departures in either direction required an uphill start.

The company also operated the 135½ mile line from Cork to Rosslare, a twisting route that abounded in short, sharp gradients, especially between Dungarvan and Rosslare. Traffic over this line could be heavy with boat and cattle trains being the most important. It was the need to cope with increasing loadings over the Dublin-Cork and Cork-Rosslare routes that determined the pattern of the GSWR's express locomotive development. Up until 1912, an extended family of 4-4-0s of progressively larger size was developed to handle these services. Thereafter efforts were directed towards introducing six-coupled express locomotives, albeit with little success prior to the amalgamation.

Secondary, goods and branch line services were mainly handled by 0-6-0 tender locomotives, almost exclusively the remarkable Class 101 (J15) which accounted for one third of the GSWR fleet. This was a long-lived general utility design and, despite later goods engines in the form of 2-6-0s and 4-6-0s, the Class 101 was never supplanted. Smallish tank engines of the 2-4-2, 4-4-2 and 0-4-4 varieties worked suburban and shunting duties; there were also some 0-6-2Ts and 0-6-0Ts, the latter type being comparatively scarce in Ireland.

With 538 route miles, the Midland Great Western Railway was the second largest constituent company. Its main line ran from Dublin to Galway and then on to the west coast at Clifden. Other important routes branched off this line in a northerly direction to Cavan and Sligo from the junction at Mullingar, and to Westport, Achill and Killala from the junction at Athlone. Traversing the largely flat country of mid-Ireland, there were no gradients of the severity found on the GSWR. Nonetheless, tightly-timed trains conveying cattle to Dublin over mainly single-line routes (totalling 370 miles) for onward transit to the British market presented a significant operating challenge.

By 1924, the fleet profile of the MGWR was broadly similar to that of the GSWR, ie express passenger services in the hands of 4-4-0s and with goods services worked by 0-6-0s. There was also a long-lived class of 2-4-0s, which had the distinction of being considered Ireland's first mixed-traffic design.

A reflection of the trunk line nature of the railway was that the MGWR only owned two classes of tank locomotive, aggregating a mere 17 engines, in 1924. Shortly before the amalgamation, the MGWR broke with tradition by ordering the first batch of Woolwich moguls in kit form. These were the only outside-cylindered locomotives associated with the company, although their entire operational history was under the auspices of the GSR and its successor.

The third largest constituent company was the Dublin & South Eastern Railway with 157 route miles. Its main line ran from two Dublin termini to Wexford with a branch to Shillelagh. A branch from Macmine Junction offered an alternative means of reaching Waterford via New Ross from Dublin. The railway served Dublin's populous and comparatively wealthy southern suburbs, and the quite densely populated coastal counties further south. Mainly a passenger carrying railway, its commuter services constituted an important share of revenue. At the amalgamation,

DSER 4-4-0 No 56 *Rathmines*, later GSWR Class 450 No 451. In original condition shewn, they were attractive but ineffective. The design proportions were incorrect being under-boilered or alternatively over-cylindered. Rebuilding of all four class members before the amalgamation with Belpaire boilers improved performance. No further modification occurred and they were comparatively short-lived 4-4-0s (by Irish standards) with the final survivor being withdrawn in 1940 after a mere 44 years' service. *IRRS collection*

CBSCR 0-6-0ST No 5, later GSR Class 475 No 475. The best-known Beyer Peacock products sold to this railway were the famous 4-6-0Ts but five attractive 0-6-0STs were also delivered between 1881 and 1894. Although there were several detail differences among these engines, they were of a standard Beyer type that dated from 1867. No 475 is seen shunting on the quays at Cork.

Real Photographs Co Ltd

suburban services were handled by a rather motley collection of four coupled tank locomotives. Longer distance services were catered for by the usual Irish combination of 4-4-0s and 0-6-0s.

The fourth constituent was the Cork Bandon & South Coast Railway whose routes fanned out from Cork in a south-westerly direction, reaching four important coastal centres by means of lines both owned and leased. The total route mileage worked by CBSCR was 95 miles. All services were handled by tank locomotives, the best known of which were the distinctive 'Bandon' 4-6-0Ts.

The route mileages of the 5' 3" gauge minor companies were:

Cork & Macroom Direct Railway – 24½

Timoleague & Courtmacsherry Light Railway (including the section to Ballinascarthy) – 9

Waterford & Tramore Railway– 7¼

The 3' 0" gauge companies contributed the following mileages:

Cavan & Leitrim Railway (including the full extent of the Arigna tramway) – 52½

Cork Blackrock & Passage Railway – 16

Cork & Muskerry Light Railway – 26½

Schull & Skibbereen Light Railway – 15

Tralee & Dingle Light Railway – 38¼

West Clare Railway – 52¾

A particular feature of the four main constituent networks (and the minor companies) was that they were virtually discrete. Much of the Irish railway system had been built in the aftermath of the Irish Potato Famine whose depredations had left the hinterland under-populated and impoverished. Railway construction in many areas was a prolonged and tortuous affair. There was neither potential traffic nor sufficient capital to sustain the duplication of routes that so burdened the grouped companies in Britain. The constituents' networks were mostly complementary rather than competing. Where companies' services shared routes, this was exercised through the more financially efficient means of running powers.

The GSR made comparatively few changes to the network infrastructure. The most significant concerned the singling, for reasons of economy, of certain double track routes. Mileages so affected were: 154 miles of ex-MGWR route, most importantly portions of the main line between Clonsilla (near Dublin) and Galway; 32½ miles of ex-GSWR route, mainly Cherryville Junction to Carlow; six miles of the ex-DSER route between Newcastle and Wicklow. Outright route closures were focused on narrow gauge lines: Cork Blackrock & Passage section – 16 miles (total mileage) in 1932; Cork & Muskerry section – 26½ miles (total mileage) in 1934; Tralee & Dingle section: Castlegregory Branch – six miles in 1939.

Thus was set the GSR's corporate structure and network which remained largely intact for 20 years. The company connected all the major towns and cities in the Irish Free State with the notable exceptions of Drogheda and Dundalk which were served by the GNR(I)'s cross-border route. In addition, good coverage was afforded to many rural areas.

Decline in revenue

The adverse international economic conditions of the inter-war years had a major impact on Ireland. Growth of personal wealth was limited, the population declined through emigration, and there was a trend that saw people leaving the country for the towns. Although the company was the principal mover of people and goods, the incursion of road vehicles into the transport market was continuous:

Year	No of licensed private cars	No of licensed lorries
1925	16,211	4,950
1938	48,599	10,406

The period up to 1940 was one of steady decline and financial stringency that was to exert constant pressure on the company's investment policies, and hence on its locomotive fleet. Annual revenues during the life of the company are detailed in Appendix A but the following data demonstrate the trends:

£000s	1925	1931	1939
Passenger receipts	1,991	1,347	1,275
Freight receipts	2,273	2,144	2,050

With this decline, it is understandable why funds available for improvements and new development were limited. Looking back from this distance, it seems that for several years it was hoped that matters would eventually improve. For example, the annual stock returns show that the fleet of passenger carriages, post office, parcel and brake vans comprised 1,670 vehicles in 1925 and that this figure had shrunk only to 1,614 in 1934 by which time the utilisation factor must have deteriorated radically. The annual revenue per item of passenger rolling stock was £1,193 in 1925 and a mere £774 in 1934. The later 1930s saw some stabilisation in revenue levels but even in 1939, the GSR's last year of normal operations, total revenue (including that from hotels etc) stood at £3,349,000 or 78% of that earned in 1925.

Much of the GSR's activities between 1925 and 1939 were devoted to providing what would now be termed a public service obligation. Nonetheless the broad statistics indicate that rationalisation did have beneficial effect. During that period, the locomotive fleet fell from 563 to 508 units while passenger vehicles reduced from 1,670 to 1,584.

However, the absolute figures tell only part of the story. Comparison with other railway operations can yield a more objective assessment of progress and in this regard, measurement against the performance of the Great Northern Railway (Ireland) during those years draws some surprising conclusions. The GNR(I) was the second largest railway company in Ireland, and being generally regarded as a professionally managed concern, it provides a valid yardstick for measurement.

The two companies were exposed to similar economic trends and changing market circumstances, although the GSR was spared the cross-border operating frustrations that impeded the northern company.

MGWR 4-4-0 Class A No 127 *Titanic*, later GSWR Class 545 No 545. Depicted here at Broadstone in original condition with saturated Belpaire boiler and slide valves, this locomotive was superheated with piston valves in 1920 and reclassified As. This modernisation did not prevent withdrawal in 1933, but it was reinstated the same year. In 1937 it reverted to saturated condition and worked on until 1955.

IRRS collection

MGWR 2-4-0 Class K No 27 *Clifden*, later GSR Class 650 No 666. Perhaps the most distinctive feature of any Irish locomotive design was Atock's 'fly away' cab, the last example of which was not replaced with a more conventional design until 1941. The purpose of this unusual styling has never been apparent. It was an improvement on earlier weatherboards that afforded little protection for the crew. The 'fly away' arrangement must have been uncomfortable in conditions of following wind and rain, or when working tender-first.

IRRS collection

There is no doubt that the GNR(I) performed better financially during the years 1925 to 1927. This would be expected given the backlog of repairs facing the GSR and the re-organisational issues with which the newly formed company had to cope. However from 1928 onwards, the GSR consistently earned a better rate per train mile on its passenger and goods services. On the other hand, revenue per passenger vehicle showed that the GNR(I) was achieving better value for money out of its proportionately smaller fleet.

With locomotives, the figures are also unexpected. Most GNR(I) locomotives were considered modern and efficient and in the 1925-1927 period, revenue earned per locomotive was better than that on the GSR. Thereafter the average GSR locomotive annually generated more revenue than did its northern counterpart. In fact, the average statistics for the period 1925-1939 contradict the general perception that the GSR was financially a mediocre performer:

Annual average 1925-1939	**GSR**	**GNR(I)**
Passenger services:		
Revenue per train mile	£0.24	£0.20
Revenue per vehicle	£900	£968
Freight services:		
Revenue per train mile	£0.43	£0.41
Revenue per vehicle	£166	£116
Total traffic revenue	£3,437,000	£1,275,000
Locomotive fleet size	527	198
Revenue per locomotive	£6,718	£6,436

These calculations are drawn from the Annual Reports of both companies; actual annual figures and a more detailed commentary appear in **Appendix F**.

A further aspect of motive power efficiency emerged in the report by Sir James Milne in 1948 on the future of Irish transport. It was noted that GSR (by then Córas Iompair Éireann) steam locomotives were habitually clocking up 125,000 miles between general repairs. This is relatively speaking a high figure and might be prone to differing interpretation as to what a general repair actually comprised as opposed to a light repair. It could be that a significant amount of interim repair work was conducted at running sheds. Also the combination of relatively low speeds, light loads and modest gradients doubtless minimised stresses on locomotives.

Government legislation and the Ingram Report

Although the GSR had been established as a private sector venture, it was not long before governmental intervention in the inland transport market was evident with the intention of favouring the company's situation against the general trend. In 1927, railway companies were given power to establish road transport services in competition with existing independent operators. This power was reinforced by further legislation in 1932 which also introduced regulatory measures over the activities of bus and lorry operators. Most significantly, concurrent legislation gave the GSR power to close or reduce railway services over routes that had been constructed partly or wholly out of public monies.

In May 1932, the GSR represented to the government that its existence was under threat, despite having reduced expenditure on permanent way and rolling stock to the barest minimum, and that further protection was needed. The following year, significant measures concerning personnel employment terms were implemented. These included reductions in remuneration levels of between 7½% and 10%, and the institution of holidays without pay. A three day strike in April 1933 resulted, unlike the nine week strike that

GSR 2-2-2T No 483, formerly WTR No 1. The most unusual and interesting contribution to the GSR's ranks from the minor companies was undoubtedly the pair of 2-2-2Ts from the Waterford & Tramore. While No 484 was an early withdrawal by the GSR, No 483 worked on until being sadly damaged beyond economic repair in 1935. GSR livery was supposedly all-enveloping and drab but here is evidence that No 483 still retains some of its pre-amalgamation gaiety, while standing at Waterford Manor Street.

IRRS collection

halted railway traffic in Northern Ireland over broadly similar issues.

These overtures to the government led to the Road Transport Act 1933 which effectively prevented the issue of new passenger and freight road transport licences. In 1932, independent operators had carried 46% of the total road passenger journeys whereas their share of an enlarged market had shrunk to less than 1% by 1938. During this period, the number of independent road transport licensees fell from 1,356 to 851 while 50 new licences were issued for routes over which the GSR was unwilling to provide its own road services.

Under the Railways Act 1933, the GSR was allowed to reduce its share capital and debenture stock, and certain of its debts were written off. In addition, the GSR closed some routes entirely as detailed above and terminated passenger trains up to 1939 over another 115½ miles. By 1938, it was apparent that these measures had not solved the GSR's difficulties and in that year a Tribunal of Inquiry on Public Transport under the chairmanship of Joseph Ingram was convened by the Department of Industry and Commerce. Key recommendations of the Tribunal's report, published 1939, included the closure of 862 miles of branch lines out a total of 2,340 track miles, and significant investment in replacement passenger and freight road services to be run by statutory transport companies. It was also proposed that the remaining private transport licences should be compulsorily acquired by those companies. The Ingram Report was published in August 1939; within less than a month the situation in Europe completely changed the prospects for transport. Fuel rationing halted the growth of road transport and the railway system re-assumed its dominance.

The World War II years (known in Ireland as 'the Emergency')

Operating conditions from 1940 onwards were anything but normal and considerable ingenuity was necessary to sustain any form of railway service at all. The GSR became the principal means of transport in the south as fuel rationing forced passengers and goods back to the railway system. Total revenue in 1943 exceeded the 1925 level for the first time but the GSR was prevented from capitalising on the intrinsic attractions of rail transportation because of problems with fuel. Almost all services were steam-hauled, fuelled by imported coal that was in short supply. Ireland's indigenous coal resources are limited, and of poor quality, so recourse to substitute fuels became unavoidable.

The fuel related difficulties and the means by which they were overcome are described in Chapter 13, together with the post-GSR oil-burning project. How extreme operating conditions became in those years was shown in a 1942 report of a Dublin-Cork express hauled by No 800 *Maedhbh* and piloted by an Aspinall 4-4-0. This train took 4 hours to cover 51 miles to Maryborough at which point a 20 minute stop for a 'blow-up' was necessary. The train continued its journey after a more modern 4-4-0 had been added as a second pilot. In fact triple-heading of heavier trains was not uncommon during this period.

In 1944, several routes were closed to all traffic while passenger services elsewhere were withdrawn. From April that year, most of the remaining lines (except suburban services) enjoyed passenger services on Mondays and Thursdays only. Passenger

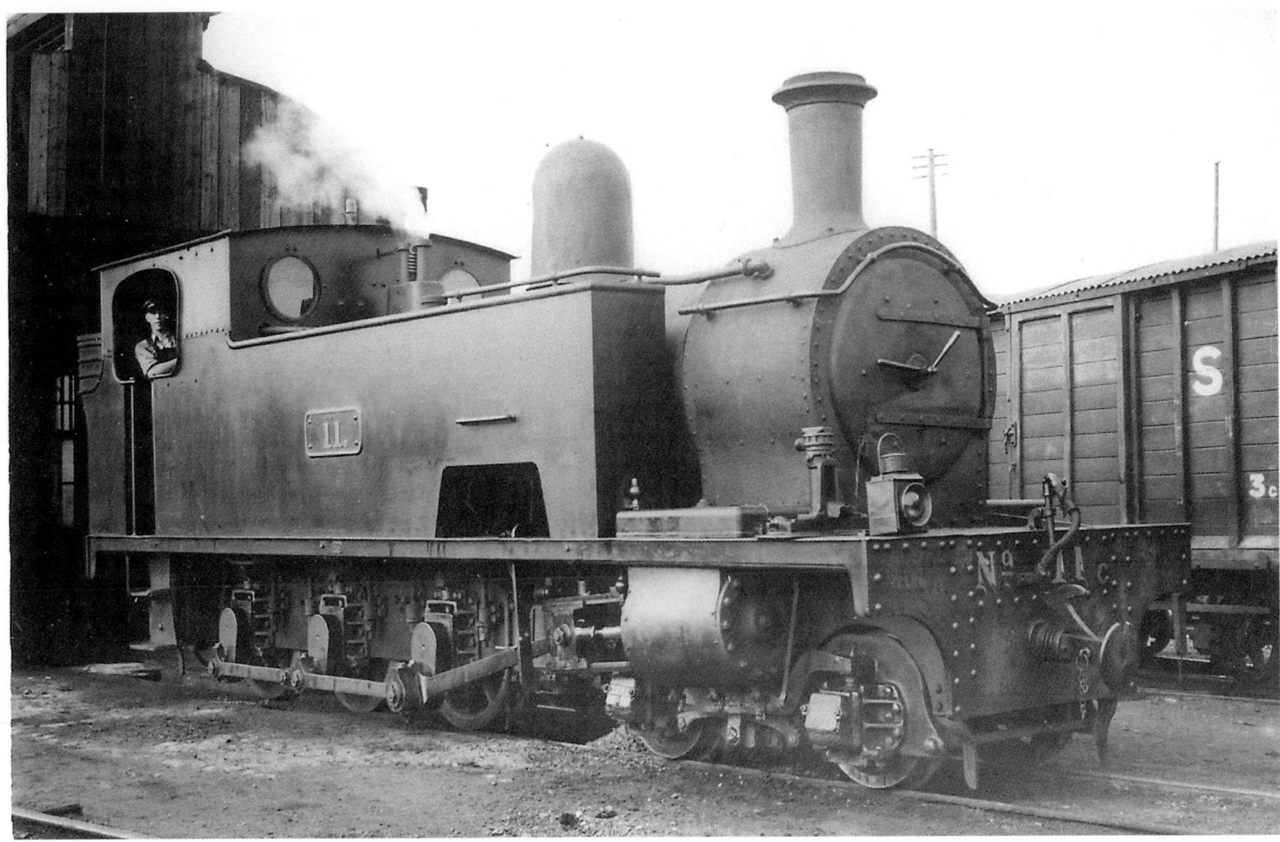

West Clare Railway No 11, later GSR No 11c. This was the second of five 4-6-0Ts delivered to this extensive narrow gauge system, and the first to be considered fully satisfactory. Delivered in 1908, No 11 worked until 1953. On shed at Ennis, April 1938. *WA Camwell*

accommodation was strictly limited with pre-booking essential. A daily Dublin-Cork passenger service was maintained by addition of carriages to mail and perishable goods trains that continued to operate. Access to these services was restricted to people with a priority claim to travel.

It was ironic that by 1944, the main railway system of one of Europe's few neutral countries was suffering as much disruption as the systems of the belligerent nations. Indeed the scarcity of services in certain areas was greater than in some occupied countries. Thus, through no fault of its own, the GSR had little opportunity to show off the inherent advantages of rail travel to a captive clientele during this period. Infrequent or non-existent services linked with inordinate delay of those that did work, provided strong inducement to the travelling public to seek other forms of transport when permitted by improved conditions.

Despite increased revenue during the war years, operating costs continued to rise and the future of the GSR as an independent entity was under threat. The first sign of changes to come was the appointment by the Government of a new company Chairman, AP Reynolds, under an Emergency Powers Order on 24 February 1942. The nominee for this position was the Managing Director of the Dublin United Transport Company (formerly Dublin United Tramway Company). Four other directors were appointed to represent the interests of the private shareholders. In addition, the Minister for Industry & Commerce directed that there was to be no increase in the meagre passenger services then provided without his consent. During 1943-1944 extensive political debate on the future of the GSR culminated in the 1944 Transport Act by which control passed along with that of the DUTC into the hands of a new corporate body, Córas Iompair Éireann. Under this legislation, the GSR was wound up with effect from 1 January 1945, just over 20 years after the company had commenced its life in the traumatic period of the early 1920s.

Chapter 2
Motive power development

The difficulties faced by the Great Southern Railways throughout the company's existence severely constrained both replacement of older locomotives and opportunities for fresh design initiatives. With the exception of the Midland Great Western Railway which had exercised a policy of locomotive renewal on a 20 year cycle, Irish companies had a tradition of extracting many years of service from their motive power fleets by process of ad hoc re-building. In such cases it might be doubtful how much of the original machine remained, but essential design characteristics changed little so that many engines at the 1924/25 amalgamation exhibited the styling and elegance of an earlier era. The late retention of so many elderly locomotives added much to the fascination of Irish railways for the enthusiast observer, if rather less for those who had to work with such aged equipment.

The operation of a railway network with a fleet in which old and small locomotives predominated meant generally relaxed journey times. A survey of services in 1925 noted that, while improvement had been achieved since the early 1900s, schedules were undemanding:

Section	Route	Distance (miles)	Best journey time (minutes)	Average Speed (mph)	Average journey time (minutes)	Average speed (mph)
Ex-GSWR	Dublin-Cork	165.5	220	45.1	271	36.6
	Dublin-Limerick via Nenagh	123.75	185	40.1	215	34.5
	Dublin-Waterford via Abbeyleix	110.25	195	34	227	29.2
Ex-MGWR	Dublin-Galway	126.5	220	34.5	236	32.2
	Dublin-Sligo	134.25	250	32.2	265	30.4
Ex-DSER	Dublin-Wexford	92.75	195	28.5	215	25.9

Source: Railway Magazine Vol LVIII 1926

Three of the constituent companies had routes long enough to warrant the use of tender locomotives and these were generally used to greater extent than was normal in Britain. Two factors favoured this preference. In many parts of Ireland, the water quality is very hard making it unsuitable for locomotive boilers, and often necessitating greater distances between favoured locations for replenishment of supplies. Also, small tender engines with modest axle loadings had advantages for use on secondary routes laid with light rail.

At the 1924/25 amalgamation, the tender locomotives of the Great Southern & Western and the Midland Great Western railways were mainly of two wheel arrangements – 4-4-0s for main line passenger traffic and 0-6-0s for goods and branch line services. By this time, with the exception of a long-lived class on the MGWR and a few ex-GSWR survivors, the 2-4-0 type had been largely phased out. The Dublin & South Eastern Railway's tender locomotives followed the same pattern although with this company, tank locomotives were more common as much of its income derived from the south Dublin commuter traffic. The Cork Bandon & South Coast Railway, the minor broad gauge companies, and the narrow gauge companies

GSWR 4-4-2T Class 269 (later C5) No 271. Originally WLWR No 18 built in 1897, this class was generally considered to be the very first of JG Robinson's large engine designs. No 271 survived until 1949.

IRRS collection

were all solely reliant on tank locomotives.

From 1900 onwards, increasing traffic led to the introduction of progressively larger designs still centred on the 4-4-0 for passenger work and on the 0-6-0 for goods. These classes retained many of the traditions established in the previous century. The GSWR explored the potential for larger goods locomotives in the form of inside-cylindered 2-6-0s and 4-6-0s but only because weight restrictions dictated the need for leading wheels.

To meet greater demands with shorter-distance passenger work, there were two significant initiatives in the 1900s. The CBSCR came to rely mainly on inside-cylindered 4-6-0Ts that proved adequate for that line's needs throughout the remainder of the steam era. The DSER more conventionally retained four-coupled drive but introduced Ireland's first 4-4-2Ts, a configuration that was later to have extensive application on other railways.

Mention should also be made of the locomotives of the minor companies that joined the GSR fold. The three broad gauge lines made colourful and individualistic motive power contributions, very much in the heterogeneous spirit of Irish steam power, of which the palm must go to the delightful 2-2-2WTs of the Waterford & Tramore.

The six narrow gauge companies also made their mark by providing no fewer than nine different wheel arrangements among a total of 43 tank locomotives (it was reported in 1929 that they shared 18 different types of boiler). The oldest locomotive dated from 1886, albeit heavily modified in the interim, while a pair of 4-6-0Ts were delivered as late as 1922 to meet burgeoning traffic demands on the West Clare Railway. The slow decline of the narrow gauge routes rendered a surplus of available motive power, obviating the need for any new construction after the amalgamation.

GSWR 4-4-2T Class 37 (later C7) No 319. The Inchicore style was evident in this Ivatt design, seen at Cork Glanmire Road. Although not apparent from the looks, this locomotive was actually four years younger than Robinson's WLWR No 18 depicted on page 21. It worked unaltered until 1950.

IRRS collection

GSWR 'Kerry Bogie' 4-4-0 Class 2 No 44. As built with round-topped raised firebox. The characteristic Inchicore double smokebox doors were quite a long-lived feature of a number of ex-GSWR locomotives. This locomotive gained fame from the poem *The Gallant 44* which recorded its exploits as pilot to a more modern locomotive on an express service.

IRRS collection

Although motive power policy remained essentially conservative in character, progress elsewhere was not ignored. The first company in these islands to own a locomotive with a Belpaire firebox was the Schull & Skibbereen Light Railway (from 1888), but this was something of an aberration. Provision of Belpaire fireboxes on the GSWR and MGWR started around the turn of the century but did not really gain momentum for several years. Between 1904 and 1908, the GSWR built a number of new 4-4-0s with tapered boilers and rebuilt some others to conform. Later these locomotives all received parallel boilers and no more of the tapered variety were built in Ireland.

The MGWR did investigative work into superheating in the 1900s and from 1915 initiated an active fitting programme. WH Morton who managed this exercise formed the view that superheating could be efficiently pursued without the need to convert from slide to piston valves. This conclusion, which was contrary to conventional wisdom in Britain, was to prove significant during GSR days when budgetary constraints limited development. The GSWR followed a little later with superheating when three new classes during the Maunsell/ Watson era were introduced. The DSER experimented with a superheated 0-6-0 in 1911 which showed encouraging results but did not lead to further installations until 1922.

In 1913, Maunsell on the GSWR introduced No 341, a 4-4-0 of a size that took this wheel arrangement to the limits then permitted by weight and axle loading restrictions. There were several interesting features to this locomotive, including the unique combination of inside cylinders with inside Walschaerts valve gear. Apart from an earlier, short-lived experiment with Marshall's valve gear on another GSWR 4-4-0, Stephenson's link motion had until then been almost exclusively applied to broad gauge locomotives. The only exceptions were the power units of steam rail motors where space limitations dictated the use of outside Walschaerts valve gear.

On the 3' 0" gauge, outside cylinders were used exclusively. Stephenson's link motion was mainly employed although six Tralee & Dingle and two West Clare railways' locomotives were fitted with outside Walschaerts valve gear. Also, two locomotives on the latter system were equipped with inside Bagnall-Price valve gear.

Watson, Maunsell's successor on the GSWR, was imbued with a large engine philosophy. His first effort was an inside-cylindered 4-8-0T design (No 900), a specialised exercise that yielded a large yet simple machine, but one that made no lasting impact on design practice. In contrast, Watson's other design (No 400) was a four-cylinder 4-6-0 dating from 1916 that had a substantial influence upon the motive power policy of the GSR.

No 400 was the first of a group of 39 locomotives in four classes and of two wheel arrangements that are treated separately in Chapter 9 'Locomotives of the transitional period'. In this context, 'transition' refers not only to the background factors of the time, ie the amalgamation and the preceding events, but also to the revolutionary nature of these machines in the Irish context. They were the first that were unequivocally of the modern era – superheated with Belpaire fireboxes and outside Walschaerts valve gear. The four-cylinder locomotives in original condition proved a false start in this endeavour. However, through an extended process of rebuilding, the seven survivors were eventually to come close to matching the standards of the other twenty-nine of this group which were competent performers.

GSWR 0-6-0 Class 101 (J15) No 179. In 1933 this locomotive was re-framed and fitted with a Z type superheated Belpaire boiler – a good engine made even better. The tender is a Type A (authors' classification), as originally introduced around the time this class first appeared, but has been modified with side plates that extend around the rear. It is seen standing at Waterford shed.

IRRS collection

Right: GSWR 4-4-0 Class 333 No 337 (D4). This was the penultimate GSWR 4-4-0 class, fitted with smaller 5' 8½" driving wheels for service between Cork and Rosslare. No 337 appears here in later condition with Type O saturated boiler and modern cab but retaining slide valves. A feature of the last four members of this class was the unusual outside framed bogie, intended to prevent overheating of the journals. This arrangement was later proved unnecessary but it was nevertheless perpetuated on GSR Class 342 (D4), a derivative of the type introduced in 1936.

IRRS collection

GSR locomotive policy

While the transitional designs covered the GSR's needs for larger locomotives well into the 1930s, there was a substantial amount of change and modification with the medium and smaller sized designs. The logic behind some of the decisions is not always easy to fathom at this distance which adds an intriguing element to what is known of GSR motive power policy.

Corporate mergers tend to produce internal stresses but in this case, the situation was more acute as a result of the arrears of routine repairs, the urgency of making good Civil War damage, and the sheer complexity and diversity of the locomotive fleet that the new organisation had inherited. Furthermore, several of the senior management appointments were taken up by ex-MGWR personnel. Thus when it came to the position of Chief Mechanical Engineer, to restore a measure of 'balance', Bazin of the GSWR was appointed although Morton, who became his deputy, had a stronger claim to the job.

It is apparent that there was conflict of views between the two men, in the matter of superheating. At an Officers' Conference convened on 14 January 1925, Morton pointed out that the proportion of superheated locomotives was much less than on other railways, quoting the following statistics:

LMS – 24%; GWR – 41%; GNR(I) – 42%; MGWR – 43%; GSWR – 6%

As superheating had passed the experimental stage and had been proven to be economical, it was suggested that the fitting programme should be accelerated. If 25 locomotives a year were fitted, it was estimated that £2,500 would be saved in the first year, rising to £15,000 in the sixth and subsequent years. The meeting recommended adoption "subject to its being found practicable to carry out the work economically within the time suggested".

With the backlog of repairs and the need to re-organise mechanical engineering affairs, Bazin might have had grounds for delay but over time it became evident that he intended to ignore this decision, particularly with respect to older, smaller locomotives. Effectively the superheating programme did not really get under way until after Bazin's retirement in 1929, as is apparent from official GSR figures drawn up in 1938:

Number of superheated locomotives in stock by year:

Type	1925	1926	1927	1928	1929	1930	1931	1932	1933	1934	1935	1936	1937
4-6-0	13	13	13	12	10	10	10	10	10	10	10	10	10
4-6-0T											1	1	1
4-4-0	18	19	19	19	21	30	33	44	55	54	60	67	69
2-4-0	12	12	18	18	17	17	17	17	19	19	18	13	11
0-6-0	39	39	39	39	39	43	50	64	82	92	106	112	116
2-6-0	8	14	17	20	23	29	29	30	30	32	34	34	35
0-6-2T									5	5	5	5	5
2-6-2T				1	1	1	1	1	1	1	1	1	1
Total	**90**	**97**	**106**	**109**	**111**	**130**	**140**	**166**	**202**	**213**	**235**	**243**	**248**

The increase in the period to 1929 was due to the assembly of Woolwich Mogul kits, and to completion of the superheating programme of Class 650 (G2) 2-4-0s, which had been started by the MGWR in 1919. The small size of the latter locomotives definitely placed them beyond the scope of Bazin's policy. This would appear to have been a gesture of independence by the team at 'the Broadstone' – the term commonly used for Broadstone Works in Dublin.

With Bazin's departure, the prohibition on the superheating of smaller locomotives was dropped. In 1930, the first Type Z superheated Belpaire boiler was fitted to a member of Class 101 and by 1953, a further 66 had been so treated. From the amalgamation until 1930, the class had been subject to steady attrition with 11 withdrawals. After superheating had commenced, the GSR was to withdraw only two more (one saturated and one superheated), and only a further two were taken out of service before 1953.

While the greater share of GSR traffic revenue derived from freight services (see Appendix A Table 1), much locomotive development was directed at passenger machines (improvement of Class 400, experiments with No 500, and the new Classes 850, 670, 342 and 800). Apart from specialised shunting engines and Class 700 (J15a) which was a synthesis of existing spare parts, the only new build initiative with overtly goods locomotive intentions was Class 710 (J15b). Even so, this was rated a mixed traffic design and when it was found incapable of matching Class 101 performance levels, superheating of the latter, which had been held in abeyance during 1934, was resumed. The longevity of Class 101 has been lauded many times but perhaps it has not been fully appreciated just how critical was the marriage of the superheated Type Z boiler to this small mid-19th century design in sustaining the company's revenue base.

Reversion to saturated boilers occurred with other classes, but this practice seems to have been a case of budgetary constraints dictating use of whatever suitable boiler was available, rather than any basic change of heart.

The MGWR-derived view that superheaters and slide valves could happily co-exist was welcome in the minimisation of modernisation costs. The use of piston valves was therefore not as widespread as might have been expected, the following classes being so fitted:

Left: GSR 4-4-0 Class 342 (D4) No 346. The similarity with GSWR Class 333 is evident although the later version introduced a new style of cab with side window. It had been GSR policy to attach old tenders to new locomotives but with this class was inaugurated a new style of 3450 gallons capacity. The new tender body profile was a precursor to that adopted with the large 4-6-0s of Class 800. Behind the water column can just be seen the roof of the present headquarters of the IRRS at Kingsbridge, now Heuston Station, Dublin.

IRRS collection

Class (number of locomotives fitted in brackets):	Ex-GSWR	Ex-DSER	Ex-MGWR	GSR.
	257 (8)	461 (2)	540* (5)	342 (5)
	332* (1)		545* (6)	372 (20)
	338* (1)		567* (1)	393 (6)
	341 (1)		619* (4)	500 (2)
	400 (10)		623 (23)	670 (5)
	500 (1)		646* (4)	710 (10)
				800 (3)
				850 (1)
Total number of engines	**(22)**	**(2)**	**(43)**	**(52)**

* Piston valves fitted after original construction.

GSR 4-6-0 Class 402 (B2a) No 406. As rebuilt in two cylinder form in 1930 with new frames and Caprotti valve gear. The Inchicore-built trio Nos 401, 402 and 406 were more extensively rebuilt than the surviving Armstrong-Whitworth engines which were so treated later. It is questionable whether the extra cost of Caprotti valve gear was justified. During rebuilding, a more modern cab, known as the 'Class 500 cab' was fitted.

IRRS collection

The two ex-GSWR 4-4-0s (Nos 332 and 338) proved inferior in performance and riding compared with their slide valve counterparts. The critical factor was most likely retention of short-lap valves as the advantages afforded by long-lap valves were not properly recognised at the time.

The Class 400 4-6-0s represented the initial step towards significantly larger express passenger locomotives but despite the alleged Swindon influence, this design appeared with short-lap valves, a factor that adversely affected performance. In 1916, the year of No 400's construction, the advantages of long lap valves were appreciated fully only by the Great Western Railway. Maunsell, by then with the South Eastern & Chatham Railway, and under the influence of a GWR-trained assistant, adopted the standard a year later with the 2-6-0 design that became the prototype of the Woolwich moguls. In searching for a better performance level than the Class 400 could offer, Bazin through collaboration with Maunsell or possibly his old colleagues at Doncaster, introduced the long travel valve to the GSWR, and thus to the GSR, through No 500. Class 700 (J15a) was the only post-amalgamation design fitted with slide valves.

In other respects, policy seems to have been administered in rather haphazard fashion. The most pressing needs concerned the ex-DSER section which saw several initiatives to up-date motive power, none of which fully met prevailing needs. The solitary P1 2-6-2T No 850 was an interesting design and fully in the spirit of contemporary trends as initiated with the two cylinder 4-6-0s and 2-6-0s. Nonetheless, it proved to be a dead end so far as GSR policy was concerned. The only other attempt at a purpose-designed steam locomotive for this section, Class 670 (I3), was regressive by comparison. This was a traditional 0-6-2T that by 1933 would elsewhere have been considered obsolescent.

The disappointing outcome of the two GSR 0-6-0 classes (700 and 710) raises a key question about new build policy generally. If further 0-6-0s were needed, why was the GSWR Class 257 not used as a template? This Maunsell design was the last GSWR 0-6-0 type introduced, and was highly regarded. For a company in financial straits, it would have provided a tried and proven (and thus more economical) solution to the company's needs. Similar questions might also be asked about two other competent pre-amalgamation designs – the ex-DSER Class 461 (K2) 2-6-0 for goods work and Class 458 (C3) 4-4-2T for suburban services. This determination to ignore proven pre-amalgamation designs could not have been in the best interests of the shareholders. It suggests 're-invention of the wheel' and an element of expensive ego on the part of the responsible CMEs.

Against this apparent policy to ignore sound designs of an earlier era, the sole exception – the Class 342 4-4-0 – looks all the more paradoxical. Four of the larger ex-GSWR 4-4-0s were withdrawn in 1927/ 8 and one more in one 1933. Their numerical replacement by five new engines in 1936 was a twist in the complex story of the ex-GSWR 4-4-0s that suggested deficiency in forward planning. Class 342, which was intended for duties not dissimilar to those undertaken by Woolwich Moguls, suggested a further exercise in regression. This aspect was exacerbated by retention of certain design features that years earlier had been proven as unnecessary.

If enthusiasts found motive power policy up to 1939 rather unexciting, the introduction of the Class 800 4-6-0s that year offered a welcome change and a promise of great things to come. As a flagship design, and as an icon of railway progress, No 800 certainly fitted the bill. A number of commentators have questioned the rationale, and have suggested that the GSR's needs might have been better served by an up-dated version of Class 500. Whether these reservations were justified will never be known because the operating environment for which these impressive machines had been intended was soon to change for ever.

Whatever may be the view about the suitability of individual GSR designs, there is no doubt that overall, a serious motive power crisis was evolving between 1925 and 1939. It was GSR policy to ascribe a 40 year working life to locomotives and carriages, and 30 years to wagons. Based on this premise, official GSR figures for the period 1925 to 1937 make dismal reading:

Year	Locomotive stock	Actual renewals	Renewals needed for 40 year average life	Annual arrears	Cumulative arrears	% Total fleet
1925	575	8	14	6	6	1
1926	575	6	14	8	14	2
1927	573	3	14	11	25	4
1928	540	4	14	10	35	6
1929	540	7	14	7	42	8
1930	531	6	13	7	49	9
1931	520		13	13	62	12
1932	520		13	13	75	14
1933	516	5	13	8	83	16
1934	516	5	13	8	91	18
1935	516	5	13	8	99	19
1936	511	5	13	8	107	21
1937	511		13	13	120	23

By the same measure, the situation for rolling stock was rather worse. As at 1937, the cumulative renewal arrears with carriages was 439 or 28% of a total fleet of 1,588 vehicles and with wagons was 3,364 or 27% of a total fleet of 12,345 vehicles. (Source: Figures submitted by the GSR to the Ingram Tribunal).

The GSR was to introduce only three more steam locomotives following the Ingram submission. That these should be of Class 800, a specialised express type with limited route availability, looks curious against the evolving fleet renewal problem. The case for a truly modern mixed traffic type that combined reasonable power with moderate axle loading was much stronger, and must raise doubts about just how cohesive was the GSR's management structure and thinking. Ostensibly this was a situation reminiscent of difficulties experienced, for example, in the early years of the London Midland & Scottish Railway where the CME was responsible for locomotive construction and overhaul, while authority for operations rested elsewhere. However the GSR's mechanical engineering hierarchy was not so compromised; the CME was responsible for workshops, running sheds and a total of some 4,800 personnel. In a properly functioning management structure, new design work should be well integrated with the present and expected future demands of operators. There must be doubt whether this was the situation at Inchicore during the 1930s. The GSR organogram defining the structure of the CME's department, and the number and grades of personnel, is quite clear. An abridged version as at 1935 is set out below:

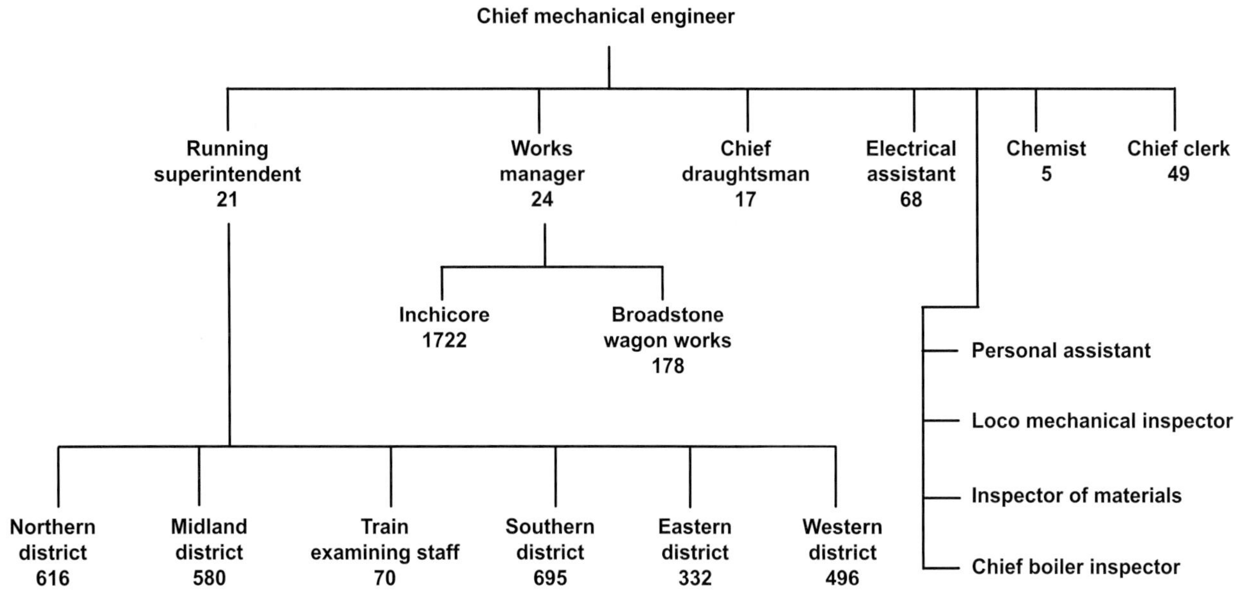

The principal locomotive depots by division were:

Northern:	Inchicore, Broadstone, Grand Canal Street, Bray, Kildare
Eastern:	Waterford, Maryborough (Portlaoise), Wexford, Rosslare
Southern:	Thurles, Limerick Junction, Mallow, Cork, Skibbereen, Tralee
Western:	Limerick, Ennis, Tuam
Midland:	Athlone, Mullingar, Galway, Westport, Sligo, Ballinamore

GSR 4-6-0 Class 400 (B2) No 405, as rebuilt in two cylinder form in 1933. This locomotive was originally built by Armstrong-Whitworth with four cylinders for the GSWR; the rebuilding was less comprehensive and therefore cheaper than that given to Class 402 (B2a). Despite being rebuilt, No 405 retains the original style of cab. At Cork, Glanmire Road. *IRRS collection*

GSR 4-6-0 Class 500 (B1) No 501, built 1925. Unlike the 400 series, there was much less variety among Class 500, although No 500 was subjected to a number of experiments. Intended as mixed traffic engines, they proved to be sound performers from the start. They were excellent passenger locomotives and little used on goods work, at least before 1940. The tender was one of only two of Type F (authors' classification) introduced for use with Nos 501 and 502 and in style quite unlike anything that had been built for the GSWR.

IRRS collection

GSR 2-6-2T Class 850 (P1) No 850. The modern locomotive as exemplified by Classes 400 and 500 found expression also in this thoroughly up-to-date tank locomotive built in 1928 for suburban work on the ex-DSER section. No 850 was criticised for a tendency to run hot and to roll at speed. Some crews found it difficult to work. This was the first pure GSR design, but minimal effort seems to have been made to eliminate its shortcomings. It remained the sole example of its type, and thus a dead end in Irish motive power development.

Authors' collection

The unanswered questions concerning the rationale for introduction of Class 800 suggest that political/promotional motives were allowed to outweigh specific operational demands and the need to conserve scarce investment funds.

The GSR was an independent company but one that had been created under considerable government persuasion against the alternative of outright nationalisation. It is tempting to speculate that governmental authority was not above giving informal yet influential direction on certain issues, and that the GSR's board and management never enjoyed complete freedom of action. This possibility was most evident in the GSR's experience with the Drumm Battery trains.

The economics of train operation came under increasing scrutiny in the 1920s and 1930s. Pursuit of better returns led to various essays by several railway companies into fixed formation, self-propelled passenger units. Two of the GSR's initiatives were conventional in the adoption of steam railcars, and one was reasonably successful within the limitations of the concept. However it was soon apparent that non-steam power had to be an essential element in the equation. This was a period in which railway companies elsewhere were exploring internal combustion engines and electricity supplied by third rail or overhead wire. Apart from a minor and mainly unsuccessful foray into small petrol-engined railcars, the GSR's main thrust was uniquely in the field of battery electric power.

The Drumm Battery electric train project started out as one where any untoward cost was to be underwritten by the government. It ended with all of the residual cost, and the considerable research and development risk, falling upon the GSR's shareholders. It is easy to be critical in retrospect but the project was a considerable act of faith based on unproven technology. For all the attractions of modernity, cleanliness and technological innovation, the Drumm project was by the criteria of rigorous investment analysis, a commercial failure for the GSR.

While some experimental work took place involving a member of Class 400 after 1939, to all intents and purposes motive power development ceased that year. The ageing fleet was presented with a fresh series of challenges during the War years. Initially there was a sharp growth in traffic loadings but services were later increasingly restricted in the face of shortages of good coal, and the substitution of low-grade alternatives.

The challenges of the 1940s

This decade was to prove an exceptionally difficult period for the GSR and its successor from 1 January 1945, Córas Iompair Éireann. A feature of the GSR's constituent companies had been fleet expansion by means of small batches of locomotives of varying designs. The thirty-two locomotives introduced by the GSR (ie excluding those originated on the initiative of the constituent companies) were in eight different classes, and thus continued this tradition of diversity. Under normal pre-World War II conditions, these standards were not particularly efficient but could be accommodated within a relatively relaxed operating environment. During the 1939-45 period and in the post-war world, running viability demanded high levels of availability, interchangeability of parts, and minimal periods out-of-service. These objectives could only be achieved with extensive standardisation. While the GSWR and MGWR had applied a considerable measure of standardisation with their fleets, there was little evidence of any continuation in this vein by GSR management.

GSR 0-6-2T Class 670 (I3) No 670. Following the disappointment with No 850, this was the GSR's second attempt at a suburban tank engine. The design was regressive by comparison and in 1933, the year of its introduction, it was almost an obsolete type. Performance on the road was adequate; poor layout of frames and motion made servicing difficult. *IRRS collection*

GSR Sentinel Steam Railcar No 355. The GSR sponsored several forays into fixed formation trains employing steam, diesel and battery electric power. The Sentinel units were reasonably successful, within the inherent limitations of this type of vehicle, being introduced for branch and rural duties in 1927. The Sentinel fleet was used on branch lines in the west and south. No 355, seen here on shed at Limerick, was withdrawn in 1942 although it had not worked for a couple of years beforehand. *IRRS collection*

Declining revenues would have discouraged new investment. On the other hand, this situation also allowed continued use of unsuitable types eg 4-4-0s with 6' 3" and 6' 7" driving wheels on secondary services. Programmes to re-boiler some ageing and, by contemporary standards, mediocre types were hardly an efficient use of scarce financial resources. Other than No 850 and Class 800, designs introduced under GSR auspices were unenterprising, and out-of-date when compared with contemporary trends in other countries. The GSR's core need was for a simple, rugged, go-anywhere type that could be produced in large numbers, just as the GSWR had done in the 19th century with its Class 101. Outside cylinders and motion would also have contributed much to operational efficiency. A smaller Woolwich mogul designed to take full advantage of the more generous Irish loading gauge and embracing many of the modern design features that were to emerge with the Ivatt LMS Class 2 would have met many pressing needs.

Sadly such progressive thinking was not to be. Although by 1944 the number of classes had been significantly reduced, there had been no priority to reduce variety within them, and several classes still consisted of five or less members. This point is underlined by **Appendix C** which records an extraordinary diversity of dimensions and types of locomotive boilers.

The Milne Report of 1948 concluded that the fleet numbers were excessive, that too many locomotives were out of service at any one time, and that workshop repairs were taking too long. The vicissitudes of that period and delays in deliveries of raw material and manufactured components were certainly contributory factors. The long-term structural inefficiency of the fleet compounded the problems. Further, acceptable returns on investment rely in large part on 'making the assets sweat' ie high levels of utilisation. In this context, average annual mileages achieved by members of Class 800 were in the region of 50-60% of the comparative figures achieved by their opposite numbers in Britain. If this disparity is evident with top-line locomotives one may only speculate just how dismal was the utilisation factor among the excessive numbers of smaller and older types engaged on secondary work.

At the end of the GSR regime and in the early days of Córas Iompair Éireann, the motive power situation was so severe as to require drastic action. Views varied over the best solution and an uncomfortable compromise resulted whereby a fleet of ageing steam locomotives worked on for longer than was desirable. Their continued service was necessary to cover for problems arising from the poor reliability of British-sourced diesel locomotives, and in retrospect the decision to allow the condition of the steam fleet to run down was premature. The protracted demise of steam was a sad affair with the last members of the GSR fleet being retired some 21 years after the company itself had ceased to exist.

Chapter 3
Classes, numbers and names

The numbering and classification systems of the Great Southern Railways were quite complex, and can easily confuse the process of establishing the identity or origin of a particular locomotive. To provide clarification, this chapter explains the numbering sequences, the two classification disciplines, the load class systems and the naming policy. The simplest means of identification is by the locomotive number but this will not always readily indicate the relative class. Hence the number and classification Keys 1 and 2 at the end of the chapter are provided to help trace individual origins and classes. Explanation of the manner in which information is tabulated on individual classes and the conventions used in the recording of leading dimensions are set out in Notes on motive power details, immediately before the Keys.

Number schemes

Following creation of the Great Southern Railway on 12 November 1924, through amalgamation of the Great Southern & Western, Midland Great Western and Cork Bandon & South Coast railways, the number series planned for broad gauge constituent locomotives was:

Ex-GSWR: 1–371, 400–409, 500–509, 900, 901

Ex-CBSCR: 510–529

Ex-MGWR: 530–670

No action was taken on the basis of this plan as a revised scheme was prepared following the second amalgamation as at 1 January 1925 which included the Dublin & South Eastern Railway in the creation of the Great Southern Railways proper. The new number series comprised:

Ex-GSWR: 1–371, 400–409, 500–509, 900, 901 (plus five locomotives unnumbered)

Ex-DSER: 422–462 (plus one locomotive unnumbered)

Ex-CBSCR: 463–482

Ex-WTR: 483–486

Ex-CMDR: 487–491

Ex-TCLR: (two locomotives unnumbered)

Ex-MGWR: 530–668 plus 233 & 234

It would seem that the CBSCR allocation was changed so as to allow space for possible extension of the 500 series beyond 510. Nos 410 to 421 were apparently initially allocated for the first batch of Woolwich moguls.

In the event, no renumbering of locomotives or livery changes took place until April 1925. This delay seems to have allowed opportunity for a final MGWR flourish with the first Woolwich mogul to be assembled. This locomotive, which had been originally intended as the first of MGWR Class D2, emerged from the Broadstone as No 49 in gloss black with red lining, the final livery of that company. It was photographed in this condition, and then returned to the workshops to be repainted and photographed in workshop grey as GSR No 410. Not long later it started service in standard GSR grey livery and numbered 372.

Broad gauge numbers

The historian's task is eased by the comparative scarcity of renumbering other than the treatment given to non-GSWR locomotives following the amalgamation. In the later years of the DSER, two older locomotives had been renumbered but neither was transferred to the GSR fleet. Some MGWR locomotives had been renumbered within that company's own series in 1922 and 1924. There also occurred the MGWR No 49/ GSR No 410 & 372 exercise with the Woolwich mogul mentioned above. Post-1925, the numbers of the two GSR Sentinel shunters were altered shortly after their introduction. A few of the GSR's smaller tank locomotives were named but not numbered. All these details are recorded in the relevant sections of the text, as are the original Waterford Limerick & Western Railway numbers of that company's locomotives surviving in 1925.

At the formation of the GSR, the largest constituent locomotive fleet was from the GSWR and no renumbering of that company's engines took place. As indicated above, numbers carried were 1 to 371 (with gaps in sequence), 400 to 409, 500, and 900. Three locomotives under construction at the time of the amalgamation retained their originally allocated numbers (501, 502 and 901) under GSR ownership.

The DSER took the numbers in the block 422 to 462. Several additional locomotives were physically acquired from this railway but never entered in the GSR lists as they had already been withdrawn but not scrapped, or were withdrawn early in 1925 as deemed

Left: The ubiquitous Irish 0-6-0 is depicted here in GSWR Class 101 (J15) No 121. Always a saturated locomotive, No 121 had by this time received a 4' 4" diameter boiler with modern smokebox door.

IRRS collection

Below: The Class 101, like most other pre-amalgamation 0-6-0s, was intended for goods duties but these engines were usually employed as mixed traffic engines. Here No 138 works a mixed train along Wexford quays in September 1944, three months before the demise of the GSR.

JM Robbins

unfit for further service. An exception in this group was DSER No 44 which was scheduled for early withdrawal but worked on in normal service until 1927, although never re-numbered or classified by the GSR.

The treatment given to the CBSCR locomotives with numbers in the block 463 to 482 contained no exceptional features. Likewise the renumbering of the nine locomotives from the Waterford & Tramore and Cork & Macroom Direct railways in the 483 to 491 series was straightforward. On the other hand the Timoleague & Courtmacsherry Light Railway's locomotives never carried numbers and merely retained their names.

The fleet of the MGWR (except for the Woolwich moguls) was quite logically allocated the numbers 530 to 668 except for a pair of 0-6-0s that were given Nos 233 and 234. They were placed in the ex-GSWR sequence as they had been constructed for the WLWR but were opportunistically purchased by the MGWR, during a dispute between the manufacturers and the WLWR. Perhaps Inchicore still felt strongly on the matter, believing it was time they were 'brought home' although they appear to have worked out their careers on the ex-MGWR section

The remaining locomotives built, assembled or acquired by the GSR were allocated numbers 1 & 2 (soon changed to 280 & 281), 342 to 346, 372 to 391, 393 to 398, 495, 670 to 674, 700 to 704, 710 to 719, 800 to 802 and 850. The numbers 1 and 2 were replaced as these duplicated those of two ex-GSWR locomotives still in service. Nos 342 to 346 were a continuation of a GSWR type and logically fitted within that company's series. The Woolwich moguls (Nos 372 to 391 and 393 to 398) were slotted into gaps in the ex-GSWR sequence. The number 495 was allocated for no apparent reason. The numbers 670 upwards were applied with gaps in sequence obviously to allow for possible additions to each type.

The GSR also maintained a fleet of departmental service locomotives, some of which were switched back and forth between departmental and normal service stock. As they retained their normal service number/name, identification of which locomotives were actually in the departmental category at any one time is largely conjectural. One source states that 12 locomotives were listed as being in this category in 1925, reportedly being six 0-6-0s, one 0-6-4T (presumably one of Class 203),

Sunday passenger trains could be quite heavy. The inaugural Inchicore-Bray service on Whit Sunday, June 1952 is entrusted to ex-DSER 0-6-0 Class 442 (J8) No 444, awaiting departure from Inchicore platform.

JM Robbins

one 0-6-0T, one 0-4-4T, and three 0-4-2Ts. The total had apparently fallen to three by 1927.

In response to an enquiry in 1929, Morton (later CME) advised that there were only three departmental locomotives: 0-4-2ST *Sambo* as Inchicore works shunter; 0-6-4T rail motor No 92 for staff use between Kingsbridge and Inchicore; and a member of 0-6-0 Class 623 (J5) to work the track-relaying train. A year later, a 2-6-0 Class 355 (K3) was reported on the departmental list, presumably in substitution for the Class 623 (J5). As the track-relaying train worked all over the system, locomotives with lower axle loadings than Class 623 (18 tons) were necessary on these duties in some areas.

The following locomotives seem to have been considered departmental for most if not all of their GSR careers: No 92, *Sambo* (always used as Inchicore shunter), *Sprite*, and *Fairy*. The transfer of *Jumbo* to the list in 1944 while still engaged as Waterford goods yard shunter, a duty it undertook for many years, casts doubt on what selection criteria were applied, and on the nature of the duties considered to be 'departmental'.

The numbers (and name-only engines) carried in GSR days are listed in Key 1 at the end of this chapter, together with the relevant classifications, which are described below.

The GSR Class system

The GSWR method of type classification, which dated back to around 1860-1870, was retained by the GSR. This relied on the lowest running number borne by any member of the class. This was not necessarily the first of the type built as exemplified by 0-6-0 No 101 which was actually the 78th member of Class 101 to be constructed. However, there were exceptions to this principle as with Class 52 which bore numbers between 1 and 98 (with gaps in sequence). In this case, the class designation conformed with the number of the first example introduced.

Confusion might arise with some older locomotives where the class designation was changed following withdrawal of that locomotive whose number had been first adopted to identify the class. For example, eight 2-4-0s numbered 10, 20, 22, 23, 43, 44, 47 & 48 were acquired from the WLWR which duly became GSWR Nos 263, 273, 275, 276, 290, 291, 292 & 293 in that order; they were logically designated Class 263 on acquisition. However, Nos 263, 273, 275 & 292 were withdrawn between 1907 and 1915 and the class was later re-designated 276, in accordance with the lowest numbered example then in service. The actual date of this change is unknown but it probably took place concurrent with the assimilation of the other companies' locomotives at the amalgamation.

Locomotives absorbed from the other companies and renumbered sequentially in the GSWR series were given class designations based on the 'lowest number' principle. Application of the GSR classification discipline was sometimes exaggerated as with five ageing but essentially similar CBSCR saddle tanks that were placed in three different classes (472, 474 and 475) on grounds of small variations in driving wheel diameters. In contrast, there was significant variety among the ex-GSWR's most numerous type but this was always known simply as Class 101.

The Inchicore Class system

The GSWR had introduced an additional, albeit little used, classification system that was based on alpha-numeric principles. This was modified and expanded to become the Inchicore Class system following the amalgamation. The GSWR (later GSR) Classes, and the relevant the GSWR alpha-numeric Classes, and the later Inchicore Classes are summarised below:

GSWR class	GSWR alpha-numeric class	Inchicore class	GSWR class	GSWR alpha-numeric class	Inchicore Class
900	A1	A1	203	H1	H1
500	B1	B1	92	H2	H2
400	B2	B2/ B2a	213	I - no suffix	I1
362	B3	B3	211	J1	J3
27	C1	C4	257	J2	J4
269	C2	C5	351	J3	J9
37	C3	C7	201	J4	J11
333	D1	D2/ D3/ D4	204	J5	J12
337	D2	D2/ D3/ D4	JUMBO	J6	J13
341	D3	D1	101	J7	J15
321	D4	D2/ D3	235	J8	J22
309	D5	D3/ D10	222	J9	J25
301	D6	D11	ERIN	J10	J27
305	D7	D12	299	J11	J28
60	D8	D13/ D14	91	J12	J29
296	D9	D15	90/ 99/ 100	J13	J30
52	D10	D17	279	K1	E1
2	D11	D19	295	K2	E2
356	E1	K3	47	K3	E3
355	E2	K4	FAIRY	L1	L4/ L5
267	F1	F4	SPRITE	L2	L4/ L5
33	F2	F6	SAMBO	L3	L2
276	G1	G3	IMP	M1	M1/ M2
21	G2	G4	228	M2	n/a

The MGWR also maintained a fleet of 0-6-0s for its goods traffic. Class L No 67 *Dublin* is standing at Broadstone locomotive depot. This photograph was taken in GSR days but No 67 (GSR Class 594/ J19 No 605) is still in MGWR condition, retaining its name and number plates.

IRRS collection

Left: A major element of the MGWR's goods traffic involved livestock movements. 0-6-0 Class 573 (J18) No 585, formerly MGWR No 131 *Atlas*, is engaged on such work. The photograph is undated but seems to have been taken in CIÉ days. The locomotive is certainly showing its age.

IRRS collection

Opposite: The GSR added its own 0-6-0s to the fleet, initially with Class 700 (J15a) which numbered only five members. They were used on mixed traffic duties, and No 704 is seen hauling a passenger train which proves that diversity was not limited to the locomotive fleet.

IRRS collection

The 'Inchicore Class' system used an alpha-numeric formula derived from that started by the GSWR. Ivatt on the Great Northern Railway (England) had introduced a system using similar principles in 1900 and this was developed by Gresley to embrace most of the locomotives acquired on formation of the London & North Eastern Railway in 1923. As an ex-Doncaster man, Bazin would have been conscious of the clarity offered by alpha-numeric classification. He is believed to have introduced this system to the GSWR around 1919 to 1921, and seems to have followed in part the English GNR/ LNER precedent.

The Inchicore Class system, instigated in 1925, had the objective of categorising all types absorbed by the GSR on a unified basis. In this case, the prefix letter denoted the wheel arrangement while the suffix number reflected the notional power rating based on nominal tractive effort ie the lower the suffix, the higher the tractive effort. This varied from the LNER methodology in drawing no distinction between tender or tank types, or between originating constituent companies. The GSR's wheel arrangement-related prefixes were:

A	4-8-0	I	0-6-2
B	4-6-0	J	0-6-0
C	4-4-2	K	2-6-0
D	4-4-0	L	0-4-2
E	0-4-4	M	0-4-0
F	2-4-2	N	2-2-2
G	2-4-0	P	2-6-2
H	0-6-4		

There were some inconsistencies in the manner in which the Inchicore Classifications were managed. For example, the convoluted rebuilding programmes applied to the ex-GSWR 4-4-0 classes numbered 301 to 314 and 321 to 340 resulted in changes to Inchicore Class designations that must have been of limited use at the time, and certainly serve to confuse the historian. There were also two cases of rather obscure reclassifications with Classes Imp and Sprite. On the other hand, the superheating program of Class 101 which improved significantly the power output of those so treated was left unrecognised. A curiosity concerned C1 which was never used although under the GSWR alpha-numeric system there had been a Class C1 (GSWR/ GSR Class 27 – Inchicore Class C4). It is likely that this classification was set aside for the proposed Class 380 4-4-2T of February 1925 which if built would have had a higher tractive effort than that of ex-DSER Class 455 (C2).

In working practice, railwaymen rarely used the Inchicore system and this was doubtless partly due to the minimal allocation of locomotives away from their native systems. Further, Inchicore Works never used the system on records such as drawings; apparently it only appeared on official lists which tabulated locomotives by classes together with their principal dimensions. Reliance continued to be placed on the time-honoured pre-amalgamation nomenclature, certainly so far as ex-GSWR locomotives were concerned. Conversely, enthusiasts (especially those over the water) have tended to rely more on the Inchicore class system. Perhaps the coincidence of the LNER having its own J15s of similar size and popularity had something to do with it!

The orderliness of the Inchicore classification system was upset with some later designs. The rebuilding of Class 400 resulted in a new sub-division B2a for those

which had a higher tractive effort, the remainder staying as B2. The reverse occurred with the Woolwich moguls. Those with 5' 6" driving wheels (GSR Class 372) were given Class K1 but the larger wheeled version with its lower tractive effort should have received a higher suffix. However, in view of the intended express duties of these later engines (GSR Class 393), they were given the compromise classification of K1a. Sub-suffixes were used again with the two attempts (GSR Classes 700 and 710) to improve upon the venerable Class 101 (J15) resulted in J15a and J15b respectively. Compromise was evident also with the new 4-6-0s of 1939. They were given the little-used B1a designation; in practice they were better known as the Class 800 or commonly, yet incorrectly, as 'the Queens'. In the text, the convention of the GSR class followed by the Inchicore class has been adopted where appropriate.

How the Inchicore classifications related to the GSR classifications and locomotive number series is tabulated in Key 2 at the end of this chapter.

Allocation policy

In practice, the degree of inter-sectional motive power transfer implied by the system-wide classifications never really eventuated. In 1929 the pre-amalgamation flavour to 5' 3" gauge locomotive allocations was evident in an official divisional list provided by the GSR:

	Loco types:						
	Ex-GSWR	**Ex-DSER**	**Ex-CBSCR**	**Ex-MGWR**	**Ex-Small Cos**	**Transitional Types**	**GSR**
Eastern (Waterford) District	39	6	–	2	–	1	–
Midland District	3	–	–	47	–	–	–
Western (Limerick) District	50	1	–	–	–	1	1
Southern (Cork) District	67	–	–	–	–	3	1
Northern (Inchicore) District	61	–	–	1	–	15	1
Grand Canal St & Bray	12	24	–	–	–	–	–
Broadstone	1	–	–	57	–	6	–
CBSCR Section	4	–	17	–	4	–	–

(An additional 70–odd locomotives were in the works at this time, together with another five 'sundry' small tank engines that do not seem then to have had a specific allocation. Only three GSR–acquired locomotives were in service by then and Woolwich moguls were still being assembled).

The pattern remained essentially unchanged in 1938 (early 1945 figures in brackets) when more detailed information (shed as opposed to divisional/ district allocations) was available:

	Loco types: Ex-GSWR	Ex-DSER	Ex-CBSCR	Ex-MGWR	Ex-Small Cos	Transitional Types	GSR.
Ex-GSWR sheds:							
Inchicore	59 (60)	–	–	– (2)	–	11 (12)	13 (15)
Limerick	51 (47)	–	–	– (1)	–	–	2 (2)
Waterford	39 (45)	– (4)	1 (–)	– (4)	–	1 (–)	1 (1)
Waterford Manor	–	–	–	2 (–)	1 (–)	–	–
Rosslare	2 (–)	–	–	–	–	1	–
Cork	47 (30)	– (1)	–	1 (1)	–	11 (9)	1 (–)
Limerick Junc	4 (4)	–	–	–	–	–	–
Thurles	3 (7)	–	–	– (1)	–	– (2)	– (1)
Mallow	– (14)	–	–	– (1)	–	– (1)	–
Tralee	14 (20)	–	–	–	–	–	– (1)
Ex-CBSCR sheds:							
Rocksavage	7 (13)	1 (2)	9 (6)	2 (1)	2 (2)	–	1 (–)
Ex-DSER sheds:							
Grand Canal St	1 (1)	17 (14)	–	–	–	–	3 (3)
Bray	4 (7)	6 (–)	– (1)	– (3)	–	–	3 (3)
Ex-MGWR sheds:							
Broadstone	– (1)	–	–	49 (50)	–	11 (10)	–
Athlone	– (1)	–	–	27 (29)	–	–	–
Mullingar	–	–	–	15 (10)	–	–	–
Sligo	1 (–)	–	–	7 (5)	–	–	–
Galway	1 (2)	–	–	2 (3)	–	–	–
Westport	3 (–)	–	–	4 (3)	–	–	–

Class 700 (J15a) No 701 is seen on goods work at Islandbridge junction in CIÉ days. It was coupled to a 19th century tender of Type A (authors' classification), which had been modernised by provision of side plates. The two cabins to the left of the photograph are located where Heuston Station's platform 10 now stands.

IRRS collection

The most pronounced pre-amalgamation character was retained on the ex-MGWR system, leavened only by a modest contingent of ex-GSWR locomotives. The transitional types were all Woolwich moguls, and their number suggests that the MGWR's original order for a dozen was not far off the mark.

Equally, the MGWR made little impact on the ex-GSWR shed allocations where a greater proportion of transitional era types and pure-GSR designs were evident. The most cosmopolitan allocations were apparent on the ex-DSER and ex-CBSCR systems, the former reflecting the attempts to modernise motive power on the Dublin-Bray services.

Load classes

The year 1925 saw the adoption of yet another method of classification. The GSWR had employed a system which divided its locomotive fleet into seven different categories for maximum permitted loadings. Appendices to the Working Timetables included tables advising the maximum loads that could be handled over specified routes for each category. The GSR refined and extended these principles to embrace the complete network. All but a few small tank locomotives were given Load Classes.

The 1925 allocation seems to have been made on the sole criterion of nominal tractive effort. Individual ratings were assessed in terms of the maximum permitted number of unloaded wagons that could be attached to locomotives in each load class so that the haulage capacity of individual types would be apparent system-wide:

Load Class	B	C	E	F	H	J	K	L	M	N	O	P	Q	R	S	T	U
GSR Class	900	211	351	201	341	101	455	321	222	301	423	27	267	52	2	299	90
	646	213	447	204	441	203	463	332	235	305	427	60	295	486	21	477	91
	372	257	461	614	850	545	573	475	333	309	428	269	422		33	482	483
	500	355	400			563	594	540	338	310		276	491		37	485	St Molaga
		362				567			440	434		279	530		47	487	
		368							472	450		296	536		Erin	Argadeen	
		442							234	454			551		471		
		448								458			650		479		
		619								490							
		623															

In 1931, the Load Class system was revised in the light of operating experience as nominal tractive effort alone is an insufficient basis for comparison in day-to-day working conditions. Load Class categories were reduced in number but were split between tender and tank locomotives with the addition of the 'T' suffix to identify the latter. This delineation was made presumably also to distinguish the lower braking power of a tank locomotive. The 1931 categories for tender locomotives were:

Load Class	A	B	C	E	J	L	M	O	R
GSR Class	372	393	257	211	101 234	222	301	60	2
		500	355	249	321 441	332	305	276	52
		646	368	338	540 545	333	310	296	530
			400	351	567 573	536	450	650	
			461	442	594 700	342	454		
			619	448	710				
				623					

(A special category H was added later for Class 800.)

Left: The GSR's second attempt at an 0-6-0 was the superheated Class 710 (J15b) which was also a general duties type. The policy of using old tenders with new locomotives – in this case No 715 – is evident here with the 1864 gallon version, modernised with side and rear plates. At Bray shed.

IRRS collection

Below left: Pursuit of larger 0-6-0 types by the GSWR and the DSER led to weight problems, and to the need to install pony wheels. The inside cylindered mogul was a relatively unusual type in these islands. GSWR 2-6-0 Class 368 (K4) No 369 was built as a mogul in 1909 but the earlier Class 355 (K3) had started life as an 0-6-0 type before conversion. GSWR cabs were not noted for the efficiency of their weather protection; here the cut-out has been reduced to improve comfort for the crew. At Cork, Glanmire Road.

IRRS collection

The 1931 Load Classes for tank locomotives were:

Load Class	FT	HT	KT	MT	NT	OT	PT	RT	ST	TT
GSR Class	201	463	203	434	423	27	267	33	299	90
	204	850	456	458	427	269	295	37	Argadeen	483
	213		472	490	428	279	491	47		485
	614		475				551	477		St Molaga
			670					479		280
								486		495

Opposite page: The unusual inside-cylindered 2-6-0 type was not restricted to tender locomotives, as evident with the Timoleague & Courtmacsherry Light Railway's *Argadeen* at Cork Rocksavage. The TCLR route was noted for being partly a roadside tramway, and for its sharp curves and indifferently-laid track. *Argadeen* is apparently provided with suitable survival gear – a jack on the front running plate and a bell on the cab.

IRRS collection

The Appendix to the Working Timetables specified the limits measured in maximum number of laden wagons that could be hauled by locomotives in each category with an overall constraint that no train should ever exceed 65 wagons. There were also overall limits on specific routes, regardless of locomotive type: Dublin-Wexford (45 wagons), Macmine–Waterford (30), Waterford–Fermoy (35), Ennis–Collooney (35).

The following wagon limits are quoted by way of example as appearing in the 1935 issue of the *Appendix to the Working Timetable*:

Load class:	A	B	C	E	FT	HT	J	KT	L	M	MT	NT	O	OT	PT	R	RT
Limerick–Nenagh	60	55	55	50	39	34	40	31	40	34	29	26	25	21	17	18	15
Thurles–Clonmel	–	–	45	43	33	31	35	27	29	28	24	22	25	21	20	19	16
Listowel–Tralee	–	–	–	–	–	–	35	–	35	–	24	–	25	21	18	18	16

The blanks indicated that all locomotives in the respective load classes were prohibited from those sections on grounds of axle loading. There were also more detailed limitations imposed on specific routes eg in respect of the heavy transfer goods duties between Dublin Docks at North Wall and Dublin, Kingsbridge.

One intention of the Inchicore and Load Class formulae was to provide a standard means of establishing accurately the capacity of locomotives working away from 'home territory' or in the hands of unfamiliar crews. In normal service conditions, locomotives rarely strayed far from home territory. However, the annual beet 'campaign' (the annual sugar beet harvest) called for numerous special workings with a wide variety of locomotives appearing at strange locations.

Load Classes were also used in the Working Timetables to describe operating procedures for specific types of locomotive. For example, the *Green Appendix* to the 1935 edition stipulates that where a locomotive from group J was to be used to assist a main line passenger train hauled by a locomotive of Classes 321, 372, 393, 400 or 500, the assisting engine was to be placed next to the train (ie coupled inside). There is plenty of photographic evidence to show that this was not always the case.

Fleet summaries

To draw together numbers, wheel bases, and GSR and Inchicore classifications, the composition of the respective components of the ultimate GSR fleet are summarised below, commencing with the GSWR locomotives:

Type	GSWR/ GSR No	GSR Class	Inchicore Class
4-4-0	2/ 5-8/ 10/ 13/ 15/ 43-46	2	D19
2-4-0	21/ 22/ 26/ 66-68	21	G4
4-4-2T	27/ 30-32	27	C4
2-4-2T	33-36/ 41/ 42	33	F6
4-4-2T	37/ 38/ 317-320	37	C7
0-4-4T	40/ 47-49/ 51/ 70/ 72-78/ 80/ 81/ 83	47	E3
4-4-0	1/ 3/ 4/ 9/ 11/ 12/ 14/ 16/ 18/ 20/ 52-59/ 97/ 98	52	D17
4-4-0	60-65/ 85-89/ 93-96	60	D13/ D14
0-6-0T	90/ 99/ 100	90	J30
0-6-0ST	91	91	J29
0-6-4T	92	92	H2
0-6-0	101-188/ 190-200/ 223/ 229/ 232/ 240-243/ 253- 256	101	J15

Type	GSWR/ GSR No	GSR Class	Inchicore Class
0-6-0T	201/ 202/ 207-210/ 217-220	201	J11
0-6-4T	203/ 205/ 206	203	H1
0-6-0T	204	204	J12
0-6-0	211/ 212	211	J3
0-6-2T	213/ 214	213	I1
0-6-0	222/ 237-239	222	J25
0-4-0ST	228	228	-
0-6-0	235/ 236	235	J22
0-6-0	257-264	257	J4
2-4-2T	267	267	F4
4-4-2T	269-271/ 274	269	C5
2-4-0	276/ 290/ 291/ 293	276	G3
0-4-4T	279	279	E1
0-4-4T	295	295	E2
4-4-0	296-298	296	D15
0-6-0ST	299	299	J28

Type	GSWR/ GSR No	GSR Class	Inchicore Class
0-6-0ST	(300) *Erin*	Erin	J27
4-4-0	301-304	301	D11
4-4-0	305-308	305	D12
4-4-0	309-314	309	D10/ D3
4-4-0	321-332	321/ 332	D2/ D3/ D4
4-4-0	333-340	333/ 338	D2/ D3/ D4/ D4a
4-4-0	341	341	D1
0-6-0	249-252/ 351-354	351	J9
2-6-0	355-361	355	K3
4-6-0	362-367	362	B3
2-6-0	368-371	368	K4
4-6-0	400-409	400/ 402	B2/ B2a
4-6-0	500/ 501*/ 502*	500	B1
4-8-0T	900/ 901*	900	A1
0-4-0T	*Imp*	Imp	M1/ M2
0-6-0T	*Jumbo*	Jumbo	J13
0-4-2ST	*Sambo*	Sambo	L2
0-4-2T	*Sprite/ Fairy*	Sprite	L4/ L5

* Introduced to service after the demise of the GSWR.

The Dublin & South Eastern Railway's locomotives which had borne numbers between 3 and 67 were renumbered in the block 422 to 462. DSER locomotive classes bore no specific designation and several engines of the same type/ class were not numbered sequentially:

Type	DSER No	GSR No	GSR Class	Inchicore Class
2-4-0	24	422	422	G7
2-4-0T	49, 9, 47, 7	423-426	423	G1
2-4-0T later 0-4-0T	69	Elf	Imp	M2 later M1
2-4-2T	64	427	427	F3
2-4-2T	3, 10, 11, 28, 45, 46	428-433	428	F2
2-4-2T	8, 12, 27, 29, 30, 40	434-439	434	F1
0-6-0	17	440	440	J20
0-6-0	36	441	441	J14
0-6-0	13, 14, 18, 65, 66	442-446	442	J8
0-6-0	50	447	447	J7
0-6-0	4, 5	448	448	J1

Type	DSER No	GSR No	GSR Class	Inchicore Class
4-4-0	55 to 58	450-453	450	D9
4-4-0	67	454	454	D8
4-4-2T	20, 34, 35	455-457	455	C2
4-4-2T	52, 54, 53	458-460	458	C3
2-6-0	15, 16	461, 462	461	K2

The locomotives of the Cork, Bandon & South Coast Railway were allotted the series 463 to 482 following on immediately after those of the DSER. No specific class designations were used by the CBSCR, nor were all locomotives of a particular type sequentially numbered:

Type	CBSCR No	GSR No	GSR Class	Inchicore Class
4-6-0T	4, 8, 11, 13-15, 19, 20	463-470	463	B4
4-6-0T	10	471	471	B5
0-6-0ST	6, 17	472	473	J24
0-6-0ST	12	474	474	J23
0-6-0ST	5/ 16	475/ 476	475	J21
4-4-0T	2/ 7	477/ 478	477	D18
4-4-2T	3/ 9/ 18	479-481	479	C6
2-4-0T	1	482	482	G6

The next block of numbers (483 to 491) was allocated to the locomotive stock acquired from the Waterford & Tramore and Cork & Macroom Direct Railways. Two named locomotives acquired from the Timoleague & Courtmacsherry Light Railway never carried numbers, nor were given GSR classifications. The numbers in brackets noted below were allotted purely for accounting purposes.

Rly Co	Type	Original No	GSR No	GSR Class	Inchicore Class
WTR	2-2-2WT	1/ 2	483/ 4	483	N1
WTR	0-4-2WT	3	485	485	L3
WTR	0-4-2T	4	486	486	L1
CMDR	2-4-0T	2 to 4	487-489	487	G5
CMDR	0-6-2T	5	490	490	I2
CMDR	2-4-2T	6	491	491	F5
TCLR	2-6-0T	*Argadeen*	(844)	–	K5
TCLR	0-4-2T	*St Molaga*	(845)	–	L6

Nos 530 to 668 were taken up by locomotives of the Midland Great Western Railway. This organisation differed from the other participants in the amalgamations in that it had a more or less orderly system of classification and apart from its solitary petrol powered rail car, no examples of the single locomotive class phenomenon.

Type	MGWR Class	MGWR No	GSR No	GSR Class	Inchic Class
0-6-0	W	141, 142	233, 234	234	J25
4-4-0	D/ Ds	1, 4-6, 2, 3	530-535	530	D16
4-4-0	C/ Cs	12, 20, 25, 26	536-539	536	D7
4-4-0	C/ C1	7-11	540-544	540	D6
4-4-0	A	127/9/5/ 6/8/4	545-550	545	D5
0-6-0T	E	106-117	551-562	551	J26
0-6-0	Ln	49-54	563-568	563	J16
0-6-0	L/ Lm	76, 78, 83-85 80, 135, 74, 86, 79, 64, 73, 82, 130-34 77, 136–139 75, 81	569-573 574-576 577-579 582-588 589-593 612, 613	573	J18
0-6-0	L	55-60, 61-63 65-72/140	594-602 603-611	594	J19
0-6-0T	P	100-103, 105	614-618	614	J10
0-6-0	H	96-99	619-622	619	J6
0-6-0	F/ Fa/ Fb	35, 87-95 39-41 36-38 42-48	623-632 633-635 636-638 639-645	623	J5
0-6-0	B	143-146	646-649	646	J2
2-4-0	K	14/6/8/9 28-30, 33/4 13/5/7, 21-24 27, 31/2	650-653 654-658 659-665 666-668	650	G2

The GSR introduced the following locomotives (plus Nos 901/ 501/ 502 as noted above in the GSWR list):

Type	GSR No	GSR Class	Inchicore Class
0-4-0T	1, 2 (later 280, 281)	280	M1
4-4-0	342-346	342	D4
2-6-0	372-391	372	K1
2-6-0	393-398	393	K1a
0-4-0ST	495	495	M3
0-6-2T	670-674	670	I3
0-6-0	700-704	700	J15a
0-6-0	710-719	710	J15b
4-6-0	800-802	800	B1a
2-6-2T	850	850	P1

Narrow gauge numbers and classifications

The principles of the GSR and Inchicore classifications were extended to the narrow gauge fleet, albeit in a different series. Locomotives retained the numbers applied by their pre-amalgamation owners but a letter suffix was added to denote their parent system, thus:

		Suffix
Cavan & Leitrim Railway	(CLR)	L
Cork Blackrock & Passage Railway	(CBPR)	P
Cork & Muskerry Light Railway	(CMLR)	K
Schull & Skibbereen Light Railway	(SSLR)	S
Tralee & Dingle Light Railway	(TDLR)	T
West Clare Railway	(WCR)	C

However, certain examples never received the allocated suffix, as noted in the respective sections

Apart from the 4-4-2T type, other four coupled wheel arrangements were also popular for passenger work. By 1925, the 2-4-0T was largely obsolete but Class 423 (G1) No 424 (ex-DSER No 9) was one of three hardy survivors that outlived the GSR Seen at Broadstone in 1952 with the saturated Belpaire Type T boiler which was fitted in 1934.
IRRS collection

in Chapter 8. Some narrow gauge locomotives were renumbered on transfer between sections. The CBPR 2-4-2Ts Nos 4P to 7P became Nos 10L to 13L, respectively, on transfer to the CLR in 1933. CMLR No 6K became 6S on transfer to the SSLR. An exception occurred with the transfer of TDLR locomotives: Nos 3T, 4T & 5T to the CLR; No 6T to the WCR and then on to the CLR; No 8T to the WCR. On transfer all TDLR locomotives retained their numbers and 'T' suffixes.

The resultant lowest number was used to create the relative class designation. Thus TDLR 2-6-0T No 1 became GSR No 1T of Class 1T. In addition, the disciplines of Inchicore Class system were adopted but with 'N' inserted between the letter and figure. Therefore TDLR No 1 also became part of Class KN2. If this abundance of classifications seems extravagant for a group of 43 rather diverse tank locomotives working on non-contiguous systems, at least they were spared inclusion in the 1925/ 1931 Load Class designations.

The fleet summary of the narrow gauge sections was thus:

Type	Owner	Orig Nos	GSR Nos	GSR Class	Inchicore Class
4-4-0T	CLR	1 to 8	1L-8L	1L	DN2
0-6-4T	CLR	9	9L	9L	HN1
2-4-2T	CBPR	4 to 7	4P-7P	4P	FN1
4-4-0T	CMLR	1, 2	1K, 2K	1K	DN6
0-4-4T	CMLR	5, 6	5K, 6K	5K	EN1
4-4-0T	CMLR	7	7K	7K	DN3
4-4-0T	CMLR	8	8K	8K	DN7
4-4-0T	CMLR	4	4K	4K	DN1
0-4-0T	SSLR	2	2S	2S	MN1
4-4-0T	SSLR	4	4S	4S	DN5
4-4-0T	SSLR	1, 3	1S	1S	DN4
2-6-0T	TDLR	1-3, 6, 8	1T-3T, 6T, 8T	1T	KN2
2-6-0T	TDLR	4, 7	4T, 7T	4T	KN1
2-6-2T	TDLR	5	5T	5T	PN2
4-6-0T	WCR	1	1C	1C	BN4
2-6-2T	WCR	2, 4, 8, 9	2C, 4C, 8C, 9C	2C	PN1
4-6-0T	WCR	3, 7	3C, 7C	3C	BN3
0-6-2T	WCR	5, 6	5C, 6C	5C	IN1
4-6-0T	WCR	10	10C	10C	BN1
4-6-0T	WCR	11	11C	11C	BN2

The MGWR Class E 0-6-0T turned up in many different locations in the guise of GSR Class 551 (J26). Usually employed in shunting or branch line work, No 561 of this popular class is seen piloting an ex-DSER Class 442 (J8) on main line duties, working wrong road in the Dublin area, in CIÉ days. *IRRS collection*

Liveries and names

The conditions of World War I induced unprecedented austerity in the locomotive liveries of several railway companies and the GSWR was no exception. What was unusual in the case of the GSWR, as perpetuated by the GSR, was retention of this livery without any effort to return to any semblance of pre-war gaiety. The mid-grey livery was applied eventually to virtually the entire fleet; this colour was all enveloping with the only areas above footplate level definitely remaining dull black being smokeboxes and cab roofs. It would seem that running plate surfaces were grey also although there were instances where these areas were painted black. Unfortunately, photographic evidence is hard to read as black and grey blend into the same shade under the layer of dirt that so often covered GSR engines.

The only relief to this dour display was the use of GSWR-style number plates cast in white metal and affixed to cab or tank sides. The numbers were in a font similar to that used by the GWR with the initials 'GSR' in small plain letters above the numbers. (Ex-GSWR locomotives also had the words 'INCHICORE WORKS' below the number, where appropriate). The numbers, letters and edge beading were picked out in red. This was the only relief to the general grey-black décor apart from the red buffer beams (buffer stocks were black). Numbers were also painted in gold/ yellow letters on the front buffer beams of tender locomotives (but not on tender buffer beams), and front and rear on tank locomotives. Buffer beam numbers were applied on the opposite side of the coupling hook to that on which the vacuum pipe was mounted

This livery style continued unchanged until 1933 when No 670 was introduced to traffic with numbers in plain white painted figures on the tank sides. This was the first Inchicore-built locomotive to appear without a cast number plate and anticipated a style that was applied across the fleet in CIÉ days.

Rather more positive was the appearance in 1939 of No 800 (with cast bronze name and number plates) in a lined deep rich green livery (details are provided in Chapter 10). This style was not extended beyond the 800 Class under the GSR regime but green of a slightly darker shade, lined black and white, did appear on some locomotives specifically assigned to passenger duties in the late 1940s.

The GSWR had not been enthusiastic about naming its locomotives. The four members of 4-4-0 Class 301 were named when built in 1900 but they survived in this condition only until 1904. Also, locomotives that had been named on the WLWR soon lost their names after takeover of that company.

At the amalgamation, there were seven named locomotives - 4-4-0 No 341 *Sir William Goulding* (the GSWR's last chairman who continued in this role with the GSR), plus unnumbered locomotives *Sprite* (0-4-4T), *Sambo* (0-4-2ST), *Jumbo* (0-6-4T), *Fairy* (0-4-2T), *Erin* (0-6-0ST), and *Imp* (0-4-0T). After the amalgamation, the last mentioned of this group was joined by his brother who had been numbered but unnamed on the DSER, and was now unnumbered by the GSR but named *Elf*. A further machine, a four wheeled 'locomotive' built specially to work the coal gantry at Cork and named *Pat* (very likely unofficially) was always treated as plant.

When originally built by the South Eastern & Chatham Railway, the type that was to become known as the Woolwich Mogul was intended to be goods locomotive. Both in Ireland and Britain, they soon took on a much broader range of duties but Class 372 (K1) No 374 seen here is on a type of work for which the class was originally conceived, in this case the 4.00 pm Kingsbridge-Cork goods in August 1946.

JM Robbins

The 2-4-2T with its greater fuel capacity supplanted the 2-4-0T Class 428 (F2) No 432 started life as a 2-4-0T in 1886 and was given greater fuel capacity through rebuilding as a 2-4-2T in 1910. In a further rebuilding in 1939, it received a saturated Belpaire Type T boiler in which condition it was photographed at Rocksavage, Cork in 1954. The GSR style number plates are still in place; No 432 remained in service for another three years.

IRRS collection

Right: A later example of the 2-4-2T, Class 434 (F1) No 436 (formerly DSER No 27) is seen at Bray coaling plant. This locomotive was built with a Belpaire boiler but in 1926 was fitted with a saturated Class 101 4' 4" boiler as shown, which it retained until withdrawal as the last of its class in 1953.

D Murray

Below right: The 0-4-4Ts of the GSWR had a distinctly antique appearance but not so the Robinson version of this wheel arrangement. Ex-WLWR No 27 started life as one of a class of four 0-4-2's in 1876. As the sole survivor of that class, it was rebuilt in 1895 as an 0-4-4T It later became GSR Class 279 (E1) No 279 and despite its uniqueness, the GSR saw fit to rebuild it with larger cylinders and heating surfaces in 1927. It is seen here close to the end of its career at Broadstone, having lost none of its Robinson elegance.

IRRS collection

In contrast, the MGWR had been keen on locomotive names with their 0-6-0 Class F (GSR Class 623/ J5) introduced 1921-24 being unique in never being so adorned. The names used were an eclectic and attractive grouping of Irish place names, ships, animals, insects, planetary bodies, and classical connotations. A few might have been politically offensive in a new nation state but their wholesale removal in the GSR spirit of austerity must have caused regret. MGWR names were generally removed concurrent with the application of GSR numbers and livery. This was a process that took several years and the dates of livery changes are recorded in individual class summaries.

The DSER also applied names to most of its locomotive fleet, in this case relying mainly on Irish saints and place names plus a couple of references to royalty, but almost all of these names had been removed before the amalgamation. The CBSCR, WTR and CMDR did not believe in naming their locomotives whereas the entire fleet of Timoleague & Courtmacsherry Light Railway (two locomotives) carried names (which were retained) with local connotations, but no numbers.

On the narrow gauge sections, the fleets of Cavan & Leitrim, Cork & Muskerry, Schull & Skibbereen, and the West Clare were all named, and most were removed in parallel with the broad gauge policy. Exceptions were ex-CLR No 1 *Isabel*, and ex-SSLR Nos 1 *Gabriel* and 3S *Kent* which retained their names until withdrawal. A further, rather surprising, exception was ex-CLR No 9 *King Edward* which still carried its name at withdrawal in 1934, although this late survival might be explained by this locomotive's minimal use.

The austere naming policy of the GSWR was continued by the GSR so far as main line locomotives were concerned and admitted retention only of No 341 *Sir William Goulding*. This could well have been purposely in memory of Sir William, who died in office as Chairman on 12 July 1925. Also, this locomotive might still have been in GSWR livery when withdrawn in 1928 so that the question of name removal à la MGWR engines might not by then have arisen.

At the other end of the power scale, the GSR sustained the perverse policy of the GSWR by leaving some of its smallest locomotives bereft of numbers while adorning them with names. Within what was an unimaginative tradition, the names *Elf*, *Imp*, *Fairy* and *Sprite* were cheeky exceptions with a nice touch of humour.

Above: After withdrawal in 1949, GSR Class 530 (D16) No 532 worked for another eight years, albeit in the humble task of boiler wash out duties at Broadstone. Seen here still at work in March 1957, and informally named 'Mayflower' on the bufferless buffer-beam. *Author' collection*

Below: Unsuitable work for a superheated express 4-4-0. A variety of motive power was used on the ex-DSER section and in this case, Class 536 (D7) No 539 was found at Bray on a two coach suburban service. Formerly MGWR Class Cs No 26, the performance of this locomotive was improved by a reduction in cylinder size (1917) and by fitting of a superheater within the original boiler (1924). Further boiler changes involving Belpaire fireboxes were to follow in 1935 and 1939. *JM Robbins*

Against this sparse background, the announcement that the lined green livery of the Class 800 was to be complemented by a truly inspired selection of names must have been widely welcomed. No 800 was first given nameplates depicting *Maeve* in Roman Script. This was soon changed to replacements using Old Irish Script, the Roman equivalent of which is *Maedhbh*. Nos 801 and 802 also received nameplates in the same style; these names would appear as *Maca* and *Tailte* if 'converted' to Roman script although a more direct translation yields English equivalents of *Macha* and *Tailtiu*. An explanation of these names in Celtic mythology is provided in Appendix J

Some sources have speculated about other names that might have been used if more of Class 800 had been built. As if to make up for past neglect of locomotive names, particular care was taken in the design of the nameplates themselves. The combination of bronze lettering using the classic characters and the blue background was most distinctive against the green of the boiler. With justification these nameplates have been considered by many as among the most beautiful ever to grace a steam locomotive.

Despite being intended for express passenger trains, later in their careers Class 400 (B2) did find work on goods duties. No 405, which was fitted with a Type K boiler in 1937 is seen passing Clondalkin on a down evening goods in 1954, a year before withdrawal. The tender is one of the two (Type F – authors' classification) introduced to traffic with locomotives Nos 501 and 502.

IRRS collection

Above: The last design for Dublin-Cork services was GSR Class 800 (B1a). No 802 *Tailte* is passing Inchicore on a down express in CIÉ days.

IRRS collection

Left: GSR Class 800 (B1a) No 801 *Macha* coasts through Clondalkin with the up Mail. The van immediately behind the engine contains the mails from the Kerry road and would have been added in the 'big shunt' at Mallow. That van and the next (the Cork mails van) were then worked round to the harbour pier at Dun Laoghaire.

IRRS collection

Left: Unfortunately, there are few good photographs of the last and largest GSWR 4-4-0 at work. GSR Class 341 (D1) No 341 *Sir William Goulding* at Mountrath.

Kelland collection

Below: The 4-4-0 classes remained on main line duties well in to the autumn of their careers. GSR Class 310 (D10) No 313 was piloting Class 402 (B2a) No 401 on 'The Enterprise' on departure from Dublin Amiens Street for Cork in August 1953.

IRRS collection

Notes on motive power details

The following format has been adopted in the layout of information on motive power units.

Chapters 4 to 7 describe the locomotives of the constituent companies on a type-by-type basis in the numerical order of the relevant GSR class designation. Individual locomotives are therefore listed and described in broadly numerical order, although in several instances there were cases of numbering out-of-sequence.

Chapter 8 covers the locomotives of the narrow gauge companies, appearing on a pre-amalgamation company-by-company basis, listed in alphabetical order. The locomotives are set out in chronological order of introduction to service within each company section.

Chapters 9 and 10 describe each class in the chronological order of introduction to service.

To help the cross-referencing of individual steam locomotive numbers against relative GSR or Inchicore class designations, the following keys appear at the end of this section:

Key 1: Locomotive No → GSR Class → Inchicore Class

Key 2: Inchicore Class → GSR Class → Locomotive No

Chapter 12 reviews motive power units other than conventional steam locomotives in sections in the order of:

- steam rail motors
- petrol-engined inspection units and rail cars
- battery electric trains.

Individual types within each section appear in the chronological order of introduction.

Leading dimensions, quoted in each Class section, are those in place at the time of the amalgamation, or at the time of construction if after 1 January 1925. These dimensions have been checked against locomotive diagrams, GSR locomotive records and the archives of RN Clements. Comparison with later diagrams issued by the GSR sometimes indicates variations in the dimensions of heating surfaces, which are usually greater in the later record. Most of these differences are relatively minor and can usually be attributed to alternative methods of measurement (eg internal as opposed to the external diameters of tubes). This certainly appears the case with ex-DSER locomotives. Reference should also be made to the **Appendix C** concerning boiler dimensions.

If all members of a constituent company class were rebuilt prior to absorption by the GSR, then the 'original' dimensions recorded are those existing as at 1 January 1925; ie dimensions when new are excluded.

Some classes were the subject of rebuilding programmes that were in process but incomplete on formation of the GSR. In such cases, pre-amalgamation dimensions are included for those locomotives still to be rebuilt plus details of all subsequent rebuildings. In a few instances, rebuildings took place soon after amalgamation and dimensions as at 1 January 1925 plus those in subsequent rebuildings are recorded eg DSER No 69 (GSR *Imp*), which was converted from a 2-4-0T to an 0-4-0T early in 1925, is in this category.

Definition of 'rebuild' is open to debate with some MGWR locomotives, due to that company's accounting practices. An example is Class H Nos 96-99 (later GSR Class 619) which were nominally new locomotives built 1906 to 1908 but used the frames and other parts of earlier engines. By the criterion of frame retention they would normally be considered rebuilds. On the other hand, it was practice on occasion to fund a completely new replacement locomotive out of revenue and record it as a rebuild.

With rebuildings or other modifications, only changed dimensions are recorded. Thus if locomotives received boiler modifications only, then the revised heating surfaces are recorded but as these dimensions would not have effected the nominal tractive effort, the latter dimension is not repeated.

Tractive effort for two-cylinder locomotives is expressed in lbs and calculated on the standard formula ie 85% of boiler pressure *multiplied* by the square of the cylinder diameter in inches *multiplied* by the cylinder stroke in inches *divided* by the driving wheel diameter in inches. The result of that sum has been *multiplied by two* to correct for four cylinder engines, and *divided by 0.667* to correct for three cylinder engines. Tractive efforts thus calculated have been rounded to the nearest 10 lbs.

Locomotive weights are quoted in working order, where known (but see comments below); wheel bases are recorded from the front axle of the locomotive; tube and superheater surfaces are based on the external diameters; boiler diameters are based on external dimensions excluding lagging etc; firebox and grate dimensions are also calculated on external dimensions but including cladding. Lengths have been taken from relevant diagrams. Where diagrams have not been traced, this dimension has been estimated by reference to scale drawings from other sources. 'Length' is subject to differing interpretation depending on company of origin:

Ex-GSWR and ex-DSER locomotives: The distance between the front buffer face and the rear face of the frames on tender locomotives, and from front buffer face to rear buffer face on tank locomotives.

Ex-CBSCR and minor companies' locomotives: The distance between the front and rear buffer face.

Ex-MGWR locomotives: The distance between front buffer face and the rear edge of the tender buffing gear which typically stood nine inches proud of the locomotive frame ends (except for MGWR class W/ GSR Class 234 where the measurement is to the rear of the locomotive frames) . With the two tank engine classes, length was from the front buffer face to rear buffer face.

Narrow gauge locomotives: The estimated distance (where known) between front and rear buffer beam faces.

The introduction of the 4-6-0 fleet by the GSWR, and its improvement and expansion by the GSR was focused on Dublin-Cork express services. Readily identifiable by its unique flush footplate, class favourite No 402 of Class 402 (B2a) is seen at Clondalkin with an express whose consist has been augmented with some vintage stock.

IRRS collection

Left: The most important Dublin-Cork services were the mail trains, in this case in the hands of Class 402 (B2a) No 406. This locomotive was one of two members of Class 400 to be fitted with Caprotti valve gear when rebuilt in 1930 and the only one to retain this equipment until withdrawal – in 1957.

IRRS collection

Transitional locomotives: The distance between front buffer face and the rear face of the frames.

GSR locomotives: The distance between front buffer face and the rear end of the frames on tender locomotives and from front buffer face to rear buffer face on tank locomotives.

In many cases, different 'weights' are recorded for the same type or class, with later notations usually being progressively heavier. The convention has been adopted of quoting the heaviest recorded weight for each version/ condition of a class. Wherever practicable, this has been reconciled with the highest quoted axle loading. Anomalies have been identified with some reported weights of narrow gauge locomotives in Inchicore records. Those which seem unrealistically high have been ignored in favour of more logical weights recorded in other sources.

For tender locomotives, the coal and water capacities are those provided for each class when new. Changes of tender type were quite common. While the recorded information in this area is not complete, the general pattern of tender changes is described in Chapter 11.

Care is needed in interpretation of withdrawal dates which are recorded by year only. All withdrawal dates appearing in the class descriptions and the relevant appendices have been taken from official company records and returns. There are cases where actual year of withdrawal differed from the official year of withdrawal. Five examples illustrate the scope for confusion on this topic:

(i) DSER No 44 was officially withdrawn in 1925 with the rest of its class. It was never allocated a GSR number or classification but actually remained in ordinary revenue-earning service until 1927.

(ii) MGWR No 87A was never allocated a GSR number but actually continued in service until October 1925.

(iii) Ex-CBSCR (GSR Class 471/ B5) No 471 stood out-of-service for several years before it was formally withdrawn.

(iv) Ex-MGWR Class B (GSR Class 646/ J2) No 649 was actually taken out of service in 1933 and officially withdrawn the following year but nominally returned to stock in 1935 before final withdrawal in 1939.

(v) Ex-GSWR Class 301 (GSR Class D11) No 301 was withdrawn and apparently derelict from mid-1960. It was resurrected for work in March 1961 on duties between Ennis and Limerick which route was seriously flooded (where diesel locomotives could not operate). It then worked ordinary services for a period in the Dublin area.

1948 assessment

In connection with concerns over the backlog of repairs and the high level of boiler failures, a summary review of the broad gauge fleet was drawn up, apparently by the CIÉ Running Department, of the performance and effectiveness of each class. Although falling outside the specific GSR period, these review comments are quoted verbatim, including apparent grammatical and factual errors, as being useful in providing a comparative assessment of each class, comparatively late in the steam era.

Key 1

Loco No	GSR class	Inchicore class
1	52	D17
2	2	D19
3, 4	52	D17
5 to 8	2	D19
9	52	D17
10	2	D19
11, 12	52	D17
13	2	D19
14	52	D17
15	2	D19
16	52	D17
17	vacant	
18	52	D17
19	vacant	
20	52	D17
21, 22	21	G4
23 to 25	vacant	
26	21	G4
27	27	C4
28, 29	vacant	
30 to 32	27	C4
33 to 36	33	F6
37, 38	37	C7
39	vacant	
40	47	E3
41, 42	33	F6
43 to 46	2	D19
47 to 49	47	E3
50	vacant	
51	47	E3
52 to 59	52	D17
60 to 65	60	D13/ D14
66 to 68	21	G4
69	vacant	
70	47	E3
71	vacant	
72 to 78	47	E3
79	vacant	
80, 81	47	E3
82	vacant	
83	47	E3
84	vacant	
85 to 89	60	D13/ D14
90	90	J30
91	91	J29
92	92	H2
93 to 96	60	D13/ D14
97, 98	52	D17

Loco No	GSR class	Inchicore class
249 to 252	351	J9
253 to 256	101	J15
257 to 264	257	J4
265, 266	vacant	
267	267	F4
268	vacant	
269 to 271	269	C5
272, 273	vacant	
274	269	C5
275	vacant	
276	276	G3
277 to 278	vacant	
279	279	E1
280 to 281*	280	M1
282 to 289	vacant	
290 to 291	276	G3
292	vacant	
293	276	G3
294	vacant	
295	295	E2
296 to 298	296	D15
299	299	J28
(300) Erin	*300*	J27
301 to 304	301	D11
305 to 308	305	D12
309 to 314	309	D10/ D3
315, 316	vacant	
317 to 320	37	C7
321 to 332	321/ 332	D2/ D3/ D4
333 to 340	333/ 338	D2/ D3/ D4/ D4a
341	341	D1
342 to 346	342	D4
347 to 350	vacant	
351 to 354	351	J9
355 to 361	355	K3
362 to 367	362	B3
368 to 371	368	K4
372 to 391	372	K1
392	vacant	
393 to 398	393	K1a
399	vacant	
400 to 409	400	B2/ B2a
410 (temporary)	372	K1
411 to 421	vacant	
422	422	G7
423 to 426	423	G1
427	427	F3
428 to 433	428	F2

Loco No	GSR class	Inchicore class
496 to 499	vacant	
500 to 502	500	B1
503 to 529	vacant	
530 to 535	530	D16
536 to 539	536	D7
540 to 544	540	D6
545 to 550	545	D5
551 to 562	551	J26
563 to 566	563	J16
567	563 later 567	J16
568	563	J16
569 to 579	573	J18
580, 581	vacant	
582 to 593	573	J18
594 to 611	594	J19
612, 613	573	J19 later J18
614 to 618	614	J10
619 to 622	619	J6
623 to 645	623	J5
646 to 649	646	J2
650 to 668	650	G2
669	vacant	
670 to 674	670	I3
675 to 699	vacant	
700 to 704	700	J15a
705 to 709	vacant	
710 to 719	710	J15b
720 to 799	vacant	
800 to 802	800	B1a
803 to 840	vacant	
*841** Jumbo*	Jumbo	J13
*842** Sambo*	Sambo	L2
843	vacant	
*844** Argadeen*	n/a	K5
*845** St. Molaga*	n/a	L6
846 to 849	vacant	
850	850	P1
851 to 899	vacant	
900 to 901	900	A1
Unnumbered:		
Imp/ Elf	Imp	M1 later M2
Fairy	Sprite	L4
Sprite	Sprite	L5 later L4

Loco No	GSR class	Inchicore class
99	99 later 90	J30
100	100 later 90	J30
101 to 188	101	J15
189	vacant	
190 to 200	101	J15
201, 202	201	J11
203		H1
204	204	J12
205, 206	203	H1
207 to 210	201	J11
211, 212	211	J3
213, 214	213	I1
215, 216	vacant	
217 to 220	201	J11
221	vacant	
222	222	J25
223	101	J15
224 to 227	vacant	
228	228	not allocated
229	101	J15
230, 231	vacant	
232	101	J15
233, 234	234	J17
235, 236	235	J22
237 to 239	222	J25
240 to 243	101	J15
244 to 248	vacant	

Loco No	GSR class	Inchicore class
434 to 439	434	F1
440	440	J20
441	441	J14
442 to 446	442	J8
447	447	J7
448, 449	448	J1
450 to 453	450	D9
454	450/ 454	D8
455 to 457	455	C2
458 to 460	458	C3
461, 462	461	K2
463 to 470	463	B4
471	471	B5
472, 473	472	J24
474	474	J23
475, 476	475	J21
477, 478	477	D18
479 to 481	479	C6
482	482	G6
483, 484	483	N1
485	485	L3
486	486	L1
487 to 489	487	G5
490	490	I2
491	491	F5
492 to 494	vacant	
495	495	M3

* Sentinel Nos 280 & 281 numbered 1 & 2 for short period in 1927

Narrow Gauge Loco No	GSR class	Inchicore class
1C	1C	BN4
2C	2C	PN1
3C	3C	BN3
4C	2C	PN1
5C, 6C	5C	IN1
7C	3C	BN3
8C, 9C	2C	PN1
10C	10C	BN1
11C	11C	BN2
1K, 2K	1K	DN6
4K	4K	DN1
5K (later 6S)	5K 6K(later 6S)	EN1
7K	7K	DN3
8K	8K	DN7
1L to 8L	1L	DN2
9L	9L	HN1
4P to 7P (later 10L to 13L)	4P (later 10L)	FN1
1S	1S	DN4
2S	2S	MN1
3S	1S	DN4
4S	4S	DN5
1T to 3T	1T	KN2
4T	4T	KN1
5T	5T	PN2
6T	1T	KN2
7T	4T	KN1
8T	1T	KN2

NB Not all narrow gauge locos carried the suffix

** for accounting purposes

Key 2

Inchicore class	GSR class	Loco No
A1	900	900 901
B1	500	500 to 502
B1a	800	800 to 802
B2	400	400 to 409
B2a	402	401/ 402/ 406 (from 1927/ 1930)
B3	362	362 to 367
B4	463	463 to 470
B5	471	471
C2	455	455 to 457
C3	458	458 to 460
C4	27	27, 30 to 32
C5	269	269 to 271/ 274
C6	479	479 to 481
C7	37	37 to 38/ 317 to 320
D1	341	341
D2/ D3/ D4/ D4a	333	333 to 340
D2/ D3/ D4	321	321 to 332
D4	342	342 to 346
D5	545	545 to 550

Inchicore class	GSR class	Loco No
D6	540	540 to 544
D7	536	536 to 539
D8	454	454
D9	450	450 to 453
D10/ D3	309/ 321	309 to 314
D11	301	301 to 304
D12	305	305 to 308
D13/ D14	60	60 to 65/ 85 to 89/ 93 to 96
D15	296	296 to 298
D16	530	530 to 535
D17	52	1/ 3/ 4/ 9/ 11/ 12/ 14/ 16/ 18/ 20/ 52 to 59/ 97/ 98
D18	477	477 478
D19	2	2/ 5 to 8/ 10/ 13/ 15/ 43 to 46
E1	279	279
E2	295	295
E3	47	40/ 47 to 49/ 51/ 70/ 72 to 78/ 80/ 81 /83
F1	434	434 to 439

Inchicore class	GSR class	Loco No
F2	428	428 to 433
F3	427	427
F4	267	267
F5	491	491
F6	33	33 to 36/ 41 to 42
G1	423	423 to 426
G2	650	650 to 668
G4	21	21 to 22/ 26/ 66 to 68
G3	276	276/ 290/ 291/ 293
G5	487	487 to 489
G6	482	482
G7	422	422
H1	203	203/ 205/ 206
H2	92	92
I1	213	213 to 214
I2	490	490
I3	670	670 to 674
J1	448	448/ 449
J2	646	646 to 649
J3	211	211 to 212
J4	257	257 to 264
J5	623	623 to 645
J6	619	619 to 622
J7	447	447
J8	442	442 to 446
J9	351	249 to 252/ 351 to 354
J10	614	614 to 618
J11	201	201/ 202/ 207 to 210/ 217 to 220
J12	204	204
J13	n/a	*Jumbo*
J14	441	441
J15	101	101 to 188/ 190 to 200/ 223/ 229/ 232/ 240 to 243/ 253 to 256
J15a	700	700 to 704
J15b	710	710 to 719
J16	563 (later 567)	563 to 568
J17	234	233 to 234
J18	573	569 to 579/ 582 to 593/ 612/ 613
J19	594	594 to 611
J20	440	440
J21	475	475 to 476
J22	235	235/ 236
J23	474	474
J24	472	472/ 473
J25	222	222/ 237 to 239
J26	551	551 to 562
J27	n/a	*Erin*
J28	299	299
J29	91	91
J30	90	90/ 99/ 100
K1	372	372 to 391
K1a	393	393 to 398
K2	461	461 462
K3	355	355 to 361
K4	368	368 to 371
K5	n/a	*Argadeen*
L1	486	486
L2	n/a	*Sambo*
L3	485	485
L4	n/a	*Sprite*
L5		*Fairy*
L6	n/a	*St. Molaga*
M1 Sentinel	280	280 281
M1 (later M2)	n/a	*Elf/ Imp*
M3	495	495
N1	483	483/ 484
P1	850	850
Not allocated	228	228

Narrow Gauge Locomotives

Inchicore class	GSR class	Loco No No
BN1	10C	10C
BN2	11C	11C
BN3	3C	3C/ 7C
BN4	1C	1C
DN1	4K	4K
DN2	1L	1L to 8L
DN3	7K	7K
DN4	1S	1S 3S
DN5	4S	4S
DN6	1K 2K	1K
DN7	8K	8K
EN1	5K 6K (later 6S)	5K (later 6S)
FN1	4P (later 10L)	4P to 7P (later 10L to 13L)
HN1	9L	9L
IN1	5C	5C, 6C
KN1	4T	4T/ 7T
KN2	1T	1T to 3T/ 6T/ 8T
MN1	2S	2S
PN1	2C	2C/ 4C/ 8C/ 9C
PN2	5T	5T

NB Not all narrow gauge locomotives carried the suffix

Chapter 4
Locomotives of the Great Southern and Western Railway

By far the largest constituent company in terms of size of locomotive and rolling stock fleets, and of route mileage, the Great Southern & Western Railway was the 'senior' partner at the amalgamation. GSWR locomotives retained their numbers and classifications, and the works at Inchicore became the engineering headquarters for the Great Southern Railways, an importance enhanced with the closure of the ex-Midland Great Western Railway works at the Broadstone in 1933.

As at 1 January 1925 the ex-GSWR fleet comprised 327 locomotives, together with two 4-6-0s of Class 500 under construction:

Type	No of classes	No of locomotives	Built since 1900	Rebuilt since 1900
4–6–0	3	17	17	–
2–6–0	2	11	11	–
4–4–0	10	85	31	4
2–4–0	2	10	–	–
0–6–0	6	134	30	96
4–8–0T	1	2	2	–
0–6–4T	2	4	–	–
0–6–2T	1	2	–	2
0–6–0T	7	18	–	5
4–4–2T	3	14	–	8
2–4–2T	2	7	–	–
0–4–4T	3	18	–	–
0–4–2T	3	3	1	–
0–4–0T	2	2	–	–
Total	**47**	**327**	**92**	**115**

With the exception of Class 101 (J15) which numbered 110 locomotives, the fleet was a proliferation of classes containing ten members or less. Many dated from the 19th century, as it had been customary to rebuild rather than replace existing locomotives. This contributed to a strong sense of lineage and consistency in styling. The company made extensive use of 4-4-0s for main line and secondary passenger services, a wheel arrangement that McDonnell introduced to Ireland in 1877 as an advance on the preceding 2-4-0 type. Between then and 1891, his successors (Aspinall and Ivatt) added more 4-4-0s by introducing classes of progressively larger dimensions but sharing a strong familial resemblance. All the 4-4-0s of this vintage survived into GSR stock but by 1925, the few remaining 2-4-0s were basically obsolete, although one ex-Waterford Limerick & Western Railway example survived until 1959.

There were certain distinguishing features with Inchicore-built locomotives from this period that outlived the GSR. Cabs had large rectangular spectacle plates and, with tender locomotives, the amount of weather protection that they afforded crews was meagre. The profile of the forward part of the side sheeting on tank locomotive cabs followed that on tender engines but the roof curved downwards at the rear to form the backplate. The rear half of the cab had no side sheeting at all.

Running plates were curved upwards to provide clearance for coupling rod cranks. The most distinctive feature, though, was the archaic double-doored smokebox front which was usually set vertically but in several cases sloped backwards. This feature was unique to the GSWR and could not have been efficient as it would have made maintenance of an air-tight seal difficult. Nonetheless, some of these smokeboxes survived until quite late. No dates have been traced for their replacement on individual locomotives but it may be assumed that this coincided with the first boiler rebuild, at least in GSR days. Also, there were cases of double-doored smokebox fronts appearing on a few ex-Dublin & South Eastern Railway locomotives following overhaul at Inchicore.

A more modern style of 4-4-0 type was inaugurated by Coey in 1900 and a pattern of progressive enlargements followed. Between then and 1906, 26 4-4-0s appeared in four separate classes and 22 survived into the 1950s. They had been intended as express locomotives but were relegated to secondary duties upon the arrival of the 2-6-0s and 4-6-0s in the 1920s. The standard express driving wheel diameter of 6' 7" was hardly suitable for such work but their retention was possible because of the comparatively light trains on which they were mainly, but not exclusively, used in later years. Coey introduced a further eight 4-4-0s in 1907-8, fitted with 5' 8½" driving wheels which made them more practical for mixed traffic work.

Maunsell, as Coey's successor, continued in this vein, but the limits of power and weight that could be encompassed satisfactorily within the 4-4-0 format were being reached. Inchicore started to introduce tapered boilers and the commensurate weight increases were not much to the liking of the Civil Engineer. To compensate, the frames of some of the later Coey 4-4-0s were lighter than desirable, necessitating a re-framing programme within 15-20 years of introduction. The Coey/Maunsell No 341, the GSWR's last and largest 4-4-0, suffered no such constructional defects but certainly aroused the Civil Engineer's suspicion.

While there are grounds for believing that four-coupled locomotives could have handled top-link GSWR services for some time to come, the case for something larger was becoming stronger by the First World War. Watson, Maunsell's successor, by-passed consideration of a 4-4-2 and went a step further in pursuit of larger locomotives. The mixed fortunes of the two 4-6-0 types that resulted from this policy are related in Chapter 9 as their modifications and most of their working lives form an integral part of GSR locomotive history.

GSWR goods locomotives were mainly traditional 0-6-0s, the oldest of which at the amalgamation were of Class 101 (J15). This was by far the most numerous class of Irish steam locomotive, and their small size and modest axle-loading made them well suited for branch line work. However, this was an extraordinarily versatile, reliable and good-steaming example of the 0-6-0 type. Throughout its long working life to the virtual end of steam, it was considered a standard type – in itself a world record. The inherently sound qualities of the Class 101 made it a genuine mixed-traffic machine, including pilot work on express passenger trains.

Apart from some 0-6-0s acquired from the Waterford, Limerick & Western Railway, Class 101 covered virtually all freight requirements until the 1900s, when some larger designs were introduced. Two types of 0-6-0, Class 351 and 257 with eight locomotives each, were introduced in 1903 and in 1913 respectively. They were more modern examples of the genre and the later type was particularly competent. Also in 1903, the company sought yet larger designs of goods locomotive and the results were mixed. A large 0-6-0 type met with axle loading and weight distribution problems which were eventually solved by provision of a pony truck. Before this solution emerged, an alternative tactic was attempted with Ireland's first 4-6-0, which also had inside cylinders, but this was not successful. These efforts, and indeed the later GSR attempts to introduce new 0-6-0s, did nothing to dislodge Class 101 from its pre-eminence.

The relatively long distances covered by many of the GSWR secondary services and the poor water quality at many stations militated against employment of tank locomotives. Where used for branch and secondary passenger services, they were mainly of the 2-4-2T, 4-4-2T and 0-4-4T wheel arrangements, some of which enjoyed long working lives. They were augmented by a few similar types acquired from the WLWR.

Six-coupled tanks were never common and the GSWR's examples were mainly used for shunting and specialised duties. The small GSWR tank locomotives had a peculiar fascination, with a distinctly vintage flavour reflecting their 19th century origins. The GSWR's penultimate tank was an 0-4-2ST built as late as 1914 for specialised shunting duties at Inchicore, apparently out of spare parts. Finally, there was Watson's 4-8-0 heavy shunting tank whose length and bulk were decidedly 'un-Irish', as was its short operating life.

Despite the proliferation of types and wheel arrangements, there was significant standardisation of leading dimensions:

Driving wheel diameters:	**Used by classes:**
4' 6½"	201, 203, 204, 211, 213, 900
5' 1¾"	101, 257, 351, 355, 362, 368
5' 8½"	2, 21, 27, 33, 37, 47, 333, 338, 500
6' 7"	60, 301, 305, 309, 310, 321, 341, 400
Bogie/ pony/ radial/ trailing wheel diameters:	
3' 0"	2, 27, 37, 52, 60, 333, 338, 341, 355, 362, 368, 400, 500, 900
3' 6"	301, 305, 309, 310, 321
3' 9"	27, 33, 47, 203, 213

With respect to cylinder dimensions, the 16" x 20" size was shared by five classes, the 18" x 24" size by five, and the 18" x 26" by seven.

Nevertheless, much of the fleet at the amalgamation retained many features of 19th century practice. Superheating had been applied only to Classes 257, 341, 400 & 500, the only locomotives equipped with piston valves. Tapered boilers had appeared with three classes of larger 4-4-0s but this feature was not perpetuated.

In early GSR days, financial constraints limited improvements mainly to the fitting of new boilers, usually with Belpaire fireboxes. The Bazin doctrine had held that the superheating of smaller or older locomotives was financially unjustifiable. Accordingly in the period before his retirement, there was a delay of about four years before superheating became widespread. Thereafter, many ex-GSWR locomotives were superheated but the substitution of piston valves for slide valves was limited.

In the late 19th century, the GSWR livery was quite exotic with locomotives painted in olive green lined red/ yellow/ red with panels edged in black. Shortly after 1900, Coey changed the livery to overall black, lined white and red, and this continued until World War One. With the exigencies of wartime conditions, the austerity livery of overall grey was introduced. This has been described as a mid-grey with a bluish tinge which looks smart on models and must have appeared handsome on the real thing when freshly painted. Unfortunately, it is an excellent colour for camouflaging dirt, and would not have encouraged efforts to maintain clean locomotives.

As described in Chapter 3, the grey livery was relieved by cab side cast white metal number plates. The number font was similar to that used on GWR locomotives, with the initials 'GSWR' above and 'INCHICORE WORKS' below. The background was black with the numbers, letters and edge beading burnished. In later GSR days, these features were often painted vermilion.

Dramatis personae

The trait for competent engineers to travel extensively in their work was exemplified by **Alexander McDonnell**. Born in Dublin in 1829, he gained an MA at Trinity College before starting in his profession as a pupil of Charles Liddell on railway building in England and Wales. At the age of 28 he became Locomotive Superintendent of the Newport, Abergavenny & Hereford Railway. Not long after that concern became part of the West Midland Railway, he moved in 1862 to Eastern Europe to establish the locomotive department of the Danube & Black Sea Railway before moving to Inchicore in 1864 as Locomotive Engineer. Shortly after his arrival in Ireland, changes in management led to his appointment as Locomotive Superintendent. McDonnell was an excellent organiser and he is credited with the modernisation of Inchicore Works, improvement in production methods, and reduction in operating costs. In rationalising the heterogeneous GSWR locomotive fleet, he was able to reduce waste by retaining parts from obsolete machines for re-use.

Although not a noted locomotive designer, McDonnell is remembered for introducing the swing-link bogies from the USA to the British Isles, and also as being responsible for introduction of Class 101. The precise origins of this class are uncertain. Some sources note its similarity to the contemporary Dx Class 0-6-0 of the London & North Western Railway but the weight of authority favours the view that it was a Beyer Peacock creation. What is certain is that McDonnell identified the need for a small, versatile locomotive with a broad operational capacity and he sponsored an excellent solution.

McDonnell left Inchicore for the North Eastern Railway in 1883, to be succeeded by **JAF Aspinall** (later Sir John Aspinall). During his short period in office, Aspinall was responsible for the introduction of three notable classes – the 4-4-0 Classes 52 and 60, and the 0-4-4T Class 47. These types had low axle loadings and were employed on a wide range of duties. Construction continued after his departure for the Lancashire & Yorkshire Railway in 1886 and like so many Irish designs of the late 19th century, they enjoyed a long working life.

The soundness of Aspinall's work meant that the only fresh designs introduced by his successor, **HA Ivatt**, were tank locomotives, principally 0-6-0T Class 207, 2-4-2T Class 33, and 4-4-2T Class 37. Ivatt stayed at Inchicore for ten years before moving to the English GNR in 1896 where his talents as a designer were to flower.

At around this time, Inchicore was developing an enviable reputation as a well-run and efficient institution. This was largely the achievement of **Robert Coey** who succeeded Ivatt and who built a competent team that included Robert Maunsell as Works Manager, EE Joynt as Chief Draughtsman, and HW Crosthwait as Running Superintendent. The Coey years were marked by the introduction of larger and more modern designs for both passenger traffic (4-4-0 Classes 301, 305, 309, 321 and 333) and goods traffic (2-6-0 Classes 355 and 368, and 4-6-0 Class 362).

In 1901, the formation of the GSWR was completed with the acquisition of the Waterford Limerick & Western Railway. In 1884, when **JG Robinson** was recruited from Swindon as Assistant Locomotive Superintendent, this company had a modest fleet of ageing locomotives to work 280 route miles of track. Four years later, he became Locomotive Superintendent and over the next twelve years managed the expansion and rejuvenation of the WLWR fleet. Some 33 new engines were introduced in twelve classes and with no fewer than nine different wheel arrangements. Robinson was responsible for all ex-WLWR locomotives that survived into GSR stock except for one 60-year old 0-4-0ST.

His WLWR designs looked more modern than contemporary GSWR types and they exhibited the first signs of the trademark Robinson elegance. Through a chance encounter with SW Johnson, Locomotive Superintendent of the Midland Railway (England) at Limerick in 1900, he became aware that the Great Central Railway was looking for a successor to Harry Pollitt. Robinson went on to considerable fame as Locomotive Superintendent of the GCR but later stated "the happiest years of my life were spent at Limerick".

In mid-1911 Coey retired through ill-health and was succeeded by **REL Maunsell**, a native of Dublin who had trained at Inchicore before taking up appointments with railways in England and India. He returned to Ireland in 1896 and rejoined the staff of the GSWR, but only held the position of Locomotive Superintendent for two years before moving on to become CME of the South Eastern & Chatham Railway. His short superintendency yielded just two fresh designs; 4-4-0 Class 341 (for which he shared the credit with his predecessor) and 0-6-0 Class 257.

Maunsell's principal impact on the GSR locomotive story was to come after he had left Ireland. His 1917 design of Class N mogul for the SECR formed the prototype for the famous 'Woolwich Moguls' initially ordered by the Midland Great Western Railway and later expanded to a fleet of 26 useful locomotives on the GSR. Maunsell was an excellent engineer and an equally accomplished administrator. He was a straight-talking individual who displayed the common touch with subordinates on the shop floor.

The congenial atmosphere that had evolved under the Coey/ Maunsell regimes ended with the appointment of **EA Watson**, a native of Clones, Co Monaghan and not English, as several eminent commentators have claimed. The early details of Watson's career are not recorded but it is known that he worked for a number of years on the Pennsylvania Railroad and also with the American Locomotive Company. During the 1900s, the Great Western Railway was closely studying best overseas practices with particular interest in American and French developments. He appears to have been recruited by the GWR for his American workshop know-how, initially as an Inspector and later as Assistant Works Manager, Swindon. This experience must have made him appear an attractive candidate to become Works Manager at Inchicore in 1911 at the early age of 30 years. He succeeded Maunsell as Locomotive Superintendent in 1913 (re-designated Chief Mechanical Engineer in 1919).

From contemporary accounts, Watson's reputation is one of a difficult man with dogmatic ideas. His designs showed a preference for large locomotives which certainly accords with his pedigree. This policy seems to have brought him into conflict with Joynt who had worked so effectively under Maunsell. Hearsay records that Watson was unpopular at Swindon in introducing American practices, and that he was similarly received at Inchicore. In mitigation, it is not unusual for the introduction of fresh ideas into a conservatively-minded community to induce fear and resentment.

Watson is widely believed to have copied GWR practices in his four-cylinder 4-6-0 but in reality there was little in common with the Swindon model, not least in performance. His only other design was an inside-cylindered heavy 4-8-0 shunting tank that was a blend of components from existing designs, but not very successful. The restrictions imposed by the First World War limited opportunities for new designs during Watson's tenure, and shortages of materials delayed introduction of the other 4-6-0s. His views seem to have been grandiose in relation to prevailing traffic demands. His departure to become General Manager of Beyer Peacock, where his large engine ideas might have been more appreciated, does not appear to have been much mourned. Watson suffered from poor health and died not long after moving to Manchester; perhaps he deserves more sympathy than history has accorded him.

The last CME of the GSWR was **JR Bazin** who had started his career on the English Great Northern Railway at Doncaster in 1897. His acceptance as a premium apprentice (then the 'fast track' to a senior appointment) followed an interview with HA Ivatt. Premium apprentices received a broad range of training experience and Bazin was no exception. He undertook a variety of duties at Doncaster works, served as a locomotive fireman, and later held several important appointments. These included Assistant District Locomotive Superintendent at the important Peterborough depot and Assistant Works Manager at Doncaster. In 1909 he applied unsuccessfully for the position of Running Superintendent on the Great Northern Railway (Ireland), and three years later was short-listed for the job of Locomotive Superintendent with the same company, losing out to GT Glover. Having been responsible for the English GNR's carriage and wagon stock for three years, in 1919 he secured the appointment of Running Superintendent on the GSWR. In November 1921, he succeeded Watson as CME at Inchicore, retaining this role with the GSR. His only design for the GSWR was the mixed traffic 4-6-0 No 500 (described in Chapter 9).

GSWR/ GSR Class 2 'Kerry Bogie' — 4-4-0 — Inchicore Class D19 1925/ 1931 Load Class S/ R

GSWR/ GSR No	Built	Rebuilt	Withdrawn
2	5/1877	1932*	1953
5	6/1877	1932*	1949
6	8/1877	1943*	1952
7	9/1877	1932*	1953
8	7/1880	–	1945
10	7/1880	1939*	1951

GSWR/ GSR No	Built	Rebuilt	Withdrawn
13	10/1880	1930 or 1931¶/ 1933*	1953
15	9/1880	1937*	1951
43	6/1878	1932*	1945
44	7/1878	1930¶/ by 1936§/ 1943*	1950
45	10/1878	1931*	1945
46	11/1878	–	1935

Designer: McDonnell **Built at Inchicore**

GSWR/ GSR Class 2/ D19 No 44. From 1930, this locomotive carried a flush round-topped firebox but by 1936 had reverted to the raised type, similar to that with which it had been fitted originally. At Enniscorthy, April 1938.
WA Camwell

All locomotives originally carried round-topped raised fireboxes.

Rebuilt by GSR with boiler type:
¶ flush round-topped firebox
* saturated Belpaire firebox type U
§ reverted to round-topped raised firebox

Boiler pressure – 150 lbs/ sq in
Cylinders – 16" x 20"
Bogie wheels – 3' 0"
Driving wheels – 5' 8½"
Wheel base – 5' 3" + 5' 6¾" + 7' 11"
Locomotive length – 25' 3"

Heating surfaces:
tubes – 757 sq ft
firebox – 83.8 sq ft
grate – 16.0 sq ft

Tractive effort – 9,530 lbs
Coal capacity – 4 tons
Water capacity – 1864 gal
Locomotive weight – 31 tons 8 cwt
Adhesive weight – 20 tons 12 cwt
Max axle loading – 10 tons 6 cwt

¶ As rebuilt with flush-topped firebox: leading dimensions unchanged. Also see comments on Class 47 E3.

** As rebuilt with saturated Belpaire firebox type U:*

Heating surfaces:
tubes – 675 sq ft
firebox – 82.6 sq ft
grate – 16.3 sq ft

Locomotive weight – 32 tons 10 cwt
Adhesive weight – 21 tons 7 cwt
Max axle loading – 10 tons 15 cwt

Top: GSWR/ GSR Class 2/ D19 No 44 as rebuilt in 1930 with flush round-topped firebox. The tender is an earlier version of the 1864 gallon type, without side plates.

IRRS collection

Right: GSWR/ GSR Class 2/ D19 No 43 as rebuilt with Belpaire firebox, seen here at Inchicore in 1936.

L&GRP

In 1873, McDonnell had introduced the Class 21 2-4-0 for branch line passenger service but it was found that the wheelbase was too rigid for the severe curves of the branches in Kerry, leading to excessive flange wear. To overcome the problem, Class 2 was introduced. This was dimensionally similar, except for the provision of an American pattern swing link bogie. The GSWR rebuilt the entire class between 1894 and 1901 with two ringed boiler and raised firebox. Boiler, wheels and motion were fully interchangeable between Classes 2 and 21.

This was McDonnell's last passenger class, the first 4-4-0 type in Ireland, and one of the earliest designs with this wheel arrangement in these islands. The Kerry bogies were originally intended for service between Mallow and Tralee but were used all over the GSWR system, except on principal main line services. They were an excellent design and well-liked, as evidenced by their long operating life.

1948 assessment: *Quite a good design of very light passenger engine, but for which there is an ever decreasing demand. They are used between Limerick and Sligo but are too low in power even for that service. Useful for assisting trains.*

GSWR/ GSR Class 21 — 2-4-0 — Inchicore Class G4, 1925 Load Class S

GSWR/ GSR No	Built	Withdrawn	GSWR/ GSR No	Built	Withdrawn
21	6/1873	1928	66	3/1876	1928
22	7/1873	1928	67	3/1876	1928
26	10/1873	1928	68	5/1876	1928

Designer: McDonnell **Built at Inchicore**

GSWR/ GSR Class 21/ G4 No 68, at Limerick. *Real Photographs Co Ltd*

Boiler pressure – 150 lbs/ sq in	*Heating surfaces:*	*Tractive effort – 21,020 lbs*
Cylinders – 16" x 20"	*tubes – 770 sq*	*Coal capacity – 4 tons*
Bogie wheels – 3' 8"	*firebox – 83.8 sq ft*	*Water capacity – 1864 gal*
Driving wheels – 5' 8½"	*grate – 16.0 sq ft*	*Locomotive weight – 30 tons*
Wheel base – 6' 0" + 7' 11"		*Adhesive weight – 20 tons*
Locomotive length – 22' 11" (estimated)		*Max axle loading – 10 tons*

Designed for secondary main line and branch line duties. By 1925, they were engaged on light passenger duties such as Portarlington to Athlone, and Ballybrophy to Nenagh and Limerick. These were the last GSWR-built 2-4-0s in service and were not altered during their short GSR career.

GSWR/ GSR Class 27 — 4-4-2T — Inchicore Class C4 — 1925/ 1931 Load Class P/ OT

GSWR/ GSR No	Built	Withdrawn	GSWR/ GSR No	Built	Withdrawn
27	11/1900	1953	31	12/1900	1953
30	12/1900	1950	32	6/1901	1951

Designer: Coey

Built at Inchicore

GSWR/ GSR Class 27/ C4 No 27 at Cork, Rocksavage.
Real Photographs Co Ltd

GSWR/ GSR Class 27/ C4 No 32 at Cork. The locomotive is in later condition with extended bunker and modern smokebox. There is no record any changes in boiler type with this class so presumably the key boiler dimensions are unchanged from those of No 27 depicted above.
Kelland collection

Boiler pressure – 160 lbs/ sq in
(later reduced to 150 lbs/ sq in)
Cylinders – 17" x 22"
Bogie wheels – 3' 0"
Driving wheels – 5' 8½"
Trailing wheels – 3' 9"
Wheel base – 5' 3" + 9' 0¾" + 7' 9" + 6' 0"

Heating surfaces:
tubes – 753.9 sq ft
firebox – 97.1 sq ft
grate – 17.5 sq ft

Tractive effort – 11,830 lbs
Coal capacity – 3 tons
Water capacity – 1,425 gal
Locomotive weight – 54 tons 15 cwt
Adhesive weight – 30 tons 18 cwt
Max axle loading – 15 tons 10 cwt
Locomotive length – 35' 10¾"

By the mid-1930's, Nos 30 to 32 worked regularly on the ex-CBSCR section.

1948 assessment: *Small obsolete tank passenger engine, used mainly on Cork-Bandon and Cork-Cobh lines.*

GSWR/ GSR Class 33 — 2-4-2T — Inchicore Class F6

1925/ 1931 Load Class S/ RT

GSWR/ GSR No	Built	Withdrawn	GSWR/ GSR No	Built	Withdrawn
33	10/1892	1957	36	4/1894	1957
34	12/1892	1957	41	12/1892	1957
35	2/1894	1959	42	1/1893	1963

Designer: Ivatt — **Built at Inchicore**

Nos 33, 34, 41, 42:

Boiler pressure – 150 lbs/ sq in
Cylinders – 16" x 20"
Pony wheels – 3' 9"
Driving wheels – 5' 8½"
Trailing wheels – 3' 9"
Wheel base – 6' 0" + 7' 11" + 6' 0"
Locomotive length – 30' 11½"

Heating surfaces:
tubes – 770 sq ft
firebox – 83.8 sq ft
grate – 16.0 sq ft

Tractive effort – 9.530 lbs
Coal capacity – 2 tons 5 cwt
Water capacity – 1250 gal
Locomotive weight – 46 tons 12 cwt
Adhesive weight – 25 tons 2 cwt
Max axle loading – 12 tons 13 cwt

Nos 35, 36:

Heating surfaces:
tubes – 757.1 sq ft
firebox – 83.8 sq ft
grate – 16.0 sq ft

Coal capacity – 3 tons
Water capacity – 1130 gal
Locomotive weight – 46 tons 2 cwt
Adhesive weight – 25 tons 2 cwt
Max axle loading – 12 tons 12 cwt

Left: GSWR/ GSR Class 33/ F6 No 36 in CIÉ at Cork, fitted with extended bunker and modern smokebox. The cut-away section of the side tanks accounts for the lower water capacity than that quoted for No 41 shown below.

CP Friel collection

Below: GSWR/ GSR Class 33/ F6 No 41 at Cork in April 1938.

WA Camwell

These locomotives were introduced for service on the Kerry branch lines. By the mid-1930s No 33 was working on the ex-CBSCR section. Nos 33 and 42 were fitted with a bell for working the Cork City Railway which was mainly a road tramway between Cork Glanmire Road, and the CBSCR at Albert Quay.

1948 assessment (33/ 37 classes):
Small passenger tank engines of obsolete design. Used on Cork and Bandon Section.

GSWR/ GSR Class 37 — 4-4-2T — Inchicore Class C7, 1925/ 1931 Load Class S/ RT

GSWR/ GSR No	Built	Withdrawn	GSWR/ GSR No	Built	Withdrawn
37	7/1894	1954	318	6/1901	1953
38	10/1894	1950	319	6/1901	1950
317	6/1901	1955	320	6/1901	1954

Designer: Ivatt/ Coey

Built at Inchicore

Nos 37 and 38:

Boiler pressure – 160 lbs/ sq in
Cylinders – 16" x 20"
Bogie wheels – 3' 0"
Driving wheels – 5' 8½"
Trailing wheels – 3'9"
Wheel base – 5' 3" + 5' 4¾" + 7' 11" + 6' 0"
Locomotive length – 34' 1¾"

Heating surfaces:
tubes – 757 sq ft
firebox – 83.8 sq ft
grate – 16.0 sq ft

Tractive effort – 9,530 lbs
Coal capacity – 3 tons 0 cwt
Water capacity – 1130 gal
Locomotive weight – 48 tons 10 cwt
Adhesive weight – 25 tons 0 cwt
Max axle loading – 12 tons 10 cwt

Nos 317 to 320, as for Nos 37 and 38 except:

Water capacity – 1245 gal
Locomotive weight – 49 tons 12 cwt
Adhesive weight – 26 tons 8 cwt
Max axle loading – 13 tons 6 cwt

Representatives of this class were allocated to Grand Canal Street shed for use on suburban services to Bray, but by the mid 1930s, Nos 317-320 had migrated to Cork where they worked local services to Youghal and Queenstown.

1948 assessment (33 & 37 classes):
Small passenger tank engines of obselete design. Used on Cork and Bandon Section.

GSWR/ GSR Class 37/ C7 No 37 at Cork.
Real Photographs Co Ltd

GSWR/ GSR Class 37/ C7 No 318 at Inchicore about 1904.
Real Photographs Co Ltd

GSWR/ GSR Class 47 — 0-4-4BT — Inchicore Class E3
1925/ 1931 Load Class S/ RT

GSWR/ GSR No	Built	Rebuilt	Withdrawn	GSWR/ GSR No	Built	Rebuilt	Withdrawn
40 *	7/1879	–	1936	74	6/1887	1919	1930
47	5/1883	1906/ 1921/ 1925	1945	75	9/1887	1912	1931
48	7/1883	1917	1930	76	9/1887	1907	1931
49 ¶	8/1883	1909	1945	77	91886	–	1931
51	4/1884	1905	1934	78	9/1886	1913	1945
70	6/1884	1904	1940	80	10/1886	1905	1931
72	12/1884	1906	1940	81	8/1884	–	1934
73	6/1887	–	1928	83	9/1884	–	1928

* Built as part of Class 28 (four locomotives – the remainder withdrawn between 1906 and 1916) but later included in Class 47 as it was dimensionally similar, except for a longer wheelbase of *6' + 12' 0½" + 5' 5"*

¶ Cab fitted with side-window

Designer: McDonnell **Built at Inchicore**

Boiler pressure – 150 lbs/ sq in
Cylinders – 16" x 20"
Driving wheels –5' 8½"
Bogie wheels – 3' 9"
Wheel base – 6' 0" + 10' 11½" + 5' 5"
Locomotive length – 33' 6½"

Heating surfaces:
tubes – 677 sq ft
firebox – 78.5 sq ft
grate – 15.25 sq ft

Tractive effort – 9,530 lbs
Coal capacity – 2 tons 15 cwt
Water capacity – 1044 gal (back tank)
– 135 gal (side tanks)
Locomotive weight – 41 tons 16 cwt
Adhesive weight – 23 tons 4 cwt
Max axle loading – 11 tons 12 cwt

Although the pre-amalgamation dates (some doubtful) of rebuilding are noted, no details have been traced concerning what this process entailed. The class originally had boiler pressure of 160 lbs /sq in but all had been reduced to 150 lbs/ sq in by 1925. No other significant dimensional changes have been traced.

The 1925 rebuilding of No 47 is believed to have involved the fitting of a larger boiler (designated 47R) which proved too heavy. This boiler was later fitted to Class 2/ D19 No 44, apparently between 1930 and 1936 (another source states removal in 1938). This boiler was of the flush round-topped variety with a higher centre line but no other details have been traced.

Class 47 originally comprised 20 locomotives (excluding No 40) and was the GSWR's numerically largest tank class. They were built principally for branch line passenger work in the Cork area, and on services between Dublin and Kildare/ Kilkenny. They were later relegated to minor branch work. In 1929 No 75 was allocated to Tralee as relief for GSR Sentinel locomotive No 1 (later No 280) which was then the regular motive power for the Castleisland branch. Later No 47 was used on these duties in replacement of ex-Cork & Macroom Direct Railway 2-4-0T Class 487 (G5) No 488 which was withdrawn in 1934.

The official wheel arrangement of 0-4-4BT ('back tank') was a rare designation, denoting that the water supply for these engines was contained in a single tank at the base and rear of the bunker.

GSWR/ GSR Class 47/ E3 No 40 This locomotive was the 100th built at Inchicore since the advent of McDonnell. For the attendant celebrations it was temporarily renumbered 100, but probably never worked in service with this number.

RN Clements collection

GSWR/ GSR Class 47/ E3 No 49 in ex-works condition in 1933. This photograph clearly depicts the all-enveloping nature of the GSR grey livery. This locomotive was unique in having a cab side-window.

L&GRP

GSWR/ GSR Class 52/ D17 No 14 with raised round-topped firebox, at Limerick in 1931.

L&GRP

GSWR/ GSR Class 52 — 4-4-0 — Inchicore Class D17, 1925/ 1931 Load Class R/ R

GSWR/ GSR No	Built	Rebuilt	Withdrawn	GSWR/ GSR No	Built	Rebuilt	Withdrawn
1	3/1890	1930¶/ date unknown#	1955	52	11/1883	1923§/ 1931*	1949
3	3/1890	1953*	1957	53	12/1883	1900§	1925
4	4/1888	1933*	1957	54	11/1883	1903§/ 1930*	1959
9	12/1886	1904§/ 1951*	1955	55	12/1884	1899§/ 1932*	1955
11	4/1888	-	1949	56	12/1888	1932*	1951
12	5/1890	1932*	1949	57	10/1888	1950*	1957
14	5/1888	1932*	1957	58	10/1888	1903§/ 1930¶/1934#/1950*	1953
16	12/1886	1905§/ 1933*	1959	59	10/1888	1911§	1955
18	6/1888	1921§/ 1933*	1959	97	2/1887	1902§	1930
20	6/1890	1941*	1959	98	2/1887	1904§/ 1930¶/ 1936#	1954

Rebuilt: § two ringed boiler with raised round-topped firebox instead of original three ringed boiler
* with superheated Belpaire firebox type X
# with saturated boiler with raised round-topped firebox
¶ with saturated boiler with flush round-topped firebox

Designer: Aspinall — **Built at Inchicore**

Boiler pressure – 160 lbs/ sq in
Cylinders – 17" x 22"
Bogie wheels – 3' 0"
Driving wheels – 6' 7"
Wheel base – 5' 3" + 6'5¼" + 7' 9"
Locomotive length – 27' 6½"

Heating surfaces:
tubes – 835 sq ft
firebox – 96 sq ft
grate – 17.5 sq ft

Tractive effort – 10,940 lbs
Coal capacity – 4 tons 10 cwt
Water capacity – 2730 gal
Locomotive weight – 36 tons 8 cwt
Adhesive weight – 24 tons 10 cwt
Max axle loading – 12 tons 8 cwt

§ # ¶ As rebuilt with saturated boiler with raised/ flush round-topped firebox:
Heating surfaces
tubes – 754 sq ft
firebox – 97.1 s ft
(Sources state that the boilers fitted to Nos 58 and 98 were MGWR type ex-Class Lm but fitted with a GSWR-style double door smoke box in 1930)

*** As rebuilt with superheated Belpaire firebox type X:**
Boiler pressure – 150 lbs/ sq in

Heating surfaces
tubes – 655 sq ft
firebox – 110 sq ft
superheater – 112 q ft
grate – 16 sq ft

Tractive effort – 10,260 lbs
Locomotive weight – 39 tons 1 cwt
Adhesive weight – 25 tons 18 cwt
Max axle loading – 13 tons 5 cwt

The styling and design of these locomotives was in the tradition established by the Kerry Bogies. They were the first 4-4-0s built for express passenger services and were typically capable of taking loads of around 150 tons from Dublin to Cork in about four hours. When displaced from these duties by the later Class 60, they were relegated to branch line work.

No 59 was the star of the film *The Quiet Man* released in 1952, a Republic Production that co-starred John Wayne, Maureen O'Hara and Barry Fitzgerald.

1948 Assessment: *Similar to Class 2. Suits Kildare/ Kilkenny and Sligo/ Limerick. Too small.*

GSWR/ GSR Class 52/ D17 No 20 with superheated Belpaire firebox, at Inchicore. *Kelland collection*

GSWR/ GSR Class 52/ D17 No 1. This photograph was taken at Limerick in April 1938, by which time it had received a raised round-topped firebox. Nos 1, 58 and 98 carried boilers with flush round-topped fireboxes, fitted in 1930. It has not been possible to trace a photograph of any of these three locomotives in this condition but they would have looked similar to GSWR/ GSR Class 2 No 44 as depicted on page 60 (top).

WA Camwell

Class 60 — 4-4-0 — Inchicore Class D14 (plus one example D13) 1925/ 1931 Load Class P/ O

GSWR/ GSR No	Built	Rebuilt	Withdrawn	GSWR/ GSR No	Built	Rebuilt	Withdrawn
60	10/1891	1908#/1934*	1957	87	1886	1898#/ 1949*	1957
61	11/1891	1935*	1955	88	1886	1904#/ 1925¶/ 1935*	1957
62	12/1891	1903#/ 1925¶/1939*	1959	89	1886	1925§/ 1936*	1960
63	12/1891	1920#	1955	93	6/1885	1933*	1960
64	10/1895	1901#/ 1941*	1959	94	8/1885	1903#/ 1934*	1959
65	10/1895	1903#/ 1931¥	1959	95	10/1885	1898#/ 1941*	1955
85	1886	1903#/ 1952*	1959	96	11/1885	1905#/ 1935*	1959
86	1886	1904#/ 1937 or 1938*	1957				

Rebuilt: # by GSWR with modified boiler

* with type Z Belpaire superheated boiler

¶ with new frames, raised running plate in straight line over coupling rods and canopy cab (often referred to as 'Bazin' cab) – No 89 also received Belpaire saturated boiler of type later used in Class 700/ D13 until 1939

§ with new frames, running plate in straight line over coupling rods, large cab and Belpaire saturated boiler of type which was later used in Class 700: Inchicore Class D13 until 1939

¥ with Class 700 type saturated boiler and canopy cab

Designer: Aspinall — **Built at Inchicore**

As originally built:

Boiler pressure – 150 lbs/ sq in
Cylinders – 18" x 24"
Bogie wheels – 3' 0"
Driving wheels – 6' 7"
Wheel base – 5' 3" + 6' 10⁷/₈" + 8' 3"
Locomotive length – 28' 6¹/₈"

Heating surfaces:
tubes – 938 sq ft
firebox – 112.5 sq ft
grate – 18.8 sq ft

Tractive effort – 12,540 lbs
Coal capacity – 3 tons 10 cwt
Water capacity – 2730 gal
Locomotive weight – 39 tons 10 cwt
Adhesive weight – 25 tons 18 cwt
Max axle loading – 12 tons 19 cwt

GSWR/ GSR Class 60/ D14 No 60 with 1864 gallon tender, at Inchicore. *R Conway*

 # Rebuilt by GSWR with modified boiler:

Boiler pressure – 160 lbs/ sq in	*Heating surfaces:*	*Tractive effort – 13,400 lbs*
	tubes – 878.6 sq ft	*Locomotive weight – 39 tons 10 cwt*
	firebox – 112.5 sq ft	*Adhesive weight – 26 tons 11 cwt*
	grate area – 18.8 sq ft	*Max axle loading – 13 tons 9 cwt*

These locomotives subsequently had their boiler pressures reduced to 150 lbs/ sq in

¶ Nos 62, 88 as rebuilt with new frames & running plates, extended smokebox, new and new cab but retaining original boiler:

Boiler pressure – 150 lbs/ sq in	*Heating surfaces:*	*Tractive effort – 12,540 lbs*
	tubes – 878 sq ft	*Locomotive weight – 42 tons 9 cwt*
	firebox – 110.5 sq ft	

§ No 89 rebuilt similar to Nos 62 & 88 but with Belpaire saturated boiler; classified as D13 from 1925 until 1933:

Boiler pressure – 160 lbs/ sq in	*Heating surfaces:*	*Tractive effort – 13,400 lbs*
	tubes – 878 sq ft	*Locomotive weight – 45 tons 9 cwt*
	firebox – 110.5 sq ft	

*** As rebuilt with type Z Belpaire superheater:**

Boiler pressure – 160 lbs/sq in	*Heating surfaces:*	*Tractive effort – 13,400 lbs*
	tubes – 662 sq ft	*Locomotive weight – 42 tons 18 cwt*
	firebox – 112 sq ft	*Adhesive weight – 25 tons 18 cwt*
	superheater – 112 sq ft	*Max axle loading – 13 tons 3 cwt*
	grate area – 18.8 sq ft	

¥ No 65 as rebuilt in 1931:

Fitted with 700 Class boiler with heating surfaces as D13 and new canopy cab.

Effectively an enlargement of the Class 52, these locomotives were a further example of the design/ styling tradition started by McDonnell, and proved to be yet another long-lived GSWR 4-4-0 class. From their introduction, they took over principal main line duties from the Class 52, including the Killarney expresses which were then the fastest trains in Ireland, and remained on this class of work until arrival of Class 305 in 1902. Their competence led to substantial reductions in Dublin-Cork journey times. They were used largely on branch line services and on the DSER section in their later careers, but were still to be seen on the main line, piloting expresses. With excursion trains, often quite heavy, they were popular as pilot engines to Class 101 (J15).

An example of the measures adopted by the GSR to preserve ageing boilers is contained in a report dated 1929 advising that No 60 was operating with a boiler pressure reduced to 125 lbs/ sq in. Presumably it continued in this condition until its rebuilding in 1934. No 94 was fitted in 1930 with a new smokebox but retaining the GSWR-style double-doors. No 64 ran for a period in the mid-1930s with an extended smokebox but not otherwise altered.

In 1949, No 61 received lined green livery as one of a small group of smaller locomotives specifically allocated to passenger services. It must have been the oldest locomotive to receive this preferential treatment and was kept in sparkling condition for a couple of years before being changed to plain black, although with wear the green re-emerged from underneath the black in later years!

1948 assessment: *Small passenger engine, fast and reliable. Suitable for Branch passenger trains and trains such as former Newspaper trains. An ideal engine with which to double head a train.*

Right: GSWR/ GSR Class 60/ D14 No 86 with 3345 gallon tender (coal rails with back plate), at Inchicore in 1936.

L&GRP

Left: GSWR/ GSR Class 60/ D13 (later D14) No 88, as rebuilt with canopy cab. It is seen at Limerick in 1930.

Real Photographs Co Ltd

Below: GSWR/ GSR Class 60/ D14 No 64 with Belpaire superheated boiler, at Inchicore.

NC Simmons

GSWR/ GSR Class 60/ D14 No 65, with canopy cab, and saturated Class 700 saturated boiler. Seen on 18 September 1953 taking water at Mallow, as No 405 arrives on the 6.40 am Mail from Dublin, Kingsbridge.

Authors' collection

Above: GSWR/ GSR Class 60/ D14 No 89, at Limerick.

Real Photographs Co Ltd

Opposite bottom: GSWR/ GSR Class 90/ J30 No 100. Although No 99 was originally given a different classification, research indicates that it was visually similar to No 100. The same GSWR diagram covered Nos 90, 99 and 100.

L&GRP

GSWR/ GSR Class 90/ 99/ 100 — 0-6-0T — Inchicore Class J30
Later all Class 90 — 1925/ 1931 Load Class U/ TT

GSWR/ GSR No	Built	Rebuilt	Withdrawn
90	9/1875	1915*	1959 Preserved
99	12/1890	–	1930
100	1/1891	–	1959

Designer: McDonnell/ Aspinall — **Built at Inchicore**

* Originally delivered to Castleisland Railway as an 0-6-4T combined locomotive and carriage; rear bogie and carriage portion removed at rebuilding

Boiler pressure – 150 lbs/ sq in	*Heating surfaces:*	*Tractive effort – 5,160 lbs*
Cylinders – 10" x 18"	*tubes – 310 sq ft*	*Coal capacity – not recorded*
Driving wheels – 3' 8½"	*firebox – 52 sq ft*	*Water capacity – 430 gal*
Wheel base – 5' 0" + 5' 11"	*grate – 10 sq ft*	*Locomotive weight – 23 tons 8 cwt*
Locomotive length – 22' 3½"		*Max axle loading – 7 tons 18 cwt*

Locomotive No 100 was equipped with 12" x 18" cylinders between 1918 and 1925.

Nos 99 and 100 were introduced for the Mitchelstown and Fermoy Railway where the maximum axle loading permitted was eight tons. Following its rebuilding, No 90 which was dimensionally similar was included in the class. No 90 has the distinction of being one of the very few ex-GSWR locomotives to have survived into preservation.

Above: GSWR/ GSR Class 90/ J30 No 90 at Rocksavage, Cork.
Real Photographs Co Ltd

After the amalgamation, Nos 90 and 100 were employed on the Timoleague and Courtmacsherry branch which had also had an eight tons axle-loading restriction. They continued at work on this section until 1954 when displaced by ex-MGWR Class E (J26) 0-6-0Ts. They were then used as shunters on the Cork Quays and at Albert Quay station. Occasionally they returned to the Timoleague and Courtmacsherry section, a journey they could only cover from Cork 'light engine' in view of their small water capacity and the fact that the first water supply was at Crossbarry (13¼ miles from Cork).

1948 assessment: *Kept specially for small, very low axleload branches in Cork District, useless for anything else.*

GSWR/ GSR Class 91 — 0-6-0ST — Inchicore Class J29 1925 Load Class U

GSWR/ GSR No	Built	Rebuilt	Withdrawn
91	4/1881	1924 or 1925	1930

Designer: McDonnell **Built at Inchicore**

GSWR/ GSR Class 91/ J29 No 91 at Inchicore. *Lens of Sutton*

Boiler pressure – 150 lbs/ sq in	*Heating surfaces:*	*Tractive effort – 5,160 lbs*
Cylinders – 10" x 18"	*tubes – 317 sq ft*	*Coal capacity – 10 cwt*
Driving wheels – 3' 8½"	*firebox – 51 sq ft*	*Water capacity – 410 gal*
Wheel base – 5' 0" + 5' 11"	*grate – 10 sq ft*	*Locomotive weight – 23 tons 8 cwt*
Locomotive length – 22' 3½"		*Max axle loading – 7 tons 18 cwt*

Originally built as an 0-6-4T combined locomotive and carriage; rear bogie and carriage portion removed, and saddle tanks installed in place of side tanks at rebuilding.

GSWR/ GSR Class 92 Combined locomotive & carriage

0-6-4T

Inchicore Class H2
Not classified for loads

GSWR/ GSR No	Built	Withdrawn
92	2/1881	1945

Designer: McDonnell

Built at Inchicore

GSWR/ GSR Class 92/ H2 No 92 'The Cab'. *R Conway*

Boiler pressure – 140 lbs/ sq in	*Heating surfaces:*	*Tractive effort – 4,810 lbs*
Cylinders – 10" x 18"	*tubes – 317 sq ft*	*Coal capacity – 10 cwt*
Driving wheels – 3' 8½"	*firebox – 51 sq ft*	*Water capacity – 370 gal*
Bogie wheels – 3' 1½"	*grate – 10 sq ft*	*Locomotive weight – 26 tons 7 cwt*
Wheel base – 5' 0" + 5' 11" + 7' 6" + 5' 6"		*Adhesive weight – 19 tons 0 cwt*
Combined locomotive and carriage length – 34' 10"		*Max axle loading – 6 tons 5 cwt*

Originally, Nos 90 to 92 were all 0-6-4T combined locomotives and carriages but this was the only example to retain this configuration unchanged until withdrawal. The carriage portion comprised a single saloon and this equipage was employed in the movement of officials between Kingsbridge station and Inchicore, being known as 'The Cab'. It was also used occasionally to move coaching stock to and from Inchicore works.

GSWR/ GSR Class 101/ J15 No 114. The second member of the class to carry this number. Seen with 4' 4" boiler and tender in original condition at Rosslare shed.

Real Photographs Co Ltd

GSWR/ GSR Class101 — 0-6-0 — Inchicore Class J15 1925/1931 Load Class J/ J

(Numbers and dates in italics refer to locomotives withdrawn pre-GSR; included here for completeness)

GSWR/ GSR No	Built	4' 4" boiler fitted	New frames	Z type boiler	Withdrawn	Comments
101	9/1882	1924	–	1940	1962	
102	1/1873	1904	–	1947	1962	
103 (first)	*8/1867*	–	–	–	*1886*	
103§	8/1889	1921	–	–	1957	
104	1/1873	1913	–	1930	1965	
105 (first)	*5/1868*	–	–	–	*1895*	
105§	6/1896	1910	–	1949	1963	
106	1/1874	1921	1937	1937	1965	
107	2/1881	by 1921	–	1935	1957	
108	2/1875	1922	1937	1931	1959	
109	1/1877	1912	–	–	1964	
110 (first)	*7/1868*	–	–	–	*1890*	
110§	12/1890	1922	–	1930	1963	
111 (first)	*9/1867*	–	–	–	*1888*	
111§	3/1891	by 1913	–	–	1963	
112	6/1866	1911 or 1912	–	–	1929	
113	12/1866	1903	–	–	1930	
114 (first)	*8/1869*	–	–	–	*1885*	*Short wheelbase*
114§	8/1889	1907	–	1948	1961	
115	10/1869	–	–	–	1929	Short wheelbase
116	8/1896	by 1908	–	–	1964	
117	3/1874	1904	–	–	1930	
118 (first)	*5/1867*	–	–	–	*1890*	
118§	5/1891	by 1928	–	1933	1966	
119	1/1877	by 1926	–	–	1962	
120	2/1877	by 1921	–	1935	1955	
121	2/1877	by 1913	–	–	1963	
122	9/1882	1901	–	1942	1963	

GSWR/ GSR No	Built	4' 4" boiler fitted	New frames	Z type boiler	Withdrawn	Comments
123	7/1881	by 1911	–	1932	1963	
124	9/1881	1901	–	1948	1965	
125	10/1881	1915	–	1949	1965	
126	11/1881	1901	–	1938	1959	
127	2/1882	by 1917	–	by 1933	1963	
128	3/1882	1914	–	1933	1963	
129	9/1889	1907	–	1933	1940	
130	12/1882	1902	–	1947	1965	
131	12/1882	1909	–	–	1963	
132	12/1888	1905	–	1941	1965	
133	6/1885	1904	–	–	1963	
134	6/1885	1922	–	–	1961	
135	9/1885	1903	–	–	1957	
136	12/1888	1905	–	1931	1962	
137	12/1888	1902	–	by 1933	1960	
138	12/1888	1903	–	1947	1962	
139	4/1881	1909	–	1932	1961	
140	5/1881	1909	–	1942	1961	
141	5/1881	by 1923	–	1939	1959	
142	3/1875	1907	–	–	1928	
143	12/1877	1906	1923	1936	1960	
144	2/1878	1910	–	1932	1954	
145	2/1878	by 1923	–	–	1926	
146	2/1878	1912	–	1930	1955	
147 (first)	*5/1867*	–	–	–	*1888*	*Beyer Peacock No 747*
147§	5/1891	1907	–	1941	1956	
148	6/1867	1907	–	1932	1953	Beyer Peacock No 748
149 (first)	*6/1867*	–	–	–	*1887*	*Beyer Peacock No 749*
149§	10/1889	1903	–	1933	1962	
150	6/1867	by 1921	–	–	1957	Beyer Peacock No 750
151	3/1868	1904	–	1950	1965	Beyer Peacock No 780
152	3/1868	1901	–	–	1959	Beyer Peacock No 781
153	3/1868	1904	–	1932	1954	Beyer Peacock No 782
154	3/1868	by 1915	–	1941	1962	Beyer Peacock No 783
155	2/1871	–	–	–	1929	Short wheelbase
156	4/1871	–	1935	1935	1961	Short wheel base
157	3/1872	by 1918	–	–	1963	
158	4/1872	1905	1923	1941	1957	
159	9/1871	1912	–	1933	1949	
160	10/1871	1907	1932	1932	1955	
161	10/1871	by 1927	–	–	1963	
162	12/1871	1909	–	–	1963	
163	7/1872	by 1923	1936	1936	1955	Sharp Stewart No 2155
164	8/1872	1924	1932	1932	1963	Sharp Stewart No 2156
165	8/1872	1921	–	–	1945	Sharp Stewart No 2157
166	8/1872	1923	1923	1933	1963	Sharp Stewart No 2158
167	3/1873	by 1916	–	–	1960	
168	4/1873	by 1921	1935	1935	1962	
169	3/1874	1921	–	–	1928	
170	4/1874	1917	–	1941	1963	
171	7/1874	by 1924	–	1933	1961	

GSWR/ GSR No	Built	4' 4" boiler fitted	New frames	Z type boiler	Withdrawn	Comments
172	8/1874	1906	–	1949	1963	
173	9/1874	1902	–	–	1933	
174	11/1874	by 1927	–	1933	1953	
175	8/1873	1924	–	1933	1956	Sharp Stewart No 2310
176	8/1873	1922	1922	–	1959	Sharp Stewart No 2311
177	12/1873	1921	–	–	1927	Beyer Peacock No 1251
178	12/1873	by 1909	–	–	1926	Beyer Peacock No 1252
179	4/1875	1920	1933	1933	1965	
180	5/1875	1912	–	–	1928	
181	8/1879	1920	1937	1937	1959	
182	9/1879	by 1927	–	1939	1962	
183	1/1880	by 1927	–	1932	1965	
184	2/1880	1921	–	–	1962	Preserved
185	8/1879	by 1918	1936	1933	1959	Sharp Stewart No 2837
186	11/1879	by 1910	1935	1932	1965	Sharp Stewart No 2838, Preserved
187	3/1882	by 1927	–	–	1963	
188	7/1882	by 1923	–	1932	1959	
189	*5/1881*	*1904*	–	–	*1923*	*Beyer Peacock No 2029* *Civil war loss*
190	5/1881	by 1918	–	–	1963	Beyer Peacock No 2030
191	10/1885	1914	–	–	1962	
192	9/1898	1908	–	1950	1956	
193	9/1898	1910	–	1948	1963	
194	11/1898	1908	–	1933	1959	
195	12/1898	1909	–	–	1965	
196	5/1899	1911	–	1953	1961	
197	6/1899	1911	–	by 1931	1965	
198	6/1899	1910	–	1933	1965	
199	11/1899	by 1912	–	1931	1954	
200	2/1903	as built	–	1941	1960	
223	2/1903	as built	–	–	1960	
229	3/1903	as built	–	–	1962	
232	3/1903	as built	–	–	1963	
240	10/1902	as built	–	–	1957	
241	12/1902	as built	–	–	1957	
242	12/1902	as built	–	–	1957	
243	1/1903	as built	–	–	1955	
253	1903	as built	–	–	1963	
254	1903	as built	–	1933	1961	
255	1903	as built	–	1936	1963	
256	1903	as built	–	1931	1959	

Designer: McDonnell **Built at Inchicore except where stated otherwise**

§ In spite of the usual GSWR practice of rebuilding and renewal, after an investigation, R N Clements concluded that these eight replacement locomotives were completely new builds. The situation with the first No 111 was ambiguous in that it was similar to but never formally absorbed into Class 101. This notwithstanding, it is for all practical purposes considered one of the total of 119 locomotives of the class.

All built at Inchicore, except for those locomotives annotated above as built by Beyer Peacock (twelve locomotives) and Sharp Stewart (eight locomotives), with relative makers' numbers. The Beyer Peacock engines, GSWR Nos 147 to154, were of their order number 2045 and were always known to the makers as their '2045 Class'. They were identical with Beyer's engines of 1872 built for the Dublin & Belfast Junction Railway. The Beyer Peacock engines GSWR Nos 177, 178, 189 & 190 were referred to by the makers as their '2960 Class'. Apart from the eight locomotives withdrawn during the 19th century and the single Civil War loss, the class was intact at the amalgamation, comprising 110 locomotives and making it numerically the largest in Ireland.

There is some dispute over origins, although the consensus holds that it was a Beyer Peacock design dating from 1866, albeit with superficial similarity to the London & North Western Class Dx 0-6-0 Goods. It is thought that McDonnell commissioned Beyer Peacock to draw up the original design and that he actually constructed three locomotives (Nos 112, 113, and 118) in 1866–1867 in general conformity therewith, using parts from withdrawn engines. This was prior to the first newly-built members of the class delivered by Beyer Peacock the following year.

With construction continuing at intervals over the next 37 years, the class never presented a homogeneous appearance. The leading dimensions in the early days were:

Boiler pressure – 140 lbs/ sq in
(later increased to 150 lbs/ sq in)
Driving wheels – 5' 1¼"
(later 5' 1¾" with thicker tyres)
Cylinders – 17" x 24"
Wheel base – 7' 3" + 8' 3"
Except Nos: 114(first)/ 115/ 155/ 156 with wheel base 7' 3" + 7' 9"
Locomotive length – 24' 9¾"

Heating surfaces:
tubes – 843 sq ft
firebox – 93 sq ft
grate – 17.5 sq ft

Tractive effort – 13,480 lbs
(14,320 lbs)
Coal capacity – 4 tons
Water capacity – 1864 gal
Locomotive weight – 30 tons 14 cwt
Max axle loading – 11 tons 6 cwt

GSWR/ GSR Class 101/ J15 No 156 with original boiler and short wheel base, at Limerick in 1930. *Elf* can be seen in the background.

Real Photographs Co Ltd

A number of changes were progressively introduced. Boiler pressure was increased comparatively early on to 150 lbs/ sq in, and later to 160 lbs/ sq in. Driving wheel diameters were increased by half an inch with the fitting of thicker tyres.

The most significant change was the introduction of 18" diameter cylinders in 1874 with steam ports enlarged from 1⅜" to 1½" on new locomotives. Replacement of 17" cylinders where necessary continued until 1885 but thereafter all replacement cylinders were 18" and eventually the whole class as inherited by the GSR had the larger size.

The variations in numbers and sizes of tubes are too numerous to record, and surviving records are not complete anyway. However, the trend was to increase heating surfaces and linked with fitting of 18" cylinders, there were resultant weight increases. The heaviest variant noted during the early period was locomotive weight – 33 tons 10 cwt; maximum axle loading – 12 tons 2 cwt.

4' 0" diameter boiler rebuilds:

In 1882, a programme commenced to install larger boilers and 59 locomotives were so fitted. At the amalgamation, only eight locomotives still retained these boilers. Nos 115 and 155 were withdrawn in this condition in 1929. Nos 119, 161, 174, 182 & 183 had all received 4' 4" boilers by 1927. No 156 was notable in retaining its 4' 0" boiler as late 1935 when it received a Z type boiler. The leading dimensions with the 4' 0" boiler as originally introduced:

Boiler pressure – 150 lbs/ sq in	*Heating surfaces:*	*Tractive effort – 16,050 lbs*
Cylinders – 18" x 24"	*tubes – 764 sq ft*	*Coal capacity – 4 tons*
Driving wheels – 5' 1¾"	*firebox – 96 sq ft*	*Water capacity – 1864 gal*
Wheel base – 7' 3" + 8' 3"	*grate – 17.5 sq ft*	*Locomotive weight – 33 tons 10 cwt*
		Max axle loading – 11 tons 15 cwt

4' 4" diameter boiler rebuilds:

This boiler type was introduced in 1901 appearing first on the Class 217 0-6-0T. The first Class 101 to be fitted was No 124 later that year in a programme that eventually almost covered the whole class then surviving. The only exceptions were Nos 115, 155 and 156 which were the remaining short wheel base variants, and presumably were too short to accept the larger boiler. Leading dimensions:

	Heating surfaces:	*Locomotive weight – 35 tons 16 cwt*
	tubes – 925 sq ft	
	firebox – 116 sq ft	
	grate – 19.3 sq ft	

New frames:

It says much for the robust nature of the original construction that only 15 locomotives required new frames during their long working lives. In 8 cases, new frames accompanied the fitting of the Z type boiler and there were two instances of new frames accompanying the 4' 4" boiler.

Z-type boiler rebuilds:

Morton, by then CME of the GSR, commenced the installation of superheated Belpaire Z-type boilers with the fitting of Nos 104 (built 1873) and 146 (1878). This programme concluded as late as 1953 with No 196 by which time a total of 67 locomotives had been so treated. Details of fitting and withdrawal dates are tabulated opposite.

GSWR/ GSR Class 101/ J15 No 105 with 4' 4" boiler and tender with side plates, at Tralee shed. *L&GRP*

	Saturated locomotives withdrawn	Locomotives fitted with superheaters	Total saturated locomotives	Superheated Locos withdrawn	Total Superheated Locomotives	Class total	*Superheated as % of Total*
1925			110			110	-
1926	2		108			108	-
1927	1		107			107	-
1928	3		104			104	-
1929	3		101			101	-
1930	2	3	96		3	99	*3*
1931		5	91		8	99	*8*
1932		9	82		17	99	*17*
1933	1	17	64		34	98	*35*
1934			64		34	98	*35*
1935		4	60		38	98	*39*
1936		3	57		41	98	*42*
1937		2	55		43	98	*44*
1938		1	54		44	98	*45*
1939		2	52		46	98	*47*
1940		1	51	1	46	97	*47*
1941		6	45		52	97	*54*
1942		2	43		54	97	*56*
1943			43		54	97	*56*
1944			43		54	97	*56*
1945	1		42		54	96	*56*
1946			42		54	96	*56*
1947		3	39		57	96	*59*
1948		3	36		60	96	*63*
1949		3	33	1	62	95	*65*
1950		1	32		63	95	*66*
1951		1	31		64	95	*67*
1952			31		64	95	*67*
1953		1	30	2	63	93	*68*
1954			30	3	60	90	*67*
1955	1		29	4	56	85	*66*
1956			29	3	53	82	*65*
1957	6		23	2	51	74	*69*
1958			23		51	74	*69*
1959	2		21	8	43	64	*67*
1960	2		19	3	40	59	*68*
1961	1		18	7	33	51	*65*
1962	4		14	8	25	39	*64*
1963	11		3	12	13	16	*81*
1964	2		1		13	14	*93*
1965	1		0	12	1	1	*100*
1966			0	1	0	0	

Some inferences can be drawn from these figures concerning the evolvement of GSR locomotive policy. In the years 1925 to 1930, a steady withdrawal programme involved eleven locomotives, as would be expected on time-expired criteria with machines of this vintage. The lifting of the embargo on the superheating of small locomotives brought about a fundamental change of heart; only four of the class were taken out of service over the next 22 years. Significantly, no superheating occurred in 1934, the year in which Class 710 (J15b) appeared. By the following year though, Class 710 having shown no significant advance performance-wise over Class 101, superheating of the latter recommenced.

The absence of any further fitting of superheaters in the years 1943 to 1946 can be explained by the exigencies of that period. Restoration of the programme in 1947 by CIÉ emphasises that the authorities were in no doubt of the operating and financial advantages to be achieved.

Viewed from this perspective, the programme had an immense impact. It extended the overall longevity of the class (the average working life of the 110 locomotives acquired by the GSR was 75 years – an extraordinary figure). A further distinction was that thirteen locomotives (Nos 104, 106, 150 to 152, 154, 156, 157, 161, 162, 164, 166 & 179) were in service for 90 or more years, with No 151 clocking up 97 years.

More importantly for the GSR fleet renewal programme as a whole, the company was relieved of the financial burden of construction of significant numbers of new locomotives. The rejuvenation of Class 101 filled an important gap in the ranks of general purpose machines necessary to keep the railway system as a whole on the move. A feature of GSR policy was the degree to which so much attention was focused on a small group of express passenger locomotives while the greater share of traffic revenue derived from goods services. Part of the answer lies in the fact that much of this goods revenue was earned by reliable, low cost machines of Class 101 (and also the slightly less distinguished MGWR standard goods 0-6-0s of the L/ Lm/ Ln family).

It is easy to understand therefore why Class 101 is the best known and most revered of all classes in the GSR fleet, and has with full justification been the subject of complete publications in its own right.

The modest axle loading gave these locomotives access to virtually the entire GSWR system, which remained their sphere of activities in GSR days although they were used in the 1920s and 1930s on ex-DSER routes, including the Dublin-Bray commuter trains. The shed allocations in later GSR days and early in the CIÉ regime indicate that their principal activities remained fairly constantly in old GSWR territory. They were absent from ex-MGWR sheds where reliance was placed on the local equivalent, the L/ Lm/ Ln family of 0-6-0s.

Shed allocation of Class 101:	**1938**	**1945**
Limerick	21	21
Waterford	17	21
Rosslare	2	–
Cork	16	10
Thurles	1	4
Mallow	–	7
Tralee	10	12
Inchicore	16	19
Grand Canal Street	1	–
Bray	2	–
Wexford	2	–

Their robust, simple construction made them great favourites with locomotive crews and shed staff, while their reliability and economy in operation pleased the financial managers. They continued in a broad range of duties, fundamentally unchanged throughout their long working careers and were to be found on every type of work, including express passenger where they were often called upon to act as pilot engines especially on the departure from Cork. An example of the high regard in which the class was held at operating level comes from a report dated August 1936 concerning the working of main line trains between Wexford and Dublin. These duties were shared between ex-DSER 4-4-0 No 454, ex-GSWR 4-4-0s Nos 302 and 306, and No 111.

Opposite left: GSWR/ GSR Class 101/ J15 No 176, with 4' 4" boiler fitted with modern smokebox, seen at at Cork Glanmire shed.
CP Friel collection

Top right: GSWR/ GSR Class 101/ J15 No 104 with Z-type superheated Belpaire boiler at Waterford shed in 1931.
L&GRP

Lower right: GSWR/ GSR Class 101/ J15 No 137 with Z-type superheated Belpaire boiler and Class 342 tender at the Broadstone.
CP Friel collection

At the other end of the operating spectrum, Class 101 was the preferred motive power for working the difficult, steeply-inclined Castlecomer branch to the Deerpark colliery. Special operating instructions applied on this section, but only one class member (No 150) received any particular modification for this work. It was equipped with a tender cab constructed out of timber which was merely bolted in place. Further, it worked as a 2-4-0 on these duties with the front connecting rods temporarily removed.

Despite the provision of larger boilers and Belpaire fireboxes, these locomotives retained their charming 19th century styling and appearance until the end; No 184 was the last to lose its characteristic double-doored smoke box (in 1948).

1948 assessment: *The general purpose small Goods engine can work over most lines. There are many variations within the class. Will also work Branch Passenger trains and, where assisted, Sunday Specials off low axleload branches.*

GSWR/ GSR Class 101/ J15 No 111 at Waterford on arrival from Macmine Junction. *HC Casserley*

An English Postscript

McDonnell left Inchicore in 1883 for the North Eastern Railway where he quickly deployed his administrative talents in re-organising that company's works at Darlington and Gateshead, rather in the fashion of what he had done for the GSWR years earlier. His efforts seem to have been resented for his stay with the NER was short and unhappy, but he did find time to introduce the 59 Class of 0-6-0s which eventually totalled 44 locomotives (32 built in four batches of eight by the NER and twelve by R Stephenson). There were several differences between the batches but some resembled a larger version of Class 101 – curved running plate over leading and centre driving wheels, GSWR-style cab and tender, left hand drive. Most prominent was the backward-sloping smokebox front profile with antiquated double smoke box doors, a pure GSWR feature that was unique among NER classes. Allocated Class J22 by the LNER, the last survivor was withdrawn in 1930.

McDonnell died on 4 December 1904 at the Railway Hotel, Holyhead *en route* to Ireland for his brother's funeral.

GSWR/ GSR Class 201 — 0-6-0T — Inchicore Class J11 / 1925/ 1931 Load Class F/ FT

GSWR/ GSR No	Built	Withdrawn	GSWR/ GSR No	Built	Withdrawn
201	12/1895	1963	210	1887	1959
202	12/1895	1955	217	1901	1961
207	1887	1959	218	1901	1959
208	1887	1959	219	1901	1955
209	1887	1949	220	1901	1959

Designer: Ivatt

Built at Inchicore

Locomotives built 1887:

Boiler pressure – 150 lbs/ sq in
Cylinders – 18" x 24"
Driving wheels – 4' 6½"
Wheel base – 7' 3" + 8' 3"
Locomotive length – 29' 11"

Heating surfaces:
tubes – 938 sq ft
firebox – 112.5 sq ft
grate – 18.8 sq ft

Tractive effort – 18,200 lbs
Coal capacity – 2 tons
Water capacity – 945 gal
Locomotive weight – 40 tons 4 cwt
Max axle loading – 15 tons 0 cwt

Locomotives built 1895:

Boiler pressure – 160 lbs/ sq in
(later reduced to 150 lbs/ sq in)

Heating surfaces:
tubes – 823 ft
firebox – 112.5 sq ft
grate – 19.3 sq ft

Tractive effort – 19,400 lbs
Coal capacity - 1 ton 10 cwt
Water Capacity – 730 gal
Locomotive weight – 42 tons 15 cwt
Max axle loading 15 tons 0 cwt

GSWR/ GSR Class 201/ J11 No 207 at Cork Glanmire Road Shed. *CP Friel collection*

Locomotives built 1901:

Boiler pressure – 160 lbs/ sq in (later reduced to 150 lbs/ sq in)	*Heating surfaces tubes – 934 sq ft: firebox – 105 sq ft grate – 19.3 sq ft*	*Tractive effort – 19,400 lbs Coal capacity – 1 ton 10 cwt Water capacity – 730 gal Locomotive weight – 43 tons 16 cwt Max axle loading -15 tons 10 cwt*

GSWR/ GSR Class 201/ J11 No 202 fitted with more modern smokebox and converted to run as an 0-4-2T; no details of this conversion have been traced.

WA Camwell

These locomotives were built for shunting work at Kingsbridge and Cork yards. A similar locomotive was created around 1914 but this remained classified as Class 204/ J12. In 1938–39, No 202 was noted working at Inchicore as an 0-4-2T. This was achieved by means of removing the coupling rods between driving and trailing wheels, and the locomotive was reportedly substituting for *Sambo*.

Nos 201 and 208 were noted in 1939 on the ex-CBSCR section, mainly used for shunting, although most unusually they were also used on passenger services.

1948 assessment (classes 201/ 204): *Powerful tank shunting engines, eminently suitable for heavy goods yard and banking of trains. Used mainly on Kingsbridge-North Wall and Cork-Rathpeacon services.*

GSWR/ GSR Class 203 — 0-6-4T — Inchicore Class H1

1925/ 1931 Load Class J/ KT

GSWR/ GSR No	Built	Rebuilt	Withdrawn
203	12/1879	–	1940
205	4/1880	1914§	1928
206	5/1880	–	1928

Designer: McDonnell **Built at Inchicore**

Boiler pressure – 150 lbs/ sq in	*Heating surfaces:*	*Tractive effort – 18,200 lbs*
Cylinders – 18" x 24"	*tubes – 900 sq ft*	*Coal capacity – 2 tons 10 cwt*
Driving wheels – 4' 6½"	*firebox – 103.5 sq ft*	*Water capacity – 1540 gal*
Bogie wheels – 3' 9"	*grate – 18.8 sq ft*	*Locomotive weight – 51 tons 6 cwt*
Wheel base – 7' 3" + 8' 3" + 4' 10½" + 5' 5"		*Adhesive weight – 35 tons 13 cwt*
Locomotive length – 36' 5"		*Max axle loading – 12 tons 13 cwt*

§ Rebuilt with Class 60 boiler

Boiler pressure – 150 lbs/ sq in	*Heating surfaces:*	*Locomotive weight – 49 tons 11 cwt*
	tubes – 878.6 sq ft	*Adhesive weight – 36 tons 19 cwt*
	firebox – 112.5 sq ft	*Max axle loading – 12 tons 10 cwt*
	grate area – 18.8 sq ft	

Built as goods shunters and later used on transfer goods duties, these locomotives were generally similar to the first Class 201 0-6-4T of 1876 (see 0-6-0T *Jumbo* Class J13).

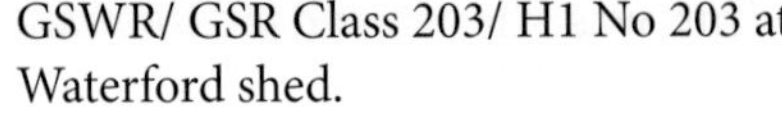

GSWR/ GSR Class 203/ H1 No 203 at Waterford shed.

Real Photographs Co Ltd

GSWR/ GSR Class 203/ H1 No 205 as rebuilt with Class 60 boiler, on a North Wall-Kingsbridge transfer goods working.

KA Murray

GSWR/ GSR Class 204 0-6-0T Inchicore Class J12 1925/ 1931 Load Class F/ FT

GSWR/ GSR No	Built (as an 0-6-4T)	Rebuilt (as an 0-6-0T)	Withdrawn
204	12/1879	1914	1952

Designer: McDonnell **Built at Inchicore**

Boiler pressure – 160 lbs/ sq in	*Heating surfaces:*	*Tractive effort – 19,400 lbs*
Cylinders – 18" x 24"	*tubes – 823 sq ft*	*Coal capacity – 1 ton 10 cwt*
Driving wheels – 4' 6½"	*firebox – 112.5 sq ft*	*Water capacity – 1130 gal*
Wheel base – 7' 3" + 8' 3"	*grate – 18.8 sq ft*	*Locomotive weight – 48 tons 10 cwt*
Locomotive length – 29' 2¼"		*Max axle loading – 17 tons 19 cwt*

GSWR/ GSR Class 204/ J12 No 204 at Inchicore, in early condition with sloping smokebox front.

Real Photographs Co Ltd

This was the second of four locomotives built as member of Class 203 (GSR H1). However, in the 0-6-4T form, the frames were prone to bending when the locomotives were lifted for repairs, so Maunsell had No 204 rebuilt as an 0-6-0T and fitted with a Class 60 boiler in 1914. The result was dimensionally similar to Class 201/ J11 but always treated as a separate class. In 1938 this locomotive was employed as banker for heavier trains out of Kingsbridge as far as Inchicore.

1948 assessment (classes 201/ 204): *Powerful tank shunting engines, eminently suitable for heavy goods yard and banking of trains. Used mainly on Kingsbridge-North Wall and Cork-Rathpeacon services.*

GSWR/ GSR Class 211 0-6-0 Inchicore Class J3 1925/ 1931 Load Class C/ E

GSWR/ GSR No	Built (as 0-6-2T)	Makers' No	Rebuilt (as 0-6-0)	Withdrawn
211	12/1903	16021	1907	1949
212	12/1903	16022	1907	1951

Designer: Coey **Built by North British Locomotive Co**

Boiler pressure – 160 lbs/ sq in	*Heating surfaces:*	*Tractive effort – 21,020 lbs*
Cylinders – 18" x 26"	*tubes – 1129 sq ft*	*Coal capacity – 5 tons 10 cwt*
Driving wheels – 4' 6½"	*firebox – 118 sq ft*	*Water capacity – 2730 gal*
Wheel base – 7' 7" + 8' 6"	*grate – 20.4 sq ft*	*Locomotive weight – 44 tons 0 cwt*
Locomotive length – 26' 9¾"		*Max axle loading – 15 tons 3 cwt*

GSWR/ GSR Class 211/ J3 No 211 at Tralee shed. *CP Friel collection*

Originally Nos 211 to 214 were built as 0-6-2Ts for use on the Drumcondra link line but proved too heavy for this route. Nos 211 and 212 were accordingly rebuilt as 0-6-0s. Class 211 and their derivatives, Class 213, were always known as the 'Scotch engines'. Both variants were always heavy on coal and water.

1948 assessment: *On paper very powerful but power obtained by too small wheels (or low gear) with the result they have a short economic life. Suitable only for Goods on undulating lines such as DSER, Waterford-Mallow and Mallow-Tralee sections. Only two in class.*

GSWR/ GSR Class 213 — 0-6-2T — Inchicore Class I1, 1925/ 1931 Load Class C/ FT

GSR No	Built	Makers' No	Withdrawn
213	12/1903	16023	1952
214	12/1903	16024	1949

Designer: Coey

Built by North British Locomotive Co

Boiler pressure – 160 lbs/ sq in	*Heating surfaces:*	*Tractive effort – 21,020 lbs*
Cylinders – 18" x 26"	*tubes – 1040 sq ft*	*Coal capacity – 2 tons 5 cwt*
Driving wheels – 4' 6½"	*firebox – 118 sq ft*	*Water capacity – 1050 gal*
Trailer wheels – 3' 9"	*grate – 20.4 sq ft*	*Locomotive weight – 58 tons 0 cwt*
Wheel base – 7' 7" + 8' 6" + 6' 0"		*Adhesive weight – 47 tons 7 cwt*
Locomotive length – 35' 2"		*Max axle loading – 17 tons 3 cwt*

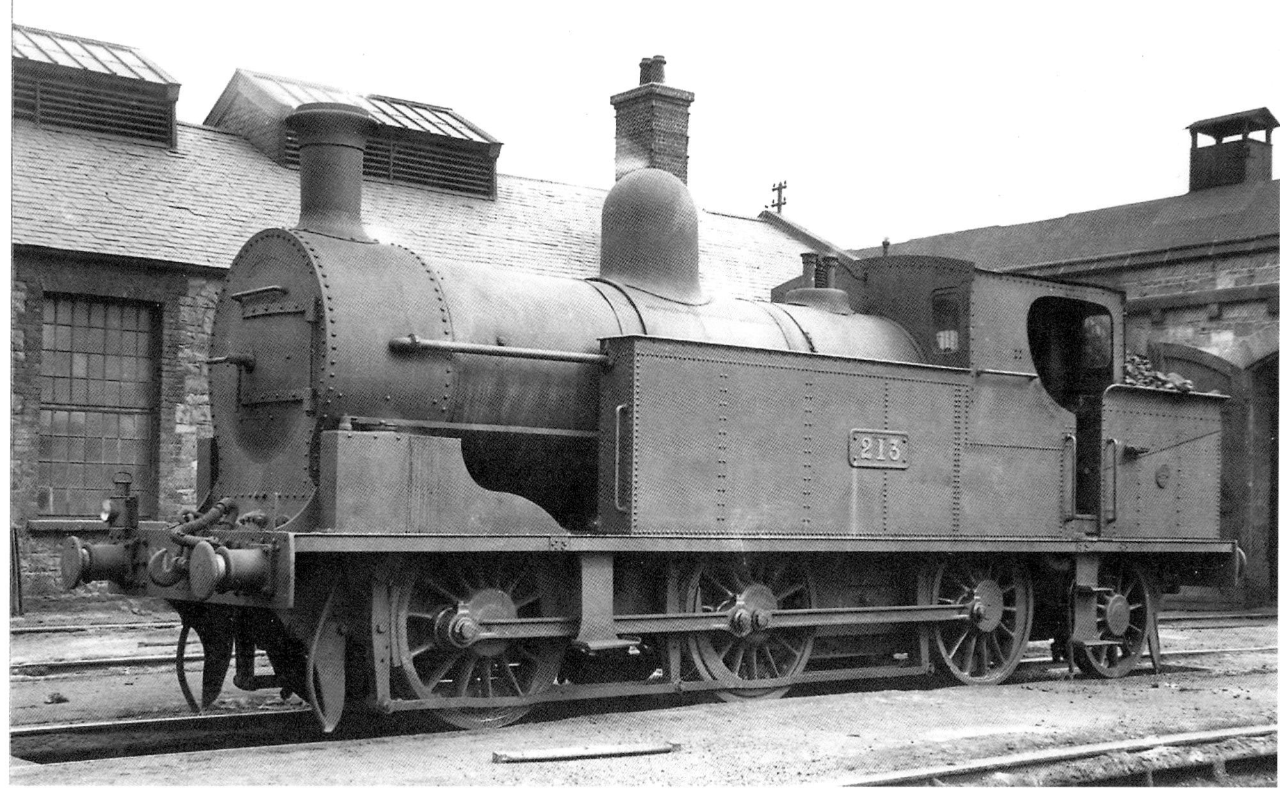

GSWR/ GSR Class 213/ I1 No 213 at Inchicore in 1936. *L&GRP*

Originally Nos 211 to 214 were built as 0-6-2Ts for use on the Drumcondra link line but proved too heavy for this route. Nos 213 and 214 were retained on these duties after having the water capacity reduced to lower the overall working weight. Following withdrawal of 4-8-0T Class 900, they found additional work as bankers on heavy goods trains as far as Clondalkin.

1948 assessment: *A tank engine edition of the 211 class. Primarily a shunter but used as expedient on Cork/ Bandon section, being a tank engine and low* (sic) *axleload.*

GSWR/ GSR Classes 222 — 0-6-0 — Inchicore Class J25
1925/ 1931 Load Class M/ L

GSWR/GSR No	Built	Makers' No	Rebuilt	Withdrawn
222 (2 *Shannon*)*	3/1900	3908	1924	1949
237 (56 *Thunderer*)*	1897	3691	1926	1951
238 (57 *Cyclops*)*	1897	3692	1925	1934
239 (58 *Goliath*)*	1897	3693	1925	1949

* Original WLWR number and name in brackets – see comments below

Designer: Robinson — **Built by Kitson**

GSWR/ GSR Class 222/ J25 No 237 at Inchicore in 1932. *HC Casserley*

No 222 as built:

Boiler pressure – 150 lbs/ sq in
Cylinders – 17" x 24"
Driving wheels – 5' 2"
Wheel base – 7' 6" + 8' 3"
Locomotive length – 26' 0"

Heating surfaces:
tubes – 873 sq ft
firebox – 108 sq ft
grate – 17.8 sq ft

Tractive effort – 14,270 lbs
Coal capacity – 4 tons
Water capacity – 2000 gal
Locomotive weight – 40 tons 14 cwt
Max axle loading – 13 tons 14 cwt

Other sources state weight 41 tons 4 cwt and max axle loading 14 tons 2 cwt)

No 237-239 as built:

Boiler pressure – 150 lbs/ sq in
Cylinders – 17" x 24"
Driving wheels – 5' 2"
Wheel base – 7' 6" + 8' 3"

Heating surfaces:
tubes – 991 sq ft
firebox – 107 sq ft
grate – 19.8 sq ft

Tractive effort – 14,270 lbs
Coal capacity – 4 tons
Water capacity – 1900 gal
Locomotive weight – 37 tons 0 cwt
Max axle loading – 11 tons 13 cwt

All as rebuilt:

Heating surfaces:
tubes – 918 sq ft
firebox – 99 sq ft
grate – 19.8 sq ft

Locomotive weight – 39 tons 16 cwt
Max axle loading – 13 tons 14 cwt

(Although the WLWR names were removed soon after the GSWR takeover, they are included here because confusion does arise over the names and identities of these four engines, and the two members of MGWR Class W (GSR Class 233) which were identical).

The WLWR had ordered two more this type but prior to delivery a dispute arose with Kitson about the method of payment in the face of the pending takeover by the GSWR. Before settlement could be reached, the pair was sold to the MGWR where they were numbered 141 and 142, and allocated Class W. At the amalgamation, they were given numbers 233 and 234 within the ex-GSWR number block and the same Inchicore classification but were allocated separate GSR Class 234, despite being identical with Class 222.

No 222 was a machine of distinction. It was provided from new with a Belpaire boiler, being the first Robinson engine and first broad gauge Irish railway locomotive to carry this feature. Further, it was the first locomotive to be adorned with the characteristically graceful chimney which was to become the Robinson trademark.

Their activities were confined to goods haulage between Limerick, Tuam and Waterford, on which work they were considered around eight wagons weaker than the Class 101 (J15). Throughout their lives they carried timber buffer beams, back and front.

1948 assessment: *These are similar to the Standard Goods* (ie Class 101) *but smaller. Their loads are, of course, less and they are only suitable for small branches or specials.*

GSWR/ GSR Class 228 — 0-4-0ST — Inchicore Class not allocated

GSWR/GSR No	Built	Makers' No	Withdrawn
228 (29)	1865	1653	1925

Built by Sharp Stewart

Boiler pressure – 120 lbs/ sq in	*Heating surfaces:*	*Tractive effort – 6,070 lbs*
Cylinders – 12" x 17"	*total – 344.5 sq ft*	*Coal capacity – not recorded*
Driving wheels – 4' 0"	*grate – 8.7 sq ft*	*Water capacity – 320 gal*
Wheel base – 7' 4½"		*Locomotive weight – 20 tons 18 cwt*
Locomotive length – 20' 5½"		

This was the only WLWR locomotive acquired by the GSWR that had not been introduced during the Robinson era. After an earlier career as a branch line engine, it was confined to yard duties from 1880. The disposal of this locomotive, which carried the unofficial name of 'Darkie', is obscure. It was supposedly scrapped in 1928 but was reportedly unofficially in use as a shunter in various sidings around Limerick until the early 1930s.

GSWR/ GSR Class 228 (No Inchicore class) No 228 at Limerick. *IRRS collection*

GSR Class 235 (Previously GSWR Class 233) — 0-6-0 — Inchicore Class J22, 1925/ 1931 Load Class M/ L

GSWR/GSR No*	Built	Makers' No	Rebuilt	Withdrawn
235 (49)	1895	3222	1924	1927
236 (50)	1895	3223	1925	1951

* Original WLWR number in brackets

Designer: Robinson

Built by Dubs, Glasgow

Boiler pressure – 150 lbs/ sq in	*Heating surfaces:*	*Tractive effort – 15,240 lbs*
Cylinders – 17½" x 24"	*tubes – 991 sq ft*	*Coal capacity – 3 tons 5 cwt*
Driving wheels – 5' 1½"	*firebox – 107 sq ft*	*Water capacity – 1900 or 2000 gal*
Wheel base – 7' 6" + 8' 3"	*grate – 17.75 sq ft*	*Locomotive weight – 37 tons 0 cwt*
Locomotive length – 26' 7"		*Max axle loading – 12 tons 16 cwt*

As rebuilt:	*Heating surfaces:*	*Locomotive weight – 39 tons 16 cwt*
	tubes – 918 sq ft	*Max axle loading – 13 tons 14 cwt*
	firebox – 99 sq ft	
	grate – 19.8 sq ft	

GSR Class 235 (previously GSWR Class 233)/ J22 No 236 at Ennis in 1931. *L&GRP*

These were basically the same as Class 222 (J25) but were more powerful on account of their larger cylinders, rating them as haulage capacity equal to that of Class 101 (J15).

GSWR/ GSR Class 257 0-6-0 Inchicore Class J4 1925/ 1931 Load Class C/ C

GSWR/ GSR No	Built	Rebuilt	Withdrawn	GSWR/ GSR No	Built	Rebuilt	Withdrawn
257	10/1913	1934*	1960	261	11/1914	1948*	1965
258	10/1913	1937*/ 1952§	1963	262	11/1914	1934*	1965
259	11/1913	1935*	1959	263	12/1914	1936*	1962
260	11/1913	1931*/ 1948§	1962	264	12/1914	1932*	1960

Designer: Maunsell **Built at Inchicore**

Rebuilt with boiler type: * Belpaire superheated
§ round-topped, as originally built

Boiler pressure – 160 lbs/ sq in	*Heating surfaces:*	*Tractive effort – 20,680 lbs*
Cylinders – 19" x 26"	*tubes – 844 sq ft*	*Coal capacity – 7 tons*
Driving wheels – 5' 1¾"	*firebox – 118 sq ft*	*Water capacity – 3345 gal*
Piston valves – 8"	*superheater – 224 sq ft*	*Locomotive weight – 47 tons 5 cwt*
Wheel base – 7' 7" + 8' 6"	*grate – 20.4 sq ft*	*Max axle loading – 17 tons 0 cwt*
Locomotive length – 28' 2¼"		

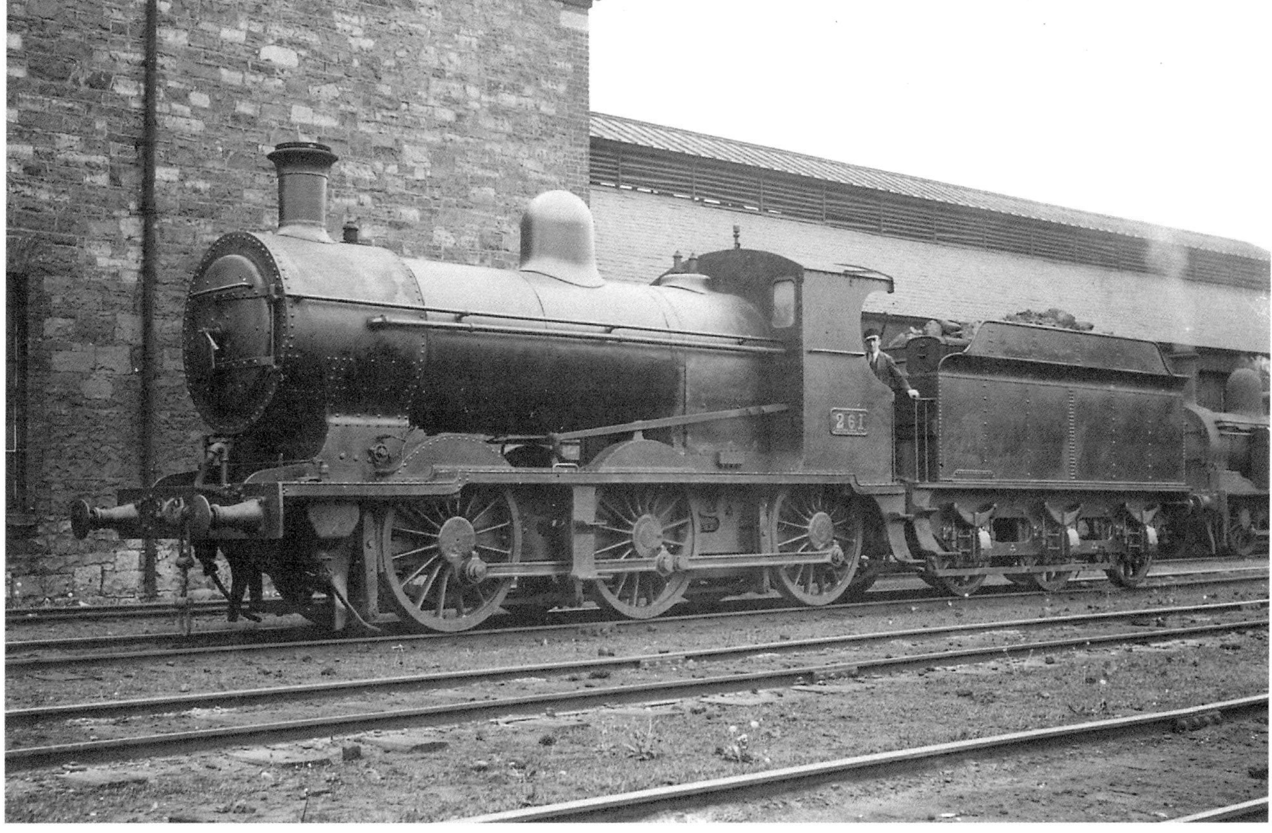

GSWR/ GSR Class 257/ J4 No 261 in original condition at Inchicore in 1938. *CP Friel collection*

*** As rebuilt with Belpaire superheated boiler:**

Heating surfaces:	Locomotive weight – 46 tons 11 cwt
tubes – 708 sq ft	Max axle loading – 16 tons 11 cwt
firebox – 120 sq ft	
superheater – 168 sq ft	
grate – 19.5 sq ft	

GSWR/ GSR Class 257/ J4 No 261 as rebuilt in CIE days with superheated Belpaire type N boiler and seen at Cork. The tender appears to be a hybrid, comprising an ex-GSWR Type A chassis and a non-standard body.

Real Photographs Co Ltd

These locomotives were a development of the Class 351 (J9) but encompassed more modern design principles being the first locomotives on the GSWR with superheaters and piston valves. Nos 257-261 were equipped with Schmidt superheaters while the remainder had Inchicore-modified superheaters. The 1914-built examples were actually completed in Watson's time and were fitted with snifting valves.

This class was highly regarded, being effective in working both goods and secondary passenger services. These locomotives, noted for their distinctive staccato-like exhaust, were much in demand for working goods and seasonal beet trains over the difficult Rosslare route. The one exception was No 263, always regarded as a poor engine and a perpetually reluctant steamer; when based at Waterford, it was known as the 'whistling gipsy' because of its peculiar whistle on the fourth beat. Even in the last days of steam, they continued to give a good account of themselves. In 1947, No 264 was the first steam locomotive to be converted to oil-firing. No 261 was the last working steam locomotive on CIÉ, albeit in the humble role of stationary boiler at Kingsbridge, until 1966.

1948 assessment: *These are a very good engine for Goods working, economic and with a long life. Axle load gives them a wide range. I would like to see half the 101 class scrapped and many other stray Goods classes, and replaced by this design.*

GSR Class 267 (Previously GSWR Class 266) — 2-4-2T — Inchicore Class F4, 1925/ 1931 Load Class Q/ PT

GSWR/ GSR No*	Built	Makers' No	Withdrawn
267 (14)	1891	1316	1935

* Original WLWR number in brackets

Designer: Robinson — **Built by Vulcan Foundry**

See also Cork & Macroom Direct Railway

Boiler pressure – 150 lbs/ sq in	*Heating surfaces:*	*Tractive effort – 11,870 lbs*
Cylinders – 16" x 24"	*tubes – 780 sq ft*	*Coal capacity – 2 tons*
Pony wheels – 3' 6"	*firebox – 88 sq ft*	*Water capacity – 1200 gal*
Driving wheels – 5' 6"	*grate – 15 sq ft*	*Locomotive weight – 45 tons 0 cwt*
Trailing wheels – 3' 6"		*Adhesive weight – 24 tons 0 cwt*
Wheel base – 7' 8" + 7' 6" + 6' 3"		*Max axle loading – 12 tons 10 cwt*
Locomotive length – 34' 0" (estimated)		

GSR Class 267 previously GSWR Class 266/ F4 No 267 at Inchicore in 1938. *R Conway*

The two locomotives of this type were built for passenger work between Limerick and Tralee. They were reportedly modelled on Aspinall's numerous Class 5 2-4-2Ts for the Lancashire & Yorkshire Railway, although there was little similarity in the leading dimensions. They came into GSWR stock with the acquisition of the WLWR in 1900, but sister locomotive No 266 was sold to the Cork & Macroom Direct Railway in 1914, becoming that railway's No 6. At the amalgamation, the GSR failed to recognise the similarity between the two locomotives and so CMDR No 6 became No 491 of Class 491, Inchicore Class F5 (withdrawn 1934).

Although officially withdrawn in 1935, No 267 provided hot water for boiler wash-out facilities at the Broadstone from 1933 until 1938.

GSWR/ GSR Class 269 — 4-4-2T — Inchicore Class C5, 1925/ 1931 Load Class P/ OT

GSWR/ GSR No*	Built	Makers' No	Rebuilt	Withdrawn	GSWR/ GSR No*	Built	Makers' No	Rebuilt	Withdrawn
269 (16)	1896	3616	1925	1957	271 (18)	1897	3689	1926	1949
270 (17)	1896	3617	1926	1949	274 (21)	1897	3690	1924	1949

* Original WLWR number in brackets

Designer: Robinson **Built by Kitson**

Boiler pressure – 150 lbs/ sq in
Cylinders – 16" x 24"
Bogie wheels – 3' 6"
Driving wheels – 5' 6"
Trailing wheels – 3' 6"
Wheel base – 5' 6" + 6' 11" + 7' 6" + 6' 3"
Locomotive length – 36' 10½"

Heating surfaces:
tubes – 780 sq ft
firebox – 88 sq ft
grate – 15 sq ft

Tractive effort – 11,870 lbs
Coal capacity – 1 ton 15 cwt
Water capacity – 1040 gal
Locomotive weight – 47 tons 10 cwt
Adhesive weight – 26 tons 0 cwt
Max axle loading – 13 tons 15 cwt

As rebuilt:

Heating surfaces:
tubes – 800 sq ft
firebox – 94 sq ft
grate – 15.8 sq ft

Water capacity – 1200 gal
Locomotive weight – 50 tons 12 cwt
Adhesive weight – 26 tons 15 cwt
Max axle loading – 13 tons 15 cwt

(In 1944, No 271 was fitted with 15½" diameter cylinders, reducing the tractive effort to 11,140 lbs)

This is considered to be Robinson's first essay into 'large engine' design and to some extent foreshadowed his Class 9K and 9L 4-4-2Ts for the Great Central Railway. These locomotives were ordered particularly for use on the Sligo extension of the WLWR but in GSR days found employment elsewhere, being noted at Wexford, Rocksavage (Cork) and on ex-DSER section suburban traffic. No 269 was the last Robinson tank engine in Ireland.

1948 assessment (269/ 295 classes): *Obsolete small passenger engines suitable only for small branches and Cork-Bandon section: light shunting. Used as an expedient rather than by choice.*

GSWR/ GSR Class 269/ C5 No 271 at Inchicore.
CP Friel collection

GSR CLASS 276 (Previously GSWR Class 263) — 2-4-0 — Inchicore Class G3, 1925 Load Class P

GSWR/ GSR No*	Built	Makers' No	Rebuilt	Withdrawn
276 (23)	3/1892	2881	1925	1949
290 (43)	6/1893	3025	1926	1951
291 (44)	6/1893	3026	1925	1959
293 (48)	6/1894	3110	1925	1954

* Original WLWR numbers in brackets

Designer: Robinson

Built by Dubs, Glasgow

As built:

Boiler pressure – 150 lbs/ sq in
Cylinders – 17" x 24"
Radial wheels – 4' 0"
Driving wheels – 6' 0"
Wheel base – 7' 4" + 8' 6"
Locomotive length – 26' 2½"

Heating surfaces:
tubes – 991 sq ft
firebox – 107 sq ft
grate – 18 sq ft

Tractive effort – 12,280 lbs
Coal capacity – c.160 cu ft
Water capacity – 1900 or 1940 gal
Locomotive weight – 36 tons 9 cwt
Adhesive weight – 24 tons 14 cwt
Max axle loading – 12 tons 10 cwt

As rebuilt:

Heating surfaces:
tubes – 918 sq ft
firebox – 99 sq ft
grate – 19.8 sq ft

Locomotive weight – 38 tons 11 cwt
Adhesive weight – 26 tons 9 cwt
Max axle loading – 13 tons 9 cwt

This class was the first designed by Robinson for express passenger service and originally comprised eight members, the first four (GSWR Nos 263, 273, 275 and 292) of which were withdrawn between 1906 and 1913. The survival of the remainder until well after World War II was therefore all the more remarkable. The GSWR had used the class on secondary passenger duties and in GSR days they worked in the west; eg on the Loughrea Branch, and were found at Claremorris and Limerick. No 290 was attached to the Waterford area and worked from there to Enniscorthy and Rosslare.

1948 assessment: *A very light passenger engine suitable only for Branch lines or Pilots. Obsolete type.*

GSWR/ GSR Class 276/ G3 No 290 at Waterford in 1931.
L&GRP

GSWR/ GSR Class 279 0-4-4T Inchicore Class E1
1925/ 1931 Load Class P/ OT

GSWR/GSR No*	Built	Makers' No	Rebuilt	Withdrawn
279 (27)	1876	1127	1899§/ 1927¶	1953

* Original WLWR number in brackets

§ Built originally as an 0-4-2 and rebuilt as an 0-4-4T in 1899

¶ Rebuilt with larger cylinders

Designer: Robinson **Built by Avonside Engine Co**

As built:

Boiler pressure – 150 lbs/ sq in
Cylinders – 16" x 24"
Driving wheels – 5' 4"
Bogie wheels – 3' 6"
Wheel base – 7' 10" + 8' 5" + 5' 6"
Locomotive length – 34' 7"

Heating surfaces:
tubes – 808 sq ft
firebox – 88 sq ft
grate – 15.8 sq ft

Tractive effort – 12,240 lbs
Coal capacity – 2 tons 10 cwt
Water capacity – 1200 gal
Locomotive weight – 49 tons 19 cwt
Adhesive weight – 28 tons 12 cwt
Max axle loading – 15 tons 3 cwt

As rebuilt in 1927:

Cylinders 17" x 24"

Heating surfaces
tubes – 853 sq ft
firebox – 92 sq ft
grate – 15.8 sq ft

Tractive effort – 13,820 lbs

GSWR/ GSR Class 279/ E1 No 279 on the turntable at Broadstone. *CP Friel collection*

This locomotive was the last survivor of a class of four 0-4-2s built in 1876. The rationale for its rebuilding with larger cylinders and another boiler when it was already 51 years old and a singleton is unclear.

1948 assessment: *Completely obsolete.*

GSR Class 295 (Previously GSWR Class 294) — 0-4-4T — Inchicore Class E2, 1925/ 1931 Load Class Q/ PT

GSWR/GSR No*	Built	Makers' No	Rebuilt	Withdrawn
295 (52)	1895	3588	1926	1954

* Original WLWR number in brackets

Designer: Robinson — **Built by Kitson**

As built:

Boiler pressure – 150 lbs/ sq in
Cylinders – 16" x 24"
Driving wheels – 5' 6"
Bogie wheels – 3' 6"
Wheel base – 7' 6" + 8' 9" + 5' 6"
Locomotive length – 33' 2"

Heating surfaces:
total – 868 sq ft
grate – 15.8 sq ft

Tractive effort – 11,870 lbs
Coal capacity – 1 ton 10 cwt
Water capacity – 1000 gal
Locomotive weight – 43 tons 0 cwt
Adhesive weight – 26 tons 16 cwt
Max axle loading – 13 tons 12 cwt

As rebuilt

Heating surfaces:
tubes – 930 sq ft
firebox – 88 sq ft
grate – 15.8 sq ft

Water capacity – 1100 gal
Locomotive weight – 43 tons 0 cwt
Adhesive weight – 26 tons 4 cwt
Max axle loading – 13 tons 4 cwt

GSWR/ GSR Class 295/ E2 No 295 at Limerick in 1933. *L&GRP*

No 295 was the survivor of a pair of locomotives ordered for service on the Athenry and Tuam Extension to Claremorris Light Railway Company (the 'ATECLRC') and specifically designed to cope with the sharp curves on that route. In later years it operated from Limerick shed, but is believed to have finished its days in Dublin as a replacement for No 279.

1948 assessment (269/ 295 classes): *Obsolete small passenger engines suitable only for small branches and Cork-Bandon section: light shunting. Used as an expedient rather than by choice.*

GSWR/ GSR Class 296 4-4-0 Inchicore Class No D15 1925/ 1931 Load Class P/ O

GSWR/GSR No*	Built	Makers' No	Rebuilt	Withdrawn
296 (53)	3/1896	3618	1923¶/ 1939§	1949
297 (54)	4/1896	3619	–	1928
298 (55)	5/1897	3694	1927¶	1949

* Original WLWR number in brackets

Designer: Robinson **Built by Kitson**

As built:

Boiler pressure – 150 lbs/ sq in
Cylinders – 17" x 24"
Bogie wheels – 3' 6"
Driving wheels – 6' 0"
Wheel base – 5' 9" + 6' 8" + 8' 2"
Locomotive length – 28' 4½"

Heating surfaces:
tubes – 887.4 sq ft
firebox – 107 sq ft
grate – 19.8 sq ft

Tractive effort – 12,280 lbs
Coal capacity – 4 tons
Water capacity – 1940 or 2000 gal
Locomotive weight – 40 tons 0 cwt
Adhesive weight – 26 tons 10 cwt
Max axle loading – 13 tons 10 cwt

¶ As rebuilt:

Heating surfaces:
tubes – 918 sq ft
firebox – 99 sq ft
grate – 19.8 sq ft

Locomotive weight – 40 tons 16 cwt
Adhesive weight – 26 tons 12 cwt
Max axle loading – 13 tons 7 cwt

§ As rebuilt

Cylinders – 16½" x 24"

Tractive effort – 11,570 lbs

GSWR/ GSR Class 296/ D15 No 298 at Ennis in 1932. *HC Casserley*

This was Robinson's last design for the WLWR and used on that company's main line between Waterford and Limerick. Their principal intended use was the hauling of boat trains in connection with steam packets of the Great Western Railway that worked the Waterford-Milford service.

At the time of No 53's introduction in 1896, a press report stated that it to be the first of a class of ten locomotives. Presumably any intention to produce the remaining seven died with the takeover by the GSWR. In 1939/ 40 one of the survivors was still working from Limerick while the other was on secondary duties on the Birr branch.

1948 assessment: *Similar remarks to those re 234 and 276 classes: obsolete type.*

GSWR/ GSR Class 299 — 0-6-0ST — Inchicore Class J28, 1925/ 1931 Load Class T/ ST

GSWR/ GSR No	Built	Name	Makers' No	Withdrawn	
299	1892	*(Shamrock)*	557	1957	**Built by Hunslet Engine Co**

Boiler pressure – 120 lbs/ sq in	*Heating surfaces:*	*Tractive effort – 6,960 lbs*
Cylinders – 12" x 18"	*tubes – 356 sq ft*	*Coal capacity – 47 cu ft*
Driving wheels – 3' 2"	*firebox – 45 sq ft*	*Water capacity – 500 gal*
Wheel base – 5' 4" + 5' 2"	*grate – 7.4 sq ft*	*Locomotive weight – 23 tons 0 cwt*
Locomotive length – 22' 5"		*Max axle loading – 7 tons 9 cwt*

This locomotive was supplied to TH Falkiner apparently for use in construction of the Kenmare line, and was later sold to the Tralee and Fenit Pier and Harbour Company. It was acquired together with the WLWR locomotive stock on the acquisition of that railway. The name Shamrock was removed at the time the locomotive acquired its GSWR number.

It continued to be used at Fenit Pier until the closure of that facility in 1941 when it moved to Limerick. Later No 299 was found at Rocksavage Cork from where it was used to haul beet trains on the Courtmacsherry branch.

1948 assessment: *Completely obsolete.*

GSWR/ GSR Class 299/ J28 No 299 at Inchicore in 1938.

WA Camwell

GSWR/ GSR Class *Erin* (nominally 300) — 0-6-0ST — Inchicore Class J27, 1925 Load Class S

GSWR/ GSR No	Name	Built	Makers' No	Withdrawn	
(300)	*Erin*	o/1894	610	1930	**Built by Hunslet Engine Co**

Boiler pressure – 130 lbs/ sq in	*Heating surfaces:*	*Tractive effort – 9,280 lbs*
Cylinders – 14" x 18"	*tubes – 520 sq ft*	*Coal capacity – 44 cu ft*
Driving wheels – 3' 6"	*firebox – 54 sq ft*	*Water capacity – 580 gal*
Wheel base – 5' 4" + 5' 5"	*grate – 8.25 sq ft*	*Locomotive weight – 25 tons 18 cwt*
Locomotive length – not recorded		*Max axle loading – 9 tons 1 cwt*

This was a contractors' locomotive built for Messrs Rowland and Cartland for use in the construction of the Wexford and Rosslare Railway. It was taken into stock by the GSWR in 1898 from the Waterford & Wexford Railway and allocated the number 300 which it never carried, just retaining its name. Before withdrawal it was working in the Tralee area.

GSWR/ GSR Class 'Erin'/ J27 *Erin* (No 300).

L&GRP

GSWR/ GSR CLASSES 301 — 4-4-0 — Inchicore Class D11
1925/ 1931 Load Class N/ M

GSWR/ GSR No	Name*	Built	Rebuilt	Withdrawn	GSWR/ GSR No	Name*	Built	Rebuilt	Withdrawn
301	*Victoria*	4/1900	1931§	1960	303	*Saint Patrick*	6/1900	1932§	1959
302	*Lord Roberts*	4/1900	1932§	1957	304	*Princess Ena*	6/1900	1933§	1959

* All names removed relatively early, believed to be in 1906.

§ Rebuilt with Belpaire superheated boiler type N

Designer: Coey — **Built at Inchicore**

Boiler pressure – 160 lbs/ sq in
Cylinders – 18" x 26"
Bogie wheels – 3' 6"
Driving wheels – 6' 7"
Wheel base – 6' 4" + 6' 10" + 8' 6"
Locomotive length – 29' 10¾"

Heating surfaces:
tubes – 1011.75 sq ft
firebox – 116 sq ft
grate – 20.4 sq ft

Tractive effort – 14,500 lbs
Coal capacity – 7 tons
Water capacity – 3345 gal
Locomotive weight – 47 tons 0 cwt
Adhesive weight – 30 tons 11 cwt
Max axle loading – 15 tons 19 cwt

NB As built the heating surfaces were recorded as tubes – 1100 sq ft, firebox – 120 sq ft but apparently they were altered to the dimensions quoted above some time before 1925.

GSWR/ GSR Class 301/ D11 No 302 as built. *Real Photographs Co Ltd*

§ As rebuilt with Belpaire superheater boiler type N:

	Heating surfaces:	*Locomotive weight – 47 tons 0 cwt*
	tubes – 708 sq ft	*Adhesive weight – 30 tons 11 cwt*
	firebox – 120 sq ft	*Max axle loading – 16 tons 9 cwt*
	superheater – 168 sq ft	
	grate – 19.5 sq ft	

The Bob Clements archives include references to Nos 301 and 302 which indicate that these two engines might have been subject to modification by the GSWR There is a note that they were fitted with piston valves but that the slide valve version (presumably Nos 303 and 304) achieved higher mileages, and also that Belpaire fireboxes might have been fitted. No dates or other details are given to indicate the dates on which piston valves/ Belpaire fireboxes were fitted and removed, nor why the modifications were made. There is a further note that an undated diagram had been seen purportedly relating to No 301 with the following dimensional differences:

Boiler pressure – 175 lbs/ sq in	*Heating surfaces:*	*Tractive effort – 15,860 lbs*
Wheel base – 6' 4" + 7' 1" + 9' 0"	*tubes – 1278 sq ft*	*Locomotive weight – 49 tons 0 cwt*
	firebox – 131 sq ft	*Adhesive weight – 32 tons 0 cwt*
		Max axle loading – 16 tons 0 cwt

GSWR/ GSR Class 301/ D11 No 304 as rebuilt with superheated Belpaire type-N boiler. At Limerick.

CH Hewison

No other information is provided; the notation of No 301 might simply have been a clerical error. However the dimensions do not accord with those of later 4-4-0s, so the reliability of this data is questionable.

--- o O o ---

This was Coey's first express design and a marked move away from the traditional GSWR 4-4-0. They were designed for main line work but were used 1906-7 on Cork-Rosslare services before moving to secondary main line work.

No 301 was the last surviving ex-GSR 4-4-0 and stood semi-derelict in Limerick for some time. Serious flooding at Ballycar between Limerick and Ennis in December 1960–January 1961 led to interruption of services until 10 March when services were restored using steam power only. The next day, despite having been withdrawn, No 301 appeared at work on this section (where it exceeded the permitted maximum axle loading), and was later seen on other duties in the Ennis area. It then worked for period in the Dublin area before becoming a stationary boiler at Inchicore, at least until mid-1962.

1948 assessment (covers classes 301/ 309/ 310): *Perform almost similar work. Suit local passenger trains in the Districts. Not much use for Goods trains. Given suitable load can run quite fast.*

GSWR/ GSR CLASS 305 — 4-4-0 — Inchicore Class D12, 1925/ 1931 Load Class N/ M

GSWR/ GSR No	Built	Rebuilt	Withdrawn	GSWR/ GSR No	Built	Rebuilt	Withdrawn
305	6/1902	1906*/ 1930§	1957	307	6/1902	1906*/ 1937§	1959
306	6/1902	1906*/ 1931¶/ 1935§	1959	308	6/1902	1904*	1933

Rebuilt with boiler type: * Tapered saturated
§ Belpaire superheated
¶ Large diameter Belpaire superheated

Designer: Coey **Built at Inchicore**

*** As rebuilt with tapered saturated boiler:**

Boiler pressure – 160 lbs/ sq in
Cylinders – 18" x 26"
Bogie wheels – 3' 6"
Driving wheels – 6' 7"
Wheel base – 6' 4" + 6' 10" + 8' 6"
Locomotive length – 29' 10¾"

Heating surfaces:
tubes – 1283.9 sq ft
firebox – 128.1 sq ft
grate – 21 sq ft

Tractive effort – 14,500 lbs
Coal capacity – 7 tons
Water capacity – 3345 gal
Locomotive weight – 49 tons 15 cwt
Adhesive weight – 31 tons 9 cwt
Max axle loading – 15 tons 15 cwt

In this condition, No 308 had a unique boiler which 5 5/8" longer on the front ring which increased the tube heating surface by 82 sq ft. No dates are recorded but presumably it was carried from 1904 until withdrawal.

§ As rebuilt with Belpaire superheated boiler (Type O):

Boiler pressure – 180 lbs/ sq in

Heating surfaces:
tubes – 1084 sq ft
firebox – 136.7 sq ft
superheater – 224 sq ft
grate – 21 sq ft

Tractive effort – 16,320 lbs
Locomotive weight – 51 tons 1 cwt
Adhesive weight – 31 tons 14 cwt
Max axle loading – 15 tons 17 cwt

¶ As rebuilt with large diameter Belpaire superheated boiler (Type N):

Boiler pressure – 160 lbs/ sq in

Heating surfaces:
tubes – 708 sq ft
firebox – 120 sq ft
superheater – 168 sq ft
grate – 19.5 sq ft

Tractive effort – 14,500 lbs
Locomotive weight – 47 tons 0 cwt
Adhesive weight – 30 tons 11 cwt
Max axle loading – 15 tons 19 cwt

On introduction, this class was very similar to Class 301 but with slightly larger heating surfaces. The first rebuilding of No 308 involved the installation of the first tapered boiler in Ireland, resulting in a locomotive that was overweight. The heavy running plate/ dragbox was replaced with a fabricated built-up arrangement, lightening holes were drilled in the frames, and all other surplus metal was cut away. The required weight reduction was thus achieved and the remainder of the class were similarly treated in 1906. This formula was adopted with the later 321 class.

The 1930 rebuilding of No 305 included the fitting of an improved cab, the raising of the running plates over the coupling rods and apparently the replacement of the frames with a set intended for further members of Class 341 (D1). However this is speculative and has not been confirmed.

Initially used for express passenger services, the class was relegated to branch line work in about 1910. No 308 was noted with cracked frames on the Inchicore scrap bank in 1931 and did no further work, being scrapped two years later.

1948 assessment: *They are suitable for medium passenger trains, such as Waterford-Limerick, Mallow-Tralee etc.*

GSWR 4-4-0 Class 305 (D12) No 308. Two years after being built in 1902, this locomotive was the first in Ireland to be fitted with a tapered boiler. The boiler was unique in being 5½" longer on the first ring than those fitted later to the other three members of the class. No 308 was not altered again and remained in this condition until 1933 when it was withdrawn. Inchicore pioneered use of tapered boilers in the early 1900s but there was no later development of this feature. Tapered boilers did not appear again on any locomotive of Irish origin. *IRRS collection*

GSWR/ GSR Class 305/ D12 No 305 as rebuilt with superheated Belpaire type-O boiler. In all-enveloping grey livery at Inchicore in 1930. *Real Photographs Co Ltd*

GSWR/ GSR CLASSES 309/ 310 4-4-0 Inchicore Class D10/ D3 1925/ 1931 Load Class N/ M

GSWR/ GSR No	Built	Maker's No	Rebuilt	Withdrawn	GSWR/ GSR No	Built	Maker's No	Rebuilt	Withdrawn
309	6/1903	6313	1913*/ 1935§	1959	312	6/1903	6316	1920*/ 1931§	1959
310	6/1903	6314	1932§	1957	313	6/1903	6317	1934§	1957
311	6/1903	6315	1930#/ 1936§	1959	314	6/1903	6318	1930§	1957

Designer: Coey **Built by Neilson Reid & Co**

Rebuilt with boiler type: * Tapered saturated type 321

Tapered with extended smokebox, believed to be from one of Nos 328-332; also received raised running plates over the coupling rods

§ Belpaire superheated type N; reclassified Class 310 on rebuilding

Boiler pressure – 160 lbs/ sq in
Cylinders – 18½" x 26"
Bogie wheels – 3' 6"
Driving wheels – 6' 7"
Wheel base – 6' 4" + 6' 10" + 9' 0"
Locomotive length – 30' 4¾"

Heating surfaces:
tubes – 1110 sq ft
firebox – 135.25 sq ft
grate – 23 sq ft

Tractive effort – 15,320 lbs
Coal capacity – 7 tons
Water capacity – 3345 gal
Locomotive weight – 49 tons 10 cwt
Adhesive weight – 30 tons 18 cwt
Max axle loading – 16 tons 0 cwt

Left: GSWR/ GSR Class 309/ D3 No 310 in original condition, at Cork.

Real Photographs Co Ltd

Below: GSWR/ GSR Class 309/ 321/ D3 No 309 as rebuilt with tapered saturated boiler. At Ballybrophy.

Real Photographs Co Ltd

* As rebuilt with tapered saturated boiler (then identical with Class 321):		
	Heating surfaces:	*Tractive effort – 15,320 lbs*
	tubes – 1283.9 sq ft	*Locomotive weight – 52 tons 1 cwt*
	firebox – 145 sq ft	*Adhesive weight – 33 tons 10 cwt*
	grate – 23 sq ft	*Max axle loading – 16 tons 16 cwt*

§ As rebuilt with Belpaire superheated type N boiler:		
Cylinders – 18" x 26"	*Heating surfaces:*	*Tractive effort – 14,500 lbs*
	tubes – 708 sq ft	*Locomotive weight – 48 tons 4 cwt*
	firebox – 120 sq ft	*Adhesive weight – 30 tons 8 cwt*
	superheater – 168 sq ft	*Max axle loading – 16 tons 4 cwt*
	grate – 19.5 sq ft	

With the first rebuilding of No 309 (with tapered saturated boiler) in 1913, this became part of Class 321 and the remaining five locomotives were re-designated Class 310, assuming Inchicore Class D10 at the amalgamation. No 312 was also re-designated Class 321, following its 1920 rebuilding. In 1926 together with Class 321, Nos 309 and 312 became Inchicore Class D3, and then D11 in 1930. This pair of locomotives rejoined the ranks of Class 310 (D10) on receiving Belpaire superheated boilers in 1935 and 1931 respectively. The 1930 rebuilding of No 311 included the installation of frames from one of the Class 321 locomotives that by then had been withdrawn.

Construction of these locomotives was contracted out due to a strike at Inchicore Works. When introduced, this class was very similar to Class 305 (D12), except for the cylinder diameter. Employed for many years on express passenger trains, they were later relegated to secondary main line and branch line duties.

1948 assessment (covers classes 301/ 309/ 310):
Perform almost similar work. Suit local passenger trains in the Districts. Not much use for Goods trains. Given suitable load can run quite fast.

Above right: GSWR/ GSR Class 309/ 310/ D3 No 312, as rebuilt with superheated Belpaire Type N boiler, at Inchicore in 1931.

L&GRP

Right: GSWR/ GSR Class 309/ 310/ D3 No 311 as rebuilt with superheated Belpaire Type N boiler.

L&GRP

GSWR/ GSR Classes 321/ 332 (See comments below) — 4-4-0 — Inchicore Classes D2/ D3/ D4 1925/ 1931 Load Class L/ J

GSWR/ GSR No	Built	Rebuilt	Withdrawn	GSWR/ GSR No	Built	Rebuilt	Withdrawn
321	12/1904	1924*/ 1933¶	1957	327	6/1905	1922#/ 1935*	1959
322	1/1905	1924*/ 1937¶	1960	328	6/1905	1922#/ 1929*/ 1932¶	1959
323	1/1905	1924*/ 1932¶	1955	329	11/1906	1921#/ 1929*/ 1930¶	1960
324	2/1905	–	1928	330	12/1906	1919#/ 1929*/ 1939¶	1957
325	5/1905	–	1928	331	10/1906	1918#/ 1929*/ 1933¶	1959
326	6/1905	1912§/ 1916§	1927	332	10/1906	1919#/ 1927¥	1959

Designer: Coey **Built at Inchicore**

Rebuilt with boiler type: * Belpaire saturated
¶ Belpaire superheated
§ Schmidt superheater and 20” x 26” cylinders (first GSWR superheated locomotive) with extended smokebox installed; reverted to original condition in 1916 but extended smokebox retained. The 1912 rebuilding was directly supervised by Maunsell and he used this experience in the design of No 341 described later.

Fitted with heavier frames ¥ Fitted with piston valves, superheated and re-designated class 332

As built in 1905 with round-topped tapered boiler:

Boiler pressure – 160 lbs/ sq in
Cylinders – 18½" x 26"
Bogie wheels – 3' 6"
Driving wheels – 6' 7"
Wheel base – 6' 4" + 6' 10" + 9' 0"
Locomotive length – 30' 4¾"

Heating surfaces:
tubes – 1283.9 sq ft
firebox – 145 sq ft
grate – 23 sq ft

Tractive effort – 15,320 lbs
Coal capacity – 7 tons
Water capacity – 3345 gal
Locomotive weight – 52 tons 1 cwt
Adhesive weight – 33 tons 10 cwt
Max axle loading – 16 tons 16 cwt

(Nos 321 to 328 had heating surfaces: tubes – 1366 sq ft)

GSWR/ GSR Class 321/ D2 No 321 in original condition with tapered boiler. This locomotive was rebuilt by the GSWR in 1924 but Nos 324 and 325 were in this condition at the amalgamation.

Real Photographs Co Ltd

 # As rebuilt in 1919-1922 (Nos 327 to 332):

(Deeper thicker frames, extended smokebox, raised running plates as detailed below)

Boiler pressure – 170 lbs/ sq in

Tractive effort – 16,280 lbs
Locomotive weight – 54 tons 10 cwt
Adhesive weight – 35 tons 10 cwt
Max axle loading – 18 tons 0 cwt

GSWR/ GSR Class 321/ D2 No 329 retaining original tapered saturated boiler but as rebuilt in 1922 with deeper, thicker frames, extended smokebox and raised footplate. At Inchicore. *Real Photographs Co Ltd*

*** As rebuilt in 1924-1930 (Nos 321 to 323, 328 to 331)**

(Nos 321 to 323 with deeper thicker frames as for Nos 327 to 332, extended smokebox, raised running plates. All locomotives fitted with saturated Belpaire type W boiler as detailed below)

Boiler pressure – 180 lbs/ sq in

Heating surfaces:
tubes – 1355 sq ft
firebox – 148 sq ft
grate – 22.5 sq ft

Tractive effort – 17,240 lbs
Locomotive weight – 55 tons 0 cwt
Adhesive weight – 35 tons 10 cwt
Max axle loading – 17 tons 15 cwt

¥ As rebuilt in 1927 (No 332):

(Belpaire type W boiler but in superheated form; 8" piston valves fitted; boiler centre line raised by 9")

Boiler pressure – 160 lbs/ sq in
(later 180 lbs/ sq in)
Locomotive length – 30' 5 ⅝"

Heating surfaces:
tubes – 1060 sq ft
firebox – 148 sq ft
superheater – 250 sq ft
grate – 22.5 sq ft

Tractive effort – 15,320 (17,240) lbs
Locomotive weight – 55 tons 10 cwt
Adhesive weight – 34 tons 16 cwt
Max axle loading – 17 tons 16 cwt

¶ As rebuilt in 1927 (No 321 to 323, 328 to 331):

(Belpaire type W boiler but in superheated form; slide valves retained)

Boiler pressure – 180 lbs/ sq in

Tractive effort – 17,240 lbs
Locomotive weight – 55 tons 6 cwt
Adhesive weight – 34 tons 19 cwt
Max axle loading – 17 tons 12 cwt

GSWR/ GSR Class 321/ D2 No 322 as rebuilt in 1924 with Belpaire saturated boiler. At Inchicore in 1936.

L&GRP

GSWR/ GSR Class 321/ D2 No 322 in CIE days with vintage tender attached. At Broadstone.

CP Friel collection

GSWR/ GSR Class 321/ D2 No 327 as rebuilt in 1922 with Belpaire saturated boiler, at Inchicore in 1938.

WA Camwell

GSWR/ GSR Class 321/ D2 No 327 in CIE days as rebuilt in 1937 with Belpaire superheated boiler

A Donaldson, courtesy WT Scott

The twelve original members of Class 321 were based on the configuration inaugurated with the rebuilding of No 308 with a tapered boiler in 1904. Main differences from the earlier locomotive were larger diameter cylinders and a longer firebox. To off-set the resultant weight increases and keep within the prevailing axle loading restriction of 17 tons, the frames were of lighter construction than had been used previously.

Being subject to a variety of rebuildings, the subsequent history of this class was complex. In 1912, No 326 was the first GSWR engine to be experimentally fitted with a Schmidt superheater, larger cylinders and greater heating surfaces. Following fracturing of the cylinders in 1916, the locomotive reverted to standard form but retained its extended smokebox. Apart from the smokebox, No 326 was then in original form together with Nos 324 and 325 at the amalgamation, as shown with the dimensions set out above.

The measures that had been adopted to reduce the overall weight in the earlier Class 305 were applied in the design of this class. The result was unsatisfactory with cracked frames plus loose bolts and rivets. As soon as weight restrictions were eased, measures were taken to provide stronger, more reliable frames. Between 1918 and 1922, Nos 327 to 332 were rebuilt with new frames of 1⅛" thickness (as opposed to the 1" thickness previously used).

In 1924, Nos 321 to 323 were given frame treatment similar to Nos 327 to 332 but in addition received canopy ('Bazin') cabs. More significantly, these engines were provided with parallel saturated Belpaire boilers (see **Appendix C** Type 327 for dimensional details). The boiler pressure was raised to 180 lbs/ sq in and the locomotive weight was then 55 tons.

It is alleged that frames cut but not used for additional members of Class 341 (D1) were employed in this re-framing exercise. While not definitely confirmed, this might explain why three engines were withdrawn in original condition after a mere 25 years' service ie only a limited number spare frame sets were available. Concurrent with the fitting to Nos 321 to 323 of new frames, extended smokeboxes and running plates raised over the coupling rods were also installed. Tapered boilers were retained and their dimensions were unchanged but the working pressure was increased to 170 lbs / sq in, and the weight was up to 54 tons 10 cwt. During the rebuilding programmes, modern canopy cabs were fitted except for No 327 which was not so fitted until 1950.

In addition, two members of Class 309/ 310 became part of this class following their rebuilding with taper boilers: No 309 in 1913 and No 312 in 1920.

In summary, at the amalgamation there were five distinct 'strains' within this class of fourteen locomotives:

Nos	Version
321-323	Heavier frames, parallel Belpaire boiler
324, 325	Original condition
326	Original condition but with extended smokebox
327-332	Heavier frames, tapered Belpaire boiler
309, 312	Original frames, tapered Belpaire boiler

In 1928/9, Nos 328-331 were rebuilt with heavier frames and parallel Belpaire boiler in conformity with Nos 321-323. From 1932 onwards, Nos 321-323 and 328-331 were provided with superheaters (see **Appendix C**).

GSWR/ GSR Class 332/ D2 No 332 as rebuilt with Belpaire superheated boiler and piston valves. At Inchicore.
Kelland collection

In 1927, installation of superheating commenced with No 332 (see type 327 in **Appendix C**). This locomotive was uniquely fitted with piston valves and the boiler pressure reduced to 160 lbs/ sq in. In this condition it was re-designated Class 332; it was considered sluggish and rough riding, and was thus less popular than the other superheated locomotives. Finally, No 327 which had retained its tapered boiler was superheated in 1932.

The original Inchicore classification of these locomotives was D4. All were re-designated D3 in 1926 and then D2 (and Load Class M) concurrent with the installation of Belpaire superheated boilers between 1927 and 1932 (Nos 324-26 remained D3 to withdrawal).

This class was the GSWR's principal express class until the introduction of No 341 and the Class 400 4-6-0s. Although reputed to be heavy on coal, they did well on the express passenger services for which they had been designed, and continued on these duties on occasions into GSR/ CIÉ days with notable performances on heavy trains that should have justified 4-6-0 haulage. A restriction on the sphere of operations was the long coupled wheel base which prevented them from working on the ex-DSER section beyond Dun Laoghaire, the curve at Sandycove being too tight.

One of the most remarkable performances by this class was by No 328 in September 1917 with a load of four bogies and two six-wheelers weighing 137 tons from Cork to Dublin. Limerick Junction (58½ miles from Cork) was passed in 60 minutes and from there to Thurles an average of 74 mph was maintained resulting in 78¾ miles being covered in 76 minutes. Following the stop at Thurles to take water, the 85¼ miles from there to passing Islandbridge were covered in 79 minutes and the train reached Amiens Street, Dublin (90½ miles) in 88 minutes.

In 1928, No 329 in saturated form took a special from Limerick Junction to Kingsbridge (107 miles) in 104 minutes. The load was believed to have been five bogies but to have covered that distance with the contents of a 3345 gallon tender was an excellent performance.

1948 assessment: *A good medium passenger engine, capable of similar work to 333 class, but has larger wheel and boiler, consequently faster, but higher axleload is a disadvantage.*

GSWR/ GSR Class 333/ 338 (See comments below) — 4-4-0 — Inchicore Classes D2/ D4/ D4A/ D3 1925/ 1931 Load Class M/ L

No	Built	Rebuilt	Withdrawn	No	Built	Rebuilt	Withdrawn
333	6/1907	1930*/ 1932#	1955	337	6/1908	1932#/ 1938*	1955
334	6/1907	1932#	1955	338	6/1908	1927§/ 1945¶	1959
335	6/1907	1933#	1955	339	6/1908	1933#	1959
336	6/1907	1932#/ 1938*	1957	340	6/1908	1932#	1955

Designer: Coey — **Built at Inchicore**

§ Rebuilt with parallel Belpaire superheater boiler type O, piston valves and canopy ('Bazin') cab; re-designated Class 338 and Load Class changed to J

* Rebuilt with parallel Belpaire saturated boiler type O, retained slide valves

Rebuilt with parallel Belpaire superheated boiler type O but retained slide valves and original cab

¥ Rebuilt with parallel Belpaire superheated boiler converted to superheated condition

¶ Rebuilt with 17" diameter cylinders

As originally built:

Boiler pressure – 160 lbs/ sq in
Cylinders – 18" x 26"
Bogie wheels – 3' 0"
Driving wheels – 5' 8½"
Wheel base – 6' 4" + 6' 10" + 8' 6"
Locomotive length – 29' 7¾"

Heating surfaces:
tubes – 1283.9 sq ft
firebox – 128.1 sq ft
grate – 21 sq ft

Tractive effort – 16,730 lbs
Coal capacity – 7 tons
Water capacity – 3345 gal

	Loco weight	*Adhesive wt*
Nos 333-336:	*50 tons 2 cwt*	*31 tons 18 cwt*
Nos 337-340:	*50 tons 6 cwt*	*32 tons 0 cwt*

Max axle loading – 16 tons 5 cwt

(See notes for explanation of weight variances)

GSWR/ GSR Class 333/ D2 No 334 as originally built with tapered saturated boiler. The purpose of the brackets on the smokebox door is unknown. Seen at Bray.

Kelland collection

GSWR/ GSR Class 333/ D2 No 339 with tapered boiler. Photographed at Inchicore in 1931.

L&GRP

§ As rebuilt with Belpaire superheater Type O boiler, 18½" diameter cylinders, piston valves and canopy cab:

Boiler pressure – 180 lbs/ sq in
Cylinders – 18½" x 26"
Piston valves – 8"

Heating surfaces:
tubes – 1068 sq ft
firebox – 136.7 sq ft
superheater – 250 sq ft
grate – 20 sq ft

Tractive effort – 19,880 lbs
Locomotive weight – 52 tons 10 cwt
Adhesive weight – 32 tons 16 cwt
Max axle loading – 16 tons 18 cwt

*** As rebuilt with Belpaire saturated boiler:**

Boiler pressure – 180 lbs/ sq in
Cylinders – 18" x 26"

Heating surfaces:
tubes – 1355 sq ft
firebox – 136.7 sq ft
grate – 20 sq ft

Tractive effort – 18,820 lbs
Locomotive weight – 51 tons 15 cwt
Adhesive weight – 32 tons 15 cwt
Max axle loading – 16 tons 15 cwt

Right: GSWR/ GSR Class 333/D2 No 333 as rebuilt with Belpaire saturated boiler, piston valves but retaining original cab. Shunting at Mallow in 1953.

Authors' collection

Below: GSWR/ GSR Class 333/ D2 No 335 as rebuilt with Belpaire superheated boiler but retaining slide valves and original cab. At Limerick in 1938. Just visible behind the tender is a member of Sentinel Class 280.

WA Camwell

Opposite upper right: GSWR/ GSR Class 338/ D2 No 338 as rebuilt with parallel Belpaire superheater boiler Type O, piston valves and canopy cab. Load class changed to J and re-classified 338. At Inchicore.

Real Photographs Co Ltd

 # As rebuilt with Belpaire superheater Type O boiler and canopy cab but retained 18" diameter cylinders and slide valves (except Nos 333/ 336/ 337 which retained original cabs):

Boiler pressure – 180 lbs/ sq in
Cylinders – 18" x 26"

Heating surfaces:
tubes – 1068 sq ft
firebox – 136.7 sq ft
superheater – 250 sq ft
grate – 20 sq ft

Tractive effort – 18,820 lbs
Locomotive weight – 52 tons 10 cwt
Adhesive weight – 32 tons 16 cwt
Max axle loading – 16 tons 18 cwt

¶ As rebuilt with 17" x 26" cylinders	*Tractive effort – 16,790 lbs*

Other than the Woolwich moguls, this was the last GSWR/ GSR class to be introduced to traffic with tapered boilers. The process of replacing tapered boilers with a saturated parallel version commenced some time before 1925 with Nos 333, 6 & 7. These engines resembled the Class 321, of which they were a mixed traffic variant with smaller driving wheels. They were built specially for services between Cork and Rosslare where they were concentrated until displacement by Woolwich moguls. They were then moved to secondary services and excursion traffic, although at least one was allocated to Grand Canal Street for working mail and main line services (Nos 334, 336 & 338 were noted on these duties in 1928-29).

The rebuilding of No 338 in 1927 resulted in a locomotive that was effectively under-boilered, although the piston valves reputedly performed better than those on No 332. To redress the imbalance between cylinder/ valve capacity and the ability of the boiler to generate adequate steam, smaller diameter cylinders were fitted in 1945.

Nos 333 to 336 were equipped with conventional bogies while the remainder (Nos 337 to 340) had bogies with outside frames and bearings to improve riding qualities on the difficult Cork-Rosslare route. A further objective was to avoid overheating of the bogie journals, a problem that had plagued the first four engines. The need for outside bogie frames (which slightly increased the overall weight) was found to be unnecessary around 1909 as a result of using a different lubricant and making some minor modifications to the axleboxes. (This unnecessary outside frame design was also adopted on the similar five members of Class 342 (D4) constructed by the GSR in 1936 – see Chapter 10).

The original D2 Inchicore classification was changed to D4 in 1926. As a consequence of its rebuilding with piston valves in 1927, No 338 was re-designated Class D4a the following year, and then D3 in 1937.

1948 assessment (333/ 338/ 342 classes): *Similar* (ie all three classes) – *valuable because they are fairly powerful and can travel most lines with their 16 ton* (sic) *axleload. Very useful for passenger specials. Reasonably fast, 342 Class completed about 1936.*

Left: GSWR/ GSR Class 338/ D2 No 338. Standing at the coaling plant at Inchicore.

Real Photographs Co Ltd

GSWR/ GSR Classes 341 4-4-0 Inchicore Class D1

Built	No	Name	Withdrawn
1913	341	*Sir William Goulding*	1928

Designer: Coey/ Maunsell **Built at Inchicore**

Boiler pressure – 160 lbs/ sq in – (later 175 lbs/ sq in)
Cylinders – 20" x 26" (later 19" x 26")
Piston valves – 9"
Bogie wheels – 3' 0"
Driving wheels – 6' 7"
Wheel base – 6' 4" + 7' 11" + 9' 11"
Locomotive length – 32' 1¾"

Heating surfaces:
tubes – 1364.9 sq ft
firebox – 155.9 sq ft
superheater – 335.1 sq ft
grate – 24.8 sq ft

Tractive effort – 17,910 lbs – later (17,680 lbs)
Coal capacity – 7 tons
Water capacity – 3345 gal

Locomotive weight – 60 tons 3 cwt
Max axle loading – 19 tons 2 cwt

Left: GSWR/ GSR Class 341/ D1 No 341 *Sir William Goulding* when new.
L Hyland collection

Below: GSWR/ GSR Class 341/ D1 No 341 at Cork in 1914.
K Nunn

Design of this locomotive was initiated by Coey, shortly before his retirement through ill-health. Final design work and completion is attributed to Maunsell making this his only express passenger design for the GSWR, and the last 4-4-0 built by the company. No 341 was significantly heavier than the preceding classes mainly due to its large diameter boiler, which was equipped with a Schmidt superheater. In view of its size and its being one of the GSWR's first superheated locomotives, it attracted much interest. The technical press noted that it was to be the first of a new class and some sources have suggested that frames were indeed cut for more engines. It has been suggested that ten examples were planned (numbered 341 to 350), but no confirmatory evidence has been found in GSWR records. Uniquely for the GSR and its constituents, No 341 was equipped with inside Walschaerts valve gear.

The Civil Engineer was concerned about No 341's weight and axle loading. Confined to the Dublin-Cork route, it was re-weighed at regular intervals to check that limits were not being exceeded. Popular with locomotive crews, this design was about as far as the 4-4-0 type could be developed without revision of weight restrictions. Maunsell's successor, Watson, showed little interest in its potential as he was concerned with even larger engines equipped with six or more coupled wheels. However, Watson's first 4-6-0 shared duties with this locomotive and there were allegations that he sought to down play No 341's competence as it showed up the indifferent performance on the road of his own design. Apart from the reduction in cylinder diameter, there were no other major modifications. The scrapping of this locomotive raised adverse comment among observers as being unreasonably premature for such a useful and competent machine.

GSWR/ GSR Class 351 (249) 0-6-0 Inchicore Class J9
1925/ 1931 Load Class E/ E

GSWR/ GSR No	Built	Rebuilt	Withdrawn	GSWR/ GSR No	Built	Rebuilt	Withdrawn
249	4/1912	1932*	1963	351	11/1903	1930*	1963
250	5/1912	1934*/ 1949¶	1963	352	12/1903	1938¶ / 1951*	1955
251	5/1912	1937*	1964	353	12/1903	1930*	1931
252	6/1912	1931*/ 1954¶	1961	354	12/1903	1935*	1962

Designer: Coey **Built at Inchicore**

Rebuilt with boiler type: * Belpaire superheated
§ Belpaire saturated
¶ Class 257 type

Nos 249 to 252 as originally built:

Boiler pressure – 160 lbs/ sq in
Cylinders – 18" x 26"
Driving wheels – 5' 1¾"
Wheel base – 7' 7" + 8' 6"
Locomotive length – 27' 11¾"

Heating surfaces:
tubes – 1040 sq ft
firebox – 118 sq ft
grate – 20.4 sq ft

Tractive effort – 18,560 lbs
Coal capacity – 5½ tons
Water capacity – 2730 gal
Locomotive weight – 45 tons 1 cwt
Max axle loading – 16 tons 3 cwt

GSWR/ GSR Class 351/ J9 No 250 in original condition with flush firebox. At Inchicore in 1933.

L&GRP

GSWR/ GSR Class 351/ J9 No 354, as rebuilt in 1935 with superheated Belpaire boiler. At Maryborough (Portlaoise) in 1939.

CP Friel collection

Nos 351 to 354 as originally built:		
Locomotive length – 26' 9¾"	*Heating surfaces:* *tubes – 1129 sq ft* *firebox – 118 sq ft* *grate – 20.4 sq ft*	*Locomotive weight – 43 tons 16 cwt* *Max axle loading – 15 tons 12 cwt*

*** As rebuilt with Belpaire superheated boiler:**

Heating surfaces:
tubes – 708 sq ft
firebox – 120 sq ft
superheater – 168 sq ft
grate – 19.5 sq ft

¶ As rebuilt with round topped superheated boiler (ex-Class 257):

Heating surfaces:
tubes – 844 sq ft
firebox – 118 sq ft
superheater – 224 sq ft
grate – 20.4 sq ft

GSWR/ GSR Class 351 J9 Nos 251. Maunsell version with raised running plate over driving wheels, at Inchicore in 1936. *L&GRP*

Nos 249 to 252 were originally allocated Class 249 on introduction but were de-designated Class 351 in 1923.

Introduced in the year that the last Class 101 was built, this goods class represented a significant increase in size and weight at the expense of versatility and route availability. They were popular on goods and seasonal beet trains on the Rosslare route. Maunsell introduced a number of design changes with the 1912-built locomotives. Running plates were raised over the coupling rods unlike the Class 101 style adopted with the first four locomotives. Also larger cabs and extended smokeboxes were fitted. No 353 was withdrawn as a result of damage sustained in a collision at Monasterevan in 1930. No 354 was fitted with 'McAllister' experimental firebars in November 1942 but these were not successful and were removed after a short time.

1948 assessment: *Comparable in size with Class 257, but a bad design of valve gear makes them heavy on coal, and sluggish. They have a short economic life in consequence.*

GSWR/ GSR Class 355 — 2-6-0 — Inchicore Class K3, 1925/ 1931 Load Class C/ C

GSWR/ GSR No	Built as 0-6-0	Makers' No	Converted to 2-6-0	Rebuilt	Withdrawn
355	11/1903	15943	by 1907	1914¶	1928
356	11/1903	15944	1908	1925#	1957
357	12/1903	15945	by 1907	1930§/ 1935*	1931 (reinstated 1935), 1960
358	12/1903	15946	1907	1930§/ 1934*	1957
359	12/1903	15947	1908	1930§/ 1934*	1959
360	12/1903	15948	1906	1921¶/ 1929§/ 1937*	1955
361	12/1903	15949	1907	1923§/ 1930*	1959

Designer: Coey — **Originally built by North British Loco** — Converted to 2-6-0s at Inchicore

Rebuilt with boiler type: ¶ Belpaire saturated Class 368 type boiler
Belpaire superheated; also equipped with leading Bissel truck
* Belpaire superheated
§ Belpaire saturated

Boiler pressure – 160 lbs/ sq in	*Heating surfaces:*	*Tractive effort – 20,680 lbs*
Cylinders – 19" x 26"	*tubes – 1318 sq ft*	*Coal capacity – 7 tons*
Radial wheels – 3' 0"	*firebox – 132 sq ft*	*Water capacity – 3345 gal*
Driving wheels – 5' 1¾"	*grate – 24.8 sq ft*	*Locomotive weight – 52 tons 15 cwt*
Wheel base – 5' 0" + 8' 0" + 9' 0"		*Adhesive weight – 46 tons 4 cwt*
Locomotive length – 31' 3¾"		*Max axle loading – 16 tons 0 cwt*

GSWR/ GSR Class 355/ K3 No 358 as rebuilt as a mogul in 1907. At Inchicore.

Real Photographs Co Ltd

GSWR/ GSR Class 355/ K3 No 361 in CIE days as rebuilt in 1930 with Belpaire superheated boiler.

CP Friel collection

¶ As rebuilt with Class 368 type boiler:		
	Heating surfaces: *tubes – 1446 sq ft* *firebox – 138.5 sq ft*	*Weights not recorded*

§ As rebuilt with saturated boiler:		
Boiler pressure – 180 lbs/ sq in	*Heating surfaces:* *tubes – 1498 sq ft* *firebox – 139 sq ft*	*Tractive effort – 23,250 lbs* *Locomotive weight – 57 tons 2 cwt* *Adhesive weight – 48 tons 12 cwt*

*** As rebuilt with superheated boiler:**		
Boiler pressure – 180 lbs/ sq in	*Heating surfaces:* *tubes – 1180.5 sq ft* *firebox – 139 sq ft* *superheater – 290 sq ft* *grate – 24.8 sq ft*	*Tractive effort – 23,250 lbs* *Locomotive weight – 57 tons 2 cwt* *Adhesive weight – 48 tons 12 cwt* *Max axle loading – 16 tons 10 cwt*

 # As rebuilt with superheated boiler and leading Bissel truck:
Wheel base – 6′ 6″ + 8′ 0″ + 9′ 0″

Right: GSWR/ GSR Class 355/ K3 No 356 as rebuilt with Belpaire superheated boiler and equipped with Bissel truck giving longer overall wheelbase. At Inchicore.

Real Photographs Co Ltd

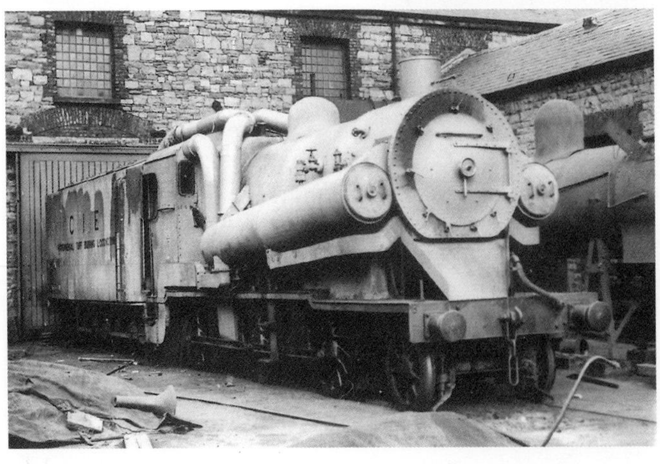

Below: GSWR/ GSR Class 355/ K3 No 356 in June 1952, as modified by Bulleid in connection with turf-burning experiments.

D Murray

Growing traffic demands dictated the need for a larger goods locomotive but the Inchicore strike meant that the order had to be placed with an outside builder. These locomotives were an entirely fresh initiative in GSWR design practice. Unfortunately they were front-end heavy with the leading axle loading exceeding the then permitted maximum of 16 tons, and they were prone to derailment. No 361 was experimentally rebuilt with a pony radial axle, five feet ahead of the leading driving axle. This modification was sufficiently successful for the remainder of the class to be rebuilt similarly but with smokebox extended by 15 inches. Concurrent with the fitting of a new boiler in 1925, No 356 was equipped with a Bissel truck in place of the radial truck, with the pony axle 6' 6" in front of the leading driving axle; this locomotive was considered superior to the others and was used occasionally on the Dublin-Cork night mails.

In 1949, Nos 356 and 357 were equipped with an automatic ash-ejection system. Steam jets were installed in the smokebox and when operated, they blasted ash into two down pipes leading from the smokebox floor. These pipes were set diagonally outwards so that ash was deposited on each side of the track. Doors were installed at the entrance to the pipes with the intention of keeping the smokebox air-tight when the system was not in operation. In practice, air leaks were fairly constant which upset the draught through the firebox. The system was unpopular with crews who found ways of plugging the pipes (including jamming a sugar beet in the pipe during the beet campaign!) thus defeating the object of the exercise. It was not long before the equipment fell into disuse and was removed. The system was also tried at this time with similar results on three ex-DSER locomotives – 4-4-2Ts Nos 455 and 457, and 2-6-0 No 462.

In 1952, No 356 had the further distinction (or indignity) of being chosen by Bulleid as the guinea pig for the initial turf-burner experiments, and was not used again in ordinary service.

1948 assessment (355 and 368 classes): *Very useful heavy goods engine, powerful and with a low axleload enabling them to be worked over many lines. A type which should have been developed.*

GSWR/ GSR Class 362 — 4-6-0 — Inchicore Class B3
'Long Tom' — 1925 Load Class C

GSWR/GSR No	Built	Withdrawn	GSWR/GSR No	Built	Withdrawn
362	12/1905	1928	365	12/1905	1928
363	12/1905	1928	366	6/1907	1931
364	12/1905	1928	367	6/1907	1928

Designer: Coey **Built at Inchicore**

Boiler pressure – 160 lbs/ sq in	*Heating surfaces:*	*Tractive effort – 21,210 lbs*
Cylinders – 19¼" x 26"	*tubes – 1467 sq ft*	*Coal capacity – 7 tons*
Bogie wheels – 3' 0"	*firebox – 133 sq ft*	*Water capacity – 3345 gal*
Driving wheels – 5' 1¾"	*grate – 24.8 sq ft*	*Locomotive weight – 57 tons 16 cwt*
Wheel base – 5' 3" + 5' 1¾" + 6' 9" + 7' 9"		*Adhesive weight – 44 tons 18 cwt*
Locomotive length – 33' 6¼"		*Max axle loading – 15 tons 18 cwt*

GSWR/ GSR Class 362/ B3 No 365 at Inchicore.
Real Photographs Co Ltd

GSWR/ GSR Class 362/ B3 No 363 at Inchicore. *IRRS collection*

This design was an attempt to produce a goods locomotive more powerful than the preceding Class 355 (at that time still with 0-6-0 wheel arrangement) but with a leading bogie to keep within the prevailing 16 tons axle loading limit. The first Irish 4-6-0 was the result and the GSWR was sufficiently proud of the increase in size to exhibit No 366 at the 1907 Dublin Exhibition. Although the increased power expectations were realised, these locomotives proved unpopular through their rough riding qualities. Like the Class 355 in 0-6-0 form, they were prone to derailment although for the opposite reason, being too light at the front end. Nos 363 and 367 carried extended smokeboxes.

Another drawback was that they were too long for some turntables. Class 355, following their rebuilding as 2-6-0s, proved to be just as capable so that the inside cylinder 4-6-0 type was not developed further. For these reasons, the Long Toms were early candidates for withdrawal.

Nicknames were not common for Irish locomotives and some sources have doubted the provenance of 'Long Tom'. Around the time of their introduction, Ivatt introduced a heavy goods 0-8-0 for the English GNR which was definitely known in this fashion.

GSWR/ GSR Class 368/ K4 No 368 in original condition. This locomotive was not rebuilt before withdrawal. No 371 received a slightly different boiler in 1923, but externally would have looked the same. *IRRS collection*

GSWR/ GSR Class 368 — 2-6-0 — Inchicore Class K4
1925/ 1931 Load Class C/ C

GSWR/GSR No	Built	Rebuilt	Withdrawn	GSWR/GSR No	Built	Rebuilt	Withdrawn
368	9/1909	–	1928	370	9/1909	1935§	1957
369	9/1909	1934§	1957	371	9/1909	1923*	1928

Designer: Coey **Built at Inchicore**

Rebuilt with boiler type: * saturated Belpaire boiler type
§ superheated Belpaire boiler and piston valves

Boiler pressure – 160 lbs/ sq in	*Heating surfaces:*	*Tractive effort – 20, 680 lbs*
Cylinders – 19" x 26"	*tubes – 1446.5 sq ft*	*Coal capacity – 7 tons*
Bogie wheels – 3' 0"	*firebox – 138.5 sq ft*	*Water capacity – 3345 gal*
Driving wheels – 5' 1¾"	*grate – 24.8 sq ft*	*Locomotive weight – 53 tons 1 cwt*
Wheel base – 5' 9" + 7' 3" + 8' 9"		*Adhesive weight – 44 tons 18 cwt*
Locomotive length – 31' 3¾"		*Max axle loading – 15 tons 11 cwt*

GSWR/ GSR Class 368/ K4 No 370 as rebuilt in 1935 with Belpaire superheater boiler and piston valves. At Killarney in 1939, while on ballast train duties.

CP Friel collection

*** As rebuilt with saturated Belpaire boiler (type unspecified):**

Boiler pressure – 180 lbs/ sq in	*Heating surfaces:*	*Tractive effort – 23,250 lbs*
	tubes – 1416.5 sq ft	
	firebox – 138.5 sq ft	
	grate – 24.8 sq ft	

§ As rebuilt with superheated Type Q Belpaire boiler and piston valves:

Boiler pressure – 180 lbs/ sq in	*Heating surfaces:*	*Tractive effort – 23,250 lbs*
Piston valves – 8"	*tubes – 1068 sq ft*	*Locomotive weight – 54 tons 10 cwt*
	firebox – 136.7 sq ft	*Adhesive weight – 47 tons 10 cwt*
	superheater – 250 sq ft	*Max axle loading – 16 tons 0 cwt*
	grate – 24.8 sq ft	

Following the success of the Class 355 in mogul form, another four of the type appeared with this class. These engines were basically similar to the earlier 2-6-0s except that the leading driving axle was set nine inches further back and the coupled wheel base was reduced by one foot in length. More visibly significant was the first fitting by Inchicore of Belpaire fireboxes.

1948 assessment: *As for Class 355.*

GSWR/ GSR Class 900 — 4-8-0T — Inchicore Class A1, 1925 Load Class B

GSWR/GSR No	Built	Withdrawn	Remarks
900	9/1915	1928	Later altered to 4-6-2T
901	12/1924	1931	–

Designer: Watson **Built at Inchicore**

GSWR/ GSR Class 900/ A1 No 901 at Kingsbridge. *CP Friel collection*

Boiler pressure – 175 lbs/ sq in	*Heating surfaces:*	*Tractive effort – 26,300 lbs*
Cylinders – 19¼" x26"	*tubes – 1426.5 sq ft*	*Coal capacity – 3½ tons*
Bogie wheels – 3' 0"	*firebox – 138.5 sq ft*	*Water capacity – 1500 gal*
Driving wheels – 4' 6½"	*grate – 24.8 sq ft*	*Locomotive weight – 80 tons 15 cwt*
Wheel base – 6' 4" + 7' 6¼" + 5' 1"+ 5' 1" + 5' 1"		*Adhesive weight – 62 tons 9 cwt*
Locomotive length – 37' 10¾"		*Max axle loading – 17 ton 4 cwt*

The background and development of this class has particular interest because it was the first attempt in Ireland to create a broad gauge locomotive that was demonstrably in the large engine league. In June 1912, the GSWR Board approved the construction of a three-cylinder 0-8-2T heavy shunter for use at Kingsbridge yard. It was intended that all cylinders should connect with the second driving axle and while drawings had been prepared, little tangible progress had been achieved by the time of Maunsell's departure. This is believed to have been due to an inability to create a workable derived motion to operate the inside valves in conjunction with the inclined inside cylinder. This was before emergence of the Holcroft-Gresley conjugated valve gear arrangement which was to overcome this problem.

(As an aside, this was the first of three attempts by Maunsell to produce an eight-coupled shunter. In 1919 a class of six three-cylinder 2-8-0Ts, with 4' 8" driving wheels and using Holcroft valve gear was approved by the Locomotive Committee of the South Eastern & Chatham Railway. Construction was delayed because

GSWR/ GSR Class 900/ A1 No 900 in later years running as a 4-6-2T, at Kingsbridge goods yard.

Real Photographs Co Ltd

of increased cost and eventually cancelled following the 1923 Grouping. Seventeen years after the first initiative on the GSWR, eight members of Maunsell's highly-regarded three cylinder 0-8-0T 'Z' class were built at Brighton).

With no solution to the valve gear problem in sight, Watson discarded Maunsell's plans and opted for a much simpler design with No 900. In general appearance radically different from any previous design, it actually shared a number of features with other GSWR classes. The cylinders and bogie were common with Class 362 while the boiler, motion, connecting rods, crank and coupled axles, and axle boxes were interchangeable with Class 368. The inside cylinders, unusually, drove the leading coupled axle which gave the front end an ungainly aspect. Use of inside cylinders – in contrast to Watson's later No 400 where access to motion was a prominent feature – was presumably determined by loading gauge clearance considerations.

These locomotives were prone to derailment, leading to banishment from certain sharply-curved sidings. This shortcoming was commonly attributed to the long rigid wheelbase which the use of thin flanges on the second and third driving wheel sets failed to alleviate. From November 1927, No 900 ran as a 4-6-2T, achieved by the simple means of removing the coupling rods between the third and fourth driving wheels. This measure converted approximately 15 tons of adhesive weight into dead weight.

However, the rigid wheel base may not have been the cause of the problem as this was actually three inches shorter than that of Class 101 (J15). It seems more likely that derailments resulted from the interaction of poorly ballasted sidings with the heavy axle loading on the leading driving wheels (two tons more than on the second coupled axle).

Apart from shunting work, Nos 900 and 901 were also used to bank goods trains between Kingsbridge and Inchicore during the day and at night, heavy goods trains as far as Clondalkin. The type was a marked departure from what had preceded in GSWR practice, but had no influence on later designs, particularly as trends in goods traffic reduced the need for a heavy shunter. While a powerful design, it was not considered a success, and Bazin's decision to add a second example (which differed only in bunker profile) nine years after the first is something of a mystery.

They were the only-eight coupled locomotives on the Irish Broad Gauge, and No 901 had the further distinction of being the only locomotive introduced to traffic in the short period of the Great Southern Railway before creation of the Great Southern Railways on 1 January 1925.

GSWR/ GSR Class *Imp* 0-4-0T Inchicore Class M1/ later M2

Not classified for loads

For details of this locomotive, refer to DSER section describing that company's Nos 69 and 70 (later GSR Elf *and* Imp *respectively).*

GSWR/ GSR Class *Jumbo* 0-6-0T Inchicore Class J13

Load Class: 1925 not classified/ 1931 FT

GSWR/GSR No	Name	Built	Withdrawn
(841)	*Jumbo*	9/1896	1957

Designer: Ivatt **Built at Inchicore**

Boiler pressure – 150 lbs/ sq in	*Heating surfaces:*	*Tractive effort – 18,200 lbs*
Cylinders – 18" x 24"	*tubes – 900 sq ft*	*Coal capacity – 1 ton 10 cwt*
Driving wheels – 4' 6½"	*firebox – 84.5 sq ft*	*Water capacity – 730 gal*
Wheel base – 7' 3" + 6' 0"	*grate – 18.8 sq ft*	*Locomotive weight – 37 tons 3 cwt*
Locomotive length – 28' 8¾"		*Max axle loading – 13 tons 16 cwt*

GSWR/ GSR Class 'Jumbo'/ J13 *Jumbo*. Trouble in store! If the (young, inexperienced) fireman allowed the boiler to blow off as pictured here, the pressure would slump to 75 lbs/ sq in or lower, usually to the intense annoyance of the driver. At Waterford.

Real Photographs Co Ltd

Two 0-6-4Ts, Nos 201 & 202, were built in 1876 as back tanks with side tanks fitted additionally later. In 1897 their numbers were removed and they were named *Jumbo* and *Negro* respectively, and transferred to the duplicate list. *Negro* was withdrawn in this condition as an 0-6-4T in 1910 while *Jumbo* was converted to an 0-6-0T in 1896. These locomotives are sometimes confused with Nos 201 and 202 of Class 201 built 1895.

Jumbo was a long term resident of Waterford (over 60 years) where it worked as the goods yard pilot. After overhaul at Inchicore in 1929, it was reported to have received a slightly larger boiler but no details have been traced. This locomotive never bore a number but for accountancy purposes only, it was referred to in the books as No 841.

1948 assessment: *Saddleback(?) engine which shunts Quays in Waterford. Suitable.*

GSWR/ GSR Class *Sambo* 0-4-2ST Inchicore Class L2 Load Class RT (after 1931)

GSWR/GSR No	Name	Built	Withdrawn
(842)	*Sambo*	6/1914	1962

Designer: Maunsell **Built at Inchicore**

Boiler pressure – 150 lbs/ sq in	*Heating surfaces:*	*Tractive effort – 11,980 lbs*
Cylinders – 16" x 20"	*tubes – 685 sq ft*	*Coal capacity – 1 ton 10 cwt*
Driving wheels – 4' 6½"	*firebox – 83.8 sq ft*	*Water capacity – 467 gal*
Radial wheels – 3' 9"	*grate –16 sq ft*	*Locomotive weight – 34 tons 13 cwt*
Wheel base – 6' 0" + 7' 11"		*Adhesive weight – 23 tons 4 cwt*
Locomotive length – 25' 7"		*Max axle loading – 11 tons 12 cwt*

GSWR/ GSR Class 'Sambo' L2 *Sambo* at Inchicore in 1931. An interesting comparison in cab design with No 701 in the background. *L&GRP*

This locomotive was reputedly assembled largely out of spare parts. It was employed originally as the Inchicore works shunter, known as the 'premises pilot', and the short, flexible wheelbase allowed it to work over all of the work's tight curves and shop sidings. On closure of Inchicore to steam it moved to the Broadstone to work as wagon shops pilot. Following closure of Broadstone shed to steam, it was re-allocated to the old GNR(I) shed at Amiens Street from where it did some general shunting.

There was a tradition that the Inchicore pilot should always be known as Sambo; it never bore a number but for accountancy purposes only, it was referred to in the books as No 842.

GSWR/ GSR Class *Sprite* 0-4-2T Inchicore Class L4/ L5

Not classified for loads

GSWR/GSR No	Name	Built	Withdrawn
–	*Sprite*	1/1873	1927
–	*Fairy*	1894	1927

Designer: McDonnell **Built at Inchicore**

Boiler pressure – 150 lbs/ sq in	*Heating surfaces:*	*Tractive effort – 2,020 lbs*
Cylinder s – 8" x 15"	*tubes – 220 sq ft*	*Coal capacity – 1 ton*
Driving wheels – 5' 0"	*firebox – 53.5 sq ft*	*Water capacity – 500 gal*
Trailing wheels – 3' 6"	*grate – 10.5 sq ft*	*Locomotive weight – 21 tons 10 cwt*
Wheel base – 5' 6" + 7' 10¼"		*Adhesive weight – 14 tons 8 cwt*
Length – see comments below		*Max axle loading – 7 tons 4 cwt*

Sprite was built as a combined engine and carriage – separated in 1889. Subsequently it was used with a close-coupled four-wheeled coach to form the paymaster's train. Apparently the coupling was permanent as the Locomotive Diagram includes the coach with additional dimensions:

Coach wheels – 3' 7¼"; Wheel base: radial wheels/ leading coach wheels – 7' 10"; coach – 10'; Combined locomotive and carriage length – 41' 9"

The Working Timetables for the period refer to the Northern and Southern pay carriages but it is not known which locomotive was allocated to which service. The pay carriage system was abolished in 1926, leading to the withdrawal of the pair the following year. By this time *Sprite* was recorded as having run 1,221,257 miles, a remarkable figure for such a diminutive machine. However, the authorities seemed reluctant to lose its services as it was retained for a further six years on the Inchicore boiler wash-out before being finally broken up.

Fairy was built to the same design but operated in the normal fashion as an independent locomotive. There was a reluctance also to dispense with this locomotive as it was not scrapped for some considerable period following its withdrawal. The estimated length of Fairy was 21' 2" (front buffer face to rear buffer beam).

Fairy was given Inchicore Class L4 and *Sprite* was originally allocated Class L5, but this was later changed to L4.

GSWR/ GSR Class 'Sprite'/ L5, later L4, *Sprite*, at Inchicore in 1914.

K Nunn

GSWR/ GSR Class 'Sprite'/ L4, *Fairy*.

IRRS collection

Chapter 5
Locomotives of the Dublin and South Eastern Railway

The Dublin & South Eastern Railway was formed on 1 January 1907, following resolution of a long-running dispute between the Dublin Wicklow & Wexford Railway and the Dublin & Kingstown Railway, and was the third largest of the GSR's constituent partners. Significantly smaller than both the Great Southern & Western and the Midland Great Western railways in route mileage and locomotive fleet size, it was predominantly a passenger-carrying line with more tank than tender locomotives. A significant portion of revenue was earned from commuter traffic between Dublin and Bray which was in the hands of four-coupled tank locomotives. Longer distance passenger services were handled by a small fleet of 4-4-0s, with goods services mainly worked by traditional style 0-6-0s.

New locomotives were only ever acquired in modest batches, either purchased from outside manufacturers or constructed by the company in the old DWWR workshops – 'the Factory' at Grand Canal Street, Dublin. This was a two-storey converted distillery and far from ideal for locomotive engineering. There was no crane for lifting locomotives; such operations were carried out by use of hydraulic jacks deployed to raise one end at a time. Heavy parts and components were moved by hand cranes and there were numerous ingenious arrangements to overcome the building's inappropriate layout and the lack of modern workshop equipment. Although new locomotives were built at the Factory, the term 'assembled' might be more accurate. It was normal practice to buy in boilers, cylinders, wheels, axles, frames, heavy forgings, iron castings and boiler fittings from outside specialist manufacturers. The GSR quickly recognised the shortcomings of the Factory by closing down the entire facility in 1926.

For all the innovation displayed by workshop personnel, the building's poor layout and inadequate equipment made it increasingly problematic for the Factory to cope with the larger locomotives that were introduced in the later years of the DSER's existence. This situation worsened with greater locomotive mileages worked during the First World War, and with extensive damage sustained through the activities of malicious elements during the Civil War. Arrangements were made for the overhaul of six locomotives by the GNR(I) at Dundalk in 1922-3; 2-4-2Ts Nos 3, 10 & 27, and 2-4-0T No 44 were so treated. 2-4-2Ts Nos 10 & 46 were scheduled also for this treatment but these plans were cancelled, possibly because of the pending amalgamation. No 51, which had been heavily damaged during the Civil War, was also to have been repaired at Dundalk. However, following the costing of this work at £2,700 it was concluded that construction of a new locomotive would be preferable.

Ostensibly there were 62 locomotives on the system as at 1 January 1925, accounted for as follows:

Wheels	Number	Wheels	Number
0-4-2	5	0-4-2T	1
0-6-0	11	4-4-2T	6
4-4-0	6	2-4-0T	13
2-4-0	4	2-4-2T	13
2-6-0	2		
Total	28		33

In addition, a contractor's 0-6-0T named *Blackburn* in the care of, but not owned by, the company was not included in the last annual return for the DSER, dated 31 December 1924.

Of the total fleet, the actual number considered operable was significantly less. The first block of numbers allocated by the GSR (Nos 410 to 462) obviously anticipated that 53 ex-DSER locomotives would be taken into the new company's stock list. The actual number officially absorbed by the GSR was:

Wheels	No of classes	No of locomotives	Built since 1900	Rebuilt since 1900
2-6-0	1	2	2	–
4-4-0	2	5	1	4
2-4-0	1	1	–	–
0-6-0	5	10	6	3
4-4-2T	2	6	6	–
2-4-2T	3	13	6	6
2-4-0T	2	5	–	1
Total	**16**	**42**	**22**	**13**

Reconciliation of the fleet composition is complicated by confusion over those locomotives deemed not fit for further service. Some had been damaged beyond economic repair in the Civil War while others were considered obsolete or worn out.

The GSR seemed to approach the DSER fleet with suspicion. Forty-two locomotives were sent to Inchicore for survey on 28-29 January 1925. The position reported to the GSR Board on 20 February 1925 stated that of 61 DSER locomotives, 20 should be scrapped immediately, while another 20 were in need of complete overhaul. Bazin recommended that Inchicore personnel be put on eight hours per week overtime to complete this overhaul programme at an incremental cost of £6,000. A review of traffic demands concluded that 52 locomotives were required to maintain ex-DSER services so that nine of the fleet total of 61 need not be replaced. Thus it was proposed that 12 new tank engines would cover the DSER's net requirements and also meet other needs on the enlarged system as there was a general shortage of suitable suburban tank locomotives. The intentions to build a new 4-4-2T are discussed in Chapter 10.

In reality, 16 members of the DSER fleet were immediately withdrawn, and a further six were scrapped shortly afterwards. Although several of these locomotives were unserviceable, at least without major works attention, this action might have been precipitate, and could have been influenced by residual resentment over the DSER's reluctance to join the newly-formed GSR. On pure engineering grounds, the withdrawals might have been justified but little consideration seems to have been given to prevailing commercial demand. The traffic pattern of the DSER was unlike anything on the GSWR, and the MGWR. In many respects, it was the mirror of the GNR(I) with which the company had wished to merge, and which would have created an organisation with a strong operational logic.

What is certain is that the ex-GSWR/MGWR hierarchies had limited recent experience of tank locomotive designs and no experience at all in coping with the needs of a commuter rail service. More particularly, the DSER had established a tradition of brisk working between Dublin, Westland Row and Dun Laoghaire. Over a distance of six miles, average timings were 18 minutes with six station stops, and 19 minutes with eight stops. This was helped by the practice of setting locomotive valves to maximise accelerative ability at the expense of speed, although non-stop runs over this route frequently exceeded 50 mph, and sometimes 60 mph.

The DSER had given consideration to electrification of its commuter services but nothing tangible resulted. The GSR sought to redress the motive power shortfall by drafting in locomotives from elsewhere of varying suitability, by at least three attempts at more modern steam power, and by application of battery electric trains. A comprehensively satisfactory solution took almost 60 years to materialise. This was in the form of the Dublin Area Rapid Transit overhead electric trains into which were integrated services over the ex-GNR(I) commuter routes northwards to Howth and Malahide.

At the amalgamation, the DSER's motive power fleet reflected the traditional conservatism found in Irish locomotives at that time. With the exception of the ex-railcar 2-4-0T, all had inside cylinders. Only the 2-6-0s were superheated and fitted with piston valves, although an 0-6-0 had experimentally carried Phoenix equipment from 1911 to 1915. One area where the DSER had led was in introducing the first 4-4-2T in Ireland, a type that was to prove popular on other railways for passenger work.

The DSER had no formal system for classifying locomotives. In several cases, the concept of 'class' was loosely interpreted as there was much diversity within small groups of locomotives of ostensibly the same basic type. The rebuilding programme of a particular type/ class could be extended over a number of years and take different forms with individual locomotives. This is readily apparent with the family of 2-4-0Ts and 2-4-2Ts. This penchant for individuality could have been a by-product of the engineering challenges imposed by the physical restrictions at the Factory. Nonetheless, variety in the rebuilding of locomotives persisted under GSR management with adverse implications for standardisation and operating costs. One feature common to most small DSER locomotives was a noise when working known as the 'Grand Canal Street wheeze'. This infuriated residents living near the line but reputedly did not adversely affect performance.

It should be noted that apart from the modifications described in the individual class sections, there were numerous other changes of detail. With the early closing of the Factory, ex-DSER locomotives were mainly repaired at Inchicore. Thus GSWR detail features such as chimneys appeared sooner than on ex-MGWR types that were still repaired at the Broadstone into the early 1930s.

The following Key is provided to help trace the GSR classifications allocated to individual DSER locomotives:

DSER No	GSR No	GSR Class	Wheel Arrangt	DSER No	GSR No	GSR Class	Wheel Arrangt	DSER No	GSR No	GSR Class	Wheel Arrangt
3	428	428	2-4-2T	**18**	444	442	0-6-0	**49**	423	423	2-4-0T
4	448	448	0-6-0	**20**	455	455	4-4-2T	**50**	447	447	0-6-0
5	449	448	0-6-0	**24**	422	422	2-4-0	**52**	458	458	4-4-2T
7	426	423	2-4-0T	**27**	436	434	2-4-2T	**53**	460	458	4-4-2T
8	434	434	2-4-2T	**28**	431	428	2-4-2T	**54**	459	458	4-4-2T
9	424	423	2-4-0T	**29**	437	434	2-4-2T	**55**	450	450	4-4-0
10	429	428	2-4-2T	**30**	438	434	2-4-2T	**56**	451	450	4-4-0
11	430	428	2-4-2T	**34**	456	455	4-4-2T	**57**	452	450	4-4-0
12	435	434	2-4-2T	**35**	457	455	4-4-2T	**58**	453	450	4-4-0
13	442	442	0-6-0	**36**	441	441	0-6-0	**64**	427	427	2-4-2T
14	443	442	0-6-0	**40**	439	434	2-4-2T	**65**	445	442	0-6-0
15	461	461	2-6-0	**45**	432	428	2-4-2T	**66**	446	442	0-6-0
16	462	461	2-6-0	**46**	433	428	2-4-2T	**67**	454	454	4-4-0
17	440	440	0-6-0	**47**	425	423	2-4-0T	**69**	Elf	Imp	2-4-0T

The following locomotives were withdrawn as a result of the cull at Inchicore in January 1925. Some were irreparable following Civil War damage but sources vary on which machines were actually lost through malicious action, and those which were merely worn out. The DSER had already taken some out of service the previous year:

DSER No	Wheel Arrangt	Comments	DSER No	Wheel Arrangt	Comments
1	2-4-0T		**33**	2-4-0	
2	2-4-0T		**38**	0-4-2	
6	2-4-0T		**39**	0-4-2	Civil War loss
10	2-4-2T	GSR No 429 - not carried	**41**	2-4-0T	
15A	0-4-2		**42**	2-4-0T	
19	0-4-2	Civil War loss	**43**	2-4-0T	
22	0-4-2	Previously 20/ 20A	**44**	2-4-0T	Worked until 1927
21	0-4-2		**51**	0-6-0	Civil War loss*
25	2-4-0	Civil War loss	**68**	4-4-0	Civil War loss*
26	2-4-0T		**(Blackburn)**	0-6-0T	Not owned by DSER
32	2-4-0				

* Destroyed in a maliciously staged head-on collision with each other.

Nos 1, 2, 6, 25, 26, 32, 33, 38, 39, 42, 43 & 44 were originally intended to take the GSR numbers 410 to 421 in that order.

Locomotive livery from around 1870 was described as green of a shade similar to that of light, fresh ivy leaves. Boiler bands, side tanks, cabsides, and tenders were lined black, edged on either side by a yellow pencil line so that the combined lining was about 2" wide. Reportedly during the Grierson period (1894-97), there was a move to change to a brown livery that would 'harmonise' with carriages but no other details are known. The green continued until 1907 when Cronin replaced it with all-over black, lined ⅛" wide yellow pencil line/ 1" wide red band/ ⅛" wide yellow pencil line. There was a ⅛" gap between the pencil lines and the red band.

Concurrent with introduction of the black livery, Cronin started to remove the names which he had introduced on new and rebuilt locomotives since 1898. In most cases, names had been painted on tank sides or centre splashers but the four Beyer Peacock locomotives of 1905 (0-6-0s Nos 65 & 66 and 4-4-0s Nos 67 & 68) were embellished with handsome brass name plates incorporated within ornate brass splasher beading. At the amalgamation these names were still in place together with those of Nos 2 , 21 & 33 (all three withdrawn in 1925 together with No 68). The other three Beyer Peacock locomotives (Nos 65, 66 & 67) very likely retained their names until physically removed prior to repainting in standard GSR grey livery. (Names removed prior to the amalgamation appear in brackets in the class sections). Conversely No 69, which was unnamed in DSER days both as a tank locomotive and in its earlier career as part of a steam rail motor, did not receive a GSR number but was christened *Elf*.

Dramatis personae

The oldest active locomotives in the DSER fleet at the amalgamation reputedly dated from the Locomotive Superintendency of **W Meikle** (1864–1865) on the DWWR but it is doubtful how much of the original machines survived in 1925. In a paper read by G H Wild in March 1948, he pointed out that quite often rebuilds were "actually or practically" new locomotives utilising suitable parts, if any, from the original.

Meikle retired through ill health not long after his appointment. He was succeeded by **John Wakefield** in 1865 who in turn was followed in 1882 by his nephew **William Wakefield**. The two Wakefields had broadly similar attitudes to motive power needs which were satisfied by reliance on small locomotives of wheel arrangements such as 2-2-2WT, 2-4-0, 2-4-0T and 0-4-2. William Wakefield's closing years, however, saw introduction of larger locomotives more able to cope with contemporary demands in the form of the DWWR's first 0-6-0s and 4-4-2Ts.

In the early 1890s, the DWWR's financial condition was unsatisfactory. In 1893 the Board commissioned an inspecting engineer, WC Furnivall, to review the company's position, to establish where excessive costs were being incurred, and to recommend corrective action. The Furnivall Report *inter alia* was very critical of the cramped and primitive working conditions of the Factory, and of the methods used in managing locomotive affairs. This led to the resignation of a number of senior officers early in 1894. In February of that year, **T Grierson** was appointed Chief Engineer with authority over William Wakefield. The latter found this situation untenable and resigned the following August.

With Wakefield's departure, and presumably in pursuit of economies, the position of Locomotive Superintendent was abolished. Locomotive matters were considered as subordinate to the Civil Engineer's Office where Grierson was in charge. It was soon clear though that his grasp of mechanical engineering was inadequate. Two designs were ordered during this period from British manufacturers and both were sufficiently flawed to need significant modification to become satisfactory (later GSR Classes 448 and 450).

In December 1896, the Board acknowledged that the position of Locomotive Superintendent should be restored and a suitably qualified individual recruited for the role. After a careful assessment of candidates, **R Cronin**, principal foreman at the Inchicore Works of the GSWR, was appointed in May 1897. This proved to be a sound choice as Cronin, undeterred by the problems imposed by the Factory, set about improving affairs with great energy. He conducted a major re-organisation and modernisation of locomotives and rolling stock over the next 20 years. He successfully replaced 2-2-2WTs and 0-4-2s that were 30–40 years old with more capable 4-4-0s and 2-4-2Ts for passenger duties, and 0-6-0s for goods work. He was responsible for the introduction of 20 new locomotives (12 of which were built at the Factory), for the rebuilding of 35 others at that location, and for introducing a degree of standardisation.

In April 1916 **GH Wild**, who until then had been District Superintendent of the GNR(I) at Londonderry, was appointed as assistant to Cronin. A year later, he became Locomotive Superintendent upon Cronin's retirement and he served in this position throughout the company's final years. For the reasons described above, this was a difficult period but Wild introduced a pair of goods 2-6-0s built by Beyer Peacock that were greatly valued by the GSR and its successor.

GSR Class 422 — 2-4-0 — Inchicore Class G7
DSER Nos 24, 25, 32 & 33 — 1925 Load Class Q

GSR (DSER) No		Name	Built	Makers' No	Withdrawn	
422	(24)	*(Glenmore)*	3/1864	1478	1928	
–	(25)	*(Glenart)*	3/1864	1479	1925	*Civil War loss*
–	(32)	*(Glenmalure)*	1873	2304	1925	
–	(33)	*Glendalough*	1873	2305	1925	

Designer: Meikle/ John Wakefield — **Built by Sharp Stewart**

Boiler pressure – 150 lbs/ sq in	*Heating surfaces:*	*Tractive effort – 11,140 lbs*
Cylinders – 16" x 22"	*tubes – 786 sq ft*	*Coal capacity – 4 tons*
Pony wheels – 3' 7½"	*firebox – 102 sq ft*	*Water capacity – 2100 gal*
Driving wheels – 5' 4½"	*grate – 15.9 sq ft*	*Locomotive weight – 32 tons 4 cwt*
Wheel base – 6' 5" + 8' 1"		*Adhesive weight – 23 tons 0 cwt*
Locomotive length – 29' 0" (estimated)		*Max axle loading – 11 tons 10 cwt*

The original dimensions of Nos 32 & 33 were marginally different: heating surface – 879 sq ft; weight – 32 tons 0 cwt.

No 32 is an example of the uncertainties concerning Civil War losses. This engine was derailed and ended up in the River Slaney in November 1922. It was recovered with some difficulty but how much work it undertook thereafter is not recorded. Notwithstanding these adventures, it is not considered a Civil War loss. On the other hand, No 18 (GSR Class 442/J8) had similarly gone swimming in the same river two weeks earlier; it was also recovered and worked for another 35 years.

The main use of No 422 during its short GSR career was on the Shillelagh branch. This line had traditionally been home to the DSER's weakest tank locomotives; after the amalgamation it was operated on the one-engine-in-steam principle. The tender (DSER No 24/ GSR No 422) attached to this locomotive was the oldest in service with the GSR.

DSER No 26 (Makers' No 1480) was another of this type until it was rebuilt as a 2-4-0T in 1900 (see section below listing DSER locomotives acquired in 1925 but not taken into GSR stock).

DSER No 33 *Glendalough* (No GSR number allocated to this locomotive, but No 24 of the same type became GSR Class 422/ G7 No 422).

L&GRP

GSR Class 423 — 2-4-0T — Inchicore Class G1
DSER Nos 49, 9, 47, 1, 2, 6 & 7 — 1925/ 1931 Load Class O/ NT

GSR (DSER) No		Name	Built	Rebuilt	Withdrawn
423	(49)	*(Carrickmines)*	1891	1914*/ 1930¶	1955
424	(9)	*(Dalkey)*	1890	1916*/ 1930¶/ 1934#	1952
425	(47)	*(Stillorgan)*	1889	1912*/ 1933#	1953
(426)	(7)	*(Foxrock)*	1895	–	1926
–	(1)	–	1891	–	1925
–	(2)	*Glenageary*	1885	1914*	1925
–	(6)	*(Greystones)*	1894	–	1925

Designer: William Wakefield

Built at Grand Canal Street

*** As rebuilt:**

Boiler pressure – 150 lbs/ sq in	*Heating surfaces:*	*Tractive effort – 12,700 lbs*
Cylinders – 17" x 24"	*tubes & firebox*	*Coal capacity – 1 ton 10 cwt*
Pony wheels – 3' 8"	*– 986 sq ft*	*Water capacity – 800 gal*
Driving wheels – 5' 6"	*grate – 15.3 sq ft*	*Locomotive weight – 40 tons 0 cwt*
Wheel base – 6' 6" +7' 10"		*Adhesive weight – 28 tons 10 cwt*
Locomotive length – 29' 8"		*Max axle loading – 14 tons 10 cwt*

At withdrawal, Nos 1/ 6/ 7 reportedly still carried original boilers which were slightly larger but with 140 lbs/ sq in pressure.

¶ Rebuilt with boiler that might have been similar to that used on Class 267 but no details available

 # As rebuilt with T type Belpaire saturated boiler:

Boiler pressure – 150 lbs/ sq in	*Heating surfaces:*	*Tractive effort – 12,700 lbs*
	tubes – 853 sq ft	*Locomotive weight – 41 tons 13 cwt*
	firebox – 105 sq ft	*Adhesive weight – not stated*
	grate – 15.1 sq ft	*Max axle loading – not stated*

Numerically this was the DSER's largest class, originally comprising 11 examples. Seven (DSER Nos 2, 9, 28, 45–47 and 49) were built between 1885 and 1891, of which Nos 28, 45 and 46 were rebuilt as 2-4-2Ts between 1909 and 1911 (see GSR Class 428/ F2). A second batch of four locomotives (DSER Nos 1, 6, 7 and 10) with detail differences were introduced between 1892 and 1896, of which No 10 was rebuilt in 1903 as a 2-4-2T and also became part of GSR Class 428/ F2.

No 7 was reportedly rebuilt in 1921 but this might have been an overhaul as the locomotive was deemed not fit for further service four years later. No 47 was the first DSER locomotive to be renumbered (in August 1925 as GSR No 425) at which time it was presumably repainted in standard GSR livery.

In 1929–30, the surviving class members were still regularly used on boat trains to and from Kingstown, often loaded up to 200 tons. On one occasion,

DSER No 9/ GSR Class 423/ G1 No 424 at Grand Canal Street in 1931.

L&GRP

No 424 hauling six bogie coaches and seven six-wheeled coaches (heavily loaded – minimum 272 tons) lost only 30 seconds on the 13 minute schedule from Dublin Westland Row to Dun Laoghaire Pier.

1948 assessment: (423/ 428 classes): *All these engines (DSER and occasionally one or two on Cork-Bandon or shunting at Mallow) are obsolete in every way. They are slow and high in coal consumption. The number in service limits the performance of the whole DSER local service.*

GSR Class 427 — 2-4-2T — Inchicore Class F3
DSER No 64 — 1925/ 1931 Load Class O/ NT

GSR (DSER) No	Name	Built as 2-4-0T	Rebuilt as 2-4-2T	LNWR Running No	Purchased second-hand	Withdrawn
427 (64)	*(Earl of Bessborough)*	*1877*	1896	2251	o/1902	1936

Designer: F W Webb — **Built by LNWR, Crewe**

Boiler pressure – 150 lbs/ sq in	*Heating surfaces:*	*Tractive effort – 13,050 lbs*
Cylinders – 17" x 20"	*tubes – 742.5 sq ft*	*Coal capacity – 2 tons 10 cwt*
Pony wheels – 3' 4"	*firebox – 107.5 sq ft*	*Water capacity – 1480 gal*
Driving wheels – 4' 9½"	*grate – 15.3 sq ft*	*Locomotive weight – 51 tons 7 cwt*
Trailing wheels – 3' 4"		*Adhesive weight – 28 tons 15 cwt*
Wheel base – 6' 9" + 7' 9" + 6' 9"		*Max axle loading – 14 tons 12 cwt*
Locomotive length – not recorded		

No 64 was the last Irish survivor of six locomotives purchased for £1500 each in 1902 from the London & North Western Railway. It was originally constructed as a 2-4-0T in 1877 (Crewe Works No 2002) and on rebuilding as a 2-4-2T in 1896, acquired new Works No 3605. All six locomotives purchased were converted to 5' 3" gauge at Crewe by means of fitting reinforced extended axle bosses (3¼" long), the frames remaining unchanged. The other five locomotives (Nos 59 to 63) returned to Britain in 1916-1917 and following re-gauging were sold to sundry users to help alleviate a general wartime shortage of motive power.

No 64 had been rebuilt with a new boiler in 1914 and new cylinders (the latter provided by the LNWR) which doubtless accounted for its retention by the DSER. It was encased in steel plating for use in an armoured train during the Civil War with the name *Faugh-a-ballagh** painted on its side, but had returned to normal condition by the time of the amalgamation.

* In English, *'Clear the way'*

These locomotives are believed to have been the only examples in Ireland equipped with Allan's straight link valve gear. They were mainly used on suburban services between Harcourt Street and Bray, but were unpopular with crews who claimed to prefer the earlier single-driver tank locomotives. No 427 left the DSER section in 1933 and worked at Mallow beet factory sidings before moving to Westport immediately before withdrawal. After withdrawal, it continued to serve until 1945 or 1946 on boiler wash-out duties at Inchicore.

DSER No 64/ GSR Class 427/ F3 No 427 at Grand Canal Street in 1931.

L&GRP

GSR Class 428 — 2-4-2T — Inchicore Class F2
DSER Nos 3, 10, 11, 28, 45 & 46 — 1925/ 1931 Load Class O/ NT

GSR No (DSER)	Name	Built as 2-4-2T	Built as 2-4-0T	Rebuilt as 2-4-2T	Subsequent boiler rebuildings	W'dwn
428 (3)	*(St. Patrick)*	1898	–	–	1934¶	1952
(429) (10)	*(St. Senanus)*	–	1896	1903	–	1925
430 (11)	*(St. Kevin)*	1896	–	–	1917*/ 1935¥/ 1945§/ 1948¶	1952
431 (28)	*(St. Lawrence)*	–	1887	1909	1930π/ 1940§/ 1944π	1950
432 (45)	*(St. Kieran)*	–	1886	1910	1939¶	1957
433 (46)	*(Princess Mary)*	–	1888	1910	1914*/ 1932#/ 1936§/ 1943¶/ 1948π	1957

Designer: William Wakefield — **Built at Grand Canal Street**

Nos 3/ 11 built as new as 2-4-2T with round-topped saturated boiler:

(There were detail differences between these two locomotives in springs, and shape of cab and bunker)

Boiler pressure – 160 lbs/ sq in	*Heating surfaces:*	*Tractive effort – 14,300 lbs*
Cylinders – 17" x 24"	*tubes – 823 sq ft*	*Coal capacity – 2 tons 10 cwt*
Pony wheels – 3' 9"	*firebox – 128 sq ft*	*Water capacity – 1500 gal*
Driving wheels – 5' 6"	*grate – 15.1 sq ft*	*Locomotive weight – 52 tons 0 cwt*
Trailing wheels – 3' 9"		*Adhesive weight – 28 tons 2 cwt*
Wheel base – 6' 6" + 7' 10" + 6' 0"		*Max axle loading – 14 tons 10 cwt*
Locomotive length – 33' 6"		

No 10 rebuilt as 2-4-2T with round-topped saturated boiler:

(The conversion of this locomotive involved only the lengthening of frames and bunker; remaining dimensions are as for 2-4-0T when originally built)

Boiler pressure – 150 lbs/ sq in	*Heating surfaces:*	*Tractive effort – 12,700 lbs*
Cylinders – 17" x 24"	*tubes & firebox*	*Coal capacity – 2 tons 10 cwt*
Pony wheels – 3' 9"	*– 986 sq ft (total)*	*Water capacity – 800 gal*
Driving wheels – 5' 6"	*grate – 15.3 sq ft*	*Locomotive weight – not recorded*
Trailing wheels – 3' 9"		*Adhesive weight – not recorded*
Wheel base – 6' 6" +7' 10" + 6' 0"		*Max axle loading – not recorded*
Locomotive length – 33' 10"		

DSER No 11 (As built for DWWR) in original condition. This locomotive was rebuilt in 1917 with a larger round-topped boiler, but DSER No 3 remained in the condition shown until 1934. DSER No 11 became GSR Class 428/ F2 No 430.

L&GRP

Nos 28, 45 and 46 rebuilt as 2-4-2T with round-topped saturated boiler:
(These conversions received more extensive treatment than that given to No 10, involving complete new frames, boilers and side tanks. Dimensions as for Nos 3/ 11 above except tank capacity was 1430 gallons)

Boiler rebuilds:

* Fitted with boilers of approximately 3" greater diameter and pitched 6½" higher; tube heating surfaces were presumably increased but details not recorded

# 4'0" Class 101 boiler:	*Heating surfaces:* *tubes – 764 sq ft* *firebox – 96 sq ft* *grate – 17.5 sq ft*

In this condition, this locomotive carried a typical GSWR double-doored smokebox

¶ Type T saturated Belpaire boiler:	*Heating surfaces:* *tubes – 853 sq ft* *firebox – 105 sq ft* *grate – 15.1 sq ft*
§ Round-topped saturated boiler ex-Class 573:	*Heating surfaces:* *tubes – 970 sq ft* *firebox – 95 sq ft* *grate – 16.5 sq ft*

¥ Fitted with an alternative boiler, details of which are unknown; believed to have been either an ex-DSER or a 4' 0" diameter Class 101 type.

π Fitted with boiler of type used on Class 267:	*Heating surfaces:* *tubes – 780 sq ft* *firebox – 88 sq ft* *grate – 15 sq ft*

Apart from No 433 noted above, Nos 428 and 431 appear to have worked with old GSWR-type smokeboxes during the 1930s. It is notable that two examples of this class were rebuilt (with different types of boiler) as late as 1948, when, in the same year, such an adverse official judgement (see below) should have been formed of their capacities.

No 430 was on loan to the Belfast & County Down Railway from July 1941 to October 1945 at a rental of £15 per week. It was used only as a relief engine, mainly on the Ballynahinch branch and other light duties.

1948 assessment: (423/ 428 classes): *All these engines (DSER and occasionally one or two on Cork-Bandon or shunting at Mallow) are obsolete in every way. They are slow and high in coal consumption. The number in service limits the performance of the whole DSER local service.*

Left upper: DSER No 28/ GSR Class 428/ F2 No 431. As rebuilt with round-topped boiler at Grand Canal Street. *CH Hewison*

Left lower: DSER No 29/ GSR Class 428/F2 No 432 as rebuilt with Type T saturated Belpaire boiler at Rocksavage, Cork. *Authors' collection*

GSR Class 434 — 2-4-2T — Inchicore Class F1
DSER Nos 8, 12, 40, 27, 29 & 30 — 1925/ 1931 Load Class N/ MT

GSR (DSER) No	Name	Built	Original boiler	Rebuilt	Withdrawn
434 (8)	*(St. Brendan)*	1903	Round-top	1925*	1950
435 (12)	*(St. Brigid)*	1901	Round-top	1925*	1950
436 (27)	*(St. Aidan)*	1907	Belpaire	1926*	1953
437 (29)	*(St. Mantan)*	1906	Belpaire	1932*	1951
438 (30)	*(St. Iberius)*	1909	Belpaire	1930#/ 1933¶/ 1937*	1952
439 (40)	*(St. Selskar)*	1902	Round-top	1925*/ date unknown§	1952

Designer: Cronin — **Built at Grand Canal Street**

Rebuilt with boiler type:
* 4' 4" diameter Class 101
# Round-topped boiler ex-No 440
¶ Belpaire saturated (probably one of those fitted when new)
§ Round-topped saturated (probably one of those fitted when new)

DSER No 40/ GSR Class 434/ F1 No 437 as rebuilt Class 101 4' 4" round-topped boiler. At Grand Canal Street 1933.

L&GRP

As built with round-topped boiler:

Boiler pressure – 160 lbs/ sq in (later reduced to 150 lbs/ sq in)
Cylinders – 17" x 24"
Pony wheels – 3' 8"
Driving wheels – 5' 6"
Trailing wheels – 3' 8"
Wheel base – 6' 6" + 8' 1" + 6' 0"
Locomotive length – 33' 0"

Heating surfaces:
tubes – 823 sq ft
firebox – 128 sq ft
grate – 15 sq ft

Tractive effort – 14,300 lbs (13,400 lbs)
Coal capacity – 2 tons 10 cwt
Water capacity – 1500 gal
Locomotive weight – 53 tons 0 cwt
Adhesive weight – 28 tons 2 cwt
Max axle loading – 14 tons 10 cwt

DSER No 40/ GSR Class 434/ F1 No 439 This locomotive carried two types of round-topped boiler; the original until 1925 and a Class 101 4' 4" type from then until a date unknown, at which it is believed to have reverted to original type. Here it is believed to be carrying the Class 101 4' 4" type boiler. At Grand Canal Street in 1933.

L&GRP

As built with Belpaire boiler:	*Heating surfaces*	*Locomotive weight – 54 tons 0 cwt*
	tubes – 834 sq ft	*Adhesive weight – 28 tons 15 cwt*
	firebox – 105 sq ft	*Max axle loading – 14 tons 12 cwt*
	grate – 17 sq ft	

(The equipping of these locomotives with Belpaire boilers required frames 3" longer at the front than the round-topped version)

*** As rebuilt with 4' 4" diameter Class 101 saturated boiler:**

Boiler pressure – 150 lbs/ sq in	*Heating surfaces:*	*Locomotive weight – 51 tons 10 cwt*
	tubes – 818 sq ft	*Adhesive weight – 28 tons 14 cwt*
	firebox – 109 sq ft	*Max axle loading – 14 tons 7 cwt*
	grate – 19.3 sq ft	

 # As rebuilt with round-topped boiler ex-No 440:

Boiler pressure – 150 lbs/ sq in	*Heating surfaces:*	*Locomotive weight – not recorded*
	tubes – 799.2 sq ft	*Adhesive weight – not recorded*
	firebox – 95 sq ft	*Max axle loading – not recorded*
	grate – 17.75 sq ft	

In response to a specific enquiry, Bredin confirmed that the round-topped boilers used in the rebuilding programme were the same as those fitted to Class 101 (although reported heating surfaces differ). Modification to frame cross-members was necessary to accommodate the larger firebox.

In 1936, No 438 was running with a GSWR type double door smokebox (none of the remainder were so fitted). Members of this class were employed on the Shillelagh branch in the 1940s.

1948 assessment: *Obsolete DSER passenger engine.*

GSR No 440 DSER No 17

0-6-0

Inchicore class J20
1925 Load Class M

GSR (DSER) No		Name	Built	Withdrawn
440	(17)	*(Wicklow)*	1899	1929

Designer: Cronin

Built at Grand Canal Street

DSER No 17/ GSR Class 440/ J20 No 440. Depicted here as DSER No 17 *Wicklow*.
Real Photographs Co Ltd

Boiler pressure – 160 lbs/ sq in	*Heating surfaces:*	*Tractive effort – 15,720 lbs*
Cylinders – 17" x 24"	*tubes – 799.2 sq ft*	*Coal capacity – 4 tons*
Driving wheels – 5' 0"	*firebox – 95 sq ft*	*Water capacity – 1850 gal*
Wheel base – 7' 0" + 7' 9"	*grate – 17.75 sq ft*	*Locomotive weight – 37 tons 16 cwt*
Locomotive length – not recorded		*Max axle loading – 13 tons 10 cwt*

This locomotive is sometimes referred to as a rebuild of an 0-4-2 dating from 1864 but sufficient new material was used in 1899 to make this effectively a new machine. It achieved notoriety in February 1900 when its brakes failed while hauling a cattle train from Enniscorthy into Dublin, Harcourt Street station, resulting in its running through the buffer stops and retaining wall, and ending up suspended 30 feet above Hatch Street. The provision of a larger boiler in 1920 did not prevent comparatively early withdrawal; this boiler found further use with 2-4-2T No 438.

GSR Class 441 **0-6-0** **Inchicore class J14**
DSER No 36 **1925/ 1931 Load Class H/ J**

GSR (DSER) No		Name	Built	Withdrawn
441	(36)	*(Wexford)*	1901	1935

Designer: Cronin **Built at Grand Canal Street**

DSER No 36/ GSR Class 441/ J14 No 441 at Waterford shed.
L&GRP

Boiler pressure – 160 lbs/ sq in	*Heating surfaces:*	*Tractive effort – 17,630 lbs*
Cylinders – 18" x 24"	*tubes – 799.2 sq ft*	*Coal capacity – 4 tons*
Driving wheels – 5' 0"	*firebox – 95 sq ft*	*Water capacity – 1850 gal*
Wheel base – 7' 0" + 7' 9"	*grate – 17.75 sq ft*	*Locomotive weight – 41 tons 0 cwt*
Locomotive length – not recorded		*Max axle loading – 14 tons 10 cwt*

The DSER considered this locomotive to be in the same class as its No 17 (GSR 440) but the GSR recognised sufficient dimensional differences to warrant separate classification. No 36 was fitted with a Phoenix superheater from 1911 until 1915. It was tested in this condition against No 17 on goods duties, and found to be 20% more powerful. Despite these encouraging results, no further superheating took place until Nos 15 and 16 (later GSR Nos 461 and 462) which were introduced in 1922.

GSR Class 442 — 0-6-0 — Inchicore class J8
DSER Nos 13, 14, 18, 65 & 66 — 1925/ 1931 Load Class C/ E

GSR (DSER) No		Name	Built	Makers' No	Rebuilt	Withdrawn
442	(13)	*(Waterford)*	1904	–	1925*	1930
443	(14)	*(Limerick)*	1905	–	1926*	1955
444	(18)	*(Enniscorthy)*	1910	–	1943§/ 1947*	1957
445	(65)	*Cork*	1905	4647	1926*/ 1949#	1957
446	(66)	*Dublin*	1905	4648	1940§/ 1951*	1957

Designer: Cronin

Nos 13, 14 and 18 built at Grand Canal Street
Nos 65/ 66 built by Beyer Peacock

Rebuilt with boiler type: * Class 351 § Class 451 # Original Class 442 restored

Above: DSER No 65/ GSR Class 442/ J8 No 445 at Grand Canal Street in 1931 *L&GRP*

DSER Nos 13, 14, 65, 66 as built:

Boiler pressure – 160 lbs/ sq in	*Heating surfaces:*	*Tractive effort – 18,790 lbs*
Cylinders – 18" x 26"	*tubes – 1074.7 sq ft*	*Coal capacity – 3 tons 10 cwt*
Driving wheels – 5' 1"	*firebox – 118.5 sq ft*	*Water capacity – 2600 gal*
Wheel base – 7' 3" + 8' 10"	*grate – 20 sq ft*	*Locomotive weight – 43 tons 6 cwt*
Locomotive length – not recorded		*Max axle loading – 15 tons 17 cwt*

DSER No 18 as built:

Driving wheels – 4' 11½"	*Tractive effort – 19,260 lbs*
	Locomotives weight 42 tons 7 cwt
	Max axle loading – 15 tons 11 cwt

(Four of these wheels came from old No 18, an 0-4-2 withdrawn in 1908. This locomotive was one of the earliest in Ireland to carry Ross pop safety valves).

*** As rebuilt with Class 351 type Belpaire saturated boiler:**

Boiler pressure – 160 lbs/ sq in	*Heating surfaces:*	*Tractive effort – 18,790 lbs*
	tubes – 1040 sq ft	*Locomotive weight – not stated*
	firebox – 118 sq ft	*Max axle loading – not stated*
	grate – 20.4 sq ft	

§ As rebuilt with Class 450 type Belpaire saturated boiler:

Boiler pressure – 160 lbs/ sq in	*Heating surfaces:*	*Tractive effort – 18,790 lbs*
	tubes – 993 sq ft	*Locomotive weight – not stated*
	firebox – 101 sq ft	*Max axle loading – not stated*
	grate – 18.5 sq ft	

DSER No 18/ GSR Class 442/ J8 No 444. The only example not fitted with a sliding window cab.

CP Friel collection

These locomotives were very popular with crews, being comfortable to work on with spacious well laid-out cabs, equipped with sliding windows except for Nos 442 and 444 which had large sliding cab sheets. They rode well, being volute-sprung throughout, and were good steamers. They only ever worked on the DSER system, sometimes on passenger services and excursions but principally goods services between Waterford and Wexford via Macmine, and the day goods between Dublin and Wexford.

1948 assessment: *DSER edition of Standard* Goods (Class 101)*: quite good.*

GSR Class 447 — 0-6-0 — Inchicore Class J7
DSER Nos 50/ 51 — 1925 Load Class E

GSR (DSER) No		Name	Built	Makers' No	Rebuilt*	Withdrawn	
447	(50)	*(Arklow)*	5/1891	1310	1912	1930	
–	(51)	*(New Ross)*	5/1891	1311	1915	1925	*Civil War loss*

Designer: William Wakefield — **Built by Vulcan Foundry**

Boiler pressure – 150 lbs/ sq in	*Heating surfaces:*	*Tractive effort – 18,850 lbs*
Cylinders – 18" x 26"	*tubes & firebox*	*Coal capacity – 4 tons*
Driving wheels – 4' 9"	*– 1028 sq ft (total)*	*Water capacity – 2600 gal*
Wheel base – 7' 3" +8' 9"	*grate – 18 sq ft*	*Locomotive weight – 39 tons 10 cwt*
Locomotive length – 30' (estimated)		*Max axle loading – not recorded*

*** As rebuilt with Belpaire boiler**

Boiler pressure – 160 lbs/ sq in	*Heating surfaces:*	*Locomotive weight – 42 tons 16 cwt*
	tubes – 840.5 sq ft	*Max axle loading – 15 tons 10 cwt*
	firebox – 84.3 sq ft	
	grate – 18.5 sq ft	

In GSR days, the survivor was used mainly on Shillelagh branch goods services.

DSER No 50/ GSR Class 447/ J7 No 447.

Authors' collection

GSR Class 448 (DSER Nos 4 & 5) — 0-6-0 — Inchicore Class J1, 1925/ 1931 Load Class C/ E

GSR (DSER) No		Name	Makers' No	Built	Rebuilt	Withdrawn
448	(4)	*(Lismore)*	3686	1897	1908*/ 1924¶	1950
449	(5)	*(Clonmel)*	3687	1897	1908*/ 1926¶	1940

* Rebuilt from 0-6-2Ts, which carried the same numbers

¶ Rebuilt with saturated Belpaire boiler

Designer: Grierson/ Cronin — **Built by Kitson**

*** As rebuilt in 1908:**

Boiler pressure – 160 lbs/ sq in
Cylinders – 18½" x 26"
Driving wheels – 4' 9"
Wheel base – 7' 7" +7' 11"
Locomotive length – not recorded

Heating surfaces:
tubes – 1142 sq ft
firebox – 107 sq ft
grate – 21 sq ft

Tractive effort – 21,230 lbs
Coal capacity – 4 tons
Water capacity – 2000 gal
Locomotive weight – 47 tons 0 cwt
Max axle loading – not recorded

¶ As rebuilt with Belpaire boiler:

Heating surfaces:
tubes – 1142 sq ft
firebox – 107 sq ft
grate – 21 sq ft

Locomotive weight – 46 tons 15 cwt
Max axle loading – 16 tons 4 cwt

These locomotives were ordered during the Grierson period, and were intended for main line goods duties. The choice of 0-6-2Ts for such work at that time was unusual and apparently resulted from Grierson's belief that tenders were uneconomic ie surplus weight that had to be hauled. The leading dimensions were similar to Kitson-built 0-6-2Ts supplied to the Lancashire Derbyshire & East Coast Railway between 1895 and 1900 (LNER Class N6).

DSER No 5/ GSR Class 448/ J1 No 449 at Grand Canal Street in 1933. *LGRP*

Unfortunately the axle loading exceeded the permitted maximum and the trailing axle boxes had a tendency to run hot. They were therefore rebuilt by Cronin as 0-6-0s with new tenders built at Grand Canal Street. In this form they were powerful and able to cope with heavy loads but had a voracious appetite for coal and water. Being difficult to fire and liable to stall on a gradient, they nevertheless had no difficulty in re-starting once boiler pressure had been restored.

The Belpaire boiler for No 4 was installed at the Factory, making this the last rebuilding undertaken at that works. This locomotive was further distinguished as being the last in DSER livery, not becoming GSR No 449 until 1930.

1948 assessment: *A DSER edition of Standard Goods* (Class 101). *Quite good but only two* (sic) *in class.*

GSR Class 450 (DSER Nos 55 to 58) — 4-4-0 — Inchicore Class D9, 1925/ 1931 Load Class N/ M

GSR (DSER) No		Name	Built	Rebuilt	Makers' No	Withdrawn
450	(55)	*(Rathdown)*	9/1895	1923*	1448	1929
451	(56)	*(Rathmines)*	10/1895	1911*	1449	1934
452	(57)	*(Rathnew)*	2/1896	1906*	1455	1933
453	(58)	*(Rathdrum)*	2/1896	1915§	1456	1940

Designer: Grierson — **Built by Vulcan Foundry**

DSER No 55/ GSR Class 450/ D9 No 450 at Waterford shed in 1928 *Kelland collection*

DSER No 58/ GSR Class 450/ D9 No 453. *Authors' collection*

*** As rebuilt with Belpaire saturated boiler (Inchicore Class D9:**

Boiler pressure – 160 lbs/ sq in
Cylinders – 18" x 26"
Bogie wheels – 3' 3"
Driving wheels – 6' 1"
Wheel base – 5' 3" + 7' 3" + 8' 3"
Locomotive length – 34' 0" (estimated)

Heating surfaces:
tubes – 995 sq ft
firebox – 101 sq ft
grate – 18.25 sq ft

Tractive effort – 15,700 lbs
Coal capacity – 4 tons
Water capacity – 2600 gal
Locomotive weight – 43 tons 15 cwt
Adhesive weight – 29 tons 11 cwt
Max axle loading – 15 tons 0 cwt

No 57 was fitted with 17" x 26" cylinders yielding a tractive effort of 14,000 lbs

§ As rebuilt with Belpaire saturated boiler (Inchicore Class D8):

Boiler pressure – 165 lbs
Wheel base – 6' 0" + 6' 9" + 8' 10"

Heating surfaces:
tubes – 1019.8 sq ft
firebox – 124 sq ft
grate – 19.7 sq ft

Tractive effort – 16,190 lbs
Locomotive weight – 48 tons 3 cwt
Adhesive weight – 33 tons 0 cwt
Max axle loading – 16 tons 10 cwt

These locomotives were supposedly ordered by the DWWR to a design that had been prepared for an English railway which had specified cylinders of dimensions 17" x 26". It has been suggested that the railway concerned was either the Midland or the Lancashire & Yorkshire but confirmation is lacking. The DWWR (presumably through Grierson's lack of familiarity with mechanical engineering issues) insisted on a 1" increase in diameter. Without any commensurate increase in boiler capacity, poor steaming resulted. Cronin rebuilt them with larger saturated Belpaire boilers which resulted in a reasonably competent design; in this process, No 57 (GSR No 452) was the first DSER locomotive fitted with a Belpaire boiler.

The treatment given to No 58 (GSR No 453) was more comprehensive with a different type of boiler with longer firebox, new frames with modified wheelbase, and other new components making it effectively a new locomotive. Because of the dimensional differences with this locomotive some sources record it as being in separate Class 453, although it officially remained part of Class 450 (D9).

GSR Class 454 (DSER Nos 65 & 66) — 4-4-0 — Inchicore Class D8 — 1925/ 1931 Load Class N/ M

GSR (DSER) No		Name	Built	Makers' No	Rebuilt	Withdrawn	
454	(67)	*Rathmore*	6/1905	4645	1922*/ 1935§/ 1939¶	1949	
–	(68)	*Rathcoole*	6/1905	4646	–	1925	*Civil War loss*

Designer: Cronin — **Built by Beyer Peacock**

Boiler pressure – 160 lbs/ sq in	*Heating surfaces:*	*Tractive effort – 15,700 lbs*
Cylinders – 18" x 26"	*tubes – 1074.5 sq ft*	*Coal capacity – 3 tons 10 cwt*
Bogie wheels – 3' 3"	*firebox – 118.5 sq ft*	*Water capacity – 2600 gal*
Driving wheels – 6' 1"	*grate – 20 sq ft*	*Locomotive weight – 45 tons 6 cwt*
Wheel base – 6' 0" + 6' 9" + 8' 10"		*Adhesive weight – 29 tons 18 cwt*
Locomotive length – 33' 0" (estimated)		*Max axle loading – 15 tons 0 cwt*

Rebuilds: * Similar to original boiler but locomotive weight increased to 45 tons 19 cwt
§ Believed to have been fitted with Class 450 Belpaire boiler
¶ Believed to have been fitted with Class 453 Belpaire boiler

No 68, the preferred of the pair, was wrecked and severely damaged in a head on collision with No 51 at Palace East in January 1923. It was still in existence at the amalgamation, but was scrapped soon thereafter.

No 67 required a new front tube plate after only four years' service. From an exchange with the builders' representative, it transpired that it had been constructed cheaply at the request of the user.

1948 assessment: *A nondescript engine and only engine of class, consequently difficult to place: otherwise it is a fair medium powered passenger engine.*

Above: DSER No 67/ GSR Class 454/ D8 No 454 at Woodenbridge in 1938.
WA Camwell

Right: DSER No 20/ GSR Class 455/ C2 No 455 at Bray in 1938.
WA Camwell

GSR Class 455 **4-4-2T** **Inchicore Class C2**
DSER Nos 20, 34 & 35 **1925/ 1931 Load Class K/ KT**

GSR (DSER) No		Name	Built	Makers' No	Rebuilt	Withdrawn
455	(20)	*(King George)*	1911	–	1932*/ 1951¥	1959
456	(34)	–	9/1924	6204	1935*/ 1938§/ 1941#	1955
457	(35)	–	9/1924	6205	1936¶/ 1941#	1959

Rebuilt with boiler type: * Class 351 round topped saturated ¶ DSER round-topped
§ Belpaire saturated (original or similar type restored)
# Class 351 type boiler restored ¥ Class 451 Belpaire saturated

Designer: Cronin

Built: No 20 at Grand Canal Street
Nos 34/ 35 by Beyer Peacock

No 20 as built with round-topped boiler:

Boiler pressure – 160 lbs/ sq in
Cylinders – 18" x 26"
Bogie wheels – 3' 3"
Driving wheels – 6' 1"
Trailing wheels – 3' 9"
Wheel base – 6' 0" + 6' 9" + 8' 10" + 6' 8"
Locomotive length – not recorded

Heating surfaces:
tubes – 1074.7 sq ft
firebox – 118.5 sq ft
grate – 20 sq ft

Tractive effort – 15,920 lbs
Coal capacity – 3 tons
Water capacity – 1700 gal
Locomotive weight – 61 tons 10 cwt
Adhesive weight – 31 tons 10 cwt
Max axle loading – 15 tons 15 cwt

Nos 34 & 35 as built with Belpaire boiler:

Heating surfaces:
tubes – 1065 sq ft
firebox – 118.5 sq ft
grate – 20 sq ft

Locomotive weight – 63 tons 0 cwt
Adhesive weight – 31 tons 12 cwt
Max axle loading – 15 tons 17 cwt

*** As rebuilt with Class 351 round-topped boiler:**

Boiler pressure – 160 lbs/ sq in
(initially 150 lbs/ sq in)

Heating surfaces:
tubes – 1129 sq ft
firebox – 118 sq ft
grate – 20.4 sq ft

Locomotive weight – 64 tons 16 cwt
Adhesive weight – 32 tons 10 cwt
Max axle loading – 16 tons 5 cwt

¶ As rebuilt with DSER round-topped boiler:

Boiler pressure – 175 lbs/ sq in

Heating surfaces:
tubes – 1065 sq ft
firebox – 118.5 sq ft
grate – 20.24 sq ft

Tractive effort – 17,170 lbs
Locomotive weight – not stated
Adhesive weight – not stated
Max axle loading – not stated

¥ As rebuilt with Class 451 type Belpaire saturated boiler:

Boiler pressure – 160 lbs/ sq in

Heating surfaces:
tubes – 993 sq ft
firebox – 101 sq ft
grate – 18.5 sq ft

Locomotive weight – 63 tons 11 cwt
Adhesive weight – 35 tons 10 cwt
Max axle loading – 17 tons 15 cwt

Left: DSER No 34/ GSR Class 455/ C2 No 456 with round-topped boiler at Grand Canal Street 1935.

L&GRP

At the time this class appeared, the 4-4-2T type had become fashionable following the exploits in power and economy of the London Brighton & South Coast Railway Class I3.

No 20 was intended for express passenger work but there was no real need for a tank locomotive with 6' 1" driving wheels. Route availability was restricted by the relatively heavy axle loading. With insufficient work, its daily mileage rarely exceeded 90. Further it was considered a poor performer, often having difficulty in starting heavy trains and working them to time over the steeper gradients. There were also frequent failures with the mechanical lubrication leading to hot axle boxes. For these reasons the decision to obtain two more, albeit heavier and with improved features, was surprising.

Despite apparent unsuitability for such duties, in GSR days the class was virtually confined to suburban work, being allocated to Grand Canal Street shed. Despite these adverse views, rebuilding must have had a beneficial effect to yield the favourable 1948 assessment. In 1949, Nos 455 and 457 were briefly and unsuccessfully fitted with an ash ejection system, fuller details of which are provided in the notes on ex-GSWR Class 355.

No 20 was the last locomotive built at Grand Canal St and the only bogie type built there; its boiler was manufactured by Kitson. Nos 34 and 35 were the last locomotives built for the DSER.

Below: DSER No 20/ GSR Class 455/ C2 No 455 fitted with ash ejection equipment on the turntable at Amiens Street.

Authors' collection

1948 assessment: *DSER heavy passenger engines.* (When) *well maintained, not at all bad. Essential to local service.*

DSER No 35 / GSR Class 455/ C2 No 457 as rebuilt with Belpaire boiler at Amiens Street in 1935.

L&GRP

GSR Class 458 — 4-4-2T — Inchicore Class C3
DSER Nos 52-54 — 1925/ 1931 Load Class N/ MT

GSR (DSER) No		Name	Built	Makers' No	Rebuilt	Withdrawn
458	(52)	*(Duke of Connaught)*	1893	3909	1920*	1955
459	(54)	*(Duke of Leinster)*	1893	3911	1913*	1953
460	(53)	*(Duke of Abercorn)*	1893	3910	1926§	1960

Designer: William Wakefield — **Built by Sharp Stewart**

DSER No 52/ GSR Class 458/ C3 No 458 at Grand Canal Street in 1931. *L&GRP*

Boiler pressure – 150 lbs/ sq in
Cylinders – 18" x 26"
Bogie wheels – 3' 1½"
Driving wheels – 5' 3"
Trailer wheels – 3' 9"
Wheel base – 5' 6"+ 6' 9" + 8' 6" + 7' 0"
Locomotive length – 36' 7"

Heating surfaces:
tubes – 1120 sq ft
firebox – 106.5 sq ft
grate – 17.8 sq ft

Tractive effort – 17,050 lbs
Coal capacity – 2 tons 10 cwt
Water capacity – 1400 gal
Locomotive weight – 55 tons 0 cwt
Adhesive weight – 31 tons 0 cwt
Max axle loading – 15 tons 15 cwt

*** As rebuilt:**

Heating surfaces:
tubes & firebox
– 992 sq ft (total)
grate – 17 sq ft

Water capacity – see below
Locomotive weight – 57 tons 0 cwt
Adhesive weight – 30 tons 12 cwt
Max axle loading – 15 tons 10 cwt

On rebuilding, No 54 only acquired a greater water capacity (1530 gallons by increasing the back tank by 130 gallons), a larger chimney and a larger cab with rounded roof

§ As rebuilt:

Heating surfaces:
tubes – 865 sq ft
firebox – 108 sq ft
grate – 17.5 sq ft

Locomotive weight – not stated
Adhesive weight – not stated
Max axle loading – not stated

On rebuilding, No 460 acquired a lower pitched boiler and forward extension to its flat-roofed cab

DSER No 53/ GSR Class 458/C3 No 460 at Amiens Street in 1928. *Kelland collection*

These locomotives were acquired particularly to work boat trains between Kingstown Pier and Kingsbridge following the opening of the City of Dublin Junction Railway. An awkward feature was the lever reverse which could be difficult, possibly dangerous, to operate as the linkage became worn. It was often necessary to shut off steam before attempting to change the cut-off.

Despite these difficulties, the type was considered quite successful and was aided by a driving wheel diameter that was more suitable for traffic requirements than that fitted to Class 455. Several commentators have opined that an up-dated version of Class 458 would have been the best solution to the demands of the DSER section under GSR management.

1948 assessment: *DSER heavy passenger engines – quite good even with certain inherent troubles.*

DSER No 15/ GSR Class 461/ K2 No 461 at Grand Canal Street. *CH Hewison*

GSR Class 461 | **2-6-0** | **Inchicore Class K2**
DSER No 15 & 16 | | **1925/ 1931 Load Class E/ C**

GSR (DSER) No	Built	Makers' No	Rebuilt	Withdrawn	
461 (15)	12/1922	6112	1944*	1965	Preserved by RPSI
462 (16)	12/1922	6113	1940*/ 1944¶	1963	

Designer: Wild — **Built by Beyer Peacock**

Rebuilt with boiler type: * Belpaire superheated type N
¶ Original Belpaire superheated type restored

DSER No 15/ GSR Class 461/ K2 No 462 at Wexford Shed in 1938. *WA Camwell*

Boiler pressure – 175 lbs/ sq in	*Heating surfaces:*	*Tractive effort – 22,890 lbs*
Cylinders – 19" x 26"	*tubes – 952 sq ft*	*Coal capacity – 5 tons*
Piston valves – 8"	*firebox – 134 sq ft*	*Water capacity – 2600 gal*
Pony wheels – 3' 0"	*superheater –164 sq ft*	*Locomotive weight – 50 tons 1 cwt*
Driving wheels – 5' 1"	*grate – 20 sq ft*	*Adhesive weight – 43 tons 9 cwt*
Wheel base – 5' 6" + 7' 3" + 8' 10"		*Max axle loading – 15 tons 1 cwt*
Locomotive length – 33' 0" (estimated)		

*** No 462 as fitted with N type Belpaire superheated boiler**

Boiler pressure – 160 lbs/ sq in	*Heating surfaces:*	*Tractive effort – 20,930 lbs*
	tubes – 708 sq ft	
	firebox – 120 sq ft	
	superheater – 168 sq ft	
	grate – 19.5 sq ft	

DSER No 15 or 16 / GSR Class 461/ K2 No 462 fitted with ash chutes to smokebox. At Grand Canal Street.

GW Sharpe

The external dimensions of the N-type boiler were slightly smaller than those of the original; weights would have been lower than in original condition but details are not recorded. The two boilers alternated between the two locomotives after 1944. In 1949, No 462 was briefly and unsuccessfully fitted with an automatic ash-ejection system, fuller details of which are provided in the notes on ex-GSWR Class 355.

These locomotives were originally conceived as 0-6-0s and as an enlargement of Class 442 which shared the same rather unusual coupled wheelbase. However, with an extended smokebox and the superheater increasing the front end weight, Wild recognised during construction that in this state they would exceed the DSER's maximum permitted axle loading. They were therefore modified before delivery by provision of a pony truck and a reduction in boiler diameter. A constraint on the design was the size of the turntable at Dublin, Harcourt Street. Delivered during the Civil War they were stored in Adelaide Shed, Belfast and only reached their native system after cessation of hostilities. In 1925, No 15 was overhauled at Limerick, returning to duty retaining its DSER livery and original number but with 'GSR' replacing 'DSER' on the number plates.

These were the only DSER locomotives to carry superheaters throughout their existence. No 461, always the more popular, survived in normal service on goods duties at Rosslare until early 1964 and then served as a stationary boiler at Inchicore for about a year. Unfortunately the DSER boiler had been scrapped with the earlier withdrawal of No 462. Nevertheless No 461's late survival led to its preservation, first as a static exhibit and later as a working locomotive operated by the Railway Preservation Society of Ireland on steam specials.

They were popular and widely respected locomotives – even by ex-GSWR and ex-MGWR crews which underlined their competence. Their large comfortable cabs yielded good weather protection which was much appreciated on the exposed seaside section between Bray and Wicklow. No 461 was allocated to Wexford and No 462 to Grand Canal Street from which sheds they worked the heavy night goods services for over 30 years. During the day, No 461 was used on local passenger services between Wexford and Rosslare Harbour, while No 462 helped out on Dublin suburban services. With the closure of Grand Canal Street, No 462 moved to the Broadstone and occasionally also worked goods services on the ex-MGWR main line, proving equally popular in that area. By the nature of their respective duties, it was most unusual to see the pair together throughout their careers.

This is one of the few pre-amalgamation classes that in the authors' opinion should have been multiplied in GSR days as providing a better solution to the company's motive power needs than some of the classes that actually appeared.

1948 assessment: *One of the best Goods on the system, very powerful and reliable with low axleload. Unfortunately only two in class.*

--- o O o ---

During 1923, Wild and the DSER Board discussed a proposal for two more locomotives from Beyer Peacock as a 4-4-0 passenger version of the moguls. The concept was to use wheel diameters and wheel base similar to Nos 67 and 68, mogul-type superheated boiler, piston valves, 18½" x 26" cylinders, and mogul-type tender. The project was deferred in October 1923 and never revived.

GSR Class *Imp* 0-4-0T/ 2-4-0T
DSER Class Nos 69 & 70

Inchicore Class M1/ M2
Load class not allocated

DSER/ DBST No	Built	Makers No	GSR Name	Withdrawn
(ex-DSER No 69)	7/1906	1692	*Elf*	1931
(ex-DSER No 70/ ex-DBST No 2)	8/1906	1693	*Imp*	1928

Designer: Cronin

Built by Manning Wardle

Boiler pressure – 160 lbs/ sq in
Cylinders – 12" x 16"
Driving wheels – 3' 7"
Wheel base – 8' 0"
Locomotive length – 17' 11"

Heating surfaces:
tubes – 441 sq ft
firebox – 45 sq ft
grate – 9.5 sq ft

Tractive effort – 7,400 lbs
Coal capacity – 1 ton
Water capacity – 500 gal
Locomotive weight – 26 tons 14 cwt
Max axle loading – 13 tons 7 cwt

Left: DSER No 69/ GSR 'Imp' Class/ M2 *Elf* as a 2-4-0T In this poor quality photograph, it is just possible to discern the leading wheels and also the front running plate extension. The GSR nameplate was obviously fitted before its conversion back to an 0-4-0T in 1925.

CP Friel collection

Below: DSER No 69/ GSR 'Imp' Class/ M2 *Elf* following reconversion to 0-4-0T at Limerick.

IRRS collection

As 2-4-0T (*Elf* only) between 1914 and 1925:

Leading wheels – 2' 0" | *Locomotive weight – 28 tons*
Wheelbase – 5' 11" + 8' 0"

These two locomotives were originally the engine units of DSER steam rail motors Nos 1 and 2. They were separated from their carriage sections and converted into 0-4-0T's Nos 69 and 70 respectively in 1908. In this process, heavy weights were fitted at the rear to counterbalance excessive front-end loading resulting from removal of the carriage sections.

DSER No 69 (later GSR *Elf*) was fitted from new with outside Walschaerts valve gear. It was rebuilt in 1914 as a 2-4-0T and was in this condition at the amalgamation. It was reconverted to 0-4-0T at the Broadstone in 1925, to its original dimensions. During GSR days, *Elf* was allocated to Limerick as station pilot.

DSER No 70 (later GSR *Imp*) differed from No 69 in being equipped with Marshall's valve gear from new, but it is not known whether this was retained in GSR days. It was sold to the Dublin & Blessington Steam Tramway in 1918 which company allotted it No 2. The DBST found that it was too heavy for the track, so sold it on to the GSWR in 1921, in exchange for 0-4-0T *Cambria*. The GSWR chose not to give it a number but merely to christen it *Imp*, which was also its official GSR classification. After withdrawal, *Imp's* boiler was fitted to ex-Timoleauge & Courtmacsherry Light Railway 2-6-0T *Argadeen* at the Broadstone.

As steam rail motors Nos 1 and 2 had suffered from riding qualities that were so bad that intending passengers would first enquire whether the next service would be an SRM before buying a ticket. If so, they would leave and catch a tram instead. As 0-4-0T's, the riding was little better and this was ascribed to the combination of the 6' 2" distance between cylinder centres and the 8' 0" coupled wheelbase. The conversion of *Elf* to 2-4-0T was apparently in the hope of overcoming this problem.

At the amalgamation, the GSR recognised the common origins of *Imp* and DSER No 69 by including the latter in the 'Imp' class and giving it the name *Elf*, but again no running number. The Inchicore classification of M1 was given to both locomotives, as Elf was rebuilt as an 0-4-0T soon after the amalgamation. Both were relegated to M2 following introduction of GSR Sentinel shunters Nos 280 and 281.

The following locomotives did not receive GSR numbers and were not included in either the GSR or Inchicore classification systems. It is doubtful whether under GSR control, they undertook any work in revenue earning service, with the exception of No 44. Their only movement of the others was most likely transfer to Inchicore for assessment prior to withdrawal and breaking up.

DSER No 48 — 0-4-2

DSER No	Name	Built	Makers' No	Withdrawn
48 (15 until 1922)	*(Barrow)*	1860	1210	1925

Designer: Haughton **Built by Sharp Stewart**

DSER No 15 *Barrow*. No GSR class or number was allocated. *CP Friel collection*

Boiler pressure – 150 lbs/ sq in	*Heating surfaces:*	*Tractive effort – 12,740 lbs*
Cylinders – 16" x 24"	*tubes & firebox*	*Coal capacity – not stated*
Driving wheels – 5' 1½"	*– 940 sq ft (total)*	*Water capacity – 1600 gal*
Trailing wheels – 3' 7½"	*grate – 15 sq ft*	*Locomotive weight – 26 tons 3 cwt*
Wheel base – 7' 2" + 6' 10"		*Adhesive weight – 18 tons 3 cwt*
		Max axle loading – 9 tons 3 cwt

No 15 was the last survivor of a series of three locomotives built by Sharp Stewart (Nos 15 and 16 in 1860, and No 37 in 1876 or 1877). It ran with a four-wheeled tender until around 1900 when it was swapped with the six-wheeled tender of sister engine No 37. This latter engine was withdrawn and scrapped in 1923 together with its tender which was the last four wheeler in service on the DSER, and probably in Ireland.

Sources differ concerning the renumbering history of No 15. Some indicate that it was renumbered 15A in 1922 (to make way for the first Beyer Peacock 2-6-0) but others state that it was allocated No 48 in the same year. As it was taken out of service around the same time, neither of these changes might have had any practical use. Nevertheless, the locomotive physically came into GSR hands and was finally scrapped in March 1925. It should be noted that the number 48 was also borne by a member of the type described next.

DSER Nos 19, 22, 38, 39 & 48 — 0-4-2 — No GSR Class

DSER No	Name	Built	Makers' No	Withdrawn
19	–	2/1864	1483	1925 *Civil War loss*
22 (20/ 20A until 1913)	–	2/1864	1490	1925 *Civil War loss. See comments below*
38	*(Nore)*	1876	2654	1925
39	*(Suir)*	1876	2655	1925 *Civil War loss*
(48)	–	1889	–	1913 (*See comments below*)

Designer: Meikle — **Built by Sharp Stewart (except No 48 – see below)**

DSER Sharp Stewart 0-4-2 No 19. No GSR class or number was allocated *Real Photographs Co Ltd*

Boiler pressure – 150 lbs/ sq in	*Heating surfaces:*	*Tractive effort – 15,520 lbs*
Cylinders – 17" x 24"	*tubes & firebox*	*Coal capacity – not stated*
Driving wheels – 4' 9"	*– 1124 sq ft (total)*	*Water capacity – 1400 gal*
Trailing wheels – 3' 9"	*grate – 17.25 sq ft*	*Locomotive weight – 28 tons*
Wheel base – 6' 11" + 7' 4"		*Adhesive weight – 20 tons 1 cwt*
Locomotive length – not recorded		*Max axle loading – 10 tons 10 cwt*

These locomotives were in process of being withdrawn at the time of the amalgamation, Nos 19 and 22 being beyond economic repair.

No 22 had been numbered 20 when built but this was amended to 20A in 1911 upon introduction of 4-4-2T *King George* (see Class 455/ C2). Nos 38 and 39, and possibly 48, had thicker tyres yielding a driving wheel diameter of 4' 10½" and a slightly larger cab which increased the weight to about 30 tons.

No 48 was the first tender locomotive built at Grand Canal Street. It lay disused outside Wexford shed for some years prior to withdrawal in 1913. It was broken up shortly thereafter and frames and other parts were used for re-building of No 19. Strangely, the number 48 remained officially on the strength of the DSER until, or shortly before, the amalgamation when the anomaly was rectified by finally expunging it from the books! This number then seems to have been 're-allocated' to No 15 (or possibly by then No 15A) described in the previous section.

DSER No 21 — 0-4-2T — No GSR Class

DSER No	Name	Built	Makers' No as 0-4-2	Rebuilt as 0-4-2T	Withdrawn
21	*Kilcoole*	2/1864	1489	1905	1925

Designer: Meikle — **Built by Sharp Stewart**

Boiler pressure – 150 lbs/ sq in	*Heating surfaces:*	*Tractive effort – 15,120 lbs*
Cylinders – 17" x 24"	*tubes & firebox*	*Coal capacity – 1 ton 15 cwt*
Driving wheels – 4' 10½"	*– 985 sq ft (total)*	*Water capacity – 960 gal*
Trailing wheels – 3' 9"	*grate – 17.25 sq ft*	*Locomotive weight – 42 tons 0 cwt*
Wheel base – 6' 11" + 8' 4"		*Adhesive weight – 24 tons 7 cwt*
		Max axle loading – 19 tons 1 cwt

This locomotive was similar to 0-4-2s Nos 19, 22, 38 and 39 prior to rebuilding. There are doubts about certain recorded dimensions: ie the extended wheelbase between trailing driving axle and trailer axle, and also the weight distribution. The loading of 19 tons 1 cwt on the trailing axle seems excessive; an alternative record indicates a more reasonable 16 tons.

DSER 0-4-2 T No 21 *Kilcoole*, as rebuilt in 1905. No GSR class or number was allocated.
CP Friel collection

DSER No 26 — 2-4-0T — No GSR Class

DSER No	Name	Built as 2-4-0	Makers' No	Rebuilt as 2-4-0T	Withdrawn
26	(Blackrock)	3/1864	1480	1900	1925

Designer: Meikle — **Built by Sharp Stewart**

Boiler pressure – 140 lbs/ sq in	*Heating surfaces:*	*Tractive effort – 9,140 lbs*
Cylinders – 15" x 22"	*tubes & firebox*	*Coal capacity – 1 ton 15 cwt*
Leading wheels – 3' 7½"	*– 1032 sq ft (total)*	*Water capacity – 700 gal*
Driving wheels – 5' 4½"	*grate – 15.9 sq ft*	*Locomotive weight – 38 tons*
Wheel base – 6' 5" + 8' 1"		*Adhesive weight – not stated*
Locomotive length – 29' 8"		*Max axle loading – not stated*

This locomotive was converted from a 2-4-0 type in 1900 (see DSER Nos 24, 25, 32 & 33 – GSR Class 422/ G7) and employed as Shillelagh branch locomotive following withdrawal of single drivers from that route.

DSER 2-4-0T No 26 *Blackrock* at Grand Canal Street. No GSR class or number was allocated.

IRRS collection

DSER No 41 2-4-0T

DSER No	Name	Built	Withdrawn
41	*(Delgany)*	1/1882	1925

Designer: William Wakefield **Built by Dublin Wicklow & Wexford Railway**

DSER No 41. No GSR class or number was allocated.

IRRS collection

Boiler pressure – 140 lbs/ sq in	*Heating surfaces:*	*Tractive effort – 10,640 lbs*
Cylinders – 16" x 22"	*tubes& firebox*	*Coal capacity – not stated*
Leading wheels – 3' 8"	*– 986.5 sq ft (total)*	*Water capacity – not stated*
Driving wheels – 5' 3"	*grate – 18.15 sq ft*	*Locomotive weight – 38 tons (est.)*
Wheel base – not stated		*Max axle loading – not stated*
Locomotive length – not recorded		

Originally built for passenger service between Harcourt Street and Bray, this locomotive was taken out of use around 1913. It stood for many years at Grand Canal Street but was not categorised as ready for scrapping until 1924.

DSER Nos 42 to 44 (GSR Class not allocated) 2-4-0T Inchicore/ Load Class not allocated

DSER No	Name	Built	Makers' No	Withdrawn
42	*(Ballybrack)*	3/1883	2261	1925
43	*(Shanganagh)*	3/1883	2262	1925
44	*(Dunleary)*	3/1883	2263	1927

Designer: William Wakefield **Built by Beyer Peacock**

DSER Nos 42 to 44. No 44 *Dunleary* as running in DSER days at Kingstown (now Dun Laoghaire). No GSR class or number was allocated.

Real Photographs Co Ltd

Boiler pressure – 145 lbs/ sq in	*Heating surfaces:*	*Tractive effort – 11,290 lbs*
Cylinders – 16" x 22"	*tubes& firebox*	*Coal capacity – 1 ton 9 cwt*
Leading wheels – 3' 10"	*– 962 sq ft (total)*	*Water capacity – 900 gal*
Driving wheels – 5' 1½"	*grate – 17 sq ft*	*Locomotive weight – 38 tons 0 cwt*
Wheel base – 7' 4" +7' 6"		*Adhesive weight – 29 tons 18 cwt*
Locomotive length – not recorded		*Max axle loading – 14 tons 19 cwt*

These locomotives were highly regarded on the DSER and were capable of heavier work than their modest dimensions might suggest. No 44 was extensively overhauled by the GNR(I) at Dundalk in 1923 and was then employed on the 5.15 pm Greystones express which regularly comprised six bogie carriages. It was very likely the good condition of this locomotive that ensured its continued use until 1927, although it was never accorded a GSR or Inchicore classification. Given the haulage capacity of these engines, it might be assumed that the decision on their early withdrawal by the GSR was premature.

(DSER) *Blackburn* 0-6-0ST

Built 8/1888 by Manning Wardle & Co
Makers' No 1099

Boiler pressure – not recorded	*Heating surfaces:*	*Tractive effort – not recorded*
Cylinders (inside) – 14" x 20"	*tubes & firebox*	*Coal capacity – 1 ton 10 cwt*
Driving wheels – 3' 6"	*– 655 sq ft (total)*	*Water capacity – 600 gal*
Wheel base – 5' 11" + 6' 1"	*grate – 8.5 sq ft*	*Locomotive weight – 27 tons 0 cwt*
		Max axle loading – not stated

This locomotive was a Manning Wardle Class Special Q, built for contractors Messrs TA Walker (Order No 27050) and used on several projects, most notably the Manchester Ship Canal. It was sold to Messrs Fisher and LeFanu in 1894 and converted to 5' 3" gauge by Manning Wardle prior to shipment to Ireland in 1894. It was used on four railway building contracts in Ireland

(i) Claremorris to Collooney Junction

(ii) The connecting line from Collooney (Waterford Limerick & Western Railway) to Collooney (Sligo, Leitrim & Northern Counties Railway)

(iii) Cashel - Goold's Cross and

(iv) Ballyroney to Newcastle line of the GNR(I). Between 1899 and 1904, it was known to have been stored on the Sligo Leitrim and Northern Counties Railway at Manorhamilton.

It was then used by the contractors on ballasting work for the GNR(I) between Newcastle and Ballyroney, and then unsuccessfully offered for sale at the latter location in 1906. Its history is then unclear as some sources state that it was later used by Messrs Fisher and Le Fanu on a contract for the Derwent Valley Water Board in Derbyshire. However, this would have required a further re-gauging (back to 4' 8½"). It is more likely that these reports confused it with another Manning Wardle tank locomotive, and that *Blackburn* remained in Ireland.

Blackburn was later acquired by Messrs Naylor Bros of Huddersfield, contractors for deviation work on the DSER in the Bray/ Greystones area and worked on that contract between 1911 and 1915. Following default by the contractors, *Blackburn* was taken over the DSER and used by another contractor to complete the deviation work. It was not formally taken into DSER stock but was later used by that company as a departmental locomotive.

It was still with the DSER at the amalgamation and noted at Inchicore in June 1925, retaining its original green livery with plenty of brasswork. On 21 August 1925, the GSR Board approved acceptance of an offer by a scrap metal dealer of £77 for the locomotive, on condition that it was cut up for transportation in wagons. The CME estimated the cost of this work at £17 yielding a net value of £60 which he felt was reasonable. That such a minor asset disposal should require Board attention suggests lingering concerns over who was actually the legal owner of *Blackburn*.

(DSER) *Blackburn* 0-6-0T
No GSR class or number.

Fred W Harman collection

Chapter 6
Locomotives of the Cork Bandon and South Coast Railway and the minor companies

Although connected by the ¾ mile long Cork City Railway through the streets of Cork over which a little-used passenger service operated for a period, the Cork Bandon & South Coast Railway was largely physically remote from the Great Southern & Western network. CBSCR locomotives had a distinctive character; at the amalgamation they were exclusively tank engines although earlier in the company's history, 2-2-2, 0-4-2 and 2-4-0 tender locomotives had been used.

The locomotives absorbed by the Great Southern Railways totalled 20 units which were divided into the following classes and wheel arrangements:

Wheels	Classes	Locos	Built since 1900	Rebuilt since 1900
4-6-0T	2	9	8	1
0-6-0T	3	5	–	–
4-4-0T	1	2	1	1
4-4-2T	1	3	1	–
2-4-0T	1	1	–	–
Total	**8**	**20**	**10**	**2**

Up until 1874, the company had relied mainly on second-hand machinery, a policy that led to unreliability and heavy expense. In that year matters started to improve with the purchase of the first of five new 2-4-0Ts. Two of these were still in service at the amalgamation although one had been rather inexplicably rebuilt as a 4-4-0T. These five locomotives alerted management to the benefits of uniformity as the next significant purchases concerned five examples of a standard type of Beyer Peacock 0-6-0ST. Nonetheless, individuality was sustained by ensuring that three driving wheel sizes were employed leading to three different GSR/ Inchicore classifications. Conversely, despite significant variations in leading dimensions, sharing of the same driving wheel diameter led to Nos 2 and 7 being placed together in Class 477.

As at 1 January 1925, thirteen members of the fleet had been built by Beyer Peacock, of which eight were the famed 4-6-0Ts – the 'Bandon Tanks'. Additionally there were four locomotives built by Dubs & Co, and two by Neilson Reid & Co. The company claimed credit for construction of the remaining locomotive (4-4-0T No 7) at its Rocksavage Works. How much of this was a genuine new-build, and how much an assembly of existing spare parts and bought-in components is questionable.

Production of this locomotive and fleet maintenance was quite an achievement in the company's cramped workshops at Rocksavage, close to the throat of the Albert Quay terminus and set at 90 degrees to the running lines. The workshops comprised a two-road building, 290 feet long in which all locomotive repairs were undertaken; facilities were so confined that operable locomotives were stabled in the loco yard across the line. This yard area was known as 'The Quarry', being hemmed in on two sides by cliffs, and did not even boast covered accommodation. Although locomotive repairs ceased in early GSR days, the Quarry continued to provide *al fresco* locomotive storage and was a favourite location for enthusiasts seeking motley combinations of tank locomotives patiently awaiting their next duties. Under GSR management, activities at the Rocksavage works were restricted to carriage and wagon repairs.

The oldest locomotives inherited by the Great Southern Railways were delivered during the Locomotive Superintendency of **Thomas Conran** (1857-1887). He was succeeded by **John Johnstone** who held the position for about 12 months in what seems to have been a temporary situation, pending the appointment of his son, James. From 1888 until the amalgamation, **James Johnstone** served as Locomotive Superintendent, being responsible for No 7 (GSR No 478), the sole 'new product' of Rocksavage.

It is uncertain how much hand the locomotive superintendents had in the design of the remainder of the fleet as they were fairly standard examples of the respective builders. The styling of the 4-6-0Ts was classically Beyer Peacock but selection of the unusual wheel arrangement suggests that there must have been significant local input into the design.

Information on CBSCR locomotive liveries is sparse with the body colour described variously as olive or sage green. Lining is reported to have been in black and vermillion. Study of black-and-white photographs suggests that the format was a black line, say 1" to 1½" thick edged with a thin vermilion line on both sides. Two 0-6-2STs imported from the USA (withdrawn well before 1925) were supposedly in sage green and adorned with a single yellow line with areas outside the lining panels painted black. However photographic evidence suggests that this style may have been applied to at least one of the 20 locomotives acquired by the

GSR (see Class 471). A report dated 1930 states that all CBSCR locomotives had been repainted in GSR grey except for Nos 473, 477 and 479 which had been renumbered but not repainted. Of this trio, only No 473 remained in service beyond that year.

Apart from use on the DSER section (usually one 4-6-0T at a time), CBSCR engines seem to have remained on their native system during GSR days. The 4-6-0Ts all out-lived the GSR but only one other CBSCR locomotive (an 0-6-0ST) survived as late as 1940. Replacement motive power came in a variety of four- and six- coupled tank locomotives from the three larger constituent companies, but with ex-GSWR machinery predominating.

GSR Class 463 — 4-6-0T — Inchicore Class B4
CBSCR Nos 4, 8, 11, 13, 14, 15, 19 & 20 — 1925/ 1931 Load Class H/ HT

GSR (CBSCR) No	Built	Makers' No	Rebuilt	Withdrawn
463 (4)	12/1919	5954	1943§/ 1950¶	1963
464 (8)	11/1920	6034	1946§	1963
465 (11)	5/1906	4752	-	1945
466 (13)	11/1920	6077	1947§	1961
467 (14)	3/1909	5265	1935§	1959
468 (15)	10/1910	5413	1944§/ 1948¶/ 1950§	1961
469 (19)	6/1914	5822	-	1945
470 (20)	12/1912	5616	-	1961

Designer: Johnstone — **Built by Beyer Peacock**

Rebuilt with boiler: § Belpaire superheated type R.
¶ Round-topped saturated (as original)

CBSCR No 4/ GSR Class 463/ B4 No 465.

Real Photographs Co Ltd

CBSCR No 19/ GSR Class 463/ B4 No 469 at Bandon in 1938.

WA Camwell

As originally built with round-topped saturated boiler:

Boiler pressure – 160 lbs/ sq in	*Heating surfaces:*	*Tractive effort – 16,030 lbs*
Cylinders – 18" x 24"	*tubes – 1075 sq ft*	*Coal capacity – 2 tons 15 cwt*
Bogie wheels – 3' 0"	*firebox – 107.5 sq ft*	*Water capacity – 1100 gal**
Driving wheels – 5' 2½"	*grate – 24 sq ft*	*Locomotive weight – 56 tons 10 cwt*
Wheel base – 6' 0" + 6' 9" + 6' 3" + 6' 3"		*Adhesive weight – 42 tons 1 cwt*
Locomotive length – 36' 6½"		*Max axle loading – 14 tons 5 cwt*

§ As rebuilt with Belpaire superheated boiler type R:

Heating surfaces:
tubes – 696 sq ft
firebox – 119 sq f
superheater – 170 sq ft
grate – 22.7 sq ft

** No 11 had a tank capacity of 1000 gal, although the tank profile matched that of the other locomotives; estimated weight – 55 tons, adhesive weight – 41 tons 9 cwt*

The 'Bandon Tanks' were the best known of all CBSCR locomotives and were the only 4-6-0Ts built by Beyer Peacock. This unusual wheel arrangement is more commonly associated with the narrow gauge scene where a cramped rear end with restricted bunker capacity is less of an operating inhibition. A 4-6-2T might have been more useful but this would have been too long for the company's turntables, smokebox leading being the normal mode of operation. Fortunately the short distance journeys typical of the CBSCR presented no problem to the use of these engines. They were typically Beyer Peacock in style and were highly regarded by footplate crews. Their principal drawback was at the rear end and concerned the difficult access to the cab over the rear driving wheel splashers; this feature made descent from the cab to rail level rather tricky.

The performance of No 467 was greatly improved by its rebuilding in 1935 and contemporary accounts expressed regret that other members were not being so treated. Rebuilding did not recommence until 1943 and the programme was unfortunately never completed.

In GSR days, the class continued to work on the ex-CBSCR section but they also distinguished themselves on the Dublin-Bray commuter services. No 468 was allocated to Grand Canal Street shed for the summer of 1929 and displaced No 850 on boat trains for a period. The Bandon Tank was well received and notwithstanding reservations over the small coal capacity, they coped competently with a particular daily turn of 188 miles. From then on, there was usually at least one on these services until the summer of 1956, with Nos 466, 469 and 470 also appearing on the DSER section at different times. In 1942, No 466 returned to become a resident of Bray shed (until October 1956), and then Grand Canal Street, until withdrawal. In 1948 it was repainted in the green livery introduced around that time for the GSR class 670 0-6-2Ts (some sources also report No 467 as being similarly treated). Overall, the class performed with more consistency than No 850 and certainly better than the average possible with GSR Class 670 (I3). It has been asserted that more Bandon Tanks would have been a far better solution to the section's needs than Harty's anachronistic 0-6-2Ts.

1948 assessment: *These were English built for Bandon Railway. They are primarily small but powerful passenger engines, suitable for Cork/ Bandon Section. They also work Goods on that Section. One is on the DSER section, but is a little too small for that Section. Quite a good design.*

CBSCR Class 463 with R-type Belpaire boiler No 464 at Cork, Albert Quay in CIÉ days. The well-known railway author, RM Arnold, is standing on the cab footsteps.

IRRS collection

GSR Class 471 — 4-6-0T — Inchicore Class B5
CBSCR No 10 — 1925/ 1931 Load Class S/ RT

GSR (CBSCR) No	Built as 4-4-0T	Rebuilt as 4-4-2T	Rebuilt as 4-6-0T	Makers' No	Withdrawn
471 (10)	7/1893	1903 §	1906	3048	1933

§ *See comments*

Built by Dubs & Co, Glasgow

As 4-6-0T:

Boiler pressure – 130 lbs/ sq in
Cylinders – 16" x 22"
Bogie wheels – 3' 0"
Driving wheels – 5' 6"
Wheel base – 5' 3" + 6' 5½" + 7' 3" + 6' 3"
Locomotive length – not recorded

Heating surfaces:
tubes – 757 sq ft
firebox – 82 sq ft
grate – 14.5 sq ft

Tractive effort – 9,430 lbs
Coal capacity – 3 tons (est.)
Water capacity – 1000 gal
Locomotive weight – 47 tons 1 cwt
Adhesive weight – 36 tons 0 cwt
Max axle loading – 12 tons 10 cwt

This locomotive was built as a 4-4-0T similar to No 3 (later Class 479 (G6) No 479 also supplied by Dubs). Material was later supplied by Dubs for conversion of No 10 to 4-4-2T, and this work might have been carried out around 1903 but confirmation is lacking.

Records indicate that this locomotive was repainted in GSR grey in 1927. This conflicts with the photograph which shows lined CBSCR livery while No 10 awaiting scrapping in the 1930s. The explanation is probably that the locomotive had stood at Inchicore for so long that the GSR paint layer had weathered away.

CBSCR No 10/ GSR Class 471/ B5 No 471. This photograph clearly shows the locomotive on the scrap line (ie 1933 or later) at Inchicore with GSR number plate but still in pre-amalgamation livery. The double lining seems to be lighter in colour than the standard CBSCR vermillion edging. Hence this may have been a case of the yellow lining introduced with the US-built 0-6-0STs having been applied to other locomotives.

Real Photographs Co Ltd

GSR Class 472/ 474/ 475 — 0-6-0ST — Inchicore Class J24/ J23/ J21
CBSCR Nos 6, 17, 12, 5 & 16 — 1925/ 1931 Load Class M/ KT

GSR (CBSCR) No	GSR Class	I'core Class	Built	Makers' No	Rebuilt	Withdrawn
472 (6)	472	J24	2/1881	2046	1922	1940
473 (17)	472	J24	9/1894	3629	–	1935
474* (12)	474	J23	4/1882	2156	–	1925
475 (5)	475	J21	11/1887	2902	–	1939
476* (16)	475	J21	10/1890	3288	–	1925

* Allocated but not carried

Built by Beyer Peacock

CBSCR No 6/ GSR Class 472 / J24 No 472 at Cork Rocksavage in 1931.

L&GRP

Nos 472 (6) and 473 (17) as built:

Boiler pressure – 140 lbs/ sq in
Cylinders – 17" x 24"
Driving wheels – 4' 6"
Wheel base – 6' 9¾" + 6' 10¾"
Locomotive length – not recorded

Heating surfaces:
tubes – 823 sq ft
firebox – 77 sq ft
grate – 14 sq ft

Tractive effort – 15,290 lbs
Coal capacity – 1 ton
Water capacity – 850 gal
Locomotive weight – 35 tons 15 cwt
Max axle loading – 12 tons 10 cwt

No 472 (6) as rebuilt:

Heating surfaces:
tubes – 614 sq ft
firebox – 77 sq ft
grate – 14 sq ft

No 474 (12) as built:

Driving wheels – 4' 5"

Tractive effort – 15,580 lbs
Locomotive weight – 36 tons 12 cwt

Nos 475 (5) and 476 (16) as built:

Driving wheels – 4' 3"

Tractive effort – 16,190 lbs

Left: CBSCR No 6/ GSR Class 472/ J24 No 472. This photograph has been inserted to show the other side of this locomotive. It has not been possible to trace photographs of Nos 474 & 476 which were withdrawn in 1925, and which had detail differences.

IRRS collection

Below: CBSCR No 17/ GSR Class 472/ J24 No 473 at Bantry in 1930.

Real Photographs Co Ltd

Bottom: CBSCR No 5/ GSR Class 475/ J21 No 475 at Cork, Albert Quay.

CH Hewison

No 6 was the first locomotive supplied by Beyer Peacock to the CBSCR It was based on Beyer's '2131' class of 1867 which was supplied to several British collieries, and which was later developed into the Beyer Peacock '3064' class, considered a standard design by the company. Examples were also sold to Australia, Belgium, Sweden, the London & South Western Railway and more British collieries. On the CBSCR, the Beyer Peacock saddle tanks succeeded the 2-4-0Ts as the principal motive power.

As would be expected with five locomotives introduced over a 13-year period, there were detail variations in style of cabs, bunkers and external boiler fittings. At the rebuilding of No 6, it received a new boiler, Salter valves on the dome (the rest had Ramsbottom valves on the firebox), vertical smokebox front, and larger cab.

The reason for allocating three different classifications was based on driving wheel diameter, which was really of no consequence given the modest dimensional variations involved. Further it is thought that driving wheels sets might have been swapped between locomotives of the different classes by the simple method of using tyres with differing thicknesses.

A report states that No 474 was working at a boiler pressure of 135 lbs/ sq in before withdrawal. No 475's final duties were on the Broadstone boiler wash-out from 1939 until 1945 when it was cut up at Inchicore. No 472 was similarly employed at Inchicore in its final years.

GSR Class 477 — 4-4-0T — Inchicore Class D18
CBSCR Nos 2 & 7 — 1925/ 1931 Load Class T/ RT

GSR (CBSCR) No		Built	Builder	Makers' No	Withdrawn
477	(2)	7/1875	Dubs & Co	861	1930
478	(7)	1901	CBSCR, Rocksavage	–	1934

Designer (No 478): Johnstone

No 477 (2):

Boiler pressure – 135 lbs/ sq in	*Heating surfaces:*	*Tractive effort – 9,470 lbs*
Cylinders – 15" x 22"	*tubes – 757 sq ft*	*Coal capacity – 52 cu ft*
Bogie wheels – 2' 6"	*firebox – 77 sq ft*	*Water capacity – 500 gal*
Driving wheels – 5' 0"	*grate – 12 sq ft*	*Locomotive weight – 35 tons (est.)*
Wheel base – 4' 11½" + 6' 4" + 6' 8½"		
Locomotive length – not recorded		

No 478 (7):

Boiler pressure – 135 lbs/ sq in	*Heating surfaces:*	*Tractive effort – 9,470 lbs*
Cylinders – 15" x 22"	*tubes – 857 sq ft*	*Coal capacity – 59 cu ft*
Bogie wheels – 2' 4"	*firebox – 77 sq ft*	*Water capacity – 600 gal*
Driving wheels – 5' 0"	*grate – 12 sq ft*	*Locomotive weight – 35 tons 0 cwt*
Wheel base – 4' 11" + 6' 6" (or 6' 2") + 6' 7¾"		*Adhesive weight – 26 tons 10 cwt*
Locomotive length – 30' 2"		*Max axle loading – 13 tons 10 cwt*

No 2 was originally built as a 2-4-0T similar to No 1 in 1875 and was rebuilt as a 4-4-0T in 1908.

CBSCR No 2/ GSR Class 477/ D18 No 477. *Colling Turner Photos Ltd*

No 7 was the only locomotive built/ assembled by the CBSCR in its Cork workshops. Although entered in the records as a 'rebuild', Johnstone maintained that it was an entirely new locomotive. Views vary over the sources of this locomotive's components. It has been suggested that: the frames came from the original No 7 (an 0-4-0ST withdrawn in 1897); the boiler was a spare purchased at the auction of broad gauge equipment by the Londonderry & Lough Swilly Railway; the crank axle, cab, bunker and side tanks were new; the wheels would seem to have been new. However, there is a measure of conjecture in identifying just from where the parts actually came. It is unclear why these two locomotives should have been placed in the same class when effort was made to distinguish the variants within the 0-6-0STs.

CBSCR No 7/ GSR Class 477/ D18 No 478 at Cork in 1928. *Kelland collection*

GSR Class 479 — 4-4-2T — Inchicore Class C6
CBSCR Nos 3, 9 & 18 — 1925/ 1931 Load Class S/ RT

GSR (CBSCR) No		Built as 4-4-0T	Builder	Makers' No	Rebuilt as 4-4-2T	Withdrawn
479	(3)	6/1891	Dubs & Co	2777	1902	1930
480	(9)	11/1894	Neilson Reid & Co	4741	1898	1935
481	(18)	11/1894	Neilson Reid & Co	4740	1900	1935

No 479 (19):

Boiler pressure – 130 lbs/ sq in
Cylinders – 16" x 22"
Bogie wheels – 3' 0"
Driving wheels – 5' 6"
Trailing wheels – 3' 6"
Wheel base – 5' 3" + 6' 5½" + 7' 3" + 6' 11"
Locomotive length – 37' 0"

Heating surfaces:
tubes – 757 sq ft
firebox – 82 sq ft
grate – 14.5 sq ft

Tractive effort – 9,430 lbs
Coal capacity – 3 tons (est.)
Water capacity – 1000 gal
Locomotive weight – 51 tons 0 cwt
Adhesive weight – 28 tons 0 cwt
Max axle loading – 14 tons 0 cwt

Nos 480 (9) and 481 (18):

Boiler pressure – 140 lbs/ sq in

Heating surfaces:
tubes – 751 sq ft
firebox – 80 sq ft
grate – 14.5 sq ft

Tractive effort – 10,150 lbs
Locomotive weight – 48 tons 17 cwt
Adhesive weight – 26 tons 2 cwt
Max axle loading 13 tons 2 cwt

A second 4-4-0T was supplied by Dubs as CBSCR No 10; this locomotive was rebuilt as a 4-6-0T in 1906 – see Class 471 (B5). The makers' numbers of the Neilson Reid engines might have been reversed.

There were numerous detail differences between the Dubs and Neilson Reid versions eg the former had laminated driving wheel springs and the latter had helical springs. They also differed in cab and bunker styles and perhaps in coal and water capacities. The difference in locomotive weights appears excessive and the figures quoted for the Neilson Reid version are considered the more reliable. The material required to rebuild these three locomotives plus No 10 was supplied by Dubs.

Despite the reported official withdrawal date for No 481, this locomotive actually continued to work in normal service until the summer of 1936.

Above: CBSCR No 3/ GSR Class 479/ C6 No 479 at Cork Rocksavage in 1928. *Real Photographs Co Ltd*

Right: CBSCR No 18/ GSR Class 479/ C6 No 481 at Cork, Albert Quay. *Real Photographs Co Ltd*

GSR Class 482 CBSCR No 1 — 2-4-0T — Inchicore Class G6, 1925 Load Class T

GSR (CBSCR) No	Built	Makers' No	Withdrawn	
482 (1)	9/1874	760	1930	**Built by Dubs & Co, Glasgow**

CBSCR No 1 (later GSR Class 482/ G6 No 482). *IRRS collection*

Boiler pressure – 135 lbs/ sq in	*Heating surfaces:*	*Tractive effort – 9,470 lbs*
Cylinders – 15" x 22"	*tubes – 756.5 sq ft*	*Coal capacity – 32 cu ft*
Leading wheels – 3' 6"	*firebox – 74 sq ft*	*Water capacity – 500 gal*
Driving wheels – 5' 0"	*grate –11.2 sq ft*	*Locomotive weight – 32 tons 0 cwt*
Wheel base – 6' 8" + 6' 8"		*Adhesive weight – 26 tons 10 cwt*
Locomotive length – 26' 11"		*Max axle loading – 13 tons 10 cwt*

This was the sole survivor in 2-4-0T form of a group of five new locomotives introduced between 1874 and 1883. The design of these locomotives was derived from that of Nos 1 and 2 built by the same manufacturer (Makers Nos 17 and 18) for the Cork & Macroom Direct Railway in 1865. The CMDR locomotives differed only in having larger driving wheels and a shorter cylinder stroke (see GSR Class 487/ G5)

Prior to this it had been policy to purchase second-hand locomotives – an expensive and unreliable exercise.

Waterford & Tramore Railway

This was the most idiosyncratic of all Irish broad gauge railways. Its line was only 7¼ miles long, running south-south-west from Waterford Manor station to the seaside resort of Tramore. The railway opened in 1853 and traffic was essentially the transport of passengers to and from the seaside. The route was generally level which meant that it was feasible to operate services with small tank locomotives. For the first 46 years, four locomotives handled all traffic requirements. If this appears generous for so short a line, it should be noted that there was no physical connection with the rest of the Irish railway network. Thus any shortage could not be conveniently covered by loan of a locomotive from elsewhere. The WTR had to be totally self-sufficient and for many years, it was a case of one locomotive in service, one on stand-by and two under repair (in the open air) at The Manor (Waterford) station.

Unusually, by exploitation of a loophole in the Board of Trade regulations, between 1889 (following the Regulation of Railways Act) and 1933, passenger services were operated without continuous brakes. This ploy derived from the requirement that trains must be capable of being stopped by hand brake only on approach to a terminus. As the only stations were termini, there was no direct obligation to install continuous brakes. The GSR installed vacuum brakes in 1933 on transfer of converted ex-Clayton steam railcar vehicles but also applied a creative interpretation of the rules by piping some coaches only, without going to a universal braking system.

Locomotive livery was ornate. The body work was light green with black boiler bands, edge-lined vermillion. Frames were brown while domes and boiler fittings were polished brass, and chimneys were capped with copper. The covering up of this gaiety with the drab all-enveloping GSR grey was perhaps a step too far towards standardisation.

A feature of WTR locomotives was the provision of overall cabs that embraced the bunker, to increase the coal capacity. The ex-MGWR Class 551 0-6-0Ts imported to replace the indigenous fleet also gained this distinctive feature. Coal capacity in this condition might be considered 'variable'.

WTR No 1/ GSR Class 483/ N1 No 483 at Waterford Manor. *IRRS collection*

GSR Class 483 W&T R Nos 1 & 2 — 2-2-2WT — Inchicore Class N1 1925/ 1931 Load Class U/ TT

GSR (WTR) No		Built	Makers' No	Rebuilt	Withdrawn	
483	(1)	4/1855	*	1895	1936	
484	(2)	5/1855	*	1897	1926	Built by Fairbairn

* Fairbairn was not in the practice of affixing builders' plates to its locomotives and the sometimes quoted Nos 55 and 56 are considered unreliable.

Boiler pressure – 130 lbs/ sq in	*Heating surfaces:*	*Tractive effort – 5,600 lbs*
Cylinders – 13" x 18"	*tubes – 562.6 sq ft*	*Coal capacity – not recorded*
Leading wheels – 3' 6"	*firebox – 68.5 sq ft*	*Water capacity – 400 gal*
Driving wheels – 5' 0"	*grate – 11.25 sq ft*	*Locomotive weight – 26 tons (approx)*
Trailing wheels – 3' 6"		*Adhesive weight – 12 tons (approx)*
Wheel base – 6' 6" + 6' 6"		*Max. axle loading – 12 tons*
Locomotive length – not recorded		

The rebuilding of these locomotives involved larger boilers from Avonside Engine Co. About 1910, new bunkers, cabs and tanks were fitted at which time they assumed the general appearance depicted in the photographs. At the amalgamation, No 1 carried a new boiler supplied by Hawthorn Leslie in 1924 to the same dimensions. No 2 retained its Avonside boiler but as a precaution was working at 125 lbs/ sq in boiler pressure. In the summer of 1926, No 2 (GSR No 484) received a new firebox and tube plates, and was painted in standard GSR grey. There then appears to have been a change of heart as it was withdrawn in October of that year.

No 1 (GSR No 483) acquired vacuum brakes by 1930 and continued in service until 1935. At the ripe young age of 80 years, it was the oldest working Irish locomotive, the sole remaining Fairbairn-built engine in existence, and the last single driver in ordinary revenue-earning service in these islands. Despite its advanced years, it was still able to give a good account of itself, and was capable of working quite heavy trains up to 40-45 mph. On 24 August 1935, it was derailed at Carriglong and extensively damaged. The GSR authorities had intended to preserve No 1 in view of its historic significance. This disaster sealed its fate and it was broken up at the accident site.

WTR No 2/ GSR Class 483/ N1 No 484 *Real Photographs Co Ltd*

GSR Class 485 — 0-4-2WT — Inchicore Class L3
W&TR No 3 — 1925 Load Class T

GSR (WTR) No		Built	Makers' No	Rebuilt	Withdrawn
485	(3)	1861	452	6/1893	1930

Built by Slaughter Gruning (Bristol)
(Later Avonside Engine Co)

WTR No 3/ GSR Class 485/ L3 No 485 *Real Photographs Co Ltd*

Boiler pressure – 125 lbs/ sq in
Cylinders – 15" x 21"
Driving wheels – 5' 0"
Trailing wheels – 3' 6"
Wheel base – 7' 3½" + 6' 3¼"
Locomotive length – not recorded

Heating surfaces:
not recorded

Tractive effort – 8,365 lbs
Coal capacity – not recorded
Water capacity – 450 gal
Locomotive weight – 30 tons
Adhesive weight – 22 tons

While details of heating surfaces have not been traced, it is recorded that the boiler barrel was 3' 11" diameter and 9' 9¼" long, with firebox 3' 9" long. Performance was considered inferior to that of the 2-2-2Ts, attributed to excessive valve lap. It is believed that this locomotive retained its WTR number and livery throughout its career. Withdrawal followed the breaking of its crank axle, although the need for a new boiler (noted as early as 1924) might have been an additional factor in this decision.

GSR Class 486
W&TR No 4

0-4-2WT

Inchicore Class L1
1925/ 1931 Load Class R/ RT

GSR (WTR) No	Built	Makers' No	Withdrawn
486 (4)	1908	1137	1941

Built by Andrew Barclay & Co

WTR No 4/ GSR Class 486/ L1 No 486 at Waterford Manor. *RG Jarvis*

Boiler pressure – 150 lbs/ sq in
Cylinders – 15" x 22"
Driving wheels – 4' 6"
Trailing wheels – 3' 0"
Wheel base – 7' 0" + 7' 0"
Locomotive length – not recorded

Heating surfaces:
tubes – 845 sq ft
firebox – 73 sq ft
grate – 12 sq ft

Tractive effort – 11,690 lbs
Coal capacity – 12 cwt
Water capacity – 550 gal
Locomotive weight – 27 tons 10 cwt

This was the heaviest and most powerful of the original WTR engines but was considered sluggish compared with its older stable mates. In addition to the well tank, there appear to have been two small side tanks. A mere youngster of 33 years when withdrawn, this decision was based on the condition of its boiler and on the success of the ex-MGWR Class E 0-6-0Ts (GSR Class 551) that had been imported earlier.

Cork & Macroom Direct Railway

This company's route ran a distance of 24½ miles from its terminus at Capwell, Cork due west to Macroom. Originally, the CMDR used the Albert Quay terminus of the Cork & Bandon Railway (later CBSCR) but a history of squabbling developed between the two companies. With neighbourly relations fraught, the CMDR built its own terminus which was opened in 1879, and adopted thereafter an independent course with no physical connection with the CBSCR system. This was not rectified until intervention by the Irish Railways Executive Committee in 1918.

Although modest in size, the CMDR was profitable and wished to play no part in the 1924/5 amalgamation process. It vigorously resisted overtures to merge with the CBSCR when the amalgamation was being promoted and only reluctantly joined the GSR fold. An early GSR Board Minute (dated 2 January 1925) authorised restoration of the physical link between the ex-CBSCR and ex-CMDR sections which indicates that the CMDR must have re-imposed its physical isolation from the rest of the Irish network as soon as free from governmental control. (The same minute authorised abandonment of passenger services into the Capwell terminus so it is clear that the new owners intended wasting little time in bringing the CMDR to heel).

At the amalgamation, the locomotive livery was black with red lining. An earlier livery, dated 1903, was light green with black and yellow lining. A contemporary coloured postcard depicts No 5 (GSR No 490) in lined brick red but the authenticity of this livery is doubtful.

GSR Class 487 — 2-4-0T — Inchicore Class G5
C&MDR Nos 2–4 — 1925/ 1931 Load Class T/ RT

GSR	(CMDR) No	Built	Makers' No	Withdrawn
487	(2)	8/1865	18	1928
488	(3)	1867	235	1934
489	(4)	1881	1505	1928

Built by Dubs & Co

CMDR Nos 2 to 4/ GSR Class 487/ G5 No 489 at Broadstone.
Real Photographs Co Ltd

Boiler pressure – 130 lbs/ sq in	*Heating surfaces:*	*Tractive effort – 7,910 lbs*
Cylinders – 15" x 21"	*tubes – 700 sq ft*	*Coal capacity – 1 ton 5 cwt*
Leading wheels – 3' 9"	*firebox – 60 sq ft*	*Water capacity – 500 gal*
Driving wheels – 5' 6"	*grate – 10.5 sq ft*	*Locomotive weight – 31 tons 3 cwt*
Wheel base – 6' 8" + 6' 8"		*Adhesive weight – 22 tons 15 cwt*
Locomotive length – 26' 6"		*Max axle loading – 11 tons 14 cwt*

Revised dimensions for No 488 from 1931:

Boiler pressure – 125 lbs/ sq in

Tractive effort – 7,610 lbs
Locomotive weight – 32 tons 5 cwt
Adhesive weight – 23 tons 10 cwt
Max axle loading – 12 tons 0 cwt

Originally numbering four locomotives on the CMDR, this design with modifications was adopted by the neighbouring Cork & Bandon Railway (predecessor of CBSCR) as a standard type. CMDR locomotives remained on their native system during GSR days, except for No 488 which spent its closing years working on the Castleisland branch.

GSR Class 490 — 0-6-2T — Inchicore Class I2
C&MDR No 5 — 1925/ 1931 Load Class N/ MT

GSR (CMDR) No		Built	Makers' No	Withdrawn
490	(5)	1905	1022	1935

Built by Andrew Barclay & Co

CMDR No 5/ GSR Class 490/ I2 — *Real Photographs Co Ltd*

Boiler pressure – 160 lbs/ sq in
(150 lbs/ sq in from 1931)
Cylinders – 16" x 24"
Driving wheels – 5' 1"
Trailing wheels – 3' 7"
Wheel base – 7' 6" + 7' 0" + 6' 0"
Locomotive length – not recorded

Heating surfaces:
tubes – 959 sq ft
firebox – 87 sq ft
grate – 16 sq ft

Tractive effort – 13,700 lbs
(12,850 lbs)
Coal capacity – 1 ton 15 cwt
Water capacity – 930 gal
Locomotive weight – 45 tons 0 cwt
Adhesive weight – 36 tons 0 cwt
Max axle loading – 12 tons 10 cwt

This locomotive was a significantly larger than the initial four 2-4-0Ts and was acquired in replacement of CMDR No 1.

GSR Class 491 — 2-4-2T — Inchicore Class F5
C&MDR No 6 — 1925/ 1931 Load Class Q/ PT

(Previously GSWR Class 266)

GSR (CMDR) No		Built	Makers' No	Withdrawn
491	(6)	1891	1315	1934

Designer: Robinson — **Built by Vulcan Foundry**

See also Great Southern & Western Railway Class 266

CMDR No 6/ GSR Class 491/ F5 at Cork Rocksavage in 1931. *LGRP*

Boiler pressure – 150 lbs/ sq in (160 lbs/ sq in from 1925)
Cylinders – 16" x 24"
Pony wheels – 3' 6"
Driving wheels – 5' 6"
Trailing wheels – 3' 6"
Wheel base – 7' 8" + 7' 6" + 6' 3"
Locomotive length – 34' 0" (estimated)

Heating surfaces:
tubes – 780 sq ft
firebox – 88 sq ft
grate – 15 sq ft

Tractive effort – 11,870 lbs (12,660 lbs)
Coal capacity – 2 tons
Water capacity – 1200 gal
Locomotive weight – 45 tons 0 cwt
Adhesive weight – 25 tons 0 cwt
Max axle loading – 12 tons 10 cwt

This locomotive was one of two built for the Waterford, Limerick & Western Railway (their No 13); it later became GSWR No 266 and was sold to the CMDR in 1914. The second of this type (WLWR No 14/ GSR No 267) became the sole member of Class 267/ Inchicore Class F4 in 1925 (withdrawn 1935). Although remaining identical with Class 267, No 491, (ex-CMDR No 6/ GSWR No 266/ WLWR No 13) was accorded this totally separate classification on absorption of the CMDR.

Timoleague & Courtmacsherry Light Railway

The composition of this organisation bears out the theory of there often being an inverse relationship between the length of a railway company's title and the shortness of its route. The TCLR was actually two separate companies.

The Ballinascarthy & Timoleague Junction Light Railway was opened in 1890 and ran for six miles from Ballinascarthy on the CBSCR branch from Clonakilty Junction to Clonakilty. The remaining three miles from Ballinascarthy to Courtmacsherry was originally proposed to be a 3' 0" gauge tramway. However, this was opened in May 1891 as a road-side broad gauge tramway with many sharp curves, owned by the Timoleague & Courtmacsherry Extension Light Railway, built under the Tramways (Ireland) Act 1883. The TCLR had the distinction of being the last broad gauge light railway company in Ireland to maintain its own rolling stock.

The company operated in close co-operation with the CBSCR but remained an independent undertaking until the amalgamation. The company only ever owned three locomotives, the earliest of which was an 0-6-0ST named *Slaney*, bought from the contractor that built the line and withdrawn in 1920. The livery was plain black, relieved in the case of *Argadeen* by a brass rectangular nameplate with raised letters and vermillion background.

GSR Class 'Argadeen' — **2-6-0T** — **Inchicore Class K5**
T&CLR *Argadeen* — **1925/ 1931 Load Class T/ ST**

Name	Built	Makers' No	Rebuilt	Withdrawn	
Argadeen (844)	9/1894	611	1929*	1957	**Built by Hunslet Engine Co**

Boiler pressure – 145 lbs/ sq in	*Heating surfaces:*	*Tractive effort – 10,350 lbs*
Cylinders – 14" x 18"	*tubes – 487 sq ft*	*Coal capacity – 1 ton 10 cwt*
Pony wheels – 2' 0"	*firebox – 52 sq ft*	*Water capacity – 600 gal*
Driving wheels – 3' 6"	*grate – 10.2 sq ft*	*Locomotive weight – 28 tons 0 cwt*
Wheel base – 5' 0" + 4' 10" + 4' 3"		*Adhesive weight – 23 tons 10 cwt*
Locomotive length – 25' 5"		*Max axle loading – 8 tons 0 cwt*

*** As rebuilt with boiler from ex-GSWR 0-4-0T *Imp***

Boiler pressure – 145 lbs/ sq in	*Heating surfaces:*	*Tractive effort – 10,350 lbs*
	tubes – 578 sq ft	*Weights reported unchanged*
	firebox – 45 sq ft	
	grate – 9.5 sq ft	

This locomotive never bore a number but for accountancy purposes only, it was referred to in the books as No 844. It was sent to Inchicore in 1929 for scrapping as it had cracked cylinders. This decision was revoked when it became apparent that the boiler from *Imp* which had been withdrawn the previous year could be used (with working pressure reduced from 160 lbs/ sq in), once it had been lengthened by an additional ring butt-jointed at the front (hence the greater heating surface). The reboilering and repairs to the cylinders were carried out at the Broadstone. This exercise was worthwhile as the locomotive enjoyed another 28 years' service. The light axle loading gave *Argadeen* a wide sphere of operations.

TCLR *Argadeen*/ GSR Class Argadeen/ K5 at Cork, Albert Quay.

CH Hewison

GSR Class 'St Molaga' T&CLR *St. Molaga*

0-4-2T

Inchicore Class L6
1925/ 1931 Load Class U/ TT

Name	Built	Makers' No	Withdrawn
St. Molaga (845)	1890	520	1949

Built by Hunslet Engine Co

TCLR *St Molaga*/ GSR Class St Molaga/ L6.

IRRS collection

Boiler pressure – 140 lbs/ sq in (145 lbs/ sq in from 1931)	*Heating surfaces:*	*Tractive effort – 5,390 lbs (5,580 lbs)*
Cylinders – 10½" x 16"	*tubes – 326 sq ft*	*Coal capacity – 10 cwt*
Driving wheels – 3' 3"	*firebox – 34 sq ft*	*Water capacity – 400 gal*
Trailing wheels – 2' 0"	*grate – 6.2 sq ft*	*Locomotive weight – 21 tons 17 cwt*
Wheel base – 4' 9" + 5' 2"		*Adhesive weight – 17 tons 17 cwt*
Locomotive length – 21' 3"		*Max axle loading – 9 tons 10 cwt*

This locomotive never bore a number but for accountancy purposes only, it was referred to in the books as No 845. Its longevity was ensured by it having been re-boilered in 1922, and by its low axle-loading, making it one of the few locomotives capable of working the Courtmacsherry branch.

1948 assessment: *Light axleload engine confined chiefly to Courtmacsherry Branch.*

Chapter 7
Locomotives of the Midland Great Western Railway

The routes of the Midland Great Western Railway were largely concentrated in the flat lands of central Ireland and offered none of the operating challenges of the order confronted by the Great Southern & Western Railway. Accordingly, there was not the same impetus for pursuit of larger locomotives. Fourteen basic classes of straightforward design using sturdy, simple construction principles sufficed for the company's needs in the period before the amalgamation. Moreover, a degree of standardisation had been achieved. Modern engineering practice was evident in a higher proportion of locomotives being superheated than with any other Irish company. The decision to acquire a dozen Woolwich moguls would have endowed the company with a class of the most modern machines then available, had the amalgamation not occurred. The story of these locomotives is covered separately in Chapter 9, as their fortunes are essentially part of GSR history.

The fleet was the second-largest absorbed by the Great Southern Railways. While it lacked the variety of classes, wheel arrangements and vintages found in other parts of the network, there was nonetheless significant variation among the members of certain classes both before and after the amalgamation. For many years the company had operated a programme of class rebuilding or replacement at intervals of roughly 20 years. This cycle was delayed by the First World War; the modernity of the fleet is nonetheless apparent in its relative youth as at 31 December 1924:

Type	No of classes	No of locos	Built since 1900	Rebuilt since 1900
4-4-0	4	21	21	–
2-4-0	1	19	–	10*
0-6-0	7	82	25	27
0-6-0T	2	17	–	17
Total	**14**	**139**	**46**	**54**

*The rebuilding programme of the 2-4-0s was completed in 1927.

A major element of the company's goods traffic concerned livestock movements which were entrusted to 0-6-0s, mainly the L/ Lm/ Ln family of Standard Goods. This was the equivalent of the GSWR's Class 101, although not quite so highly regarded, and Ireland's second largest class. They were later augmented by the four locomotives of Class B which used much larger boilers; substantially more powerful, the increased weight restricted their spheres of usefulness. The two members of Class W and the four of Class H, all acquired through opportunistic purchases, proved more versatile.

Not long before the amalgamation, a new generation of 0-6-0s of the F/ Fa/ Fb family had been introduced. They were mixed traffic, rather than pure goods machines, and certain features of their design suggest that they might have been partly the product of war surplus materials bought at attractive prices.

Passenger services on the MGWR were somewhat leisurely, and were handled by four classes of 4-4-0, totalling 21 locomotives. In GSR days, MGWR 4-4-0s appeared fairly regularly in Cork and were considered straightforward, reliable machines. Secondary services were much the domain of a long-lived class of 2-4-0. The earliest examples, which dated from the 1870s, are regarded as Ireland's first mixed traffic design. They were replaced by a modernised version in the 1890s; these latter locomotives were subject to a complex re-boilering programme by the GSR but their survival in superheated form until the early 1960s was nonetheless remarkable.

At the amalgamation, the MGWR owned only two classes of tank locomotives, both of the 0-6-0 wheel arrangement. The larger was confined to shunting and banking duties while the smaller (Class E) became the most widely distributed of all MGWR classes. Although comprising a mere 12 locomotives, they found work beyond their native system on the Dublin & South Eastern, Cork Bandon & South Coast and Timoleague & Courtmacsherry sections, and also at Tralee and Fenit. Most notably, three were moved to the isolated Waterford & Tramore section where they revolutionised services.

The competence of the fleet was such that throughout GSR days, it covered almost exclusively the traffic requirements of the ex-MGWR section. There were a few withdrawals of older 0-6-0s soon after the amalgamation but essentially the fleet remained intact, aided by a constant allocation of Woolwich moguls. This was largely due to the quality of motive power management exercised at Broadstone Works, Dublin. The first locomotive to be constructed there was 0-6-0 No 49 *Marquis* in 1879 (later GSR No 563, withdrawn

1928). Thereafter, the majority of new locomotives were built there together with others assembled out of sets of parts supplied by English manufacturers. Numerous rebuilds and renewals of existing MGWR locomotives were also undertaken at the works.

Belpaire fireboxes with saturated boilers became the company standard in 1902 and, during the Cusack regime, Morton undertook experiments in superheating. Following his appointment as Locomotive Superintendent, Morton commenced a programme of installing superheaters of both Robinson and Schmidt types. In some cases, 8" diameter piston valves were installed, actuated by Stephenson link motion and accompanied by Detroit sight-feed lubrication for the cylinders.

Pursuit of this thoroughly modern configuration was not comprehensive; a number of superheated engines retained slide valves. After January 1925, this programme continued for a period (apparently counter to prevailing GSR policy) and focused on completion of the Class K 2-4-0 (GSR Class 650).

Between 1879 and 1924, a total of 120 new locomotives were built or assembled at the Broadstone, with the last being 0-6-0 Class Fb No 95 in June 1924. All locomotives built specifically for the MGWR were fitted with right-hand drive (a feature that also distinguished the products of the Woolwich Arsenal). New assembly recommenced the following year with the first Woolwich mogul kit. This was completed as No 49, in MGWR livery, in April 1925 but soon afterwards appeared in service as GSR No 372. Locomotive construction ceased with mogul No 383 in March 1927 but repairs continued until 1933 when the works closed. Repairs were then concentrated at Inchicore where a new erecting shop was completed in 1934. At the Broadstone, the last rebuild completed was that of Class As No 546 (MGWR No 129) in 1933, and the last locomotive to leave the works was 0-6-0T No 562 (MGWR No 117) in June of that year.

All types of locomotive were originally painted in lined emerald green, apparently of a shade similar to that used by the Great Central Railway in England. The green was all enveloping – boiler, cab, valances, tender frames – with only chimney, smoke box and running plate surfaces in black. The lining style was black bands edged in white. In 1902 Cusack introduced a handsome royal blue livery with lining of black bands edged in yellow. The blue was substituted on all areas that had previously been green, except that locomotives with conventional cab profiles had black cab roofs. As the blue livery did not wear well, a return was made in 1906 to green livery of a slightly lighter shade. In 1913, the livery was changed for all locomotives to plain black. From 1916, superheated passenger locomotives were embellished with a single thin red line while the insides of frames were painted red. Class F was finished in this style from new. This livery has been erroneously described as 'blue-black', resulting from the application of cleaning oil to varnished paintwork leaving a dark bluish tinge.

Except for Class F/ Fa/ Fb (GSR class 623), every MGWR locomotive was named. The names were carried on cast brass plates with a vermilion ground. On older locomotives, the plates were straight and attached to the boiler lagging usually at or near the mid-way point with tender locomotives, and centrally on the tanks of Classes E and P. Later locomotives had curved plates attached to the centre splasher. MGWR number plates were cast brass except for Class F/ Fa/ Fb which carried painted numbers only. On renumbering, standard GSR-style cast number plates were applied.

Dates, where known, for the removal of names are recorded for each class. In most, if not all, cases this was concurrent with renumbering in the GSR system and repainting in the austere GSR livery. The last MGWR locomotive to retain its pre-amalgamation livery was No 74 *Luna* of Class Lm which was not repainted until late 1931.

Dramatis personae

The MGWR motive power inherited by the GSR was introduced by three Locomotive Superintendents over a period of 53 years. The earliest examples were the work of **Martin Atock**, a prominent member of an extended railway family. Atock was born in 1836 and his early career included a spell as a draughtsman under his father who was then Carriage and Wagon Superintendent on the Eastern Counties Railway in England. In 1861 he was appointed Locomotive Superintendent of the Waterford & Limerick Railway, which position he held for eleven years – *prima facie* evidence of his competence. Between 1848 and 1861, no fewer than five individuals had held this position on the WLR together with an interregnum during which a contractor had been engaged; there were to be five short-lived successors to Atock in the position.

In 1872, Atock joined the MGWR, bringing with him James Rowe, Chief Draughtsman, from the WLR The pair started immediately upon the next generation of locomotives for the MGWR. In 1875, three pre-1860 built locomotives were renewed but, in 1879, a significant policy change came about with a decision that all locomotives, carriages and wagons should enjoy only a 20-year life before replacement.

Atock was a prolific designer of sound, competent machines that served the MGWR well. At his retirement, every locomotive in MGWR service was of his design, save Class H (GSR Class 619) for which he had recommended purchase at an attractive price. It was said that he never designed an unsatisfactory class. There were two distinctive aspects to his work – an aversion to bogie locomotives and an attachment to the extraordinary 'fly away' cab. The aerodynamics of this design must have been strange, making tender-first working uncomfortable for locomotive crews. Replacement commenced early in the Cusack regime but the last was not removed until 1941. Even towards the end of his tenure, Atock remained busy introducing new types, continuing in his harmonious working partnership with Rowe. However the latter died in late 1899 and this is believed to have been a major factor in Atock's decision to retire in 1900 at the age of 64, despite being in good health.

On receiving three months' notice of Martin Atock's intention to retire, **Edward Cusack** was appointed as first assistant locomotive engineer with Thomas Atock (Martin's son) as second assistant locomotive engineer. These appointments effectively anointed Cusack as Martin Atock's successor, which was confirmed in 1901. Concurrently, Basil Hope was recruited as first assistant locomotive engineer from the North Eastern Railway. This proved to be a flawed management structure, especially in comparison with the potency of the Martin Atock-James Rowe partnership.

Cusack's rise had been meteoric by the standards of the time. He had been appointed a junior assistant locomotive engineer at the Broadstone in 1890, following four years' apprenticeship at Kitson and two years as an improver at Crewe – but fortunately for him, he happened to be the youngest son of the MGWR's Chairman. With such slight experience, Cusack would have required strong support in his assistants. However, Hope proved something of a lightweight without any great disposition towards hard work, while Thomas Atock suffered from poor health and apparently was not one to push himself too hard.

Thus an unusual degree of responsibility came to rest on the shoulders of a young draughtsman, theoretically No 4 in the hierarchy, who had been recruited to replace the late James Rowe. This gentleman was **W H Morton**, all of whose previous experience had been with Kitson. He had approached the prospect of a career change with trepidation and uncertainty. This seems to be in keeping with a reticent and self-effacing manner that belied his stature as an engineer. Morton soon became Works Manager, and eventually rose to the position of first assistant locomotive engineer following the departures of Hope in 1907 and Thomas Atock in 1911. Cusack resigned in 1915 and Morton acted as Locomotive Engineer for six months before being appointed. The delay in confirmation of appointment was grudging treatment for a man who had supported a weak team and who had pioneered work on superheater development. (The Cusack-Morton superheater was so titled as a courtesy to his then boss).

Apart from his engineering and management competence, Morton had business acumen and a keen eye for a bargain. Three purchases orchestrated by him amply illustrate the point. In 1922–23, nineteen hopper wagons originally intended for a Spanish railway were purchased from a Belgian manufacturer for loco coal and permanent way purposes. Secondly, a pair of 20 ton travelling cranes manufactured by Cowans & Sheldon at the instigation of Ministry of Munitions for service with, but never delivered to, the British Army in Russia were purchased in 1923. These were purchases at bargain basement prices but more significant was the order for 12 kits of parts for Woolwich moguls. Clearly he was a man – in modern parlance – to think 'outside the box'.

On the formation of the GSR, Morton was the senior by date of appointment as Locomotive Engineer (Superintendent) but junior in age to Bazin of the GSWR, whose deputy he became. With Bazin's early retirement in 1929, Morton once again assumed the number one role, this time as Chief Mechanical Engineer. No new designs resulted from this second spell at the top but his work had the greatest impact on locomotive policy of any of the five CMEs of the GSR. He was appointed General Manager of the GSR in April 1932.

GSR Class 234 / MGWR Class W — 0-6-0 — Inchicore Class J17 / 1925/ 1931 Load Class M/ L

GSR (MGWR) No	Name	Built	Makers' No	Renum'd	Rebuilt	Withdrawn
233# (141)	*Limerick*	1/1901	3974	–	–	1929
234 (142)	*Athenry*	1/1901	3975	1928	1940 or 1941§	1950

GSR number allocated but not carried

Designer: Robinson (for Waterford Limerick & Western Railway) **Built by Kitson**

As rebuilt by MGWR in 1923:

Boiler pressure – 150 lbs/ sq in
Cylinders – 18" x 24"
Driving wheels – 5' 2"
Wheel base – 7' 6" + 8' 3"
Locomotive length – 26' 6 7/8"

Heating surfaces:
tubes – 873 sq ft
firebox – 108 sq ft
grate – 17.75 sq ft

Tractive effort – 15,990 lbs
Coal capacity – 4 tons
Water capacity – 2000 gal
Locomotive weight – 41 tons 4 cwt
Max axle loading – 13 tons 14 cwt

§ As rebuilt with larger round-topped saturated type S boiler:

Heating surfaces:
tubes – 918 sq ft
firebox – 99 sq ft
grate – 19.6 sq ft

Revised weights not recorded

(Another source quoted the rebuilding date as 1932 but the authors consider this unlikely)

These locomotives were ordered by the Waterford Limerick & Western Railway which had already purchased four of this type (later GSWR/ GSR Class 222). They were intended to be WLWR Nos 4 *Samson* and 11 *Dragon,* (although another source states No 4 *Shamrock* and No 11 *Samson*). Prior to delivery a dispute arose with Kitson over the method of payment in the face of the pending takeover by the GSWR. Before this could be settled, the pair was sold to the MGWR where they were the first Belpaire-boilered locomotives. In November 1924, they were initially allocated Nos 612 and 613 in the GSR list but in April 1925 were re-allocated Nos 233 and 234. These numbers were vacant in the ex-WLWR section of the GSWR number list and had been carried by locomotives of the same type which had been withdrawn in 1919 and 1911 respectively (Dubs Nos 3042 and 3043).

The second Nos 233 and 234 (ie ex-MGWR Class W) were given separate GSR and Inchicore Classifications (234/ J17) from those applied to the WLWR /GSWR batch which became GSR Class 222 (J25). This separation took place despite the two types being dimensionally similar in 1925, except for cylinder diameter.

It is presumed that Class 233 was not adopted in accordance with the convention as early withdrawal of No 233 itself was contemplated. They were not significantly dimensionally altered in the pre-amalgamation period. The rebuilding of No 234 involved installation of a round-topped firebox similar to those fitted to other ex-WLWR types. Enlargement of the cylinders from 17" to 18" diameter seems to have taken place in 1922.

These locomotives were long-term residents of Mullingar from where they were employed on goods trains to Cavan and Longford. By 1938, No 234 had moved to Sligo.

1948 assessment: *Only one of its class. Similar to Standard* (ie Class 101), *but slightly smaller. Does shunting work.* (It is interesting to note that even at this late stage, this locomotive was considered separate from Class 222).

GSR Class 234/ J17 (MGWR Class W) No 234 at Collooney in 1938. *WA Camwell*

GSR Class 530 — 4-4-0 — Inchicore Class D16
MGWR Class D/ Ds — 1925/ 1931 Load Class Q/ R

GSR (MGWR) No	Name	Built	Renum'd	Rebuilt	Withdrawn
530 (1) (36 until 1924)	*Empress of Austria*	1/1900	1925	1930*/ 1936¥/ 1939§	1949
531 (4) (25 until 1924)	*Cyclops*	3/1901	1925	1930#*/ 1934§	1945
532 (5) (26 until 1924)	*Britannia*	3/1900	1926	1930 or 1931*	1949
533 (6) (37 until 1922, 35 until 1924)	*Wolfdog*	9/1900	1927	1930* /1935¥	1953
534 (2)	*Jupiter*	3/1900	1926	1920#¶/ 1932§	1949
535 (3)	*Juno*	5/1901	1929	1919#¶/ 1929*	1949

Designer: Atock/ Cusack — **Built at Broadstone**

Rebuilt with:
¶ Round-topped superheated boiler; reclassified Ds by MGWR
# 17" x 24" cylinders
* Round-topped superheated boiler
¥ Superheater boiler
§ Belpaire superheated boiler X type plus extended smokebox

MGWR Class D No 37 Wolf Dog (Later GSR Class 530/ D16 No 532) in original condition with round-topped saturated boiler.
IRRS collection

As built:

Boiler pressure – 150 lbs/ sq in
Cylinders – 16" x 22"
Bogie wheels – 3' 6"
Driving wheels – 5' 8"
Wheel base – 5' 6" + 6' 6" + 7' 11"
Locomotive length – 28' 6½"

Heating surfaces:
tubes – 985 sq ft
firebox – 95 sq ft
grate – 16 sq ft

Tractive effort – 10,560 lbs
Coal capacity – 4 tons
Water capacity – 1600 gal
Locomotive weight – 40 tons 8 cwt
Adhesive weight – 26 tons 11 cwt
Max axle loading – 15 tons 13 cwt

¶ Rebuilt with round-topped superheater boiler:

Heating surfaces:
tubes – 610 sq ft
firebox – 95 sq ft
superheater – 113 sq ft
grate – 16 sq ft

Locomotive weight – 39 tons 17 cwt

 # Rebuilt with new cylinders:

Cylinders – 17" x 24" *Tractive effort – 13,000 lbs*

*** Rebuilt with round-topped saturated boiler, supplied by Inchicore:**

No details can be traced but presumably dimensions were unchanged from those of boilers fitted when built. Some sources state that this was a type U (saturated Belpaire) boiler but photographs of No 532 dating from the 1950s – see below – indicate that this locomotive still carried a round-topped boiler.

¥ Rebuilt with superheated boiler:

This is believed to involve fitting of superheater to the Inchicore boiler but no details can be traced

§ Rebuilt with Belpaire superheater boiler X type:

Boiler pressure – 160 lbs/ sq in	*Heating surfaces:*	*Tractive effort – 11,270 lbs*
	tubes – 655 sq ft	*Locomotive weight – 39 tons 17 cwt*
	firebox – 110 sq ft	*Adhesive weight – 24 tons 12 cwt*
	superheater – 112 sq ft	*Max axle loading – 12 tons 10 cwt*
	grate – 15 sq ft	

Nos 531 and 534 were fitted with 17" x 24" cylinders sometime between 1925 & 1931

GSR Class 530/ D16 (MGWR Class Ds) No 531 in later condition with Belpaire superheated boiler and larger tender. At Athlone in 1938. *WA Camwell*

These locomotives were complete rebuilds of six 2-4-0s constructed by Beyer Peacock in 1880-1 (Makers' Nos 1960 to 1965). Some sources attribute Atock as the designer but with his well-known aversion to bogies, it is likely that Cusack had a hand in the design. No 36 (GSR No 530) retained its Atock 'fly-away' cab until 1924; the remainder had received square cabs on becoming 4-4-0s. They were known as the 'Mayo Bogies'.

Although withdrawn in 1949, No 532 continued on wash-out duties at the Broadstone until May 1957. It then spent over three years in a siding at Ashtown, Dublin before being scrapped at Dundalk.

Intended principally for service between Mullingar and Sligo, they only occasionally appeared at Dublin, Broadstone station. In later years these locomotives were employed mainly on passenger services to Mayo.

1948 assessment: *Completely obsolete. Small passenger engine of bad design.*

GSR Class 536 / MGWR Class C/ Cs — 4-4-0 — Inchicore Class D7 / 1925/ 1931 Load Class M/ L

GSR (MGWR) No	Name	Built	Renumbered	Rebuilt	Withdrawn
536 (12)	*Shamrock*	2/1913	1925	1925*/ 1935§/ 1938¶	1951
537 (20) (9 until 1924)	*Emerald Isle*	5/1912	1926	1923 or 1924*/ 1935§/ 1940¶	1953
538 (25) (4 until 1924)	*Ballynahinch*	12/1910	1927	1915#/ 1924*/ 1936¶	1950
539 (26) (5 until 1924)	*Croagh Patrick*	5/1910	1927	1917#/ 1924*/ 1935§/ 1939¶	1952

Designer: Cusack **Built at Broadstone**

Rebuilt with reduced cylinders
Rebuilt with boiler type: * Superheater within original boiler § Belpaire superheated type X
¶ Large diameter Belpaire superheated

GSR Class 536/ D7 (MGWR Class C) No 538 in original condition with Belpaire saturated boiler in 1933. *LGRP*

As originally built:

Boiler pressure – 175 lbs/ sq in	*Heating surfaces:*	*Tractive effort – 16,710 lbs*
Cylinders – 18" x 26"	*tubes – 975 sq ft*	*Coal capacity – 5 tons*
Bogie wheels – 3' 6"	*firebox – 115 sq ft*	*Water capacity – 2500 gal*
Driving wheels – 6' 3"	*grate – 16.25 sq ft*	*Locomotive weight – 46 tons 13 cwt*
Wheel base – 5' 6" + 7' 3" + 8' 2"		*Adhesive weight – 30 tons 6 cwt*
Locomotive length – 29' 10¼"		*Max axle loading – 16 tons 7 cwt*

 # As rebuilt with reduced cylinders:

Cylinders – 17" x 26" *Tractive effort – 14,900 lbs*
(Nos 4 and 5 might have been built in this condition)

*** As rebuilt by fitment of Schmidt superheater within original boiler:**

Locomotive length – 29' 7½"	*Heating surfaces:*
	tubes – 815 sq ft
	firebox – 124 sq ft
	superheater – 206 sq ft
	grate – 16.25 sq ft

§ As rebuilt with Belpaire superheated boiler type X:

Boiler pressure – 160 lbs/ sq in

Heating surfaces:
tubes – 655 sq ft
firebox – 110 sq ft
superheater – 112 sq ft
grate – 16 sq ft

Tractive effort – 15,280 lbs
Locomotive weight – 43 tons 8 cwt

At this rebuilding No 537 received a GSWR-style cab

¶ As rebuilt with large diameter Belpaire superheated boiler Type C (as for Class A) but retaining slide valves:

Boiler pressure – 175 lbs/ sq in

Heating surfaces:
tubes – 801 sq ft
firebox – 123 sq ft
superheater – 167 sq ft
grate – 17.3 sq ft

Tractive effort – 16,710 lbs
Locomotive weight – 46 tons 4 cwt

The four locomotives of this class, and the five of Class C1 (GSR Class 540/ D6) described next, were constructed at the Broadstone from six sets of parts supplied by Kitson, plus allegedly redundant parts from three withdrawn locomotives. As built, these locomotives were not considered totally satisfactory, being somewhat over-cylindered. The boiler had the same dimensions as that of the older Class D (whose cylinders were only 16" x 22") while the working parts were identical with the larger Class A

At the first rebuilding, Class Cs/ GSR Class 536 locomotives were provided with Schmidt superheaters, while retaining slide valves but not receiving smokebox extensions. The boiler pitch was raised slightly and it is believed, but not confirmed, that 19" x 26" cylinders were fitted. The heating surfaces are believed to have been: *tubes - 679 sq ft; firebox - 115 sq ft; superheater - 180 sq ft.* Performance was significantly improved through the superheating process.

1948 assessment (both 536 and 540 classes): *These are similar and interchange-able on work. They are similar to the 545 Class except 536 Class has a smaller boiler; 540 Class slightly larger. Sluggish bad running engines. Can run on DSER section but cannot keep time.*

As Class A (GSR Class 545) (see below) was confined to the Dublin-Galway main line by virtue of excessive axle loading, Class C was introduced to handle passenger services over the routes to Mayo and Sligo. However, this class and the next described Class 540 proved unsatisfactory with poor riding qualities leading to frequent breaking of bogie springs, particularly on the Sligo route. Their large driving wheels impeded acceleration away from stops and also limited their hill-climbing capacities; they were also heavy on fuel.

They were mainly used on slower passenger services between Dublin and Galway.

GSR Class 536/ D7 (MGWR Class C) No 538 in later condition with large diameter X type superheated Belpaire boiler fitted in 1938. The extension at a smaller diameter than that of the main smokebox barrel was characteristic of superheated MGWR locomotives. At Broadstone in 1938.

WA Camwell

GSR Class 540 — 4-4-0 — Inchicore Class D6
MGWR Class C/ C1 — 1925/ 1931 Load Class L/ J

GSR (MGWR) No	Name	Built	Renumbered	Rebuilt	Withdrawn
540 (7)	*Connemara*	7/1909	1927	1917	1953
541 (8)	*St. Patrick*	6/1913	1927	1917	1959
542 (9) (6 until 1924)	*Kylemore*	1911	1926	1917	1959
543 (10)	*Faugh-a-Ballagh*	12/1909	1928	1921	1959
544 (11)	*Erin-Go-Bragh*	5/1915	1926	1926	1955

Designer: Cusack — **Built at Broadstone**

As originally built:

Boiler pressure – 175 lbs/ sq in	*Heating surfaces:*	*Tractive effort – 16,700 lbs*
Cylinders – 18" x 26"	*tubes – 975 sq ft*	*Coal capacity – 5 tons*
Bogie wheels – 3' 6"	*firebox – 115 sq ft*	*Water capacity – 2500 gal*
Driving wheels – 6' 3"	*grate – 16.25 sq ft*	*Locomotive weight – 46 tons 13 cwt*
Wheel base – 5' 6" + 7' 3" + 8' 2"		*Adhesive weight – 30 tons 6 cwt*
Locomotive length – 29' 10¼"		*Max axle loading – 16 tons 7 cwt*

As rebuilt with large diameter Belpaire superheated boiler (as for Class A) and piston valves:

Piston valves – 8"	*Heating surfaces:*	*Locomotive weight – 51 tons 1 cwt*
Locomotive length – 29' 7½"	*tubes – 815 sq ft*	*Adhesive weight – 30 tons 3 cwt*
	firebox – 124 sq ft	*Max axle loading – 19 tons 15 cwt*
	superheater – 206 sq ft	
	grate – 17.3 sq ft	

GSR Class 540/ D6 (MGWR Class C1) No 541 with type A superheated boiler and piston valves. At Broadstone in 1931. *LGRP*

This class shared its origin with that of Class Cs (GSR Class 536) and was used on similar work. However, these locomotives were rebuilt with superheaters earlier and were concurrently fitted with piston valves. Presumably the financial situation could not support the fitting of piston valves to the remaining four (Class Cs). Schmidt superheaters were fitted except with regard to Nos 10 & 11 (GSR Nos 543 & 544) which had a Robinson superheater; *reported heating surfaces: tubes – 821 sq ft; firebox – 125.5 sq ft; superheater – 211 sq ft.*

No 541 was reported in 1938 to be fitted with a boiler from 0-6-0 Class F This was initially identified by virtue of this boiler still being equipped with the connections for operating the ex-MGWR track laying machine. No 543 was reported as allocated to Tralee in the Spring of 1939, being replaced by No 541.

It is conventional wisdom that application of superheating was the more effective if accompanied by fitting of piston valves and comparison of the careers of these locomotives with those of their slide valve companions in Class 536 vindicates this view. Class 536 was subject to more rebuilding in the 1930s whereas no further significant modification of this class proved necessary. Further, the final survivor of Class 536 was withdrawn in 1953, the same year as the first of this class was withdrawn. On this evidence, the lower initial cost rendered by slide valve retention proved a false economy in the long run.

1948 assessment (both 536 and 540 classes): *These are similar and interchangeable on work. They are similar to the 545 Class except 536 Class has a smaller boiler: 540 Class slightly larger. Sluggish bad running engines. Can run on DSER section but cannot keep time.*

GSR Class 545 — 4-4-0 — Inchicore Class D5
MGWR Class A/ As/ A1 — 1925/ 1931 Load Class J/ J

GSR (MGWR) No	Name	Built	Renum'd	Rebuilt	Withdrawn
545 (127)	*Titanic*	9/1903	1926	1920*/ 1937§	With'n & reinstated 1933/ 1955
546 (129)	*Celtic*	6/1902	1927	1918*/ 1933#/1936§	1959
547 (125)	*Britannic*	1905	1926	1917*	1954
548 (126)	*Atlantic*	4/1904	1925	1925¶/ 1937§	1955
549 (128)	*Majestic*	12/1902	1926	1926¶	1931
550 (124)	*Mercuric*	1905	1928	1916*/ 1924¶	1957

* Rebuilt with Belpaire superheated boiler and 8" piston valves; re-classified As

¶ Rebuilt with Belpaire superheated boiler, 8" piston valves, new frames and cab, raised footplate; re- classified A1

§ Rebuilt with type A boiler

See notes below regarding this rebuild

Designer: Cusack — **Built at Broadstone**

MGWR Class A No 126 *Atlantic* (later GSR Class 545/ D5 No 548) at Broadstone in 1914. *Ken Nunn*

Dimensions as originally built:

Boiler pressure – 175 lbs/ sq in
Cylinders – 18" x 26"
Bogie wheels – 3' 6"
Driving wheels – 6' 3"
Wheel base – 5' 6" + 7' 9" + 9' 3"
Locomotive length – 31' 3½"

Heating surfaces:
tubes – 1213 sq ft
firebox – 150 sq ft
grate – 20 sq ft

Tractive effort – 16,700 lbs
Coal capacity – 6 tons
Water capacity – 3000 gal
Locomotive weight – 51 tons 5 cwt
Adhesive weight – 34 tons 3 cwt
Max axle loading – 18 tons 1 cwt

*** As rebuilt with Belpaire superheated boiler and 8" piston valves and reclassified MGWR Class As:**

Cylinders – 19" x 26"	*Heating surfaces:*	*Tractive effort – 18,600 lbs*
Piston valves – 8"	*tubes – 832.5 sq ft*	*Coal capacity – 5 tons*
Locomotive length – 31' 3¾"	*firebox – 150 sq ft*	*Water capacity – 2500 gal*
	superheater – 211 sq ft	*Locomotive weight – 52 tons 16 cwt*
		Adhesive weight 35 tons 6 cwt
		Max axle loading – 18 tons 18 cwt

No 127 (later 545) received a modified coupled wheelbase of 9' 6" in 1920

¶ As rebuilt and reclassified MGWR Class A1:

Cylinders – 18" x 26"	*Heating surfaces:*	*Locomotive weight – 55 tons 15 cwt*
Piston valves – 8"	*tubes – 842 sq ft*	*Max axle loading – 19 tons 0 cwt*
	firebox – 150 sq ft	*Adhesive weight – 37 tons 15 cwt*
	superheater – 170 sq ft	

This rebuilding also included new frames and cab plus raised running plate over driving wheels. (No 124 might have carried 19" diameter cylinders for a period following this rebuilding)

§ As rebuilt with type A boiler:

	Heating surfaces:	*Locomotive weight – 52 tons 0 cwt*
	tubes – 821 sq ft	*Max axle loading – 17 tons 10 cwt*
	firebox – 142 sq ft	
	superheater – 167 sq ft	
	grate – 20.5 sq ft	

Left: MGWR Class As No 124 Mercuric (later GSR Class 545/ D5 No 550). As rebuilt in 1916, at Broadstone. This locomotive was rebuilt again in 1924 but Nos 125/ 127/ 129 later GSR Nos 545 to 547 were in this condition at the amalgamation).
Real Photographs Co Ltd

Right: MGWR Class A1 No 124 Mercuric (later GSR Class 545/ D5 No 550), following its second pre-amalgamation rebuilding in 1924, at Broadstone.
Real Photographs Co Ltd

GSR Class 545/ D5 (MGWR Class As) No 545 as rebuilt in 1937. At Broadstone in 1938.

WA Camwell

GSR Class 545/ D5 (MGWR Class As) No 546. Hybrid condition resulting from 1933 rebuild showing the more modern version of cab, frame and raised footplate that had been introduced in 1924 with No 550 (124) and classified A1 by MGWR At Inchicore in 1936.

LGRP

 # The 1933 rebuild of No 546 produced a hybrid combining the wheels of No 546, frames and cab of withdrawn No 549, and boiler of withdrawn Class 646 (J2) No 646. Conventionally, the identity of this locomotive should have become No 549, ie based on identity of frames. This exercise was significant also in being the last rebuild of a locomotive carried out at the Broadstone before closure of the works.

At their rebuilding, they received the characteristic modified smokebox with the extension having a smaller diameter than the main barrel. Schmidt superheaters were installed except for No 545 (127) which was given a Robinson superheater, apparently increasing the locomotive weight to 53 tons 8 cwt. It is not clear why superheater surfaces should differ between Versions As and A1, unless a different method of measurement was applied.

Concurrent with the first four rebuildings, four tenders were exchanged with the Class H (GSR 619/ J6). It is also reported that four tender swaps were effected with Class A (GSR 646/ J2). Obviously these figures do not reconcile but what is certain is that the original larger tenders were removed from Class A as their axle boxes had a tendency to run hot. It was felt that the risk would be reduced by using these tenders with slower speed freight locomotives.

No 550 (124) was derailed and badly damaged during the Civil War at Streamstown. After lying idle for two years, it was extensively modified as detailed above to produce a more modern-looking machine, and reclassified as Class A1. Some sources suggest that the damage was so extensive that No 124 was a new locomotive rather than a rebuild. In any event, these measures provided the template for the rebuilding of Nos 548 (126) and 549 (128).

No 548 was a good example of the limbo into which locomotives could fall in GSR days. It was supposedly withdrawn for scrapping in 1934 and presumably stood idle for two to three years at Inchicore. Then it re-appeared in traffic in 1937, following the fitting of a new boiler.

These locomotives were the first that can be definitely attributed to the Cusack era although Morton was mainly responsible for the design. They introduced the royal blue livery and were the first Broadstone-built locomotives with Belpaire fireboxes, inaugurating a new MGWR standard. When new, they were the largest locomotives in Ireland and initially worked Dublin to Mullingar only, pending strengthening of the Shannon Bridge at Athlone. Later they handled the 'Limited Mail' and fastest express passenger trains through to Galway but within a couple of years, these schedules were eased. Thereafter they worked services that rarely fully extended their capacities. In GSR days, some of these locomotives spent time in the Cork and Limerick districts eg in 1938, No 548 was allocated to Cork shed.

1948 assessment: *Built as passenger engines. Their passenger loading is too small for main line work and their axleload precludes them from working branch lines such as D&SE to Wexford where the load would suit. They are used as Goods engines (chiefly cattle and special goods) but no 4-4-0 is efficient on such wok. They work local passenger trains in Cork area. A poor design.*

GSR Class 551 — 0-6-0T — Inchicore Class J26
MGWR Class E — 1925/ 1931 Load Class Q/ PT

GSR (MGWR) No	Name	Built	Builder	Makers' No	Rebuilt	Renum'd	Withdrawn
551 (106)	*Lark*	6/1891	Kitson	3370	1923*	1926	1954
552 (107)	*Robin*	1891	Kitson	3371	1913*	1927	1963
553 (108)	*Swallow*	1891	Kitson	3372	1923*/ 1941¶	1926	1955
554 (109)	*Fly*	1891	Sharp Stewart	3693	1924*	1928	1955
555 (110)	*Bat*	1891	Sharp Stewart	3694	1924*/ 1935¶	1930	1960
556 (111)	*Wasp*	1891	Sharp Stewart	3695	1923*	1928	1956
557 (112)	*Hornet*	1892	Kitson	3380	1914*	1927	1959
558 (113)	*Gnat*	1892	Kitson	3381	1923*	1926	1960
559 (114)	*Stork*	1892	Kitson	3382	1924*	1926	1960
560 (115)	*Achill*	1893	Kitson	3527	1924*/ 1932¶	1930	1963
561 (116)	*Cong*	1893	Kitson	3528	1911*	1929	1959
562 (117)	*Moy*	1893	Kitson	3529	1923*	1928	1963

Designer: Atock — **Built by Kitson/ Sharp Stewart**

* Rebuilt with 'standardised' leading dimensions
¶ Rebuilt with enlarged cab (which permitted an extra ton of coal to be carried) and modified footsteps for service on Waterford & Tramore section

There were dimensional differences between these locomotives as built:

Nos 551 to 553 (106 to 108) & 557 to 559 (112 to 114):

Boiler pressure – 150 lbs/ sq in	*Heating surfaces:*	*Tractive effort – 11,700 lbs*
Cylinders – 15" x 22"	*tubes – 667 sq ft*	*Coal capacity – 1 ton 15 cwt*
Driving wheels – 4' 6"	*firebox – 66 sq ft*	*Water capacity – 580 gal*
Wheel base – 6' 3" + 7' 0"	*grate – 13 sq ft*	*Locomotive weight – 36 tons 16 cwt*
Locomotive length – 28' 7½"		*Max axle loading – 13 tons 10 cwt*

Nos 554 to 556 (109 to 111):

Heating surfaces:	*Water capacity – 600 gal*
tubes – 668 sq ft	*Coal capacity – 1 ton 15 cwt*
firebox – 72.5 sq ft	*Locomotive weight – 35 tons 0 cwt*
grate – 13 sq ft	*Max axle loading – 13 tons 10 cwt*

Nos 560 to 562 (115 to 117):

Heating surfaces:	*Water capacity – 700 gal*
tubes – 666.9 sq ft	*Coal capacity – 1 ton 10 cwt*
firebox – 50 sq ft	*Locomotive weight – 36 tons 16 cwt*
grate – 13.1 sq ft	*Max axle loading – 13 tons 10 cwt*

*** As rebuilt:**

Heating surfaces:	*Water capacity – 700 gal*
tubes – 668 sq ft	*Coal capacity – 1 ton 5 cwt*
firebox – 72 sq ft	*Locomotive weight – 35 tons 12 cwt*
grate – 13.1 sq ft	*Max axle loading – 12 tons 10 cwt*

GSR Class 551/ J26 (MGWR Class E) No 552 at Broadstone in 1931.

L&GRP

GSR Class 551/ J26 (MGWR Class E) No 560 fitted with modified cab, bunker, front and rear footsteps for service on the Waterford & Tramore section. Depicted at Cork shed in 1962, long after it had left the WTR section.

CP Friel Collection

The 1911 to 1924 rebuilding programme produced a reasonably standardised class. However details of the 'as originally built' dimensions are included as variations within the three pre-amalgamation versions do cause confusion. There were other, minor variations with these locomotives. Apart from Nos 551, 555 and 560, they remained visually unchanged except for installation of more modern smokebox doors and shortened chimneys during their long careers.

These locomotives were intended mainly for branch line use together with shunting duties at the Broadstone. They have been called the 'Irish Terrier' tanks as they resembled the London Brighton & South Coast A1/ A1X tanks in looks, utility and, to no small extent, performance. They enjoyed similar popularity and some had working lives almost to the end of GSR steam, their size and low axle loading making them useful beyond MGWR territory.

Some were used for a period on the DSER section in 1925 where their capacities were rather stretched. They were longer term residents on the CBSCR section, and were also used in Limerick. No 556 worked on the Shillelagh branch in 1932–33 where it was unpopular (a contemporary account attributes this to ex-GSWR never having a good word to say about ex-MGWR machinery). The wanderings for which they are best remembered involved the transfer of Nos 551, 555 and 560 (along public highways!) to the isolated Waterford & Tramore route where they were a great success. The style of enlarged cab and bunker was basically similar to that applied earlier to the 2-2-2Ts of the WTR; a modified form of inset footstep was fitted because of clearance problems.

1948 assessment: *A small tank engine suitable only for shunting. Very small boiler, coal and water capacity, however, limits their use in that field. Three engines on self-contained Waterford/ Tramore section.*

GSR Class 563 / 567 0-6-0 Inchicore Class J16
MGWR Class Ln 1925/ 1931 Load Class J/ J

GSR (MGWR) No		Name	Built	Renum'd	Rebuilt	Withdrawn
563#	(49)	*Marquis*	9/1879	–	1899	1928
564#	(50)	*Viscount*	9/1879	–	1899	1925
565#	(51)	*Regent*	5/1880	–	1899	1926
566#	(52)	*Baron*	6/1880	–	1899	1927
567	(53)	*Duke*	9/1880	1925	1899, 1919¶, 1925*, 1942¥	1950
568#	(54)	*Earl*	9/1880	–	1898	1925

GSR number allocated but not carried; survivor reclassified as sole member of Class 567
¶ Fitted with experimental Cusack-Morton firebox superheater 1919; removed 1925
* Rebuilt with Belpaire boiler superheater, Robinson superheater and piston valves
¥ Fitted with type X boiler

Designer: Atock **Built at Broadstone**

As rebuilt in 1898/9:

Boiler pressure – 160 lbs/ sq in
(later reduced to 135 lbs/ sq in)
Cylinders – 18" x 24"
Driving wheels – 5' 1½"
Wheel base – 7' 0" + 7' 11"
Locomotive length – 26' 6¾"

Heating surfaces:
tubes – 970 sq ft
firebox – 95 sq ft
grate – 16.5 sq ft

Tractive effort – 17,200 (14,510) lbs
Coal capacity – 1 ton 10 cwt (approx)
Water capacity –1600 gal
Locomotive weight – 40 tons 9 cwt
Max axle loading – 13 tons 12 cwt

¶ As fitted with Cusack-Morton superheater

Boiler pressure – 175 lbs/ sq in

Heating surfaces:
(not recorded)

Tractive effort – 18,810 lbs

*** As rebuilt in 1925:**

Boiler pressure – 150 lbs/ sq in
Piston valves – 8"
Fitted with Schmidt superheater

Heating surfaces:
tubes – 644 sq ft
firebox – 168 sq ft
superheater – 115 sq ft
grate – 16.5 sq ft

Tractive effort – 16,120 lbs

¥ As fitted in 1942 with type X boiler:

Boiler pressure – 160 lbs/ sq in

Heating surfaces:
tubes – 655 sq ft
firebox – 110 sq ft
superheater – 112 sq ft
grate – 16 sq ft

The attention given to No 567 (53) during late MGWR and early GSR days suggests that this was to have been a prototype for modernisation of this class (ie superheating and piston valves), and perhaps later of Class L/ Lm. Before this programme could be implemented, Bazin's prohibition on superheating of smaller locomotives took effect, making the remainder of the class early candidates for withdrawal on the basis of age. No 567 was a casualty of the Milne Report which advocated early removal of older, single-locomotive classes.

1948 assessment: *Only one of type. Was built from 573 class* (sic) *as an experimental development which was justified, but not continued. A good engine.*

MGWR Class Ln No 49 *Marquis* (later GSR Class 563/ J16 No 563) in original condition. This was the first locomotive built at Broadstone, where it is seen in this photograph.

IRRS collection

GSR Class 567/ J16 (MGWR Class Ln) No 567 as rebuilt in 1925 with Robinson superheater and piston valves.

L&GRP

GSR Class 573/ J18 No 576 in GSR days but still appearing as MGWR Class L No 74 Luna. This photograph is undated but No 74 was the last MGWR locomotive in pre-amalgamation livery, not being re-painted until 1931.

Authors' collection

GSR Class 573 — 0-6-0 — Inchicore Class J18/ J19
MGWR Class L/ Lm — 1925/ 1931 Load Class K/ J

Note: the distinction between this class and the next class described (MGWR Class L/ GSR Class 594/ J19) is unclear as they shared the same nominal tractive effort and all other salient features, although Class 594 was rated as slightly heavier. For all practical purposes GSR classes 573 (J18), 594(J19), and 563/ 567(J16) were the same.

MGWR Class Lm:

GSR No (MGWR)	Name	Built	Renum'd	Builder	Makers' No	Rebuilt	Withdrawn
569§ (76)	*Lightning*	5/1892	–	MGWR	–	–	1925
570§ (78)	*Planet*	2/1893	–	MGWR	–	–	1925
571§ (83)	*Lucan*	1/1892	–	MGWR	–	–	1925
572§ (84)	*Dunkellan*	4/1891	–	MGWR	–	–	1925
574 (80)	*Dunsandle*	6/1891	1926	MGWR	–	1938#/ 1940*	1963
576 (74)	*Luna*	9/1891	1931	MGWR	–	1931*	1957
578§ (79)	*Mayo*	11/1892	–	MGWR	–	–	1926
582 (73)	*Comet*	8/1892	1925	MGWR	–	1918#/ 1932*	1959
583 (82)	*Clonbrock*	3/1892	1926	MGWR	–	1926#/ 1932*	1963
584 (130)	*Ajax*	4/1895	1929	Sharp Stewart	4057	1937*	1955
585 (131)	*Atlas*	4/1895	1926	Sharp Stewart	4058	–	1960
586 (132)	*Pluto*	4/1895	1926	Sharp Stewart	4059	–	1957
587 (133)	*Titan*	5/1895	1927	Sharp Stewart	4060	1927#/ 1941*	1961
588 (134)	*Vulcan*	5/1895	1927	Sharp Stewart	4061	1927#/ 1940*	1963
589 (77)	*Star*	9/1892	1925	MGWR	–	1917#/ 1941*	1962
590 (136)	*Cavan*	7/1895	1928	Kitson	3585	1928#/ 1936*	1961
591 (137)	*Maynooth*	7/1895	1927	Kitson	3586	1927#/ 1940*	1959
592 (138)	*Nephin*	8/1895	1925	Kitson	3599	1935#	1962
593 (139)	*Tara*	8/1895	1929	Kitson	3600	1929#	1965
612¶ (75)	*Hector*	10/1891	1925	MGWR	–	1925¥/ 1942#	1961
613¶ (81)	*Clancarty*	3/1893	1925	MGWR	–	1925¥/ 1940*	1963
– (135)	*Arran Isles*	6/1895	–	Kitson	3584	–	1923 *Civil war loss*

§ GSR number allocated but not carried
¶ Allocated Inchicore Class J19 in 1925; see further comments below

Rebuilt with boiler type:

¥ Spare Belpaire saturated; # Class 573 round-topped; * Belpaire superheated type X

Class Lm as built with round-topped saturated boiler:

Boiler pressure – 150 lbs/ sq in
Cylinders – 18" x 24"
Driving wheels – 5' 3"
Wheel base – 7' 0" + 7' 11"
Locomotive length – 26' 7¼"

Heating surfaces:
tubes – 970 sq ft
firebox – 95 sq ft
grate – 16.5 sq ft

Tractive effort – 15,740 lbs
Coal capacity – 4 tons
Water capacity – 2000 gal
Locomotive weight – 38 tons 0 cwt
Max axle loading – 13 tons 3 cwt

¥ As rebuilt with spare Belpaire saturated boiler:

Boiler pressure: - 150 lbs/ sq in

Heating surfaces:
tubes – 938 sq ft
firebox – 115 sq ft
grate – 16 sq ft

¥¶ Locomotives No 612 and 613 were fitted with spare boilers of a type that had been used in the rebuilding of Class L (MGWR Nos 55 to 72, 85 & 104/ later 140) between 1902 and 1913. The surviving members of Class L were allocated GSR Nos 594 to 611 following the amalgamation. As MGWR Nos 75 and 81 were rebuilt in 1925 in similar fashion to the treatment previously given to Class L, they were given Nos 612 and 613 and Inchicore Class J19, although apparently still considered part of GSR Class 573. The later rebuildings of these engines in 1942 and 1940 respectively brought them back into Class 573 (J18) proper.

 # As rebuilt with Class 573 round-topped boiler:

Heating surfaces:
total – 889 sq ft
grate – 16 sq ft

*** As rebuilt with Belpaire superheated type X boiler:**

Boiler pressure – 160 lbs/ sq in

Heating surfaces:
tubes – 655 sq ft
firebox – 110 sq ft
superheater – 112 sq ft
grate – 16 sq ft

MGWR Class L:

GSR (MGWR) No	Name	Built	Renum'd	Builder	Works' No	Rebuilt	Withdrawn
573§ (85) (95 until 1924)	*Bulldog*	8/1876	–	R Stephenson	2307	6/1895	1927
575 (135) (92 until 1924)	*Bittern*	6/1876	1926	R Stephenson	2290	1894 1930¶/1939*	1957
577 (86)	*Bullfinch*	5/1876	1925	R Stephenson	2284	1894	1928
579§ (64) (91 until 1924)	*Bear*	6/1876	–	R Stephenson	2289	5/1895	1928

§ GSR number allocated but not carried

In addition, four members of Class L were allocated duplicate numbers in 1924 by the MGWR but were officially withdrawn shortly before the amalgamation; however No 87A actually continued at work until October 1925. None of these locomotives were included in GSR stock lists, nor given GSR numbers:

MGWR No	Name	Built	Builder	Works' No	Rebuilt	Withdrawn
(87A)	*Buzzard*	5/1876	R Stephenson	2285	6/1895	1925
(88A)	*Buffalo*	5/1876	R Stephenson	2286	12/1893	1925
(89A)	*Bison*	6/1876	R Stephenson	2287	12/1895	1925
(90A)	*Beaver*	6/1876	R Stephenson	2288	1894	1925

For completeness there were two other locomotives in this series:

MGWR No	Name	Built	Builder	Works' No	Rebuilt	Withdrawn
93	*Butterfly*	8/1876	R Stephenson	2305	1894	1923
94	*Badger*	8/1876	R Stephenson	2306	1894	1923

Designer: Atock

Class L as built with round-topped saturated boiler:

Boiler pressure – 160 lbs/ sq in (later 150 lbs/ sq in)
Cylinders – 18" x 24"
Driving wheels – 5' 3"
Wheel base – 7' 0" + 7' 11"

Heating surfaces:
tubes – 970 sq ft
firebox – 95 sq ft
grate – 16.5 sq ft

Tractive effort – 16,790 (15,740) lbs
Coal capacity – 4 tons
Water capacity – 2000 gal
Locomotive weight – 38 tons 7 cwt
Max axle loading – 13 tons 15 cwt

Left: GSR Class 573/ J18 (MGWR Class L) No 593 in rebuilt condition with round-topped saturated boiler.

L&GRP

Below: GSR Class 573/ J18 (MGWR Class Lm) No 575 as rebuilt with Belpaire superheated Type X boiler in 1939. At Broadstone 1939.

WA Camwell

Left: GSR Class 573/ J18 (MGWR Class Lm) No 574 as rebuilt condition in 1940 with Belpaire superheated boiler. Note the modern round-roofed profile cab on which part of the cut-out has been plated in. At Inchicore about 1949.

A Donaldson

¶ As rebuilt with Belpaire saturated boiler (ex Class 594) and square cab:

Boiler pressure – 150 lbs/ sq in

Heating surfaces:
tubes – 938 sq ft
firebox – 115 sq ft
grate – 16 sq ft

Tractive effort – 15,740 lbs

*** As rebuilt with Belpaire superheated type X boiler:**

Boiler pressure – 160 lbs/ sq in

Heating surfaces:
tubes – 655 sq ft
firebox – 110 sq ft

Tractive effort – 16,790 lbs

Note re Nos 587, 588, 591 and 593 (all Class Lm): *Some (but not all) sources report that these locomotives were fitted with round-topped saturated boilers from Class 101, apparently in the early 1940s. However, the recorded dimensions (total tube & firebox heating surfaces – 889 sq ft, and grate area – 16 sq ft) do not accord with reported dimensions for any boilers fitted to Class 101.*

From 1891, the Broadstone added 22 locomotives to the Standard Goods Class (MGWR Nos 73 to 84, 86 to 95). These are usually considered to have been new builds although there is doubt concerning the origin of the second batch as they may have been rebuilds of earlier locomotives supplied by Robert Stephenson in 1876. If not rebuilds proper, then at least some material from the earlier machines was used in the process. Four of these locomotives were still in service at the amalgamation (MGWR Nos 95 [later 85], 86, 91 [later 64], 92 [later 135]). They were MGWR Class L but were included with members of Class Lm as GSR Class 573 (J18).

The remainder were classified Lm. Apart from the MGWR-built examples, a further ten were provided in 1895 (five each from Sharp Stewart and Kitson). One of the Kitson locomotives (No 135) was derailed in 1923 in a Civil War incident and so badly damaged that it was scrapped. As built, the Kitson engines had some small differences from the others and a weight of 37 tons 2 cwt. Otherwise, there was no significant difference between the versions, and in practice these locomotives were considered as an extension of the Class L (GSR Class 594/ J19) described next. At its height, the combined family of Class L/ Lm/ Ln totalled 58 locomotives making it Ireland's second most numerous class after the GSWR Class 101 (J15).

MGWR No 79 (GSR No 578 allocated but not carried) served for some years after withdrawal on boiler wash-out duties at the Broadstone and apparently was the penultimate locomotive to carry its MGWR name and number plate.

No 590 was equipped with special steam connections in 1928 to work with the ex-MGWR track-laying train, at which time it must have been considered a departmental locomotive.

1948 assessment (573 & 594 classes): *The Midland edition of the 101 Standard Goods. Design poor and very few of them alike. Wear too rapidly. Essential to keep working.*

GSR Class 573/ J18 (MGWR Class Lm) No 593 in CIE days. This locomotive is in similar condition to No 574 (previous illustration). Having been one of the last survivors of the L family in original condition, No 574 was the last to be rebuilt in 1951.
CP Friel collection

GSR Class 594 — 0-6-0 — Inchicore Class J19
MGWR Class L — 1925/ 1931 Load Class K/ J

GSR (MGWR) No	Name	Built	Renum'd	Rebuilt	Withdrawn
594 (55)	*Inny*	1885	1928	1902* Type B/ 1942¥	1961
595 (56)	*Liffey*	1885	1925	1902* Type A/ 1934¶	1957
596 (57)	*Lough Corrib*	1885	1925	1904* Type C/ 1935¶	1959
597 (58)	*Lough Gill*	1885	1926	1903* Type C/ 1930¶	1959
598 (59)	*Shannon*	1885	1927	1903* Type C/ 1937¶	1965
599 (60)	*Lough Owel*	1885	1929	1913* Type not known/ 1937¶	1964
600 (61)	*Lynx*	1887	1929	1913* Type not known/ 1949¶	1957
601 (62)	*Tiger*	1888	1926	1904* Type C/ 1916§/ 1931¶	1959
602 (63)	*Lion*	1888	1926	1903* Type C/ 1933¶	1959
603 (65)	*Wolf*	1888	1928	1904* Type C/ 1940¶	1965
604 (66)	*Elephant*	1889	1930	1910* Type C/ 1920§/ 1934¶	1961
605 (67)	*Dublin*	1888	1929	1903* Type C/ 1932¶	1957
606 (68)	*Mullingar*	1887	1927	1903* Type D/ 1934¶	1963
607 (69)	*Athlone*	1889	1928	1904* Type C/ 1934¶	1961
608 (70)	*Ballinasloe*	1889	1927	1902* Type C/ 1932¶	1959
609 (71)	*Galway*	1887	1926	1912* Type C/ 1935¶	1954
610 (72)	*Sligo*	1888	1925	1906* Type C/ 1931¶	1963
611# (140, 104 until 1901)	*Wren*	1886	–	1901* Type A	1925

GSR number allocated but not carried

Designer: Atock — **Built at Broadstone**

*** As rebuilt between 1902 and 1913 with Belpaire saturated boiler:**

Boiler pressure – see below
Cylinders – 18" x 24"
Driving wheels – 5' 3"
Wheel base – 7' 0" + 7' 11"
Locomotive length – 26' 1½"

Heating surfaces: see below

Tractive effort – see below
Coal capacity – 4 tons
Water capacity – 1700 gal
Locomotive weight – 39 tons 16 cwt
Max axle loading – 13 tons 15 cwt

Although all these locomotives were part of a single rebuilding programme, four types of boiler were used with differing heating surfaces. These are summarised as follows:

	Tubes	*Firebox*	*Grate*	*Boiler pressure*	*Tractive effort*
Type A	*106 sq ft*	*950 sq ft*	*16 sq ft*	*150 lbs/ sq in*	*15,740 lbs*
Type B	*115 sq ft*	*938 sq ft*	*16 sq ft*	*150 lbs/ sq in*	*15,740 lbs*
Type C	*115 sq ft*	*938 sq ft*	*16 sq ft*	*160 lbs /sq in*	*16,790 lbs*
Type D	*103 sq ft*	*910 sq ft*	*16 sq ft*	*160 lbs/ sq in*	*16,790 lbs*

All later had their boiler pressure set at 150 lbs/ sq in but dates not known. At this rebuilding, most locomotives lost their distinctive Atock 'fly away' cabs. Nos 60, 61, 71 & 72 also received heavy slide bars at this rebuilding.

¥ Rebuilt with round-topped boiler as fitted to Class 573

§ Rebuilt with odd boilers from older withdrawn locomotives; details not recorded

¶ As rebuilt with Belpaire superheated X type boiler:

Boiler pressure – 160 lbs/ sq in

Heating surfaces:
tubes – 655 sq ft
firebox – 110 sq ft
superheater – 112 sq ft
grate – 16 sq ft

Weight recorded as unchanged but this appears incorrect

GSR Class 594/ J19 (MGWR Class L) 0-6-0 No 594 with round-topped saturated boiler at Sligo in 1950.
L&GRP

GSR Class 594/ J19 (MGWR Class L) No 598 as rebuilt with Type X Belpaire superheated boiler at Broadstone in 1938.
WA Camwell

GSR Class 594/ J19 (MGWR Class L) No 603 as rebuilt with Belpaire saturated boiler, closed in valances and modified cab spectacle plates. At Broadstone in 1938.
WA Camwell

This class, also known as the Standard Goods, originally comprised 20 new locomotives built between 1885 and 1889; Nos 64 *Leopard* (Civil War loss) and 85 *Meath* were withdrawn in 1923 & 1924 respectively.

These locomotives were of the same type as GSR Class 573/ J18 and it is unclear why they should have been allocated different classifications. A possible explanation might be that they were segregated by the GSR to identify that they had been built new and did not contain major parts (eg frames) obtained from much older locomotives on being rebuilt. Thus they might have been accorded a greater operating life expectancy. In the event, there was little difference between the withdrawal dates of this class and the longer-lived examples of Class 573 (J18).

No 610 (and No 625) were the first ex-MGWR locomotives to be renumbered and repainted in GSR livery.

1948 assessment (573 & 594 classes): *The Midland edition of the 101 Standard Goods. Design poor and very few of them alike. Wear too rapidly. Essential to keep working.*

GSR Class 614 — 0-6-0T — Inchicore Class J10
MGWR Class P — 1925/ 1931 Load Class F/ FT

GSR (MGWR) No	Name	Built	Renumbered	Rebuilt	Withdrawn
614 (100)	*Giantess*	1880	1928	1901§/ 1932*/ 1937¶	1955
615 (101)	*Giant*	1880	1926	1902*/ 1937¶	1951
616 (102)	*Pilot*	1880	1927	1900§/ 1932¥/ 1941¶	1950
617 (103)	*Pioneer*	1880	1928	1903*/ 1937¶/ 1940#	1959
618 (105)	*Hercules*	1890	1928	1911*/ 1940¶	1949

Originally provided with round-topped boilers, rebuilt with boiler type: § Larger saturated
* Belpaire saturated ¥ Belpaire superheated type X ¶ Round topped saturated type Class 573
# Round-topped saturated type Class 594

Designer: Atock — **Built at Broadstone**

GSR Class 614/ J10 (MGWR Class P) No 617 in original condition with round-topped boiler at Broadstone in 1938.

WA Camwell

As built:

Boiler pressure – 130 lbs/ sq in
Cylinders – 18" x 24"
Driving wheels – 4' 6"
Wheel base – 7' 0" + 7' 11"
Locomotive length – 30' 2½"

Heating surfaces:
tubes – 978 sq ft
firebox – 95 sq ft
grate – 16 sq ft

Tractive effort – 15,910 lbs
Coal capacity – 1 ton 10 cwt
Water capacity – 880 gal
Locomotive weight – 43 tons 0 cwt
Max axle loading – 16 tons 19 cwt

§ As rebuilt with larger boiler:

No 100:

Boiler pressure – 150 lbs/ sq in

Heating surfaces:
tubes – 970 sq ft
firebox – 106 sq ft
grate – 16.5 sq ft

Tractive effort – 18,360 lbs

No 102:

Boiler pressure – 160 lbs/ sq in

Heating surfaces:
tubes – 910 sq ft
firebox – 103 sq ft
grate – 16.5 sq ft

Tractive effort – 19,580 lbs

*** As rebuilt with Belpaire saturated boiler:**		
Boiler pressure – 150 lbs/ sq in	*Heating surfaces:* *tubes – 938 sq ft* *firebox – 115 sq ft* *grate – 16 sq ft*	*Tractive effort – 18,360 lbs* *Locomotive weight – 45 tons 16 cwt* *Max axle loading – 16 tons 19 cwt*

¥ As rebuilt with Belpaire superheated type X boiler:		
Boiler pressure – 150 lbs/ sq in	*Heating surfaces:* *tubes – 655 sq ft* *firebox – 110 sq ft* *superheater – 112 sq ft* *grate – 16 sq ft*	*Tractive effort – 18,360 lbs* *Locomotive weight – not recorded* *Max axle loading – not recorded*

¶ # As rebuilt with round-topped saturated Class 573/ 594 type boilers:

The only recorded information in this condition is total heating area – 889 sq ft; grate area 16 sq ft. However, this heating surface does not accord with data listed for boilers carried by Classes 573/ 594

These locomotives were built for banking and shunting at North Wall goods yard, Dublin, where they worked their entire lives. In view of these duties, the fitting of a superheated boiler to No 616 in 1932 seems to have been extravagant. Larger cabs were fitted to Nos 615 and 617 in 1938.

1948 assessment: *Small shunting tank engine, only suitable for small yards and short banking trips. Obsolete.*

GSR Class 614/ J10 (MGWR Class P) No 618 as rebuilt with Belpaire boiler at Broadstone. Class 372/ K1 No 378 or 388 is standing behind. What appears to be a Class 540 or 545 is standing to the left.

Real Photographs Co Ltd

GSR Class 619 — 0-6-0 — Inchicore Class J6
MGWR Class H — 1925/ 1931 Load Class C/ C

GSR (MGWR) No	Name	Acquired	Makers' No§	Renum'd	Rebuilt	Withdrawn
619 (96)	*Avonside*	1/1880	1211	1926	1906*/ 1922¶/ 1936#	1949
620 (97)	*Hibernia*	1/1880	1212	1928	1907*/ 1921¶/ 1941#	1949
621 (98)	*Caledonia*	1/1880	1213	1926	1908*/ 1919¶/ 1943#	1949
622 (99)	*Cambria*	1/1880	1214	1927	1908*/ 1918¶/ 1936#	1945

§ Another source states Nos 96 to 99 had Works Nos 1211, 1213, 1212 & 1214 in that order. Built by Avonside

(Dimensional records for these locomotives as introduced are incomplete but they appear to have had 4' 9" driving wheels, 7' 6" + 7' 6" wheel base, and 17" x 24" cylinders. Photographic comparison suggests that relatively little of the originals beyond frames, cranks, wheels and tenders was retained at the first rebuilding. Therefore they might be considered new engines built 1906 to 1908).

Rebuilt with boiler type: * Belpaire saturated
¶ Belpaire superheated (Robinson) plus piston valves
# Alternative Belpaire superheated type H

GSR Class 619/ J6 (MGWR Class H) No 621 at Broadstone in 1936. *LGRP*

¶ As rebuilt with Belpaire superheated boiler plus piston valves:

Boiler pressure – 175 lbs/ sq in
Cylinders – 18" x 24"
Piston valves – 8"
Driving wheels – 4' 9"
Wheel base – 7' 6" + 7' 6"
Locomotive length – 28' 6"

Heating surfaces:
tubes – 832 sq ft
firebox – 116 sq ft
superheater – 172 sq ft
grate – 20 sq ft

Tractive effort – 20,290 lbs
Coal capacity – 7 tons
Water capacity – 3000 gal
Locomotive weight – 43 tons 17 cwt
Max axle loading – 15 tons 12 cwt

 # Alternative Belpaire superheated type H:

Heating surfaces:
tubes – 821 sq ft
firebox – 114 sq ft
superheater – 167 sq ft
grate – 20.75 sq ft

Locomotive weight – 46 tons 3 cwt
Max axle loading – 15 tons 13 cwt

These locomotives were built in 1878 by Avonside Engine Company to an order from the Waterford, Dungarvan and Lismore Railway, which company refused to accept them due to late delivery. They were purchased from the builders by MGWR at the modest price of £1600 each. Compared with contemporary locomotives built specifically for the MGWR, they had spacious and comfortable cabs, but were not fitted with vacuum brakes and, up until their first rebuilding, their duties were confined to banking work at North Wall goods yard.

The second rebuilding programme was more significant with the provision of Robinson superheaters and piston valves – further evidence of a concerted effort towards modernisation that was forestalled by GSR policy regarding secondary types. At this rebuilding, the class received larger capacity tenders transferred from Class A (GSR 545/ D5) 4-4-0s. Their unusual origin bestowed this class with driving wheels of smaller diameter than the MGWR standard of 5' 3" for goods locomotives. This feature, together with their free-steaming capacity, made them excellent for goods work, although they were also popular for slower speed passenger services; eg night mails. They were highly regarded by the GSR locomotive authorities.

No 622 broke its crank axle in the early 1940s and because of the shortage of spare parts, it never ran again. No 621 is reported not to have worked for four or five years before its official withdrawal, which indicates a poor return on its 1943 rebuilding.

Although part of MGWR rather than GSR history, No 99 was the guinea-pig for extensive trials with the Cusack-Morton patent superheater in 1915–16, until removal in 1918.

1948 assessment: *A very powerful engine, but the wheel diameter is 4' 9" from which the higher power is derived: the revolutions per mile are, therefore, excessive and the engine needs continuous heavy repair after 20,000 miles.*

GSR Class 623/ J6 (MGWR Class Fa) No 641 MGWR Sub-class F also had curved footplate over driving crank pins and open valances. At Broadstone in 1936.

G Coltas

GSR Class 623 — 0-6-0 — Inchicore Class J5
MGWR Class F/ Fa/ Fb — 1925/ 1931 Load Class C/ E

GSR (MGWR) No	MGWR Class	Built	Renumbered	Rebuilt	Withdrawn
623 (35, 86 until 1924)	Fb	1/1924 §	1927	–	1957
624 (87)	Fb	1/1924 §S	1927	–	1962
625 (88)	Fb	1/1924 §S	1928	–	1961
626 (89)	Fb	1/1924 §S	1926	1931	1961
627 (90)	Fb	2/1924 §S	1927	–	1961
628 (91)	Fb	6/1924 ¶	1928	–	1954
629 (92)	Fb	6/1924 ¶	1930	–	1954
630 (93)	Fb	6/1924 ¶	1929	–	1959
631 (94)	Fb	6/1924 ¶	1927	–	1954
632 (95)	Fb	6/1924 ¶	1929	–	1959
633 (39)	F	4/1921 ¶	1926	1931	1957
634 (40)	F	7/1921 ¶	1927	1931	1959
635 (41)	F	8/1921 §	1926	–	1957
636 (36)	Fa	7/1922 §	1926	–	1959
637 (37)	Fa	7/1922 §	1927	–	1963
638 (38)	Fa	1922 §	1927	1931	1963
639 (42)	Fa	1922 §	1928	–	1963
640 (43)	Fa	1/1923 §	1926	–	1960
641 (44)#	Fa	1922 ¶	1928	–	1959
642 (45)#	Fa	1922 ¶	1929	–	1961
643 (46)#	Fa	1922 ¶	1925	–	1955
644 (47)#	Fa	3/1923 ¶	1927	–	1957
645 (48)#	Fa	10/1923 ¶	1927	–	1955

§ Built with Schmidt superheater
§S Built with 'S type' superheater, believed to be a variant of the Schmidt type
¶ Built with Robinson superheater

No details of the 1931 rebuilding have been traced other than a reference to provision of new boilers, presumably of the same dimensions.

Designer: Morton#

All built at Broadstone, except for Nos 44 to 48 which were built by Armstrong-Whitworth – their Nos 175 to 179

Sub-class F:

Boiler pressure – 175 lbs/ sq in
Cylinders – 19" x 26"
Piston valves – 8"
Driving wheels – 5' 8"
Wheel base – 7' 1" + 7' 11"
Locomotive length – 27' 7"

Heating surfaces:
tubes – 821 sq ft
firebox – 126 sq ft
superheater – 210 sq ft
grate – 17.3 sq ft

Tractive effort – 20,530 lbs
Coal capacity – 7 tons
Water capacity – 2500 gal
Locomotive weight – 49 tons 4 cwt
Max axle loading – 18 tons 0 cwt

From the tender registers, it appears that No 633 might have been coupled later to a 2800 gallon tender of the type introduced with Sub-class Fb.

Sub-class Fa: Identical with sub-class F except for different heating surfaces, believed to be tubes and firebox combined – 939 sq ft; locomotive weight 48 tons 10 cwt; other detail differences are not known.

Sub-class Fb: Identical with Sub-class F except that running plates were raised to clear coupling rods. The tenders for these locomotives as introduced were slightly taller with 2800 gallon water capacity.

GSR Class 623/ J6 (MGWR Class Fb) No 628 at Broadstone. Similar to sub-classes F/ Fa except for raised footplate over driving wheels.
L&GRP

This was the last MGWR class to be introduced before the initial order of Woolwich mogul kits of parts. Despite the year 1922 being officially ascribed for construction of Nos 44 to 48, these were actually the first five of the class, being completed by Armstrong Whitworth the previous year. These manufacturers also supplied five sets of frames and cylinders for five other locomotives built at the Broadstone. It may be surmised that the cylinders at least for the remaining 13 examples were also supplied by these manufacturers as cylinders were never cast at the Broadstone.

Although the designer of these locomotives was recorded as Morton, it is thought that they were influenced by the availability of parts owned by the British Ministry of Supply and rendered surplus at the end of World War 1. Certainly, the driving wheel diameter of 5' 8" was an unusual choice and somewhat large for an 0-6-0. It might be possible that use of this size was influenced by the ready availability of suitable material at an attractive price (Morton's ready eye for a bargain again?) rather than use of an optimal size. Other features that set these locomotives apart from other MGWR classes were the absence of names, painted numbers as opposed to cast number plates, and left hand drive.

The involvement of Armstrong-Whitworth also may not be without significance. This company was a leading armaments manufacturer that post-war moved into commercial locomotive manufacture. Morton's involvement in this war surplus market could have been a further step towards identification of the cut-price opportunity offered by the Woolwich products.

Officially, the class was intended to take over passenger and Limited Mail services on the 84-mile Mullingar-Sligo route where speeds were generally lower and where use of rebuilt Class C 4-4-0s had encountered problems of excessive fuel consumption, poor riding and broken bogies. While being the principal motive power on this route for many years, they were also the mainstay of power for the heavy livestock traffic over the ex-MGWR system, which was often worked at moderately high speeds. They also found plenty of employment on night mail services, extra passenger services and excursion traffic.

Several of the class were fitted with special steam connections to drive the generator on the ex-MGWR Bretland track-laying train; Nos 624, 626, 627, 632 and 636 were noted with this equipment at different times. While allocated for these duties, they were presumably categorised as departmental locomotives.

Nos 625 and 610 were the first ex-MGWR locomotives to be renumbered and repainted into GSR livery.

1948 assessment: *A powerful engine, primarily used on goods work for which they are suitable. They can work passenger trains such as 372 Class work on the Midland section. On this work their life is short. All engines of class are on Midland section. Upkeep rather heavy.*

GSR Class 646 0-6-0 Inchicore Class J2
MGWR Class B 1925/ 1931 Load Class B/ B

GSR (MGWR) No	Name	Built	Makers' No	Renumbered	Rebuilt	Withdrawn
646 (143)	*Canada*	6/1904	16128	1926	1916*	1933
647 (144)	*Australia*	6/1904	16129	1929	1917¶	1930
648 (145)	*India*	6/1904	16130	1926	1918¶	1939
649 (146)	*Africa*	6/1904	16131	1928	1919¶	1939

* Rebuilt with Belpaire superheated (Schmidt) boiler and piston valves
¶ Rebuilt with Belpaire superheated (Robinson) boiler and piston valves

Designer: Cusack **Built by North British Locomotive Co**

*** With Schmidt superheater:**

Boiler pressure – 175 lbs/ sq in
Cylinders – 18" x 26"
Piston valves – 8"
Driving wheels – 5' 3"
Wheel base – 7' 4" + 8' 11"
Locomotive length – 29' 5

Heating surfaces:
tubes – 150 sq ft
firebox – 842 sq ft
superheater – 211 sq ft
grate – 20 sq ft

Tractive effort – 19,890 lbs
Coal capacity – 6 tons
Water capacity – 3000 gal
Locomotive weight – 50 tons 3 cwt
Max axle loading – 17 tons 4 cwt

*** With Robinson superheater:**

Heating surfaces:
tubes – 150 sq ft
firebox – 844 sq ft
superheater – 170 sq ft
grate – 20 sq ft

Locomotive weight – 48 tons 3 cwt
Max axle loading – 17 tons 4 cwt

Soon after introduction of the Class A 4-4-0, which was significantly larger than previous passenger locomotives, it was decided to repeat the process with Class B, a larger 0-6-0 which shared the same size boiler. The result was the creation of the MGWR's most powerful goods engine which, as with Class A, was restricted by weight to operations between Dublin and Galway. These operational limitations were very likely the reason why the class was not increased and certainly they were unpopular with the GSR authorities, which accounts for their relatively early withdrawal. No 646 was actually withdrawn a year before its official withdrawal of 1933; No 648 was taken out of service in 1934. The fate of No 649 was more complex; it was actually taken out of service in 1933 and officially withdrawn the following year although nominally returned to stock in 1935 before final withdrawal in 1939. In reality both Nos 648 and 649 did little or no work after 1933, standing idle on the Inchicore scrap line.

When new, these locomotives were equipped with smaller tenders of 2500 gal capacity. Two or more of these were involved in the tender swaps described in the sections on Class A (GSR 545 / D5) Class H (GSR 619/ J6).

GSR Class 646/ J2 (MGWR Class B) No 646.
Real Photographs Co Ltd

GSR Class 650 MGWR Class K/ Ks — 2-4-0 — Inchicore Class G2 1925/ 1931 Load Class Q/ O

GSR (MGWR) No	Name	Built	Renumbered	Rebuilt	Withdrawn
650 (14)	*Racer*	6/1893	1926	1926*/ 1934§/ 1944¶/ 1947§	1959
651 (16)	*Rob Roy*	12/1895	1927	1927*/ 1935§/ 1951¶	1959
652 (18)	*Ranger*	6/1893	1926	1926*/ 1939§	1954
653 (19)	*Spencer*	1894	1926	1933§/ 1939¶/ 1942§	1963
654 (28)	*Clara*	3/1897	1926	1926*/ 1941§/ 1950¶	1962
655 (29)	*Clonsilla*	1897	1926	1926*/ 1934§/ 1954¶	1961
656 (30)	*Active*	4/1898	1926	1926*/ 1939§/ 1944¶/ 1951§	1957
657 (33)	*Arrow*	9/1898	1925	1925*/ 1939#/ 1953§	1961
658 (34)	*Aurora*	8/1898	1928	1925*/ 1935#/ 1940¶/ 1948#	1954
659 (13)	*Rapid*	6/1893	1926	1922*/ 1932§/ 1950#/ 1953¶	1961
660 (15)	*Rover*	12/1895	1928	1921*/ 1931§	1959
661 (17)	*Reindeer*	1894	1927	1923*/ 1933§/ 1950#	1959
662 (21)	*Swift*	5/1896	1925	1921*/ 1948¶	1955
663 (22)	*Samson*	9/1896	1928	1923*/ 1932§/ 1949¶	1959
664 (23)	*Sylph*	7/1896	1927	1924*/ 1930#/ 1937¶/ 1959§	1961
665 (24)	*Sprite*	1897	1928	1918*/ 1949§/ 1954#	1959
666 (27)	*Clifden*	8/1897	1926	1919*/ 1930#/ 1935§/ 1941¶/ 1949§	1957
667 (31)	*Alert*	11/1897	1927	1924*/ 1934§/ 1939¶/ 1943§	1957
668 (32)	*Ariel*	1/1898	1928	1924*/ 1935§	1959
– (20)	*Speedy*	1896	–	–	*(civil war loss)* 1923

Designer: Atock — **Built at Broadstone**

Rebuilt with boiler type:

* Round-topped superheated
§ Belpaire superheated type Y
\# Round-topped saturated (reversion to as-built condition)
¶ Round-topped superheated

MGWR Class K No 16 *Rob Roy* (later GSR Class 650/ G2 No 651) in original condition, on the Broadstone turntable in 1898.

L&GRP

As built:

Boiler pressure – 150 lbs/ sq in
Cylinders – 17" x 24"
Leading wheels – 4' 0"
Driving wheels – 5' 8"
Wheel base – 7' 0" + 8' 0"
Locomotive length – 26' 5¼"

Heating surfaces:
tubes – 1020 sq ft
firebox – 95 sq ft
grate – 16.5 sq ft

Tractive effort – 13,000 lbs
Coal capacity – 4 tons
Water capacity – 1700 or 2000 gal
Locomotive weight – 38 tons 5 cwt
Adhesive weight – circa 26 tons 3 cwt
Max axle loading – 15 tons 18 cwt

Rebuilt with boiler type:	Heating surfaces (sq ft):					
	Tubes	***firebox***	***superheater***	***grate***	***Boiler pressure***	***Weight***
* Round-topped superheated; reclassified Ks	*643*	*95*	*113*	*16.5*	*150 lbs/ sq in*	*37 tons 2 cwt to 37 tons 16 cwt*
# Round-topped saturated boiler	*835*	*99*	*–*	*16.75*	*150 lbs/ sq in*	*not recorded*
§ Belpaire superheated boiler type Y	*673*	*95*	*112*	*15.5*	*160 lbs/ sq in*	*not recorded*
¶ Round-topped superheated	*643*	*95*	*113*	*16.5*	*150 lbs/ sq in*	*not recorded*

This class comprised newly-built engines and replaced an earlier series of 2-4-0s which carried the same names. A variety of different cabs was fitted during late MGWR days and by the GSR. These are believed to be the years in which distinctive Atock 'fly away' cab was replaced:

No	Year	No	Year	No	Year	No	Year
650	1923	655	1935	660	1924	665	1928
651	1935	656	1936	661	1923	666	1930
652	1926	657	1925	662	1925	667	1924
653	1933	658	1925	663	1923	668	1924
654	1935	659	1922	664	1924		

These were Atock's last passenger locomotives and initially they worked premier services including the Limited Mails and heavy Dublin-Galway/ Sligo trains which could necessitate double-heading as far as Mullingar. Following introduction of Class A 4-4-0s they were relieved of these heavy duties and were found on a variety of work throughout the MGWR system. They were particularly associated with passenger trains on the Mayo and Sligo services until relieved by Classes C and F in the mid-1920s. They returned to the Sligo route in 1937 where they remained the principal passenger type until replaced by diesel railcars in the mid-1950s.

In their last years, they were also employed on suburban services on the ex-DSER section, and in working the Wexford Mail. They were highly regarded in that area and were remembered with considerable affection. Many considered the Class K to be the best of all MGWR designs, a view supported by the survival of some into the 1960s at which time they were among the last 2-4-0s at work anywhere in the world. They have been described as 'flying machines' when not overloaded.

1948 assessment: *Quite a good small passenger engine which will work most Midland Branches and some DSER section trains (local).*

GSR Class 650/ G2 (MGWR Class K) No 656 at Broadstone shed. As rebuilt with round-topped superheated boiler but retaining Atock 'fly away' cab. *CP Friel collection*

GSR Class 650/ G2 (MGWR Class K) No 662 as rebuilt with round-topped superheated boiler and modern cab at Inchicore in CIE days.

IRRSCollection

GSR Class 650/ G2 (MGWR Class K) No 664 as rebuilt with Belpaire saturated boiler but fitted with canopy-style cab. In ex-works condition in 1935. Although photograph was taken at Broadstone, the works there had by then closed.

G Coltas

GSR Class 650/ G2 (MGWR Class K) No 650 as rebuilt with Type Y Belpaire superheated boiler at Broadstone in 1938.

WA Camwell

Chapter 8
Locomotives of the narrow gauge companies

The narrow gauge companies originated independently to serve local needs but all shared the 3' 0" gauge which allowed the Great Southern Railways to transfer locomotives and rolling stock between systems, as required. The two companies that emanated from Cork had routes that paralleled arterial roads and, with the growth of motor transport, were early closure casualties. After about 12 months in store, the entire fleet of the ex-Cork Blackrock & Passage Railway was moved to the Cavan & Leitrim Railway Section and one of the 0-4-4Ts (No 6K) of the Cork & Muskerry Light Railway was transferred the Schull & Skibbereen Light Railway section.

With the decline of traffic on Tralee & Dingle Light Railway section, more migrations took place. In 1941, two 2-6-0Ts (Nos 3T and 4T) were transferred to the CLR, followed by the unique 2-6-2T (No 5T) in 1949. In CIÉ days, two other 2-6-0Ts of the TDLR (Nos 6T and 8T) moved to the West Clare Railway, in 1953 and 1954 respectively. One of these (No 6T) moved on again in 1957, also to the CLR. The concentration of locomotives from three pre-amalgamation railways on the CLR section, which remained exclusively steam operated until closure in 1959, made this system the focus of attention from enthusiasts. The application of number suffixes did have one practical benefit in the closing years of the CLR as Nos 3L and 4L operated alongside Nos 3T and 4T

All the locomotives of the WCR remained on that system because the size and weight of its locomotives prevented their use elsewhere. For example, the smallest WCR engine was only slightly lighter than CLR 0-6-4T No 9 which had caused much damage to that system's trackwork.

The steady and inexorable decline of the narrow gauge meant that the locomotive fleet inherited in 1925 was adequate to meet demand. No significant modifications were carried out beyond adjustment of the height of couplings in connection with transfer between systems.

Cavan & Leitrim Railway

This railway provided a cross-country link between Dromod (on the ex-MGWR route from Mullingar to Sligo) and Belturbet, the terminus of the Great Northern Railway branch from Ballyhaise on the Clones to Cavan section. There was also a branch from Ballinamore to Arigna. Work commenced on construction of the main line in 1883 and on the Arigna branch (always known as 'the tramway') in 1886. The railway opened in 1887 and the total route mileage from Belturbet to Dromod was 33¾ miles, while the branch from Ballinamore to Arigna was 14¾ miles long. A final extension of just over four miles from Arigna to the coal mines at Derreenavoggy was commenced in 1918 and completed in 1920. The main station and works were at Ballinamore.

Traffic on the main line consisted of passengers, goods and agricultural produce, usually conveyed in mixed trains. The extension to the coal mines introduced quite heavy mineral traffic to the system with up to six trains a day. Despite such traffic levels, services remained almost solely in the hands of the eight original locomotives until 1934. The arrival of the ex-CBPR 2-4-2Ts in that year greatly eased the situation, as did the later import of ex-TDLR locomotives. The railway, always steam hauled, was a late narrow gauge survivor because of the coal traffic which had to be transhipped by hand onto broad gauge wagons at either Dromod or Belturbet. Following the introduction of road transport to ship the coal from Arigna direct to industrial consumers, the section closed on 1 April 1959.

Part of the CLR has been restored at the Dromod terminus as a tourist line working over a distance of half a mile and using rolling stock from the TDLR and WCR. A small museum has been opened in the former station building at Belturbet.

GSR Class 1L — 4-4-0T — Inchicore Class DN2

C & L Nos 1 to 8

C&L No	GSR No	Name	Makers' No	Built	Withdrawn
1	1	*Isabel*	2612	4/1887	1949
2	2L	*Kathleen*	2613	5/1887	1960 Preserved
3	3L	*Lady Edith*	2614	6/1887	1959 Preserved
4	4L	*Violet*	2615	7/1887	1960
5	5	*Gertrude*	2616	9/1887	1925
6	6	*May*	2617	10/1887	1927
7	7	*Olive*	2618	11/1887	1945
8	8L	*(Queen Victoria)§*	2619	12/1887	1959

§ Name removed in 1921

Built by Robert Stephenson & Co

*Boiler pressure – 150 lbs/ sq in**	*Heating surfaces:*	*Tractive effort – 11,900 lbs*
Cylinders – 14" x 20"	*tubes – 500 sq ft*	*Coal capacity – 40 cu ft/ I ton*
Bogie wheels – 2' 1"	*firebox – 48 sq ft*	*Water capacity – 600 gal*
Driving wheels – 3' 6"	*grate – 9.0 sq ft*	*Locomotive weight – 27 tons 0 cwt*
Wheel base – 5' 0"+ 5' 9" + 6' 0"		*Adhesive weight – 16 tons 0 cwt*
		Max axle loading – 9 tons 5 cwt

** Between 1929 and 1931, the following locomotives worked at reduced boiler pressures: Nos 1/ 4 at 130 lbs/ sq in; Nos 2/ 7/ 8 at 140 lbs/ sq in. Apparently they also worked at these reduced pressures between 1946 and 1950.*

This was numerically the largest narrow gauge class in Ireland and appears to have been ideally suited to the CLR's needs. By June 1924, the average mileage of Nos 1 to 4 was about 500,000. Nos 5 to 8 which were originally mainly used on the tramway (with their driving wheels encased behind protective sheeting – removed pre-1924) had averaged about 300,000 miles by this date. These were impressive mileage figures for narrow gauge locomotives. All had operated from new without brick arches as this condition was believed to favour the poor quality Arigna coal. The GSR installed brick arches in 1925 to all of the class.

Nos 3, 5 and 6 were in poor condition at the amalgamation; only No 3 received works attention to restore it to a proper working state. No 7 was sent to Inchicore in 1939 for repairs which were not carried out; in 1940 it was cannibalised to repair No 2 but its remains were not officially scrapped for another five years. The class members that survived until 1959/ 1960 were by far the longest-lived members of the GSR narrow gauge fleet.

Cavan & Leitrim Railway No 3 *Lady Edith* (Later GSR Class 1L/ Inchicore Class DN2 No 3 (For rear view of cab, see the background to the right hand photograph on page 224).

IRRS collection

Cavan & Leitrim Railway No 7 *Olive* (Later GSR Class 1L/ Inchicore Class DN2 No 7) as originally equipped for working the Arigna roadside tramway section.

IRRS collection

GSR Class 9L **0-6-4T** **Inchicore Class HN1**

C & L No 9

C&L No	GSR No	Name	Makers' No	Built	Withdrawn
9	9	*King Edward*	3136	7/1904	1934

Built by Robert Stephenson & Co

Boiler pressure – 150 lbs/ sq in	*Heating surfaces:*	*Tractive effort – 14,600 lbs*
Cylinders – 15" x 20"	*tubes – 681 sq ft*	*Coal capacity – 70 cu ft/ 1½ tons*
Driving wheels – 3' 3"	*firebox – 66 sq ft*	*Water capacity – 700 gal*
Bogie wheels – 2' 1"	*grate – 14 sq ft*	*Locomotive weight – 36 tons 15 cwt*
Wheel base – 3' 8½" + 3' 8½" + 5' 10" + 5' 0"		*Adhesive weight – 25 tons 11 cwt*
		Max axle loading – 11 tons 5 cwt

GSR Class 9L/ Inchicore Class HN1 No 9 *King Edward* (Cavan & Leitrim Railway No 9).

IRRS collection

This locomotive was designed to haul loads of 132 tons up a 1 in 30 gradient at 12 mph. It was intended to cope with curves as tight as two chains, and for this it was fitted with flangeless trailing driving wheels. The considerable advance in weight and power over the 4-4-0Ts was rarely realised as the long rigid wheelbase combined with the heavy axle loading caused spreading of the rails, particularly on bends. So much damage to track was caused that its use became subject to special Board permission in CLR days. The locomotive was found to work rather more satisfactorily in reverse, ie with the bogie leading, so the cow catcher was remounted below the bunker.

It was used quite frequently during the 1916-8 period, leading to much track damage and complaints from permanent way personnel. Thereafter it was virtually withdrawn, and was unsuccessfully offered for sale in 1922. Following the amalgamation, it was used only very occasionally when motive power was in short supply, and became completely surplus following the transfer of the four 2-4-2Ts from the Cork Blackrock & Passage section.

Cork Blackrock & Passage Railway

Originally a broad gauge line seven miles long from Cork Albert Street to Passage which opened in 1850, the decision was taken in 1896 to extend the route and convert it to 3' 0" gauge. The route re-opened as a narrow gauge line, 16½ miles long from Cork via Passage and Monkstown to Crosshaven. The CBPR was a suburban company and enjoyed some unique features for the Irish narrow gauge. An intensive timetable was operated, primarily for the transport of commuters and day trippers; goods traffic was never significant (although almost 40 coal wagons were to find their way to the ex-CLR section after closure). The railway suffered heavy damage during the Civil War with substantial interruption to timetables.

The section from Cork to the first major station of Blackrock was double track, singled by the GSR in 1927. The CBPR always faced intense competition from electric tramway and road services, which was the reason for its closure in 1932.

The first three (broad gauge) locomotives had been 2-2-2WTs numbered 1 to 3. The only narrow gauge locomotives used on the narrow gauge were the four 2-4-2Ts whose numbers continued in the series after that of the singles.

GSR Class 4P (later 10L) — 2-4-2T — Inchicore Class FN1

CBPR Nos 4 to 7

CBPR No	GSR No (First)	GSR No* (Second)	Makers' No	Built	Withdrawn* (Final)
4	4p	10L	5561	1899	1959
5	5p	11L	5562	1899	1936
6	6p	12L	5563	1899	1959
7	7p	13L	5564	1899	1954

Built by Neilson & Co

* All four locomotives were withdrawn in 1933 and stored at Inchicore; in 1934 they were renumbered, given new GSR Class 10L, and transferred to the CLR section.

Boiler pressure – 160 lbs/ sq in
Cylinders – 14½" x 22"
Pony wheels – 3' 0"
Driving wheels – 4' 6"
Trailing wheels – 3' 0"
Wheel base 6' 6" + 8' 0" + 6' 6"
Locomotive length – 34' (estimated over buffer beams)

Heating surfaces:
tubes – 721 sq ft
firebox – 80 sq ft
grate – 12 sq ft

Tractive effort – 11,650 lbs
Coal capacity – 2½ tons
Water capacity – 1200 gal
Locomotive weight – 37 tons 3 cwt
Adhesive weight – 21 tons 17 cwt
Max axle loading – 11 tons 11 cwt

GSR Class 4P (later 10L)/ Inchicore Class FN1 (Cork Blackrock & Passage Railway No 5P) at Cork Albert Street in 1931. *L&GRP*

Part of the fascination of the Cavan & Leitrim section in later years was the variety of motive power that was transferred there. An unidentified ex-CBPR 2-4-2T stands at Ballinamore in company with ex-Cavan & Leitrim No 3L The rundown condition of the C & L fleet in its later years is readily apparent. *Author's collection*

These were noteworthy in being of modern design with the largest driving wheel diameter on the Irish narrow gauge lines. As a result they were able to work at relatively high speeds.

They might have appeared unsuitable for the C&L section, a rural system with quite significant goods traffic, but in fact they performed well on the main line (Belturbet to Dromod). Shortly their after arrival, No 13L was tested on the tramway section from Ballinamore to Arigna but encountered severe difficulties, which led to the type being banned from that route.

Cork & Muskerry Light Railway

This was a partly urban and partly rural light railway, while also providing convenient access to the tourist destination of Blarney Castle. The railway was planned as a main line to Blarney (8½ miles from Cork) which opened in 1887. The city terminus was at Western Road and for four miles followed the public highway. For a little more than half of this distance, this road was also used also by the electrified Cork City Tramway whose services competed directly with those of the CMLR. A branch off the Blarney route to Coachford (15½ miles from Cork) opened in 1888. A further 8½ mile branch from St Anne's to Donoughmore was opened in 1893.

A notable incident occurred on 6 September 1927 when the 7.45 am mixed train from Donoughmore hauled by 4-4-0T No 8 had a violent collision with a steam roller engaged on repairs of the adjoining road between Carrigrohane and Victoria Cross station (quite close to Cork City). There were no injuries but considerable damage was caused to the train, with derailment of two coaches – and also to the steam roller.

Despite the apparent traffic potential offered by it serving the republic's second largest city, the railway was exposed to intense road competition. Further, having to make use of four miles of public highway into the city itself did not help its case. Competition from omnibuses became increasingly acute and this was the principal reason for closure of the system in 1934.

GSR Class 1K — 4-4-0T — Inchicore Class DN6

CMLR Nos 1 & 2

CMLR No	GSR No	Name	Makers' No*	Built	Withdrawn
1	1K	*City of Cork*	137	1887	1934
2	2K	*Coachford*	136	1887	1934

Built by Falcon Railway Plant Works

(No 3 *St. Annes* was also supplied by Falcon in 1887, Works No 138*; withdrawn 1924)

* Order of works numbers is uncertain

GSR Class 1K/ Inchicore Class DN6 No 1k (Cork & Muskerry Light Railway No 1) at Cork, Western Road in 1931.
L&GRP

*Boiler pressure – 140 lbs/ sq in**	*Heating surfaces:*	*Tractive effort – 6,720 lbs*
Cylinders – 11½" x 18"	*tubes & firebox – 472 sq ft*	*Coal capacity – 1 ton*
Bogie wheels – 2' 0"	*grate – 8.25 sq ft*	*Water capacity – 500 gal*
Driving wheels – 3' 6"		*Locomotive weight – 28 tons 0 cwt*
Wheel base – 4' 10½" + 4' 4½" + 6' 0"		*Adhesive weight – 16 tons 0 cwt (est.)*
		Max axle loading – 9 tons 0 cwt (est.)

** From 1929, No 2K worked at 145 lbs/ sq in*

These locomotives were built as 2-4-0Ts for the opening of the railway but were converted to 4-4-0Ts in about 1889. They were fitted with Joy's valve gear.

GSR Class 5K (later 6S) 0-4-4T Inchicore Class EN1

CMLR Nos 5 & 6

CMLR No	GSR No (First)	GSR No (Second)	Name	Makers' No	Built	Withdrawn
5	5K	see comments	*Donoughmore*	180	1892	1935
6	6K	6S	*(The) Muskerry*	200	1893	1954

Built by Thomas Green & Sons (Leeds)

GSR Class 5K (later 6S)/ Inchicore Class EN1 No 6S (Cork & Muskerry Light Railway No 6). This photograph depicts the locomotive after transfer to the Schull & Skibbereen section.

Real Photographs Co Ltd

Boiler pressure – 140 lbs/ sq in	*Heating surfaces:*	*Tractive effort – 11,100 lbs*
Cylinders – 14" x 20"	*tubes & firebox – 600 sq ft*	*Coal capacity – 1 ton*
Driving wheels – 3' 6"	*grate – 10.5 sq ft*	*Water capacity – 500 gal*
Bogie wheels – 2' 0"		*Locomotive weight – 23 tons 19 cwt*
Wheel base – 6' 0" + 5' 2½" + 3' 8"		*Adhesive weight – 16 tons 12 cwt*
		Max axle loading – 8 tons 8 cwt

These locomotives were built for the Donoughmore Extension Railway. In 1935 they were transferred to Inchicore and dismantled. Some sources claim that No 5K was later reconditioned for service on the Tralee & Dingle section and renumbered 9T. However, this was a transfer on paper only as the locomotive was withdrawn that year and some of its components were used in the reconditioning of 6K which was then transferred to the Schull & Skibbereen section as No 6S.

On the SSLR, this locomotive encountered problems and had to be returned to Inchicore for modification. The coupling heights had to be adjusted to match the indigenous rolling stock and the corners of the buffer beams were trimmed off to provide adequate clearance at platforms and goods/ cattle docks. The bunker was too small and a suitable extension was added (the increased capacity is not recorded). A curiosity was the fitting of dual brake hoses at the bunker end as the original single hose would not reach the train hoses when traversing a sharp bend. Once these difficulties had been overcome, No 6S did useful work up to closure in 1947, and was the last locomotive in use.

GSR Class 7K 4-4-0T Inchicore Class DN3

CMLR No 7

CMLR No	GSR No	Name	Makers' No	Built	Withdrawn
7	7K	*Peake*	274	1898	1935

Built by Brush Electrical Engineering
(successors to Falcon Railway Plant Works)

GSR Class 7K/ Inchicore Class DN3 No 7K (Cork & Muskerry Light Railway No 7). *Real Photographs Co Ltd*

Boiler pressure – 140 lbs/ sq in	*Heating surfaces:*	*Tractive effort – 10,690 lbs*
Cylinders – 14" x 22"	*tubes – 590 sq ft*	*Coal capacity – 1 ton 5 cwt*
Bogie wheels – 2' 3"	*firebox – 56 sq ft*	*Water capacity – 700 gal*
Driving wheels – 4' 0"	*grate – 10.5 sq ft*	*Locomotive weight – 28 tons 0 cwt*
Coupled wheel base – 6' 0"		*Max axle loading – not recorded*
Total wheel base – 17' 5"		

This was the largest locomotive in the fleet and fitted with outsized chimney and dome.

GSR Class 8K — 4-4-0T — Inchicore Class DN7

CMLR No 8

CMLR No	GSR No	Name	Makers' No	Built	Withdrawn
8	8K	*Dripsey*	307	1904	1935

Built by Brush Electrical Engineering
(successors to Falcon Railway Plant Works)

GSR Class 8K/ Inchicore Class DN7 No 8K (Cork & Muskerry Light Railway No 8). *Real Photographs Co Ltd*

Boiler pressure – 140 lbs/ sq in	*Heating surfaces:*	*Tractive effort – 6,430 lbs*
Cylinders – 12" x 18"	*tubes – 590 sq ft*	*Coal capacity – 1 ton 5 cwt*
Bogie wheels – 2' 3"	*firebox – 56 sq ft*	*Water capacity – 700 gal*
Driving wheels – 4' 0"	*grate – 10.5 sq ft*	*Locomotive weight – 29 tons 0 cwt*
Wheel base – 4' 6" + 5' 9" + 6' 0"		
Total wheel base – 17' 5"		

This locomotive was similar to No 7 but smaller in some dimensions. It achieved fame by colliding with a steam roller, as described above.

GSR Class 4K — 4-4-0T — Inchicore Class DN1

CMLR No 4

CMLR No	GSR No	Name	Makers' No	Built	Withdrawn
4	4	*Blarney*	1200	1919	1927

Built by Hunslet Engine Co

Cork & Muskerry Light Railway No 4 as built (later GSR Class 4K/ Inchicore Class DN1). *Real Photographs Co Ltd*

Boiler pressure – 160 lbs/ sq in	*Heating surfaces:*	*Tractive effort – 10,950 lbs*
Cylinders – 13" x 20"	*tubes – 402 sq ft*	*Coal capacity – 1 tons*
Bogie wheels – 2' 0"	*firebox – 65 sq ft*	*Water capacity – 600 gal*
Driving wheels – 3' 6"	*grate – 8.25 sq ft*	*Locomotive weight – 28 tons 0 cwt*
Coupled wheel base – 6' 0"		*Adhesive weight – 19 tons 17 cwt*
Total wheel base – 15' 6"		*Max axle loading – 10 tons 10 cwt*

This locomotive was ordered before World War One but with delayed delivery, it actually did very little work. The shortness of its life was unusual by Irish standards and it has been speculated that either the design was in some way unsuitable for CMLR conditions or the axle loading was excessive for bridges that had been damaged during the Civil War. Had it survived until the programme of inter-system transfers commenced, its virtually new condition might have guaranteed it a working career elsewhere. Some sources state its number as '9' as this engine was the company's 9th and last. The first No 4 *Blarney* (an 0-4-2T) on the CMLR had been withdrawn in 1911.

Schull & Skibbereen Light Railway

This was the most southerly of the narrow gauge railways, making a connection with the Cork Bandon & South Coast Railway by means of an awkwardly laid out interchange station at Skibbereen. From there it ran in a westerly direction to Schull, with a short extension on to a pier beyond the terminus. Total route mileage was just over 15 miles. Much of the line, which was poorly and lightly laid, ran immediately adjacent to the public Skibbereen-Schull road with some stiff gradients and sharp curves. Its close proximity to a main arterial road for most of its route made its comparatively late survival remarkable. The line was closed because of fuel shortages from April 1944 until December 1945; services were suspended for the last time in January 1947 but it was not formally abandoned until early 1952.

GSR Class 2S — 0-4-0T — Inchicore Class MN1

SSLR No 2

SSLR No	GSR No	Name	Makers' No	Built	Withdrawn
2	2	*Ida*	B	1886	1926

Built by Dick, Kerr (Kilmarnock)

(The reported works number is considered unreliable)

Boiler pressure – 140 lbs/ sq in	*Heating surfaces:*	*Tractive effort – 5,730 lbs*
Cylinders – 9½" x 16"	*not recorded*	*Coal capacity – not recorded*
Driving wheels – 2' 6"		*Water capacity – 355 gal*
Wheel base – 6' 0"		*Locomotive weight – 18 tons 0 cwt*

One of the Schull & Skibbereen 0-4-0T tram engines in original condition.

IRRS collection

This was the last survivor of three fully enclosed tramway-type locomotives built for the opening of the line. In original form these locomotives had encountered numerous difficulties. Rebuilding of No 2 in 1905 created a more practical machine and resulted in its outliving the others by several years. At the rebuilding, it was fitted with a larger boiler with Belpaire firebox and extended smokebox, supplied by Nasmyth, Wilson & Co. Some of the body cladding was removed, giving it a slightly more conventional appearance. Where the rebuilding work took place is unknown but it has been suggested that the Cork Bandon & South Coast Railway might have been involved. In its rebuilt form, No 2 was a substantially improved locomotive and was noted at the head of some quite heavy trains. By 1925, it was used only in emergencies. Some sources state that it was not taken into GSR stock although this conflicts with the allocation of GSR/ Inchicore classifications.

GSR Class 2S/ Inchicore Class MN1 No 2 *Ida* (Schull & Skibbereen Light Railway No 2) at Skibbereen in 1924. The locomotive appears to have been pulled out of its shed especially to be photographed.
K Nunn

GSR Class 4S — 4-4-0T — Inchicore Class DN5

SSLR No 4

SSLR No	GSR No	Name	Makers' No	Built	Withdrawn
4	4S	*Erin*	341*	1888	1954

Built by Nasmyth, Wilson & Co

* Other sources state 342

GSR Class 4S/ Inchicore Class DN5 No 4S (Schull & Skibbereen Light Railway No 4) in 1938.
HC Casserley

Boiler pressure – 150 lbs/ sq in	*Heating surfaces:*	*Tractive effort – 8,260 lbs*
Cylinders – 12" x 18"	*tubes – 453 sq ft*	*Coal capacity – 10 cwt*
Bogie wheels – 1' 10"	*firebox – 56 sq ft*	*Water capacity – 500 gal §*
Driving wheels – 3' 4"	*grate – 9 sq ft*	*Locomotive weight – 24 tons 6 cwt*
Wheel base – 4' 3" + 5' 4½" + 5' 6"		*Adhesive weight – 18 tons 10 cwt*
		Max axle loading – 9 tons 11 cwt
		§ GSR diagram states 600 gal

Relaxation of tramway regulations permitted the use of more conventional designs by the time this locomotive was introduced. No 4 was a great improvement over the tram engines in riding qualities and haulage capacity; it had the distinction of being the first in the British Isles to carry a Belpaire firebox.

GSR Class 1S — 4-4-0T — Inchicore Class DN4

SSLR Nos

SSLR No	GSR No	Name	Makers' No	Built	Withdrawn
1	1	*Gabriel*	1085	5/1906	1937
3	3S	*Kent*	1356	3/1914	1954

Built by Peckett

GSR Class 1S/ Inchicore Class DN4 No 1 *Gabriel* (Schull & Skibbereen Light Railway No 1)
Real Photographs Co Ltd

GSR Class 1S/ Inchicore Class DN4 No 3S No 3S *Kent* (Schull & Skibbereen Light Railway No 3) in 1936.
IRRS collection

Dimensions of No 1:

Boiler pressure – 160 lbs/ sq in
Cylinders – 12" x 18"
Bogie wheels – 2' 0"
Driving wheels – 3' 0½"
Wheel base – 4' 0" + 5' 6" + 5' 6"
Length – 26' 2½"

Heating surfaces:
tubes – 492 sq ft
firebox – 83 sq ft
grate – 8 sq ft

Tractive effort – 9,650 lbs
Coal capacity – 1 ton 5 cwt
Water capacity – 600 gal
Locomotive weight – 26 tons 10 cwt
Adhesive weight – 20 tons 15 cwt
Max axle loading –10 tons 15 cwt

Dimensions of No 3S as for No 1, except:

Length – 24' 11"

Heating surfaces:
tubes – 454 sq ft
firebox – 60 sq ft
grate – 7.6 sq ft

Coal capacity – 18 cwt
Water capacity – 600 gal
Locomotive weight – 25 tons 10 cwt
Adhesive weight – 20 tons 0 cwt
Max axle loading – 10 tons 5 cwt

The 4-4-0T type had proved satisfactory on the SSLR but significant improvements were introduced with No 1 including more appropriate wheel diameters, greater tractive effort, and better adhesive weight. No 1 *Gabriel* was introduced to replace the original tramway 0-4-0T No 1 *Marion* while No 3 was a direct replacement of the original tramway 0-4-0T No 3 *Ilen*.

The name borne by No 3 was subject to local political disputation. It was originally named *Conciliation* but the alternative of 'Hibernia' was soon proposed and then rejected. Then it was re-titled *Kent*, the nameplate being manufactured by a SSLR fitter – one Paddy Murphy – out of brass boiler tubing. A peculiar feature was the unusual shape of the 'K' which was attributed to the fitter being unfamiliar with this letter (there is no 'K' in the Irish language).

No 1 was worn out by 1936 and following withdrawal, its cylinders were fitted to No 3.

Tralee & Dingle Light Railway

Construction commenced in 1888 to open up the remote Dingle Peninsula. Services started in 1891 over a distance of 32¼ miles from Tralee to Dingle together with a six mile branch from Castlegregory Junction to Castlegregory. The gradient profile made it a difficult line to work. The first ten miles from Tralee to Castlegregory Junction were level, but prone to flooding in parts. From the latter point the line climbed 650 feet in four miles with gradients as steep as 1 in 29.

There was a short branch to the pier at Dingle which fell into disuse around 1935. The railway survived on a minimum of track maintenance with a full service until roads in the area were metalled in the late 1930s, and traffic moved to competing buses and lorries. The Castlegregory branch closed completely in 1939 concurrent with the withdrawal of passenger services on the main line. A daily goods train ran from then until 1947 when coal shortages led to its withdrawal. A monthly cattle special for Dingle Fair was later restored and ran until June 1953 when the ex-TDLR section closed completely.

Over forty years later, part of the route was re-laid from a new station called Tralee Basin to Blennerville Windmill for tourist trains, hauled by 2-6-2T No 5 which had been recovered from the USA and fully restored.

--- o O o ---

Contrary to the usual policy of changing number and/ or suffix on transfer to another section, none of the running numbers borne by TDLR locomotives were changed.

Dates of transfers: No 3T to CLR – 1942; No 4T to CLR – 1946; No 5T to CLR – 1950; No 6T to WCR 1953 then to CLR 1957; No 8T to WCR – 1954.

GSR Class 1T **2-6-0T** **Inchicore Class KN2**

TDLR Nos

TDLR No	GSR No	Makers' No	Built	Withdrawn
1	1T	477	2/1889	1954
2	2T	478	2/1889	1954
3	3T	479	5/1889	1959
6	6T	677	7/1898	1960
8	8T	1051	1910	1955

Built by Hunslet Engine Co

GSR Class 1T/ Inchicore Class KN2 No 3T (Tralee & Dingle Light Railway No 3). At work on the Cavan & Leitrim section in 1957.

DG Coakham

GSR Class 1T/ Inchicore Class KN2 No 6T (Tralee & Dingle Light Railway No 6). Rear view of ex-Cavan & Leitrim No 2L in background.

Authors' collection

Boiler pressure – 150 lbs/ sq in	*Heating surfaces:*	*Tractive effort – 10,630 lbs*
Cylinders – 13" x 18"	*tubes – 494 sq ft*	*Coal capacity – 1 ton 10 cwt*
Pony wheels – 2' 0"	*firebox – 66 sq ft*	*Water capacity – 750 gal*
Driving wheels – 3' 0½"	*grate – 9.75 sq ft*	*Locomotive weight – see below*
*Wheel base – 6' 10" + 4' 3" + 4' 6"**		*Adhesive weight – 23 tons 16 cwt*
		Max axle loading – 8 tons 10 cwt

** Another source states 6' 11" + 4' 3½" + 4' 6"*

These locomotives were fitted with outside Walschaerts valve gear and flangeless centre drivers. They were the main source of motive power for the TDLR and are remembered for their sterling work during the final years of operations. The design weight was 30 tons 15 cwt, which may have risen to 32 tons. The Inchicore recorded weight of 38 tons is generally believed to be incorrect.

GSR Class 5T — 2-6-2T — Inchicore Class PN2

TDLR Nos

TDLR No	GSR No	Makers' No	Built	Withdrawn
5	5T	555	1892	1959 Preserved

Built by Hunslet Engine Co

GSR Class 5T/ Inchicore Class PN2 No 5T (Tralee & Dingle Light Railway No 5) at Ballinamore.
Authors' collection

Boiler pressure – 150 lbs/ sq in	*Heating surfaces:*	*Tractive effort – 11,460 lbs*
Cylinders – 13½" x 18"	*tubes – 531 sq ft*	*Coal capacity – 17 cwt*
Pony wheels – 2' 0"	*firebox – 70 sq ft*	*Water capacity – 750 gal*
Driving wheels – 3' 0½"	*grate – 10.7 sq ft*	*Locomotive weight – 39 tons 0 cwt*
Trailing wheels – 2' 0"		*Max axle loading – not recorded*
Wheel base – 6' 11" + 4' 6" + 4' 6" + 5' 3"		

This was the first inside framed 2-6-2T built for a narrow gauge line in these islands. Originally equipped as an oil burner with Holden apparatus in which form it was successful, it was converted to coal firing in 1893. No 5 was worked very hard during the 1930s and 1940s and was the favoured locomotive for the daily goods service. In 1944, it was the subject of unsuccessful turf-burning experiments and by 1948 was stored in run-down condition at Tralee shed awaiting general overhaul. Following overhaul in 1949, No 5 was transferred to the CLR section where it was again heavily used. After withdrawal it survived in preservation as described above.

GSR Class 4T — 2-6-0T — Inchicore Class KN1

TDLR Nos

TDLR No	GSR No	Makers' No	Built	Withdrawn
4*	4T	836	1903	1959
7	7	800	1902	1928

Built by Kerr, Stuart

* Originally No 8; renumbered in 1908

Tralee & Dingle Light Railway No 7 (later GSR Class 4T/ Inchicore Class KN1 No 7) at Castlegregory Junction in 1924. *K Nunn*

GSR Class 4T/ Inchicore Class KN1 No 4 (Tralee & Dingle Light Railway No 4). Depicted in CIE days at Ballinamore. *Photomatic Ltd*

As originally built:

Boiler pressure – 140 lbs/ sq in
Cylinders – 12½" x 20"
Pony wheels – 2' 0"
Driving wheels – 3' 0"
Wheel base – 6' 0" + 4' 6" + 4' 6"

Heating surfaces:
tubes – 431 sq ft
firebox – 47 sq ft
grate – 7.5 sq ft

Tractive effort – 10,330 lbs
Coal capacity – 1 ton
Water capacity – 750 gal
Locomotive weight – 31 tons 0 cwt
Max axle loading – not recorded

No 4T as modified:

Boiler pressure – 160 lbs/ sq in
Cylinders – 13½" x 20"

Tractive effort – 13,770 lbs

Nominally more powerful than the Hunslet 4-4-0Ts, these standard products of Kerr, Stuart were unpopular on the TDLR. They proved inferior in performance and, most importantly for this hilly line, in brake power. Their inside Stephenson's link motion was hard to service compared with the ready accessibility of the outside Walschaerts motion of the Hunslet locomotives. Before 1908, No 4 was modified with higher boiler pressure and larger diameter cylinders but these measures brought no noticeable improvement in performance; No 7 was thus left in original condition.

Both locomotives were used as little as possible on the TDLR section and No 7 was withdrawn when re-boilering was due. No 4 continued in service being used mainly on the Castlegregory branch and then only when absolutely necessary following closure of that route. On transfer to the ex-CLR section, it was unpopular at first due to the unsuitability of Arigna coal in the small narrow firebox. However once enginemen mastered a different firing technique, No 4 was used intensively on passenger services and lasted long enough for employment on demolition trains.

West Clare Railway

This railway was incorporated in 1884 and the first section opened from Ennis (where it connected with the broad gauge) to Miltown Malbay in 1887, a distance of 27 miles. Later extensions from Miltown Malbay, owned by the associated South Clare Railway, took the main route to Moyasta Junction where a connection was made with the Kilkee-Kilrush line of that railway. Ennis to Kilkee was considered the main line; Moyasta junction was the only triangular narrow gauge junction in these islands. The complete network (total mileage of 52¾ miles) was open by 1892, and for all intents and purposes it was known as the West Clare Railway.

Other than the first three 0-6-0Ts, the last of which was withdrawn in 1916, the locomotives on the WCR were substantially larger than those on the other narrow gauge lines. This reflected the difficult nature of the route with some steep gradients, many level crossings, and several miles in country exposed to severe Atlantic gales. Steam survived until 1955 when the line was completely dieselised but this modernisation programme did not ensure long term survival as the entire section closed in 1961.

In 1984, a society was formed to preserve remnants of the WCR at Moyasta junction and to create an interpretative centre recording the history of the railway. In 1990, sufficient funding became available to purchase the station house, rebuild the platform, relay 600 yards of track, and reconstruct the signal boxes. Two replica carriages have been constructed to be operated in due course with the restored 0-6-2T No 5.

--- o O o ---

The GSR inherited 11 locomotives in six different classes from the WCR, all in the large engine category by narrow gauge standards. Most of the fleet was in good condition with two locomotives less than three years old. Despite the diversity of types, the two surviving 0-6-2Ts and the four 2-6-2Ts shared many leading dimensions and had interchangeable boilers. Of the 4-6-0Ts, all but No 10 shared the same size boiler. Generally speaking the boilers and fireboxes were in good condition, although the mechanical condition of some engines was poor. Nonetheless, apart from two early withdrawals of 2-6-2Ts in 1925 and 1928, the remaining fleet was able to cope well with all traffic until dieselisation of the system in the 1950s. This was in contrast to the CLR system where in the final years, services could only be sustained with locomotives cascaded from other, closed sections.

GSR Class 5C — 0-6-2T — Inchicore Class IN1

WCR Nos 5, 6

WCR No	GSR No	Name	Makers' No	Built	Withdrawn
5	5C	*Slieve Callan*	2890	1892	1959 Preserved
6	6C	*Saint Senan*	2891	1892	1956

Built by Dubs (Glasgow)

(No 7 *Lady Inchiquin* was also supplied by Dubs in 1892, Makers' No 2892; withdrawn 1922)

Boiler pressure – 150 lbs/ sq in
Cylinders – 15" x 20"
Driving wheels – 3' 6" (previously 4' 0")
Trailing wheels – 3' 6" (previously 4' 0")
Wheel base – 4' 9" + 4' 9" + 5' 6"
Locomotive length – 30' 4"

Heating surfaces:
tubes – 627 sq ft
firebox – 75 sq ft
grate – 11.18 sq ft

Tractive effort – 13,660 lbs (previously 11,950 lb)
Coal capacity – 2 tons
Water capacity – 938 gal
Locomotive weight – 35 tons 12 cwt
Max axle loading – 9 tons 3 cwt

Left: GSR Class 5C/ Inchicore Class IN1 No 6C (West Clare Railway No 6).
Authors' collection

These locomotives were nominally introduced for service on the South Clare Railway but were used indiscriminately with the earlier 0-6-0Ts throughout the West and South Clare network. They were the first of the large engines to work on the system. Certain features were modern for their time, with screw reverse and twin injectors rather than pumps. At first the riding was poor and these locomotives were hard on the track making them unpopular with the civil engineer. Some improvement was achieved by the reduction in wheel diameters and later by adjustments to the springing. There is no definite information to confirm when these modifications were carried out but they were possibly completed by 1914. It is known that 3' 6" wheels were considered in the original design process. The use of trailing wheels with the same diameter as the drivers was a most unusual feature.

The open sided cabs were uncomfortable in the face of Atlantic gales and the front part of the cut-out was reduced by the semi-permanent installation of a timber shutter. The early troubles were mainly associated with No 5, which apparently did not afflict Nos 6 and 7. Nonetheless, No 5 turned out to be a survivor and worked right through to the end of steam whereas No 7 had been withdrawn prior to the amalgamation.

GSR Class 2C — 2-6-2T — Inchicore Class PN1

WCR Nos 2, 4, 8, 9

WCR No	GSR No	Name	Builder	Makers' No	Built	Rebuilt	Withdrawn
2	2C	*Ennis*	Thos Green (Leeds)	234	10/1900	1950	1955
4	4	*Liscannor*	Thos Green (Leeds)	236	6/1901	–	1928
8	8	*Lisdoonvarna*	Dubs (Glasgow)	3169	1894	–	1925
9	9C	*Fergus*	Thos Green (Leeds)	229	11/1898	–	1954

Nos 2, 4, 9:

Boiler pressure – 150 lbs/ sq in
Cylinders – 15" x 20"
Pony wheels – 2' 6"
Driving wheels – 3' 6"
Trailing wheels – 2' 6"
Wheel base – 4' 3" + 4' 3" + 5' 0" + 4' 6"

Heating surfaces:
tubes – 666.5 sq ft
firebox – 74 sq ft
grate – 11.18 sq ft

Tractive effort – 11,900 lbs
Coal capacity – 2 tons
Water capacity – 900 gal
Locomotive weight – 36 tons 12 cwt
Adhesive weight – 26 tons 14 cwt
Max axle loading – 9 tons 7 cwt

Locomotive length over buffer beams – 27' 0" plus 1' 3" bunker overhang (estimated)

From 1927, Nos 2 and 4 were working with boiler pressures at 145 lbs; in 1939 No 4 was restored to 150 lbs/ sq in. No 9 was reduced to 145 lbs/ sq in before 1939 and remained in this condition.

WCR No 4 ***Liscannor*** (Later GSR Class 2C/ Inchicore Class PN1 No 4) *IRRS collection*

No 8 as above except:	*Heating surfaces:* *tubes – 666 sq ft* *firebox – 75.8 sq ft* *grate – 11.12 sq ft*	*Coal capacity – 1 ton 10 cwt* *Locomotive weight – 36 tons 9 cwt*

No 2 as rebuilt:

Used by Bulleid as a guinea pig for experiments with an all-welded steel firebox.

Heating surfaces:
tubes – 482 sq ft
firebox – 74 sq ft

As Nos 5 to 7 were insufficient to cope with growing traffic demands, No 8 was ordered from Dubs with modifications based on experience gained from the earlier engines. Several features and dimensions were the same but riding was improved by installation of a pony truck. The cab design was changed to give better protection against cross winds. The later engines from Thomas Green differed only in minor details but had the useful advantage of a larger coal capacity.

Despite being an improvement on the 0-6-2Ts, two were early withdrawals by the GSR due to their poor mechanical condition.

Right: GSR Class 2C/ Inchicore Class PN1 No 9C (West Clare Railway No 9) at Ennis.
Authors' collection

GSR Class 10C — 4-6-0T — Inchicore Class BN1

WCR No 10

WCR No	GSR No	Name	Makers' No	Built	Withdrawn
10	10C	*Lahinch*	818	1903	1952

Built by Kerr, Stuart

West Clare Railway No 10 (later GSR Class 10C/ Inchicore Class BN1 No 10C). *Kerr Stuart*

Boiler pressure – 160 lbs/ sq in	*Heating surfaces:*	*Tractive effort – 17,000 lbs*
Cylinders – 15" x 20"	*tubes – 620.5 sq ft*	*Coal capacity – 1¾ tons*
Bogie wheels – 2' 0"	*firebox – 79.5 sq ft*	*Water capacity – 800 gal*
Driving wheels – 3' 0"	*grate – 12.0 sq ft*	*Locomotive weight – 76 tons 10 cwt*
Wheel base – 4' 6" + 6' 6" + 4' 0" + 4' 0"		*Max axle loading – tons cwt*
Locomotive length over buffer beams – 25' 8"		

This was a totally new departure in design from anything that had preceded on the WCR. It was a type recommended by the Board of Works for narrow gauge lines and it is likely that Barrington, consultant engineer to the WCR, liaised with the Board in drawing up the specification. There were several design shortcomings with No 10 which are believed to have been the fault of the specification supplied to the makers, rather than the fault of Kerr, Stuart themselves. Principally, the connecting rod drove the leading driving wheels which meant that the central driving wheels were positioned very awkwardly under the ash pan. Also, the slide valves were located over the cylinders – not an unusual practice – but they would have been more effective if placed between the cylinders where plenty of space was available.

No 10 was the most powerful locomotive on the line, although a rather slow due to its small driving wheels. It formed the basis for the remaining locomotives supplied to the WCR and some of the design shortcomings were unfortunately carried forward to them.

GSR Class 11C — 4-6-0T — Inchicore Class BN2

WCR No 11

WCR No	GSR No	Name	Makers' No	Built	Withdrawn
11	11C	*Kilkee*	1881	5/1908	1953

Built by Bagnall

Boiler pressure – 160 lbs/ sq in	*Heating surfaces:*	*Tractive effort – 14,570 lbs*
Cylinders – 15" x 20"	*tubes – 622 sq ft*	*Coal capacity – 1 ton 15 cwt*
Bogie wheels – 2' 3"	*firebox – 74 sq ft*	*Water capacity – 860 gal*
Driving wheels – 3' 6"	*grate – 11.5 sq ft*	*Locomotive weight – 36 tons 0 cwt*
Wheel base – 4' 9" + 6' 0½" + 4' 2" + 4' 2"		*Max axle loading – not recorded*
Locomotive length over buffer beams – 26' 4" (estimated)		

This was considered a very satisfactory locomotive and an improvement on No 10. It was unusually fitted with Bagnall-Price valve gear.

Right: GSR Class 11C/ Inchicore Class BN2 No 11C (West Clare Railway No 11) at Ennis

CH Hewison

GSR Class 1C — 4-6-0T — Inchicore Class BN4

WCR No 1

WCR No	GSR No	Name	Makers' No	Built	Withdrawn
1	1C	*Kilrush*	1098	1912	1953

Built by Hunslet Engine Co

Boiler pressure – 160 lbs/ sq in	*Heating surfaces:*	*Tractive effort – 13,600 lbs*
Cylinders – 15" x 20"	*tubes – 530 sq ft*	*Coal capacity – 1¾ tons*
Bogie wheels – 3' 9"	*firebox – 74 sq ft*	*Water capacity – 800 gal*
Driving wheels – 2' 3"	*grate – 11.5 sq ft*	*Locomotive weight – 40 tons 0 cwt*
Wheel base – 4' 9" + 5' 6½" + 4' 5" + 4' 5"		*Adhesive weight – 30 tons 12 cwt*
Locomotive length – 26' 4" (estimated)		*Max axle loading – 10 tons 4 cwt*

This locomotive was almost an exact copy of No 11, but the larger driving wheels meant that the driving wheel base had to be altered to accommodate the brake blocks. Surprisingly the Bagnall-Price motion was retained, though Hunslet had been amongst the earliest users of Walschaerts valve gear.

Right: GSR Class 1C/ Inchicore Class BN4 No 1C (West Clare Railway No 1) at Ennis.

CP Friel collection

GSR Class 3C — 4-6-0T — Inchicore Class BN3

WCR Nos 3 & 7

WCR No	GSR No	Name	Makers' No	Built	Withdrawn
3	3C	*Ennistymon*	1432	11/1922	1953
7	7C	*Malbay*	1433	11/1922	1956

Built by Hunslet Engine Co

Left: GSR Class 3C/ Inchicore Class BN3 No 3C (West Clare Railway No 3)
Authors' collection

Below: GSR Class 3C/ Inchicore Class BN3 No 7C (West Clare Railway No 7) at Ennis
Authors' collection

Boiler pressure – 160 lbs/ sq in	*Heating surfaces:*	*Tractive effort – 13,600 lbs*
Cylinders – 15" x 20"	*tubes – 530 sq ft*	*Coal capacity – 1¾ tons*
Bogie wheels – 2' 3"	*firebox – 74 sq ft*	*Water capacity – 860 gal*
Driving wheels – 3' 9"	*grate – 11.5 sq ft*	*Locomotive weight – 39 tons 10 cwt*
Wheel base – 4' 9" + 5' 6½" + 4' 5" + 4' 5"		*Max axle loading – 10 tons 4 cwt*
Locomotive length – 26' 4" (estimated)		

These locomotives were virtually dimensionally identical with No 1C but were fitted with outside Walschaerts valve gear, necessitating a slight alteration to the front contour of the side tank. They were the last narrow gauge engines introduced for public use in Ireland. (Bord na Mona purchased three industrial narrow gauge tank locomotives in 1949.) A riveted steel firebox was fitted in 1942 to No 7C and this was the last WCR engine in regular service, sharing goods workings with ex-TDLR No 6T.

Chapter 9
Locomotives of the transitional period

The formation of the Great Southern Railways coincided with exploration of the potential for larger locomotives by both the Great Southern & Western and Midland Great Western railways. In keeping with sentiments elsewhere, there was a belief that future traffic levels would demand greater outputs of power than could be delivered through further development of the traditional 4-4-0 which until then had borne the brunt of express passenger services. Thus the designs of this 'transitional period' directly concern the optimisation of the potential offered by six-coupled machines. A mere 39 locomotives fall within this category, and their story is one of mixed fortunes.

On the GSWR, the appointment of Watson in 1912 was to prove a watershed in Irish design practice, largely stemming from what is known of his tastes and preferences. His earlier career in America was followed by a spell at Swindon, thereby making his interest in bigger engines understandable. Equally his difficult personal nature and his apparent antipathy to local ways resulted in an iconoclastic attitude that would make change inevitable.

It can be deduced that he must have soon confronted the views of the Civil Engineer concerning locomotive weights and in particular that of No 341, the GSWR's last and largest 4-4-0. Intriguingly, there is no record of a 4-4-2 being considered, despite this wheel arrangement being quite common among Irish tank locomotives and despite the then still open debate elsewhere about the rival merits of 4-6-0s and 4-4-2s.

The choice of a 4-6-0 wheel arrangement was finessed by the decision to use four cylinders so as to restrict hammer blow – a further concession to the Civil Engineer's constraints. From today's viewpoint, the four-cylinder 4-6-0 was to prove a comparatively unsuccessful concept, except on the Great Western Railway. However, in 1916 this trait would not have been universally evident and, in the circumstances, Watson's determination on this type had a certain logic.

Watson is known to have studied contemporary four cylinder 4-6-0s – the Claughton Class of the London & North Western Railway and the GWR's Star Class. Because of his time at Swindon and because he was able to obtain a full set of general arrangement drawings, it is widely believed that Watson set out to emulate the Star with his No 400 although it seems that his staff did not necessarily share the same enthusiasms. The actual design work was undertaken by EE Joynt, the Chief Draughtsman at Inchicore, who had enjoyed a warm and fruitful working relationship with Maunsell but not so with his successor. Joynt nevertheless found the process an interesting exercise in itself but apparently firmly believed that the 4-6-0 was inappropriate for GSWR conditions. This was not the only point of disharmony between the two men, a factor that would not have helped a consensus approach to what was an unprecedented step for the company.

A curious aspect of GSWR management was the apparent lack of enquiry at board level about the wisdom of investment in larger locomotives. On completion, No 400 went straight to work on the service for which it was designed, the principal Dublin-Cork expresses. A single daily journey of 165½ miles was made with the corresponding reverse working in the hands of No 341, the locomotive that Watson had ignored as a basis for further development. The timings were not demanding but No 400 soon demonstrated a capacity for fast running although it was not long before several significant design flaws became apparent. Even more embarrassing, locomotive crews who reputedly disliked Watson as much as did his immediate colleagues, found that No 341 generally performed better than No 400. There were even (unsubstantiated) claims by footplatemen that Watson negatively modified No 341 to camouflage the lacklustre nature of the 4-6-0's work.

With the basic design far from satisfactory, the approval for nine more of the type was remarkable. In Britain the Stars and to a lesser extent the Claughtons, were performing well on more demanding duties. Study of contemporary timetables indicate that it would have been hard to keep ten locomotives fully employed at the relaxed schedules obtaining on the Dublin-Cork line, the only route open to them. The performance of No 341, working in partnership with No 400, should have alerted someone in authority to question why more of the larger type should be required. Without needing to look over the water, that same person might have also asked how the Great Northern Railway (Ireland) was able to cope so well with its own family of 4-4-0s (and was to continue to do so until the end of steam)

With Watson's departure to Beyer Peacock in 1921 as General Manager, Bazin inherited a situation with nine members of the 400 Class then in course of construction but also in need of improvement. Some sources indicate that he was initially enthusiastic about the 400s but he seems soon to have changed his opinion. The programme to make performance acceptable was to prove a drawn out affair with a number of different modifications tried. This exercise was never completed as three locomotives were withdrawn as early as 1929–1930.

The core of Bazin's plans for improvement lay in the propagation of ideas first manifest in his No 500. The GSWR was only the second company to introduce a type that was to become so predominant in these islands, the mixed traffic two (outside) cylinder 4-6-0. This accords No 500 a historic significance that is rarely acknowledged. This locomotive quickly demonstrated a broader range of competence than its mixed traffic role implied. There are several photographs from around 1930 showing the class at work on the most prestigious services, including mail trains.

The satisfaction given by No 500 created the template for Bazin's plans to improve Class 400 which was first manifest with the rebuilding of No 402 in 1927. Before this though, there had been an intention to expand the Class 500 to ten members, suggesting the objective of a fleet of at least twenty 4-6-0s of small and large wheeled varieties. If this had come to pass, then regular use of 4-6-0s beyond the boundaries of the GSWR (eg on the MGWR main line) might have become a reality in GSR days, provided that suitable bridge strengthening etc was effected.

Classes 400 and 500 remained restricted throughout their careers to the Dublin-Cork and Mallow-Killarney routes, and the provision of thirteen 4-6-0s to cover these rather limited traffic requirements was generous. At a time when top line locomotives were achieving 40,000 to 50,000 miles per annum in other countries, recorded mileages at withdrawal were modest (see examples below). This factor raises questions about adequacy of return on investment in the original construction and the subsequent modifications, and about what justification there could have been for seven more of Class 500 that were planned but never built.

Locomotive	Total mileage	Annual average
No 405	1,089,021	33,001
No 500	881,975	28,451
No 501	900,226	31,042

(Nos 401 & 406, following rebuilding with Caprotti valve gear, did rather better with annual average mileages of 38,500 and 33,400 between 1930 and 1939).

The GSWR handed over to the GSR a fleet of 17 4-6-0s (including Class 362) of which only No 500 could be considered completely satisfactory. The decision to build no more of Class 500, after the two under construction as at 1 January 1925, stemmed from the pre-amalgamation purchasing activities of the MGWR, a bargain-conscious company that was an active buyer in the war surplus market. The impact on Irish locomotive practice of its 1924 decision to buy 12 kits of parts for Woolwich 2-6-0s was far reaching and deferred a perceived need for more 4-6-0s until the late 1930s.

The unusual and rich pedigree of the moguls yielded a thoroughly modern design. Accessibility to working parts was excellent; superheating was joined with long-lap valves, a potent combination that was yet to be fully acknowledged elsewhere; the tapered boiler was Swindon-inspired and a potent steam raiser. The Woolwich moguls had offered a radical move away from MGWR design traditions when ordered and they delivered a startling advance in operating performance when in service. Enginemen were surprised and delighted at the amount of power these moderately sized engines could produce. Managers were grateful that this power was available over a much wider range of routes than were open to the heavier 4-6-0s.

The GSR acknowledged their worth by acquiring another 15 kits of parts and the resultant cost per kit at approximately £2,000 was an extraordinarily good deal. It was indeed unfortunate that a little more money was not spent on them to improve the frame bracing, to provide a more commodious cab, and to fit smoke deflectors.

GSWR/ GSR Class 400/ 402 4-6-0 Inchicore Class B2/ B2a 1925/ 1931 Load Class E/ C

As four-cylinder locomotives:

GSWR/ GSR No	Built	By	Works' No	Superheated	Rebuilt with 2-cylinders	Withdrawn in 4-cylinder condition
400	8/1916	GSWR Inchicore	–	as built	–	1929
401	4/1921	GSWR Inchicore	–	as built	1930	
402	8/1921	GSWR Inchicore	–	as built	1927	
403	6/1923	Armstrong Whitworth	188	as built	1934	
404	6/1923	Armstrong Whitworth	189	as built	1935 (carrying No 409)	
405	6/1923	Armstrong Whitworth	190	as built	1933	
406	11/1921	GSWR Inchicore	–	as built	1930	
407	6/1923	Armstrong Whitworth	185	1925	1938	
408	6/1923	Armstrong Whitworth	186	1924	–	1930
409	6/1923	Armstrong Whitworth	187	1924	–	1930 (carrying No 404)

Designer: Watson **Built by Inchicore/ Armstrong Whitworth**

No 400 as built:

Boiler pressure – 175 lbs/ sq in
Cylinders – (4) 14" x 26"
Piston valves – 8" diameter
Bogie wheels – 3' 0"
cwt Driving wheels – 6' 7"
Wheel base – 6' 4" + 5' 6" + 7' 0" + 8' 3"
Locomotive length – 36' 8¾"

Heating surfaces:
tubes – 1614 sq ft
firebox – 158 sq ft
superheater – 440 sq ft
grate – 28 sq ft

Tractive effort – 19,190 lbs
Coal capacity – 7 tons
Water capacity – 3345 gal
Locomotive weight – 70 tons 14
Adhesive weight – 50 tons 14 cwt
Max axle loading – 17 tons 6 cwt

GSWR/ GSR Class 400/ B2 No 400 in as-built condition. *Real Photographs Co Ltd*

Watson, as Assistant Locomotive Superintendent and Works Manager under Maunsell, was fully aware of the Civil Engineer's attitude towards weights and axle loadings from the debate that had attended the introduction of No 341 (Class D1). He therefore set an alternative development course by pursuing the four-cylinder 4-6-0 concept to reduce axle loading and hammer blow. The degree to which he was influenced by the GWR Star class in the light of his earlier Swindon experience has been much discussed in the general, but erroneous, belief that No 400 was an attempt to produce an improved version of the former.

In reality, No 400 owed little to the Swindon design school. Despite Inchicore's earlier experience in building tapered boilers, it carried a parallel boiler paired with a firebox dimensionally similar to that used on the Class 368 2-6-0 of 1909. This decision might have been based on the need to contain weight and to minimise construction cost but it denied the opportunity to exploit the carefully fashioned structural profile that helped make the Swindon tapered boiler such a splendid steam raising vessel. Boiler pressure at 175 lb/ sq in (the highest yet applied at Inchicore) and high degree superheat were features similar to those employed on the LNWR Claughton and quite inconsistent with the Swindon tradition of 225 lbs/ sq in and lower degree superheat.

The cylinder layout was the same as that used on the Star to accommodate divided drive; ie the inside cylinders were set further forward to drive the front coupled axle. Outside Walschaerts valve gear with the inside valves actuated by rocker levers was the reverse of the GWR layout and a more modern concept that made the motion easily accessible. (Despite the apparent attraction of this arrangement, its only other use in these islands was with London Midland & Scottish Railway 'Princess' Class 4-6-2 No 6205 *Princess Victoria*).

Another divergence was the use of 1⅛" thick frame plating as opposed to the GWR standard of 1¼". More significantly, the Star-type cylinder layout meant that the frames were cut away to accommodate the rear bogie wheels at the point where they also supported the outside cylinders. The stresses imparted at this point required hefty cross-bracing of the frames which, on the Stars, greatly hampered access to the inside motion. On No 400, the cross bracing was noticeably flimsy by comparison, despite the absence of inside motion, and this led to undue flexing of the frames and fractured steam pipes. Another shortcoming was the failure to exploit a potential benefit of the high-pitched boiler by providing a more generously-sized ashpan in the space available.

Perhaps the most important departure from Swindon standards concerned use of short travel valves. In full gear, the valve travel was 5¼" with a 1¼" lap, whereas the GWR standard lap was 1.63". Two years earlier, Maunsell by then with the South Eastern & Chatham Railway, had consulted Joynt at Inchicore about valve design. The latter had recommended reduction in lap from 1¼" to ⅞" and it is apparent that Joynt's views remained firmly in the short travel camp. The adoption of a 1¼" lap for No 400 seems to have been a Watson/ Joynt compromise and, crucially, far short of the tested and proven Swindon dimension. This feature linked with the Schmidt wide-type single piston ring (a component later to be discredited in connection with the original LMS Royal Scots), led to a voracious appetite for fuel and water as mileage built up.

Orders for more of the class were instigated in 1918 but wartime shortages in materials and pressures on workshop facilities meant that completion of the remaining nine locomotives was much delayed. The three Inchicore-built locomotives (Nos 401, 402 & 406) were introduced in 1921. The Armstrong-Whitworth versions (Nos 403 to 405 and 407 to 409) were completed in 1922 but not delivered until the following year because of the Civil War situation. At this stage, there were four dimensional variations between the ten locomotives, although the remaining nine all had substantially heavier frames than the prototype:

Nos 401, 402 and 406, as built, had differing dimensions:

Heating surfaces	*Locomotive weight – 76 tons 7 cwt*
tubes – 1590 sq ft	*Adhesive weight – 55 tons 4 cwt*
firebox – 158 sq ft	*Max axle loading – 18 tons 11 cwt*
superheater – 350 sq ft	
grate – 28 sq ft	

Nos 403 to 405 as built had differing dimensions:

	Heating surfaces:	*Coal capacity – 8 tons*
	tubes – 1614 sq ft	*Water capacity – 4500 gal*
	(later 1590 sq ft)	
	firebox – 158 sq ft	*Locomotive weight – 76 tons 7 cwt*
	superheater – 366 sq ft	*Adhesive weight – 55 tons 4 cwt*
	grate – 28 sq ft	*Max axle loading – 18 tons 11 cwt*

Nos 407 to 409 as built (saturated) had differing dimensions:

Boiler pressure – 225 lbs/ sq in	*Heating surfaces:*	*Tractive effort – 24,680 lbs*
	tubes – 1870 sq ft	*Coal capacity – 8 tons*
	firebox – 158 sq ft	*Water capacity – 4500 gal*
	grate – 28 sq ft	*Weights not recorded*

(On conversion to superheated condition, Nos 407 to 409 became identical with Nos 403 to 405)

GSWR/ GSR Class 400/ B2 No 407 in original condition with four cylinders but fitted with external main steam pipes. This was the last surviving four-cylinder Class 400. The small tender had presumably been swapped from an Inchicore-built locomotive. At Inchicore in 1936.
Real Photographs Co Ltd

(There was a further, less obvious, variation between Nos 401, 402 and 406. During construction of Nos 401 and 402, an error occurred in the drilling of the frames with holes being inserted in the wrong places and yielding a small weight reduction as compared with No 406).

The disappointing results with No 400 led to a number of changes with Nos 401 to 409: there were modifications to the superheater design (where fitted); three-feed Detroit lubricators were installed; the internal steam pipes (which had been poorly laid out in No 400) were simplified and enlarged; the motion and framing was strengthened. No 400 also remained unique in retaining a different cab cut-out and footplate profile; a canopy ('Bazin') cab was provided in 1924.

The reason for ordering Nos 407 to 409 in saturated form has been much discussed, as by 1918 there was little doubt elsewhere about the performance advantages imparted by superheating. Bazin was averse to conversion of medium and smaller locomotives on the grounds that any improvement in performance could not justify the cost. However this rationale could not be extended to what was the largest GSWR express design. Further the contract specification with the manufacturers was actually signed by Watson who apparently had no doubts about the advantages of superheating. The most logical explanation for this paradox is that Watson, aware of his forthcoming departure to Beyer Peacock, was content to be influenced in the knowledge that Bazin would have to live with the consequences. Alternatively, with so many emerging problems with the design, perhaps it was thought that part of the solution might just lie in the higher boiler pressure/ saturated option. The dismal performance of the saturated trio soon settled that particular argument.

All the Armstrong-Whitworth locomotives had laminated springs on all driving wheels connected by compensating levers. They were later converted to conform with the Inchicore arrangement which had helical springs on the centre driving wheels. A further difference was provision of a new type of larger tender with 4500 gallons water capacity (described as Tender Type E in Chapter 11). This type was later rotated among the GSWR-designed tenders allocated to other members of this class (and also of Class 500).

Once the superheating programme was completed, the class achieved an almost homogeneous condition with the only visible differences being those apparent on No 400. The later engines were an improvement on the prototype but by no means satisfactory. Although capable of high-speed running at times, they were generally sluggish and with increasing mileages still had a ferocious appetite. The saturated engines were the worst and used only *in extremis* before their conversion.

The employment of four cylinders yielded a higher initial capital cost and increased maintenance expenses which must have been particularly frustrating with performance falling short of what contemporary four-cylinder 4-6-0s were achieving elsewhere. More directly, Bazin had the evidence that his cheaper, simpler two-cylinder 4-6-0 Class 500 was easily out-performing Class 400. On a different plane, the first Woolwich moguls were showing what was possible with a moderately sized, properly designed, modern locomotive. By the late 1920s it seems that it was hard to find work for the fleet of thirteen 4-6-0s. It was reported in 1929 that Nos 403 and 404 had for some time been lying dismantled at Inchicore, before reassembly and return to duty in very dirty condition.

On 12 February 1926, the General Manager submitted estimates to the Locomotive, Permanent Way and Works Committee for the cost of conversion of one 4-cylinder Class 400 into a Class 500, and of the savings in operating costs that would result. While details of these figures are not recorded, Bazin estimated that if all ten members of Class 400 were to be converted to Class 500, then operating costs of £4,000 per annum could be achieved. As a result of these proposals, conversion of one locomotive was approved.

The two-cylinder conversion programme started in 1927 with No 402 and is described below. However, efforts continued to improve performance of the four-cylinder engines, directed at the four post-1930 Armstrong Whitworth survivors (Nos 403, 405, 407, 409). Trial modifications included revised steam pipes and additional horizontal cross stays between the frames. Unfortunately, these measures did not solve the problem of pipe fractures. Another arrangement was introduced in 1930 whereby the steam pipes emerged from the smokebox side and connected with a tee-junction. At this point one pipe went forward to feed the inside cylinders and the other back to the outside cylinders. It was a clumsy and inelegant arrangement with the pipes fully exposed to the air – 'super-cooling' perhaps to off-set any advantages from superheating?

Recognising that something radical had to be done, Bazin passed a full set of drawings to Maunsell, by then CME with the Southern Railway, with a plea for advice. Maunsell handed the problem on to his technical assistant, Harry Holcroft, who had been involved in the design process that led to the Woolwich moguls.

GSWR/ GSR Class 402/ B2a No 402 as rebuilt (1927) with two cylinders and showing flush footplate over driving wheels which was unique among the two cylinder conversions; fitted with Class 500-type cab. At Cork shed.

C P Friel collection

Holcroft's studies and recommendations formed the basis for conversion to two cylinders. However during this programme, it was decided that three locomotives were surplus to requirements. Nos 400 (in original condition with all its associated deficiencies) and 408 were scrapped in 1929 and 1930 respectively.

The fate of the third casualty was unusual as instructions issued for No 404 to be withdrawn in 1930 were ignored. This was considered the best of the remaining four-cylinder engines and so on a local and totally unofficial initiative, its identity was switched with that of No 409. Thus No 404 masquerading as No 409 was able to survive until 1958. On the other hand, the original No 409 which had seen little use before it was superheated in 1925 was withdrawn a mere five years later. This tragically short – and expensive – career was remarkable by any standard and quite of out character with the Irish tradition of operational longevity.

Finally, before describing this class in its two cylinder state, it is a reflection of the financial situation of the GSR that the rebuilding programme commenced with No 402 in 1927 but was not completed until August 1938 with No 407 (by then the Cork spare engine and little used since early 1937).

The two cylinder conversions:

GSR No	Rebuilt as two-cylinder	Valve gear	Later rebuilt	Withdrawn
401	1930	Caprotti	1939#/ 1949¥/ 1954§	1961
402	1927	Walschaerts	1946#/ 1953§	1961
403	1934	Walschaerts	1936#	1957
405	1933	Walschaerts	1937#	1955
406	1930	Caprotti	–	1957
407	1938	Walschaerts	1949#	1955
409 (ex-404)	1935	Walschaerts	1939¶/ 1952#/ 1955§	1958

Rebuilt as follows:
Fitted with large diameter superheated Belpaire boiler type K
¥ Reverted to Walschaerts valve gear
§ Reverted to original sized superheated Belpaire boiler
¶ Fitted with Lemaitre multiple-jet blast pipe; removed 1941

Re-designation to Class 402 (B2a): No 402 in 1927, Nos 401 and 406 in 1930

GSWR/ GSR Class 402/ B2a No 401 as rebuilt in 1930 with two cylinders and Beardmore-Caprotti valve; high-set footplate over valves; low main footplate; deep splashers; Class 500-type cab; K type boiler. At Inchicore.

C P Friel collection

No 402 as rebuilt:

Boiler pressure – 180 lbs/ sq in
Cylinders – 19½" x 28"
Piston valves – 10" diameter
Bogie wheels – 3' 0"
Driving wheels – 6' 7"
Wheel base – 6' 4" + 6' 0½" + 7' 0" + 8' 3"
Locomotive length – 37' 0¼"

Heating surfaces:
tubes – 1590 sq ft
firebox – 158 sq ft
superheater – 350 sq ft
grate – 28 sq ft

Tractive effort – 20,620 lbs
Coal capacity – 8 tons
Water capacity – 4500 gal
Locomotive weight – 73 tons 10 cwt
Adhesive weight – 54 tons 17 cwt
Max axle loading – 18 tons 10 cwt

No 401 & 406 as rebuilt:

Similar leading dimensions to No 402 but fitted with Beardmore-Caprotti valve gear which required the footplate to be stepped higher over the cylinder area.

Nos 403, 405, 407, 409 as rebuilt:

Frame renewal was restricted to provision of longer and deeper plates in front of the leading driving wheels which were riveted to the existing frames. This configuration resulted in the running plate being stepped down behind the slide bars. Boiler dimension, wheel base, adhesive weight and maximum axle loading were as for No 402.

Cylinders – 19½" x 26"
Wheel base – 6' 4" + 5' 6" + 7' 0" + 8' 3"
Locomotive length – 37' 0¼"

Tractive effort – 19,150 lbs
Locomotive weight – 73 tons 8 cwt

 # As rebuilt with type K boiler:

Heating surfaces:
tubes – 1606 sq ft
firebox – 171 sq ft
superheater – 350 sq ft
grate – 28 sq ft

Locomotive weight – 75 tons 10 cwt
Adhesive weight – 54 tons 17 cwt
Max axle loading – 18 tons 10 cwt

GSWR/ GSR Class 402/ B2a No 406 as rebuilt in 1930 with two cylinders and Beardmore-Caprotti valve; high-set running plate over valves removed ; K-type boiler; Class 500-type cab; later 4500 gallon tender. At Limerick Junction in 1932.

Kelland Collection

Above: GSWR/ GSR Class 400/ B2 No 405 as rebuilt in 1937 with modifications to front end of frames only; fitted with K type boiler; original profile cab.
CH Hewison

Right: GSWR/ GSR Class 400/ B2 No 403 with original profile cab at Cork, Glanmire Road.
OS Nock

Holcroft's verdict was that radical rebuilding was necessary involving new 28" stroke cylinders, lengthened wheel base, new frames and wheel centres, and long-lap valves thereby creating a larger wheeled version of the Class 500. This was to all intents and purposes a new locomotive retaining the original boiler. These proposals were accepted and implemented with No 402 in 1927. A successful locomotive resulted that was faster, more powerful and more economical than the four-cylinder version. Regarded as the most effective of all the rebuilding exercises undertaken with the class, No 402 was re-classified Class 402 (B2a) and was the favourite right through to its withdrawal in 1961. No 402 was immediately distinguishable from all the other two-cylinder rebuilds in being the only one with a straight running plate from the smokebox saddle back to the cab. The reputation of this locomotive was enhanced by its working a non-stop special train (albeit of only 95 tons) conveying the first US Ambassador to Ireland from Cork to Dublin on 20 March 1934 at an average speed of 67.5 mph (Limerick Junction-Dublin pass-to-stop at an average of 73.7 mph).

In 1930, Nos 401 and 406 were also rebuilt with two cylinders. However in these cases, Beardmore-Caprotti poppet valve gear which gave infinitely variable cut-off was adopted. Also the smokebox was slightly shorter than the standard six feet, although this was later brought into line with the rest of the class. In this form, these locomotives were competent and considered even more economical than No 402, although No 401 reverted to Walschaerts valve gear in 1949. A further advantage was that over this period, the valve gear proved remarkably durable, retaining most of its original parts.

The benefits gained by rebuilding are reflected in mileage figures for No 406. In the period 1921–1930 it was reported as running a mere 60,318 miles in four-cylinder condition whereas in the succeeding ten years it covered 334,257 miles. The work of the Caprotti locomotives could be impressive as was apparent on 9 August 1930, when No 401 hauled a load of 375 tons from Portlaoise to Dublin at an average speed of 58.7 mph for the 50.9 miles.

Against these gains, these conversions were expensive (conversion of the Caprotti engines together cost £14,000, or the equivalent of about seven Woolwich mogul kits of parts). In the prevailing economic conditions, the financial feasibility of such extensive treatment was questionable. It is believed that a deal was struck with Beardmore so that the full cost was not borne by the GSR but details cannot be verified (see Dabeg feedwater heater fitted to Class 372 No 389 described below). However, if Bazin's estimates that rebuilding would save £400 per locomotive in annual operating expenses were correct, then the payback on more rebuilding similar to that of Nos 401 and 406 would have been 17½ years in addition to amortisation of the original construction cost.

GSWR/ GSR class 400/ B2 No 409 (alias 404) with Le Maitre exhaust and smoke deflectors. *Father Browne/ Davison & Associates*

Also, the essay into Caprotti valve gear was an extravagant and unnecessary move away from standardisation when No 402 with Walschaerts valve gear had proven to be such a good performer. A further disadvantage was that drivers, raised on short travel valve locomotives, were reluctant to work these engines at the optimum recommended by the valve gear manufacturers (ie fully open regulator with very short cut-off) to minimise fuel and water consumption without detriment to performance.

No satisfactory explanation has been provided as to why the Inchicore-built engines should have received preferential treatment, although inferior build quality with the remainder might have been a factor. On 3 June 1927, the Board had authorised investigation of legal action in respect of the failure of the driving wheel tyres on all six Armstrong Whitworth-built engines.

Conversion of the remainder, which remained Class 400 (B2), was delayed until 1934 and was not completed for another three years. In this case, the rebuilding was less comprehensive than that given to the Inchicore trio. New cylinders of the type inaugurated with the rebuilding of No 402 were used but with 26" stroke. This was achieved by fitting special cylinder covers and by making some modifications to the motion. These changes necessitated frame extensions in front of the leading driving axle, secured by riveting patch plates inside and outside; the original wheelbase was retained. The running plate profile differed from that of No 402 as it stepped down immediately after the motion bracket. No 405 is reported as being the first member of the class to have its single wide Schmidt piston valve rings replaced with the more efficient narrow type. These four locomotives were theoretically less powerful, based on tractive effort, and they were generally considered to be not as strong as Class 402 (B2a). Nonetheless they proved capable thereby justifying the economies implemented with the less comprehensive conversion.

Up until this stage, the boiler dimensions had remained more or less unchanged, in contrast to the differing cylinder volumes that the rebuildings had yielded:

Original four-cylinder	14" x 26"	16,010 cu ins
1929/ 30 two-cylinder	19½" x 28"	16,716 cu ins
1934-1938 two-cylinder	19½" x 26"	15,530 cu ins

Yet further changes were inaugurated in 1936 when the original boiler on No 403 was replaced with the larger K class boiler, a type that was eventually fitted to all but one of the survivors. This boiler was pressed to 175 lb/ sq in but with the capacity to be increased to 225 lb/ sq in, although this never took place. Nos 401 and 402 reverted to the original type of boiler in 1952 and 1953 respectively, although No 401 reverted yet again to a K class boiler in 1953.

In 1939, the performance of No 409 was greatly improved with the fitting of the Lemaitre multiple-jet blastpipe. This imparted a capacity for exhilarating acceleration but, at moderate steaming rates which by then were order of the day, coal consumption increased substantially. Some improvement was achieved through modification in 1941 (when smoke deflectors were also added). However under easy schedules and with reasonably light loads, the normal 400s were considered economical and given the traffic conditions by then prevailing, the speed and haulage capacities of which No 409 had proven capable were no longer justified. The ordinary chimney and blastpipe were soon restored.

Externally, there were numerous detail differences. For example, the rebuilding process that resulted in Class 402 saw these locomotives provided with Class 500 type cabs, although No 401 on receiving the K class boiler was also provided with a cab similar to that used on Class 342, albeit without the side window. There was also much variety in chimneys, smokebox saddles and doors, and tenders.

The timing of the introduction of Nos 401 to 409 was unfortunate. The circumstances of the Civil War not only delayed their introduction but also led to severe service interruptions which meant that it was some time before they could be fully extended in express work. Then throughout the remainder of the 1920s there was a steady decline in passenger train usage. The combination of these factors meant that by 1929, there was insufficient work to keep fully employed a class of ten locomotives equipped with 6' 7" driving wheels, specifically designed for express work, and with limited route availability.

Loadings did show some slight increase in the mid-1930s and on occasions, recourse was taken to triple heading of heavier trains on the difficult start out of Cork. The number and diverse nature of the modifications to the seven locomotives that survived the cull of 1929/1930 torpedoed the notion of 'class'. A retired driver commented that they were more an amalgamation of individual locomotives, each of which had unique characteristics requiring special handling to achieve optimal performance. This situation would have conspired against crews getting the best out of them although in their final state they were considered economical, easy to maintain, and reliable steamers. With good Welsh steam coal, the 400's did well, but they also steamed freely on second-rate fuel in the form of phurnacite ovoids, or briquettes. After all the troubles of their earlier years, it is nice to be able to record that the extended programme of conversions eventually yielded seven locomotives which, for all their individual quirks, performed well during a crisis period. These factors must have been greatly welcome to the GSR management in the difficult closing years of the company, and to its successor, CIÉ.

Even so, the effort necessary to rectify the early problems was costly. One of the most brilliant locomotive design engineers of the 20th century had worked out the optimal means of improving the class in two-cylinder form yet only one example followed his recommended format (No 402). The adoption of Caprotti valve gear, despite its inherent efficiency, for the next two (Nos 401 and 406) was a pointless exercise, given the substantial additional cost involved and the injection of more variety into this small class. The introduction of the K type boiler was another modification where the operational advantages must have been outweighed by the disadvantages of still more variety.

In conclusion, there are grounds for thinking that the post-1930 history of this class was influenced as much by pre-amalgamation prejudices as by changing circumstance. By 1930, the GSR had six competent two-cylinder 4-6-0s on its books comprising Nos 401, 402 and 406 and the three members of Class 500 (described next). Significantly, during Morton's tenure as CME (1930-1932) no further modification work was undertaken on the 400s, and there were sound reasons

The four Class 400s built by Armstrong-Whitworth that survived after 1930 received less extensive rebuilding as two cylinder engines and retained the Class 400 (B2) designation. No 409 is seen standing at Cork after arrival with the 6.40 am Mail Train in 1954.
Author' collection

for this. The superheating programme for smaller locomotives, particularly Class 101, was then under way and this would have absorbed surplus workshop resources.

Also, passenger traffic receipts had collapsed. As a percentage of 1925 revenue levels, the annual figures were alarming: 1930 (74%); 1931 (68%); 1932 (66%). The provision of 10 large wheeled and 3 smaller wheeled 4-6-0s might have been considered generous in 1925 but at least there were then hopes that the market would remain stable, if not grow. Morton would have been well justified in acknowledging that:

(1) The case for more expenditure on express passenger locomotives was non-existent;

(2) The money spent on fitting Nos 401 and 406 with Caprotti valve gear had been an unwarranted extravagance that did not offer a legitimate path for future motive power development;

(3) The six 2-cylinder 4-6-0s, supported as necessary by Woolwich moguls and 4-4-0s, were adequate for Dublin-Cork traffic requirements;

(4) His attention was more profitably focused on improving motive power for goods services which up to 1930 had exceeded the 1925 level, and had only fallen to 94% by 1931.

Rebuilding of the remaining four-cylinder engines was initiated by Harty (another ex-GSWR man) in 1933. Although this was a simpler and cheaper exercise than the earlier programme, passenger receipts continued to hover around 65% of 1925 levels for the remainder of the 1930s. The competence of Class 500 in passenger work had been a contributing factor in the redundancy of a like number of Class 400 in 1929-30, based on traffic levels of the 1920s. By 1933, a strong argument could be made for withdrawal rather than rebuild of some, if not all, the surviving four-cylinder 4-6-0s. Nonetheless, conversion did proceed with the last (that of No 407) taking place concurrent with the construction of Class 800 (see Chapter 10). Thus by 1939, the GSR's last normal year of operations, there were twelve 4-6-0s of limited route availability (with one more to come) to service a traffic sector that was earning 64% of 1925 revenue levels.

No 406 was involved in the Straboe accident on 20 December 1944 at milepost 46¾ while working the down Mail to Cork. Having passed a signal at danger, it ran into the rear of a cattle train hauled by Class 101 No 184 that had been stationary for about 30 minutes for bailing out (see Chapter 13 for information on this ritual). A post office sorter was killed in the accident, the only on-train fatality to occur throughout the history of the GSR. No 406 sustained only minor damage and was back at work early in 1945.

1948 assessment: *Can work main line trains up to load of 20, Night Mails or Goods. Given a high maintenance standard and load of 12-14, could run fast. They are not all of a standard design.*

GSWR/ GSR Class 500/ B1 No 502 at Inchicore in 1936. *L&GRP*

GSWR/ GSR Class 500 4-6-0 Inchicore Class B1 1925/ 1931 Load Class B/ B

GSR No	Built	Withdrawn
500	4/1924	1955
501	2/1926	1955
502	3/1926	1957

Designer: Bazin **Built at Inchicore**

Boiler pressure – 180 lbs/ sq in	*Heating surfaces:*	*Tractive effort – 23,780 lbs*
Cylinders – 19½" x 28"	*tubes –1590 sq ft*	*Coal capacity – 8 tons*
Piston valves – 10" diameter	*firebox – 158 sq ft*	*Water capacity – 3850 gal*
Bogie wheels – 3' 0"	*superheater – 350 sq ft*	*Locomotive weight – 74 tons 10 cwt*
Driving wheels – 5' 8½"	*grate – 28 sq ft*	*Adhesive weight – 53 tons 17 cwt*
Wheel base – 6' 8" + 5' 10½" + 7' 0" + 7' 4"		*Max axle loading – 18 tons 10 cwt*
Locomotive length – 37' 1¼"		

The evolution of the modern two-cylinder 4-6-0 with long-lap valves was pioneered by the GWR early in the early 20th century culminating in the Saint Class. RW Urie, Locomotive Superintendent of the London & South Western Railway, recognised the potential of the Saint concept and developed it further by using outside Walschaerts valve gear in preference to the GWR's inside Stephenson motion. In this mode, he introduced three standardised types of 4-6-0 (for express, mixed traffic and goods work) that were rugged, simple and reliable, with excellent accessibility to moving parts. Their main drawback was that they were sometimes indifferent steamers.

On inheriting this locomotive family at the formation of the Southern Railway, Maunsell as CME quickly set about improving the steaming and added more of the express version (the King Arthur class) and its goods counterpart (the S15) as standard types for the newly Grouped company. These Urie/ Maunsell locomotives were a major milestone in the steam locomotive story as progenitors of a type that was to see extensive application by the LMS and LNER, but Class 500 was the first example of the genre outside the LSWR/ Southern Railway.

The introduction of ten examples of Class 400 had been at the behest of Watson, and it was clear to Bazin that this design in its original condition was too flawed to provide a format for any derivatives. The circumstances therefore facing Bazin on the GSR and Maunsell in Britain were coincidentally similar, although Bazin's problems were the more acute. Maunsell's improvements with ex-LSWR engines involved provision of long lap valves, and given his continuing close relationship with his erstwhile colleagues at Inchicore, it might be surmised that exchange of ideas with Bazin had an influence on No 500.

An alternative source of influence might have come from the LNER. Bazin retained close relations with his old colleagues at Doncaster and would have known that Gresley's large boiler Class K3 2-6-0 of 1920 had been built for similar work to that intended for No 500. An important feature of the K3 was use of piston valves with 6 ⅜" travel and 1½" lap.

In determining the valve dimensions for his new 4-6-0, Bazin therefore had the comfort of informed technical support from two independent sources. He might have consulted one or both, although Maunsell supported by his technical assistant Harry Holcroft (an ex-GWR man) would have offered the greater body of empirical evidence. In any event, the decision to adopt a valve travel of $6^{3}/_{16}$" and a 1½" lap was unusual by the standards of the time but proved key to the performance of the design. The only drawback was use of the inefficient Schmidt wide-type single piston ring although this was rectified in due course.

Envisaged as a mixed traffic type (with a boiler interchangeable with Class 400), the prototype appeared in GSWR days. Once proven on the road, plans were formulated to add to the type but only two more were actually built. This reduction was a reflection more of the GSR's financial condition than of any defect in the design. A solution to the Class 400 dilemma had still to be found and implemented, and this would be expensive. Further, the first of the Woolwich moguls purchased by the MGWR the previous year, emerged from the Broadstone in April 1925. The competence of these 2-6-0s, their greater router availability and their low purchase price militated against construction of any more of the smaller wheeled 4-6-0s.

Over the years, Class 500 was consistently well regarded by all who worked with these engines. Despite their intended mixed traffic use, they were rarely used on freight work in their early days, being preferred for passenger work. They had no difficulty in working to the fastest express passenger schedules then prevailing. In contrast to the 400s, except for one modification to No 500 described below, they were not rebuilt or materially changed during their careers. They were among the first 4-6-0s to be withdrawn by CIÉ, a policy that many observers felt to be misguided in view of their competence, and suitability for a wider range of duties than the Class 400, or the later Class 800.

The only substantial modification was the equipping in 1928 of No 500 with the Bredin-Burnell feed-water heater system. (Messrs Bredin and Burnell were then Works Manager and Chief Chemist respectively of the GSR). Briefly, water was drawn from the tender by means of Weir pumps and discharged into a pre-heater located between the frames to which exhaust steam was admitted. The condensed water from the expended exhaust steam was discharged through the blast pipe through an ingenious system of valves. Meanwhile the heated water then passed to waste gas heaters housed in rectangular tanks either side of the smokebox. Significant internal modifications were made to the smokebox to accommodate the operation of these heaters. Operation of the system was flexible as the locomotive could be worked with either or both the exhaust steam and waste gas heaters in use, or by reversion to conventional injector feed.

The system was modified by removal of the waste gas heaters in 1932 which restored the smokebox to conventional profile. The remainder of the equipment was removed in 1940 when No 500 reverted to standard injector feed.

1948 assessment: *Can work today any train worked by 400 class. Have in the past worked Cork Mail but smaller diameter wheels renders them quite unsuitable for such work. Better on Goods work than Passenger, except on Night Mails.*

Left: GSWR/ GSR Class 500/ B1 No 500 as fitted with full Bredin-Burnell feed water heater system in 1928. At Inchicore.

Lens of Sutton

Below: GSWR/ GSR Class 500/ B1 No 500 fitted with Bredin-Burnell feed water heater system but following the removal (in 1932) of the waste gas heaters from either side of smokebox. At Cork in 1938. The purpose of the small cab-side plate 'O T' above the number plate is thought to denote 'on test'.

HC Casserley

GSR Class 372 (MGWR Class D2) — 2-6-0 — Inchicore Class K1

1925/ 1931 Load Class B/ A

GSR No	Built	Withdrawn	GSR No	Built	Withdrawn	GSR No	Built	Withdrawn
372§¶	4/1925	1960	379	12/1926	1959	386	2/1928	1959
373	9/1925	1959	380	12/1926	1959	387	11/1928	1959
374	11/1925	1959	381	12/1926	1959	388	12/1928	1962
375	2/1926	1957	382	1/1927	1955	389 #	12/1928	1955
376	3/1926	1961	383	3/1927	1959	390	5/1929	1955
377	3/1926	1960	384	1/1928	1960	391	5/1929	1957
378	10/1926	1959	385	1/1928	1960			

Designer: Maunsell

Kits of parts built at Woolwich Arsenal; Nos 372 to 383 assembled at Broadstone; the remainder at Inchicore.

§ Completed as MGWR No 49 in glossy black and red lined livery but immediately repainted in works grey and renumbered No 410; then changed to No 372 before entering traffic in standard GSR grey.

GSR Class 372/ K1 No 380 with original SECR-style smokebox door at Inchicore in 1930. This locomotive carries a top lamp bracket which would have been part of the 'kit' for expected use in Britain but was superfluous on the GSR. Locomotives appearing in photographs on pages 248, 252 and 253 also carry this unnecessary feature.

Real Photographs Co Ltd

Boiler pressure – 180 lbs/ sq in¶
Cylinders – 19" x 28"
Piston valves – 10" diameter
Pony wheels – 3' 1"
Driving wheels – 5' 6"
Wheel base – 8' 10" + 7' 3" + 8' 3"
Locomotive length – 33' 8 5/8"

Heating surfaces:
tubes – 1390.5 sq ft§
firebox – 135 sq ft
superheater – 285 sq ft
grate – 25 sq ft

Tractive effort – 23,430 lbs
Coal capacity – 5 tons
Water capacity – 3500 gal
Locomotive weight – 61 tons 0 cwt
Adhesive weight – 47 tons 18 cwt
Max axle loading – 17 tons 4 cwt

¶ *Boiler pressure on No 372 was 200 lbs/ sq in until August 1925 – tractive effort 26,040 lbs (all locomotives later increased to 200 lbs/ sq in)*

No 389 fitted with Dabeg feed-water heater, approved by GSR Board on 3 June 1927 on the basis of 'no cost to the GSR'; removed 1939.

§ Ten boiler tubes were later removed, reducing the tube surface by 59 sq ft.

The history of this type really began in 1910 with Harry Holcroft, who as a draughtsman at Swindon, had visited America and had been impressed with the utilitarian, maid-of-all-work character of the many outside-cylindered moguls in use. This led to his designing the 43XX class moguls, the first of the large numbers of medium sized, mixed traffic 2-6-0s to work in Britain. Two years later, Maunsell left the GSWR to become Chief Mechanical Engineer of the South Eastern & Chatham Railway. The mechanical engineering situation on the SECR was then at low ebb, and Maunsell needed help to re-organise Ashford Works, rationalise the motive power fleet, and introduce new designs. Holcroft was one of a small group of talented personnel recruited to help in this exercise and given his pride in the 43XX, it was no surprise that the mogul type should play a role in the SECR's refurbishment programme.

In January 1915, the SECR board approved the building of ten mixed-traffic 2-6-0s and six express 2-6-4 tanks. The two types shared most key parts but wartime conditions delayed construction with one of each not appearing until mid-1917. The first 2-6-0, numbered 810 and designated Class N, reflected Swindon influence with a tapered boiler (of classic GWR style), Belpaire firebox, high working pressure, top feed, smokebox regulator and long-travel valve gear. Midland Railway influence was evident in styling of chimney, cab, smokebox and tender. Maunsell made his personal mark by insisting on maximum accessibility, so outside Walschaerts valve gear was employed. Smaller details also adopted the best practices of other railways, resulting in a flexible, easily maintained, general utility locomotive. On the road, No 810 distinguished itself as the SECR's best freight engine by far. An important ingredient in the performance was that the 10" diameter piston valves followed the Swindon formula with a travel of 6⅞", a lap of 1½" and a lead of $^5/_{16}$". These dimensions applied also to the later examples of the type that came to Ireland.

In 1917, the UK government asked the Association of Railway Locomotive Engineers (ARLE) to prepare standard 2-6-0, 2-8-0, 4-4-0, 4-6-0, and 2-8-2T designs for use throughout the country by a post-war nationalised railway system. ARLE comprised the senior mechanical engineers of the major railway companies and this project soon foundered on conflicting egos and rivalries. With the 1918 Armistice, interest waned and the project was wound up in late 1919, with work most advanced on the 2-6-0 and 2-8-0 designs.

The British government was concerned that in peacetime, work should be found for redundant munitions manufacturers and it was proposed that their factories be used to produce steam engines. In November 1919, the Ministry of Munitions placed an order with the Woolwich Arsenal for construction of fifty 2-6-0s and fifty 2-8-0s conforming with the ARLE designs. Unfortunately the drawings proved incomplete, so the order was amended to 100 locomotives of the SECR Class N 5' 6" design, as being the closest available to the ARLE-sponsored concept.

The capacity of Woolwich successfully to build the locomotives was soon called into question. Boiler construction was contracted out to established manufacturers, North British, Kitson and Robert Stephenson who delivered on time and in accordance

with specifications. However construction and assembly progress was slow as a result of poor production planning, inadequate costing, and lack of knowledge of steam locomotive practice. Efforts to market the locomotives were equally unsuccessful. The opening asking price had been £14,000 for an engine and tender but with minimal buyer interest, the price soon started to fall. The first buyer was the MGWR with 12 sets of parts in March 1923 costing £24,000.

Even before the first mogul kit had been assembled, the GSR expressed interest in adding to the type. The minutes of the Officers' Conference of 13 March 1925 record a recommendation to inspect the following materials: 15 more kits of parts, 26 separate boilers, and 18 separate pairs of cylinder castings. Two years later, plans were more modest and the purchase was completed of 15 more sets of parts and four spare boilers for £34,000. Eventually the MGWR/ GSR created 26 moguls at bargain basement prices (hence the 'Woolworth' nickname) with the purchase cost averaging out at about £2,200 per engine set whereas Woolwich Arsenal had paid £3,375 average for each boiler alone in 1921! Further evidence of the GSR's commitment to the type is the decision in February 1926 to purchase a set of patterns from Woolwich Arsenal.

A curiosity is that the Board minute dated 20 February 1925 authorising assembly of six locomotives in 1925 and five in 1926 (assembly of No 410, later 372, was already in hand) notes that each completed locomotive would cost £4000. This is believed to include the original cost of the kit.

The Board minute dated 2 December 1927 authorised the assembly of eight more of the type in the 1928 renewal programme (actually not completed until 1929). The recommendation for this programme was justified by the expectation that £2,136 per annum would be saved as a result but frustratingly there is no indication of how this was calculated.

To accommodate the 5' 3" gauge, it was necessary to provide new frame stays, smokebox saddles, axles and exhaust pipe distance pieces. The footplate was widened by 6½" to 8' 10½" and the distance between the cylinder centres was increased by a similar amount to 7' 2½". The cab dimensions remained unchanged, a feature that was to lead to criticism from footplate crews who found the interior cramped by Irish standards, and who also disliked the unfamiliar right-hand drive (except for those used to ex-MGWR locomotives).

Another shortcoming was rough riding as mileages built up after repairs, a characteristic that was not unusual with outside-cylindered moguls. However, this trait seems to have been more extreme with the Irish version than with the British version and is attributed to two factors. Firstly, the greater distance between the cylinders would have exacerbated lateral movement. Secondly, whereas the British locomotives had a very stiff frame construction resulting from stays consisting of horizontal flanged plates fitted top and bottom, a short-sighted economy was introduced with the Irish version through reliance on a single new horizontal flanged plate (obviously longer to accommodate the wider gauge) fitted approximately midway between top and bottom of the frames.

(Locomotives introduced to service as Classes N & U with the Southern Railway, at the same time as their Irish counterparts, increasingly suffered from fractured frames. Because they were expected to continue at work into the 1960s, a number were re-framed and extensively rebuilt in the period 1955 to 1961 by British Railways).

The amount of power that these modestly-sized locomotives could generate was a pleasant surprise to footplatemen. This reflects the moderate expectations that had been engendered hitherto by the conservative

Opposite: GSR Class 372/ K1 No 385 with original SECR-style smokebox door at Inchicore in 1931.

L&GRP

Right: GSR Class 372/ K1 No 389 with original SECR-style smokebox door and fitted with Dabeg feed-water heater.

C P Friel Collection

and rather dated Irish engineering practices. Apart from No 500, this was the first completely competent type of the new era to be put to work in Ireland, and thus the first of a new generation of steam power. The reduction of No 372's working pressure to 180 lbs/ sq in could be explained by the wish to prolong boiler life but less charitable reports state that this measure was taken to prevent this locomotive overshadowing the ex-GSWR 4-6-0s. Certainly the instant effectiveness of the Woolwich moguls in 1925 stood in stark contrast to the difficulties that were afflicting Class 400. Later in their careers, the boilers were restored to 200 lbs/ sq in working pressure. Specific dates are not recorded but this programme was completed during the 1930s.

There were few later changes to these locomotives beyond replacement of the SECR-style smokebox door with the centre-handle style employed with the Class 500, and from around 1933 onwards, the piston tail rods were removed. The SECR-style chimneys were replaced by a larger diameter cast iron one-piece chimney of Inchicore design on all except Nos 379 and 393 (latter of Class K1a described below).

There was contention among locomotive crews about the competence of the type. They do not seem to have been overly popular on the ex-GSWR section, in the early years at least, but ex-MGWR crews were fulsome in their praise, stating that services over their section could not be maintained without them. These varying views might be attributed to pre-amalgamation rivalry as the Woolwich was considered an MGWR-inspired type, and because of its 'foreign' origins. Other sources disputed that there had been any significant criticism, alleging that they were vital in helping meet the GSR's motive power demands.

The brake system was of pure Ashford layout with a steam brake on the locomotive powered by two 7½" diameter steam cylinders below the footplate. The tender was equipped with vacuum brake, powered by a single cylinder mounted below the running plate at the front end. Concern was expressed about deficiency in brake power when working non-fitted goods trains and several runaways occurred including that of No 390 at Cork in 1939 and of No 394 (see Class K1a below) near Inchicore on an up goods in 1954. The worst runaway involved No 375 working a Bridgetown-Thurles beet train at Cahir in December 1955 which ended up on the bank of the River Suir, killing the driver and fireman. Braking problems were identified early on with the British locomotives leading to the fitting of an additional brake cylinder on the tender; similar modifications were never instituted in Ireland.

One definite operating disadvantage stemmed from the chimney top being lower than the cab, so that exhaust often obscured forward visibility. As a result, smoke could swirl around the footplate making them dirty engines to work and leaving footplate crews looking like chimney sweeps. In Britain, this was overcome by fitting of smoke deflectors beside the smokebox; despite several recommendations, this useful modification was never applied in Ireland. A further cause of discomfort was that while the original design had included lagging and clothing of the firebox backplate, this feature was not fitted (in common with Inchicore's standard practice) leading to very hot footplate conditions.

It should be remembered that the type was originally intended for freight work in the south-east of England so their continued employment on express passenger services was stretching their riding and steaming capacities. There are reports that they had to be thrashed to keep time with heavier express passenger trains. Apart from the problems with riding discussed above, steaming suffered as fuel quality deteriorated. The Swindon-inspired firebox did not take kindly to ovoids, slack and duff. In the CIÉ oil-burning programme, all but four (and all the 6' 0" version described below) were converted, although not all actually worked in this condition.

The potential offered by fitting larger boilers (parallel in this case) was recognised by inclusion of several in the new boiler order that was cancelled as a result of the Milne Report (see Chapter 14). A substantial increase would have been achieved:

	Existing	**Proposed**
Boiler pressure	180 lbs/ sq in	200 lbs /sq in
Heating surfaces:		
tubes	1390.5 sq ft	1255 sq ft
firebox	135 sq ft	144 sq ft
superheater	285 sq ft	340 sq ft
grate	25 sq ft	27.5 sq ft
Tractive effort	23,430 lbs	26,040 lbs

In view of the stresses imparted to the existing structure, frame renewal or strengthening would have seemed inevitable with a significant weight increase and concomitant reduction in route availability.

A further option allegedly proposed around this time was that the moguls should be rebuilt as 3-cylinder 4-6-0s with the larger boilers, or with a smaller version to keep down overall weight. It is unclear whether this was a serious exercise or merely a flight of fancy but the idea seems to have had little merit. Rebuilding as a 4-6-0 would have involved creation of a virtually new locomotive with perhaps limited route availability,

GSR Class 372/ K1 No 372 with later GSR-style smokebox door standing in front of the water-softening plant at Inchicore in 1936. *L&GRP*

and would have added more engines of a wheel arrangement of which there was already an adequate supply. A more effective, and much cheaper alternative could have been created by fitting larger cabs, smoke deflectors and better cross-frame bracing.

In service, the type's axle loading gave it a much broader scope of operations compared with the 4-6-0s. On the ex-MGWR system, they could go almost anywhere bar a number of minor branch lines. On the ex-GSWR system, apart from the Dublin-Cork main line, they were also permitted on the Cork-Rosslare, Portlaoise-Waterford, Limerick to Ballybrophy, Limerick-Waterford, and Mallow-Killarney routes. They were allowed as far as Bray on the ex-DSER system under a 30 mph speed restriction, and they are remembered for working an annual excursion from Bray to Claremorris (for Knock).

They were used on the principal express passenger services on the ex-MGWR main line to Galway when in good condition, and also on similar services between Cork and Rosslare. As mileages increased, they were rotated onto goods services (where the rough riding would present fewer problems), mainly working out of Cork.

In the closing phase of CIÉ steam, these locomotives continued in an active role. Recognising that they would be needed for some time to come on heavier passenger and goods traffic on the ex-MGWR section, on the Rosslare expresses, on goods work around Cork and Tralee, and on certain special trains, it was decided in 1954 to give 20 of them heavy repairs. In the event, only Nos 372, 373, 376, 377, 383, 385 and 388 were so treated (and none of the larger-wheeled version). Like other late steam survivors, they were in deplorable condition by the end.

As a footnote, in 1963 during a clear-out of surplus parts and scrap metal at Inchicore, a set of Woolwich frames was discovered. Obviously intended for the 'missing' No 392 and clearly forgotten, this set might otherwise have found use in reframing one of the operating locomotives that was showing signs of wear.

1948 assessment (both 372 and 393 classes): *Primarily goods engines but suitable for passenger trains. The only difference in the classes is the 393 have larger wheels. They work Galway passenger trains but are too overloaded to run fast: also Sligo passenger and Rosslare Expresses, Up and Down Cork Night Mails. The boilers were built for British gauge and are too small for Irish requirements. Their axleload is much in their favour because they can go over sections that other large engines cannot. A good general purpose engine not requiring excessive repair.*

GSR Class 393 — 2-6-0 — Inchicore Class K1a, 1931 Load Class B

GSR No	Built	Withdrawn	GSR No	Built	Withdrawn	GSR No	Built	Withdrawn
393	9/1930	1954	395	9/1930	1957	397	11/1930	1957
394	9/1930	1959	396	10/1930	1959	398	12/1930	1955

Designer: Maunsell

Kits of parts built at Woolwich Arsenal; assembled at Inchicore.

Boiler pressure – 180 lbs/ sq in (later 200 lbs/ sq in)
Cylinders – 19" x 28"
Piston valves – 10" diameter
Pony wheels – 3' 1"
Driving wheels – 6' 0"
Wheel base – 8' 10" + 7' 3" + 7' 9"
Locomotive length – 33' 8 5/8"

Heating surfaces:
tubes – 1390.5 sq ft
firebox – 135 sq ft
superheater – 285 sq ft
grate – 25 sq ft

Tractive effort – 21,480 lbs (later 23,870 lbs)
Coal capacity – 5 tons
Water capacity – 3500 gal
Locomotive weight – 62 tons 11 cwt
Adhesive weight – 51 tons 11 cwt
Max axle loading – 17 tons 10 cwt

GSR Class 393/ K1a No 396. Distinguishable from Class 372/ K1 by small driving wheel splashers. *L&GRP*

The genesis of the Woolwich moguls has been described in the section on Class 372. Allowing for the mysterious gap of No 392 in the number series, the final six kits of parts were assembled with six-foot driving wheels. Just as Class 372 had its British counterpart in Southern Railway Class N, so Class 393 was the Irish equivalent of SR Class U. The remarks about performance, riding etc concerning Class 372 apply equally to these locomotives. The only additional modification concerned adjustments to the frames to accept the 6' 0" diameter driving wheels and the provision of small splashers. The boiler centre line was pitched three inches higher. The increase in driving wheel diameter was intended to make these engines more suitable for express work and they were considered faster runners although more prone to rolling at speed. In keeping with Class 372, boiler pressure was increased to 200 lbs/ sq in during the 1930s.

Some sources claim that Morton, when with the MGWR, had intended that six of the original order for 12 locomotives should be assembled with 6' 0" driving wheels, and that it was only after taking over as CME that he was able to fulfil this plan. This is borne out by the 'D2' classification apportioned by the MGWR in 1924 to the first 5' 6" Woolwich moguls. Presumably 'D1' had been set aside for the 6' 0" driving wheel version which eventually was to materialise as Class 393.

GSR Class 393/ K1a No 398 in CIE days with new style smokebox door and number. At Inchicore.

C P Friel Collection

A report dated 1931 states that the Rosslare Boat express was being worked exclusively by these engines but later they appear to have shared duties indiscriminately with the smaller-wheeled version and it must be questionable whether provision of larger driving wheels was worthwhile. It may be significant that Nos 393 and 398 were the first of all the Woolwich moguls to be withdrawn, that overall these engines had shorter working lives than those of Class 372, and that none were selected for the 1954 heavy repair programme.

1948 assessment (both 372 and 393 classes): *Primarily goods engines but suitable for passenger trains. The only difference in the classes is the 393 have larger wheels. They work Galway passenger trains but are too overloaded to run fast: also Sligo passenger and Rosslare Expresses, Up and Down Cork Night Mails. The boilers were built for British gauge and are too small for Irish requirements. Their axleload is much in their favour because they can go over sections that other large engines cannot. A good general purpose engine not requiring excessive repair.*

Chapter 10
Great Southern Railways' Locomotives

As at 1 January 1925, the fleet of the Great Southern Railways, immediately following absorption of the Dublin & South Eastern Railway, stood at 602 steam locomotives. Withdrawal of locomotives deemed unfit for repair or unsuitable for future traffic needs commenced that year. In spite of the new locomotives introduced by the GSR, through process of steady attrition the fleet total had shrunk by 17% to 503 by the end 1944.

The pattern of withdrawals was irregular. In several cases, numerically small classes became smaller by the scrapping of one to three locomotives in the 1920s and 1930s, with the remainder staying at work into the 1950s (eg Classes 222, 234, 296, 305, 321, 351, 355, 368 and 545). Reboilering programmes added diversity to some classes by use of different boiler types (eg Class 650). Thus while the number of different classes was reduced, confusing variety within some remained. Despite this complexity, some general trends can be identified.

The years **1925 to 1927** were typified by re-organisation and consolidation. In addition to the start of the withdrawal programme, works facilities were rationalised with the closure of the Factory at Grand Canal Street, Dublin and the ending of locomotive repairs at Rocksavage, Cork. Apart from the purchase of two Sentinel shunters, introduction of new motive power was restricted to the first 12 Woolwich moguls, which were the last locomotives built or assembled at the Broadstone. A landmark rebuilding in 1927 was the conversion of No 402 to two-cylinder propulsion.

A change of emphasis was noticeable between **1928 and 1930**. The assembly of Woolwich moguls was switched to Inchicore, and completed in 1930. Bazin authorised the installation of superheaters and piston valves on two ex-GSWR 4-4-0s, signalling a possible change of policy towards second-string power. No 850, the first pure GSR design and the most advanced tank locomotive on the system, appeared, and with it the prospect of modernisation on a broader front. The year 1928 was also notable for the withdrawal of 35 locomotives, the largest annual cull in the history of the GSR. Pursuit of modernity was interrupted with the introduction of the out-dated Class 700 the following year. Two more Class 400's were rebuilt as two-cylinder locomotives. Bazin retired and was succeeded by Morton.

The period **1930 to 1932** was a watershed in motive power affairs. Morton had an open attitude towards superheating, which was timely in view of the deteriorating economic situation. He introduced no new designs to the GSR and did nothing about converting more Class 400s. However his programme of modernising older locomotives, particularly Class 101, relieved the company of the necessity of building new engines. This exercise was of immense economic benefit, and was to continue for a number of years.

The most significant event during Harty's tenure from **1932 to 1937** was the opening of a new erecting shop at Inchicore, following closure of Broadstone Works the previous year. Locomotive development during this period was limited, if not regressive. The three new classes that appeared were all out-dated with some poor design features (Classes 670, 710 and 342). Class 710 was intended as a replacement for Class 101, modernisation of which was suspended in 1934. The following year, the superheating programme for Class 101 recommenced after the new locomotives were found to fall short of the mark. Completely out of character with this lack of enterprise, work started on the design of Class 800 in the final stages of Harty's tenure.

Bredin's appointment in **1937** opened a period of great promise, focused around the arrival of No 800 and the hope that this would lead to further progress in fleet rejuvenation. Before construction of the new 4-6-0s could be completed, aspirations for further progress were frustrated by the war years, a period when keeping any sort of service going was a considerable achievement.

In summary, the efforts to introduce a new generation of motive power were essentially unsuccessful. Only two GSR designs could be considered contemporary with modern trends – Classes 850 and 800 – and neither made any lasting impact on operations at large. The former suffered from lack of any concerted attempt to improve performance, or to develop its potential. The latter, for all its technical brilliance, was focused at a narrow spectrum of motive power needs, and could at best have had only marginal impact on the company's revenue base.

It was a disappointment that the initiatives in new motive power should have yielded such peripheral benefits. The company had a growing need for reliable, dependable types that could fill multi-functional roles with extensive route availability. The classes that came closest to filling these vital needs ironically had pre-amalgamation antecedents – the superheated Class 101 and the Woolwich mogul.

GSR Livery

The dour image of the GSR locomotive era was sustained by retention of the GSWR unlined grey livery. While practical and reasonably smart when fresh, this colour did nothing to enhance looks, as grime and dirt built up. The actual shade used is debatable. It has been described as 'battleship grey' which seems unlikely as being too light, and is not borne out by study of contemporary models which are in a definite mid-grey. Confusion also stems from the practice of cleaning with a type of oil that left a greenish tinge. Further, it is possible that the paint composition varied over time, and that the shade changed with ageing.

The grey was all-enveloping with only cab roofs, smokebox barrels and saddles, running plate surfaces, and buffer stocks in black. Numbers and number plate beading were painted red against a black background, although there were cases of numbers being painted white; eg Nos 462 & 464 after overhaul in 1931. Parts that normally would be expected to be black were actually grey – running plate valances, footsteps and frames. This livery style was also applied to locomotives acquired from the constituent companies although apparently to save expense, only a single layer of grey paint was applied, or perhaps thinned paint was used.

The grey livery was not popular, at least among enthusiasts. In 1930, the GSR revised its coach livery with a lighter shade of chocolate below the waist and cream upper panels. This style was well received and led to hopes that there would be an improvement in locomotive liveries. The first change was modest being the application of painted white numbers from new on the side tanks of Class 670, the only Inchicore-built locomotives not to be provided with cast number plates.

Arrival of No 800 brought more promise, as green livery was applied, although there is some doubt about the detail of this livery. A contemporary account describes it as "medium blue-green colour with black bands and yellow lines". However, the lining was actually a light shade of bluish-green (officially *eau de nil*) which might have appeared to be yellow in black and white photographs. Boiler bands were lined narrow *eau de nil* / broad black/ narrow *eau de nil*. The lining for cabsides and tender was a single narrow *eau de nil* line with the area between that and the body edge painted black. Just as most GSR locomotives had hitherto been enveloped in grey, green was liberally applied to Class 800 – boiler and firebox, cab front and sides, splashers, cylinder cladding and end covers, piston valve end covers, frame above running plate level on front fall plate, valances, footsteps, bogie and driving wheel spokes and rims, tender sides and rear, tender frames. The smokebox and saddle, cab roof, main and bogie frames, boiler hand rails, regulator linkage, vacuum brake exhaust pipe, running plate surfaces and footstep treads were black. Against the green tender frames, the springs, hangers and axle boxes were painted black.

Mention has already been made of the distinctive and beautiful bronze name and number plates with their blue background. The tender was adorned with the initials 'G S' with the GSR crest equidistant between the two letters. The crest used was similar to that which adorned maroon-liveried GSR carriages and was actually mounted on a timber board attached to the tender side. These locomotives were thus unique in displaying evidence of GSR ownership, beyond the small letters that adorned the number plates of machines introduced after 1925.

No 800 was repainted and smartened up while in store at Inchicore and was then repainted on arrival at the museum premises at Witham Street, Belfast. It is in this condition that it is displayed at the Ulster Folk and Transport Museum at Cultra. Great effort was made to copy the original livery and in its present condition it looks very fine. However, there are some errors: the bogie frames and main frames below running plate level should be black and not green; the lining cream is paler than *eau de nil*; study of contemporary photographs suggests that the there was no single line around the cut-outs in the tender frame as now appears. Regarding the 'G S' initials on the tender, the font is rather too thick compared with the original and the company's crest is missing. Finally there is debate over the shade of green applied as personal recollection states that it was lighter and slightly bluer than the present colour. However, this is difficult to judge as the subtlety of the actual shade is lost within the artificial lighting in the museum hall.

To help identify the correct shade of green, reference should be made to the locomotive models of the late Drew Donaldson on display at Cultra. Although not prototypically authentic liveries, models of Nos 63, 133, 321, 545, 648 and 651 actually carry paint (suitably thinned) of the batch used for No 800 and obtained by Drew from Inchicore.

Dramatis personae

The first two Chief Mechanical Engineers had served with the two principal constituent companies, and both were British by birth. Company mergers can evoke bitter rivalry among senior officials competing for key positions. **JR Bazin** had been appointed on the GSWR in 1921 and was on home ground as GSR mechanical engineering was headquartered at Inchicore. However Morton, who was younger, had led the MGWR locomotive department since 1915, as well as being a significant presence at the Broadstone for 10-15 years before that. On this basis he would have had a stronger claim to the top job but as some other senior positions went to ex-MGWR men, Bazin was preferred so as to 'create balance'.

There is no direct evidence of significant dissent between the two but the situation could not have been easy for either man. An immediate point of difference between them concerned superheating. Morton's proposal to continue the superheating programme was accepted and then ignored by Bazin. Apart from starting the programme of improvements on the Class 400s, Bazin is best known on the GSR for his efforts to develop a new strain of suburban tank locomotive.

Bazin retired in 1929, serving as President of the Institution of Locomotive Engineers in 1930, and was succeeded by **WH Morton**. During his second spell in the top engineering role, he introduced no fresh designs, but his contribution was undoubtedly the most substantial of the GSR's five CMEs, as he focused on improving the fleet as a whole. His lifting of the embargo on the superheating of smaller locomotives, led to the eventual conversion of 66 members of Class 101 (J15). This programme, which is analysed in the section describing that class (Chapter 4), meant that the GSR avoided the expense of building more new general purpose machines. Superheating of other classes was also commenced or re-started – ex-GSWR Classes 52, 301, 305, 309, 321, 333, 351 and 355 and ex-MGWR Classes 530, 545, 573 and 594. Others received Belpaire fireboxes for the first time eg ex-GSWR Classes 2 and 257 and ex-MGWR Class 650. He was CME for only three years before becoming General Manager of the GSR in 1932. It was then rare for a CME to accede to the even more important appointment of Chief Executive Officer, although Bredin also was to be elevated to this office.

Following Morton's promotion, **AW Harty** was appointed CME in 1932. A native of Cork, he was educated there and then became an apprentice in 1894 with the GSWR in that city. He completed his apprenticeship at Inchicore during the time that Coey was Locomotive Engineer. Following a period in a number of different positions, he was appointed Locomotive Works manager at Limerick in 1904, and then District Locomotive Superintendent at Waterford four years later. He returned to Limerick in 1911 in a similar capacity and was promoted to Chief District Locomotive Superintendent for Waterford and Limerick in 1916. At the formation of the GSR, he became Running Superintendent for the whole system, and then was CME from 1932 until retirement in 1937. Although the Class 800 is widely credited to his successor, much of the preliminary design work was undertaken during his period of office.

EC Bredin, who succeeded Harty in 1937, is best known as the designer of the Class 800, having followed in the then established pattern of being a long-term Irish railways employee. Nonetheless, after completing his schooling in Dublin, of which he was a native, he undertook two years' engineering training with Fielding & Platt in Gloucester before joining the GSWR as a pupil in their Carriage & Wagon works in 1907. He moved to the Locomotive Engineer's office at Inchicore in 1909 with special responsibility for monitoring coal consumption, and later became Junior Assistant to the Running Superintendent. In 1911, he became Shed Foreman at Rosslare where his duties were wider than this job title implied, as he was also responsible for the local electricity generating station, gas works, and electric pier cranes. After three years, he became Assistant to the Running Superintendent, and later District Locomotive Superintendent, Northern District.

He was appointed Assistant Works Manager in 1916, and then Works Manager in 1921. His responsibilities increased significantly after the amalgamation, as he was required to reorganise the various locomotive workshops, and then to supervise their co-ordinated working. He held the position of Works Manager for sixteen years before succeeding Harty in 1937. He became Deputy General Manager in 1941, and succeeded Morton as General Manager in 1942, retiring from this position at the end of 1946. Bredin might have felt some frustration with the way his career had worked out. Following the amalgamation, there had been few redundancies as would be the case with a modern day corporate merger, and this had left GSR top-heavy with management. His long wait for advancement in the 1920s and early 1930s was followed by a truncated period of progress in the No 1 position before everything changed in the War years.

The last occupant of the CME's seat was **M J Ginnetty** who had joined the MGWR as Chief Draughtsman

1911, having started his career on the GNR(I). He later became Works Manager at the Broadstone and then, in 1922, he was appointed Running Superintendent of the MGWR. In 1925 he became District Superintendent, of the Northern District, GSR. He followed Bredin but only in an acting capacity, presumably because he was due for retirement in late 1944. The position of CME then stood vacant for the short remaining period of the GSR's existence and for several years following under Córas Iompair Éireann.

Finally, mention should be made of **C F Tyndall** who began training with the GSWR at Inchicore in 1916, becoming Junior Assistant to the Works Manager in 1923. Two years later, he was appointed Senior Assistant to the Running Superintendent of the GSR. In 1929 he became Assistant District Locomotive Superintendent for the Cork area and in 1937, took control of the Waterford district. After becoming Running Superintendent in 1942, he was appointed Mechanical Engineer with effect from 1 January 1945 upon formation of CIÉ his position being re-titled Chief Motive Power Engineer in 1947. His particular contribution to the GSR locomotive story concerns his work with alternative fuels during the war years.

GSR Class 280 — 0-4-0T — Inchicore Class M1, 1931 Load Class TT

No	Built	Makers' No	Withdrawn
280	5/1927	6846	1948
281	5/1927	6847	1948

Built by Sentinel Waggon Co

Boiler pressure – 275 lbs/ sq in	*Heating surfaces:*	*Coal capacity – 10 cwt*
Cylinders – (2) 6¾" x 9"	*tubes – 35 sq ft*	*Water capacity – 300 gal*
Driving wheels – 2' 6"	*firebox – 36.5 sq ft*	*Estimated weight – 20 tons 5 cwt*
Wheel base – 6' 2"	*grate – 5.1 sq ft*	*Max axle loading – 10 tons 8 cwt*
Coupled by internal chain drive		
Locomotive length – 21' 1¼"		

GSR Class 280/ M1 No 1 (later No 280) in as new condition in 1927.

Real Photographs Ltd

During 1926, the GSR placed enquiries with Sentinel concerning the supply of 20 ton and 27 ton steam locomotives, and also steam railcars. An order for two steam locomotives, costing £1,590 each, was placed in conjunction with that for two Steam Railcars in December 1926. Further details are provided in the commentary on the Steam Railcars in Chapter 12.

Initially the numbers 1 and 2 respectively were allocated to these locomotives but they were renumbered in the company's books soon after introduction. However reports indicate that they were still carrying their original numbers in 1928/9.

These locomotives were standard Sentinel products with a vertical boiler placed above the frames inside the cab, and surrounded by bunker and water tanks. Feed water passed through a preheater which was fed by exhaust steam before admission to the boiler by means of a clack valve. The steam was superheated by passage through coils placed inside the smoke chute above the boiler. The two cylinders were mounted vertically between the axles which were powered by two roller chains on sprockets at the end of the crankshaft. Adjusting rods tied the axle boxes to the frames at the centre on each side and by this means it was possible to compensate for chain wear. The locomotive weight was borne by eight steel pads that rested on the ends of the four springs, which allowed movement of the axles when the chain tension was adjusted.

The reversing lever was a simple arrangement with a mere five notches: forward start at 80% cut-off – forward fast at 30% – intermediate or 'neutral' – reverse fast at 30% – reverse start at 80%.

Braking was possible by steam, hand and counter pressure. The latter was achieved by placing the reversing handle in the opposite direction to that of travel. Then by use of a special valve operated by a foot pedal, air was admitted to and then compressed within the cylinders. Vacuum braking was also fitted to haul passenger stock. The boiler layout and mechanical specification was very similar to that used in Sentinel steam railcars Nos 354 to 357.

Their low operating cost, minimal axle loading, and short wheelbase made them economical shunters suitable for lightly-built lines, and thus of interest to the cash-starved GSR. They were initially allocated to Cork and Tralee and one was tried out on the Castleisland branch. By the summer of 1931, both were at Tralee but in 1932 they moved to Limerick although still used on occasion in the Tralee area. At Limerick they worked the Market siding but when that facility closed in 1940, they lay out-of-service until withdrawal. It is curious that despite their efficiency and economy, no further work was found for them during the difficult period of the fuel crisis.

GSR Class 280/ M1 No 281 at Limerick in 1935.

L&GRP

GSR Class 850 2-6-2T

Early proposals:

The decision taken in January 1925 to withdraw a major portion of the DSER fleet confirmed that there would be insufficient indigenous locomotives available for the Dublin-Bray commuter services. There was immediate recognition of the importance of finding suitable replacements; several proposals and other apparently conflicting ideas were forthcoming:

1) Within a month the GSR Locomotive Committee recommended the construction of ten new 2-6-2Ts in replacement. The key dimensions for the proposed class were to be:-

Boiler pressure – 180 lbs/ sq in	*Heating surfaces:*	*Coal capacity – 3½ tons*
Cylinders – 17" x 26"	*tubes – 938 sq ft*	*Water capacity – 2030 gal*
Pony wheels – 3' 0"	*firebox – 112.5 sq ft*	*Estimated weight – 61 tons*
Driving wheels – 5' 1¾"	*grate – 18.8 sq ft*	
Trailing wheels – 3' 0" (Boiler as for 60/ 101 classes)		
Wheel base – 7' 9" + 6' 0" + 7' 3" + 7' 0"		

No other details are known but it would seem that in the design mode for medium-sized locomotives that had prevailed on the GSWR, they would have been inside-cylinder engines. Precisely why the class did not eventuate is unknown but revised plans soon drawn up would have been relevant.

2) Rumours circulated around this time of proposals to rebuild members of the GSWR Classes 301 and 305 as 4-4-2Ts. This concept certainly followed in the DSER tradition but a likely constraint was that the axle loadings of the resultant conversions would have been too heavy.

3) Another solution explored was the transfer in of ex-CBSCR Class 463 (B4) 4-6-0Ts. One was tried out and performed well, proving popular with crews. Apparently, however, it could be spared only for short periods by its native system and it was not until 1929 that a single example of this class was allocated almost continuously to Dublin-Bray services.

4) By 20 February 1925, the Locomotive, Permanent Way & Works Committee seems to have revised its views as it then recommended construction of ten examples of a 4-4-2 tank locomotive. The Board adopted this recommendation a month later. (The minute is interesting as it also speculates about seeking trade union co-operation in working a night shift at Inchicore so that the ten locomotives could be introduced to traffic by the end of 1926 – evidence of how important the need for new locomotives was felt at this time).

This was the most concrete proposal for a new design to relieve the situation and a diagram appeared for the planned Class 380 4-4-2T. The drawing is undated but allocation of the number 380 suggests that it was prepared between mid-February 1925 and mid-April 1925. (The first Woolwich Mogul was allocated 372 in April, with the expectation that the number series of the first dozen would end at No 383.) The leading dimensions from the diagram are:

Boiler pressure – 180 lbs/ sq in	*Heating surfaces:*	*Tractive effort – 19,150 lbs*
Cylinders – 17½" x 28"	*tubes – 708 sq ft*	*Coal capacity – 2 tons 15 cwt*
Pony wheels – 3' 0"	*firebox – 120 sq ft*	*Water capacity – ??? gal*
Driving wheels – 5' 8½"	*superheater – 168 sq ft*	*Estimated weight – 62 tons*
Trailing wheels – 3' 6"	*grate – 19.5 sq ft*	*Adhesive weight – 31 tons 10 cwt*
Wheel base – 6' 8" +7' 8" + 8' 0" + 7' 0"		*Max axle loading – 15 tons 15 cwt*
Length – 39' 2½"		

The boiler was a standard GSR Type N Belpaire superheated. The driving wheel diameter was the GSWR standard for mixed traffic locomotives but would have been unduly large for a locomotive intended to make frequent station stops and then accelerate swiftly away. The outside cylinders and Walschaerts valve gear indicates a modern design and resembles that of the later 2-6-2T No 850. Location of the driving wheels fore and aft allowed for a generous ash pan in between. The need was originally estimated at twelve of the type but by the time the project had reached this stage, it had been reduced to ten locomotives. The 4-4-2T was well-known on the ex-DSER section and Class 380 seems to have been intended as a modernised version of this type.

Two other variations on the 4-4-2T theme followed not long after the diagram for No 380 had been prepared. Notional running numbers allocated to these designs were 280 and (confusingly) 850. The known leading dimensions were:

No 280:

Wheel base – 6' 8" +8' 2" + 8' 6" + 7' 9"
Estimated weight – 60 tons

No 850 (as 4-4-2T):

Wheel base – 6' 8" +8' 2" + 8' 0" + 7' 0"
Estimated weight – 64 tons

Other than the temporary transfer of a member of Class 463, none of these plans and ideas bore fruit. Precisely why they did not eventuate is unclear but the workload arising from the amalgamation and the need to make good Civil War damage would have been relevant factors. In the interim, surplus locomotives from elsewhere were drafted in to make up the shortfall and despite their heterogeneous backgrounds, they seem to have allowed local footplate crews to cope. New locomotives to the design of DSER Nos 52 to 54 (Class 458/ C3) might have provided a more logical and effective solution, but GSR locomotive policy did not favour further locomotives to proven pre-amalgamation designs.

--- o O o ---

Three years later than originally contemplated, the first example of the new generation appeared and it turned out to be the only example of its type:

GSR Class 850 — 2-6-2T — Inchicore Class P1 — 1925/ 1931 Load Class H/ HT

No	Built	Withdrawn
850	9/1928	1955

Designer: Bazin — **Built at Inchicore**

GSR Class 850/ P1 No 850 at Amiens Street in 1930 *L&GRP*

Boiler pressure – 160 lbs/ sq in
Cylinders – 17½" x 28"
Piston valves – 8"
Bogie wheels – 3' 1"
Driving wheels – 5' 6"
Trailing wheels – 3' 0"
Wheel base – 8' 7" + 6' 9" + 6' 6" + 7' 3"
Locomotive length – 39' 2½"

Heating surfaces:
tubes – 697 sq ft
firebox – 119 sq ft
superheater – 240 sq ft
grate – 19.75 sq ft

Tractive effort – 17,700 lbs
Coal capacity – 3 tons
Water capacity – 1700 gal
Locomotive weight – 71 tons 10 cwt
Adhesive weight – 47 tons 10 cwt
Max axle loading – 16 tons 0 cwt

Left: GSR Class 850/ P1 No 850 at Amiens Street.

Authors' collection

Below: GSR Class 850/ P1 No 850 In CIE days with modified smokebox saddle at Amiens Street.

Kelland collection

No 850 was the first passenger tank locomotive to be built at Inchicore since 1902. It was a significant step in GSR policy as the first tangible effort towards new generation motive power on the DSER system, as the largest locomotive to work the Dublin-Bray-Greystones services, and as the first pure GSR steam design.

It was an impressive-looking machine and contemporary with 1920s trends, as evidenced by outside cylinders, Walschaerts valve gear, superheated Belpaire boiler, piston valves and three-feed Detroit vacuum lubricator. The engine was equipped with vacuum brake in the normal Inchicore fashion, powered by two brake cylinders below the footplate, each with its own vacuum reservoir just in front of the firebox. Although some features of the locomotive's styling (eg the cab and bunker design) marked a new departure for Inchicore, others were very traditional. Examples of the latter were the design of cab windows, and the single filler for bunker and side tanks which was located at the rear of the bunker in a style that had stayed unchanged with Inchicore-built tank engines since 1869.

Being significantly more modern in concept than any other tank locomotive on the GSR, it evoked much interest. Bazin used to visit Kings Cross from time to time and recorded that his old colleague, HN Gresley, paid close attention to the design and performance of No 850 during the period that the LNER Class V1/ V3 2-6-2T was being planned.

Contemporary accounts hinted that it was to be first of a class intended for Dublin-Bray services, the ex-CBSCR route, and other sections with short-distance passenger traffic. It has been suggested that main line work was also contemplated as it was given trials on Dublin-Thurles and Limerick-Waterford passenger trains. In the event, No 850 remained a long-time resident of Grand Canal Street shed and worked almost exclusively between Dublin and Bray, other than for a short period on Waterford-Limerick services during the early 1930s. When working from Dublin, No 850 was a frequent performer on the 17.07 Greystones Express or the Dun Laoghaire pier train.

In service, No 850 seems to have been received with mixed feelings by loco crews as some footplatemen found it awkward to operate. The locomotive was capable of good work, proving fast and powerful although with a propensity to roll at speed. When freshly out of the shops, it performed well but tended to become problematic as mileage built up, with a proneness to failure. There appeared to be an Achilles heel with the original lightweight motion which had a tendency to run hot. This problem was reduced, but not completely eradicated, by replacement with motion of more normal construction.

Whether the crew's criticisms were fully justified is questionable. The locomotive was quite unlike anything that had worked over the ex-DSER section before, and as often occurred elsewhere, coming to terms with a new design could be challenging, particularly with numerically small classes where the opportunity for many crews to build up experience was limited.

References have been found to the cutting of three sets of frames and while these are unsubstantiated, it is reasonable to assume that No 850 was intended as the prototype of a new class. What was strange was the apparent disinterest in development and improvement of the design. The GSWR/ MGWR dominated mechanical engineering department had limited experience with tank locomotives generally (most of which dated from the 19th century), and none of what was best for a tightly timed suburban commuter service with frequent stops. It would have been most unusual for such a radical new departure in design practice not to have encountered teething problems. However, apart from the installation of a smokebox saddle of revised design at its last general overhaul in 1948, No 850 was not significantly modified or improved during its working life.

There has been speculation about use of material for the 27th Woolwich mogul kit (represented by the 'missing' No 392 in the locomotive list) in the construction of No 850. The driving wheel diameter was certainly that of the K1 moguls and on the large side for a locomotive required to accelerate quickly away from frequent station stops. Few of the other major dimensions were shared with the tender locomotive, and the consensus view now is that the pony and driving wheels, and maybe some minor parts only were used. Consideration might have been given to more comprehensive use of the spare mogul parts to create a 2-6-4T rather as Armstrong Whitworth had done for the Metropolitan Railway in 1925 but the resultant maximum axle loading of 19 tons plus would have been excessive for the ex-DSER route.

No 850 was an infrequent visitor to the Harcourt Street line. On 17 August 1946, it ran into the turntable pit at that station and this proved to be its last visit.

1948 assessment: *Built 1928 for DSER* (section) *only one of class. Quite powerful, but needs altogether excessive repair but it is not replaceable at present.*

GSR Class 700 — 0-6-0 — Inchicore Class J15A, 1931 Load Class J

No	Built	Withdrawn	No	Built	Withdrawn
700	11/1929	1963	703	12/1929	1960
701	11/1929	1959	704	12/1929	1960
702	11/1929	1955			

Designer: Bazin

Built at Inchicore

GSR Class 700/ J15a No 701 at Inchicore in 1931. *L&GRP*

Boiler pressure – 160 lbs/ sq in	*Heating surfaces:*	*Tractive effort – 17,130 lbs*
Cylinders – 18" x 24"	*tubes – 887 sq ft*	*Coal capacity – 7 tons*
Driving wheels – 5' 1¾"	*firebox – 126 sq ft*	*Water capacity – 3345 gal*
Wheel base – 7' 3" + 8' 3"	*grate – 19.1 sq ft*	*Locomotive weight – 41 tons 0 cwt*
Locomotive length – 25' 3¾"		*Max axle loading – 14 tons 7 cwt*

The idea of a new 0-6-0 class seems to have been mooted in 1927 as a replacement for older locomotives on secondary and branch services. The only details available are driving wheels of 5' 1¾" diameter, 15' 0" wheelbase and an estimated weight of 44 tons 10 cwt. The inference is that this design would have replaced ageing members of Class 101 and other types of similar vintage. The practicality of the idea seems limited as the estimated weight was some 11 tons heavier than a Class 101 with 4' 0" diameter boiler, which presumably is why the proposal did not proceed.

Two years later, comparatively few 0-6-0s had yet been withdrawn and, with declining traffic levels, there was little need for more of this wheel arrangement. However, in 1924-5 Inchicore had built eight new boilers classified as Type 60/ 101 and intended for use on those two classes. In fact, only one boiler was fitted to a member of Class 60 and none to Class 101. It has been claimed that the only purpose for Class 700 was to make use of these boilers.

This was Bazin's last design and reflected his conservative policy regarding smaller locomotives in

GSR Class 700/ J15a No 704 at Inchicore in 1938. *WA Camwell*

the combination of saturated boiler and slide valves. Other traditional features were wheels, axles, cylinders and motion which were identical with those of Class 101 (J15). One concession to modernity was the use of underslung springs – laminated for the front and rear drivers, and helical for the centre drivers. The boiler was of greater diameter than the largest saturated boiler fitted to Class 101, yet had a smaller heating surface. Within two years of the introduction of Class 700 (J15a), the fitting of the Z-type superheated boilers to Class 101 commenced. In contrast, the Class 700 was never superheated and there is no record of any substantive effort to improve performance, although No 700 may have operated for a period in 1930 at a boiler pressure of 170 lbs/ sq in.

Despite the dimensional similarities, visually the class was quite different from Class 101. This was due to the higher-pitched, larger saturated boiler with Belpaire firebox, a more modern cab with extended roof supported at the rear by pillars, and the running plate raised clear of the coupling rods. When new they were given old GSWR 3345-gallon tenders declared redundant in 1928 following withdrawal Class 362 4-6-0s. These tenders were later swapped for other old tenders on visits to the workshops.

The lack of specific need for this class was apparent in their allocation to sundry passenger and goods services on an *ad hoc* basis. The modest axle-loading gave these locomotives a potentially wide sphere of operations although this feature was not really exploited. Shortly after introduction, No 701 was at work between Harcourt Street/ Westland Row and Bray but the class was mainly allocated to Inchicore and Waterford, and used on the Dublin-Cork main line. Viewed as a reasonable design promising a marginal improvement over the saturated Class 101, they were considered decidedly mediocre (with a heavy appetite for coal and water) when compared with the superheated Class 101, making them unpopular with locomotive crews. In 1941, No 702 was used on a turf-burning test between Dublin and Athlone, consuming 9 tons on the return trip.

1948 assessment: *Built in 1929 as an addition to 101 class, but from running point of view it did not compare with older design.*

GSR Class 495 — 0-4-0ST — Inchicore Class M3, 1931 Load Class TT

No	Makers' No	Built	Purchased	Withdrawn
495	1556	6/1920	1930	1949

Built by Peckett

GSR Class 495/ M3 No 495 at Cork, Rocksavage in 1938. *WA Camwell*

Boiler pressure – 160 lbs/ sq in	*Heating surfaces:*	*Tractive effort – 6,181 lbs*
Cylinders – 10" x 15"	*tubes – 274 sq ft*	*Coal capacity – 6 cwt*
Driving wheels – 2' 9"	*firebox – 40 sq ft*	*Water capacity – 475 gal*
Wheel base – 5' 0"	*grate – 5.6 sq ft*	*Locomotive weight –18 tons 0 cwt*
Locomotive length – 19' 5½" (est.)	*Boiler size – 8' 0" x 2' 11 5/8"*	*Max axle loading – 9 tons 0 cwt*

This locomotive was a standard Peckett product (their 'Beaufort' type) built in June 1920 and acquired from Allman & Co, Distillers, Bandon. It was a typical contractor's saddle tank locomotive with outside cylinders and open-backed cab. Following purchase, it was despatched to Rocksavage on the former CBSCR system for shunting work on the Victoria Quay siding, the line to the Ford motor works, and the sharply-curved line to Anderson's Quay. It was the only engine permitted to work the latter line but does not seem to have been greatly used by the mid-1930s. A 1939 report stated that it was in store not having worked at all for the previous 18 months.

This engine was a colourful exception to the dour GSR livery policy. Throughout its life it retained the colour scheme applied by the makers - olive green cab and tank, lined in black and yellow. The frames were red.

1948 assessment: *Bought from a Brewery for special purpose of shunting Albert Quay-Cork, for which work it is especially suited, but not often required.*

GSR Class 670 — 0-6-2T — Inchicore Class I3, Load Class KT

No	Built	Withdrawn
670	12/1933	1959
671	12/1933	1959
672	12/1933	1959
673	1/1934	1962
674	12/1933	1959

Designer: Harty

Built at Inchicore

GSR Class 670/ I3 Nos 670 and 674 at Amiens Street. *Kelland Collection*

Boiler pressure – 160 lbs/ sq in
Cylinders – 18" x 24"
Piston valves – 8"
Driving wheels – 5' 6"
Trailing wheels – 3' 1"
Wheel base – 7' 6" + 8' 3" + 6' 9"
Locomotive length – 35' 6½"

Heating surfaces:
tubes – 662 sq ft
firebox – 112 sq ft
superheater – 112 sq ft
grate – 18 sq ft

Tractive effort – 16,020 lbs
Coal capacity – 3 tons
Water capacity – 1500 gal
Locomotive weight – 57 tons 10 cwt
Adhesive weight – 45 tons 10 cwt
Max axle loading – 15 tons 15 cwt

GSR Class 670/ I3 Nos 670 at Bray in 1935 *L&GRP*

This class represented the final attempt by the GSR to introduce a tank locomotive specifically to handle the Dublin-Bray-Greystones commuter services. Rather than try to develop the latent potential of the modern No 850, Harty chose to take a regressive step with these engines. The design was undeniably conservative although economy was achieved by combining the competent Z type boiler (as used in the rebuilding of Classes 60 and 101) with frames and running gear that were to appear later with the Class 710. Although generally considered adequate performers, early reports on the activities of these engines were not favourable as they appeared to have difficulty in keeping time on the demanding Dublin-Bray section.

Further, repairs and maintenance work were time-consuming because little thought had been given to maximising the accessibility of the inside motion and working parts. In this regard, they were a departure from normal Inchicore practice in that the valves were pitched at an angle to the line of the cylinders so as to achieve direct drive. The cross-heads were carried by four slide bars that were supported centrally in the motion plate. The cramped and awkward layout compared unfavourably with the excellent accessibility of No 850. An unusual feature was that the superstructure was welded; No 673 uniquely was riveted after the original welding cracked.

Very little change took place with these locomotives. Following a collision between Nos 670 and 674 at Bray in September 1934, soon after their introduction, where both sustained rear end damage, their bunkers were extended into the cab space to increase the coal capacity to 3 tons 10 cwt. The remaining three were similarly modified later. When built, cast-iron chimneys were provided although about 1950, Nos 673/ 4 were equipped with the standard built-up type. From new, they broke with GSR convention in carrying large painted numbers on their tank sides, the first locomotives built at Inchicore without the traditional cast cab-side number plates.

Throughout their career, they worked commuter trains on Dublin-Bray-Greystones services. Their most notable duty was to work the Wexford Mail between Bray and Westland Row, as it was normal practice to change engines on this service at Bray. In June 1936, No 673 worked as far as Wexford but this was an isolated occurrence. From 1948 onwards, they appeared in the lined green 'passenger' livery.

1948 assessment: *This is a tank edition of 710 class tender engine used entirely on DSER section. They are slow and need too much repair. Could not, however, work DSER section without them.*

GSR Class 710 — 0-6-0 — Inchicore Class J15b, Load Class J

No	Built	Withdrawn	No	Built	Withdrawn
710	10/1934	1959	715	4/1935	1959
711	10/1934	1962	716	5/1935	1961
712	10/1934	1959	717	6/1935	1959
713	11/1934	1959	718	6/1935	1959
714	12/1934	1959	719	6/1935	1962

Designer: Harty **Built at Inchicore**

Boiler pressure – 160 lbs/ sq in
Cylinders – 18" x 24"
Piston valves – 8"
Driving wheels – 5' 1¾"
Wheel base – 7' 6" + 8' 3"
Locomotive length – 27' 6¾"

Heating surfaces:
tubes – 662 sq ft
firebox – 112 sq ft
superheater – 112 sq ft
grate – 18 sq ft

Tractive effort – 17,130 lbs
Coal capacity – 7 tons
Water capacity – 3345 gal
Locomotive weight – 43 tons 0 cwt
Max axle loading – 14 tons 17 cwt

Left: GSR Class 710/ J15b No 716 at Clara in 1938.

WA Camwell

Below: GSR Class 710/ J15b No 718. A young engine with an old tender at Inchicore.

Real Photographs Ltd

This was the final 0-6-0 type introduced to the GSR and effectively a smaller wheeled tender version of Class 670 0-6-2T. The intention seems to have been to create a locomotive somewhere between Class 101 (J15) and Class 257 (J4). An ex-driver has stated that this design was "a mule without the strength of a mule but with all the stubbornness of that animal".

Little more popular with crews than the preceding Class 700/ J15a, they were at least more modern in being superheated and fitted with piston valves. They had the reputation of being poor steamers with a heavy appetite for coal and water, although curiously these complaints were not levelled at their tank locomotive counterparts. The frames were extended at the rear to support a very deep cab which gave good weather protection but seemed to fulfil no other purpose. This feature meant that the fireman had quite a hike between the tender coal space and the firebox door. Unusually, they were fitted with steam sanding gear.

When introduced they were equipped with second-hand late-period GSWR 3345-gallon tenders, but a number were used on suburban services on the DSER section, for which work they were given the archaic 1864-gallon tenders with springs mounted above the running plate. They were used on a wide variety of secondary duties, but without any particular distinction.

1948 assessment: *Intended as a modern addition to 101 class. Reasonably good.*

GSR Class 342 4-4-0 Inchicore Class D4 Load Class L

GSR Class 342/ D4 No 346 at Broadstone with No 89 standing behind. *WA Richards*

In 1927, it is reported that consideration was given to a new class of 4-4-0s for secondary services. Proposed dimensions were: bogie wheels – 3' 0"; driving wheels – 6' 3"; wheelbase – 6' 0" + 6' 7½" + 8' 3"; estimated weight 45 tons. Quite why it was felt that such a type was needed is unclear. The driving wheel diameter was a MGWR standard and large for secondary services. The weight would have been similar to that of MGWR Classes C/ C1/ Cs, albeit with a longer wheelbase implying a smaller boiler. The design does not seem very practical nor would it have satisfied any pressing traffic requirement.

In fact GSR policy towards 4-4-0s seem to have been rather confused in the late 1920s and early 1930s. Some good pre-amalgamation classes of other wheel arrangements were ignored for further development, in preference for new designs. The one exception to this policy was the decision to build five new 4-4-0s based on ex-GSWR Class 333/ 338, in the form of Class 342 (D4).

This decision casts doubt over the rationale for certain aspects of GSR motive power planning and deployment. In 1927, some of the ex-GSWR Class 321 (D4) 4-4-0s dating from 1904-6 received new boilers and strengthened frames. However three of this class were withdrawn in 1927–28, together with the solitary Class 341 (D1), although none were unduly old by Irish standards. A further early withdrawal involved Class 305 (D12) No 308 which was taken out of service with cracked frames around 1931. These withdrawals can be directly attributed to the growing number of Woolwich moguls at work. However, excluding No 341 whose field of operations was limited to the Dublin-Cork route, the scrapping of the other 4-4-0s with their wider route availability seems odd. Perhaps with better allocation of available motive power, those premature withdrawals and their numerical replacement through the later Class 342 (described below) might have been rendered unnecessary.

No	Built	Rebuilt	Withdrawn	No	Built	Rebuilt	Withdrawn
342	9/1936	–	1959	345	12/1936	–	1959
343	10/1936	–	1959	346	12/1936	1940*	1960
344	11/1936	1940*	1959				

Designer: Harty **Built at Inchicore**

Boiler pressure – 180 lbs/ sq in
(later – 160 lbs/ sq in)
Cylinders – 18" x 26"
Piston valves – 8"
Bogie wheels – 3' 0"
Driving wheels – 5' 8½"
Wheel base – 6' 4" + 6' 10" + 9' 0"
Locomotive length – 30' 1¾"

Heating surfaces:
tubes – 1080 sq ft
firebox – 136.7 sq ft
superheater – 252 sq ft
grate – 20 sq ft

Tractive effort – 18,820 lbs
(later – 16,730 lbs)
Coal capacity – 7 tons
Water capacity – 3450 gal
Locomotive weight – 51 tons 10 cwt
Adhesive weight – 32 tons 0 cwt
Max axle loading – 16 tons 0 cwt

*** As rebuilt:**

Boiler pressure – 175 lbs/ sq in
Cylinders – 17" x 26"

Tractive effort – 16,320 lbs
Locomotive weight – not recorded

All the Coey 4-4-0s built for the GSWR had the standard express 6' 7" driving wheel diameter, except for Class 333 which had been intended primarily for the difficult Cork-Rosslare route. No 338 was extensively rebuilt in 1927, and equipped with superheating and piston valves. No other member of Class 333 was as extensively rebuilt and No 338 remained unique with a revised Load Class.

In its rebuilt condition, No 338 formed the template for Class 342 although with some detail differences, principally in the cab design. This was more angular than the rounded canopy fitted to No 338, and was equipped with side windows. A Wakefield mechanical lubricator was fitted on the left hand side.

A prominent feature of Class 342 was the use of bogies with outside frames and bearings, a style that had been adopted in 1908 on Nos 337 to 340. The intention was to avoid overheating of the bogie journals, a problem that had plagued Nos 333 to 336. However, the need for outside bogie frames had soon been found unnecessary (around 1909) by using a different lubricant and making some minor modifications to the axleboxes. As No 338 still retained its outside framed bogie when the specification for Class 342 was drawn up, this design feature was included although the related problem had actually been rectified about 28 years earlier.

There were a number of variations within Class 342. No 346 had Hoffman roller bearing axleboxes on its bogie wheels. About 1940, Nos 344 and 346 were rebuilt with 17" diameter cylinders and the boiler pressure was reduced to 175 lbs/ sq in while the remainder had their boiler pressure reduced to 160 lbs/ sq in but retained their original sized cylinders. The modifications were reputedly introduced to reduce a proneness to slipping.

Apart from the oversight concerning the bogie design, there were other curiosities about these locomotives. The fitting of 5' 8½" driving wheels promised allocation to Rosslare-Cork services but there is no evidence of their particular use on this route. Before the War, they were concentrated on services southwards from Dublin, and were favourites for working 'mystery tour' trains, reaching a variety of destinations. In CIÉ days, they also worked Dublin-Waterford/ Rosslare, between Waterford and Limerick, and also on the ex-MGWR section to Sligo, Westport, and occasionally Galway. Why five new mixed-traffic type 4-4-0s should be needed as late as 1936 against the continuing decline in traffic levels and the general competence of the Woolwich moguls is unclear.

No 346 was lent to the GNR(I) in 1947 to work the Bundoran Express between Dublin and Dundalk only. The purpose was to assess the design in connection with the planning of that company's Class VS three-cylinder 4-4-0 which was introduced the following year. At the time No 346 was an oil burner and it is believed that the opportunity was also taken for comparative testing against GNR(I) oil burners.

1948 assessment (333/ 338/ 342 classes): *Similar* (ie all three classes) – *valuable because they are fairly powerful and can travel most lines with their 16 ton axleload. Very useful for passenger specials. Reasonably fast, 342 Class completed about 1936.*

GSR Class 800 — 4-6-0 — Inchicore Class B1a, Load Class H

No	Name	Built	Withdrawn	
800	*Maedhbh*	4/1939	1962	Preserved
801	*Macha*	11/1939	1957	
802	*Tailtiu*	6/1940	1955	

(Names appeared in Old Gaelic Script; these are the equivalents when printed in Roman type).

Designer: Bredin

Built at Inchicore

GSR Class 800/ B1a No 801 *Macha* with original double chimney on a down train at Mallow. *Real Photographs Ltd*

Boiler pressure – 225 lbs/ sq in (later – 180 lbs/ sq in)
Cylinders – (3) 18½" x 28"
Piston valves – 9"
Bogie wheels – 3' 0"
Driving wheels – 6' 7"
Wheel base – 7' 8" + 5' 6" + 7' 3" + 8' 6"
Locomotive length – 40' 11¾"

Heating surfaces:
tubes – 1,670 sq ft
firebox – 200 sq ft
superheater – 468 sq ft
grate – 33.5 sq ft

Tractive effort – 34,785 lbs (later 27,830 lbs)
Coal capacity – 8 tons
Water capacity – 5000 gal
Locomotive weight – 84 tons 4 cwt
Adhesive weight – 63 tons 0 cwt
Max axle loading – 21 tons 0 cwt

By the mid-1930s, heavier loadings on the principal Dublin-Cork services were felt to be stretching the capacities of the existing fleet of 4-6-0s, particularly on the difficult climb out of Cork where multiple locomotives were sometimes deemed necessary. In 1936, triple-heading was reported on several occasions. In one case the combination was two 4-4-0 plus an 0-6-0 and in two other instances, it was 0-6-0 + 4-4-0 + 4-6-0 (which a leading commentator of the time considered extravagant for a load of 11 bogies). Nonetheless, operators believed there was a need for a significantly larger locomotive that could cope with these trains unaided, at higher overall average speeds, in part achieved by elimination of the stop to remove pilot engines.

The decision to proceed with a larger design could

not have been straightforward. Inchicore had been responsible for all of Ireland's 4-6-0 tender locomotives. Of this small yet diverse group (inside two-cylinder, outside two-cylinder, and four-cylinder versions), only Class 500 was satisfactory from the start. There would have been full awareness of the risks arising from any repeat of the Class 400 saga. Some commentators have remarked that it would have been wiser to play safe with a modernised, larger boilered version of Class 500. The post-war experience of British Railways with large two-cylindered express locomotives (the Britannia class), and with the high-speed capacity of small-wheeled engines (the Class 9F 2-10-0) would certainly support this view. However in the 1930s the belief remained that a multi-cylindered locomotive with six feet plus driving wheels was to be preferred for express work.

A further argument in support of three cylinders (actuated by three sets of Walschaerts valve gear) derived from weight and size considerations. Reportedly some thought was given to developing a pacific in the mid-1930s. Use of a trailing axle would have helped keep the maximum axle loading within acceptable limits but the resultant locomotive would have been too long for the turntables on the Dublin-Cork route. A compromise was therefore struck with the Civil Engineer to the effect that a 4-6-0 with a 21 ton axle loading would be acceptable, provided that it had three cylinders thereby allowing improved balancing of the motion and reduced hammer blow.

It was over 10 years since No 502 had entered traffic. In the interval steam locomotive design had progressed elsewhere whereas Irish practice had stagnated. The GSR's only previous attempt to build a truly modern locomotive (No 850) had led nowhere and the pedestrian Classes 670, 700 and 710 that followed were obsolescent. Against this track record, the design that emerged in 1939 was a truly startling break with this uninspiring tradition. In fact, so many features were unprecedented in Ireland that planning and execution of the new venture must have relied heavily upon study of foreign practice. However just where outside help came from is not immediately apparent.

As no three-cylinder simple expansion express locomotive had been built in Ireland, any relevant British experience would have been of interest at the start of the project. Reviewing the principal features of the Class 800 and by process of elimination, it can be deduced that there was significant influence derived from British practice in the design. Firstly, it is easy to discount the GWR and LNER. Swindon never built a three-cylinder machine and the only major point of similarity was the firebox. Doncaster was well versed in three-cylinder propulsion but the divided drive, three sets of Walschaerts valve gear, and Belpaire firebox were manifestly out-of-step with contemporary LNER thinking. The visual similarity between Class 800 and the rebuilt LMS Royal Scot is striking but this was coincidental rather than intentional. In 1937, the rebuilding of Royal Scots was still six years in the future and the only example of this genre then in service was No 6170 *British Legion*. This was a one-off rebuild of an experimental engine and would not then have been sufficiently prominent to warrant close examination by the Inchicore team.

There is a further reason for discounting the LMS influence. At that time Stanier was deeply embroiled in his re-stocking programme and had confronted problems in the boiler design of his own three-cylinder 4-6-0, the Jubilee Class. Although by 1937, these difficulties had been largely resolved, these circumstances make it unlikely that the LMS would have been an immediate point of reference at the time plans were being drawn up for No 800.

By this process, there is left the remaining member of the Big Four and here the circumstantial evidence is powerful. Richard Maunsell had retired from the Southern Railway in 1937. He had been popular during his short tenure as Locomotive Superintendent of the GSWR and was known to have visited the Inchicore drawing office in retirement. During his time away, his personal standing would have been enhanced by the presence of the Woolwich moguls.

His English experience on the South Eastern & Chatham Railway, and later on the Southern Railway, had been wide-ranging despite the actual number of locomotives bearing his imprimatur being comparatively fewer than those of his peers with the larger companies. He had created a family of potent rebuilt and new inside-cylindered 4-4-0s; he had been responsible for the design of the Woolwich moguls; he had introduced three-cylinder versions of both 5' 6" and 6' 0" variants of this type. These three-cylinder developments had been the brainchild of his brilliant assistant, Harry Holcroft, who had been consulted years before about how to improve the Class 400. Holcroft's recommendations had led directly to the rebuilding of No 402.

In 1926, Maunsell had introduced the four-cylinder 4-6-0 Lord Nelson class which briefly had been the most powerful express design in Britain – on paper at least. In fact, the Lord Nelsons joined that list of British four-cylinder 4-6-0 designs that did not fully meet expectations, an accusation that could not be levelled at his final design – the three-cylinder 4-4-0 Schools Class.

GSR Class 800/ B1a No 802 *Tailte* with single chimney at Inchicore in 1951, and carrying Belfast-Dublin-Cork Enterprise headboard.

Kelland Collection

By any standard, the Schools were simply magnificent, persistently performing on arduous services to a standard that the GNR(I) large 4-4-0s would have been stretched to emulate. The combination of circumstance and the Mogul/ Lord Nelson/ Schools history makes a compelling case for Maunsell's informal yet influential involvement in the creation of the Class 800.

Another positive influence was also present. Apart from the use of long-lap piston valves, it is known that the Inchicore Drawing Office studied the pioneering work of André Chapelon in the streamlining of steam passages, and that these principles were put to good use. Officially, while the design process commenced under Harty's regime, his successor EC Bredin has always been accredited as the designer. This is probably fair as there seems to have been little in Harty's career and background to suggest that he would have been motivated to lead such a startlingly progressive initiative of his own volition shortly before retirement.

That Chapelon should have had an influence suggests a broad determination to make the design as modern as possible. Just as Class 500 has never received the acclamation that was perhaps its due as one of the earliest examples of the modern two-cylinder long lap 4-6-0, so Class 800 has enjoyed little recognition for one particular noteworthy design feature. Post-war, the fitting of double chimneys became commonplace in Britain but at the time of No 800's introduction, this feature was still a novelty. The class was designed for high-speed running and it had very likely not passed notice at Inchicore that the LNER a year earlier had achieved a world speed record with No 4468 Mallard, one of only four Class A4s then fitted with double chimneys.

Class 800 was provided with twin blast pipes and a double chimney where the inside cylinder exhausted through the forward chimney and the outside cylinders through the rear chimney. This unique arrangement has been described as a curiosity whose purpose was unclear. The explanation was most likely quite simple – there were very few double chimneys in use anywhere at the time, so this layout might then have seemed as logical as any other. This feature nonetheless made the class distinctive as being the first in these islands to have been exclusively fitted with double chimneys from new. As an indication of the locomotive's size, the whistle had to be mounted horizontally on the firebox to clear the loading gauge.

The arrangement may not however, have given the satisfaction expected. No 802 carried a single chimney for 1949 to 1951, and No 801 was equipped with a similar chimney from 1954 until withdrawal. In their

GSR Class 800/ B1a No 801 *Macha* with single chimney and additional brackets on smokebox door. At Cork.
CP Friel Collection

last years, Nos 800 and 802 are understood to have carried double chimneys with conventional blast pipe arrangements

Other features reflected modern practices. A MeLeSco superheater with 28 elements and Wakefield 12 feed lubricator were fitted. The valve dimensions were unquestionably modern: lap – 1½"; travel – 6¾"; lead – $^{3}/_{10}$". As well as intended to haul heavy loads, Class 800 was designed for high speed running but rather curiously, the exhaust clearance was nil.

The bogie and tender wheels had roller bearings, needle roller bearings were used on quadrant links, a multiple valve regulator was fitted, and mechanical lubrication applied to slidebars and axle boxes. The cab was modern and spacious, being nine feet wide, and the roof was extended rearwards to reduce air turbulence that would otherwise suck coal forward on to the footplate.

In memory of the problems with flexing of frames in the Class 400 as built, efforts were made to prevent recurrence of these difficulties by massive construction. For comparison, the Lord Nelsons and Royal Scots used frame plating of 1" and 1⅛" thickness respectively, whereas the frames of No 800 were of 1¼" high tensile steel. With the intention of sustained high speed running, care was taken to provide adequate brake power. Two large 24" diameter vacuum cylinders were mounted on the locomotive and two more on the tender. In service, it was noted how effectively these locomotives could reduce speed quickly if required.

The combination of stronger frames and exploitation of the larger Irish loading gauge casts suspicion on the reported weight of 84 tons on introduction of No 800. This was close to the working weights of the Lord Nelsons (83 tons 10 cwt) and the Royal Scots (83 tons). There is a report from an unofficial visit to Inchicore when No 800 was actually being weighed that it turned the scales at just over 90 tons. Other sources have suggested that the weight could have been understated by as much as 10 tons which would suggest a maximum axle loading of in the region of 22-23 tons, although use of three cylinders would have significantly reduced the hammer blow. There seems little doubt that any possible objections from the civil engineer were overlooked in the determination to create a prestigious locomotive that would be a response to the large express designs for which the LMS and LNER had been responsible in the 1930s.

In keeping with the iconic role that the class was to fulfil, Bredin issued special instructions regarding the care of these locomotives. He made the following remarks … *"the fire irons should be kept in the space provided along the right trailing splasher so that tender paintwork is not damaged"* and *"a good deal of expense and trouble has been undertaken to give these engines an attractive appearance, which every Driver will take a pride in preserving. Care in working will preserve the paint from damage when filling sandboxes, filling oil pumps and such other work …"*

Despite the care taken with design and appearance, there are some features that do not complement the overall presentation. The regulator rodding was mounted externally on the right-hand side of the boiler, despite the locomotives being left-hand drive. This was a practical but austere measure rather more typical of post-war British design practice. The cab side windows seem disproportionately small for the size of the locomotive and their plain brass framing does not sit comfortably on the cab side. Viewed from the front, the buffer heads seem somewhat undersized for so large an engine while the smokebox has a slightly lop-sided air. This arises from the hand rail on the right side being set at the centre line of the boiler whereas that on the left side is lower to allow for the vacuum brake exhaust pipe which runs along the centre line from the cab to discharge into the smokebox at the mid-way point.

These are minor criticisms, though, that do not detract significantly from what is a most impressive-looking machine with a truly classical mating of a large Belpaire firebox with a stylish taper boiler profile (actually a parallel boiler hidden beneath tapered sheeting and lagging). After all the trials and tribulations with the 400 Class, there must have been a strong desire to see a flagship introduced that would be a determined Irish response to locomotive developments elsewhere and a focus of corporate, and indeed national, pride. No 800 does not seem to have been found wanting in those respects and more importantly, early trials indicated that performance matched the looks. During a visit by senior locomotive engineers from the LMS in 1940, No 801 was placed at their disposal. These engineers were lavish in their praise for its speed and haulage capacity, and for its comparatively modest appetite for fuel. This visit was not publicised at the time but the notion of the mighty LMS seeking guidance from the GSR is an amusing reversal of the popular notion that the Royal Scots were somehow the progenitors of the 800s!

By 1942, there was growing evidence to support these favourable early impressions. On one occasion, No 800 reputedly lifted 17 bogies out of Cork unassisted and reportedly performed as far as Rathpeacon better than a pair of class 400s could have managed. Another time, No 802 hauling a late-running mail train of ten bogies covered 51 miles from Maryboro' to Kingsbridge in 43 minutes at an average speed of 71 mph. For six to eight miles, speed was sustained at around 95 mph

GSR Class 800/B1a No 800 *Maeve* at Cork, Glanmire. *OS Nock*

and the view was formed that in better condition, and presumably with better quality fuel, attainment of 100 mph which such a load would be quite possible. During the visit of a fuel expert from Britain who was investigating how well GSR locomotives were doing with alternative fuels, No 800 averaged 70 mph from Ballybrophy to Dublin (a distance of 66¾ miles).

Post war, their use was inevitably more limited and restrained in comparison with their brief but brilliant debut. From the late 1940s all three worked with a boiler pressure of 180 lbs/ sq in although No 801 reverted to its original working pressure before withdrawal. Also around that time, Nos 800 & 801 (and possibly No 802) carried speedometers, while No 801 had a vacuum operated windscreen wiper (which was of little practical use) on the driver's spectacle plate.

There are, however, some questions about the class that remain unresolved. In normal conditions, loadings on Dublin-Cork services rarely exceeded 300 tons and schedules, while brisk, were not unduly demanding for the existing fleet of 4-6-0s. The start from Cork was difficult but not impossible for a Class 500. After all, Stanier Class 5 4-6-0s regularly took loads of around 300 tons out of Inverness unassisted on the 22-mile climb, mainly at 1 in 60 to 1 in 70, to Slochd Summit. By comparison, the Class 800 seems to have been a rather extravagant solution to what might be viewed as a comparatively modest operational difficulty.

The actual number of Class 800s originally planned has been a matter of conjecture. Reports about a new class of large locomotives being planned at Inchicore suggested that five would be built but as there was uncertainty whether the wheel arrangement would 4-6-0 or 4-6-2, little credence can be placed on such speculation. Separate sources provide lists of names selected. Apart from listing names that clearly were not of Irish queens, the fact that Grainne appears in one list and not the other suggests that these names were speculative only.

On the other hand, four boilers were constructed under Order No 3056 and the boiler register as at 8 September 1946 states:

Boiler No 958 (mileage 255,000), No 959 (230,000), No 960 (192,000), No 961 (135,000). In all cases the ages of the boiler and firebox was recorded as seven years. There would have seemed little point in building a spare boiler from new and the contention that a fourth locomotive was intended is supported by a 1938 report during the building of No 800 and 801 expressing doubt whether money would be available for "two other engines of the class" as "all four are required for the Cork Mail turns".

What is definite is that the timing of the introduction of these locomotives could not have been worse. When new, No 800 was put to work on its intended duties between Dublin and Cork and had no difficulty in keeping to a schedule that had been reduced by 22 minutes. However there was little time left for such exploits. Nos 800 and 801 were to enjoy a short period of normal operating conditions, while No 802 was not completed until 1940. Nonetheless there was an obvious determination to put these engines to good use as by April 1941, No 800 had clocked up 148,000 miles, a not-insignificant figure. By 1949-50, the cumulative mileages of Nos 800–02 were 372,000, 351,000 and 428,000 respectively.

Slower schedules during the war years were at first a matter of operating convenience but soon became a necessity as the fuel supply situation reached crisis levels. These conditions continued for several years and, for all their distinguished status, many must have considered the trio to be white elephants. Oliver Bulleid, despite being a late champion of steam, was dismissive of the design although this might simply have been reflective of his iconoclastic attitude towards some of his predecessors' work.

In the post-war period, the continuing fuel crisis prevented the Class 800 from re-establishing its pre-eminence on express work although all three members played their full part on the heaviest trains. On 2 October 1950, CIÉ's principal express service was revised to operate Belfast-Dublin-Cork, thus slightly expanding the operating range. The Enterprise called at Dublin Amiens Street for locomotive change and train reversal. Over the southern leg, the new train was often assigned to 800s which worked to Amiens Street over the line from Islandbridge Junction. The train ran non-stop from Dublin to Limerick Junction, the first regular non-stop working over GSR/ CIÉ metals of over 100 miles.

With the introduction of the first-generation diesel locomotives, the class was soon relegated to secondary work and often quite menial duties. Nonetheless, despite their brief pre-war career and their sad closing years, there is evidence to support the belief that these locomotives were every bit as good as their English counterparts.

In fact, the Class 800 is considered by many to rank alongside the most powerful 4-6-0s in these islands, and worthy of consideration in the same light as the GWR King class and the LMS rebuilt Royal Scots. Essentially based on a design dating from 1907, the Kings are widely considered to have been out-performed by the Scots in their later form so that the Irish design had some tough competition. Early mileages between repairs were impressive but changing circumstances meant that there was never an opportunity to test the Class 800 thoroughly over an extended period. By comparison the Kings and Royal Scots were kept hard at work on front line duties until their demise in 1962 and 1965 respectively. Also, the 800s were limited by use as is apparent when comparing annual mileages:

Locomotive(s)	Built	Withdrawn	Total mileage	Average annual mileage
GSR No 801	1939	1962	641,000	27,870
King Nos: 6000/ 1/ 3/ 4/ 9/ 10/ 12/ 13/15/ 19	1927/8	1962	1,900,000+	55,000+

Regarding the Royal Scots, even in their less successful original form, they averaged 54,973 miles in 1927 and by 1936, the annual average of this class of 70 locomotives had risen to 72,242 miles. Once again, dismal annual mileage figures raise questions about whether the GSR/ CIÉ ever achieved a satisfactory return on investment in its top line express locomotive fleet.

The remaining valediction of the design came in a test to which the Kings and Royal Scots were never subjected. Constrained to operate with sub-standard fuel of types described in Chapter 13, the class was not spared the obligation of having to stop regularly for 'bailing out', but the boilers showed a consistent ability to raise steam in difficult circumstances. This was in large part due to the generous area of the grate – almost 20% larger than the Class 400 – and to the superior qualities of the Belpaire firebox. In fact when in post-war years, CIÉ moved to relieve the fuel crisis by converting locomotives to oil fuel, no consideration was given to converting the 800s, such was their acknowledged steaming capacity.

Nonetheless, the key question "Why were they built?" remains unanswered. The original intention to build four examples would have yielded a 40% increase in a 4-6-0 fleet with limited route availability. Although the three that appeared were a substantial increase in power over the ten 4-6-0s then in service, there was no compensating withdrawal of older locomotives. This meant that the overall utilisation factor of the 4-6-0 fleet, already poor compared with the work and mileages demanded of express locomotive elsewhere, declined even further. As already raised in Chapter 9 concerning Class 400, there is the subsidiary question "Why were thirteen 4-6-0s needed principally for the Dublin-Cork services, a route of 165¼ miles?"

At around £12,000 each, the 800s were expensive to build, the more so for a company in poor financial condition. The alleged need to overcome double-heading out of Cork must surely have been possible using a cheaper solution. (Ironically, local trade union interests insisted that they be assisted out of Cork in CIÉ days, despite the acknowledged power of these locomotives). Some changes in operating rules, allowing a pair of Class 101 0-6-0s to loose bank heavy trains, would have overcome the difficulty. This would also have freed up scarce funds to meet more pressing demands such as a medium-sized standard utility design to cope with the demands of Dublin-Bray services.

Nevertheless, the presence of Class 800 had a great impact on staff morale. The GSR and its employees were very proud of them as a statement of their ability to create and operate locomotives of the first rank, comparable with the best that Britain could then produce. They were commonly depicted in all types of GSR (and later CIÉ) publicity and publications, making them well known to the Irish public at large. Nonetheless, the operating rationale and commercial justification for these majestically impressive machines will for ever remain one of those great mysteries of the steam locomotive story.

1948 assessment: *Good fast engine, needing little repair. Only three, however, in the class which reduces their value.*

GSR Class 820 (Proposed) 4-6-2T

During 1940, work started on a design, the only known dimensions for which were:

Boiler pressure – 200 lbs/ sq in	*Heating surfaces:*	*Tractive effort – 18,960 lbs*
Cylinders – (3) 14" x 26"	*tubes – 1084 sq ft*	*Coal capacity – 5 tons*
Driving wheels – 5' 8½"	*firebox – 136.7 sq ft*	*Water capacity – 2500-2700 gal*
	superheater – 252 sq ft	
	grate – 21 sq ft (Boiler as for 342 Class)	

Ten locomotives were proposed, fitted with three cylinders presumably in the format inaugurated with Class 800. Just how firm was this proposal is open to question as the intended duties for so many locomotives are not immediately obvious. (One source refers to plans for six 3-cylinder express tank locomotives, for use on ex-DSER section suburban trains interspersed with Waterford services).

An unattributed sketch drawing exists which indicates a large tank locomotive of awkward layout with a 16' 3" coupled wheelbase. All three cylinders drive the leading axle, which is set far back, just in front of the ashpan. The centre driving wheels are behind the ashpan under the cab and the rear set under the forward part of the bunker. This layout has little in common with Class 800 and one feels that substantial revision would have been needed to create an effective locomotive. In fact, a change to a 2-6-4T wheel arrangement would have been a sensible early modification.

Design work seems to have been halted fairly early on in view of the worsening international situation and the adverse implications for the GSR's operations. The significance of these plans lies in the suggestion that Class 800 was to have been the first of a new locomotive generation, and in providing a glimpse of how locomotive thinking might have developed in the closing years of the GSR

Chapter 11
Tenders

All weights quoted in this chapter are laden weights unless stated otherwise.

The water quality in many parts of Ireland is poor with a high lime content making it generally unsuitable for use in locomotive boilers. Water troughs were never used anywhere in the country although their installation was investigated on the Dublin-Cork main line. Unfortunately, it was not possible to identify a stretch of level track that was sufficiently close to a good quality water supply to make such an investment feasible. During the era of the Great Southern Railways the only water softening plant was at Inchicore, first proposed in April 1926 and eventually established in late 1927. (Further water treatment plants were installed later in Córas Iompair Éireann days at other locations).

The comparative scarcity of places where suitable water could be taken on, made it desirable to exploit the greater operating range afforded by the use of tenders. Throughout the history of the GSR, tender locomotives comprised 69% or more of the company's operating fleet, and they were used on many services that could have otherwise been handled by tank engines. Also, lightly-laid track in some places made it preferable to use tender locomotives with lower axle loadings.

The only constituent companies using tender locomotives at the amalgamation were the Great Southern & Western, Midland Great Western and Dublin South Eastern railways. The variety that characterised the GSR's locomotives was also evident with the tender fleet. The number of different types at the amalgamation and built/ acquired subsequently was:

Ex-Great Southern & Western Railway:	8
Ex-Waterford Limerick & Western Railway:	10
Ex-Dublin & South Eastern Railway:	8
Ex-Midland Great Western Railway:	11
Great Southern Railways:	3

Many tenders were of considerable antiquity. Some were modified to increase capacity but others worked until retirement in essentially original condition. Larger locomotives, heavier trains and faster speeds meant that later designs were progressively of greater fuel and water capacities. This trend was most pronounced with the GSWR which in 1924 still used a few of 1600 gallons capacity, in contrast to its most modern 4500 gallon tenders, with two of 4670 gallons capacity under construction.

Of the constituent companies, the GSWR's fleet was numerically speaking the largest, and if the vehicles acquired from the WLWR are excluded, it was the most standardised. The greater variety among the tenders of the other companies stemmed from the acquisition of locomotives in small batches from different manufacturers.

Diversity persisted even with comparatively late tenders. As an example, MGWR Classes F/ Fa/ Fb (GSR Class 623) built 1921-1924 were provided with two types of tender; the difference involved water capacity, which was only apparent in a quite subtle difference in the side profile of the body. Also, the last nine tenders built/ ordered by the GSWR were of three quite distinctive types and capacities.

Variety was also evident among tenders of the same type. This usually involved the provision of side rails or side extension plates to increase coal capacity. The difficulties with fuel supplies in the 1940s led to a spate of makeshift timber extensions to increase fuel capacity still further. A later short term modification was the installation of oil tanks in the coal space for use with oil-burning locomotives; on reversion to coal, most of these vehicles retained the ladders that had been fitted on the tender sides towards the rear. This useful modification greatly eased access to the water/ oil fillers from rail level.

Excluding the GSWR-designed locomotives Nos 501 & 502 and their tenders, the GSR built/ assembled 34 tenders and 49 tender locomotives. The shortfall was made up by use of older tenders rendered surplus by the steady contraction in locomotive numbers. The size of tender selected would depend on the nature of the duties contemplated. Thus Class 710 (J15b) locomotives, introduced in 1934, would work with 3345 gallon ex-GSWR tenders on rosters involving longer journeys. On the other hand, aged 1864 gallon tenders might be used if the locomotive was allocated to short distance suburban work over the ex-DSER route.

Of the three tender types introduced new by the GSR, two worked only with the locomotive classes with which they first appeared (the Woolwich moguls and Class 800). The third type introduced with locomotive Class 342 worked with a variety of other engines, including even Class 101.

The steady reduction in locomotive numbers

rendered a continuing surplus of tenders that found use in other areas. The running frames of some were used to transport materials at Inchicore and other works locations. Others enjoyed secondary careers in 'tender trains' which were used to supply water to remote locations. The use of old tenders for this purpose largely fell away under CIÉ, on installation of the water softening plants mentioned earlier. A final variation in the tender story involved the creation of a limited number of hybrids out of old tenders; this process involved the marriage of a running frame with a non-original body. Two of these curiosities appear in photographs on page 291.

The information set out below is drawn from the GSR Tender Registers of 1929, 1940 and 1944, cross-checked against the records of RN Clements and other sources, and retrospectively corrected back to 1925. Certain anomalies in the list that cannot be explained are suitably annotated.

Numbering methodology

The GSWR's numbering system, judging by the run of the numbers, seems to have been established around 1870, possibly as part of McDonnell's re-organisation programme. Existing tenders were given the same number as that of the corresponding locomotives to which they were then coupled, and new tenders carried the number of the first locomotives with which they worked. So far as can be determined this methodology remained largely in place until the introduction of the Class 400 locomotives. When No 400 appeared it was coupled to an existing 3345 gallon tender of older vintage; the six Armstrong Whitworth-built locomotives (Nos 403–05, 407–09) appeared with tenders numbered 400 to 405; the Inchicore trio, Nos 401, 402 and 406, initially ran with earlier 3345 gallon tenders. Locomotive No 500 appeared with unique tender No 406.

Following the amalgamation, ex-GSWR tenders retained their numbers. The Great Southern Railways re-numbered those tenders absorbed from the MGWR and DSER, as part of the number series previously maintained by the GSWR – ie in parallel with the renumbering of locomotives of non-GSWR origin. The Tender Registers identify them by the number they carried in pre-amalgamation days, helpfully suffixed 'D' (for DSER) and 'M' (for MGWR). Ex-Waterford, Limerick & Western Railway tender numbers were suffixed 'WL', presumably dating from the earlier absorption of that company's fleet by the GSWR. On transfer into the GSR fleet numbering system, the DSER and MGWR tenders were given the same new numbers that were allocated to their related locomotives.

With one fleeting exception, none of the tenders that appeared new under GSR auspices was given a number that related to the first allocated locomotive. An attempt was made to revert to the GSWR-derived system with the Woolwich mogul tenders that were numbered 410 to 435, the first mogul having briefly carried the number 410. Tenders built after 1925 were all numbered within the series that eventually ran from 1 to 440, with gaps in sequence.

Ex-DSER tenders were numbered 422, 440–54, 461 and 462. Ex-MGWR tenders were numbered 240, 241 and 530–668 (with gaps in sequence). There are uncertainties with the gaps in the MGWR list, resulting from numbering anomalies.

Two tender numbers were allocated twice by the GSR. The tender coupled to ex-DSER 2-4-0 No 24 (GSR Class 422 No 422) was given the related GSR locomotive number. This locomotive was withdrawn in 1928 and the number was subsequently carried by a Woolwich mogul tender. Also, ex-DSER 0-6-0 No 17 (GSR Class 440 No 440) received the related GSR locomotive number. This locomotive was withdrawn in 1929 and the number subsequently re-appeared on a tender behind a member of GSR Class 342 (D4).

Tenders were identified by a single cast number plate, mounted centrally on the rear of the body, just above the buffer beam.

Great Southern & Western Railway Tenders

A few, old tenders of 1500 to 1608 gallon capacity remained in service in the 1930s and early 1940s. It is known that locomotive No 13, based at Kenmare, was coupled during that period to what was reported as a 1320 gallon tender with 10' 4" wheelbase, but no other information has been traced. (The capacity was more likely to be 1500 gallons but this is conjecture). Other early tenders identified as having survived into GSR service are listed below. No dimensional details have been found but in general style, they may have been slightly smaller versions of the 1864 gallon standard Type A tender described later. They were built and numbered as follows:

Built	Nos	Gallons
1870*	41, 42	1500
1873	21 to 26	1608
1876	66 to 69	1608

** Construction date uncertain*

GSWR 'standard' types

There were five standard types of GSWR tender at the amalgamation with another introduced shortly afterwards. A feature of most GSWR tenders was the use of snap-head rivets that made cleaning of the body more difficult. Later types introduced for service with 4-6-0s used a combination of welded seams and flush-head rivets to create smooth body sides. Also, the tender shovelling plate was set below the level of the footplate boards which made stooping necessary to reach the coal. It was not until the introduction of a new tender style with Class 342 in 1936 that the shovelling plate was raised on Inchicore-designed tenders to overcome this awkward characteristic.

GSWR Type A tender with capacity increased by fitting of side and rear plate extension. *Real Photographs Co ltd*

For convenience, these types are labelled Types A to F – a notation system that is an unofficial device of the authors to help with cross-referencing. The GSWR applied a considerable measure of standardisation through its tender classes which, linked with the numbering system, helps to identify types and, in many cases, the locomotive with which each initially worked.

Type A

This type was apparently introduced more or less concurrently with Class 101, and was attributed to McDonnell as an adaptation of an existing Beyer Peacock design. Construction was conventional, using a six-wheeled chassis with a 12' 4" wheelbase, with equally spaced wheels of 3' 9" diameter. Laminated springs were mounted on the running plate which restricted the width of the body and hence the carrying capacity. Tender sides and rear were flared outwards at the top. Official carrying capacities were four tons of coal and 1864 gallons of water, with a weight of 24 tons. Many of these tenders survived well into GSR days without visible modification. The most significant change was the fitting of side plates, and sometimes rear extension plates, to increase the coal capacity, and to reduce the risk of spillage.

A total 116 of these tenders were built, mostly at Inchicore. The following were built by outside contractors:

Nos	Builder	Dates
151–54	Beyer Peacock	between 1868 and 1873
175	Sharp Stewart	1874
176	Sharp Stewart	1873
177, 178	Beyer Peacock	1873
185, 186	Sharp Stewart	1879
189, 190	Beyer Peacock	1881

(Tenders Nos 163 to 166 were built at Inchicore although the corresponding locomotives of the same numbers were built by Sharp Stewart).

Type A tenders were built and numbered as follows:

Built	Numbers
1867	62/ 3
1868	56/ 7, 151/ 3/ 4
1869	114/ 5
1870	60/ 1
1871	155/ 6/ 159–62
1872	58, 158/ 163–66
1873	102/ 4, 152, 167, 175–78
1874	168–75
1875	64/ 5/ 108, 157, 179, 180
1876	59, 106, 117
1877	2, 5–7, 43–46, 109, 119–21, 143
1878	144–46
1879	181/ 2/ 5/ 6
1880	8, 10/ 3/ 5, 110, 147, 183/ 4
1881	107, 112/ 3/ 123–26/ 139–42/ 8/ 9, 189, 190
1882	101/ 5, 111, 122/ 7/ 8, 130/ 1, 150, 187/ 8
1885	133–35, 191
1887	103
1888	4, 11/ 4 / 8, 132, 136–39
1889	129
1890	118

GSWR Type A tender with coal capacity increased by installation of side plates, and further timber side extension.

Authors' collection

GSWR Type B tender in original condition

IRRS collection

Type B

In 1885, a modernised version of Type A appeared initially with those members of Class 52 used on night mail and certain other main line trains that ran longer non-stop distances. The overall chassis dimensions were unchanged from Type A, but the laminated springs were mounted on the outside frames, directly above the axle boxes. Viewed from the side, the body profile was unchanged but relocation of the springs enabled a wider body to be fitted, thereby increasing the carrying capacity to 5 tons 10 cwt and 2730 gallons. A later modification was the provision of a side plate extending from the front right along the side and around the rear in one solid piece. The official weight of the Type B tender, which was usually referred to as the '2700-gallon express type', was 28 tons 5 cwt.

As Class 52 was relegated to less arduous duties, all members of that locomotive class reverted to the smaller Type A tenders. Type B tenders were then transferred to Class 60 while the last examples appeared with locomotive Class 305. Type B comprised 28 vehicles. They were built and numbered as follows:

Built	Numbers
1884	1, 3, 9, 12/ 6/ 7/ 9, 20, 52–55
1885	93–96
1886	85–89
1895	97, 98

GSWR Type B tender after fitting of side plates to increase coal capacity. Ladders were retained from when the tender was equipped for oil-burning.

Authors' collection

GSWR Type C tender. Back plate has been fitted to coal rails. This tender has been converted back from oil-burning to coal. The warning white circle remains, as do the ladders fitted to aid re-filling of oil tank. Retention of this facility also greatly helped the taking on of water.

Authors' collection

Type C

This type (the first of which was numbered 194) appeared with the introduction of the first Coey 4-4-0 in 1900, and was the most common among the GSWR's later and larger locomotives. Chassis dimensions remained unchanged (3' 9" wheel diameters and 12' 4" evenly spaced wheel base). The tender body shape followed the same style as Type B but was taller. Measurement of several different drawings suggests that the length over buffers was 22' 0". Capacity was increased to 7 tons and 3345 gallons, with the weight at 32 tons 10 cwt. Known as the '3300-gallon express tender', this design remained unaltered except for slight modification to the brake gear and the later addition of three coal rails above the coal space. These rails were supported within a frame that followed a similar profile as that used on the plates fitted to Type A, with concave curved ends, and supported by four vertical stanchions.

From about 1911, it became practice to install plates behind the coal rails although there is a photograph of No 400 as new in 1916 with an open coal rail version. A later development saw the coal rails replaced altogether with a plain side plate with the same profile. Although nine tenders of larger capacities than 3345 gallons were introduced later, these did not completely supplant Type C from use with the ex-GSWR 4-6-0s. A 1937 photograph of No 407, the last remaining four-cylinder engine, depicts a Type C tender while a 1949 picture shows a similarly-equipped No 500 departing on an express from Kingsbridge. There was a total of 67 Type C tenders in service; they were built and numbered as follows:

Built	Numbers
1899	194–99
1903	301–04, 309–14, 355–61
1904	305–08, 321–24
1907	325–28
1908	329–36
1909	337–40
1910	351–54, 362
1911	363–69
1917	370–73
1922	374–77

GSWR Type C tender with coal rails and backing plate

IRRS collection

GSWR Type C tender with slightly different profile side plates. The Inchicore penchant for snap head rivets can be clearly seen. This tender seems to have had a hard life, judging by the patches to the body sides.

Authors' collection

GSWR Type C Tender with side plates.

Authors' collection

GSWR Type D tender No 406.

The Railway Gazette

The following Type C were built by contractors in 1903: Nos 309 to 314 (Neilson, Reid) and Nos 355 to 361 (North British).

Type D

Mixed traffic 4-6-0 No 500 was introduced with a unique tender, No 406. It was built in 1922 and the last in the traditional GSWR form. The side plates above the flared sides were deeper and than on the fender-fitted variant of Type C and the body sides were extended at the front by an additional panel. The length over buffers was 21' 8¾" (ie almost unchanged from Type C). Wheelbase remained the standard at 12' 4" evenly spaced but the carrying capacity was increased to eight tons and 3870 gallons, with a weight of 42 tons.

Type E

The Type C tender fitted to locomotive No 400 seemed disproportionately small compared with the locomotive, a feature that was also apparent once its voracious appetite became evident. The other three Inchicore-built members of the class (Nos 401, 402 and 406) were introduced with the modern version of Type C tender but the six Armstrong-Whitworth engines came with a completely fresh design – Type E

The standard 3' 9" diameter wheels were used but the wheelbase was extended to 15' 2", evenly spaced. Sides and rear were flared at the top and a solid fender was fitted that stretched almost the full length of the side. Capacity was increased to seven tons and 4500 gallons, and a tender more appropriate to the size of the locomotive resulted. The weight was 48 tons and length over buffers was 25' 11½" as opposed to approximately 22' 0" for Type C

The Type E tenders were built by Armstrong-Whitworth in 1922, numbered 400 to 405, and were delivered with locomotives Nos 403 to 405 and 407 to 409. Some sources imply that Inchicore built at least three more of this type around 1923/ 4 but this was not the case, as confirmed by the GSR Tender Register. An article in *The Locomotive* for 15 November 1928 which describes the rebuild of No 402 with two cylinders states that a larger tender had been attached, the inference being that previously the locomotive had been working with a Type C tender.

Type F

This version consisted of two tenders completed in 1925 and numbered 407 and 408. They were intended for use with Nos 501 and 502, having been ordered by the GSWR but completed by the GSR. The styling was quite different from the tenders introduced in GSWR days having plain flat sides and a flat top with no railings or side plates. The coal space was contained within raves inset from the sides, which would have aided rearward vision. They were nicknamed 'biscuit tins'.

When introduced, these were the largest tenders in Ireland, having a capacity of 4670 gallons and seven tons, ten cwt. The wheelbase was 13' 0", evenly spaced, and the weight was 49 tons.

GSWR Type E tender, manufactured by Armstrong Whitworth.

Kelland collection

GSWR Type F tender, known as the 'biscuit tin'. Fitted with ladders.

Authors' collection

Ex-Waterford, Limerick & Western Railway Tenders

At least nineteen WLWR-built tenders were still in service with the GSWR at the amalgamation, although in six cases the corresponding locomotive had been scrapped earlier. Presumably these six vehicles were working with Inchicore-built locomotives but it has not been possible to identify which.

Sources conflict over the water capacities of some of the ex-WLWR tenders but most were of around 2000 gallons, although there seems to have been differences in the capacities of tenders of ostensibly the same size but built by difference manufacturers. Tender No 39 (GSR No 289) would appear to have been a late survivor from a class of 2-4-0s dating from 1874-1882, the last locomotive member of which was withdrawn in 1911.

The tenders known to have passed into GSR stock were numbered as follows:

Built	WLWR No	GSWR No	Builder	Built	WLWR No	GSWR No	Builder
1881	8	261	Vulcan Foundry	1895	49	235	Dubs
1881	36	286	Vulcan Foundry	1895	50	236	Dubs
1882	39	289	Vulcan Foundry	1896	53	296	Kitson
1884	1	193	R Stephenson	1896	54	297	Kitson
1892	22	275	Dubs	1897	55	298	Kitson
1893	43	290	Dubs	1897	56	237	Kitson
1893	44	291	Dubs	1897	57	238	Kitson
1893	45	233	Dubs	1897	58	239	Kitson
1894	47	292	Dubs	1900	2	222	Kitson
1894	48	293	Dubs				

The following remaining ex-WLWR tenders might have survived until GSR days but no details have been traced, so this list is largely speculative:

Built	WLWR No	GSWR No	Builder	Built	WLWR No	GSWR No	Builder
1874	30	281	Vulcan Foundry	1886	9	262	Dubs
1876	19	272	Avonside	1889	10	263	Dubs
1881	37	287	Vulcan Foundry	1892	23	276	Dubs
1883	41	231	Vulcan Foundry	1893	46	234	Dubs

The dimensions of ex-WLWR tenders known to have survived post-1925 are:

WLWR Tender Nos	GSR Tender Nos	Loco: GSR Class	Weight	Wheelbase	Wheel diam	Water	Coal	Builder
1	193	???	???	???	???	2000 gal	???	R Stephenson
2	222	222	27t 8c	4'10" + 4'10"	3' 9"	2000 gal	4 tons	Kitson
8	261	???	???	5' 3" + 5' 3"	3' 6"	1585 gal	4 tons	Vulcan Foundry
22	275	???	28t 5c	5' 3" + 5' 3"	3' 6"	1940 gal	4 tons	Dubs
36	286	???	???	5' 3" + 5' 3"	3' 6"	1585 gal	4 tons	Vulcan Foundry
39	289	???	???	5' 3" + 5' 3"	3' 6"	1630 gal	4 tons	Vulcan Foundry
45	233	235	???	5' 3" + 5' 3"	3' 6"	1900 gal	160 cu ft	Dubs/ Kitson
43, 44	290/ 1	276	28t 5c	5' 3" + 5' 3"	3' 6"	1900 gal	160 cu ft	Dubs/ Kitson
47, 48	292/ 3	276	28t 5c	5' 3" + 5' 3"	3' 6"	1940 gal	160 cu ft	Dubs/ Kitson
49, 50	235/ 6	235	28t 5c	5' 3" + 5' 3"	3' 6"	1900 gal	160 cu ft	Dubs/ Kitson
53	296	296	27t 8c	9' 8" overall	3' 6"	1940 gal	4 tons	Kitson
54, 55	297/ 8	296	28t 5c	9' 8" overall	3' 6"	2000 gal	4 tons	Kitson
56–58	237–39	236	28t 5c	5' 3" + 5' 3"	3' 6"	2000 gal	3¼ tons	Dubs/ Kitson

NB Because of uncertainties concerning with which locomotives classes these tenders worked, it has not been feasible to allocate 'types' in the Authors' type system.

It should be noted that tender No 2 (GSR No 222) was the same type as GSR Nos 240 and 241 attached to ex-MGWR 0-6-0s Nos 141 and 142 (GSR Class 234/ J17).

Right: WLWR/ GSWR tender associated with 0-6-0s Nos 2, 56 to 58 and MGWR Nos 141 & 142 (GSWR/ GSR Classes 222 – J25 and 234 – J17). Referred to as Type Q in the MGWR tender list.

IRRS collection

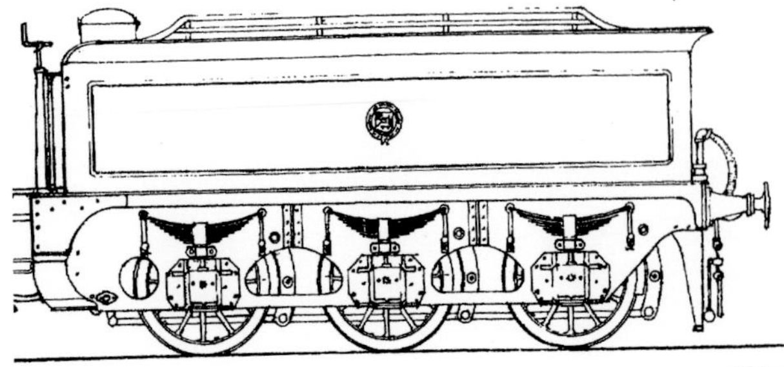

Below left: WLWR/ GSWR tender believed to have been purchased with 4-4-0s Nos 53-55 (GSWR/ GSR Class 296 – D 15).

Stephenson Locomotive Society

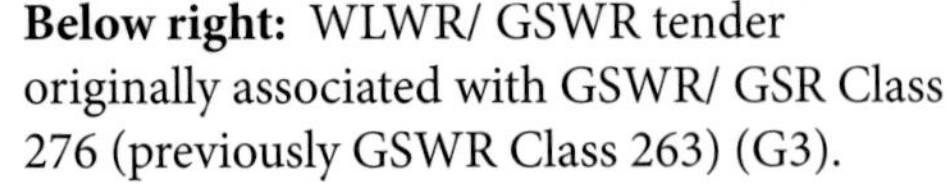

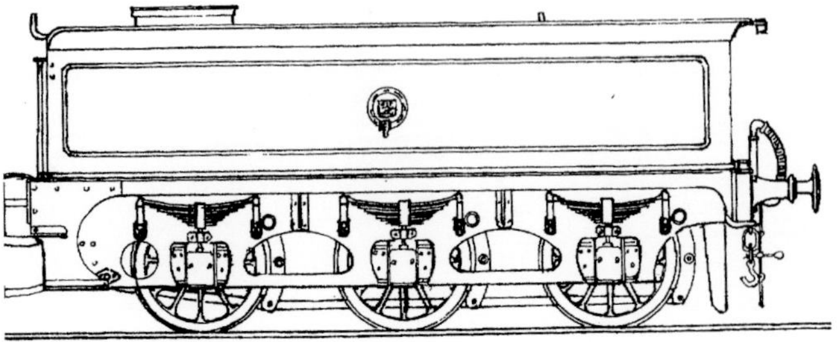

Below right: WLWR/ GSWR tender originally associated with GSWR/ GSR Class 276 (previously GSWR Class 263) (G3).

Stephenson Locomotive Society

Dublin & South Eastern Railway Tenders

The DSER tender fleet was substantially smaller than that of the GSWR but proportionately more diverse. From contemporary accounts, it seems that tender exchanges were relatively unusual with DSER locomotives. The tenders acquired by the GSR had been built as follows:

Built	DSER No	GSR No	Builder	Built	DSER No	GSR No	Builder
1864	24	422	Sharp Stewart	1905	14	443	Grand Canal Street
1891	50	447	Vulcan Foundry	1905	65	445	Beyer Peacock
1895	55	450	Vulcan Foundry	1905	66	446	Beyer Peacock
1895	56	451	Vulcan Foundry	1905	67	454	Beyer Peacock
1896	57	452	Vulcan Foundry	1908	4	448	Vulcan Foundry
1896	58	453	Vulcan Foundry	1908	5	449	Vulcan Foundry
1899	17	440	Grand Canal Street	1910	18	444	Grand Canal Street
1900	36	441	Grand Canal Street	1922	15	461	Beyer Peacock
1904	13	442	Grand Canal Street	1922	16	462	Beyer Peacock

In addition, some sources record that the following 1600 gallon tenders built by Sharp Stewart were acquired from the DSER as spares:

Built	DSER No	GSR No
1873	32	554
1873	33	553
1877	39	552

The accuracy of this information is doubtful. The GSR numbers are in the ex-MGWR number series (albeit the locomotives carrying these numbers were tank engines). However the GSR registers indicate that Nos 552 to 554 were 3000 gallon tenders (of ex-MGWR Type T), although no reference is made to what numbers were allocated in pre-amalgamation days. (Ex-MGWR Type T 3000 gallon tender No 551 is preserved with GSR locomotive No 461).

Type	DSER Tender No	GSR Tender No	Loco: GSR Class	Loco: I'core Class	Weight	Wheel-base	Wheel diam	Water	Coal	Builder
G	24	422	422	G7	23t 0c	5' 9" + 5' 9"	3' 6"	2100 gal	4 tons	Sharp Stewart
H	17, 36	440/ 1	440/ 441	J20/ J14	22t 0c	5' 9" + 5' 9"	3' 6"	1850 gal	4 tons	Grand Canal St
J	13/ 4	442/ 3	442	J8	23t 0c	5' 9" + 5' 9"	3' 6"	2600 gal	4 tons	Grand Canal St
K	18, 4, 5	444/ 8/ 9	442/ 448	J8/ J1	25t 0c	5' 9" + 5' 9"	3' 6"	2000 gal	4 tons	Grand Canal St
L	65/ 6/ 7	445/ 6/ 54	442/ 454	J8/ D8	30t 10c	5' 9" + 5' 9"	3' 8½"	2600 gal	4½ tons	Beyer Peacock
M	50	447	447	J7	25t 15c	5' 9" + 5' 9"	3' 6"	2600 gal	4 tons	Vulcan Foundry
N	55-58	450-453	450	D9	27t 0c	5' 3" + 5' 3"	3' 7½"	2600 gal	4 tons	Vulcan Foundry
P	15/ 6	461/ 2	461	K2	32t 10c	6' 0" + 6' 0"	3' 8½"	2600 gal	5 tons	Beyer Peacock

There are certain discrepancies over recorded water capacities. The GSR Tender Register states that the capacity of DSER Nos 4 and 5 (GSR tender Nos 448 and 449 respectively) was 2000 gallons, and of DSER No 18 (GSR No 444) was 2600 gallons. There is no record of modifications to tender tanks; the changes might have been resulted from capacities being re-measured.

Type G tender as associated with DSER Locomotive No 24 (GSR No 422).

Real Photographs Ltd

Believed to be Type H Tender as associated with DSER Locos Nos 14 and 36 (GSR Nos 440 and 441).

Real Photographs Ltd

DSER Type J Tender, as supplied with DSER Nos 13 & 14 (GSR Class 442/ J8 Nos 442 & 443).

CP Friel collection

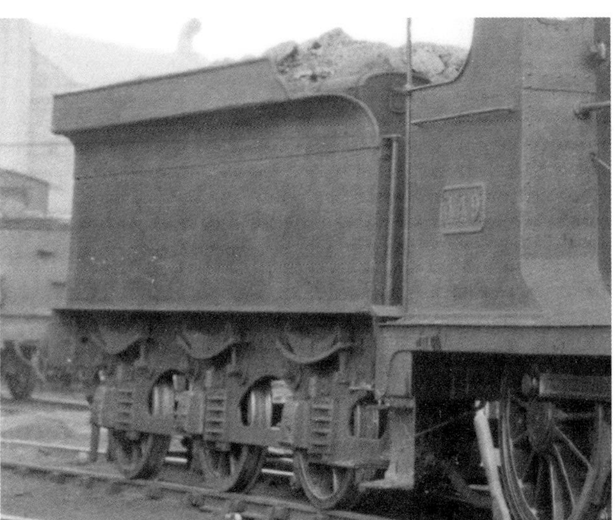

DSER Type K tender associated with Class 444 (J8) and Class 448 (J1).

L&GRP

DSER Type L Tender. *L&GRP*

DSER Type M Tender. *CP Friel Collection*

DSER Type N tender. *Kelland Collection*

DSER Type P This tender was delivered by Beyer Peacock with three side coal rails which were replaced later with side plates. Additional timber side extensions were fitted during the fuel crisis. The frame at the tender front was used to support a weather sheet when working tender-first. *Authors' collection*

Midland Great Western Railway Tenders

Ex-MGWR tenders were considered superior to those designed at Inchicore. Flush head rivets were universally used giving a smoother outward appearance, and aiding cleaning. The tender shovelling plate was set at hip level and made firing less strenuous. A significant proportion of ex-MGWR tenders were of 1600-1700 gallon capacity, which necessitated more frequent water stops than was the case with ex-GSWR types.

No records have been traced of building dates for ex-MGWR tenders; the closest estimates that can be madc would be based on the construction dates of the related locomotives.

Despite this railway's attitude towards locomotive standardisation, there was considerable variety among its tender fleet, as evident in the following table:

Type	MGWR Class	GSR Class	I'core Class	Weight	Wheelbase	Wheel diam.	Water	Coal	Builder
Q	W	234	J25	27t 8c	4' 10" + 4' 10"	3' 9"	2000 gal	4 tons	Kitson
R	D/ Ds	530	D16	24t 7c	5' 6" + 5' 6"	3' 9"	1600 gal	4 tons	Broadstone
S	C/ Cs/ C1	536/ 540	D7/ D6	31t 7c	6' 0" + 6' 0"	3' 9"	2500 gal	7 tons	Broadstone
T	A/ As/ A1/ B	545/ 646	D5/ J2	35t 16c	6' 6" + 6' 6"	3' 9"	3000 gal	6 tons	Broadstone/ North British
U	L/ Lm/ K/ Ks	573/ 650	J18/ G2	22t 5c	6' 0" + 6' 0"	3' 9"	2000 gal	4 tons	B'stone/ Kitson/ S Stewart
V	Ln	563/ 567	J16	22t 17c	5' 6" + 5' 6"	3' 8"	1600 gal	4 tons	Broadstone
W	L	594	J19	22t 5c	5' 9" + 5' 9"	3' 9"	1700 gal	4 tons	Broadstone
X	H	619	J6	35t 16c	6' 6" + 6' 6"	3' 9"	3000 gal	7 tons	Avonside
Y	F/ Fa	623	J5	33t 6c	6' 0" + 6' 0"	3' 9"	2500 gal	7 tons	B'stone/ Armstrong Whitworth
YA	Fb	623	J5	33t 6c	6' 0" + 6' 0"	3' 9"	2800 gal	7 tons	Broadstone
Z	K/ Ks	650	G2	23t 0c	5' 6" + 5' 6"	3' 9"	1700 gal	4 tons	Broadstone

The MGWR actively rotated tenders among class members and between classes, which complicates identification of which type worked with which locomotive class. Particular difficulties relate to identification of the allocation of tenders in Types R/ V and W/ Z

It should be noted that the GSR discipline of tenders bearing the same number as the first corresponding locomotive was ignored with type Y/ YA as tender numbers 573–84 and 589 were allocated to the tenders with locomotives GSR Nos 633–45.

A further curiosity with the MGWR's tender numbering system was that several numbers in that company's list (specifically Nos 35, 57, 88, 89, 91, 92,

93, 94 127 and 140) were borne by two vehicles at the same time. This might have in part arisen from the partial renumbering of locomotives in 1922 and 1924. Strangely however, while confusion over tender (and locomotive) numbers could occur with older members of a fleet, eight members of the class Fb (the latest additions) were involved in these discrepancies.

Duplicated MGWR Nos	GSR Nos	Duplicated MGWR Nos	GSR Nos
35	544 & 623	92	539 & 629
57	616 & 619	93	540 & 630
88	625 & 644	94	631 & 643
89	626 & 645	127	545 & 571
91	628 & 642	140	621 & 668

Inconsistencies in the numbering of MGWR tenders pre-amalgamation seem to have continued after 1925. The GSWR/ GSR principle of allocating the number of the related locomotive could not have applied in the case of tenders Nos 551 to 554/ 614 to 618 as the related locomotives were 0-6-0Ts of Classes E (GSR class 551) and P (GSR class 614). See also comments in DSER tender section concerning possible alternative origins of vehicle Nos 552 to 554.

Further, the list of ex-MGWR tenders identifies 126 individual vehicles whereas the locomotive fleet comprised 139 locomotives at the end of 1924, of which 17 were tank engines. It is thus possible that four tender numbers have been included in the list in error.

MGWR Type R tender *Real Photographs Ltd*

MGWR Type S tender. *L&GRP*

MGWR Type T tender As later equipped with side plates in replacement of original side rails. Further timber side and rear extension fitted to coal space. *Authors' collection*

MGWR Type U tender *L&GRP*

Above: MGWR Type V tender *IRRS collection*

MGWR Type W tender in original condition. *WA Camwell*

MGWR Type X tender. *L&GRP*

Type Y in CIE days with side plates and further timber extension. For earlier version with coal rails only see the photograph on page 204. *CP Friel Collection*

MGWR Type Z tender. *IRRS collection*

It is known that some tenders were rebuilt in the form of hybrids. This vehicle has an ex-MGWR underframe and what appears to be a GSWR-style body. It is coupled to Class 573 J18 No 590. *Authors' collection*

This tender appears to be an ex-GSWR Type A underframe, carrying a body with raised sides (below the characteristic flare in the body profile). *IRRS collection*

Great Southern Railways Tenders

Under GSR auspices, the total of tender locomotives and individual tenders built or acquired were:

Locomotive Class	Locomotive Nos	Tender Nos	Number built	
500 (B1)	501, 502	407, 408	2	Described above as GSWR Type F
372 (K1)	372–91	410–29	20	
393 (K1a)	393–98	430–35	6	
700 (J15a)	700–04		n/a	No new tenders built for these engines
710 (J15b)	710–19		n/a	No new tenders built for these engines
342 (D4)	342–46	436–40	5	
800 (B1a)	800–02	80–82	3	
Total			**36**	

(There was a discrepancy in the data given to the 1938 (Ingram) Tribunal of Inquiry which stated that 27 new tenders had been acquired or built since the amalgamation. This was prior to construction of the three tenders for Class 800. The difference might be accounted for by a failure to include the six tenders assembled for use with Class 393(K1a) in the count).

Woolwich Mogul tender in as assembled condition. *Authors' collection*

Woolwich Mogul tender. Note that an additional portion has been cut out of the tender side panel, presumably to help accommodate staff exchange equipment. Retains ladders fitted for oil-burning. *Authors' collection*

Woolwich Mogul. This photograph has been selected to highlight the narrowness of the tender body (built to the British loading gauge) compared with the width of the tender frames, and of the following coach vehicle (1st/ 3rd brake No 861 built specially for the Cork-Rosslare boat express in 1906 and preserved by the Railway Preservation Society of Ireland). The fourth coach in the train is one of four Pullman cars to work in Ireland.

IRRS collection

Class 342 tender coupled behind locomotive No 344 at Cork, Glanmire Road shed.

IRRS collection

Class 800 tender (presumably No 80) displaying the board mounted GSR crest between the 'G' and 'S' on the tender side.

Real Photographs Ltd

Woolwich mogul tenders

These were unlike other types in service. When Maunsell set about re-organising locomotive affairs on the South Eastern & Chatham Railway, he recruited personnel from the Midland Railway. This led to a distinct Midland flavour to parts of the prototype SECR Class N which formed the template for the Woolwich moguls – particularly the cab and tender. These tenders were the same as the smaller standard SECR (and later Southern Railway) tenders, and were equipped with self-trimming bunkers. The wheels were of 4' 0": diameter and the wheelbase was 13' 0" evenly distributed. The carrying capacity was 3500 gallons and five tons with a weight of 30 tons 5 cwt. Other recorded dimensions are: length 21' 5½"; width 8' 10½"; height 10' 6". The first 12 Woolwich tenders were assembled at the Broadstone; the remainder were completed at Inchicore.

Research has failed to identify any examples of Woolwich moguls attached to other types of tender, or of Woolwich tenders working with other classes. Presumably the drawgear was incompatible with other locomotives/ tenders without significant modification. If these tenders were not readily interchangeable with other classes, then it would not have been necessary to assemble all 26 as a tender takes less time to repair than a locomotive.

Following the singling of the ex-MGWR main line west of Maynooth, it was necessary to fit staff exchange equipment to these tenders which necessitated the removal of the sanding gear.

Class 342 tenders

Although this class was a continuation of a GSWR type, a new style of tender was provided, numbered 436 to 440. The traditional dimensions of 12' 4" wheel base and 3' 9" wheel diameter were retained but the carrying capacities were 7 tons and 3450 gallons. No 440 was fitted with Hoffman roller bearings. The side profile was generally similar to GSWR Type C but the sides were flat and, where previously there had been an outward flare on the upper part of the body, the sides now slanted inwards. An unusual feature compared with the Class 800 tenders described next was that the bodies were welded rather than riveted.

These tenders were later used with older locomotives. For example, No 502 was recorded coupled to a Class 342 tender (*Railway Magazine* July 1969) and the type was also seen working with Class 101 0-6-0s.

Class 800 tenders

As would be expected, the tenders provided for this class were the largest used by the GSR. They were given numbers 80 to 82, which had never been used in the GSWR/ GSR tender list. In keeping with the modernity of the locomotives, the bodies of the tenders were constructed out of rustless steel. The traditional 3' 9" diameter wheels were used but the wheelbase was extended to 15' 2", evenly spaced, and roller bearing axle boxes were fitted. The carrying capacities were officially 8 tons and 5000 gallons while the length over buffers was 26' 2¾". However, the actual water capacity was reputed to exceed 6000 gallons. There are reports that the height of the tender sides combined with certain non-swivelling water cranes could make filling the tank difficult.

The general body styling initiated with the Class 342 type was repeated except that the fender cut-out was rather narrower at the front while the concave cut out at the rear was further forward and well in advance of the tender filler. The inward slant of the upper part of the tender slide was a prominent feature that did not complement the lines of the locomotive cab, but was obviously necessary in view of the high sides and the need to maintain rearward vision.

Self-weighing tenders

During the summer of 1951, three tenders (Nos 312, 414 and 547) were modified with provision of self-weighing equipment for the purpose of accurately measuring coal consumption. With plans pending for the introduction of main line diesel locomotives, it seems that this exercise was rather late in the day. Also, residual development of steam power by CIÉ was by then focused on turf-burning, with the option of changing to oil fuel. It is not known to what extent these tenders were used to measure coal consumption and no test results have been found.

The installation of equipment on a 3345-gallon ex-GSWR Type C tender was an understandable choice as this was the most common type in service with larger locomotives. It is possible that the Woolwich tender was selected in connection with CIÉ's abortive proposals to provide Classes 372 & 393 with larger boilers. On the other hand, it is hard to see what might have been achieved with self-weighing equipment on tender No 547 which worked with ex-MGWR locomotives by then engaged on secondary and not particularly demanding duties.

Redundant tenders

Certain tender numbers were recorded with an 'A' suffix, denoting their use as 'mobile oil tanks etc'. From this, it is assumed that these vehicles were also used as water carriers in the tender train. The tender numbers so recorded are: 23, 66, 162, 231/4, 262/3, 281/7, 291 but this list is very likely incomplete.

Five were also used for storage of cooling water for Diesel railcars by CIÉ (Nos 222, 241, 298, 647/8). A further two, with their centre wheels removed, were used for transporting material around Inchicore works.

Preserved tenders

The following tenders from the GSR and its predecessors survive in preservation:

No 82 (ex-locomotive No 802) is on display with locomotive No 800 in the Transport Gallery at the Ulster Folk and Transport Museum. This was the very last tender introduced to service.

No 156 (built 1871) GSWR Type A with Class 101 locomotive No 184.

No 375 (built 1922) GSWR Type C with Class 101 locomotive No 186

No 551 with MGWR Type T with Class 461 locomotive No 461

Also a 2730 gallon tender accompanied locomotive No 186 when first preserved; other details not known.

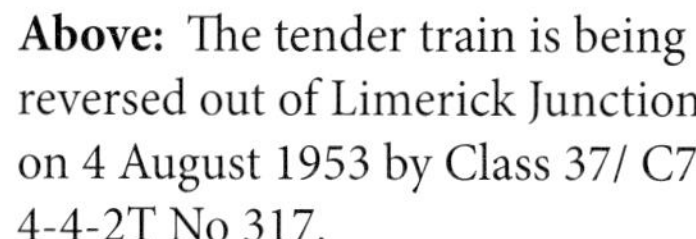

Above: The tender train is being reversed out of Limerick Junction on 4 August 1953 by Class 37/ C7 4-4-2T No 317.

Authors' collection

Left: On another occasion No 317 (just out of shot) is standing at Limerick Junction water tower. The first vehicle of this tender train has had its centre axles removed.

Authors' collection

The GSR Tender List

GSR No	Original No	Type	Capacity Gallons	Comments
1	1	B	2730	
2	2	A	1864	
3	3	B	2730	
4–8	4–8	A	1864	
9	9	B	2730	
10, 11	10, 11	A	1864	
12	12	B	2730	
13–15	13–15	A	1864	
16, 17	16, 17	B	2730	
18	18	A	1864	
19, 20	19, 20	B	2730	
21, 22	21, 22		1608	Old GSWR type
23				Vacant
24–26	24–26		1608	Old GSWR type
27–40				Vacant
41–46	41–46	A	1864	
47–51				Vacant
52–54	52–54	B	2730	
55–65	55–65	A	1864	
66				Vacant
67–69	67–69	n/a	1608	Old GSWR type
70–79				Vacant
80–82	n/a	Cl. 800	5000	Class 800
83, 84				Vacant
85–89	85–89	B	2730	
90–92				Vacant
93–98	93–98	B	2730	
99, 100				Vacant
101–15	101–15	A	1864	
116				Vacant
117–91	117–91	A	1864	
192				Vacant
193	1WL	WLWR	2000	
194–199	194–99	C	3345	
200–221				Vacant
222	2WL	WLWR	2000	
223–232				Vacant
233	45WL	n/a	1900	GSR Class 235
234				Vacant

GSR No	Original No	Type	Capacity Gallons	Comments
235	49WL	n/a	1900	GSR Class 235
236				Vacant
237–239	56–58WL	n/a	1980	GSR Class 235
240, 241	141/ 42M	Q	2000	
242–260				Vacant
261	8WL	WLWR	1585	
262–74				Vacant
275	22WL	WLWR	1940	
276–85				Vacant
286	36WL	WLWR	1630	
287/ 88				Vacant
289	39WL	WLWR	1630	
290/ 91	43/ 44WL	WLWR	1900	GSR Class 276
292/ 93	47/ 48WL	WLWR	1940	GSR Class 276
294/ 95				Vacant
296	53WL	WLWR	1940	
297/ 98	54/ 55WL	WLWR	2000	
299, 300				Vacant
301–04	301–04	C	3345	
305–08	305–08	C	3345*	
309–11	309–11	C	3345	
312	312	C	3345	Self–weighing
313/ 14	313/ 14	C	3345	
315–20				Vacant
321–40	321–40	C	3345	
341–50				Vacant
351–77	351–77	C	3345	
378–99				Vacant
400–05	n/a	E	4500	Armstrong–Whitworth
406	n/a	D	3870	Loco No 500
407/ 08	n/a	F	4670	Loco Nos 501/ 2
409	n/a	n/a		Vacant
410–13	n/a	Woolwich	3500	Class 372/ 393
414	n/a	Woolwich	3500	Class 372/ 393 self–weighing
415–21	n/a	Woolwich	3500	Class 372/ 393
422 (1st)	24D	G	2100	
422 (2nd)	n/a	Woolwich	3500	Class 372/ 393

* RN Clements records Nos 305-08 as Type B 2730 gal built 1904, which seems unlikely; GSR tender register records them as Type C 3345 gal.

GSR No	Original No	Type	Capacity Gallons	Comments
423–35	n/a	Woolwich	3500	Class 372/ 393
436–39	n/a	Cl 342	3450	Class 342
440 (1st)	17D	H	1850	
440 (2nd)	n/a	Cl 342	3450	Class 342
441	36D	H	1850	
442/ 43	13/ 14D	J	2600	
444	18D	K	2600	
445/ 46	65/, 66D	L	2600	
447	50D	M	2600	
448/ 49	4/ 5D	K	2000	
450–53	55–58D	N	2600	
454	67D	L	2600	
455–60				Vacant
461/ 62	15/ 16D	P	2600	
463–529				Vacant
530	14M	R or V	1600	
531	23M	R or V	1600	
532	26M	R or V	1600	
533–37	30–34M	R or V	1600	
538	???	R or V	1600	
539/ 40	92/ 93M	R or V	1600	
541	1M	R or V	1600	
542	17M	R or V	1600	
543	25M	R or V	1600	
544	35M	R or V	1600	
545	127M	T	3000	Self–weighing
546	97M	T	3000	
547	39M	T	3000	
548	126M	T	3000	
549	???	T	3000	
550	98M	T	3000	
551	???	T	3000	
552	???	T	3000	
553	???	T	3000	
554	???	T	3000	
555–62				Vacant
563	6M	S	2500	
564	8M	S	2500	
565/ 566	10M/ 11M	S	2500	
567	20M	S	2500	
568	???	S	2500	

GSR No	Original No	Type	Capacity Gallons	Comments
569	???	S	2500	
570	125M	S	2500	
571	127M	S	2500	
572	129M	S	2500	
573–75	36–38M	S	2500	
576–84	40–48M	S	2500	
585–88				Vacant
589	99M	Y	2800	
590	???	W or Z	1700	
591	59M	W or Z	1700	
592–96	61–65M	W or Z	1700	
597	67M	W or Z	1700	
598–606	69–77M	W or Z	1700	
607–12	79–84M	W or Z	1700	
613/ 14	2M, 3M	R or V	1600	
615	55M	R or V	1600	
616	57M	???	2100	
617	56M	R or V	1600	
618	58M	R or V	1600	
619	57M	R or V	1600	
620	85M	W or Z	1600	
621	140M	R or V	1600	
622	86M	R or V	1600	
623	35M	Y	2800	
624–632	87–95M	Y	2800	
633	13M	R or V	1600	
634/ 35	15/ 16M	R or V	1600	
636/ 37	18/ 19M	R or V	1600	
638/ 39	21/ 22M	R or V	1600	
640	24M	R or V	1600	
641	60M	R or V	1600	
642	91M	R or V	1600	
643	94M	R or V	1600	
644/ 45	88/ 89M	R or V	1600	
646–49	143–46M	T	3000	
650–52	27–29M	U	2000	
653–58	49–54M	U	2000	
659, 60	130/ 31M	U	2000	
661–68	133–40M	U	2000	
669	???	R or V	1600	

Chapter 12
Other motive power

The idea of self-propelled vehicles for passengers and restricted amounts of goods has a long history in Ireland, the first initiatives dating from around 1850. These early attempts were unsuccessful as it was soon evident that better performance and operating flexibility was possible with the conventional combination of locomotive and hauled vehicles. The Great Southern & Western Railway re-visited the idea in 1881 with the introduction of three steam carriages for branch services where traffic was light. These vehicles took the form of 0-6-4Ts with small carriage saloon bodies mounted over the trailing bogie. While adequately powered, the seating accommodation was restricted and any increase in passenger numbers necessitated the addition of a conventional carriage which defeated the object of the exercise. These vehicles (numbered 90 to 92) in the GSWR locomotive list were better suited to special duties such as conveyance of inspecting officials or working the pay carriage service. Only No 92 remained in this form in 1925.

In the early 1900s, the advent of electric tramways presented an acute challenge by encroaching on the suburban commuter market where railway companies had enjoyed a monopoly. To combat this new competition, self-propelled passenger vehicles were revived by several companies. Various designs were tried but the general principle was to use a coach, normally with a saloon-type interior, integrally and permanently connected to a small steam locomotive power unit. When running in reverse, the unit, usually known as a steam rail motor (SRM), was driven from a cab in the coach at the opposite end from the locomotive.

Passengers were largely receptive to this new form of rail transport, and there was some success in tempting them back from the tramways. However recurring problems were encountered. The poor weight distribution of some SRMs led to rough and uncomfortable riding. Where the steam power unit was within enclosed body work, servicing could be time-consuming. If the power unit was out of commission, the coach unit similarly could not be used to generate revenue. Internal and external cleanliness was a big challenge as SRMs had to be serviced in the dirty environments of locomotive depots. Further, SRMs could become victims of their own success on services where their popularity generated increased passenger numbers. If overcrowding necessitated the attachment of a coach, the additional load often overtaxed the small power unit leading to late running, or worse.

A generic shortcoming of this type of vehicle was that limited space and weight restrictions dictated the use of small boilers. Some types (eg Sentinel's products) were efficient steam raisers but as their boilers contained comparatively little steam, there was no reserve capacity to cope with adverse operating circumstances such as steep gradients. Thus SRMs were denied an important advantage of conventionally boilered locomotives – the ability to expend energy faster than it is being generated by the boiler so as to cope with unusually demanding conditions over short, finite periods (known as 'mortgaging the boiler').

At the amalgamation, SRMs (known as steam railcars in Ireland) were no longer operating but during the 1920s two British commercial manufacturers (Sentinel and Clayton) actively sought new markets by applying their expertise with steam road vehicles in railcars of their own design. The format offered the potential of covering commuter routes (mainly off-peak period services because of their limited capacity), and of replacing normal trains on lightly-used branch lines.

Initially, these units were reasonably successful but the inherent drawbacks described above soon recurred. Of the two types, the Clayton products proved the less satisfactory and their working lives were short. The Sentinels enjoyed longer careers but they had also ceased to work by about 1940. It should be noted that the London & North Eastern Railway, which had been an enthusiastic investor in Sentinel products and to a lesser extent those of Clayton, had broadly similar experiences.

The next step on from SRMs was to try internal combustion engines of the size that was increasingly being used in motor buses and lorries. Attractions included elimination of the fireman, ready availability, and more cleanliness. Drawbacks in the early days included lack of reliability and a lower power rating than even SRMs could achieve. At the amalgamation, the only non-steam motive power inherited by the GSR was a petrol-engined railcar from the Midland Great Western Railway which continued for a few years in departmental-type duties, and a three foot gauge motor rail car for inspection duties on the Tralee & Dingle Light Railway.

The second attempt by the GSR at fixed formation trains concerned two pairs of petrol-engined railcars purchased from Drewry in Britain, specifically intended for use as single units on lightly worked rural services on both broad and narrow gauge. Drewry was better known for permanent way inspection units; passenger work to fixed timetables was soon found to stretch the capabilities of the broad gauge version. The narrow gauge pair proved more successful.

Drewry also supplied to the GSR four small petrol rail cars for use by the Civil Engineer's department on inspection duties; like the solitary Tralee & Dingle unit, these units were never used in revenue earning service.

The third initiative relied on another form of motive power, and was technically the most interesting. During the 1920s, expansion of electricity supplies and establishment of a national grid linked with the Ardnacrusha hydro-electric scheme on the River Shannon was a major governmental priority. From early 1930 most of Dublin's power needs were satisfied from this source and the authorities were keen to develop the client base for electricity. The GSR was viewed as a major potential consumer.

Electrification by third rail or overhead supply would have required capital well beyond the GSR's resources. Even if funds had been available, it is doubtful that there were a sufficient routes with the requisite traffic density to provide an acceptable return on investment. A compromise solution was therefore sought through the adoption of two-car articulated electric units driven by a newly-patented power source – the Drumm Battery.

Adoption of brand-new, evolving technology to drive a public transport system in daily use was a considerable act of faith and the government provided start-up financial help in the project. Scepticism was voiced over the operating feasibility, but after initial trials with a converted Drewry unit, the first Drumm train comprising a permanently-coupled two-car set went to work on ex-DSER section commuter services in 1932. From 1939, there were four Drumm trains in use but, with the batteries requiring renewal in 1949, it was concluded that this unique form of motive power was no longer viable.

The net result of all these initiatives was that following the demise of the GSR, the rail services inherited by CIÉ were soon to revert almost exclusively to the classic steam locomotive and hauled vehicle formation, ie the situation inherited in 1925. It was to be left to the new owners to start all over again in the pursuit of the next generation of motive power, which commenced with two Sulzer diesel-electric locomotives Nos 1100 and 1101 in 1950.

Steam powered units

Sentinel railcars

A Board minute for 3 December 1926 indicates that consideration had been given to the purchase of broad and narrow gauge Steam Railcars, as well as 20 ton and 27 ton steam locomotives. The FOB prices to an English port, quoted by Sentinel were:

Broad gauge railcar	£4,275 per vehicle plus extras: curtains – £22-10s-0d; hand rails & straps – £10-10s-0d.
Narrow gauge railcar	£4,150 per vehicle plus extras as above.
20 ton locomotive	£1,590 per locomotive plus extras: steam heating – £20; finish painting – £25.
27 ton locomotive	£2,275 per locomotive plus extras as above.

A recommendation was made to purchase one broad gauge railcar and one 20 ton locomotive for trial purposes, but approval was granted to acquire two of each for early delivery. The first two vehicles were ordered concurrently with a pair of 20 ton locomotives (GSR Class 280 – Makers' Nos 6846 and 6847). There is no record of any further consideration being given to buying narrow gauge railcars, presumably the cost making them too expensive in relation to potential traffic levels.

There seems to have been considerable enthusiasm for the concept at the time because on 7 January 1927 the Board approved purchase of two more railcars, with the request that a better price be sought with the manufacturers. This resulted in the acquisition of four vehicles:

GSR No (Carriage list)	Built	Makers' No	Withdrawn
354	11/1927	6844	1941
355	11/1927	6845	1942
356	11/1927	6912	1942
357	11/1927	6913	1941

Built by Sentinel Waggon Co, Shrewsbury

The makers' numbers quoted above are from Sentinel's records. However, from personal observation recorded in the R N Clements Archives, the following number combinations were noted: GSR No 354 (Makers' No 6845); No 355 (6913); No 356 (6844); No 357 (6912).

Boiler pressure – 275 lbs/ sq in	*Heating surfaces:*	*Rated horsepower – 100 hp*
Cylinders – (2) 6¾" x 9"	*water tubes – 36.5 sq ft*	*Coal capacity – 13.5 cwt*
Power bogie wheels – 2' 6"	*firebox – 36.5 sq ft*	*Water capacity – 300 gal*
Power bogie wheelbase – 8' 6"	*superheater – not quoted*	*Weight – 24 tons 5 cwt*
Carrying bogie wheel base – 6' 6"	*grate – 18 sq ft*	
Overall length – 47' 7"		

GSR Sentinel Steam Railcar No 356 at Inchicore. Vehicle numbers have been moved to the body ends.

CP Friel collection

They were standard products of the company using the normal arrangement of engine unit articulated with the coach section and completely enclosed within the bodywork. The mechanical parts were similar to those used on the earliest Sentinel units delivered to the LNER, and to those on GSR Class 280. The power unit was derived from Sentinel's road vehicles and included a vertical water-tube superheated boiler with two cylinders, poppet valves, and chain drive to both axles. This configuration was economical; the fuel capacity yielded an operating range of 150-200 miles, and each SRM could cover 50 miles between water refills.

The coach sections were built by Metropolitan-Cammell of Nottingham with seating accommodation for 55 third class passengers in saloons with electric lighting and heating; they were intended for branch line and rural services. A second driving cab was installed at the other end from the engine section and a speaking tube allowed for communication between driver and fireman when operating in reverse. The guard's compartment and luggage accommodation was immediately adjacent to the second driving cab. The car had electric headlamps in the vehicle ends plus buffers and draw gear, but no vacuum pipes which prevented the towing of a trailer. Steps were fitted to allow passenger access from ground level to the saloons.

GSR Sentinel Steam Railcar No 356 *L&GRP*

In 1929 it was found necessary to fit spark arresters, evidenced by box-like fittings on the roof above the power unit.

They were used mainly in the Southern and Western districts, including a period on the lightly-trafficked 5¾ miles Goold's Cross – Cashel branch, a line where the unsuccessful GSWR Steam Rail Motor No 1 had been tried in 1904. Other duties included the Foynes and Newmarket branches, and between Limerick, Nenagh and Ballybrophy.

An unusual working was noted in 1928 whereby a Sentinel railcar (or a Clayton, as described in the next section) left Mullingar at 11.10 am attached to the Cavan train. The railcar was detached at Inny junction at 11.38 am and then ran all stations to Sligo, arriving at 2.48 pm. (In view of the lack of vacuum connections, the railcar must have been fully crewed while attached to the conventional train). The balancing working was a departure from Sligo at 11.30 am, arriving at Mullingar at 2.48 pm. Other services radiating from Mullingar involved return runs within the day to Athenry and Athlone. By 1930, Nos 354, 355 and 357 were at work in the Western District and No 356 was in the Southern District.

The Sentinel units were the most successful of all the steam rail motors/ steam railcars operated by the GSR and its constituent companies, and they enjoyed the longest working careers. It is believed that they stood out-of-service at Waterford for 2-3 years before being withdrawn and scrapped.

They were painted in the standard GSR coach livery of dark purple-brown with yellow straw lining. The fleet number (in the coaching series) was carried on the body waist at mid-point on the power unit and above the rear bogie.

Clayton railcars

GSR No (Carriage list)	Built	Withdrawn	
358 to 363	All 1928	All 1932	**Built by Clayton Wagons (Lincoln)** – no makers' numbers

Boiler pressure – 300 lbs/ sq in
Cylinders – (2) 7" x 10"
Power bogie wheels – 3' 6"
Trailing bogie wheels – 3' 1½"
Bogie wheelbase (both) – 7' 0"

Heating surfaces:
water tubes – 47.2 sq ft
firebox – 23.75 sq ft
superheater – not given
grate – 4.12 sq ft

Rated horsepower – 100 hp
Capacity – 15 cwt
Water capacity – 550 gal
Weight – 28 tons (approx)

Overall lengths: Nos 358 to 361 – 59' 6¾";
Nos 362 and 363 – 57' 6½"

Perhaps encouraged by the early promise of the Sentinel units, six Clayton railcars were delivered a year later. The choice of Clayton was obviously influenced by the quoted price. At £1,800 each they cost less than 50% of that for a Sentinel unit but in practice this proved a false economy.

Nos 358 to 361 were similar to units supplied in 1928 to the LNER except that the Irish version had seating accommodation for 9 first class and 55 third class passengers, plus three tip-up seats in the luggage compartment which had a floor space of 45 square feet. The slightly shorter bodies of Nos 362 and 363 provided accommodation for five first class and 51 third class passengers, plus ten tip-up seats in the luggage compartment which had floor space of 90 square feet. Two-class accommodation was provided to allow for use also on commuter services.

Steam was raised in a vertical water tube superheated boiler to which fuel was fed from above by means of a stoking tube, an arrangement which firemen found very awkward. The cylinders were activated by piston valves and drive was to one axle by means of spur gears. The Claytons visually differed from the Sentinels in that the water tank and bunker were mounted externally on the power bogie. This had coupled driving wheels and was articulated with the coach section. A second cab was installed at the end of the coach section, with speaking tube connection to the footplate. Vacuum hoses were fitted with the intention of towing trailers. The overall appearance was rather primitive compared with the neatly enclosed Sentinels. Livery was similar to that applied to the Sentinel units with fleet numbers on the waist near the power unit end.

Some units (Nos 359, 361 and 362) were initially tried on Dublin suburban services from Westland Row to Dalkey, and from Harcourt Street to Foxrock. They were also tried on the Mullingar-Sligo, Cork-Macroom, and Cork-Clonakilty routes, but only for relatively short periods at each location as they proved markedly less successful than the Sentinel version. In 1930, Nos 358, 359 and 361 were allocated to the Midland District and No 363 to the Southern District.

Problems included a tendency to run short of steam, accessibility difficulties with the frequently-needed boiler washouts, and considerable periods out of service under repair. On Foxrock services, apart from erratic steaming it was found that the Claytons could not cope with the gradients without stopping for a 'blow up', hardly suitable performance for a heavily-worked commuter line. The frequency of breakdowns made them a liability on branch services with prolonged delays as fitters had to travel long distances to reach defective units. The makers had claimed that coal consumption would average 11 lbs per mile but in practice, this was found to vary between 19 and 25 lbs per mile. The situation worsened in 1929 when Clayton Wagons Ltd went into liquidation, leading to difficulties in obtaining spare parts. Matters really came to a head when on 7 November 1930, little more than two years after their introduction, Morton recommended to the Locomotive, Permanent Way and Works Committee that the power units be removed. It was proposed that the coach sections be converted to hauled stock and transferred to the Waterford & Tramore section where the existing rolling stock was old and in poor condition.

These modifications allowed for some loss on the original investment to be recouped. After removal of the engine units, the six carriage portions were formed into three non-powered articulated pairs, each pair weighing about 37 tons. The ex-power unit ends were adjacent with the articulating bogie located below the spaces that had been occupied by the boiler units and connected to the pinions previously used for the powered bogies. Official withdrawal was during 1932, although they very likely did little work as steam railcars after Morton had formed his judgement. They were observed at work as articulated pairs in June 1932, when all available coaching stock was mustered to handle heavy passenger traffic in connection with the Dublin Eucharistic Congress. They were then moved to the isolated Waterford and Tramore section, where they represented a considerable improvement in style and comfort over the existing passenger stock.

In articulated form they were paired: No 358 (all third) + No 359 (first/ third/ brake); No 360 (first/ third) + No 362 (all third); No 361 (all first) + No 363 (all first). Their seating accommodation was substantially changed for use on the WTR section:

Tramore end			**Waterford end**		
Coach No	**1st**	**3rd**	**Coach No**	**1st**	**3rd**
359	16	57 + brake compartment	358	-	95
360	16	69	362	-	96
361	85	-	363	96	-

Nos 359 and 360 were later converted to third class accommodation only. However the all first pair (Nos 361 and 363) was retained for 'Race Day Special' workings. These vehicles were particularly popular with punters who, hopefully having purchased return tickets in advance, liked to sample first class accommodation on their journeys to *and* from Tramore races. The ex-Claytons remained in service until 1955, although by then in severely run-down condition, when they were replaced by diesel railcars.

Above: GSR Clayton Steam Railcar No 360 at Mullingar in 1929.
HC Casserley

Right: GSR Clayton Steam Railcars with power units removed and coupled in articulated pairs of hauled carriage stock at Waterford Manor Station in 1939.
WA Camwell

Left: GSR (ex-MGWR) Petrol powered inspection vehicle No 1. This view is dated 1936 but the MGWR livery is still evident, plus the legend "Engineers Dept No 1" which had been added in 1912.
WA Camwell

Petrol powered units

In GSR days, there were ten units in this category:

Departmental vehicle No 1 (ex-Midland Great Western Railway)

Cylinders – (4) 4" bore x 5" stroke	*Power rating – 27 bhp*
Gearbox – not stated	*Unit weight – 3 tons 0 cwt (working order)*
Wheels – not stated	*Maximum speed – 33 mph*
Wheel base – 8' 0"	
Length – not stated	

This was the only non-steam powered broad gauge vehicle in the GSR motive power fleet as at 1 January 1925 being a petrol-engined railcar purchased by the MGWR from Charles Price & Sons of Manchester in December 1911. It was equipped with a 27 hp four-cylinder water-cooled engine and could be driven from either end. Petrol engines of that era were not particularly reliable and this is borne out by the need to fit a replacement engine in 1924.

The body was of a saloon type with reversible seats for eleven passengers, and space for luggage and mail bags up to a weight of four cwt. The unit was used on the Achill branch but even the modest demands of that route were beyond its capacities as by 1916, it had become a departmental vehicle for use by the Civil Engineer. In GSR days it is thought to have operated staff services between Inchicore and Kingsbridge for a period. Withdrawal might have taken place in 1926 or 1927 (no certain date has been traced). In 1936 it was noted without any engine in Inchicore yard, still in MGWR livery.

Inspection railcar No 6 (ex-Tralee & Dingle Light Railway)

Cylinders – (4) in 3.3 litre, Ford Model T engine	*Power rating – not stated*
Gearbox – two speed (?)	*Weight – not stated*
Wheels – 2' 0"	
Wheel base – 6' 6"	
Length – 10' 0"	

GSR (ex-Tralee & Dingle) Inspection Railcar No 6 at Ennis. *CH Hewison*

In 1922, the TDLR created an inspection railcar out of a Ford Model 'T' motor car engine and transmission mounted in a steel four-wheeled frame and supported by a chassis manufactured by Baguley. A four-door body, best described a 'quaint', was apparently manufactured locally and provided accommodation for the driver and three passengers. Although fitted with reverse gear, it effectively could only be driven bonnet-leading over any distance for reasons of safety and because long distances in reverse could induce overheating. It was intended for and only ever used on departmental work.

Shortly after the amalgamation, it was transferred to the West Clare section, and Ennis was its base during GSR days. Numbered 6 in the GSR departmental list, it was later fitted with a more modern Ford engine, and it travelled quite extensively over other narrow gauge sections. Its modest size and weight permitted easy transportation on a broad gauge carriage truck, and it was moved around on many occasions in this fashion. It was used several times on the Cork & Muskerry and Cork, Blackrock & Passage sections before their closure, and it paid at least four visits to the Cavan & Leitrim section in the 1950s. Its last visit to the Cavan & Leitrim was recorded shortly before the closure of that section in 1959.

If a long working life is any yardstick, then this was the most successful of all the railcars, steam rail motors, and non-steam units for it survived on the West Clare section until closure in 1961.

Inspection railcars Nos 2 to 5 (Great Southern Railways)

Vehicle No	Introduced	Makers' No	Replacement Ford Engine	Withdrawn
2	12/1926	1492	1941	1963
3	12/1926	1493	?	1963
4	3/1927	1494	1944	1963
5	5/1927	1495	1942	1963

Cylinders – (4)
Transmission – Cone clutch and Baguley 3-speed gearbox giving speeds of 8, 17 and 28 mph at 1000 rpm
Wheels – 2' 0"
Wheel base – 7' 0"
Length – 11' 8"
Power rating – 20 bhp @ 1000 rpm
Petrol tank capacity – 15 gallons
Radiator water capacity – 12 gallons
Weight – 2 tons 16 cwt (working order)
Maximum speed – 35-40 mph

The purchase of six Drewry inspection cars was first recommended to the Board on 19 June 1925 but was deferred on three occasions before it was finally agreed to seek quotes on 18 February 1926. Board approval was finally granted on 2 July to purchase four vehicles at a cost of £885 each plus £25 shipment charges; it was noted that one more might be required later.

The Drewry Car Co supplied them specifically for use by the Civil Engineer's department. They were four-wheeled, mounted on the standard Baguley Type B chassis. Being specifically intended for inspection work, the controls were located in the centre of each car, thereby allowing a clear view from seats (six in total) at either end. When the original engines wore out, they were replaced with 24 bhp Ford engines. Throughout their working lives, they were allocated to Westland Row, Cork, Limerick and Waterford. These allocations were changed around quite often. At withdrawal, No 5 had been out-of-service for some years while No 2 (usually the Dublin-based unit) was still in GSR livery.

GSR Drewry Civil Engineer's Inspection Vehicle No 5.
L&GRP

Narrow Gauge Drewry passenger railcars (Great Southern Railways)

GSR No (Carriage list)	Built	Makers' No	Withdrawn
395	8/1927	1644	1943
396	8/1927	1645	1943

Cylinders – (4) 4¾" x 6"	*Power rating – 40 hp @ 1000 rpm, 46 bhp @ 1050 rpm*
Transmission – Cone clutch and 3 speed gearbox giving speeds of 6.6, 12.8 and 23 mph @ 1000 rpm	
Wheels – 2' 0"	*Petrol tank capacity – 15 gallons*
Wheel base – 8' 9"	*Radiator water capacity – 12 gallons*
Length – 20' 6"	*Weight – 5 tons 10 cwt (working order)*
Width – 6' 9"	

These were four-wheeled single-car units with a driving cab at either end. They were basically a standard Drewry design, powered by a Baguley four-cylinder petrol engine which was mounted longitudinally at one end. In view of the gradients on the WCR section, it was deemed wise before delivery to install a 40 hp engine in preference to the 25/ 30 hp version originally intended; an increase of £45 to £1,405 cost per vehicle resulted. The estimated running cost was an economical 9d per mile.

The mainframe was constructed out of channel steel with an inner frame to carry the engine and gearbox. The lightweight bodywork had flat sides and ends, comprising a teak frame with outside steel panels and plywood lining inside up to the waist line, with windows in drop frames above. The curved roof frame was of ash, and covered with matchboard and canvas. Passenger accommodation was provided for 30 on reversible rattan seats within a single saloon.

These units were purchased complete from the manufacturers to the criticism of labour representatives who claimed that the bodywork could have been manufactured locally. This elicited a ministerial response that railcars were specialised vehicles that could not be made at Inchicore. Performance was such that speeds up to 40 mph were possible. They were also capable of coping with 1 in 75 gradients at around 25 mph, and as steep as 1 in 20 in low gear at around seven mph.

Used exclusively on the ex-West Clare Railway section, they performed with reasonable efficiency. They were not fitted with vacuum brakes, nor intended to haul trailers. However it was found that they could cope with an old WCR inspection car specially adapted to carry luggage. Also on occasions a brake van or a horse box was towed.

They usually worked off-peak services between Kilkee and Moyasta Junction. They also made a daily return trip through to Kilrush and a daily return journey over the main line to Ennis. The Kilkee-Kilrush working was especially for school children which required an early morning start-up. Apparently they were reluctant starters (the units, not necessarily the children) on cold mornings and the passengers were often recruited to push while the driver 'bump' started the engine.

Although more useful than the broad gauge pair, they were not popular with staff as their introduction had directly led to redundancies. They worked until the winter of 1936 and then stood out of use at Ennis. In 1939, they were moved to Inchicore and scrapped there in 1943.

GSR Drewry 3' 0" Gauge Railcar No 396 at Kilkee in 1933. *L&GRP*

Broad Gauge Drewry passenger railcars (Great Southern Railways)

GSR No (Carriage list)	Built	Makers' No	Rebuilt	Withdrawn
385	12/1927	1642	–	1941
386	1/1928	1643	1930	1930 (from ordinary service)/ 1941

Cylinders (6) – 5" x 6" *Power rating – 70/75 bhp @ 1000 rpm*
Transmission – Cone clutch and 3 speed gearbox giving speeds at 10.4, 18 and 35.7 mph @ 1000 rpm
Wheels – 2' 6"
Wheel base – 13' 0" *Petrol tank capacity – 40 gallons*
Length – 23' 6" *Radiator water capacity – 20 gallons*
Width – 7' 2½" *Weight – 7 tons 8 cwt (working order)*

GSR Drewry 5' 3" Gauge Railcar No 385. *Real Photographs Co Ltd*

The general design, frame and body construction was similar to narrow gauge units Nos 395/ 396 described above. The longer body, main frame and wheelbase were necessary to provide space for the larger six-cylinder Baguley engine. With the higher bhp and gear ratios, the maximum speed was rated at 40 mph on the level (20 mph on a 1 in 75 gradient). However these factors linked with the greater overall weight yielded an inferior power-to-weight ratio compared with the narrow gauge version. With uncertain performance and reliability these units were unsuccessful in ordinary passenger work. They were noted idle at Inchicore in 1929 for quite a period, having been reported on as 'useless'.

No 385 went to work on the Cashel Branch in early 1928 and later found employment at Wexford in 1930. By 1933, it was scheduled in the timetable to operate between Wexford and Duncormick on Wednesdays and Saturdays (according to the timetable, this was then No 385's only work). It later returned to the Cashel branch where it worked until 1938.

No 386 started operations between Mullingar and Boyle in October 1928 before returning to Inchicore for period in store in 1929. It does not seem to have done any further work in passenger service before withdrawal for modification in connection with the Drumm project (see below).

By 1939 No 385 was in store at the Broadstone together with No 386 which had been lying derelict there for some time. Thereafter, neither did any further work. Both were put to use after leaving the railway; No 385 as a hut in Cabra, Dublin while No 386 formed part of a bungalow at Bray, located on the formation of the pre-1915 coastal line, where it survived until about 1960.

Battery electric powered units

Drumm Electric Multiple Units

If the GSR never provided motive power that was completely satisfactory for the Dublin-Bray commuter traffic, it was not for want of trying. The most innovative attempt concerned the harnessing of battery electric power as applied in the Drumm trains.

Dr James Drumm was a talented research chemist who in the 1920s developed a new type of resistance alkaline battery. The principal advantages lay in the speed with which the battery could be charged, and in its ability to accept booster charges during use. These characteristics are familiar for example in the modern mobile telephone but were revolutionary at the time. This experimental work caught the attention of the Irish government which was then keen to find customers for the new national electricity grid. Written evidence prepared by the GSR for submission to the 1938 Railway Tribunal is the prime source for information on how the project proceeded.

Following discussions between Dr Drumm and the Irish Government, in February 1930 the Minister for Industry and Commerce sought collaboration with the GSR in order that the Drumm Battery might be subject to a practical test as a power source for a railway vehicle. The CME was duly authorised to support an experimental project, provided that "no great cost" was imposed on the GSR.

Drewry petrol mechanical railcar No 386 was converted from internal combustion traction by fitting two axle-hung 30 hp electric motors by Victory Dynamo & Motor Works, Leeds and control gear by Vlasco Clarke & Watson, Warrington. The conversion cost was £625, but this excluded the cost of the 110 volt Drumm Battery. As originally built, this unit could be driven from both ends but one end was now 'semi-streamlined' in a wedge shaped form. Other body modifications allowed for the suspension of the Drumm Battery on a specially-designed frame below the solebars (these were quite flimsy to keep weight down).

The conversion work was completed in July 1930 and the vehicle ran its first trial to Clondalkin on 30 July 1930. Trials continued until 27 August 1930 and, on 21 August, speeds of 40–50 mph were attained between Inchicore and Hazelhatch.

Above: GSR Drewry Railcar No 386 converted to Drumm Battery experimental vehicle in 1930.

L&GRP

Right: GSR Drewry Railcar No 386 as Drumm Battery experimental vehicle, out of service with batteries removed.

CH Hewison

The results were good enough to justify employment of No 386 from 1 September for the conveyance of senior railway officers, in some comfort, on a shuttle service between Kingsbridge and Inchicore. This service operated until about March 1931; No 386 was then taken out of service and stored at Inchicore.

In November 1930, a joint agreement was reached between the Department of Finance, the Drumm organisation as the patent holder, and the GSR for financial support in further tests involving regular railway operation. On 3 December 1930, Dail Éireann voted to provide £25,000 for battery development. The essence of these arrangements was that the Department of Finance would:

(a) Reimburse the GSR for the net losses arising from further tests on the Dublin & South Eastern section;

(b) Provide preferential terms for sale of the Drumm Battery to the GSR later;

(c) Allow the GSR to retain No 386 as modified in return for a nominal payment to the patent holder.

Following this agreement, two articulated two-car electric units were constructed at Inchicore and charging stations were installed at Amiens Street, Dublin and Bray stations. At Bray, a short length of energised overhead wire was slung over the two running and the bay platform lines, beneath the footbridge. Later, charging equipment was mounted on gantries beside the Martello siding, Bray. At Amiens Street, energised wire was slung beneath a footbridge. Charging was effected by means of a small pantograph, mounted on the roof at the inner end of the brake composite vehicle. The cost of this investment was:

Passenger vehicles	£18,145
Electrical equipment (excluding batteries)	£8,241
Cost of batteries and associated testing	£5,870
Sub-total: rolling stock cost	*£32,256*
Charging stations	£11,155
Total	**£43,411**

A later GSR report shows a rolling stock cost of £26,533, of which £11,500 was charged to revenue as being the estimated equivalent cost of four conventional coaches.

The proposal to operate a train over a 14½ mile route with up to 14 station stops and with gradients as steep as 1 in 48 was treated with some scepticism by the contemporary railway press. Nonetheless, construction of the first Drumm articulated two car unit (known as Train A) was completed at Inchicore in late 1931 and it ran its first trial between Amiens Street and Westland Row on 29 November. On 1 December a trial trip was made to Bray with sufficient confidence for President Cosgrave to be taken over the same route the following day. A longer trial trip was made Harcourt Street – Greystones on 3 December. Train A entered ordinary passenger service to Bray on 13 February 1932 and worked until 4 August when it was taken out of service for battery modifications.

On 3 August 1932, Train B had ran its first trial from Inchicore to Sallins, and then ran two trials to Portarlington on the 4th and 8th (the latter with President de Valera aboard). Train B then worked in ordinary service from 9 August 1932 until 14 July 1933. The technical and dimensional details were:

Train No	Vehicle Nos (Passenger coach series)	Introduced	Withdrawn
A	2500 (Brake composite)/ 2501 (Third)	2/1932	5/1949
B	2502 (Brake composite)/ 2503 (Third)	8/1932	5/1949

Built at Inchicore

Wheel diameter – 3' 7¾"	*Tare weight (both vehicles combined) – 70 tons 0 cwt (weight as built – later sources state 75 tons 0 cwt)*
Motor bogie wheelbase – 10' 0"	*Carrying bogie wheelbase – 9' 0"*
Overall length over buffers – 125' 8"	*Motors – 2 x 200 hp axle-hung electric motors supplied by British Thomson-Houston Ltd, Rugby*
Body length (each vehicle) – 60' 9"	
Body width – 9' 0"	*Control gear – supplied by Metropolitan-Vickers Electrical Co Ltd, Manchester*
Distance between bogie centres – 52' 8"	
	Maximum axle loading (author's estimate) – 17½ tons

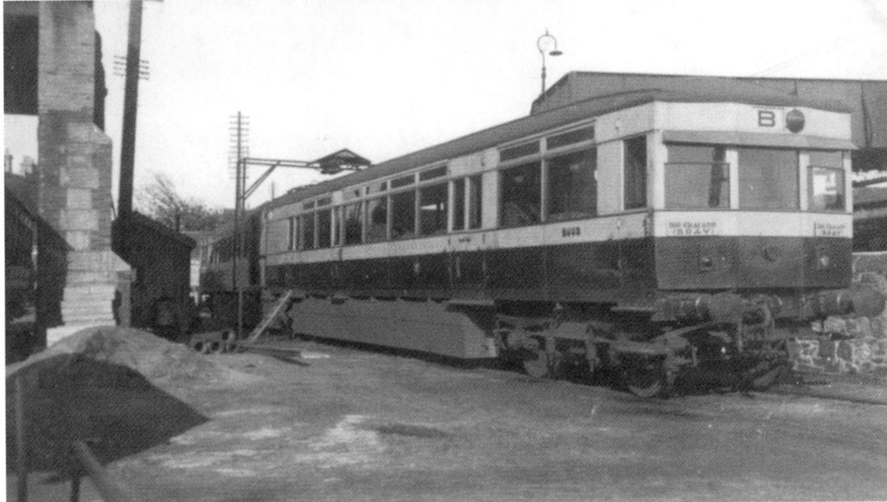

Above: Drumm train A arrives at Bray from the Dublin direction. The signal cabin, platform with canopy, and footbridge were all built by the GSR in 1927.

Courtesy of the National Library of Ireland

Left: GSR Drumm Battery Train B in original livery, standing below the charging gantry at Bray.

CP Friel collection

Articulation was effected by a centre powered bogie. The body section of the all third coach over the centre bogie contained the switch gear while a larger section at the inner end of the brake composite contained a compartment with other electrical equipment and the luggage/ guard's compartment. There was no passenger or guard access from one coach to the other.

Drumm patent batteries were mounted on carrying frames slung below the solebars of each carriage comprising 264 cells each weighing 130 lbs (ie 15 tons 7 cwt per vehicle). Each battery cell could be charged to 500 volts and the aggregate capacity was 600 ampere-hours. The rate of current discharge was 150 ampere-hours in half an hour. Electro-pneumatic remote control allowed one driver to operate both pairs in multiple from driving cabs at either end. All wheels were braked and Hoffman roller bearing axle boxes were used throughout.

As built, the seating capacities were:

Nos 2500/02: 38 first and 26 third class passengers
Nos 2501/03: 76 third class passengers

Train A was modified in 1935 and Train B in 1936, by insertion of additional doors which resulted in:

Nos 2500/02: 33 first and 26 third class passengers
Nos 2501/03: 70 third class passengers

Accommodation was divided between two first and three third class saloons, allowing for smokers and non-smokers. Electric heating and lighting was provided. Construction comprised steel underframes with relatively lightweight timber-panelled bodies to minimise the dead-weight factor. However, the bodywork proved too flimsy and in due course,

Five-car Drumm Train at Amiens Street. Compartment brake third No 1899 is inserted between Train A and B The latter has its pantograph raised to re-charge its batteries through the wire connection installed under the foot bridge. One of the disadvantages with the five-car configuration is apparent as the unit would have occupied this through platform for at least thirty minutes if a full re-charge of both battery sets was intended.

IRRS collection

additional cross-bracing became necessary. Livery was the usual passenger coach livery of purple-brown lower panels and cream upper panels.

The charging stations using equipment supplied by Brown-Boveri Company, London were installed at Amiens Street and Bray. These were capable of replenishing power at the rate of one minute for each mile to be run meaning that typically an interval of 15 minutes was necessary at each turn-around. Regenerative braking was a further means of restoring charge to the batteries while in motion.

As early as April 1932, it was reported in *The Railway Gazette* that daily mileage was limited by inability to work at peak times because of inadequate seating capacity. On 19 July 1933, Trains A and B ran on trial as a five-car set, created by insertion of non-corridor, non-gangway 60' 0" compartment brake third No 1899 which had been built in 1928.

This vehicle was adapted for this role by through wiring of the control cables connected by jumpers and sockets at each end. This was effectively a 'piped' coach with brakes inoperative; this would have been acceptable in view of the weight to brake ratio of trains A and B

Two more trial return trips were run from Amiens Street on the 20th and 21st to Rathdrum, and to Wicklow respectively. On the latter trip, President de Valera was again a passenger and there were some anxious moments as the hilly route and journey length really tested the capacity of the batteries during the return to Dublin.

Trains A and B re-entered ordinary service in links involving two, three and five-car workings from 7 August 1933. These arrangements were short-lived as operating problems arose. Concurrent re-charging of the batteries of two trains roughly doubled the interval needed between journeys thereby unduly occupying platform or siding space. Also, it was found that the towing of No 1899 by a single set heavily taxed the batteries. Therefore it was only feasible to work as a five-car set, or as two independent two-car sets with the trailer standing out of service.

On 25 June 1935, Train A was derailed and damaged by running into a collapsed wall and landslide in the Sandycove-Dun Laoghaire section. The driver, having spotted the obstruction, had made an emergency brake application but the train was still moving at around ten mph at the point of impact. The body broke away from the leading bogie and rode up over the obstruction. Despite the light construction, the leading carriage body sustained comparatively little damage and there were no casualties. However, heavy rain was falling and the track soon flooded leading to short circuits in the batteries and minor fires. Fortunately no serious fire broke out. The accident inspector made several adverse comments in his report about the design of the unit and the risks of having so many large electric batteries in close proximity to the track (10% of them were damaged in the accident). Nevertheless, Train A was returned to service on 7 January 1936 in basically original condition with some modifications, and in overall maroon livery, then described as "the new LMS lake colour".

Between January and May 1936, Train B was out of service for similar modifications (believed to be connected with the batteries) and it too acquired the lake livery during this period. Daily operating mileages were initially about 110 for each unit, soon increased to 134, on a five-day operating week. At weekends the

GSR Drum Battery Trains A and B in later livery, standing on the Martello Tower siding at Bray.
Real Photographs Co Ltd

vehicles were serviced at Bray (all Drumm Train drivers were from that shed). By July 1935, the weekly unit mileage had risen to 1000 miles, working a seven day week and the two Trains had aggregated 1.5 million revenue-earning miles between them. Railway consultants Messrs Merz and McLellan reported that the experimental phase could be considered completed. It was felt that the batteries would have a ten year working life.

During the 1930s the Drumm organisation continued development to improve the technology and in January and July 1937, Trains B and A respectively were taken out of service for battery renewal. Train B returned to work with new batteries on 18 March 1938 and Train A, with rebuilt batteries, on 5 May. Train B was again out of service from 5 October 1938 until 28 March 1939, having sustained serious damage in a collision with 0-6-2T Class 670 (I3) No 670 at Bray.

In 1937, it was decided to confine operations to the Harcourt Street-Bray route as loadings were lighter than on services out of Amiens Street/ Westland Row. Attempts to charge batteries using facilities owned by Dublin United Tramways on ex-DSER land at Hatch Street proved unsatisfactory so recharging took place only at Bray during this period. In March 1938, the transfer of the charging plant from Amiens Street to Harcourt Street was approved, a change that must have greatly improved the 'operating envelope' on return journeys.

On 14 June 1944, all Drumm services were suspended due to very dry weather conditions leading to low water levels on the River Shannon, and thus a reduced capacity to generate hydro-electric power. Train B returned to service on 15 November and Train A on 11 December that year. By 1947, increasing deterioration in performance was evident and Train A, with its rebuilt battery life-expired, was withdrawn from service on 4 October. Train B was taken out of service on 27 November 1948 and its batteries (new in 1938) were transferred to Train D (described below). It had already been agreed on 3 May 1948 that both Trains A and B should be converted to locomotive-hauled passenger coaches. The official withdrawal date for both was recorded as 18 May 1949, the day on which the CIÉ Board agreed that Drumm services should be abandoned.

In June 1949, the carriages of Train A re-entered service (still articulated) as conventional hauled passenger coaches, retaining their composite brake and all third seating configurations. They continued to work, steam hauled, on the Harcourt Street line.

The GSR/ CIÉ Carriage Stock Year Book (which dates from July 1944) clearly states that Train B, never a popular unit, was similarly treated in 1953/ 1954. However, on the authority of informed witnesses, this was aspiration rather than reality as Train B, still in GSR livery, slowly rotted away in open storage at Inchicore and never worked again. It was officially withdrawn in 1956 while the coaches Nos 2500/ 2501 (ex-Train A) survived until 1957.

--- o O o ---

Initial results with Trains A and B were sufficiently encouraging for two separate proposals from the Drumm Battery Company in June 1933 and July 1935 for financial support for more trains over a longer period of testing. The second was the more interesting as it advocated four more two-car trains. It was proposed that these be financed on hire purchase terms (presumably funded by the government) over ten years for the Drumm Batteries and 20 years for the rolling stock and electrical equipment.

Significantly, the GSR appeared unimpressed, responding in October 1935 that the initial cost of Drumm Battery trains was prohibitive unless economies were absolutely assured. It was the GSR's view that: "the cost of one battery, the life of which had yet to be ascertained, serving two coaches having a capacity of 140 passengers only is equal to the cost of a main line express locomotive having a proved life of 40 years, and capable of hauling ten bogies coaches carrying 700 to 800 passengers over the whole (sic) of the railway system".

Revised proposals were made by the Drumm Battery Company Ltd which resulted in November 1936 in a fresh agreement involving a newly formed company, Drumm Battery Sales Ltd (DBS), whereby:

(a) The GSR would construct, equip and maintain at its own expense two new trains designed in accordance with the GSR's standard carriage design principles.

(b) DBS would reimburse the GSR for work undertaken in connection with Drumm Battery development.

(c) The GSR would release the Minister for Industry and Commerce from all other claims.

(d) The GSR would purchase two new Drumm Traction Batteries to be constructed in accordance with the general recommendations of Professors Allman and Andrews (presumably independent technical experts) at a price of £6,000 each; these batteries to carry ten year guarantees.

(e) DBS would adapt, recondition and adjust the original batteries in Trains A and B in general conformity with the recommendations of Allman and Andrews. The GSR would then purchase these batteries at a cost of £3,000 each against a five year guarantee.

(f) The GSR would purchase the charging equipment etc for a sum of £27,147. (Given that the original investment cost of the charging equipment was recorded as £11,155, presumably other unspecified items were included).

(g) Several other sums, expenses and legal costs of DBS amounting to £45,000 with 5% interest to be paid by the GSR in 20 half yearly instalments of £2,925 each.

(h) The property in the old and new batteries, and in the equipment to remain the property of DBS until expiration of the term or earlier payment of the amount specified in (g).

A note appended to this summary indicates that the Electricity Supply Board had sold electricity to the Drumm organisation at a fixed preferential price since 1931 but that with effect from 31 March 1938, standard rates would apply with a rebate for off-peak consumption and a general rebate of 30% overall. How this would translate into overall running costs is not recorded but the GSR vigorously, and apparently unsuccessfully, contested the increases as they "would militate against use of the Drumm Battery Trains".

The terms of the November 1936 agreement were remarkably different from the original spirit of collaboration, and to the financial disadvantage of the GSR shareholders. Presumably other undisclosed factors were at play in the negotiations. Regarding battery performance, those fitted to Trains A and B were to be up-graded to the latest, improved specification

Model of Drumm Battery Train C in the care of the Fry Model Railway Museum, Malahide. At the time construction of this unit was authorised, Cyril Fry was an employee of the GSR and was able to obtain a copy of the first set of plans. These envisaged more streamlined ends, apparently inspired by the German 'Flying Hamburger' streamlined diesel train. The model, while generally accurate, thus depicts a styling that was not finally used.

Authors' collection

and given a fresh five-year guarantee by the Drumm organisation. New trains would be subject to a ten year guaranteed battery life.

A drawback with the first two trains was that the underframes had to be of heavy construction to bear the weight of the batteries. In a paper read by Bredin in February 1941 to the Engineering & Scientific Association of Ireland, he stated that in an attempt to reduce the overall tare weight, the alternative arrangement had been explored of a separate battery locomotive with two lightly constructed driving passenger coaches, one leading and one trailing. Despite much effort, the tare weight still exceeded that of the two-coach articulated arrangement so the idea had been abandoned.

Trains C and D were presented to the press for inspection on 20 September 1939, after which Train C moved to Bray. This unit ran an official trial between Harcourt Street and Bray on 3 October and entered passenger service two days later. Train D moved to Bay on 4 October and entered service on 6 November. Train C was equipped with new batteries whereas Train D used batteries recovered from the earlier units which had been rebuilt. (Presumably Train D had to make do with these rebuilt batteries as one of the sets of new batteries specified in the agreement of November 1936 – paragraph (d) above – was fitted to Train B which returned to duties on 18 March 1938).

The dimensional details:

Train No	Vehicle Nos (Passenger coach series)	Introduced	Withdrawn
C	2504 (Brake composite)/ 2505 (Third)	10/1939	5/1949
D	2506 (Brake composite)/ 2507 (Third)	11/1939	5/1949 **Built at Inchicore**

Tare weight (both vehicles combined) – 88 tons 0 cwt
*Maximum axle loading (*author's estimate) – 17½ tons

These were also two-car articulated units. They had the same leading dimensions, bogie layout, traction and control equipment, and motor configuration as Trains A and B. The only significant mechanical difference was a change in the springing and damping arrangements on the centre bogie. This prevented this component from being interchangeable with the earlier units.

Improvements in the specification and performance of the batteries made more robust construction methods possible. The coaches were metal-bodied with elliptical roofs and rounded driving ends. A modern outward appearance resulted together with an increase in tare weight, as noted above. The livery was lined maroon (lake) for the bodywork and grey for the roofs, as had been initiated with Train A in 1935.

Seating capacities were:

Nos 2504/06:	36 first and 22 third class passengers
Nos 2505/07:	77 third class passengers

Improved manufacturing techniques allowed use of materials of greater purity in the batteries, which it was claimed would give greater efficiency during a ten-year guaranteed working life. Each battery weighed 15½ tons and contained 272 cells with an average discharge per cell of 1.65 volts. Maximum discharge capacity on a single cycle was 400 ampere hours; charging current 400 amperes; charging current during regenerative braking 600 amperes. These units were geared to give a maximum speed of 47 mph and maximum acceleration of 0.8 mph per second. If required, they could be re-geared to a maximum speed of 55 mph and one mph per sec acceleration. Geoffrey Wigham claimed to have passed Milltown on an up train at 72 mph!

It was found that they could run non-stop Dublin to Bray in under 20 minutes, and that they had a maximum operating range on a single charge of 40 miles. Newspapers speculated that all commuter trains from Harcourt Street and Westland Row could be operated by Drumm trains but this overlooked the fact that several of these services ran through to Greystones where additional charging facilities would be needed.

The decision to equip Train D with rebuilt batteries from new proved unwise. Under wartime conditions, nickel needed for battery renewal was not available and this unit was taken out of service on 9 October 1944 as most of its battery cells were life-expired. Those that were still serviceable were transferred to Train A At this time, consideration was given to conversion of Train D to a diesel railcar but this idea was shelved.

Then on 27 July 1945, Train C was taken out of service and cannibalised to provide batteries and other parts to return Train D to work. This latter unit collided with the buffer stops at Harcourt Street on 15 January 1948; it was taken out of service for repairs and did

GSR Drumm Battery Train D *Authors' collection*

not work again as a battery electric unit. However, the process of cannibalisation was seemingly not over as Train C then returned to work on 10 July 1948, by now in CIÉ green livery, lined *eau de nil*.

After official withdrawal as Drumm trains, they were converted to hauled coaching stock, whereby removal of cabs and control equipment permitted an increase in seating capacity (Nos 2504 & 2506 – 38 first class and 44 third class; Nos 2505 & 2507 – 91 third class). These conversions (during which they retained their rounded outer ends) were carried out in 1953–54. The work included installation of through wiring and vacuum piping plus steam heating, and axle (belt) driven dynamo, and batteries.

In this modified condition they were intended for use as intermediate pairs between two pairs of AEC railcars (of the 2648-2656 number group) to form six-car sets. Trials were apparently carried out but there is no record of their having worked in ordinary service in this fashion. An informed commentator feels that the weight of the pair so modified at 64 tons might have unduly taxed the AEC railcars. Instead they were extensively used on steam hauled suburban services from Harcourt Street and Amiens Street stations until both pairs were withdrawn on 18 February 1964.

Assessment

In service, the Drumm units proved popular with passengers for their comfort and internal cleanliness. Personal reminiscences hold that acceleration away from stations was as good as that with the present day overhead-electric DART services. One small disadvantage was a noticeable jolt when the regenerative braking engaged and disengaged. More serious was that the units moved with much less noise than a steam train and as part of their route was used illegally by pedestrians as a footpath, several trespassers were struck by Drumm trains.

Early operating experience tended to confound commentators' reservations about the claimed capacity of the batteries. However, it was soon proven that the system could not cope with peak hour traffic and that reversion to steam-hauled trains at those periods was necessary. A further concession to the system's limitations was the concentration of Drumm services on the Harcourt Street line with its lighter traffic demands and shorter distance to Bray. It is alleged that Trains C and D spread the curve at Salthill, and so were unwelcome on services to and from Westland Row.

In July 1939 special charging facilities were installed at Amiens Street and a Drumm unit worked services for one day on the Great Northern Railway (Ireland) route to Malahide. This test, largely unnoticed at the time, was successful but there were no further developments.

Aggregate annual train miles run by Units A and B were recorded as:

1932	29,451
1933	30,303
1934	39,186
1935	28,298
1936	21,030
1937	11,425 (one unit only)

– which averages out per unit at around 15,500 miles per annum or 62 miles per day, unacceptably low figures in the context of modern fixed formation trains.

Although overall lifetime mileages are not available, the following figures have been traced:

Train	From	To	Total miles	Average miles: per year	per month	per day*
A	Feb 1932	Dec 1943	212,827	16,941	1,412	61
B	Aug 1932	Dec 1943	218,340	17,703	1,475	64
C	Oct 1939	Dec 1948	115,201	12,454	1,038	45
D	Nov 1939	May 1949	138,754	14,479	1,207	52

* Based on an average 23 day working month

For contemporary comparison purposes, it is objective to measure how these mileages matched with alternative fixed formation trains ie Sentinel steam railcars and Gardner two-car diesel units of the GNR(I). Mileage figures for GSR Sentinels cannot be traced but basically similar vehicles at work in the North Eastern area of LNER achieved an average mileage of 28,169 per unit in 1934. On the other hand, the Sentinels had a markedly poorer load factor (55 passengers in the GSR version against 140 in Drumm Trains A and B), significantly slower performance, and the need for an extra crew member.

Comparison with the GNR(I) Gardner two-car diesel units Nos F and G used on the Amiens Street to Howth suburban route (8¼ miles) is more telling. Over an 18 year period, the Gardners each averaged 57,000 miles per annum which indicates a far superior combination of operating flexibility and availability. Although intended for Howth services, they could be transferred instantly to other areas if circumstances so dictated, and did in fact work frequently to Balbriggan and Drogheda, and on occasions through to Belfast.

The Drumm system lost out significantly in its confinement to operations between charging stations and in the cost of those facilities. It is hard to reconcile this fundamental constraint with early promotional claims that Drumm trains would have widespread application and would be suitable for branch lines (where the axle loading would have been another limiting factor).

The Government's 1937 decision to withdraw support for the Drumm organisation would not have engendered confidence among management, and the tenor of the GSR's submission to the 1938 Tribunal suggested little enthusiasm for extension of the concept. This is understandable given that the initial agreement that the government would reimburse losses incurred in testing had metamorphosed into a situation where the GSR was carrying the prime risk on technology that was still to be proven over its projected working life. The 1940 plans for the Class 820 4-6-2T for the ex-DSER section further reflected doubts about the potential offered by more battery electric powered units.

The GSR was the most important user of Drumm batteries (apparently the only other application was in a few small commercial road vehicles eg dust carts and delivery vans). The inability of the batteries to retain the charge over time obviously dictated a need for continuing research and development, and for general technical support. With the onset of World War II, further sales prospects unfortunately evaporated and the Drumm Battery Co Ltd went into voluntary liquidation in August 1940. This had adverse implications for the efficacy of the operating guarantees that had been negotiated in the 1936 agreement.

Apart from the Sandycove accident in 1935, the Drumm trains were involved in other incidents that raised safety questions and concerns about stability of the battery cells. The most spectacular involved Train C at Bray in 1942 while the battery was being re-charged. A cell exploded injuring a workman, and a ball of flame shot out of the battery side followed by a huge volume of smoke. The metal frame of the battery was wrecked and some windows were broken with pieces of metal falling onto a nearby football ground. The explosion was heard up to a mile away. Train C was then out of service from 20 September 1942 until 14 April 1943.

For vehicles as modern and attractive as were Trains C and D, the decision to employ old, rebuilt batteries in one of them seems extraordinarily short-sighted, and presumably budgetary restrictions once again limited GSR development plans. Utilisation was unimpressive throughout the life of the project but to be reduced to cannibalisation of batteries and equipment to keep one of two trains running a mere 5 years after introduction bordered on the ludicrous.

The vulnerability of the system was exposed in another way when for around two weeks in August-September 1947, the charging station at Harcourt Street was out of order. With a shortage of substitute carriages, Drumm units were temporarily used as steam-hauled stock which given their tonnage yielded a poor weight/seating capacity ratio. In 1949 the position with the Drumm trains was fully reviewed by CIÉ management, following the complete failure of one battery set and rapid deterioration of the remainder. In May it was concluded that operations were no longer economically viable and the fleet was withdrawn immediately. (Coincidentally around this time, the remaining CIÉ electric tramcars were also withdrawn but the two events were not connected). Nevertheless, CIÉ seemed reluctant to disengage entirely from the project as in addition to the delay in conversion to hauled stock, the electric motors and control equipment were not offered for sale until 1952.

Looking at the Drumm fleet's commercial achievement, the working careers of Trains A and B spanned the years 1931 to 1948 which, notwithstanding extended intervals out of service, was notable for largely untried technology under normal operating conditions. In this regard, it must be recorded that despite any initial misgivings, once the decision was taken to go ahead, Inchicore was fully committed to helping make the system work

By comparison, Trains C and D were a significant disappointment. At the time of their introduction in October 1939, Drumm-powered vehicles had been under trial and in normal service for over 9 years. The Drumm battery had undergone considerable development, and this work should have seen the provision of a power source to match the contemporary and stylish design of the carriages. In reality, excluding scheduled periods of non-use for cleaning, regular servicing etc, the amount of time these two Trains were available for operations was poor:

	Train C	**Train D**
Started work	05/10/1939	06/11/1939
Out of service following Bray explosion	*20/09/1942*	
Returned to service	14/04/1943	
Out of service due to electricity restrictions	*14/06/1944*	*14/06/1944*
Returned to service	15/11/1944	
Taken out of service - parts cannibalised	*27/07/1945*	
Returned to service		14/09/1945
Out of service following Harcourt St collision		*15/01/1948*
Returned to service	10/07/1948	
Withdrawn from service	18/05/1949	18/05/1949
Notional operating career in days	3509	3478
Actual period available for service in days	2070	2533
Availability before time-out for scheduled repairs etc	59%	73%

Commercial success relies heavily upon the degree to which fixed assets are employed. The sad conclusion has to be drawn that – as with the fleet of 4-6-0s – the GSR failed to achieve an acceptable return on its money.

During the 1930s much pioneering work was carried out elsewhere with diesel engines for shunting locomotives and fixed formation trains. The oft-rehearsed advantages of diesel power – particularly operating flexibility and immediate availability – would have been intrinsically attractive to the GSR management yet by 1944, no experience had been gathered with this form of traction. In summary, and with all the advantages of 20/20 hindsight, the Drumm venture was one from which the GSR would have done better to remain aloof. In investment terms, development of diesel power or, as a stop-gap, provision of more suitable steam locomotives for the ex-DSER suburban services would have been a sounder financial strategy.

A Scottish postscript: After Drumm, the battery electric concept might have been considered finished but in 1957 British Railways introduced an experimental accumulator driven railcar pair. Numbered SC 79998/ 99 the vehicles were based on a standard lightweight Derby-built two-car DMU. They were officially a Driving Motor Brake Second (weight 37 tons 10 cwt) and a Driving Trailer Composite (weight 32 tons 10 cwt). The DMBS was equipped with two 100 KW Siemens-Schuckers nose-suspended traction motors powered by 216 lead acid cell batteries of 1070 amp/ hour capacity. The batteries were suspended Drumm fashion below the solebars on both vehicles. Seating capacity was 12 – 1st class, 105 – 2nd class.

The pair was used on the branch from Aberdeen to Ballater, a distance of 43 miles with a ruling gradient of 1 in 68. Acceleration was 0.75 mph per second up to 30 mph, and top speed was 60 mph. Technological progress was evident in the need for only a short charge between trips; a full charge was made overnight. The pair worked for several years but the type was not multiplied.

And last but not least…

GSWR/ GSR 'Pat'

No survey of GSWR/ GSR motive power would be complete without mention of 'Pat', a four-wheeled, 5' 3" gauge vehicle built in 1884 at Inchicore to work on the coal gantry at Cork depot. It was equipped with a small vertical boiler of cross-tube type, working at 80 lbs/ sq in; this was renewed around 1946. There were two vertical cylinders 6½" x 7½" operating a light crank shaft, a geared pinion being attached to the shaft and engaging with a large toothed gear wheel fitted to the inner side of each of the two front wheels of the engine (making it technically an 0-2-2T). The driving and trailing wheels were of 3' 7½" diameter. Overall length was 13' 4". A report dated 1959 said that faded traces of its original elaborate livery (presumably dating from 1884) were just visible. There is conjecture whether Aspinall, then Locomotive Superintendent to the GSWR had a hand in the design.

The Locomotive Department, Cork advised in 1937 that 'Pat' could haul 5 laden hopper coal wagons (approximately 120 tons) on the overhead gantry from Penrose Quay on the River Lee to the coal bunkers at Cork, Glanmire Road shed, a distance of 1,140 feet. It was last steamed on 24 June 1963 for an Irish Railway Record Society visit, and it was cut up mid-November that year.

Technically speaking, it should not appear in this volume as it was always listed as plant rather than as a locomotive. Nonetheless, 'Pat' was rail-borne, self-propelled and steam powered which in the authors' view justifies inclusion. Let the photographs speak for themselves.

GSWR/ GSR 'Pat'. Side view.

IRRS collection

GSWR/ GSR 'Pat'. End view displaying corrugated iron weather protection equipment.

Authors' collection

Chapter 13
The fuel saga

The ending of the Great Southern Railways with effect from 31 December 1944 had no immediate impact on the company's locomotive fleet, or on its obligations to keep train services moving. The final year of the GSR's existence was by far the least successful, measured by train and engine miles. Some slight recovery was possible in Córas Iompair Éireann's first year but the overall trend was profound:

Year	Passenger train miles *(000s)*	Goods train miles *(000s)*	Total train miles *(000s)*	Total engine miles
1939	5,714	3,492	9,206	12,027
1940	5,595	3,502	9,097	11,860
1941	4,135	3,417	7,552	10,368
1942	1,985	3,814	5,800	8,726
1943	2,109	3,923	6,032	8,884
1944	1,618	3,375	5,193	7,816
1945	1,716	3,642	5,358	8,102

That services should have been sustained even at this reduced level was remarkable. Ireland's recognised mineral wealth in GSR days was modest. Locally mined low-grade coal in small amounts was supplied to GSR/CIÉ but most tonnage consumed was imported and of steam grade.

In the period 1925 to 1939, the GSR purchased an average of 225,000 tons of coal per annum. Up until 1931, Britain was the exclusive supplier, apart from 1926, which was the year of the prolonged British coal miners' strike, when 135,000 tons were bought in the USA, and 13,500 tons from continental Europe. In 1932, diversification was sought through purchases from Germany but by 1936, 98% had reverted to Britain, the balance coming from Arigna in Ireland.

Cost was a dominant factor in buying British coal. A Board minute for 6 November 1925 noted that Ebbw Vale colliery was selling coal at £1 per ton whereas earlier purchases had been priced at £1-4s-0d per ton. By comparison, coal purchased from the USA during the 1926 UK miners' strike was priced at £1-11s-6d per ton.

With the outbreak of World War II, coal imports from any source involved a dangerous sea journey and, with Ireland's determination to remain neutral, supplies became erratic. In a steam locomotive, there is a direct correlation between fuel quality and the tonnage expended to raise steam. In 1939, the GSR consumed 227,000 tons of coal at the rate of 42 lbs per engine mile whereas in 1944, the relative figures were 278,000 tons of 'fuel' and 80 lbs per mile. This deterioration in consumption rates stemmed from the decline in the volume and quality of coal available, and from the poorer calorific value of substitute fuels used during this period.

Essentially, there are three key components to locomotive coal:

(1) **Volatile content** is the gaseous element that is important in the lighting up process, and in meeting sudden demands for more power when running.

(2) **Carbon content** is that element that cannot be burned as gas but reduces to coke on the fire bars thereby creating the fire bed. It generates steady continuous heat at a slower rate than the volatile content.

(3) **Ash** is the remaining component which consists of sundry non-combustible matter.

Under normal peacetime conditions, coal was screened at the pithead into various grades, depending on the proportions of the various components. Coal was purchased according to the grade required and care was taken in checking that the stipulated quality was delivered. Excessive use of the wrong category could adversely affect locomotive performance and the company's fuel bill.

An excess of volatile content meant a need to replenish the fire at a faster rate and hence greater consumption. At the other end of the scale, too much ash reduced the flow of air to the volatile and carbon contents, inhibiting the rate of combustion. Ash of a low melting point could swiftly coalesce into clinker. If unchecked, this would bond into a solid mass

GSWR/ GSR Class 60 (D14) No 96 taking water at Ennis. Fuel difficulties meant reliance on alternative combustible materials with lower calorific value and/ or lower density for which many smaller tenders had inadequate carrying capacity. A modest increase in the tender fuel capacity has been achieved by fitting a narrow timber side plate; photograph taken in 1955, long after the fuel crisis had ceased.

IRRS collection

effectively blocking the airflow through the fire bars. To avoid this problem, the fireman would break up the clinker at every available opportunity, and rake it out while the locomotive was stationary. Failure to do this could mean having to clean out the firebox completely, and to build a new fire from scratch.

The first signs of trouble were seen with declining coal quality during 1940. Wartime conditions reduced the thoroughness of coal screening at the pithead, so railway companies had to accept whatever coal was available on the market. Supply shortages meant that recourse to anthracite dust with the trade name of 'duff' became necessary. Duff had a very fine texture, a low volatile content and a slowing burning rate. It could not be used for lighting up and was best expended in augmenting a fire that had been built up and stabilised with good steam coal. As stocks of good coal dwindled, native timber was employed as a substitute source of volatile content. The best combination was a mixture of native timber and coal but this needed careful management. As the timber burned faster, it could leave the remnants of the fire to collapse on to the fire bars and to form clinker. If this condition was reached, revival of the fire using timber was virtually impossible while the clinker blocked the airflow.

Several measures were tried to overcome the disadvantages of finely textured coal dust by bonding it with other substances to defer its decomposition in the firebox. Duff bonded with pitch fashioned in the shape of briquettes had proved a satisfactory household fuel with enhanced volatile content, but the pitch generated tar that clogged the boiler tubes. Weak cement was then tried as the bonding agent. Duff and cement alone lacked the necessary volatile content, although this could be slightly enhanced by including sawdust in the mix. Experiments were also conducted with mixtures such as duff with turf mould and cement, and pitch substituted for cement in other fuel combinations.

All these variants proved unsatisfactory in practice. Apart from the clogging effect of pitch, the cement bonding quickly broke down on contact with the fire, reducing the duff back to its original fine dust consistency. Alternatively the volatile content burned too quickly, in turn splitting the briquette and again reducing the fuel to dust. Experiments with various combinations of locally available combustible materials were urgently conducted throughout 1941 because train services were rapidly deteriorating.

At one point, the GSR had only three days' supply of coal in hand, despite a reduction of services in July 1941 followed by a further reduction in October. At the low point, locomotive depots in Dublin and at some county locations were within 5-6 hours of complete failure. The Irish government eased this crisis by releasing some of its own coal, pending further deliveries by ship. The distribution of these emergency fuel stocks led to an extraordinary ad hoc operation by motor lorry and horse-and-cart that was an epic in itself.

By March 1942, generally regarded as the peak point of the crisis, the entire GSR system was on the brink of collapse. Journeys of five hours duration by the timetable were taking up to three days to complete. Locomotives were either running out of fuel, or out of steam through fireboxes blocked by clinker in mid-journey. Stranded locomotives and trains littered the system. Locomotive crews were reluctant to leave a station or passing loop before they had raised steam to a level that promised safe arrival at the next section without stalling. Inordinate delays to schedules occurred while crews 'bailed out' at each stop; ie cleaned out the firebox of non-combustible clinker, and rebuilt the fire. Frustrating though this practice was for both passengers and railwaymen, it was preferable to failing within a single track section (eg on the ex-MGWR main line) and thus paralysing other trains up to 40 miles distant.

GSR Class 650 (G2) No 668, formerly MGWR Class Ks No 32, is also equipped with a narrow timber side plate extension. On Broadstone turntable.

IRRS collection

A further complication was a 60% reduction in availability of empty wagons for loading as many were tied up on heavily delayed journeys while laden, or in working back empty. With schedules virtually non-existent the system of load classes went by the board as it became a matter of using whatever locomotive was in steam and available for the next departure.

These operational difficulties were in contrast to the situation on the Great Northern Railway (Ireland). Northern Ireland had ready access to coal mined in Britain and while not of pre-war standard, the GNR(I) did not face the shortages that afflicted the GSR. Operating practices were modified to ensure that there was always sufficient coal in the tender from the north to cover all cross-border workings. Even so the GNR(I), like the British Big Four companies was not immune from post-war shortages. In the crisis of 1947 both Irish companies took recourse to oil-burning.

In these circumstances, criticism was levelled at the GSR on the premise that, in other countries, satisfactory services were maintained by steam locomotives that consumed low grade coal or inferior substitutes. However, practically speaking, the degree of possible corrective action was limited. The majority of the fleet reflected design standards of the late 19th and early 20th centuries, a period when good quality coal had been plentiful. Satisfactory steaming had thereby been possible with fireboxes of modest proportions and small grate areas, as was particularly characteristic of larger-wheeled 4-4-0s. Further, traditional use of lower grade coal in other countries dictated the need for a large firebox and grate supported by a trailer truck or bogie, which was not a feature of Irish design practice.

Another limitation imposed by the fleet profile was that little real progress had been made with rationalisation. With 503 locomotives in 78 different classes, it was simply not possible to design a boiler better suited to contemporary fuel quality that could have widespread application. The GSR experienced the hard way what had become apparent elsewhere – standardisation was an essential ingredient in modern motive power management.

In citing examples of countries where inferior coal was typically used, critics also overlooked the fact that this was usually in briquetted form. The manufacture of briquettes is a science of its own as not all coal and duff is suitable for compacting. Also, the process requires constant monitoring and adjustment to take account of variables such as moisture content.

The Laboratory and Testing Department at Inchicore was continuously engaged in monitoring fuel quality as and when it became available. From the spring of 1942, this data was essential for the operation of several second-hand briquetting plants that the GSR had been able to acquire. With intensive use of this equipment and in the light of experience, the annualised production rate of briquettes rose from 30,000 to 80,000 tons. Some of the binding agents used earlier were involved in this process plus recovered smokebox ash. Production rates were closely monitored as briquettes were acknowledged as key to overcoming operating difficulties. Footplate crews soon recognised their value, and would plead for as many as possible, hoarding and hiding any surplus provided!

Not all needs could be met by briquetted coal and recourse was made to other fuels. The relatively poor-grade coal from Arigna was sometimes of better quality than that available through imports but nonetheless had a high ash content resulting in copious quantities of clinker. Where the coal had a low volatile content, it was sometimes mixed with loose pitch, but this practice was usually restricted to lighting-up, and to the sometimes tricky matter of re-lighting a fire after removal of clinker and ash.

Turf was also used but in a conventional, unmodified steam locomotive it had limited success. In 1944, the estimated average BTU (British Thermal Unit) of imported coal was 13,000 whereas turf had a rating of 9,500 BTU. Typically the composition of turf was volatile content – 75%, carbon content – 25% and ash – 5%. The excess of volatile element meant that achieving combustion was not difficult but when there was demand for extra steam, the consumption rate became very high. Another drawback was that turf had a moisture content of 28% to 40% yielding a bulk density that was excessive for the available tender or bunker capacity. Briquetted turf naturally had a lower moisture content (around 12%) and was significantly less bulky but it was not available in large quantities. This type of fuel was used on the DSER section being distributed to Grand Canal Street and Bray only, but not with any economy resulting. Trials in August 1944 on Dublin-Bray-Greystones services with briquetted turf showed a consumption rate of 100 to 105 lbs per mile, typically 25 lbs per mile more than the consumption rate with the poor quality imported coal.

The best results between Harcourt Street and Bray were achieved with locomotive No 455 where the consumption rate came down to 73 lbs per mile (ie roughly the same as with poor coal) but only after extensive modification to the blast pipe. Gains were largely offset by the need to fit a spark arrester.

Phurnacite, a high carbon fuel designed for enclosed smokeless stoves, was also used. It was expensive and supplies were limited but when it was available, a strong fire resulted and fire cleaning was hardly ever necessary. A drawback was that it could break up in the tender when exposed to continuous vibration as was typical with a locomotive on the move.

Experiments were conducted with pulverised coal which required physical modifications to both tender and firebox, resulting in a fuel feed process not dissimilar to that in an oil-burning locomotive. Coal in fine dust form was loaded into a special hopper on the tender and then fed into a small-diameter pipe partly by gravity and partly by a worm drive at the bottom of the hopper. From this small-diameter pipe, the coal dust was then passed into a larger-diameter pipe, driven by an air blast. From there it passed through a flexible coupling between locomotive and tender, through a further large-diameter pipe under the footplate and into the firebox at ash pan level through a circular plate perforated with hundreds of small holes. The firebox was brick lined and the fire was lit by ignition of waste matter or by directing the fuel jet upon a small wood fire. Once steam pressure had reached 30-50 lbs/sq in, there was sufficient pressure for the process to become self-sustaining ie to drive the auxiliary engines that operated the hopper screw and worked the fan to produce the air blast. An alternative was to take steam from another locomotive to start the auxiliaries. These arrangements represented the most advanced physical modifications to locomotives proposed as a means of overcoming the fuel crisis. The resultant steaming qualities were impressive. However the technical problems, and presumably the cost of modification and consequent maintenance, outweighed the advantages and the project was abandoned.

Three other initiatives should be noted. One was the steam injection grate which could be fitted to any locomotive and was suitable for use with coal or briquettes. The design was such that its use was discretionary ie only if the fuel quality suggested that clinker was going to cause problems. The idea was the brainchild of an engineer with the Electricity Supply Board who spent many long hours trying to perfect the system, although it eventually failed through its

In other cases a tender side plate extension was fitted, as with GSR Class 619 (J6) No 620, (formerly MGWR Class H No 97) at the Broadstone.
IRRS collection

GSR Class 623 (J5) No 634, formerly MGWR Class F No 40, still retains the deeper form of tender side plate around 1953. It is passing Glasnevin Cemetery, Dublin (North City Mills branch on the right) with the down 8.20 am Ballina goods.

IRRS collection

inability to cope with large amounts of ash. Another initiative was simpler and more effective – the drop grate which became a standard GSR/ CIÉ feature and which greatly eased the burden of fire cleaning.

The third effort was promoted by Bredin in co-operation with Mackintosh, the Assistant Locomotive Engineer for the GNR(I) at Dundalk. This contemplated the equipping of a Class 101 locomotive coupled to a large tender with a conveyor to feed turf into the firebox. Ten tons of duff and one ton of pitch were sent to Dundalk for the trials but the project was halted in October 1942 due to war-time shortages of bearings for the conveyor.

By the end of 1942, the fuel situation had stabilised. Use of briquettes and Phurnacite played an important role in this achievement, accounting for 30% of all fuel consumed. Serious delays still occurred but were no longer so extreme that it took days to complete a journey. This progress was helped by establishment of a Fuel Control Office which carefully monitored and managed fuel resources. An enlarged Laboratory and Test Department under the direction of the Chief Chemist examined the contents of every coal cargo by analysing samples from several levels in the shipment. The Laboratory collaborated closely with the Running Department, which reported daily on the quantity and quality of coal in stock at every depot. This made it possible to distribute fuel throughout the system where it could do most good. Previously distribution had been on a simple tonnage basis to wherever supplies were short, without reference to quality. Thus an unlucky depot could receive several shipments of inferior fuel over an extended period with disastrous results.

This Fuel Control discipline relied on recognition that every train was important. There was no point in supplying good coal to a main line train if branch services required to make fixed connections had to struggle with inferior fuel. Coal was graded into categories A to E with grade A fuel (briquettes, Phurnacite and better quality coal) restricted to passenger trains. Heavy goods trains received grade B fuel, lighter goods trains worked with grade C, and less important services grade D. Locomotives on pilot duties had to make do with whatever rubbish constituted grade E.

Timetables were recast to reflect contemporary reality rather than maintain the pretence that anything like the timings and frequency of 1939-1940 was still possible. In August 1942, train loads were reduced by 15% across the system and by 25% on sections known to be habitually heavily loaded. This had the benefit of reducing the number of locomotives needed for regular services (ie reduction in double-heading) while making motive power available for the special trains and one-off services that became increasingly common.

Another measure was the establishment of fire cleaning stations. Previously locomotive crews had worked as far as they thought prudent, based on their judgement of the quality of their fuel. If this took a turn for the worse as lower levels were reached in the tender, then the risk of an unscheduled stop within a section increased greatly. In these circumstances, it was usual for crews to try to punch holes through the clinker to restore draught. With a fire in this condition, the locomotive's blast could draw air through the holes in the clinker at a greater velocity. This raised the temperature in the immediate vicinity and could increase the speed at which clinker formed, thereby sealing off the air supply and leading to total failure.

Fire cleaning stations were located at locomotive depots and at points after long adverse gradients. For example, an important station was established at Sallins where fires were cleared of the considerable amounts of ash that built up during the steady climb from Kingsbridge. In some cases ash pits were installed within the running lines at starting signals, as at Thurles (mile post 86¼), Limerick Junction (mp 107) and Mallow (mp 144½). These operations helped to maintain the reduced and slower timetables, and also relieved locomotive crews of excess physical labour. This was important in view of the extended hours they were habitually required to work.

Nevertheless, crews were still frequently seen working away at this back-breaking chore whenever necessary at other locations. A direct result of their efforts was that piles of ash, clinker, and dust from bailing-out sessions littered the trackside at fire cleaning stations and many other locations. Cleaning-up was a major task and much of the detritus was moved to Hazelhatch on the Dublin-Cork main line where it virtually filled a disused quarry close to the railway.

The net effect was that seemingly against the odds, an integrated railway service was maintained by dint of the extraordinary levels of commitment by ordinary railway employees. The financial cost was also extraordinary. In 1939, the GSR's fuel bill was £338,691 whereas by 1945, CIÉ's first year, this figure had risen to over £1,055,247. This equated to a fuel cost per mile of 7.77d in 1939 compared with 2s 7.36d per mile in 1945, an increase of 303.6%.

Hard though it may be to believe, after 1942/ 3 the quality of fuel available continued to decline further but deterioration in services was halted by the measures described above. Delays were still frequent but GSR management was assiduous in following up passenger complaints and in enquiring into causes. The response by footplate crews was in the highest traditions of their profession. Drivers and firemen learned by bitter experience how to cope with strange and inferior fuels. Their accumulated knowledge of this rather esoteric subject was second to none.

Interestingly, in the planning for the Allied invasion of Nazi Europe, assessment of the ability of steam locomotives to operate military supply and troop trains with poor fuel was an important factor. It had been represented to the military planners that certain fuels would be quite unsuitable. Discreet enquiries about how the GSR was coping with these substances in everyday service provided cogent evidence to the contrary. Valuable practical advice was passed on that was put to good use from June 1944.

The immediacy of the fuel problem caused the newly formed CIÉ to lose little time in enquiring into the scale of the difficulties. A report of stoppages throughout 1944 brought forth the following data:

Cause of stoppage: / District:	Fuel	Mechanical failure	Train divide	Obstruction	Total
Kingsbridge	60	5	2	5	72
Cork	182	1	18	28	229
Limerick	162	3	28	3	196
Waterford	88	2	7	5	102
Athlone	132	1	6	38	177
Mullingar	81	7	4	16	108
Westland Row	155	1	13	9	178
Total	**860**	**20**	**78**	**104**	**1062**

While 81% of all stoppages were caused by poor fuel, the length of those delays was further analysed by time lost:

No of minutes: District:	1 to 30	31 to 45	45 to 60	61 to 75	76 to 90	91 plus	Total
Kingsbridge	27	8	9	6	1	9	60
Cork	129	18	17	4	5	9	182
Limerick	117	24	13	4	2	2	162
Waterford	49	13	10	4	4	8	88
Athlone	102	11	6	2	5	6	132
Mullingar	67	6	5	0	2	1	81
Westland Row	102	25	21	6	0	1	155
Total	**593**	**105**	**81**	**26**	**19**	**36**	**860**

The ultimate Class 101! No 185 was rebuilt with a Type Z Belpaire superheated boiler in 1933, and with new frames in 1935, and was then fitted with oil-burning equipment in 1947. A total of 17 Class 101s were fitted as oil burners. No 185 was employed as an oil burner on Dublin-Bray services, and is seen at Amiens Street in 1948. The white discs on smokebox front and tender sides are barely discernible beneath the grime.

IRRS collection

Grim though these statistics might seem, it should be noted that 69% of stoppages were of 30 minutes or less. This sort of late running could logically be attributed to the need to stop en route for bailing out. These delays must have caused much frustration but a level of operating stability had been achieved with only 9% of the total resulting in stoppages exceeding one hour. This was a considerable improvement over the havoc that had plagued the system 2-3 years earlier.

The coming of peace in Europe brought little relief to the fuel supply situation which actually worsened from late 1946. The winter of 1946-47 was one of the worst of the 20th Century. The British coal industry was struggling to meet growing demand, exacerbated by weather conditions, and the British railway system was finding it almost impossible to move coal from the pits to the customers. As with railways in Britain, CIÉ turned to oil as an alternative fuel source and started to equip locomotives with weir-type burners. Class 257 (J4) 0-6-0 No 264 had been experimentally fitted out as an oil burner in 1945 and based on this experience, a full scale programme was implemented:

Locomotives fitted in 1947:

Class 101 (J15):	102/ 6/ 7, 110, 140, 153, 160/ 6, 182, 185§, 198, 255/ 6
Class 257 (J4):	257-63
Class 351 (J9):	249, 252, 351/ 2/ 4
Class 321 (D2):	330
Class 333 (D4/ D3):	334/ 5*/ 8, 340
Class 342 (D4):	344/ 6
Class 355 (K3):	356/ 7, 361
Class 372 (K1):	372/ 4-9, 381*/ 2/ 5*, 386-91
Class 393 (K1a):	393-96/ 8
Class 400 (B2):	403/ 7/ 9
Class 402 (B2a):	401
Class 500 (B1):	500/ 1/ 2*
Class 573 (J18):	576, 583/ 7
Class 594 (J19):	595/ 7/ 8, 601/ 6/ 7
Class 623 (J5):	624-26, 628-33, 636-39, 641-43

Locomotives fitted in 1948:

Class 101 (J15):	138, 148/ 9, 170
Class 355 (K3):	360
Class 393 (K1a):	397
Class 623 (J5):	640

§ Fitted experimentally with Laidlaw-Drew apparatus.

* Although converted, these locomotives never ran in service as oil burners.

No ex-MGWR passenger locomotives were converted. Hence it was necessary to transfer temporarily ex-GSWR and ex-GSR types (Nos 330, 334, 338, 344 and 346) to Broadstone shed to cover Sligo and Mayo passenger services. All locomotives were reconverted to coal firing in 1948 except Nos 372, 397 and 401 which were so treated in 1949.

The system adopted by CIÉ involved the installation of oil storage tanks of approximately 1400 gallons capacity into selected tenders. The tanks were manufactured at Inchicore. They were of welded construction, rectangular in shape to fit neatly in to the tender coal space, and with an extension about two feet deep at the bottom front to form a sump. These converted tenders were readily identifiable by the manner in which the tanks projected above the tender sides. A further visible modification was the installation of ladders on the tender sides towards the rear, or on the tender rear. These allowed easy access from rail level so as to aid filling of the oil tanks. The ladders proved useful also for refilling the water tank, and so were retained after re-conversion to coal-burning. (The tanks were transferred to other duties later, and at the time of writing some can still be seen in departmental service, mounted on wagons).

Oil was distributed from the tank by gravity through a flexible coupling to a pipe that passed to the burner unit under what was previously the ashpan. This unit also had a live steam inlet, controlled from the footplate and directly opposite the oil inlet pipe. The burner was mounted on studs set into the bottom of the foundation ring and its position could be vertically and laterally adjusted to a limited degree. The burner faced the firebox door but at a lower level. The dimensions of the burner outlets varied according to class but oil outlets were typically 1¾" by ¾" deep, and the steam outlets slightly larger. The firebox floor was brick lined as was also the walls up to a height of about 2' 3".

To light up, burning waste was placed in the firebox and the steam jet turned on, followed by the oil jet. As oil trickled down from the inlet and came into contact with the steam jet, it was partly atomised and partly borne across the firebox by the steam. Usually steam pressure as low as 10-15 lbs/ sq in was sufficient. The burning waste immediately ignited the oil, creating a flame directed against the brick wall (the 'flash wall') just below the firebox door. Because the firebox floor was sealed by the brick lining, three dampers (approximately ten inches square in larger locomotives) were set into the floor to admit air. The locomotive blast would draw air out of the firebox thereby creating a vacuum effect; inlet of air through the dampers was thus accelerated which added to the roar of the burners.

CIÉ tried to anticipate every eventuality by designing the burner system to handle both light and heavy grade oil. For the latter, arrangements were also made to install pre-heating equipment in the tender oil tank, and adjacent to the burner, a special pre-heating unit was fitted to accelerate the lighting up process. In addition a burner-cleaner steam connection was included so that if heavy grade oil was used that might coagulate, the burner could be cleaned by the blow-through of steam under pressure.

As an alternative means of raising steam, an oil burner could be connected with another locomotive already in steam through the steam heating pipes. A special by-pass valve cut out access to the normal train steam heating system and directed steam straight to the burner. This method required great care as intense heat could be generated almost instantaneously with the risk of imparting undue stress on the boiler. It is believed that CIÉ only used light grade oil but the comprehensive nature of these measures illustrates the depth of commitment towards the project.

The footplate of an oil-burning locomotive can be intimidating on first acquaintance. The heat is often intense and can make the cab an uncomfortable place to be in warm weather. There is a fierce roar from the oil jets which produce a vivid flame unlike anything in a conventional coal firebox. However, once the firing technique is mastered, the results are usually impressive. Steaming remains rock steady under varying conditions, lighting-up is swift, the fireman is relieved of heavy labour, boiler tubes remain comparatively clear, and spark emission at the blast pipe is eliminated. In talking with a member of the locomotive department of the Welsh Highland Railway during the preparation of this book, it was learned that with the aid of compressed air, it is possible to raise full working steam pressure from cold in under 1½ hours on ex-Southern African Railways 2-6-2 + 2-6-2 Class NGG16 Garratts Nos 138 and 143.

However, oil burners on CIÉ were not entirely problem-free. Opinions differed over the optimal layout of burners, inlet dimensions, most appropriate fuel quality etc. This was hardly surprising given the slight knowledge that two to three years' practical experience yielded as compared with over 100 years of refinement in coal-burning design and techniques. Although never fully determined, there was evidence that conversion to oil did not always improve maximum steaming rates. This might have been because greater adjustments to blast pipe dimensions were necessary than would have

Above: The Swindon-inspired fireboxes of the Woolwich moguls did not take kindly to poor quality fuel making these engines prime candidates for oil-burning. Class 393 (K1a) No 394 is seen at Inchicore sporting the tell-tale white discs.

IRRS collection

.... as is also Class 393 (K1a) No 397 at Islandbridge Junction. *IRRS collection*

been considered usual in coal-burning locomotives.

It was also thought that oil-burning was more effective where the firebox provided a greater proportion of the total heating surface. This was borne out by the faster response in steaming rates to adjustments in the firebox controls and by the relative lack of heat storage in the firebox and boiler. Steaming did not become fully effective until the brick firebox lining had thoroughly heated up. This lining really provided the only means of heat retention when the oil admission was reduced to minimal level or closed off completely. Damper control was also critical when oil supply was low as excessive air admission could cool the firebox rapidly. It followed that oil-burning equipment was best fitted to locomotives likely to be in continuous use, and special rostering arrangements were prepared to this end.

Once the locomotive had ceased work, closure of

the dampers and placement of a chimney cover helped to slow heat loss. Oil-burning locomotives were not in service long enough to determine what effect faster heating and cooling cycles had on boiler and firebox life, but it was probably adverse.

CIÉ instituted an intensive driver training programme with considerable success. Apparently not a single failure was caused by inadequate or inappropriate handling by a footplate crew. In this context, the preceding troubles that crews had had to face must have engendered an especial competence and adaptability.

In the early days, the project's biggest impediment stemmed from a shortage of steel to manufacture oil storage tanks for provincial locomotive depots. With careful handling, a smaller locomotive consumed around 6 gallons of oil per mile. This meant that unless there was an oil supply at the destination, converted locomotives could only stray around 90-100 miles from Dublin to be certain of making the return journey without running short of fuel. The Woolwich moguls were much heavier on fuel, using around 11.5 gallons per mile; a range of 50 miles from Dublin was considered the safe working maximum.

By mid-summer 1947, the situation had eased as adequate material had been found to install storage tanks at Galway and other depots. Obsolete tenders were adapted to transport oil to provincial depots. Before this, it was announced that six mobile oil tanks were to be created. They were to be semi-permanently coupled behind the tender and fitted with axle-driven pumps to feed the main tender oil tank while in motion. Little has been recorded about these vehicles, and it is not certain how many were built and how much work they did. They were not continuously braked and so could only be used in non-fitted goods trains.

Apparently there were plans to create a fitted version for use on passenger services but reversion to coal-burning took place before any progress could be made. The idea was not unprecedented as South African Railways had, in 1938, inaugurated the concept of carrying auxiliary water supplies in a separate tank wagon to overcome axle loading limitations on the Class GM Garratts. Nonetheless it seems to have been the first time that the concept was seriously broached in these islands. (The idea was resurrected by the Ulster Transport Authority in the mid-1960s in an unsuccessful attempt to convert the ex-Northern Counties Committee Class WT 2-6-4T into a tender-tank type for use on Belfast-Dublin services).

In 1947, oil was becoming increasingly available on world markets. After years of struggling with poor quality coal and substitute fuels, widespread conversion to oil-burning seemed the ideal solution. Similar conclusions were reached in Britain but CIÉ converted a larger proportion of its operating fleet than was ever attempted across the water. Oil-burning locomotives were easily identifiable by large white circles, painted on the smokebox door and on tender sides. This simple device served as a warning to signalmen that the locomotive did not have to be sidelined for bailing out, but could be offered on immediately to the next section. (Incidentally, oil burner trials were conducted around 1955 with Class 101 No 197. Rather unnecessarily, white circles were applied. These remained in place after re-conversion to coal; a comedian drew a clock face on the circles, and the engine was then known as '197 o'clock').

Unfortunately in the post-war world, protection of scarce foreign currency reserves was an important priority for both Irish and British governments, through the imposition of Exchange Control regulations. Oil had to be paid for in US dollars but Ireland was within what was then known as the Sterling Area with the Irish Pound directly linked to the Pound Sterling. Under these restrictions, foreign exchange was denied for the purchase of large quantities of oil, so reversion to full coal burning status became inevitable. Fortuitously, by 1948 coal started to become more readily available and of improved quality. It was never to return, though, to the quality standards of the years in which the GSR steam fleet had been built.

After ten years of maintaining services against the odds and after termination of oil-burners, it is understandable why the idea of a steam locomotive capable of exploiting indigenous energy sources appeared so attractive. The mandate given to Oliver Bulleid to develop a turf burner (with capacity for conversion to oil) was eminently logical. Some commentators have condemned this effort as a wasteful exercise, a judgement that is unconvincing when considered in the light of the traumas of the preceding decade.

Chapter 14
Aftermath

The takeover of the Great Southern Railways by Córas Iompair Éireann at the beginning of 1945 brought no visible signs of change for some time. World War II (known in the Irish Free State as 'The Emergency') was still in progress. Materials and coal were in short supply, and would remain so through most of the 1940s. Average speeds were low because of the fuel situation, the heavy loading of the comparatively few trains that were running, and the inadequate maintenance of permanent way. The locomotive and rolling stock fleets continued to age with no prospect of early relief.

Apart from the frustrated oil-burner project of 1947–48, there was little change on the motive power front. A small gesture was made, though, that displayed a wish to improve the railways' public image. The main locomotive livery was still all-enveloping grey, except for Class 800 which remained green. However, in 1948 several engines likely to be used exclusively on passenger services were painted a slightly darker shade of green, lined white/ black/ white. The new style was complemented by the CIÉ 'flying snail' logo which was derived from the logo of the Dublin United Transport Company. This logo also appeared on other locomotives that were progressively painted all-over unlined black.

Classes 372, 393, 400, 402, 500, 670 and 850 received the green treatment plus some Dublin suburban engines. Individual examples of the latter included Nos 61, 305, 336, 433, 436, 439, 455 to 459, 466 and 467. The new livery looked very fine. Rather less encouraging was the replacement of cast GSR number plates with large plain yellow painted numbers on other locomotives that were painted plain black. A further small change occurred in 1950 with the fitting of smokebox number plates (painted white numbers on a black background) to the Woolwich moguls, plus Classes 400 and 500 in substitution for buffer beam numbers.

However, the system needed more rejuvenation than was possible with a coat of paint. There were pressing questions about how scarce investment capital was to be spent and what savings could be achieved through rationalisation. There were few genuinely modern steam locomotives at work and in truth, the efforts of twenty years of GSR locomotive development had yielded only modest progress. The dilemmas facing GSR managers in 1925 were broadly similar in 1945, except that much of the motive power and rolling stock was still in service but twenty years older. How and where to spend money efficiently was a difficult practical question, not helped by the position of Chief Mechanical Engineer having stood vacant since late 1944.

It was felt that an independent, non-biased view should help in reaching some tough decisions. To this end, the Minister for Industry & Commerce on 1 July 1948 commissioned Sir James Milne to review inland transport, to recommend measures for the integration of rail, road and canal services, and to consider ways by which the finances of the relevant bodies could be placed on a sound footing. The *Report on Transport in Ireland*, better known as the Milne Report, was produced in the short space of five months. This prevented any formal public enquiry but did allow for the submission of written evidence from 23 institutions. Milne was

The photograph on page 11 showed 0-4-4T GSWR Class 47 No 83 in pre-amalgamation days. CIÉ No 49 of the same class is seen shunting at Wexford in 1945. Despite the passage of over 20 years very little has changed except that this locomotive, uniquely, has acquired a side window cab.

JM Robbins

Left: Livestock trains continued for several years in the CIÉ period in time-honoured fashion. Here CIÉ Class J18 0-6-0s Nos 604 (pilot engine) and 597 shunt an up cattle special at Clonsilla in 1956.

IRRS collection

Below: Some express services were still handled by 4-4-0s as with GSR Class 332 (D2) No 332 seen leaving Kingsbridge in 1955 with a passenger train that would split at Mallow for Cork and Kerry.

IRRS collection

assisted by five senior railway officers and by one executive experienced in shipping and road transport. The report provided an objective, informed overview of the Irish transport situation and of the GSR's position, in the guise of CIÉ. The section concerning CIÉ's motive power is particularly interesting in offering an impartial assessment of the condition to which the ex-GSR fleet had been reduced.

The selection of Sir James was noteworthy, given his background. He had been General Manager of the Great Western Railway since 1929. As the senior chief executive officer of the Big Four railway companies at Nationalisation he had been offered, and had rejected, this position with the newly-formed British Railways. Two of his colleagues in the exercise were also ex-GWR senior officers.

The GWR had a long history of stability in motive power policy, having in 1923 come virtually unscathed through the British version of the amalgamation by which the GSR had been formed. A comprehensive Locomotive Standardisation Plan introduced in 1901 was destined to continue with but minor modifications well into the nationalised era. Between 1901 and nationalisation, only three individuals held the position of Chief Mechanical Engineer. The successors to G J Churchward, architect of the standardisation programme, saw little need to change the design precepts set by their illustrious predecessor.

The GWR's consistent attitude to locomotive design was no better illustrated than in the matter that had caused the GSR so much angst – superheating. In 1906, a two-cylinder 4-6-0 became the first locomotive in Britain fitted with a modern superheater. Having determined the optimal layout, 80 express 4-6-0s, 30 heavy freight locomotives, sundry large and medium sized tank locomotives, and virtually all of an extensive fleet of 4-4-0s had been fitted by 1913. All locomotives built new thereafter were superheated except for smaller tank engines.

The member of the Milne team charged with reviewing motive power matters was Oliver Bulleid. He held similar views on standardisation (and on boiler efficiency), although his approach was significantly more unorthodox and innovative. The position within CIÉ thus contrasted fundamentally with what had been Milne's experience although Bulleid would have been more familiar with the situation, based on his experience with the Southern Railway from 1937. His predecessor, Maunsell, had given that concern some excellent locomotives but the vast electrification programme had meant that many secondary services remained in the hands of a motley collection of ageing steam locomotives.

In Chapter 2 it was noted that, by the GSR's own estimate, the programme of locomotive replacement was some 120 machines in arrears by 1937. Now, eleven years later, the fleet had been augmented only by three specialised express locomotives with a limited field of operations. By extrapolation of the GSR's own estimates, 50% of the fleet was due for replacement by 1947. In the interim, apart from the abortive oil-burning scheme, little had changed. Given their pedigrees, it can be seen how Milne and Bulleid would have looked askance at the condition of the fleet.

Locomotive repairs were costed at 1s 5d per mile and were considered by Milne to be unacceptably high, although this figure was inflated by the backlog of repairs from the war years and the oil-burning re-conversion programme. (In normal conditions, a repair cost of 10d per mile was thought reasonable). A census of the fleet revealed that 28% was stored awaiting repair or in the workshops at any one time. The average period for a general repair had risen from 76 days in 1939 to 110 days in 1948, in large part caused by delays in procurement of materials.

As at 1 January 1948, the broad gauge fleet totalled 461 locomotives. Based on study of the structure of services, Milne calculated that the traffic requirements dictated the need for:

Summer timetable	174 locomotives in steam		
Shunting, trip working and sundry duties	49	"	"
Total	**233**	"	"

Presumably this estimate derived from British operating practice. In reality, 257 locomotives were being used on average daily which seems a reasonable variance. It was noted that the maximum number in use on one particular day was 348, although it is unclear whether this was due to poor management or to the need to cover extra seasonal and excursion traffic.

With restoration of the 1939 mean of 76 days for general repairs, about 20% of the fleet would be out-of-service at any one time. Assuming that 300 locomotives available for service would provide a safe working minimum, then a fleet of 360 would suffice. Further savings in workshop time and better operating availability arising from a modernised, standardised fleet would have further reduced the total required. There is an element of speculation in these calculations but however the figures are addressed, it was evident that the total of 461 broad gauge locomotives at the beginning of 1948 was around 80-100 more than was really needed.

Regarding the narrow gauge lines, 27 locomotives remained in service of which 11 were considered surplus to requirements. It was believed that availability of the remainder could be improved by regular shipment to Inchicore for more extensive repairs.

Another area that came in for adverse comment was the position concerning boilers. There were 37 different sizes in use (cf the GWR which used 15 sizes for 2000 plus of its locomotives). Since 1929 it had been

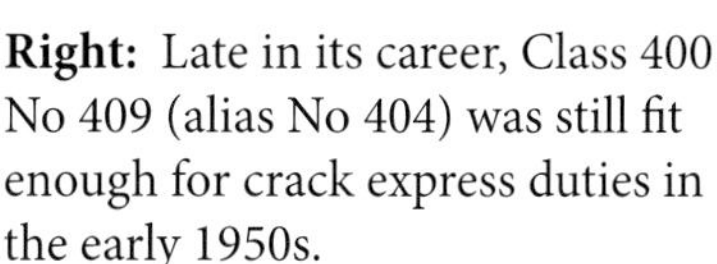

Right: Late in its career, Class 400 No 409 (alias No 404) was still fit enough for crack express duties in the early 1950s.

IRRS collection

Right: The everyday reality of the GSR persisted well into the CIÉ era. Class 101 (J15) No 150 rests at Kilkenny in 1956.

Authors' collection

policy to consider individual boilers as having a working career of 550,000 miles which was held to equate with an estimated working life of twenty years. By this formula, boilers were withdrawn on achievement of this mileage or on reaching the prescribed age regardless of their actual condition. Milne roundly condemned this "unsound and extravagant" practice which, it might be speculated, could have had its roots in MGWR policy. That company had a regime of replacing locomotives on a 20-year cycle which could mean the premature redundancy of boilers in mid-life. Milne also pointed out that installation of water treatment equipment at provincial depots where quality was poor would lengthen working lives.

CIÉ management had felt that modification of locomotives to accept new standard boilers would be the best solution. To this end, 94 boilers in six different classes (12 x type 'C', 10 x 'D', 6 x 'K', 12 x 'N', 4 x 'W' and 50 x 'Z') had been ordered in 1947 at an aggregate cost of £261,000 from British manufacturers. It was expected that a total of 148 new boilers would eventually be required. Milne recommended cancellation of this order and CIÉ agreed. This was perhaps the only piece of Milne's advice that was fully implemented – and a settlement of £31,000 in damages for breach of contract resulted.

It was Milne's view that 67 surplus boilers in stock could be refurbished for further use, if the principle of redundancy based on mileage was abandoned. He also felt that Inchicore's existing facilities had the capacity to build eight new boilers per annum. In addition he opined that it would be preferable to build new locomotives with more efficient boilers, in the process re-cycling certain materials from withdrawn engines where appropriate.

The issue of axle loadings over the GSR system raised some radical comments. It was proposed that three or four new classes with a maximum of 16 tons could handle all traffic needs except shunting and some minor branch line services. For the latter, the retention of a number of older locomotives with a 14 ton maximum could cover these requirements.

The Milne team was unimpressed with the 4-6-0 fleet, suggesting that all of Classes 400, 500 and 800 should be withdrawn at their next general repair. It was recommended that Dublin-Cork expresses should be revamped with a greater service frequency using smaller locomotives with axle loadings within the 16 ton limit. No record has been found on how these remarks were received but they could have come as bombshell, as they countered a basic premise of GSWR/GSR locomotive policy dating back to the introduction of Coey's 4-4-0 Class 309 in 1903.

Although Milne's message might have seemed heretical, it largely derived from the experiences of the war years, where poor fuel, heavy traffic loadings, and inadequate maintenance standards had dictated new trends in steam locomotive design. Common-user principles, broad spheres of operating availability, ready accessibility of working parts, easy maintenance methods, and excellent boiler design were considered essential elements to which the aged and diverse Irish fleet could not aspire.

If focus on steam power at this comparatively late date seems curious, the explanation is apparent within the report itself. Milne favoured the introduction of diesel railcars, doubtless based on the success that the GWR had enjoyed with its own fleet. However he was firmly against diesel locomotives (incidentally as had also been the GWR) on the grounds that they were expensive to purchase. Further, they needed additional investment in new workshop facilities while their performance and reliability had yet to be proven. Although diesel locomotives could potentially run at higher speeds than their steam counterparts, this advantage could only be realised after upgrades to track and signalling.

On the other hand, Milne believed that smaller steam locomotives within the 16-ton limit hauling six coach trains could do as well as diesel locomotives within prevailing constraints on the Dublin-Cork route. Milne proposed cancellation of outstanding orders for diesel locomotives (six 500 hp shunters; two 900 hp freight locomotives; six 1800 hp passenger/ freight locomotives). These recommendations were accepted, although the power units had been built. They were purchased and used later in locomotives built in the mid-1950s. The poor reliability of most of these machines, when they were eventually introduced, suggested that Milne had been right.

The tone of contemporary correspondence from Inchicore to some District Running Superintendents suggests that the Milne recommendations on rationalisation and reduction of the fleet met with resistance at operating level. Innate conservatism and the philosophy of 'having always done things a particular way' are typical barriers to the implementation of change in many organisations. Perhaps the extensive nature of the recommended withdrawals contributed to this reaction:

	Class	Original company	No in Class		Class	Original company	No in Class
4-4-2T	455	DSER	3	2-4-0T	423	DSER	3
	458	DSER	3	0-6-2T	213	GSWR	2
	27	GSWR	4	0-6-0	448	DSER	1
	269	GSWR	4		211	GSWR	2
	37	GSWR	6		619	MGWR	3
4-4-0	338	GSWR	1		442	DSER	4
	536	MGWR	4	0-6-0T	614	MGWR	5
	454	DSER	1		204	GSWR	1
	296	GSWR	2		Jumbo	GSWR	1
	530	MGWR	5	0-6-0	563	MGWR	1
	2	GSWR	8		234	MGWR	1
0-4-4T	279	GSWR	1		222	GSWR	4
	295	GSWR	1	0-4-2T	St Molaga	TCLR	1
2-4-2T	434	DSER	6	0-4-0T	495	GSR	1
	428	DSER	5	2-6-2T	850	GSR	1

The criterion for selection was elimination of classes with small numbers as emphasised by inclusion of No 850, the most modern design in the group.

No replacements were proposed on the basis that they were surplus to requirements. It was felt that withdrawal of Classes 400, 500 and 800 should follow, as and when new Inchicore-built steam locomotives within the 16-ton axle loading limit were introduced. In this respect, Milne calculated that Inchicore could construct ten new locomotives every year.

The Milne Report had only partial practical impact. Between 1949 and 1951, a total of 51 steam locomotives were withdrawn but not to the swingeing extent proposed:

	Class	Original company	Qty wd'n	No after 1951		Class	Original company	Qty wd'n	No after 1951
4-4-2T	27	GSWR	2	2	0-6-2T	213	GSWR	1	1
	37	GSWR	2	4	0-6-0	101	GSWR	1	92
	269	GSWR	3	1		211	GSWR	2	–
4-4-0	2	GSWR	4	4		222	GSWR	3	–
	52	GSWR	4	14		234	MGWR	1	–
	296	GSWR	2	–		235	GSWR	1	–
	454	DSER	1	–		448	DSER	1	–
	530	MGWR	4	1		567	MGWR	1	–
	536	MGWR	2	2		619	MGWR	3	–
4-4-0T	1L	CLR	1	4	0-6-0T	201	GSWR	1	9
2-4-2T	428	DSER	1	4		614	MGWR	3	2
	434	DSER	3	3	0-4-2T	St Molaga	TCLR	1	–
2-4-0	276	GSWR	2	2	0-4-0T	495	GSR	1	–

By the end of 1960, only 128 steam locomotives were left on the books. Earlier that year GSWR/ GSR Class 90 (J30) No 90 was shunting at Cork, Albert Quay in ominous company.

IRRS collection

The elimination of several small classes was thus achieved but that individualistic element among the ex-GSR fleet was to continue for some years to come. This situation was fascinating for the historian and enthusiast but less welcome to those wishing to minimise the range of necessary spare parts, the amount of time needed for repairs, and overall operating costs.

Study of such internal correspondence as can be traced lends support to Milne's contentions about the use and suitability of the 4-6-0 fleet. In December 1946, concerns were expressed about Class 800 locomotives as there were difficulties in rostering trains heavy enough to exploit their haulage capacity. As a result, the mileages that the class were then achieving were wastefully small. Remarks were passed about the limited route availability (Amiens Street, Dublin to Cork only) and that Class 400 was only slightly more flexible (Amiens Street to Cork plus Mallow to Killarney). Particular attention was drawn to the exclusion of 4-6-0s from the ex-DSER and ex-MGWR sections on grounds of width and axle loading. It can be inferred that there would have been a measure of concurrence among some GSR management for Milne's ideas two years later about smaller locomotives hauling more frequent and lighter trains.

Seven years on, the general deployment of the 4-6-0s again came in for criticism. As at 17 September 1953, the disposition of the locomotives was as follows:

Loco	Mileage* (000s)	Remarks
800	1,000	Ran trials 26/7/53 after general repair. Developed hot axle boxes. Returned to shops and not available since.
801	116,000	Stopped 26/5/53 with defective crank. Awaiting general repair.
802	45,000	In traffic
500	36,000	In traffic
501	70,000	In traffic
502	76,000	Stopped 15/9/53 awaiting tube plate and other repairs
401	67,000	Stopped 16/9/53, in shops for repairs to cracked smokebox saddle casting
402	119,000	In shops since 13/6/53 for general repair
403	51,000	In shops for TU (*tightening up?*) since 7/4/53
405	74,000	In traffic
406	23,000	Stopped 16/9/53 for repairs to crosshead liner
407	71,000	In traffic
409	41,000	In traffic
	*** Since last general repair**	

This might be a snapshot of a difficult period but the tenor of the Running Superintendent's remarks reflects a frustration that suggests that this was not an isolated situation. The prolonged non-availability of No 800 was an event that the Superintendent failed to understand. This class could be prone on occasions to overheating of the rear driving axleboxes (through either proximity to the ashpan or excess axle-loading) but 53 days out of service to effect adjustments or repairs is mystifying.

The elapsed time under repair of three front-line locomotives – Nos 801 (114 days), 502 (96 days) and 403 (163 days) – obviously conflicted with Milne's views on the desirability of restoring the average repair cycle to the 1939 mean of 76 days. Further, Milne had identified that a maximum of 20% of locomotives should be out of service at any on time; on the date mentioned, only six out of thirteen 4-6-0s were serviceable. One may only speculate what proportion of the less eminent members of the steam fleet was out-of-use at that time.

The files contain copies of applications for approval to scrap locomotives which include details of recorded mileages. Below are listed some of the higher mileages identified among older engines, of which Class 101 is predictably well represented, together with some samples of mileages covered by more modern types. (The mileage for *Jumbo* seems high for a shunter, and was presumably based on the convention of notional miles per hour in steam).

Class	Number	Introduced	Mileage
52	1	1890	1,706,980
52	4	1888	1,748,337
52	14	1888	1,787,047
52	55	1884	1,979,544
57	57	1888	1,627,186
60	60	1891	1,839,533
60	61	1891	1,728,462
60	63	1891	1,674,322
60	87	1886	1,956,085
60	88	1886	1,916,744
60	95	1885	1,968,169
101	107	1881	1,690,159
101	120	1877	1,783,354
101	135	1885	1,690,495
101	146	1878	1,793,266
101	158	1872	1,907,909
101	160	1871	1,797,810
101	163	1872	1,827,791
101	175	1873	1,797,185
101	192	1898	1,527,245
573	575	1894	1,554,353

Class	Number	Introduced	Mileage
Jumbo	*Jumbo*	1896	1,610,376
372	382	1927	637,467
392	397	1930	696,864
400	405	1922	1,089,021
500	500	1924	881,975
500	501	1925	900,226
700	702	1929	561,762
800	802	1939	562,877
850	850	1928	541,580

(The average annual mileages of the 4-6-0s were unimpressive:

No 405 – 33,001 miles; No 500 – 28,451 miles;

No 501 – 31,042 miles; No 802 – 35,180 miles.

By comparison, GWR Castle Class No 4080 averaged 49,362 miles pa in a working career from 1924 to 1964).

Despite the Milne view that the fleet total exceeded the optimum by 100, between the date of his report (1948) and the end of 1953, only 75 broad gauge and five narrow gauge engines were withdrawn. This perhaps was just as well given the apparently dilatory performance of the workshops. Presumably, the arrival of replacement diesel locomotives in 1955 was expected to relieve the situation, but both Bulleid and Milne seemed doubtful that this would result, particularly if British-built machines were to be employed.

A pair of main line diesel locomotives was introduced in 1950–51 and another 106 in three different classes between 1955 and 1958, together with 24 for shunting and secondary services. These units were essentially of British-based design, despite Bulleid (who was by then CME) believing that US-sourced machines would prove more satisfactory. The same Exchange Control regulations and shortage of US dollars that had stymied the oil-burning project were the cause. The uncertain reliability of these units led to use of the more successful diesel railcars on main line services rather than just the branch and suburban work for which they had been intended

This situation meant that CIÉ had to rely on steam locomotives inherited from the GSR for longer than had been expected, as is apparent from the withdrawal dates quoted in the individual class histories. Grand Canal Street shed closed to steam in March 1954, with its remaining allocation moving to the Broadstone. Inchicore's steam activities ended in September 1957 and Broadstone shed closed in May 1961. The remaining steam locomotives still at work then migrated to the ex-GNR(I) shed at Amiens Street.

In later years, the only ex-GSR works still officially

Left: Steam locomotive withdrawals were a constant fact of life. Deductively, the locomotives here are GSWR/ GSR Class 222 (J25), most likely No 237, and GSWR/ GSR Class 276 (G3), probably No 291. They await the cutter's torch in 1951 or 1952 at Inchicore. *IRRS collection*

Below: The solitary GSR prairie No 850 still looks handsome in lined green livery standing in Inchicore yard, perhaps awaiting works attention. However the engine's condition suggests another story. The coupling rods, connecting rods and valve gear are absent, the brakes are disengaged, and the locomotive is parked against a redundant tender which is acting as a stop-block. The year is very likely 1955, with cutting up the next move. *IRRS collection*

repairing steam locomotives was at Limerick. The CIÉ locomotive repair records indicate that Nos 104, 151, 179 and 183 received attention there in March 1962, while Nos 351 and 462 had been similarly treated at Waterford shed the previous month. In addition it is known that locomotive No 461 was repaired at Cork as late as June 1962 and No 599 at Limerick in August 1962. The efforts of Limerick works to keep old and increasingly decrepit engines on the move in the closing years of steam were particularly noteworthy.

Pressures on motive power had been temporarily eased by the acquisition of 83 ex-GNR(I) locomotives on the break-up of the Great Northern Railway Board on 30 September 1958. These locomotives, generally in better condition than their southern counterparts, were welcome to hard-pressed operators. They were used well beyond the boundaries of the old GNR(I) within the Republic, but their exploits do not form part of this story. Several different ex-GSR classes survived into the 1960s including, inevitably, some Class 101 (J15) engines. The last two ex-GSR steam locomotives in normal service were Nos 261 and 262 of Class 257 (J4).

The last available record of allocations/ locomotives in store was dated April 1963 and records the following engines still on the books:

could never have dre
of rail travel – the air-
acceleration away fr
of on-time arrivals
conditions with wh
once had to contend.

Limerick Junc	Mallow	Athlone	Amiens St	Sutton*	Inchicore	Thurles	Cork	Preserved	Stationary boilers (Inchicore)
106	109	574	637	132	179	104	118	184	354
125	116	593		151	183	124	251	800	464
130		599		172	249	195	262		
164		603		197	461		463		
186				198			560		
351				261					
				562					

* Ex-GNR(I) tram shed.

Left: There is no doubt about what is under way here.

A O'Toole

Below: Stranger in the camp. Ex-GNR(I) 4-4-0 Class VS No 207 *Boyne*, one of the locomotives acquired by CIÉ on the break-up of the Great Northern Railway Board, at Kildare on a trial train, Christmas 1962.

IRRS collection

It was unfortunate that Irish steam ended before the preservation movement in these islands really gathered momentum and that the efficiency of the scrapping facilities at Mullingar, Inchicore, Waterford and Dundalk meant that there was to be no Barry-style miracle. An unusual event concerned the sale and export of a number of locomotives and components to Aviles, Spain in 1958, specifically:

27/1/58 by SS *Cymbria*
Nos 34, 36(?), 41, 86, 107, 135, 158, 313, 445, 575, 576, 586 and 595, plus two spare tenders and boilers from Nos 6c, 553 and 802.

30/1/58 by MV *Spora*
No 391, a consignment of boilers and tenders from Nos 86, 158 and 445 and some ex-GNR(I) locos.

5/3/58 by MV *Lough Fisher*
Nos 395, 397 and 502, plus GNR(I) locos.

As the export of scrap metal was not then permitted, to circumvent the regulations these locomotives had to be sold in notionally working condition. This pretence was initially supported by some being driven to the North Wall yard at Dublin and by the presence of coal in their tenders, although more sense was applied with later shipments. An investigation in 1959 into the fate of these locomotives, in the hope of finding survivors, led to confirmation that all were broken up immediate upon arrival. Thus a greater sense of gratitude is felt

Knowledge and wisdom passes from one generation to the next.

A O'Toole

It is understood that preliminary dismantling of No 800 had commenced before the authorities realised the locomotive's significance, and this work was halted.

A O'Toole

Appendix A: Traffic trends and trading revenues

The history of the Great Southern Railways fell neatly into two distinct eras. The first covered the years 1925 to 1939, a 15 year period of normal, albeit difficult trading conditions. The second related to the five years 1940 to 1944 when conditions were anything but normal as the company struggled with problems forced upon it by the pressures and shortages of World War II, or the Emergency as it was known in the Irish Republic. It follows that no meaningful conclusions on trends can be drawn from the figures related to that five year period.

However, in the years up to 1939, the declining role of passenger trains in total operations was significant. Passenger train movements consistently accounted for slightly more than 50% of all movements while total annual train miles remained basically static. Further, in the period up to 1932 the total number of passenger vehicles was unchanged. Thereafter the number of vehicles showed some small decline but by the end of 1939, the fleet total was only 86 less than that in 1925.

Against this stability, passenger revenue was 46% of total revenue in 1925 but this figure had shrunk to 38% in 1939. Even more striking, the monetary value of passenger revenue in 1939 was £1,275,000 whereas this had been £1,991,000 in the GSR's first full year of operations. This meant that the passenger fleet was generating a diminished level of total revenue, that utilisation factors were declining, and that the number of vehicles (theoretically) available for service was significantly greater than the underlying level of demand.

During the same period, there had been a proportionately greater reduction in locomotive numbers, yielding an improvement in average annual locomotive miles. Nonetheless, it is apparent that utilisation of locomotives (and more so of passenger vehicles), was unacceptably poor as later endorsed by the Milne Report. The years 1930 to 1932 illustrate how badly passenger services were being managed:

Year	Passenger train miles as % of 1925 level	Average vehicle mileage as % of 1925 levels	Passenger train receipts as % of 1925 levels
1930	110%	112%	74%
1931	106%	107%	68%
1932	101%	103%	66%

In contrast, the financial performance of goods services remained robust. Apart from depressed conditions in the early 1930s, freight-based revenue remained steady and on average 1925 to 1939 accounted for 58% of total revenue while consuming only 41% of total locomotive miles.

The difficult economic and trading conditions of the period make it understandable why so little investment in new locomotives took place. What is less clear is why so much new motive power investment was directed at passenger services, and at express 4-6-0 locomotives in particular. Appendix A comprises:

Table 1 **Traffic revenues**

Table 2 **Annual route miles, passenger vehicle totals, locomotive repairs**

Table 3 **Total annual locomotive mileages**

Source: Annual reports of the GSR 1925 to 1944

Financial Accounts and Statistical Returns prepared in accordance with the First Schedule to the Railway Companies (Accounts and Returns) Act, 1911

Appendix A – Table 1 – Traffic revenues 1925-1944

	1925	1926	1927	1928	1929	1930	1931	1932	1933	1934	1935
TRAFFIC RECEIPTS £000s											
- Passenger	1497	1433	1298	1147	1071	996	869	874	795	820	846
- Mail	180	181	167	161	156	155	156	156	155	156	155
- Parcels & merchandise	314	326	341	335	329	329	322	292	275	272	277
TOTAL passenger train receipts	***1,991***	***1,940***	***1,806***	***1,643***	***1,556***	***1,480***	***1,347***	***1,322***	***1,225***	***1,248***	***1,278***
% of Total Train Receipts	46	46	42	40	39	39	38	43	43	41	41
As % of 1925 level		97	91	83	78	74	68	66	62	63	64
Goods Traffic											
- Merchandise	1538	1550	1607	1618	1585	1509	1442	1158	1103	1198	1238
- Livestock	457	461	498	537	512	496	426	292	273	248	298
- Coal, fuel & minerals	278	234	326	313	306	311	276	247	249	316	305
TOTAL goods train receipts	***2,273***	***2,245***	***2,431***	***2,468***	***2,403***	***2,316***	***2,144***	***1,697***	***1,625***	***1,762***	***1,841***
% of Total Train Receipts	53	53	57	60	60	61	61	56	57	58	59
As % of 1925 level		99	107	109	106	102	94	75	72	78	81
Misc	29	26	28	27	27	27	24	24	21	22	22
TOTAL RECEIPTS	***4,293***	***4,211***	***4,265***	***4,138***	***3,986***	***3,823***	***3,515***	***3,043***	***2,871***	***3,032***	***3,141***

	1936	1937	1938	1939	*Average 1925-1939*	1940	1941	1942	1943	1944
TRAFFIC RECEIPTS £000s										
- Passenger	852	846	844	820	***1,001***	734	866	763	1,186	953
- Mail	156	156	162	162	***161***	162	162	162	130	130
- Parcels & merchandise	287	285	280	293	***304***	302	399	341	433	382
TOTAL passenger train receipts	***1,295***	***1,287***	***1,286***	***1,275***	***1,465***	***1,198***	***1,427***	***1,266***	***1,749***	***1,465***
% of Total Train Receipts	40	40	41	38	***41***	35	36	32	37	30
As % of 1925 level	65	65	65	64		60	72	64	88	74
Goods Traffic										
- Merchandise	1,297	1,258	1,280	1,440	***1,388***	1,553	1,738	1,635	1,859	2089
- Livestock	313	297	282	301	***379***	313	297	419	405	409
- Coal, fuel & minerals	335	336	295	309	***296***	351	497	605	761	866
TOTAL goods train receipts	***1,945***	***1,891***	***1,857***	***2,050***	***2,063***	***2,217***	***2,532***	***2,659***	***3,025***	***3,364***
% of Total Train Receipts	60	59	59	61	***58***	65	64	68	63	69
As % of 1925 level	86	83	82	90		98	111	117	133	148
Misc	24	23	23	24	***25***	22	17	14	18	18
TOTAL RECEIPTS	***3,264***	***3,201***	***3,166***	***3,349***	***3,553***	***3,437***	***3,976***	***3,939***	***4,792***	***4,847***

Appendix A – Table 2
Annual route miles, passenger vehicle totals, locomotive repairs 1925-1944

	1925	**1926**	**1927**	**1928**	**1929**	**1930**	**1931**	**1932**	**1933**	**1934**
Mileage open to traffic:										
Single track	1,733	1,744	1,744	1,768	1,830	1,877	1,892	1,891	1,876	1,865
Double track	438	431	421	345	394	292	281	281	280	280
Three tracks or more	10	13	13	13	13	13	13	13	13	13
Total route mileage	**2,181**	**2,188**	**2,178**	**2,126**	**2,237**	**2,182**	**2,186**	**2,185**	**2,169**	**2,158**
% Single Track/ Total route miles	***80***	***80***	***80***	***83***	***82***	***86***	***87***	***87***	***87***	***86***
Coaching stock fleet										
Passenger Carriages	1,050	1,050	1,044	1,024	1,021	1,021	1,028	1,024	996	996
PO, luggage, parcel & brake vans	620	620	620	619	619	619	618	618	618	618
Total passenger stock	1,670	1,670	1,664	1,643	1,640	1,640	1,646	1,642	1,614	1,614
Number of locomotives										
- Renewed	8	6	5	4	7	6			5	5
- Received heavy repairs	103	133	157	160	163	172	137	157	135	151
- Received light repairs	62	45	107	105	98	109	107	93	56	150
- Under or awaiting repair	108	89	94	86	89	66	63	54	58	50

	1935	**1936**	**1937**	**1938**	**1939**	**1940**	**1941**	**1942**	**1943**	**1944**
Mileage open to traffic:										
Single track	1,784	1,784	1,786	1,760	1,759	1,753	1,753	1,753	1,753	1,753
Double track	279	279	277	277	277	277	277	277	276	276
Three tracks or more	13	13	13	13	13	13	13	13	13	13
Total route mileage	**2,076**	**2,076**	**2,076**	**2,050**	**2,049**	**2,043**	**2,043**	**2,043**	**2,042**	**2,042**
% Single Track/ Total route miles	***86***	***86***	***86***	***86***	***86***	***86***	***86***	***86***	***86***	***86***
Coaching stock fleet										
Passenger Carriages	973	977	977	974	970	970	878	837	834	831
PO, luggage, parcel & brake vans	611	611	611	614	614	614	522	520	517	506
Total passenger stock	1,584	1,588	1,588	1,588	1,584	1,584	1,400	1,357	1,351	1,337
Number of locomotives										
- Renewed	5	5			2	1				
- Received heavy repairs	171	141	145	144	128	139	165	147	146	151
- Received light repairs	168	183	237	170	159	119	131	134	188	127
- Under or awaiting repair	51	59	74	60	67	68	74	72	61	88

Appendix A – Table 3 – Total annual locomotive mileages 1925-1944

	1925	1926	1927	1928	1929	1930	1931	1932	1933	1934	1935
000s											
Passenger trains	5,642	5,672	5,954	6,033	6,220	6,226	5,948	5,680	5,545	5,723	5,759
Freight trains	3,112	3,071	3,279	3,361	3,375	3,355	3,247	2,994	3,112	3,371	3,549
Passenger shunting	260	281	292	297	284	280	293	282	282	291	289
Freight shunting	1,501	1,433	1,526	1,560	1,531	1,527	1,478	1,387	1,377	1,468	1,518
Other (light engine movements/ assisting)	891	916	967	934	941	954	808	854	959	1,012	1,077
Total mileages	11,406	11,373	12,018	12,185	12,351	12,342	11,774	11,197	11,275	11,865	12,192
- Passenger related	5,902	5,953	6,246	6,330	6,504	6,506	6,241	5,962	5,827	6,014	6,048
% total	*52*	*52*	*52*	*52*	*53*	*53*	*53*	*53*	*52*	*51*	*50*
As % of 1925 level		101	106	107	110	110	106	101	99	102	103
- Freight related	4,613	4,504	4,805	4,921	4,906	4,882	4,725	4,381	4,489	4,839	5,067
% total	*40*	*40*	*40*	*40*	*40*	*40*	*40*	*39*	*40*	*41*	*42*
As % of 1925 level		98	104	107	106	106	102	95	97	105	110
- Other movements	891	916	967	934	941	954	808	854	959	1,012	1,077
% total	*8*	*8*	*8*	*8*	*8*	*8*	*7*	*8*	*9*	*9*	*9*

	1936	1937	1938	1939	*Average 1925-39*	1940	1941	1942	1943	1944
000s										
Passenger trains	5,762	5,783	5,749	5,715	***5,827***	5,595	4,135	1,985	2,109	1,618
Freight trains	3,639	3,561	3,388	3,492	***3,327***	3,502	3,417	3,814	3,923	3,575
Passenger shunting	287	289	293	299	***287***	288	256	188	196	171
Freight shunting	1,563	1,560	1,535	1,566	***1,502***	1,556	1,647	1,834	1,843	1,682
Other (light engine					***0***					
movements/ assisting)	1,014	1,046	1,029	956	***957***	919	914	904	812	765
Total mileages	12,265	12,239	11,994	12,028	***11,900***	11,860	10,369	8,725	8,883	7,811
- Passenger related	6,049	6,072	6,042	6,014	***6,114***	5,883	4,391	2,173	2,305	1,789
% total	*49*	*50*	*50*	*50*	***51***	*50*	*42*	*25*	*26*	*23*
As % of 1925 level	103	103	102	102		100	74	37	39	30
- Freight related	5,202	5,121	4,923	5,058	***4,829***	5,058	5,064	5,648	5,766	5,257
% total	*42*	*42*	*41*	*42*	***41***	*43*	*49*	*65*	*65*	*67*
As % of 1925 level	113	111	107	110		110	110	122	125	114
- Other movements	1,014	1,046	1,029	956	***957***	919	914	904	812	765
% total	*8*	*9*	*9*	*8*	***8***	*8*	*9*	*10*	*9*	*10*

Appendix B: Motive power fleet totals

During the 20 year life of the Great Southern Railways, the company continued to submit Annual Reports in the standard format that had previously accorded with the First Schedule to the Railway Companies (Accounts and Returns) Act, 1911. These documents included statistical data on the financial condition of the company and also on the numbers of locomotives, carriages and wagons in service at each year end.

Previous commentators have had difficulty in reconciling the reported locomotive totals with the actual numbers known to have comprised the fleet at specific times. These differences might have occurred through clerical recording errors but it is likely that ambiguity in the operational status of certain locomotives also contributed to discrepancies. As was concluded in the Milne Report, the GSR's fleet size was significantly larger than average traffic levels actually demanded. With comparatively low utilisation, there must always have been plenty of locomotives on hand at depots for the work available, and it is reasonable to assume that some must have stood out of service for considerable periods. Equally there would have been a number of locomotives standing at Inchicore for long periods awaiting a decision on withdrawal, or refurbishment and return to duty. In such circumstances, uncertainty over the precise status of some locomotives would have complicated the count.

The existence of certain locomotives in this form of limbo is well known. For example, ex-CBSCR 4-6-0T No 471 stood at Inchicore awaiting its fate for around six years before withdrawal. The four ex-Cork Blackrock & Passage Railway 2-4-2Ts were officially withdrawn in 1933, then refurbished and reinstated for further work on the Cavan & Leitrim section the following year. On the other hand, ex-Cork & Muskerry Light Railway 0-4-4T No 5 was withdrawn in 1935 and several reports claim that it was then transferred to the Tralee & Dingle section, when in fact it was cannibalised to keep CMLR No 6 serviceable for use on the Schull & Skibbereen section.

Other formally recorded withdrawal and later reinstatements were comparatively few. Ex-MGWR 4-4-0 No 545 was withdrawn and reinstated during 1933, working for another 22 years. Ex-GSWR 2-6-0 No 357 stopped work in 1931 but returned to service four years later. It is reasonable to assume that others went through this cycle but were not formally recorded as such in the annual returns.

The physical count might also have been distorted by the status of locomotives on departmental duties. There was no renumbering or special type of identification for locomotives in this category and counting errors could easily have resulted. Uncertainty over departmental status is usually attributed to the otherwise inexplicable addition to the fleet of one 0-6-0 in 1944.

Table 1 below shows the figures as recorded in the annual returns. There is little point in attempting another reconciliation of the differences at this distance in time. However Table 2 summarises the withdrawals and additions to the fleet in the period 1925-1944.

These figures are based on locomotives that were allocated GSR numbers, ie recorded as such in the company's asset registers. Thus, the DSER locomotives which had already been withdrawn (or were about to be) but nevertheless came into the GSR's possession in 1925, have been excluded. Also in this category is the curiosity of DSER No 44, which was never given a GSR number but actually worked on normal duties until 1927.

Table 1 Steam locomotive fleet by wheel arrangement 1924-1944

Table 2 Steam locomotive withdrawals and additions 1925-1944

Table 3 Railcar and inspection vehicle totals 1925-1944

Table 4 Annual steam locomotive totals by originating company 1925-1944 plus Córas Iompair Éireann 1945-1965

Appendix B
Table 1 – Steam locomotive fleet by wheel arrangement 1924-1944

	1924	1925	1926	1927	1928	1929	1930	1931	1932	1933	1934	1935	1936	1937	1938	1939	1940	1941	1942	1943	1944
Type																					
4-6-0	17	19	19	19	15	14	12	10	10	10	10	10	10	10	10	12	13	13	13	13	13
4-4-0	106	111	111	109	105	104	103	102	102	100	99	98	103	103	103	103	102	102	102	102	102
2-6-0	9	17	25	28	27	29	35	35	35	35	35	36	36	36	36	36	36	36	36	36	36
2-4-0	29	30	30	30	23	23	23	23	23	23	23	23	23	23	23	23	23	23	23	23	23
0-6-0	212	213	211	211	204	204	200	198	198	196	199	204	204	204	204	203	200	200	200	200	201
Total tender locomotives	**373**	**390**	**396**	**397**	**374**	**374**	**373**	**368**	**368**	**364**	**366**	**371**	**376**	**376**	**376**	**377**	**374**	**374**	**374**	**374**	**375**
4-8-0T	2	2	2	2	1	1	1														
4-6-0T	9	9	9	9	9	9	9	9	9	8	8	8	8	8	8	8	8	8	8	8	8
4-6-0T NG		*5*	*5*	*5*	*5*	*5*	*5*	*5*	*5*	*5*	*5*	*5*	*5*	*5*	*5*	*5*	*5*	*5*	*5*	*5*	*5*
4-4-2T	17	23	23	23	23	23	22	22	22	22	22	20	20	20	20	20	20	20	20	20	20
4-4-0T	2	2	2	2	2	2	1	1	1	1	13	9	9	1	1	1	1	1	1	1	1
4-4-0T NG		*15*	*15*	*13*	*13*	*13*	*13*	*13*	*13*	*13*	*13*	*9*	*9*	*9*	*9*	*9*	*9*	*9*	*9*	*9*	*9*
2-6-2T					1	1	1	1	1	1	1	1	1	1	1	1	1	1	1	1	1
2-6-2T NG		*4*	*4*	*4*	*3*	*3*	*3*	*3*	*3*	*3*	*3*	*3*	*3*	*3*	*3*	*3*	*3*	*3*	*3*	*3*	*3*
2-6-0T		1	1	1	1	1	1	1	1	1	1	1	1	1	1	1	1	1	1	1	1
2-6-0T NG		*7*	*7*	*7*	*6*	*6*	*6*	*6*	*6*	*6*	*6*	*6*	*6*	*6*	*6*	*6*	*6*	*6*	*6*	*6*	*6*
2-4-2T	7	20	20	20	20	20	20	20	20	16	19	18	16	16	16	17	17	17	17	17	17
2-4-2T NG		*4*	*4*	*4*	*4*	*4*	*4*	*4*	*4*	*4*	*4*	*4*	*4*	*4*	*4*	*3*	*3*	*3*	*3*	*3*	*3*
2-4-0T	1	8	8	7	5	5	4	4	4	4	3	3	3	3	3	3	3	3	3	3	3
2-2-2T		2	2	2	1	1	1	1	1	1	1	1									
0-6-4T	3	3	3	3	3	3	3	1	1	1	1	1	1	1	1	1					
0-6-4T		1	1	1	1	1	1	1	1	1											
0-6-2T	2	3	3	3	3	3	3	3	3	8	8	7	7	7	7	7	7	7	7	7	7
0-6-2T NG		*2*	*2*	*2*	*2*	*2*	*2*	*2*	*2*	*2*	*2*	*2*	*2*	*2*	*2*	*2*	*2*	*2*	*2*	*2*	*2*
0-6-0T	39	37	38	38	36	36	33	35	35	35	35	34	34	34	34	33	32	32	32	32	32
0-4-4T	17	17	18	18	16	16	14	10	10	10	8	7	5	6	6	6	5	5	5	5	5
0-4-4T NG		*2*	*2*	*2*	*2*	*2*	*2*	*2*	*2*	*2*	*2*	*2*	*1*	*1*	*1*	*1*	*1*	*1*	*1*	*1*	*1*
0-4-2T		3	3	3	3	3	2	2	2	2	2	2	2	2	2	2	2	1	1	1	1
0-4-0T	2	2	2	2	1	1	2	1	1	1	1	1	1	1	1	1	1	1	1	1	1
0-4-0T NG		*1*																			
0-4-0T Sentinel				2	2	2	2	2	2	2	2	2	2	2	2	2	2	2	2	2	2
Total tank locomotives	**101**	**173**	**174**	**173**	**163**	**163**	**155**	**149**	**149**	**149**	**160**	**146**	**140**	**133**	**133**	**132**	**129**	**128**	**128**	**128**	**128**
Total fleet	**474**	**563**	**570**	**570**	**537**	**537**	**528**	**517**	**517**	**513**	**526**	**517**	**516**	**509**	**509**	**509**	**503**	**502**	**502**	**502**	**503**
Tender locos as % of total	**78.7**	**69.3**	**69.5**	**69.6**	**69.6**	**69.6**	**70.6**	**71.2**	**71.2**	**71.0**	**70.0**	**71.8**	**72.9**	**73.9**	**73.9**	**74.1**	**74.4**	**74.5**	**74.5**	**74.5**	**74.6**

Appendix B
Table 2a – Steam locomotive withdrawals 1924-1944

Ex-GSWR	Type	1925	1926	1927	1928	1929	1930	1931	1932	1933	1934	1935	1936	1937	1938	1939	1940	1941	1942	1943	1944
21	2-4-0				6																
47	0-4-4T				2		2	4			2		1				2				
52	4-4-0	1					1														
90	0-6-0T						1														
91	0-6-0T	1																			
101	0-6-0		2	1	3	3	1			1							1				
203	0-6-4T				2												1				
222	0-6-0										1										
228	0-4-0ST	1																			
235	0-6-0			1																	
267	2-4-2T											1									
296	4-4-0				1																
300	0-6-0ST						1														
305	4-4-0									1											
321	4-4-0			2	1																
341	4-4-0				1																
351	0-6-0							1													
355	2-6-0				1			1													
362	4-6-0				***5***			***1***													
368	2-6-0				2																
900	4-8-0T				1			1													
Imp	0-4-0T				1			1													
Sprite	0-4-2T			2																	
Sub total		**3**	**2**	**6**	**26**	**3**	**6**	**9**	**0**	**2**	**3**	**1**	**1**	**0**	**0**	**0**	**4**	**0**	**0**	**0**	**0**
Ex-DSER:																					
422	2-4-0				1																
423	2-4-0T			1																	
427	2-4-2T												1								
428	2-4-2T	1																			
440	0-6-0					1															
441	0-6-0											1									
442	0-6-0						1														
447	0-6-0						1														
448	0-6-0																1				
450	4-4-0					1				1	1						1				
Sub total		**1**	**0**	**1**	**1**	**2**	**2**	**0**	**0**	**1**	**1**	**1**	**1**	**0**	**0**	**0**	**2**	**0**	**0**	**0**	**0**

Ex-CBSCR	Type	1925	1926	1927	1928	1929	1930	1931	1932	1933	1934	1935	1936	1937	1938	1939	1940	1941	1942	1943	1944
471	4-6-0T									1											
472	0-6-0ST											1					1				
474	0-6-0ST	1																			
475	0-6-0ST	1														1					
477	4-4-0T						1				1										
479	4-4-2T						1					2									
482	2-4-0T						1														
Sub total		**2**	**0**	**0**	**0**	**0**	**3**	**0**	**0**	**1**	**1**	**3**	**0**	**0**	**0**	**1**	**1**	**0**	**0**	**0**	**0**
Ex-minor Cos:																					
483	2-2-2WT				1								1								
485	0-4-2WT						1														
486	0-4-2T																	1			
487	2-4-0T				2						1										
490	0-6-2T											1									
491	2-4-2T										1										
Sub total		**0**	**0**	**0**	**3**	**0**	**1**	**0**	**0**	**0**	**2**	**1**	**1**	**0**	**0**	**0**	**0**	**1**	**0**	**0**	**0**
Ex-MGWR:																					
234	0-6-0					1															
545	4-4-0						1														
563	0-6-0	2	1	1	1																
573	0-6-0	4	1	1	2																
594	0-6-0	1																			
646	0-6-0						1			1						2					
Sub total		**7**	**2**	**2**	**3**	**1**	**2**	**0**	**0**	**1**	**0**	**0**	**0**	**0**	**0**	**2**	**0**	**0**	**0**	**0**	**0**
Transitional:																					
400	4-6-0					1	2														
Narrow gauge:																					
Ex-CLR		1		1							1										
Ex-CBPR *													1								
Ex-CMLR				1							2	3									
Ex-SSLR			1											1							
Ex-TDLR					1																
Ex-WCR		1			1																
Sub total		**2**	**1**	**2**	**2**	**0**	**0**	**0**	**0**	**0**	**3**	**3**	**1**	**1**	**0**	**0**	**0**	**0**	**0**	**0**	**0**
Grand total		**15**	**5**	**11**	**35**	**7**	**16**	**9**	**0**	**5**	**10**	**9**	**4**	**1**	**0**	**3**	**7**	**1**	**0**	**0**	**0**

* Four ex-CBPR 2-4-2Ts withdrawn in 1933 but were returned to traffic on CLR section the following year.

Appendix B
Table 2b – Steam locomotive additions 1924-1944

Class:	Wheel Type	1925	1926	1927	1928	1929	1930	1931	1932	1933	1934	1935	1936	1937	1938	1939	1940	1941	1942	1943	1944
500	4-6-0		2																		
372	2-6-0	4	6	2	6	2															
393	2-6-0						6														
280	0-4-0T			2																	
850	2-6-2T				1																
700	0-6-0					5															
495	0-4-0ST						1														
670	0-6-2T									5											
710	0-6-0										5	5									
342	4-4-0												5								
800	4-6-0															2	1				
355 †	2-6-0											1									
Total		**4**	**8**	**4**	**7**	**7**	**7**	**0**	**0**	**5**	**5**	**6**	**5**	**0**	**0**	**2**	**1**	**0**	**0**	**0**	**0**
Net change		**-11**	**3**	**-7**	**-28**	**0**	**-9**	**-9**	**0**	**0**	**-5**	**-3**	**1**	**-1**	**0**	**-1**	**-6**	**-1**	**0**	**0**	**0**

† Re-instated locomotive

Appendix B
Table 3 – Railcar and inspection vehicle totals 1925-1944

Year end:	**1925**	**1926**	**1927**	**1928 -1929**	**1930 -1931**	**1932 -1938**	**1939 -1940**	**1941**	**1942**	**1943 -1944**	
Ex-TDLR inspection car	1	1	1	1	1	1	1	1	1	1	Wdn 1961
Ex-MGWR petrol car	1	1									
Sentinel railcars			4	4	4	4	4	2			
Clayton railcars				6	6						
Drewry inspection cars		2	4	4	4	4	4	4	4	4	All wdn 1963
Broad gauge Drewry Railcars*				2	2	2	2				
Narrow gauge Drewry Railcars			2	2	2	2	2	2	2		
Drumm trains						2	4	4	4	4	All wdn 1949
Total	**2**	**4**	**11**	**19**	**19**	**15**	**17**	**13**	**11**	**9**	

** One unit withdrawn from normal service in 1929 and used as an experimental vehicle for Drumm project; finally broken up with the other, 1941.*

Appendix B
Table 4 – Annual steam locomotive fleet totals by originating company 1925-1944 – plus Coras Iompair Éireann 1945-1965

5' 3" Gauge:										3' 0" Gauge:							Grand
Y/E	GSWR	DSER	CBSCR	WTR	CMDR	TCLR	MGWR	GSR	Total	CLR	CMLR	CBPR	SSR	TDLR	WCR	Total	Total
1924	326		20	4	5	2	139		**496**	9	7	4	4	8	11	**43**	**539**
1925	325	41	18	4	5	2	131	3	**529**	8	7	4	4	8	10	**41**	**570**
1926	325	40	18	4	5	2	129	10	**533**	8	7	4	3	7	10	**39**	**572**
1927	320	40	18	4	5	2	128	17	**534**	7	6	4	3	7	10	**37**	**571**
1928	294	39	18	3	3	2	125	21	**505**	7	6	4	3	7	9	**36**	**541**
1929	290	37	18	3	3	2	124	28	**505**	7	6	4	3	7	9	**36**	**541**
1930	281	35	15	2	3	2	123	35	**496**	7	6	4	3	7	9	**36**	**532**
1931	272	34	15	2	3	2	122	35	**485**	7	6	4	3	7	9	**36**	**521**
1932	272	34	15	2	3	2	122	35	**485**	7	6	4	3	7	9	**36**	**521**
1933	270	33	14	2	3	2	121	38	**483**	7	6	4	3	7	9	**36**	**519**
1934	268	32	13	2	1	2	121	40	**479**	6	4	4	3	7	9	**33**	**512**
1935	265	31	10	2		2	121	50	**481**	6	2	4	3	7	9	**31**	**512**
1936	264	30	10	1		2	121	55	**483**	6	1	3	2	7	9	**28**	**511**
1937	264	30	10	1		2	121	55	**483**	6	1	3	2	7	9	**28**	**511**
1938	264	30	10	1		2	121	55	**483**	6	1	3	2	7	9	**28**	**511**
1939	264	30	9	1		2	119	57	**482**	6	1	3	2	7	9	**28**	**510**
1940	260	28	8	1		2	119	58	**476**	6	1	3	2	7	9	**28**	**504**
1941	260	28	8			2	119	58	**475**	6	1	3	2	7	9	**28**	**503**
1942	260	28	8			2	119	58	**475**	6	1	3	2	7	9	**28**	**503**
1943	260	28	8			2	119	58	**475**	6	1	3	2	7	9	**28**	**503**
1944	260	28	8			2	119	58	**475**	6	1	3	2	7	9	**28**	**503**
1945	252	28	6			2	117	58	**463**	5	1	3	2	7	9	**27**	**490**
1946	252	28	6			2	117	58	**463**	5	1	3	2	7	9	**27**	**490**
1947	252	28	6			2	117	58	**463**	5	1	3	2	7	9	**27**	**490**
1948	252	28	6			2	117	56	**461**	5	1	3	2	7	9	**27**	**488**
1949	236	27	6			1	109	55	**434**	4	1	3	2	7	9	**26**	**460**
1950	232	23	6			1	105	55	**422**	4	1	3	2	7	9	**26**	**448**
1951	224	22	6			1	103	55	**411**	4	1	3	2	7	9	**26**	**437**
1952	222	18	6			1	101	55	**403**	4	1	3	2	7	9	**26**	**429**
1953	211	14	6			1	99	55	**386**	4	1	3	2	7	5	**22**	**408**
1954	203	14	6			1	91	54	**369**	4		2		5	4	**15**	**384**
1955	176	10	6			1	81	48	**322**	4		2		4	3	**13**	**335**
1956	173	10	6			1	80	48	**318**	4		2		4	1	**11**	**329**
1957	130	5	6				66	43	**250**	4		2		4	1	**11**	**261**
1958	129	5	6				66	43	**249**	4		2		4	1	**11**	**260**
1959	88	3	5				40	17	**153**	2						**2**	**155**
1960	77	2	5				35	9	**128**							**0**	**128**
1961	65	2	2				21	7	**97**							**0**	**97**
1962	47	2	2				20	1	**72**							**0**	**72**
1963	17	1	2				2		**22**							**0**	**22**
1964	15	1					2		**18**							**0**	**18**
1965									**0**							**0**	**0**

Appendix C1: Locomotive boilers

The Great Southern Railways' programme to modernise the constituent companies' locomotive fleets focused on replacement of time-expired boilers. There was already considerable variety among the boilers acquired in 1925 and while the concept of standardisation might have seemed attractive, limited progress to this end was achieved in the next 20 years.

A system of boiler types was introduced, mainly identified by a single letter although some were known by the GSR Class designation with which they were originally associated. Several of the boiler types were used with a single locomotive class but two types in particular – N and Z – found their way onto a number of different classes of varying vintages. It was significant that these two types were equipped with parallel boilers, Belpaire fireboxes and superheaters ie after the hiatus of 1925-1929, there was a determined effort to introduce modernity with enhanced efficiency. Nonetheless, older saturated types with round-topped fireboxes lasted well into the 1950s.

As noted elsewhere, the policy of retiring boilers on an age basis alone was criticised in the Milne Report. The inference is that the possibility of an old boiler still having years of potential operating life was discounted at the time of withdrawal. By this process, changes of boilers or of boiler types occurred more frequently than might have otherwise been necessary. It was notable that changes in boiler type could persist well into old age, as graphically illustrated with the 19 surviving members of 2-4-0 Class 650 (G2). At the creation of Córas Iompair Éireann in 1945, the programme of boiler changes which had started in the early 1920s continued unabated. As at 1 January 1945, these locomotives were aged between 48 and 51 years yet 14 more changes of boiler type were to occur, the last being as late as 1959. Pursuit of improved performance would not have been a significant criterion by that stage so replacements would have been implemented to make use of whatever was in stock and serviceable at the time.

As will have been observed in the individual class histories, some later boiler changes were regressive and of doubtful value. The Bandon 4-6-0Ts, already sound performers, were improved by installation of Type R boilers. Only five of the class were so fitted; two later reverted to round-topped saturated boilers although one of these did return to a Type R after two years.

Sometimes the number and variety of changes were bewildering. During the period 1932 to 1951, Class 455 (C2) carried six different boiler types and underwent seven different boiler changes. As this class comprised a mere three locomotives, this programme must have achieved some sort of record.

Another case of regression involved Classes 400 and 500 which originally shared the same boiler. Later, six of the surviving 400s received larger K type boilers, but three of these were carrying original type boilers at withdrawal. In view of the comparatively modest haulage demands made of this class during the 1930s, the excursion into larger boilers must have been an exercise offering a minimal financial return.

The heating surfaces quoted for the original Class 400 boilers identify a further complication. The class prototype (No 400) and the three Armstrong Whitworth superheated locomotives (Nos 403–05) shared the same heating surface areas yet the Inchicore trio (Nos 401/ 2/ 6) had smaller tube areas. Variations in tube areas resulted from use of differing numbers of small tubes, easily effected by replacement of boiler tube plates. This is the most likely explanation why the heating surfaces quoted in the table in this Appendix sometimes differ from heating surfaces for the same type of boiler recorded in some of the class histories. In several instances the differences in quoted heating surfaces are quite small and would have had little or no impact on steaming capacity. Presumably these variations, as with a number of the boiler changes, came about through monetary shortages and the necessity of using whatever suitable material was on hand.

Another difficulty lies in photographic evidence that is at odds with recorded details in class histories. For example, locomotive No 403 reportedly received a Type K boiler in 1936 which it carried until withdrawal in 1957. However a photograph shows this locomotive in CIÉ lined green livery and carrying an original type, smaller boiler. The inevitable conclusion is that even more changes of type (let alone of heating surfaces) took place than were actually recorded.

Finally, reported boiler dimensions can vary between classes that ostensibly carried the same type: For example, Belpaire superheated Boiler Type O was carried by three classes but the reported dimensions vary as follows:

Class	Heating surfaces:			No of tubes	
	Tubes	Superheater	Firebox	Small	Superheater
305	1084	224	136.7	168 x 1¾"	24 x 5⅛"
333	1068	250	136.7	168 x 1¾"	24 x 5⅛"
342	1080	252	136.7	149 x 1¾"	24 x 5⅛"

Notes on details in Tables

The dimensional details (where known) of every boiler type carried by locomotives entered in the GSR fleet lists are recorded in the Appendix Tables. The tables are set out as follows;

Table 1: Ex-GSWR Classes in numerical order with details of all boiler types carried by each class.

Table 2: Ex-DSER Classes – details as for Table 2.

Table 3: Ex-CBSCR and minor companies' Classes – details as for Table 2.

Table 4: Ex-MGWR Classes – details as for Table 2.

Table 5: Narrow gauge locomotive boilers by pre-amalgamation company. While firebox lengths are usually recorded, widths have proved to be an elusive dimension and are not included.

Table 6: GSR boiler types are listed by letters (A to Z), and cross-referenced to those classes which carried each type. This appears to have been the intended basis for a standard system of boiler classification but contains certain anomalies. The inclusion of three round topped saturated types in this system seems anachronistic. Type E which was used by Class 551 (J26) only might have been considered as suitable for other small tank classes. However, there seems little logic for Types J and S (restricted to ex-WLWR designs) which were carried by locomotives that were potentially obsolescent even in 1925, notwithstanding that some worked on for many years.

Also, it is notable that three GSR-era types were excluded from the system. No 495 (and thus its boiler) was something of an odd-ball. The boilers known as Type 60/ 101, despite only one example having been used previously (with a member of Class 60), were used with GSR Class 700 only. Finally, the boiler on No 850 remained outside any classification or Type system, and thus stayed unique like the locomotive itself.

Abbreviations and dimensions used in the tables:

The following abbreviations are used to describe the general boiler superstructure:

RT Sat Saturated boiler with round-topped firebox

RT Tap Sat Saturated tapered boiler with round-topped firebox

RT Sup Superheated boiler with round-topped firebox

Bel Sat Saturated boiler with Belpaire firebox

Bel Sup Superheated boiler with Belpaire firebox

Bel Tap Sup Superheated tapered boiler with Belpaire firebox

Regarding dimensions, the following disciplines have been applied:

A Boilers are based on the outside dimensions of the barrel, excluding lagging and outer cladding, measured in feet and inches, rounded to the nearest inch

B Fireboxes are based on external measurements, including cladding, measured in feet and inches, rounded to the nearest inch.

C With constituent company locomotives, details where known of every boiler type carried by any member of each class have been recorded. Where a later boiler change involved fitting of a GSR 'standard boiler', that change is detailed merely as the type fitted, and reference should be made to the GSR boiler list for relevant details.

D With some ex-GSWR classes, a GSR standard superheated boiler was fitted but in saturated condition; the particular variant dimensions relative to this modification are recorded in Table 2.

Appendix C1 – Table 1 – Ex-GSWR boiler types

GSR Class	TYPE	BARREL Length	Diam.	FIREBOX Length	Width	HEATING SURFACES Grate sq ft	No tubes	Tubes sq ft	F'box sq ft	
2	RT Sat	9' 4"	3' 10"	4' 8"	4' 5"	16	175 x 1¾"	770	84	Three ringed with raised RT firebox
	RT Sat	9' 4"	3' 9"	4' 8"	4' 5"	16	172 x 1¾"	757	84	Similar to above but two ringed
	RT Sat	9' 5"	4' 3"	4' 8"	4' 5"	16	???	???	???	Flush firebox
	Type U									Refer GSR list
27	RT Sat	9' 7"	4' 0"	5' 1"	???	18	167 x 1¾"	754	97	
33	RT Sat	9' 4"	3' 10"	4' 8"	4' 6"	16	174 x 1¾"	770	84	
	RT Sat	9' 4"	3' 10"	4' 8"	4' 6"	16	172 x 1¾"	757	84	
37	RT Sat	9' 4"	3' 10"	4' 8"	4' 6"	16	172 x 1¾"	757	84	
47	RT Sat	9' 4"	3' 8"	4' 8"	4' 4"	15	154 x 1¾"	677	79	
52	RT Sat	9' 7"	4' 0"	5' 1"	4' 6"	18	185 x 1¾"	835	96	Three ringed with raised RT firebox
	RT Sat	9' 7"	4' 0"	5' 1"	4' 6"	18	167 x 1¾"	754	97	Similar to above but two ringed
	Type X									Refer GSR list
60	RT Sat	9' 9"	4' 3"	5' 5"	4' 6"	19	204 x 1¾"	938	112	Three ringed with raised RT firebox
	RT Sat	9' 9"	4' 3"	5' 5"	4' 6"	19	191 x 1¾"	879	112	Two ringed
	Bel Sat	9' 10"	4' 8"	5' 0"	3' 11"	19	188 x 1¾"	887	122	Also used on Class 700
	Type Z									Refer GSR list
90/ 99/ 100	RT Sat	7' 6"	2' 9"	4' 0"	3' 6"	10	104* x 1½"	318	51	* Also 98 and 102 tube versions
91/ 92	RT Sat	7' 6"	2' 9"	4' 0"	3' 6"	10	104* x 1½"	318	51	* Also 98 and 102 tube versions
101	RT Sat	9' 10"	4' 0"	5' 1"	4' 6"	18	185 x 1¾"	856	96	Raised firebox
	RT Sat	9' 10"	4' 0"	5' 1"	4' 6"	18	165 x 1¾"	764	96	Raised firebox
	RT Sat	9' 10"	4' 3"	5' 7"	4' 6"	19	200 x 1¾"	925	116	Flush firebox
	RT Sat	9' 10"	4' 3"	5' 7"	4' 6"	19	194 x 1¾"	897	116	Flush firebox
	Type Z									Refer GSR list
201	RT Sat	9' 9"	4' 3"	5' 5"	4' 6"	19	196 x 1¾"	900	85	
	RT Sat	9' 10"	4' 3"	5' 5"	4' 6"	19	191 x 1¾"	878	90	
203	RT Sat	9' 9"	4' 3"	5' 5"	4' 6"	19	196 x 1¾"	900	14	
	RT Sat	9' 10"	4' 3"	5' 5"	4' 6"	19	179 x 1¾"	823	113	Class 60 type; different tube area
211	RT Sat	10' 4"	4' 6"	5' 10"	4' 6"	20	233 x 1¾"	1129	118	
	RT Sat	10' 4"	4' 6"	5' 10"	4' 6"	20	213 x 1¾"	1040	118	
213	RT Sat	10' 4"	4' 6"	5' 10"	4' 6"	20	233 x 1¾"	1129	118	
222	Bel Sat	10' 3"	4' 2"	5' 6"	4' 5"	18	185 x 1¾"	873	108	
	RT Sat	10' 3"	4' 5"	5' 8"	4' 6"	20	??? x 1¾"	918	99	
228	RT Sat	10' 10"	2' 11"	3' 0"	???	9	57 x 1⅞"	307	40	
235	RT Sat	10' 1"	4' 4"	5' 8"	4' 6"	20	194 x 1¾"	918	99	
257	RT Sup	10' 4"	4' 6"	5' 10"	4' 6"	20	122 x 1¾"	844	118	

GSR	TYPE	BARREL		FIREBOX			HEATING SURFACES			
Class		Length	Diam.	Length	Width	Grate sq ft	No tubes	Tubes sq ft	F'box sq ft	
257	RT Sup	10' 4"	4' 6"	5' 10"	4' 6"	20	122 x 1¾"	844	118	
	Type N									Refer GSR list
267	RT Sat	10' 3"	4' 1"	4' 8"	???	15		780	88	
269	RT Sat	10' 4"	4' 1"	4' 10"	???	15	165 x 1¾"	780	88	
	Type S									Refer GSR list
276	RT Sat	10' 0"	4' 0"	5' 10"	4' 6"	18	210 x 1¾"	1000	110	
	RT Sat	10' 3"	4' 5"	5' 8"	4' 6"	20	???	918	99	
279	RT Sat	11' 0"	4' 2"	4' 9"	4' 3"	15	156 x 1¾"	808	88	
	Type S									Refer GSR list
295	RT Sat	10' 3"	4' 3"	4' 10"	???	16	165 x 1¾"	793	88	
	Type S									Refer GSR list
296	RT Sat	10' 4"	4' 2"	5' 10"	4' 6"	20	188 x 1¾"	887	107	
	RT Sat	10' 3"	4' 5"	5' 8"	5' 6"	20	194 x 1¾"	918	99	
299	RT Sat	7' 9"	2' 11"	3' 6	3' 0"	7	83 x 1¾"	356	45	
(300) Erin	RT Sat	7 9"	3' 9"	3' 2"	???	8	129 x 1⅞"	511	52	
301	RT Sat	10' 4"	4' 6"	5' 10"	4' 8"	20	225 x 1¾"	1100	120	
	Type N									Refer GSR list
305	RT Tap Sat	10' 4"	5' 1"– 5' 7"	6' 1"	4' 6"	21	237 x 1¾"	1148	127	
	RT Sat	11' 0"	4' 6"	6' 1"	4' 6"	21	301 x 1⅝"	1366	128	No 308 only
	Type N									Refer GSR list
	Type O									Refer GSR list
309/ 310	RT Sat	10' 4"	4' 6"	6' 7"	4' 10"	23	229 x 1¾"	1110	135	
	Class 321 RT Tap Sat									See GSWR Class 321
	Type N									Refer GSR list
321/ 332	RT Tap Sat	10' 4"	5' 1"– 5' 7"	6' 4"	4' 8"	23	301 x 1⅝"	1366	145	Nos 321 to 328 only
	RT Tap Sat	10' 4"	5' 1"– 5' 7"	6' 4"	4' 8"	23	283 x 1⅝"	1284	145	Nos 329 to 332 only
	RT Tap Sat	10' 4"	5' 1"– 5' 7"	6' 4"	4' 8"	23	177 x 1⅝"	1153	145	No 326 only (Schmidt superheater)
	Type W									Refer to GSR list
	Type W but in saturated form						280 x 1¾	1355	148	Refer to GSR list
333	RT Tap Sat	10' 4"	5' 1"– 5' 7"	6' 1"	4' 8"	21	283 x 1⅝"	1284	128	
	Type O									Refer GSR list
	Type O but in saturated form						280 x 1¾"	1355	137	Refer GSR list
341	Bel Sup	11' 0"	5' 2"	7' 0"	???	25	205 x 1⅝"	1365	156	
351	RT Sat	10' 4"	4' 6"	5' 10"	4' 6"	20	233 x 1¾"	1129	118	
	RT Sat	10' 4"	4' 6"	5' 10"	4' 6"	20	213 x 1¾"	1040	118	
	Type N									Refer GSR list
	Class 257 RT Sup version									See ex-GSWR Class 257

355	RT Sat	11' 4	4' 9"	6' 4.5"	5' 4"	25	248 x 1¾"	1318	132	
	Class 368 RT Sat									See ex-GSWR Class 368
	Type Q									Refer GSR list
	Type Q in saturated form						280 x 1¾"	1498	139	Refer GSR list
362	RT Sat	14' 10"	4' 9"	7' 0"	5' 1"	25	227 x 1¾"	1467	133	
368	RT Sat	11' 3"	4' 11"	7' 0"	4' 6"	25	293 x 1⅝"	1447	139	
	Type Q									Refer GSR list
400	Bel Sup	14' 1	5' 3"	8' 0"	4' 6"	28	173 x 1¾"	1614	158	
	Bel Sup	14' 1	5' 3"	8' 0"	4' 6"	28	168 x 1¾"	1590	158	
	Bel Sup	14' 1	5' 3"	8' 0"	4' 6"	28	170 x 1¾"	1614	158	
	Bel Sat	14' 1	5' 3"	8' 0"	4' 6"	28	280 x 1¾"	1870	158	
	K Type									Refer GSR list
500	Bel Sup	14' 1	5' 3"	8' 0"	4' 6"	28	168 x 1¾"	1590	158	
	K Type									Refer GSR list
900	RT Sat	11' 3"	4' 11"	7' 0	4' 7"	25	289 x 1⅝"	1427	139	
Jumbo	RT Sat	9' 9"	4' 3"	5' 5"	4' 6"	19	196 x 1¾"	900	85	
Sambo	RT Sat	9' 4"	3' 10"	4' 8"	4' 6"	16	156 x 1¾"	685	84	
Sprite	RT Sat	7' 2"	2' 10"	4' 0"	???	11	104 x 1¾"	220	54	

Appendix C1 – Table 2 – Ex-DSER boiler types

GSR	**TYPE**	**BARREL**		**FIREBOX**			**HEATING SURFACES**			
Class		**Length**	**Diam.**	**Length**	**Width**	**Grate sq ft**	**No of tubes (small)**	**Tubes sq ft**	**F'box sq ft**	
422	RT Sat	9' 4"	4' 5"	5' 3"	???	15	164 x 1¾"	724	108	
423	RT Sat	10' 2"	4' 5"	5' 1"	4' 10"	15	185 X 1¾"	986 total		
	Type T									Refer GSR list
427	RT Sat	9' 4"	4' 5"	5' 8	5' 3"	15	164 x 1¾"	725	108	
428	RT Sat	10' 2"	4' 3"	4' 9.5"	4' 6"	15	171 x 1¾"	823	128	
	Class 101		4' 0" size							Refer GSWR list
	Type T									Refer GSR list
	Class 573									Refer GSWR list
	Class 267									Refer GSWR list
	RT Sat as for Class 434									Probable but unconfirmed
434	RT Sat	10' 1"	4' 2"	5' 3"	4' 5"	15	177 x 1¾"	823	128	
	Bel Sat	10' 1"	4' 4.5"	5' 3"	4' 5"	17	177 x 1¾"	834	105	
	Class 101	9' 10"	4' 5"	5' 7"	???	20	177 x 1¾"	818	109	Note 1.
	Class 440									See ex-DSER Class 440

GSR Class	TYPE	BARREL Length	BARREL Diam.	FIREBOX Length	FIREBOX Width	FIREBOX Grate sq ft	HEATING SURFACES No of tubes (small)	HEATING SURFACES Tubes sq ft	HEATING SURFACES F'box sq ft	
440	RT Sat	10' 1"	4' 5"	5' 8"	5' 2"	18	177 x 1¾"	800	95	
441	RT Sat	10' 1"	4' 5"	5' 8"	5' 2"	18	177 x 1¾"	800	95	
442	RT Sat	10' 3"	4' 8"	6' 0"	4' 5"	20	223 x 1¾"	1075	119	
	Class 351									Refer GSWR list
	Class 450									See ex-DSER Class 450
447	Bel Sat	10' 3"	4' 8"	5' 8"	4' 6"	19	179 x 1¾"	841	84	
448	RT Sat	11' 6"	4' 8"	6' 0"	5' 7"	21	210 x 1¾"	1142	107	Note 2.
	Bel Sat	11' 6"	4' 8"	6' 0"	???	21	210 x 1¾"	1142	107	Note 2.
450	Bel Sat	10' 3"	4' 8"	5' 7.5"	4' 4"	18	180 x 1¾"	995	101	
	Bel Sat	10' 3"	5' 0"	6' 0"	4' 4"	20	211 x 1¾"	1020	124	
454	RT Sat	10' 3"	4' 8"	6' 0"	4' 6"	20	223 x 1¾"	1075	119	
	Class 450									See ex-DSER Class 450
455	RT Sat	10' 3"	4' 8"	6' 0"	4' 5"	20	223 x 1¾"	1075	119	
	RT Sat	10' 3"	4' 8"	6' 0"	4' 5"	20	??? x 1¾"	1065	119	
	Class 351									Refer GSWR list
	Class 450									See ex-DSER Class 450
458	RT Sat	10' 2½"	4' 8"	5' 9"	4' 0½"	17	???	992 total		
	RT Sat	10' 2½"	4' 5"	5' 9"	4' 0½"	18	180 x 1¾"	865	108	
	RT Sat	10' 2"	4' 4"	5' 2"	4' 11"	18	180 x 1¾"	865	108	
461	Bel Sup	10' 3"	4' 10"	6' 0"	4' 5"	20	144 x 1¾" 18 x 6¼" *	952*	134	* +superheater 162 sq ft
	Type N									Refer GSR list
Elf	Bel Sat	5' 8"	3' 8"	4' 2"	3' 1"	9.5	175 x 1¾"	441	45	

Note 1. Dimensions are at variance with those quoted for Class 101 boilers in GSWR section.

Note 2. The identical dimensions recorded suggest that one set is in error; figures for Bel Sat version considered the more accurate.

Appendix C1 – Table 3 – Ex-CBSCR and minor companies' boiler types

GSR Class	TYPE	BARREL Length	BARREL Diam.	FIREBOX Length	FIREBOX Width	FIREBOX Grate sq ft	HEATING SURFACES No of tubes (small)	HEATING SURFACES Tubes sq ft	HEATING SURFACES F'box sq ft	
Ex-Cork Bandon and South Coast Railway										
463	RT Sat	10' 8"	4' 3"	5' 11"	4' 0"	24	214 x 1¾"	1075	107.5	
	Type R									Refer GSR list
471	RT Sat	10' 1"	4' 0"	4' 9"	4' 4"	14.5	142 x 2"	757	82	
472/ 4/ 5	RT Sat	9' 4"	4' 0"	4' 3"	4' 0"	14	187 x 1¾"	903	77	* See footnote
477 (477)	RT Sat	9' 10"	4' 0"	3' 9"	???	11.2	143 x 2"	757	74	
477 (478)	RT Sat	9' 0"	3' 11"	4' 0"	???	12	???	857	77	
479	RT Sat	9' 10	4' 0"	4' 9"	4' 4"	14.5	142 x 2"	757	82	† See footnote
482	RT Sat	9' 10	4' 0"	4' 9"	???	11.2	143 x 2"	757	74	
Ex-Waterford & Tramore Railway										
483	RT Sat	9' 3	3' 9"	???	???	11.5	113 x 2"	563	69	
485	RT Sat	9' 9"	3' 11"	3' 9"	???	???	???	???	???	
486	RT Sat	10' 0"	4' 2"	4' 0"	???	12	180 x 1¾"	845	73	
Cork & Macroom Direct Railway										
487	RT Sat	9' 10"	3' 10"	4' 0"	3' 9"	10.5	143 x 2"	700	60	
490	RT Sat	9' 4"	4' 2"	5' 0"	???	16	216 x 1¾"	959	87	
491	RT Sat	10' 3"	4' 1"	4' 8"	???	15		780	88	As for Class 267
Timoleague & Courtmacsherry Light Railway										
Argadeen	RT Sat	7' 10"	3' 9"	4' 1"	2' 7"	10.2	131 x 1¾"	487	52	
	Bel Sat	7' 10"	3' 7"	3' 6"	2' 5"	9.5	166 x 1¾"	578	45	*Ex-Imp*
St Molaga	RT Sat	8' 3"	3' 1"	3' 5"	1' 10"	6.2	78 x 1⅞"	326	34	

* There were dimensional differences in the boilers fitted to and rotated between Classes 472/ 474/ 475. Figures quoted are the most probable.

† There were small dimensional differences between the Dubs and Neilson-built locomotives.

Appendix C1 – Table 4 – Ex-MGWR boiler types

GSR Class	TYPE	BARREL Length	BARREL Diam	FIREBOX Length	FIREBOX Width	Grate Sq Ft	HEATING SURFACES No of tubes (small)	No of tubes (large)	Tubes Sq Ft	F'box Sq Ft	Super'ter Sq Ft	
234	RT Sat	10' 3"	4' 4"	5' 6"	4' 5"	17.8	178 x 1¾"		est 840	108		
	RT Sat	10' 4"	4' 4"	5' 6"	4' 5"	17.8	185 x 1¾"		873	108		
	Type S											Refer GSR list
530	RT Sat	10' 2"	4' 5"	4' 4"	3' 10"	16	230 x 1⅝"		985	95		
	RT Sup	9' 9"	4' 5"	4' 4"	3' 10"	16	80 x 1⅝"	12 x 5¼"	610	95	113	
	RT Sat	9' 10"	4' 5"	4' 4"	3' 10"	16.7	179 x 1¾"		803	99		
	RT Sup						????		???	???	???	[1] see footnote
	Type X											Refer GSR list
536	RT Sat	10' 2"	4' 5"	5' 0"	4' 6"	15.8	204 x 1¾"		975	115		
	RT Sup	10' 4"	4' 10"	5' 9	3' 8"	17.3	116 x 1¾"	18 x 5¼"	815	124	206	[2] see footnote
	Type X											Refer GSR list
	RT Sup	10' 4"	4' 10"	5' 5"	5' 5"	17	112 x 1¾"	18 x 5¼"	801	123	167	
	RT Sat	11' 0"	4' 10"	6' 3"	4' 5"	20	235 x 1¾"		1213	150		
	Bel Sup	11' 0"	4' 10"	6' 3"	4' 5"	20	112 x 1¾"	18 x 5¼"	832	150	211	
545	RT Sat	11' 0"	4' 10"	6' 3"	4' 4.5"	20	235 x 1¾"		1213	150		
	Bel Sup	11' 0"	4' 10"	6' 3"	4' 4.5"	20	112 x 1¾"	18 x 5¼"	832	150	211	
	Class 646 Bel sup											See ex-MGWR Class 646
	Type A											Refer GSR list
551	RT Sat	8' 10"	3' 11"	4' 6"	3' 10"	13	173 x 1⅝"		668	72		
	RT Sat	8' 10"	3' 11"	4' 6"	3' 10"	13	125 x 1¾"		505	82		
563	RT Sat	9' 8"	4' 5	5' 0"	4' 5"	16.5	230 x 1¾"		970	95		
567	Bel Sup	9' 2"	4' 5"	???	???	???	???	???	???	???		[3] see footnote
	Bel Sup	9' 2"	4' 5"	5' 5"	5' 5"	17	88 x 1¾"	18 x 5¼"	644	168	115	[4] see footnote
573	RT Sat	9' 9"	4' 4"	5' 0"	4' 6"	16	236 x 1¾"		920	95		
	Type X											Refer GSR list
	RT Sat	9' 8"	4' 5"	5' 0"	4' 5"	16.5	230 x 1¾"		970	95		
	Class 594	9' 8"	4' 5"	4' 10"	4' 4"	16	206 x 1¾"		938	115		[5] see footnote
594	Bel Sat	9' 8"	4' 5"	4' 10"	4' 4"	16	225 x 1⅝"		950	106		[6] see footnote
	Bel Sat	9' 8"	4' 5"	4' 10"	4' 4"	16	206 x 1¾"		938	115		[7] see footnote
	Bel Sat	9' 8"	4' 5"	4' 10"	4' 4"	16	200 x 1¾"		910	103		
	Bel Sup	9' 8"	4' 5"	4' 10"	4' 4"	16	107 x 1¾"	12 x 5¼"	655	110	112	
	Type X											Refer GSR list
	Class 573 RT Sat											See above
614	RT Sat	9' 7½"	4' 5"	5' 0"	4' 5"	16.5	230 x 1⅝"		970	106		
	RT Sat	9' 7½"	4' 5"	5' 0"	4' 5"	16.5	200 x 1¾"		910	103		

GSR Class	TYPE	BARREL Length	BARREL Diam	FIREBOX Length	FIREBOX Width	Grate Sq Ft	HEATING SURFACES No of tubes (small)	No of tubes (large)	Tubes Sq Ft	F'box Sq Ft	Super'ter Sq Ft	
	Bel Sat	9' 8"	4' 5"	5' 0"	4' 5"	16	206 x 1¾"		938	115		
	Type X											Refer GSR list
	Class 573 RT Sat											See ex-MGWR Class 573
	Class 594 Bel Sat											See ex-MGWR Class 594
619	Bel Sup	11' 0"	4' 10"	6' 3"	4' 4½"	20	105 x 1¾"	18 x 5¼"	832	116	172	
	Type H											Refer GSR list
623	Bel Sup	10' 4"	4' 10"	4' 8"	3' 8"	17.3	116 x 1¾"	18 x 4½"	821	125	210	[8] see footnote
	Bel Sup	10' 4"	4' 10"	4' 8"	3' 8"	17.3	116 x 1¾"	18 x 4½"	815	124	210	[9] see footnote
646	Bel Sup	11' 0"	4' 10"	6' 3"	4' 4½"	20	112 x 1¾"	18 x 5¼"	842	150	170	
650	RT Sat	10' 2"	4' 5"	5' 0"	4' 6½"	16.5	230 x 1⅝"		1020	95		
	RT Sat	10' 2"	4' 5"	4' 10"	4' 4"	16.5	179 x 1¾"		835	99		
	RT Sup	10' 2"	4' 5"	5' 0"	4' 6½"	16.5	86 x 1¾"	12 x 5½"	643	95	113	
	Type Y											Refer GSR list

[1] *Super'd version of 9' 10" saturated boiler - no details available.*
[2] *Robinson super'd version had 12 sq ft more total heating surface.*
[3] *Fitted with Cusack-Morton superheater.*
[4] *Fitted with Schmidt superheater*
[5] *Spare Class 594 Bel Sat - dimensions unknown.*
[6] *225 tube version might have carried a smaller boiler.*
[7] *Some 206 tube boilers had higher boiler pressure.*
[8] *Quoted for Broadstone-built locos; large tube diameter appears incorrect.*
[9] *Armstrong Whitworth-built locos.*

Appendix C1 – Table 5 – Narrow gauge boiler types

CLASS	DESCRIPTION	BARREL		FIREBOX	HEATING SURFACES			
		Length	Diameter	Length	Grate sq ft	No of tubes	Tubes sq ft	Firebox sq ft
Cavan & Leitrim Railway								
DN2	4-4-0T Nos 1 to 8	8' 6"	3' 5"	6' 3"	9	124 x 1⅞"	500	48
HN1	0-6-4T No 9	10' 11"	3' 10"	4' 8"	14	133 x 1¾"	681	66
Cork Blackrock & Passage Railway								
FN1	2-4-2T Nos 4 to 7	10' 0"	3' 8"	6' 9"	12	???	721	80
Cork & Muskerry Light Railway								
EN1	0-4-4T Nos 5 & 6	9' 10"	3' 6"	3' 5"	10.5	115 x 1¾"	600 total	–
DN1	4-4-0T No 4	6' 11"	3' 8"	???	8.25	122 x 1¾"	402	65
DN3	4-4-0T No 7	9' 0"	3' 7"	6' 0"	10.5	152 x 1¾"	590	56
DN6	4-4-0T Nos 1 & 2	7' 6"	3' 7"	4' 9"	8.25	???	472 total	–
DN7	4-4-0T No 8	8' 3"	3' 7"	5' 7"	10.5	111 x 1¾4"	590	56
Schull & Skibbereen Light Railway								
MN1	0-4-0T No 2	No details have been found						
DN4	4-4-0T Nos 1	8' 0"	3' 8"	4' 6"	8	???	492	83
	4-4-0T Nos 3	Reportedly similar to No 1 but unconfirmed			7.6	???	454	60
DN5	4-4-0T No 4	8' 0"	3' 6"	4' 6"	9	120 x 1¾"	453	56
Tralee & Dingle Light Railway								
KN1	2-6-0T Nos 4 & 7	8' 7"	3' 5"	4' 7"	7.5	107 x 1¾"	431	47
KN2	2-6-0T Nos 1 to 3/ 6/ 8	8' 0"	3' 7"	6' 2"	9.75	124 x 1¾"	494	66
PN2	2-6-2T No 5	8' 9"	3' 7"	6' 2"	10.7	134 x 1¾"	531	70
West Clare Railway								
BN1	4-6-0T No 10	9' 3"	3' 9"	6' 5"	12	142 x 1¾"	620.5	80
BN2	4-6-0T No 11	8' 9"	3' 9"	6' 4"	11.5	150 x 1¾"	622	74
BN3	4-6-0T Nos 3/ 7	8' 9"	3' 9"	6' 4"	11.5	128 x 1¾"	530	74
BN4	4-6-0T No 1	8' 9"	3' 9"	6' 4"	11.5	150 x 1¾"	530	74
IN1	0-6-2T Nos 5 & 6	9' 3"	3' 9"	6' 6"	11.1	144 x 1¾"	627	75
PN1	2-6-2T Nos 2/ 4/ 9	9' 3"	3' 9"	6' 6"	11.2	153 x 1¾"	666.5	74
PN1	2-6-2T No 2 rebuilt 1929	9' 3"	3' 9"	6' 6"	10.1	134 x 1¾"	583	77
PN1	2-6-2T No 2 rebuilt 1950	6' 6"	2' 4"	6' 0"	10.1	106 x 1¾"	482	74

Appendix C1 – Table 6 – GSR boiler types

REF	TYPE	BARREL Length	BARREL Diameter	FIREBOX Length	FIREBOX Width	FIREBOX Grate sq ft	HEATING SURFACES No tubes small	No tubes large	Tubes sq ft	Firebox sq ft	Super'ter sq ft	Carried by GSR Class:
A	Bel Sup	11' 0"	4' 10"	6' 3"	4' 5"	21	104 x 1¾"	18 x 5¼"	827	150	170	545
C	Bel Sup	10' 4"	4' 10"	5' 5"	4' 5"	17	112 x 1¾"	18 x 5¼"	801	123	167	536, 540, 623
D	Bel Tap Sup	12' 6"	4' 8"– 5' 0"	8' 0"	4' 1"	25	175 x 1¾"	21 x 5⅛"	1391	135	285	372, 393
E	RT Sat	9' 1"	4' 0"	4' 6"	4' 1"	13	126 x 1¾"		509	72	–	551
H	Bel Sup	11' 0"	4' 10"	6' 3"	4' 5"	21	104 x 1¾"	18 x 5¼"	821	114	167	619
J	RT Sat	10' 3"	4' 5"	5' 8"	4' 6"	20	185 or 194(?) x 1¾"		918	99	–	222, 234, 276, 296
K	Bel Sup	14' 6"	5' 8"	8' 0"	4' 6"	28	183 x 1¾"	24 x 5¼"	1606	171	350	400, 500
M	Bel Sup	14' 9"	6' 0"	11' 7"	4' 6"	34	143 x 2"	28 x 5½"	1670	200	468	800
N	Bel Sup	10' 4"	4' 8"	5' 10"	4' 5"	20	90 x 1¾"	18 x 5¼"	708	120	168	211, 213, 257, 301, 310, 351, 442, 454, 455, 461
O	Bel Sup	10' 4"	5' 3"	6' 1"	4' 7"	21	168 x 1¾"	24 x 5⅛"	1068	136.7	250	305, 333, 342
Q	Bel sup	11' 3"	5' 0"	7' 0"	4' 6"	25	168 x 1¾"	24 x 5¼"	1180	139	290	355, 368, 900
R	Bel Sup	10' 1"	4' 5"	6' 7"	4' 5"	23	111 x 1¾"	12 x 5¼"	696	119	112	463
S	RT Sat	10' 3"	4' 5"	4' 10"	4' 4"	20	194 x 1¾"		793	88	–	234, 269, 279, 295
T	Bel Sat	10' 2"	4' 2"	4' 10"	4' 5"	15	182 x 1¾"		853	105	–	423, 428
U	Bel Sat	9' 0"	4' 2"	5' 0"	4' 5"	16	182 x 1¾"		673	82.6	–	2
W	Bel Sup	10' 4"	5' 3"	6' 7"	4' 7"	23	168 x 1¾"	24 x 5¼"	1068	148	250	321
X	Bel Sup	9' 8"	4' 5"	5' 0"	4' 5"	16	111 x 1¾"	12 x 5¼"	655	110	112	52, 530, 536, 567, 573, 594, 614
Y	Bel Sup	10' 0"	4' 5"	5' 0"	4' 5"	16	111 x 1¾"	12 x 5¼"	673	95	112	650
Z	Bel Sup	9' 10"	4' 5"	5' 7"	4' 5"	19	111 x 1¾"	12 x 5¼"	662	112	112	60, 101, 204, 434, 670, 710
Non-classified GSR boilers:												
Class:												
495	RT Sat	8' 0"	3' 0"	2' 9"	3' 1"	5.6	72 x 1¾"		274	40	–	
700	Bel Sat	9' 10	4' 8"	5' 7"	4' 6"	19.1	188 x 1¾"		887	126	–	
							Known as Type 60/ 101 but used on one member of Class 60 only					
850	Bel Sup	10' 10"	4' 7"	5' 10"	c. 4' 6"	20	90 x 1¾"	18 x 5⅛"	697	119	240	

Appendix C2: Boilers & locomotive maintenance

The following internal memorandum is quoted verbatim to illustrate the intensity of the debate at Inchicore at the time of the Milne Report concerning the position with boiler replacements and the repair situation generally:

13th May 1948

To: Production Manager, INCHICORE
Copy: General Manager, KINGSBRIDGE

From: Asst. Running Supt., KINGSBRIDGE

Locomotive Maintenance Position, May 1948

I have your letter of 11th inst. under heading "Engine Boiler Condition".

I may say that the boiler position has developed and continues to develop, since the discussion in the General Manager's Office, at the end of 1947, that not only are the engines whose boiler life is expended a serious difficulty but such is adversely affecting the whole standard of repair because boiler life is becoming an increasing factor in determining when general repair to an engine is due and not mileage, which usually represents the true index to the economic life of an engine as well as the coal consumption. A saving of even 1 lb of coal per mile represents £15,000 per annum. The present trend is to "general repair" engines at a much lower mileage than heretofore, probably for reasons stated above, at the same time the average mileage of engines with high mileages are being continued in service regardless of condition so long as the boiler remains serviceable. This is the inevitable drift at present which it will be difficult to arrest.

The following survey will assist in an understanding of the position:-

Particulars of the number of (*broad gauge*) engines which received general and heavy repairs during the year 1940 with comparative figures for the years 1947 and 1948 to 30/4/48.

	General	Heavy	Total
1940	107	28	135
1947	59	38	97
1948 to 30/4/48	29	8	37

The average (*presumably annual*) mileage of engines in use has increased from 43,000 in 1940 to 50,000 at present.

The total number of general repairs fell very considerably in 1947 whilst the number of "heavy repairs" increased (these latter do not give the same return in service value as "general repairs").

At the moment there are 165 engines with a mileage of 60,000 or over, of which 28 are actually stopped awaiting general repairs and 6 stopped for slight repairs.

These figures must be related to the fact that in 1940 the average mileage of engines entering shops was 97,081 miles, in 1947 it was almost 20,000 miles less at 77,532, therefore, whilst the average mileage of engines in use has increased 17% the mileage of engines between general repairs has decreased 20%, added to this is the decline in the number of general repairs which will later on accentuate these figures.

Of the engines in service 36 are on boiler time limit, which indicates that they are unreliable and will fall due for repairs shortly; the significant fact is that 9 of these have mileages of less than 60,000 (actually they vary between 38,000 and 100,000 miles).

The output of general repairs for the first 4 months of the year indicates that the output for the year will be approximately 100 general repairs or possibly slightly more. The output to the 30/4/48 was 31, to this will be added approximately 26 of those on boiler time limits now or a total of 57 engines; to this must be added, say a further 15 which will stop themselves through major defects and which must be given general repairs or alternatively let them lie out of traffic, a position which could not be contemplated. The inference is that general repairs to only 30-35 engines can be carried out by direct selection; this is very important. To illustrate a practical working difficulty – the 372/ 393 class position may be mentioned there are 26 engines in the classes (interchangeable) and they are vital to the service as they are the largest engines capable of working to Cork, Waterford, Limerick, Sligo, Galway, Cavan and Claremorris; of the 15 in service only 5 are in good condition and the boiler life of the class is almost expended. One of them put into service last December is giving continuous boiler trouble at 12,000 miles, whilst nominally a new engine ex-shops it could not be used on, say, Sunday Specials. Complete failures due to Boilers represent 27% of all failures for the first three months of the year; if oil burning failures, which were abnormal, are eliminated the boiler failures were 33% of all failures. There are many other cases of partial failure causing delays.

Another matter of concern is the large number of engines stopped in Sheds for repairs of late. On Saturday the 7th inst. the number was 80, equal to approximately 30% of those working. The reason for the increase in numbers is threefold:-

1 Awaiting the supplying of material.

2 Undertaking in Sheds work which is beyond the capacity of the staff and the very poor equipment available in Sheds.

3 The reduced mechanical condition of the engine stock.

71 or 15.3% of the total stock (Broad Gauge) are at present either in Shop under repairs or stopped awaiting repairs as distinct from engines under repairs in Running Sheds.

The conversion of engines to Oil Burning and subsequent reconversion of a large number during 1947 and 1948, has, no doubt, affected the general repair programme and it seems unlikely that the arrears of general repairs will be cleared off within measurable time.

On Tuesday after the 10.00 am passenger train to Cork had left there was not a single passenger engine in Inchicore Shed which could be availed of and 23 engines stopped for repairs. There are 52 Boiler Inspectors' reports of repairs required to engines in the Cork District alone, representing overwork which cannot be undertaken at a rate that the position demands.

There can be no doubt that the present position can further develop and by early next year become serious; unless extra steps can be taken to deal with it the alternative may be that the Company may have to face a continuance of the present type of service over the next 2, 3 or more years because even if the boilers on order were delivered at the end of this year the position would arise in which the priority would again have to be given to the same engines which are now contributing to the reduced average life of engines in service and for a period would still further reduce the average life of engines in service, in considering this I am making allowance for the fact that some boilers can be changed under emergency conditions without "general repairing" an engine.

To deal with the present position I consider that it will be necessary to provide generally improved conditions for carrying out repairs in certain Districts and these facilities should not be limited to boiler repairs only, since this type of repair is usually rather slow it is imperative that the Running Department shall be in a position to maintain other engines in service to enable boiler repairs to be carried out ie to achieve a higher standard of repair on the running engines generally.

I may add that I have discussed this matter this week with the Mechanical Engineer

J.H. Dudley
Asst. Running Superintendent

Appendix D: Annual boiler mileages

In September 1946, as part of the proposed boiler renewal programme, a census of boilers was conducted by Córas Iompair Éireann, the results of which are summarised in the attached table. The number of boilers in use and spare for each class or classes was counted as at 8 September 1946, and compared with the relative average annual mileage for 1939, the last year of normal operations for the GSR. An exception related to the four boilers for Class 800, the mileage for which was calculated on an actual average basis since date of construction.

Although from the nature of the records on file, it is apparent that there was an element of estimation, some conclusions can be drawn:

1 As there were usually more boilers than relative locomotives, the estimated annual mileage per locomotive would therefore have been proportionately higher than the average mileage per boiler.

2 The 1939 mileages might have been slightly overstated as a separate analysis of the largest group, Class Z, suggests that average annual mileages over the historic life of each boiler was in the region of 21,000 to 22,000 miles.

3 Assuming a reasonable degree of accuracy in the figures, the implication is that many older, smaller types were proportionately doing more work for their living than some of the larger locomotives. It is remarkable, for example that Class 650 (G2) dating from 1893 covered an average mileage in 1939 that was 65% of the mileages achieved by Classes 400 and 500.

4 In the census, boiler types N, U, X and Z are specifically segregated into separate classes which raises the question whether these were truly standard types. Although the leading dimensions might have been the same, it could have been that other features limited the ability to rotate these boilers among different classes. For example, the version of Type X suitable for Class 52 (for which apparently no spares were held) might not have been suitable for Classes 530, 567, 573, 594 and 614. If this was the case, then this factor would also have contributed to longer periods under repair than was desirable.

5 Apart from Class 800, the high average age across-the-board is striking, as is also the few spare boiler available for some types, as exemplified with Class Z type boilers. Thus ageing boilers would have needed more maintenance, and there must have been situations where return to duty was delayed by the need to repair the boiler, there being no spare available. It is understandable in view of this data why CIÉ management was so concerned to acquire adequate replacements through the new build order in the late 1940s.

Boiler Type	Carried by GSR Class:	No of engines Sept 1946	No of boilers Sept 1946	No of spare boilers Sept 1946	Average boiler age (yrs)	Average firebox age (yrs)	Average annual mileage for 1939
A	545	5	6	1	12	9	20,000
C	536, 540, 623	32	34	2	21	9	28,000
D	372, 393	26	31	5	19	8	30,000
E	551	12	13	1	21	12	16,000
H	619	3	5	2	14	11	15,000
J	222, 234, 276, 296	11	13	2	21	15	22,000
K	400, 500	10	12	2	18	8	40,000
M	800	3	4	1	7	7	29,000*
N	211, 213, 442, 454, 455, 461	12	14	2	13	10	25,000
N	257, 301, 310, 351	25	29	4	24	13	25,000
O	305, 333, 342	16	19	3	13	11	27,000
Q	355, 368	8	9	1	19	12	18,000
R	463	6	9	3	20	18	31,000
S	269, 295	5	6	1	19	13	17,000
T	423, 428	8	9	1	13	12	22,000
U	2	8	12	4	15	15	23,000
U	33, 37	13	17	4	21	15	25,000
W	321	9	11	2	20	10	35,000
X	52	12	12	0	25	17	20,000
X	573, 594	12	17	5	24	17	20,000
X	530	3	5	2	17	17	20,000
X	567, 614	40	45	5	13	12	20,000
Y	650	19	21	2	16	14	26,000
Z	60	10	12	2	23	11	25,000
Z **	60, 101	6	8	2	18	16	25,000
Z	101	49	50	1	23	13	25,000
Z	204, 670, 710	82	87	5	13	11	25,000
Z	434	1	1	0	27	27	25,000
	Total	**446**	**511**	**65**			

** Annual average since construction*
*** Categorised as 60, 101 type*

Appendix E: Passenger routes and locomotive usage

In assessing the requirement for replacement boilers, Córas Iompair Éireann in 1948 conducted a survey of passenger routes and of the locomotive classes suitable to work over each route. The precise date of the survey cannot be traced but the results, which are quoted largely verbatim below, provide an interesting insight into where classes were used and how they were regarded by their operators. A few routes are marked as 'untested' for particular classes; it is assumed that these locomotives theoretically could work in those areas but in fact had not actually done so.

Route No	From	To	Route No	From	To
1	Kingsbridge	Cork	**27**	Bagenalstown	Palace East
2	Mallow	Waterford	**28**	Banagher	Clara
3	Waterford	Rosslare	**29**	Maryboro'	Mountmellick
4	Mallow	Killarney	**30**	Roscrea	Birr
5	Westland Row	Galway	**31**	Ennis	Collooney
6	Clonsilla	Kingscourt	**32**	Kilmessan Junc.	Athboy
7	Mullingar	Sligo	**33**	Enfield	Edenderry
8	Inny Junction	Cavan	**34**	Streamstown	Clara
9	Athlone	Westport	**35**	Crossdoney	Killeshandra
10	Kildare	Kilkenny & Waterford	**36**	Kilfree Junc.	Ballaghadereen
11	Maryboro'	Kilkenny	**37**	Manulla Junc.	Ballina
12	Ballybrophy	Limerick	**38**	Claremorris	Ballinrobe
13	Limerick	Limerick Junc. & Waterford	**39**	Loughrea	Attymon Junc.
14	Amiens Street	Wexford	**40**	Ballingrane	Tralee
15	Macmine Junc.	Waterford	**41**	Ballingrane	Foynes
16	Cork	Youghal	**42**	Headford Junc.	Kenmare
17	Killarney	Tralee	**43**	Tralee	Fenit
18	Charleville	Patrickswell & Limerick	**44**	Castleisland	Gortatlea
19	Limerick	Ennis	**45**	Farranfore	Valencia Harbour
20	Goold's Cross	Cashel	**46**	Cobh Junc.	Cobh
21	Thurles	Clonmel	**47**	Cork	Macroom
22	Kilkenny	Castlecomer	**48**	Fermoy	Mitchelstown
23	Portarlington	Athlone	**49**	Clonakilty Junc.	Clonakilty
24	Athy	Ballylinan	**50**	Drimoleague Junc.	Skibbereen
25	Rosslare	Wexford	**51**	Waterford	Tramore
26	Cork	Bantry	**52**	Sallins	Tullow

Class 800 (3 locomotives):

Route 1 and Kingsbridge–Amiens Street

Limited Kingsbridge and Cork. Suitable for high speeds (Cork 2½ hours) with a load of approximately 200 tons and economic working at that speed. Disadvantage: Only three in the class. If one was in shops and two working one fast train each way daily, it could not be replaced if unable to work return trip.

Class 400 (7 locomotives):

Routes 1 to 4 and Kingsbridge–Amiens Street

Could only work 100 tons on fast Cork Service (about 2 hours 50 mins). The heaviest engines which can work between Mallow and Killarney. Axleload suitable for Midland Section but gauge height too great. Untried as yet on Limerick to Waterford and Rosslare, or Mallow to Waterford and Rosslare routes. Would suit as heavy Goods Engines for many years. Within seven engines of the class there are two with Caprotti Valve Gear. One of same power with Walschaerts gear and four others rather similar to each other but not standard.

Class 500 (3 locomotives):

Routes 1 to 4 and Kingsbridge–Amiens Street

Originally used as Passenger Engines but only suitable for Goods Services. Could work same services as 400 class.

Class 321 (9 locomotives):

Routes 1 to 4 and 10 to 11 (2 & 3 untested), Routes 12 to 13

Useful light passenger engines capable of maximum speed of approximately 68 mph on level with a load of 100 tons. Used at present chiefly on Kingsbridge to Waterford, Kingsbridge to Limerick branches as they are one of the heaviest engines capable of working between Waterford to Maryboro' and Ballybrophy to Limerick. Useful for Newspaper Trains.

Class 333/ 346 (13 locomotives):

Routes 1 to 24 inclusive

Generally these will perform the same work as 321 class but they are especially valuable because they can work a number of 16 ton axle load branches that 321 class cannot travel over. Before 1939 there were not enough of them to meet Special Passenger Train Traffic because nearly all branch passenger specials necessitated double-heading. They are not suitable for sustained high speed except with light loads and thus employed have a short life. Too many types within the class.

Class 301/ 304 (4 locomotives):

Class 305/ 307 (3 locomotives):

Class 309/ 314 (6 locomotives):

Routes 1 to 24 inclusive

For operational purposes these engines perform similar work to the 333 class, but with smaller loads except group 309 to 314, they are 16 ton axle loads and are only useful in Cork to Waterford and Limerick Districts for local Branch Passenger Trains. They are not fast with economic load.

Class 2 (11 locomotives):

Class 52 (18 locomotives):

Class 530/ 535 (5 locomotives):

Routes 1 to 48 inclusive;

Routes 26, 49 & 50 untested

These are obsolete as their power is too slight for anything but small Branch Passenger Trains and no use for Branch Goods Working. They are at present limiting the speed of Branch Trains which must be worked by them.

Class 650 (12 locomotives):

Routes 1 to 39 and 52, (26 untested)

These are slightly better than 2/ 52/ 530 Class and for their size do good work, chiefly on Midland Section Branches but they are slow and suited for very few modern trains. Economic on small Branches for which their 14.5 ton axle load suits them. Useful on DSE local services.

Class 60 (15 locomotives):

Routes 1 to 46; (26, 49, 50 untested)

Useful for small Branch Trains but can travel fast and work Newspaper Trains with load of approximately 75 tons sustaining 60 mph for long periods. Very useful for double-heading another under-powered engine such as 333 class on a limited axle load Branch. Economic to work and maintain.

Class 536 (4 locomotives):

Class 540 (5 locomotives):

Routes 1 to 24 inclusive

Class 545 (5 locomotives):

Routes 1 to 13 inclusive

These classes are essentially the same except 536 and 540 classes have 16 ton axle load and can work over more Branches than 545 class. They are a bad design, slow and unreliable, suitable for slow stopping trains of about 150 tons. Chiefly used light auxiliary Goods during recent years, but not even suited for this because of passenger wheel arrangement.

Class 372/ 391 (20 locomotives):
Class 393/ 398 (6 locomotives):
Routes 1 to 13 inclusive

These engines were built at Woolwich after 1914 War for the British Gauge and adapted to the Irish Gauge. Their boilers are too small for our requirements–393 class was built in 1929 from the same parts but with a wheel 6" larger to work the Cork Mail. They were unsatisfactory and too slow and were withdrawn. They were suitable, however, for the Cork to Rosslare Express with limited load but still under-boilered. For some years past they work only heavy Goods and the Galway Passenger Train, occasionally to Sligo. They are the biggest passenger engines on the Midland Section but have never had an opportunity of fast running because they are always overloaded. They can also work between Limerick and Rosslare Harbour over which they worked the Boat Train in former years. They are the most powerful engines permitted Maryboro' to Waterford, Waterford to Limerick, Ballybrophy to Limerick Sections due to their favourable axle load.

Tank Engines (Passenger)

Class 423 (3 locomotives):
Routes 1 to 26 inclusive
Class 428 (5 locomotives):
Routes 1 to 50 inclusive
Class 434 (6 locomotives):
Routes 1 to 39 inclusive and 52

Much too small for even DSE Local Services and are limiting the services. Used sometimes on the Cork and Bandon Section but only as and expedient, also too under-powered for this section. With some alterations would suit as shunting pilot.

Class 670 (5 locomotives):
Routes 1 to 24 inclusive

A more modern and more powerful edition of above classes. Has worked the Wexford Mail, but they are slow and need too much maintenance. Would suit a 16-ton branch.

Class 850:
Routes 1 to 24 inclusive

The only engine of its class. Fairly powerful, works on DSE Section. Maintenance very high and engine should be scrapped as soon as it can be replaced.

Class 463 (5 locomotives):
Routes 1 to 39 inclusive, and 52

These are the largest Passenger Engines of the Cork and Bandon Section for which they are best suited. Some of them work DSE local service but they are under-powered for trains now required on that Section.

Class 455 (3 locomotives):
Routes 1 to 25 inclusive;
Class 458 (3 locomotives):
Routes 1 to 26 inclusive

DSE Passenger Local Service. A good design in most respects but not powerful enough to enable speeding up of the Local Services with loads of 6 Bogies (equivalent of up to 12–30 foot coaches).

Special Notes on axle load map

Kingsbridge to Cork	21T 800 class allowed
Islandbridge to Amiens Street	21T 800 class allowed
Amiens Street to Bray	Woolwich Class (max 17t 12c) and other engines up to 17t 12c allowed with a speed restriction of 10 mph Amiens St to Westland Row and 30 mph Westland to Bray.
Amiens St to Wexford	J4 class 16t 11c allowed
Gould's Cross to Cashel	17½t allowed with goods trains Max speed 25 mph.
Lines coloured blue (16T limit)	Speed restriction of 30 mph with 16½t axle load.
Streamstown to Clara	17½t allowed with goods trains Max speed 25 mph.
Drimoleague to Baltimore	Six coupled engines prohibited (except in emergencies)
Skibbereen to Schull	Loco 6^S, 8^T, 8^C allowed.

Map showing permitted axle loads on GSR routes

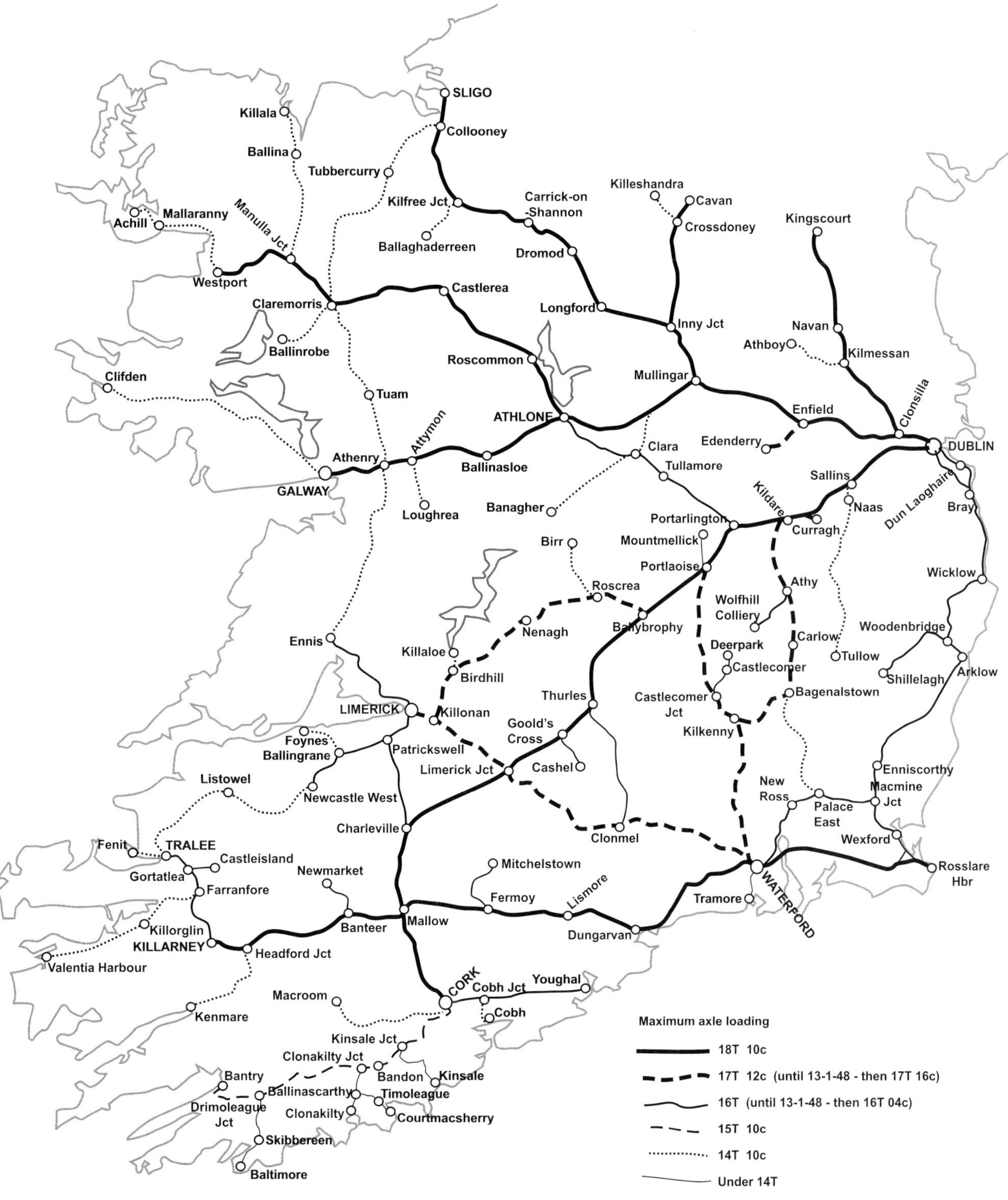

Appendix F: 1925-1940 Comparison Great Southern Railways V Great Northern Railway (Ireland)

For the first full year of operations, the Great Southern Railways stated that its Financial Accounts and Statistical Returns had been prepared in accordance with the First Schedule to the Railway Companies (Accounts and Returns) Act, 1911. This legislation had been drawn up to embrace the activities of railways in both Britain and Ireland. The GSR continued to report in this format throughout its existence, which helps comparison with reported figures for the Great Northern Railway (Ireland) which was legally obliged to report thus during this period.

The operating conditions between 1940 and 1944 were so unusual, and the trading results were so vulnerable to distortion by external factors that no useful purpose is served in considering those five years. Otherwise the two companies faced broadly similar economic circumstances in the 1920s and 1930s, plus the growing threat of road competition. There were of course some fundamental differences. The GNR(I) had to cope with unusual operating challenges in dislocation to services arising from its cross-border operations. On the other hand the GSR in its early days had to contend with a major repair programme arising from damage wrought during the Civil War. Further it was burdened with numerous branch and narrow gauge lines, several of which were lightly trafficked and inherent loss leaders.

Railway companies, as major commercial entities, had a prime obligation to earn a profit for their owners. Thus, effective use of fixed assets, of which locomotives and rolling stock formed a major part, was critical in this endeavour. The ultimate test in this regard was how much work each item did, and what revenue was generated through that use.

Compared with modern day standards, pre-war utilisation levels of locomotives and rolling stock were poor across-the-board. This is particularly evident with GSR passenger vehicles. The fleet was reduced by only 5% between 1925 and 1939 yet passenger vehicle revenue fell by 32% during this period. Thus by 1939, a major element of the GSR fleet was either on the move but empty, or standing idle in sidings. This scenario also raises a question over what element of the fleet could be truly considered to be operational.

The GNR(I) fleet worked to a better level of utilisation and on average their vehicles earned £68 more per year. However, the GSR was able to earn revenue per passenger train mile at a rate 17% better than that on the GNR(I).

With freight services, the fact that the GSR reported unchanged fleet totals over several years raises the suspicion that the company was unsure how many wagons it owned. It is likely though that the number in revenue-earning service (ie excluding unused or unserviceable vehicles) was lower than the reported level. This would have had the effect of an improvement on the reported annual revenue per freight vehicle. Based on the reported figures, GSR freight vehicles on average earned 37% more revenue per year – an extraordinary variance. The GSR held the advantage in nearly every year in revenue per freight train mile although the 15 year average was only 5% better.

Regarding locomotive usage, each member of the smaller GNR(I) fleet covered on average 12% more miles per annum than did the each GSR locomotive. This certainly bears out the contention that GSR annual locomotive mileages were unimpressive. However, for all this extra effort each GNR(I) locomotive earned 4% less per annum than did its southern counterpart.

The underlying revenue trends were in steady decline and the years 1931–34 were particularly difficult for both companies. The subsequent recovery was more robust for the GSR suggesting that this company had a more stable position within its home territory with less vulnerability to competition.

In the final analysis, the financial performance of the GSR in the revenue it was earning on its mobile fixed assets was superior, and contrary to the general impression that many observers have formed about the company's operational efficiency.

GREAT SOUTHERN RAILWAYS	1925	1926	1927	1928	1929	1930	1931	1932	1933	1934	1935
PASSENGER SERVICES:											
Passenger train mileage 000s	5,902	5,953	6,246	6,330	6,504	6,506	6,241	5,962	5,827	6,014	6,048
Passenger train receipts £000s	1,991	1,940	1,806	1,643	1,556	1,480	1,347	1,322	1,225	1,248	1,278
No of vehicles	1,670	1,670	1,664	1,643	1,640	1,640	1,646	1,642	1,614	1,614	1,584
Mileage per vehicle	3,534	3,565	3,754	3,853	3,966	3,967	3,792	3,631	3,610	3,726	3,818
Revenue per train mile £	**0.34**	**0.33**	**0.29**	**0.26**	**0.24**	**0.23**	**0.22**	**0.22**	**0.21**	**0.21**	**0.21**
Revenue per passenger vehicle £	**1,192**	**1,162**	**1,085**	**1,000**	**949**	**902**	**818**	**805**	**759**	**773**	**807**
FREIGHT SERVICES:											
Freight train mileage 000s	4,614	4,505	4,805	4,921	4,907	4,882	4,725	4,381	4,489	4,839	5,067
Freight train receipts £000s	2,274	2,246	2,426	2,460	2,403	2,305	2,114	1,697	1,625	1,763	1,881
No of vehicles	12,671	12,671	12,671	12,671	12,671	12,400	12,389	12,376	12,345	12,345	12,345
Mileage per vehicle	364	356	379	388	387	394	381	354	364	392	410
Revenue per train mile £	**0.49**	**0.50**	**0.50**	**0.50**	**0.49**	**0.47**	**0.45**	**0.39**	**0.36**	**0.36**	**0.37**
Revenue per freight vehicle £	**180**	**177**	**192**	**194**	**190**	**186**	**171**	**137**	**132**	**143**	**152**
LOCOMOTIVE USAGE & REVENUE:											
Total traffic revenue	4,294	4,213	4,260	4,140	3,986	3,811	3,485	3,043	2,871	3,061	3,141
Locomotive fleet	563	570	570	537	537	528	517	517	513	513	508
Mileage per locomotive	18,679	18,347	19,388	20,952	21,250	21,568	21,211	20,006	20,109	21,156	21,880
Revenue per locomotive £	**7,627**	**7,391**	**7,474**	**7,710**	**7,423**	**7,218**	**6,741**	**5,886**	**5,597**	**5,967**	**6,183**

GREAT NORTHERN RAILWAY (IRELAND)	1925	1926	1927	1928	1929	1930	1931	1932	1933	1934	1935
PASSENGER SERVICES:											
Passenger train mileage 000s	2,678	2,794	2,962	3,152	3,260	3,237	3,255	3,279	2,212	2,945	3,121
Passenger train receipts £000s	878	790	734	684	668	632	597	569	409	521	545
No of vehicles	688	681	680	680	680	660	660	656	631	605	600
Mileage per vehicle	3,892	4,103	4,356	4,635	4,794	4,905	4,932	4,999	3,506	4,868	5,202
Revenue per train mile £	**0.33**	**0.28**	**0.25**	**0.22**	**0.21**	**0.20**	**0.18**	**0.17**	**0.19**	**0.18**	**0.17**
Revenue per passenger vehicle £	**1,276**	**1,160**	**1,079**	**1,006**	**982**	**958**	**905**	**867**	**648**	**861**	**908**
FREIGHT SERVICES:											
Freight train mileage 000s	1,903	1,960	1,841	1,854	1,871	1,851	1,845	1,791	723	1,299	1,326
Freight train receipts £000s	920	831	883	835	839	790	739	586	372	454	494
No of vehicles	5,751	5,745	5,752	5,752	5,728	5,728	5,674	5,626	5,567	5,510	5,503
Mileage per vehicle	331	341	320	322	327	323	325	318	130	236	241
Revenue per train mile £	**0.48**	**0.42**	**0.48**	**0.45**	**0.45**	**0.43**	**0.40**	**0.33**	**0.51**	**0.35**	**0.37**
Revenue per freight vehicle £	**160**	**145**	**154**	**145**	**147**	**138**	**130**	**104**	**67**	**82**	**90**
LOCOMOTIVE USAGE & REVENUE:											
Total traffic revenue	1,798	1,621	1,617	1,519	1,509	1,422	1,336	1,155	780	975	1,040
Locomotive fleet	202	202	201	201	201	201	200	198	198	197	195
Mileage per locomotive	22,678	23,535	23,896	24,906	25,527	25,313	25,500	25,606	14,823	21,543	22,805
Revenue per locomotive £	**8,901**	**8,025**	**8,045**	**7,557**	**7,508**	**7,075**	**6,680**	**5,833**	**3,939**	**4,949**	**5,333**

GREAT SOUTHERN RAILWAYS	1936	1937	1938	1939	Average 1925-39	1940	1941	1942	1943	1944
PASSENGER SERVICES:										
Passenger train mileage 000s	6,049	6,072	6,042	6,014	*6,114*	4,883	4,391	2,173	2,305	1,788
Passenger train receipts £000s	1,295	1,287	1,286	1,275	*1,465*	1,198	1,427	1,266	1,749	1,465
No of vehicles	1,588	1,588	1,588	1,584	*1,625*	1,584	1,400	1,357	1,351	1,337
Mileage per vehicle	3,809	3,824	3,805	3,797	*3,763*					
Revenue per train mile £	0.21	0.21	0.21	0.21	*0.24*	0.25	0.33	0.58	0.76	0.82
Revenue per passenger vehicle £	816	811	810	805	*900*	756	1,019	933	1,295	1,096
FREIGHT SERVICES:										
Freight train mileage 000s	5,202	5,121	4,923	5,058	*4,829*	5,058	5,064	5,649	5,766	5,262
Freight train receipts £000s	1,943	1,891	1,857	2,050	*2,062*	2,217	2,532	2,649	3,025	3,365
No of vehicles	12,345	12,345	12,345	12,205	*12,453*	11,797	11,830	11,853	11,848	11,844
Mileage per vehicle	421	415	399	414	*388*	429	428	477	487	444
Revenue per train mile £	0.37	0.37	0.38	0.41	*0.43*	0.44	0.50	0.47	0.52	0.64
Revenue per freight vehicle £	157	153	150	168	*165*	188	214	224	255	284
LOCOMOTIVE USAGE & REVENUE:										
Total traffic revenue	3,264	3,201	3,166	3,349	*3,437*	3,976	3,929	4,792	4,847	4,847
Locomotive fleet	508	508	508	508	*527*	501	500	500	500	500
Mileage per locomotive	22,148	22,034	21,585	21,795	*20,765*	19,842	18,910	15,644	16,142	14,100
Revenue per locomotive £	6,425	6,301	6,232	6,593	*6,718*	*6,657*	*6,608*	*6,551*	*6,473*	*6,410*

GREAT NORTHERN RAILWAY (IRELAND)	1936	1937	1938	1939	Average 1925-39	1940	1941	1942	1943	1944
PASSENGER SERVICES:										
Passenger train mileage 000s	3,180	3,296	3,330	3,286	*3,066*	3,369	3,662	3,610	3,821	3,725
Passenger train receipts £000s	559	574	571	586	*621*	642	1,098	1,345	1,518	1,604
No of vehicles	598	597	589	584	*639*	585	585	593	592	576
Mileage per vehicle	5,318	5,521	5,654	5,627	*4,821*	*4,883*	*4,935*	*4,973*	*4,996*	*5,009*
Revenue per train mile £	0.18	0.17	0.17	0.18	*0.20*	0.19	0.30	0.37	0.40	0.43
Revenue per passenger vehicle £	935	962	969	1,003	*968*	1,097	1,877	2,268	2,564	2,785
FREIGHT SERVICES:										
Freight train mileage 000s	1,315	1,344	1,382	1,457	*1,584*	1,625	1,958	2,220	2,260	2,376
Freight train receipts £000s	504	492	486	585	*654*	713	1,045	1,197	1,209	1,340
No of vehicles	5,472	5,465	5,493	5,507	*5,618*	5,460	5,480	5,536	5,601	5,656
Mileage per vehicle	240	246	252	265	*281*	298	357	401	404	420
Revenue per train mile £	0.38	0.37	0.35	0.40	*0.41*	0.44	0.53	0.54	0.54	0.56
Revenue per freight vehicle £	92	90	89	106	*116*	131	191	216	216	237
LOCOMOTIVE USAGE & REVENUE:										
Total traffic revenue	1,064	1,066	1,057	1,171	*1,275*	*1,241*	*1,215*	*1,188*	*1,166*	*1,143*
Locomotive fleet	193	193	191	191	*198*	*197*	*197*	*197*	*196*	*196*
Mileage per locomotive	23,290	24,042	24,670	24,833	*23,532*	25,311	28,529	29,635	30,956	31,106
Revenue per locomotive £	5,513	5,523	5,534	6,131	*6,436*	*6,272*	*6,155*	*6,029*	*5,927*	*5,822*

Appendix G: Valve layouts and superheating

The general form of valves in steam locomotives was essentially unchanged almost from the start of the steam era. However, it was only around the time of introduction of the transitional locomotives described in Chapter 9 that the importance of the finer points of valve layouts began to be widely appreciated.

Valve design and operation are critical factors in performance. Many older engines had poorly designed valves but in an era of low speeds and modest loads, the adverse effect of this feature was not readily apparent. At the beginning of the 20th Century, heavier loads and faster speeds placed greater demands upon locomotive crews. General awareness grew of the significance of coal and water consumption as a simple yet effective means of measuring comparative efficiency.

This was graphically demonstrated in the superior performance of the Castle Class locomotive in the LNER/ GWR locomotive exchanges of 1924. The GWR locomotive on average consumed 12½% less per mile than the LNER Pacific when burning Welsh steam coal. Even more impressive, the Castle burned 6½% less when using harder Yorkshire coal (for which its firebox was definitely unsuited) on the LNER. The better performance was directly attributed to the valve layout; the LNER Pacifics were soon fitted with long travel valves and their coal consumption was radically reduced.

Valve operation

When the regulator is opened, steam from the boiler passes through the internal steam pipe (and superheater where fitted). Steam then passes through the external steam pipe to the steam chest, where the supply of steam to the cylinders is regulated by the action of the valves. Regardless of the type of valve gear fitted, valves work the following cycle:

a) Live steam admission to the cylinder up to the point at which admission is closed off (the 'cut off').

b) Expansion of steam within the cylinder before valve movement opens the exhaust port.

c) Release of the used steam from the cylinder through the exhaust port.

d) Compression after the valve has closed the exhaust port.

And usually but not always:

e) A brief period of pre-admission of live steam to the cylinder before the piston completes that stroke and starts the next.

In the cycle, the valve has three distinct duties:

i To close both steam ports when in its central position.

ii To admit steam to one end of the cylinder only at one time.

iii To open the exhaust port at one end of the cylinder before, or at least as soon as, it opens to admit steam at the other end.

Cut-off

The point at which the valve stops admission of steam to the cylinder, the 'cut-off', is measured as a percentage of the total stroke that the piston has travelled. In full forward gear, cut-off occurs when the piston has typically travelled 75% of the stroke. This cut-off, where maximum amounts of steam are admitted to the cylinder for the longest period, is used on starting or when the locomotive is working hard eg hauling a heavy load uphill. A shorter cut-off means that the valve ceases to admit steam to the cylinder earlier in the piston stroke. The work of completing the piston stroke relies thereafter on the expansive property of the steam which is trapped in the cylinder, until the valve movement opens the exhaust port. In broad terms, early cut-off means less steam consumption and hence less expenditure of coal and water in the manufacture of that steam. It follows that optimisation of the point of cut-off in relation to the nature of the work that the locomotive is required to do is fundamental to efficiency.

Lead

After the exhaust port has opened and shortly before the piston reaches the end of the stroke, the admission port (in most locomotives) also opens. This pre-admission factor is known as the valve 'lead' and is defined as the amount by which the admission port is open (usually ⅛" to 3/16") when the driving piston is static at front or back dead centre. Maximum pressure at the start of the next stroke is ensured by filling the clearance space between the cylinder end and the piston. Lead is essential with locomotives designed for high speeds, under which conditions the valve events are occurring in rapid succession. Early admission provides a cushion of live steam between the piston and the cylinder at the end of the stroke.

Lap (or travel)

The other critical element in valve efficiency is 'lap'. This is defined as the amount by which the valve overlaps each steam admission port when it is in mid-position. The greater the lap, the greater must be the travel of the valve for any given position of cut-off, and hence the greater is the maximum port opening at that cut-off. Thus 'lap' and 'travel' are different terms used to describe the same element of valve set up. A long-lap or long-travel valve allows the steam to pass more freely into and out of the cylinder, and makes for a faster, freer-running and hence more efficient locomotive. Ultra-long travel (lap) valves are inefficient because of the extra power needed to move the valve and because there is a tendency to excessive wear of the valve and/ or valve liners.

Nineteenth century locomotive worked with valve laps in the region of 1" or slightly less – now recognised as short- travel or short-lap valves. Pioneering work by the Great Western Railway identified the advantages to be gained by the long valve travel. Efficient modern steam locomotives operate with laps of around 1½" to 1⅞".

It is apparent that in the design of GSWR Class 400, the traditionalist short-travel camp at Inchicore prevailed against Watson's desire for longer travel. (EE Joynt favoured ⅞", but 1¼" was agreed as a compromise). The design was thus hamstrung from the start by this feature, quite apart from its other defects. Despite having come from Swindon, it seems that Watson had not recognised this vital point, possibly because it was yet to gain widespread recognition or possibly because he had been working on the carriage and wagon side, and may not therefore have been fully *au fait* with the latest in locomotive developments. In this context, the criticism heaped upon Watson for the shortcomings of the 400s might in part have been unfair as this vital failing in the design might simply have not been his fault.

In moving to the South Eastern & Chatham Railway at Ashford, Harry Holcroft was one of the first to preach on behalf of the long-lap valve outside Swindon, and Richard Maunsell was one of the first converts. This was to the great advantage of his prototype Class N 2-6-0 No 810, and to the derivative Woolwich moguls that followed. The authors speculate that Maunsell was instrumental in selling the long-lap message to Bazin, which was put to good use with No 500.

It is possible that Bazin might also have had in mind the long lap valves used on English GNR's 2-6-0 Classes H2, H3 and H4 (later LNER K1, K2 and K3). However it is clear that Doncaster then had yet to accept the principle as witness the short lap used on the Class O2 2-8-0s and the initial Gresley Pacifics.

To amplify, the following points should be noted:

A The maximum travel of a piston valve (and also of a slide valve) is twice the 'steam lap' plus twice the port openings whereas the minimum travel is twice the 'steam lap' plus twice the mid-gear 'lead'.

B There are actually two kinds of 'lap'. Steam lap is the amount by which the valve overlaps the port on the live steam side while exhaust lap is the equivalent amount on the exhaust side. Exhaust lap was generally given to locomotives expected to work at low speeds eg on shunting duties, the effect being to delay the exhaust of steam and to derive maximum work from its expansive properties within the cylinder.

C 'Negative exhaust lap', usually referred to as 'exhaust clearance', is the amount the port is open to exhaust when the valve is in mid position. This was sometimes given to fast-running locomotives to create a freer exhaust, and thus freer running at speed. Exhaust clearance, where used, rarely exceeded $^{1}/_{16}$"; the effect was that the cylinder ports on both sides of the piston were concurrently open to exhaust at the point the valve was passing through the mid position, which is naturally only for a tiny instant when the locomotive is in motion.

Types of valve gear

The bulk of the GSR fleet dated from the 19th century in design standards, if not actual construction date. This usually meant a combination of saturated boiler, Stephenson valve gear and slide valves.

Stephenson's valve motion has several advantages, not the least of which is the capacity for variable lead. The valve gear can be adjusted to create negative lead in full forward gear (ie steam admission commences *after* the piston has commenced the stroke) thereby imparting considerable 'punch' on starting or in slow speed slogging. At the same time, the valve gear can be set to create positive lead when running at speed on a shorter cut-off.

Walschaerts valve gear was less common on the GSR and was mainly found on later locomotives (Classes 341, 372, 393, 400, 500, 800 and 850, and sundry other applications). Unlike Stephenson's motion, the amount of lead with this valve gear is constant regardless of the position of the cut-off, making it preferable for use with locomotives more likely to be engaged in sustained high-speed running. The amount of lead, if any, should thus be set with the expected type of work the locomotive will undertake in mind. An extreme example of the effects of getting the lead wrong is found with the Baltic Tanks of the Belfast & County Down Railway. These locomotives were fitted with Walschaerts valve gear set up with constant *negative* lead. The largest engines in Ireland when introduced, they were remarkably weak for their size with an extremely heavy appetite for coal and water.

Caprotti valve gear was used with only two GSR locomotives (Nos 401 and 406). A feature of this valve gear, which permitted almost infinitely variable cut-off, was that the manufacturers recommended that working with full open regulator and very early cut-off yielded optimal performance and fuel economy. However, observations indicated that drivers did not take full advantage of this characteristic, preferring to work at later cut-offs, as was normal with engines fitted with short-lap piston valves or slide valves. This practice limited realisation of the advantages offered by these expensive rebuildings.

It was not uncommon for drivers, experienced with one type of valve gear, to drive locomotives with other types in fuel-expensive and thus inefficient fashion. Lack of standardisation meant that drivers had to be familiar with different driving techniques, and this was particularly relevant to Class 400. By 1930, the seven surviving members used three different types of cylinder/ valve set-up, each of which demanded its particular driving technique to optimise performance. Drivers who had been brought up on short-travel Stephenson valve gear were now confronted with the inherent confusion of one long-travel Walschaerts two-cylinder locomotive (No 402), two Caprotti valve gear two-cylinder locomotives (Nos 401 & 406) and four short-travel Walschaerts four-cylinder locomotives (Nos 403, 405, 407 and 409).

Saturated versus superheated steam

With a locomotive boiler that generates saturated (non-superheated) steam, slide valves work efficiently (within the inherent limitations of the external combustion engine) partly because the 'wet' nature of the steam acts as a lubricant within the valve. A superheater makes steam hotter and drier in which condition it no longer acts as a lubricant, thereby making the injection of lubricating oil essential to make the valve work properly without undue wear. It was found that piston valves could be lubricated more effectively than traditional slide valves. As a result, the replacement of slide valves with piston valves generally accompanied the installation of superheating.

Piston valves consist of two circular pistons (valve heads) fitted on to a spindle with the whole assembly reciprocating within the cylindrical steam chest, the centre line of which is usually (but not always) parallel with the centre line of the adjacent driving cylinder. The valve heads are fitted with rings to reduce steam leakage and in Irish locomotives (and the majority elsewhere) inside admission applies. With this set up, live steam is contained between the two valve heads and admitted to the driving cylinder through the steam ports at the inner edges of the valve heads. Steam is exhausted from the driving cylinder at the outer edges of the valve heads into separate passages that combine to communicate with the blast pipe.

The Midland Great Western Railway, a pioneer in this field in Ireland, concluded that superheating and slide valves could acceptably co-exist in their locomotives. This was contrary to general findings in Britain and it is surmised that this was possible because of the comparatively relaxed schedules in place in the years before the amalgamation. Certainly the harder running needed for heavier loads and faster schedules would have taxed the superheater/ slide valve combination.

Another factor that favoured retention of slide valves was cost. Installation of piston valves would have required the casting of new blocks to accommodate the boring of new cylinders and the adjacent cylindrical steam chests, plus probable modifications to frames and valve motion. A superheater alone could be conveniently fitted in conjunction with scheduled boiler repairs eg tube renewal, and this was not excessively expensive. The casting and fitting of new cylinders was financially speaking another matter entirely, particularly if the existing cylinders and slide valves had not reached the end of their working lives. Further, Broadstone Works never cast its own cylinders so replacements would have had to be purchased from commercial manufacturers in Britain.

A total of 119 GSR locomotives were equipped with piston valves, of which only 22 (two ex-GSWR and 20 ex-MGWR) were conversions from slide valves.

The ex-GSWR locomotives were 4-4-0s Nos 332 and 338, and the former in particular was noted for sluggish running and poor riding. No 338 with its smaller driving wheels was engaged on slower duties where any reluctance to run freely would have been less of an inhibition. The sluggishness most likely stemmed from retention of short valve lap rather than any inherent inferiority in the piston valve concept. Had the matter of valve lap been addressed, performance might have been radically improved, so encouraging more conversions. However, by this time the 4-4-0s were less frequently engaged on front line duties so the question was no longer that critical.

There may be significance in the year – 1927 – of these conversions. In the authors' view, this was the point at which the GSR, having completed the Civil War repair programme, could start seriously to pursue new motive power initiatives (as with the rebuilding of No 402, which included provision of long-lap valves). It is speculated that Bazin had delayed the superheating programme by giving priority to the repair back-log, and that Nos 332/ 338 were the first step towards a broader superheating programme. The disappointment with No 332 would have reinforced his reservations about the viability of converting older, smaller locomotives.

Summary

The main limitations on steam flows and hence on valve efficiency are the length of valve travel, the piston valve diameter, and the layout of steam chest and port passages. The longer the valve travel, the wider can be made the steam ports in the valve liner. The extension of the steam chest beyond the ends of the cylinder barrel enables the piston valve heads to be widely spaced so that the steam ports can be located directly at the ends of the cylinder bore, permitting direct passages between the valve ports and the cylinder. The chief advantage derived from long-lap valves is greater exhaust freedom and the ability to work the locomotive at an earlier cut-off point as the valve moves a greater distance for a given angular movement of the return crank. The initial movement of the valve is accelerated with sharper definition of the events of admission, expansion, exhaustion and compression.

The alternative scenario presented by traditional short-lap valves with awkward steam passages was that proportionately longer cut-offs were needed under all working conditions to off-set the throttling or choking effect of steam being unable to move freely through the valves and cylinders. Thus, regardless of how competently the boiler generated steam, the valves worked against that energy being put to best effect.

In the late 1930s, André Chapelon pioneered scientific investigation into ways in which efficiency could be enhanced by streamlining steam passages. The work of this genius led to a revolutionary improvement in the performance of certain French locomotives. Bredin studied Chapelon's work and adopted these principles in the streamlining of the passages of Class 800. This feature linked with use of long lap piston valves achieved memorable results.

The valve cycle

Piston valve events are explained diagrammatically as illustrated opposite:

Legend:

A Piston at end of stroke; forward valve slightly open providing lead; rearward valve fully open to exhaust steam through rearward port to blast-pipe.

B Piston has commenced next stroke; forward valve full open to admit steam; rearward valve open to exhaust steam behind piston.

C Piston stroke has reached point at which forward valve has closed (the point of cut-off) and is now being driven by expansive property of trapped steam; rearward valve is starting to close.

D Piston has covered about 75% of the stroke; forward valve has started to open to exhaust steam through forward port; exhaust has been expelled through rearward valve which is now closed producing compression in the cylinder.

E Piston has completed stroke; rearward valve slightly open providing lead; forward valve fully open to exhaust steam through forward port.

F Piston has commenced next stroke; rearward valve is opening further to admit steam; forward valve open to exhaust steam behind piston.

G Piston has covered about 75% of the stroke; rearward valve has started to open to exhaust steam through rearward port; exhaust has been expelled through forward valve which is now closed producing compression in the cylinder.

H Piston has almost completed the stroke; forward valve has started to admit lead; rearward valve is fully open to exhaust steam.

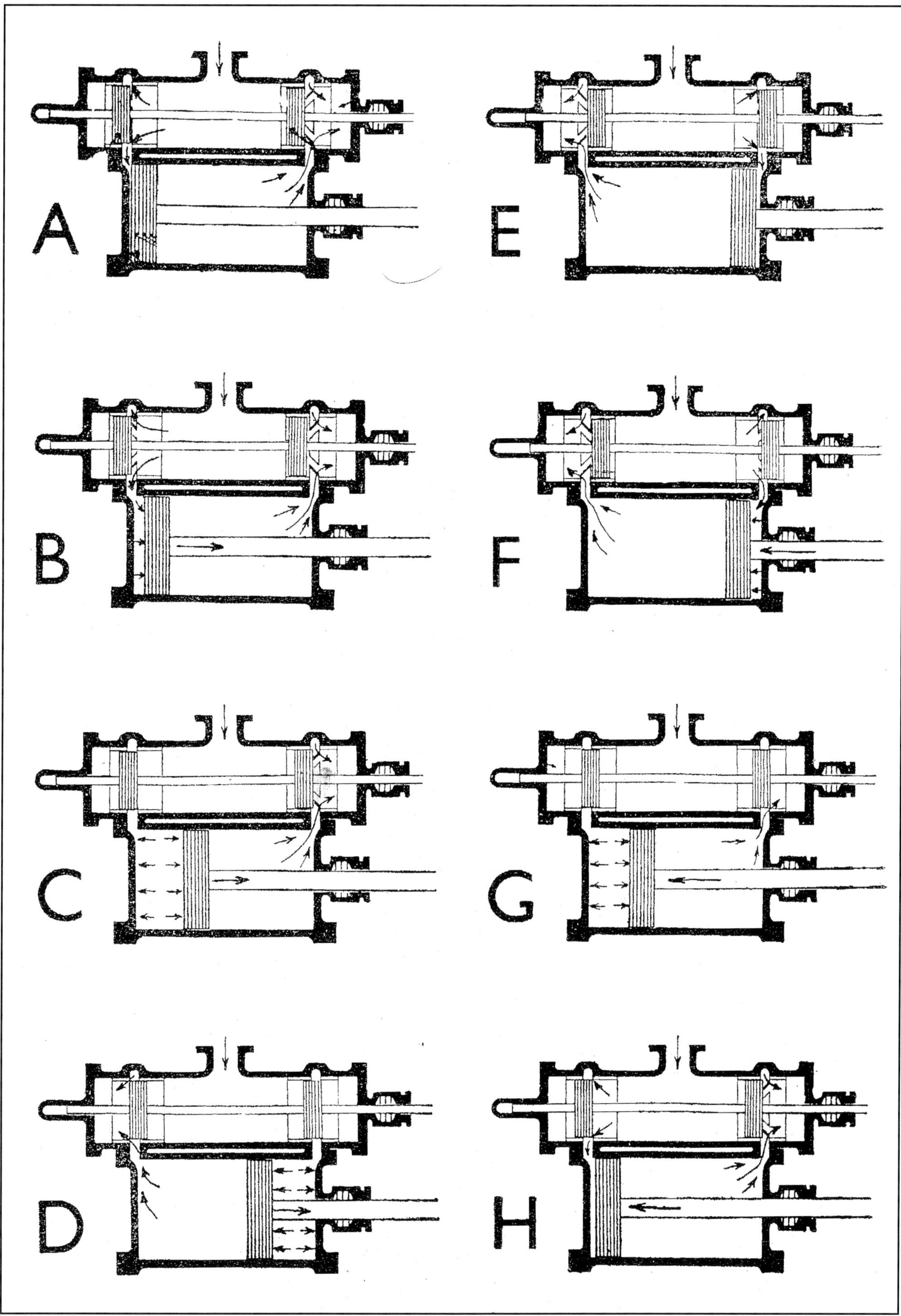
A
B
C
D
E
F
G
H

Appendix H: Locomotive allocations 1938 and 1945

1938

Athlone 234, 532, 535, 553, 574, 575, 582, 583, 588 to 590, 592, 595, 597, 598, 600, 605 to 607, 612, 627, 635, 636, 641, 642, 653, 659, 662, 667, 668

Bray 435, 436, 439, 455 to 57, 459, 466, 650, 660, 661, 670, 674, 850

Cork 4, 10, 15, 20, 33 to 36, 88, 103, 120, 127, 128, 131, 135, 146, 152, 179, 201, 208 to 210, 223, 305, 313, 317, 319, 320, 361, 370, 374, 380, 382, 389, 397, 403, 405, 407, 454, 501, 546

Cork, Rocksavage 2, 31, 32, 37, 90, 100, 207, 217, 269 to 271, 274, 299, 423, 432, 463, 464, 467, 468, 470, 475, 552, *Argadeen*, *St Molaga*

Dublin, Broadstone 279, 373, 375, 376, 381, 386, 393 to 396, 398, 536 to 545, 547, 548, 550, 556, 561, 567, 584, 585, 591, 601, 603, 608, 614 to 621, 623 to 626, 628 to 631, 633, 634, 637, 638, 640, 644, 645, 651, 652, 654, 664,666

Dublin, Grand Canal St 211, 424, 425, 428, 430, 431, 433, 434, 437, 439, 444, 445, 458, 460, 462, 671 to 673

Dublin, Inchicore 5, 41, 42, 52, 60 to 64, 86, 95, 98, 121, 122, 132, 136, 137, 143, 148, 149, 151, 159, 172, 184, 196 to 198, 200, 202, 204, 213, 214, 220, 254 to 264, 323, 327, 330 to 332, 338, 339, 342 to 346, 354, 356, 357, 372, 374, 379, 383, 390, 391, 401, 402, 406, 409, 500, 502, 530, 534, 701 to 704, 710 to 713, 716 to 719, Sambo

Galway 276, 293, 558, 586, 663

Limerick 1, 2, 6, 16, 18, 54, 55, 59, 89, 93, 96, 101, 106, 119, 123 to 125, 138, 154, 160 to 162, 164, 168, 185, 187, 190, 191, 100, 218, 219, 222, 229, 232, 239, 241, 251,253, 280, 281, 291, 295, 296, 298, 301, 303, 304, 360, 377, 559

Limerick Junction 9, 311, 312, 328

Mallow 57, 65, 133, 139, 140, 170, 182, 193, 194, 252, 307, 336, 352, 359, 397, 551

Mullingar 576, 587, 594, 596, 599, 604, 610, 632, 643, 656

Sligo 562, 593, 609, 657, 665

Thurles 30, 105, 126, 130, 195, 309, 322, 384, 385, 557, 715

Tralee 7, 13, 38, 56, 102, 104, 107 to 110, 141, 156, 175, 176, 181, 192, 311, 333, 358, 369, 714

Waterford 3, 11, 12, 14, 44, 58, 85, 87, 94, 111, 114, 116, 118, 134, 144, 147, 150, 153, 157, 163, 166, 167, 171, 174, 183, 186, 188, 212, 237, 240, 242, 243, 249, 250, 290, 303, 306, 310, 314, 334, 335, 337, 340, 351, 443, 446, 448, 461, 553, 555, 560, 602, 700, *Jumbo*

Westport 554, 655, 658

1945

Athlone 234, 532, 533, 535, 574, 575, 582, 583, 588 to 590, 592, 595, 597, 598, 600, 605 to 607, 612, 627, 635, 636, 641, 642, 653, 659, 662, 667, 668

Bray 435, 436, 439, 455 to 457, 459, 466, 850, 660, 661, 670, 674, 850

Cork 2, 10, 15, 20, 33 to 6, 88, 103, 120, 127, 128, 131, 135, 146, 152, 179, 201, 208 to 210, 223, 305, 323, 317, 319, 320, 361, 370, 374, 380, 382, 389, 397, 403, 405, 407, 454, 501, 546

Cork, Rocksavage 27, 31, 32, 90, 100, 207, 217, 269 to 271, 274, 299, 423, 432, 463, 464, 467, 468, 470, 475, 552, *St Molaga*, *Argadeen*

Dublin, Broadstone 279, 373, 375, 376, 381, 386, 393 to 396, 398, 536 to 545, 547, 548, 550, 556, 561, 67, 584, 585, 591, 601, 603, 608, 614 60 621, 623 to 626, 628 to 631, 633, 634, 637, 638, 640, 644, 645, 651, 652, 654, 664, 666

Dublin, Grand Canal St 211, 424, 425, 428, 430, 431, 433, 434, 437, 439, 444, 445, 458, 460, 462, 671 to 673

Dublin, Inchicore 5, 41, 42, 52, 60 to 64, 86, 95, 98, 121, 122, 132, 136, 137, 143, 148, 149, 151, 159, 172, 184, 196 to 198, 200, 202, 204, 213, 214, 254 to 264, 323, 327, 330 to 332, 338, 339, 342 to 346, 354, 356, 357, 374, 374, 379, 383, 390, 391, 401, 402, 406, 409, 500, 502, 530, 534, 701 to 704, 710 to 713, 716 to 719, 800 to 802, *Sambo*

Galway 279, 293, 448, 586, 663

Limerick 1, 2, 6, 16, 54, 55, 59, 89, 93, 96, 101, 106, 119, 123 to 125, 138, 154, 160 to 162, 164, 168, 185, 187, 190, 191, 199, 218, 219, 222, 229, 232, 239, 241, 251, 253, 280, 281, 291, 295, 296, 298, 301, 303, 304, 360, 377, 559

Limerick Junction 9, 311, 312, 328

Mallow 57, 65, 133, 139, 140, 170, 182, 193, 194, 252, 307, 336, 352, 359, 387, 551

Mullingar 576, 587, 594, 596, 599, 604, 610, 632, 643, 656

Sligo 562, 593, 609, 657, 665

Thurles 30, 105, 126, 130, 195, 309, 322, 384, 385, 557, 715

Tralee 7, 13, 38, 56, 102, 104, 107 to 110, 141, 156, 175, 176, 181, 192, 311, 333, 358, 369, 714

Waterford 3, 11, 12, 14, 44, 58, 85, 87, 94, 111, 114, 116, 118, 134, 144, 147, 150, 153, 157, 163, 166, 167, 171, 174, 183, 186, 188, 212, 237, 240, 242, 243, 249, 250, 290, 303, 306, 310, 314, 334, 335, 337, 340, 351, 443, 446, 448, 461, 553, 555, 560, 602, 700, *Jumbo*

Westport 554, 655, 658

Appendix J: Class 800 names and nameplates

The three locomotives of this class are frequently referred to as 'The Queens'. This title is unofficial and misleading as only *Maeve* was a lady of that rank. However, it is apparent that in Irish mythology, the three names are connected. The comments below are heavily abridged versions of entries appearing in *Brewer's Dictionary of Irish Verse & Fable* by Sean McMahon and Jo O'Donoghue (Weidenfeld & Nicolson, 2004).

No 800 *Maedhbh* (English equivalent)

A goddess who had an incarnation as the devious, acquisitive and much-married Queen of Connaught, conferring kingship on her spouses. She is chiefly associated with the epic *The cattle raid of Cooley*, a dispute over possession of a brown bull and a white bull that escalates into warfare, leading to the deaths of many warriors. One of those killed is Cúchulainn (the greatest of the epic heroes of Irish mythology) who confronts Maedhbh's enemies alone because the Ulster warriors have been debilitated by the curse of Macha.

No 801 *Macha* (English equivalent)

A goddess who appears in several incarnations: as a deity, another name for the Morrigan, the chief goddess of war and slaughter, synonymous with ghastliness in the Celtic pantheon; as the wife of Nemed, the leader of the third wave of supposed invaders of the island of Ireland; and as the mysterious wife of Cruinniue Mac Agnomian, the builder of Emain Macha (the seat of the Ulster kings) and the founder of the first hospital in Ireland.

No 802 *Tailtiu* (English equivalent)

A princess of the early inhabitants of Ireland who were enslaved by the old gods and made to carry loads of fertile earth to the rocky parts of the terrain. She became foster-mother to Lugh, one of the greatest Celtic gods (sun god and patron of art and craft). She gave her name to Tailtinn (Teltown) between Kells (a small market town in Co Meath) and Navan Fort, a late Bronze Age enclosure two miles west of Armagh city that has been identified as the site of Emain Macha (see *Macha* above).

--- o O o ---

When new, No 800 carried the name Maeve in normal Anglicised letters but this was soon changed to the Gaelic equivalent in Old Irish Script. The nameplate for No 800 displayed in the Fry Model Railway Museum at Malahide Castle, Co Dublin was cast especially for inspection and approval by the Directors of the Great Southern Railways. Once approved, two more of each were cast for fitting to the locomotive, and the moulds were then broken.

Hopefully, this explanation will satisfy the queries of many visitors to Malahide who have challenged the authenticity of the *Maedhbh* nameplate on the grounds that they have seen two more on No 800 at the Ulster Folk and Transport Museum.

Appendix K: GSR locomotives in miniature

The paucity of Great Southern Railways' locomotives in preservation adds importance to contemporary models which may be viewed at the following locations:

Think Tank Museum, Birmingham

GS&WR/ GSR No 500

This is by far the most significant model known to the authors. It was built by C R H Wilson, one time Editor of *The Locomotive* magazine. The story has it that Wilson wished to build the definitive model of a significant steam locomotive and contacted the CMEs of the Big Four UK companies to seek General Arrangement drawings etc. None showed any interest in helping so he approached JR Bazin, who did not hesitate to provide GA drawings and other technical information. The model was built to a scale of 1½" to the foot from 1929 over a period of 10 to 12 years. It is so perfect in every detail that many consider this to be the definitive model of any prototype in these islands. As a result, apparently no-one has ever had the courage to steam it. The model is not presently on show but can be viewed by special appointment with the museum authorities.

Fry Model Railway Museum, Malahide Castle, County Dublin

The Fry Collection

Cyril Fry was a prolific builder and collector of locomotive models from the 1930s until the 1970s. The models built by him add a new dimension to the term 'scratchbuilding' as he cast his own wheels and other parts. The collection on display is known to be incomplete but those on show are considered to be accurate representations of the prototype, except where noted. The Fry-built models:

GS&WR Class 47 E3 No 47 in grey livery

GS&WR Class 341 D1 No 341 in original GS&WR livery

GS&WR Class 362 B3 (incorrectly in lined GSR green livery) (not on show at time of writing)

GS&WR Class 500 B1 No 501 with Type E tender (incorrectly in lined GSR green livery)

GS&WR Class 900 A1 No 900 (incorrectly in lined GSR livery)

DSER Class 461 K3 No 461 in CIÉ black livery

WTR 2-2-2T No 2 in original livery

MGWR Class K 2-4-0 as built in original green livery

WCR 0-6-2T No 5 in original livery

WCR 2-6-2T No 8 in original livery

GSR Class 342 D4 No 342 as an oil burner in CIÉ black livery

GSR Class 372 No 372 in CIÉ green livery

GSR Class 670 I3 No 670 in CIÉ green livery (not on show at time of writing)

GSR Class 710 J15b No 710 in CIÉ livery

GSR Class 800 No 800 in CIÉ Green livery

GSR Clayton Steam Railcar

GSR Drumm Battery Train C – See photograph on page 313.

GS&WR Class 400 No 404 in as-built condition but in lined black livery. This is thought to be the only model of an Irish locomotive constructed by Bassett Lowke of Northampton; it was displayed on the GS&WR Stand at the 1924 Wembley Exhibition. At the Fry Museum, it appears on show, together with a fine rake of carriages by the respected firm of Mills Brothers.

Ulster Folk and Transport Museum, Cultra, Northern Ireland

The Donaldson Collection:

This is a collection of O Gauge clockwork-powered hand-built locomotives built by the late Drew Donaldson, a highly individualistic and well-known Irish railway enthusiast. He showed his individuality by painting all his models in green livery, as he preferred this colour to black or grey; only the real Nos 61, 409, 502, 801 and 802 were ever in green livery. The models of Nos 61, 133, 321, 545, 648 and 651 are painted in the shade of GSR light green applied to Class 800, when new. This paint was obtained from Inchicore and had to be thinned prior to use. It will be noted that the collection contains models of Nos 801 and 802 so, in a fashion, the illustrious trio live on together.

The Donaldson Collection

GSR Class	I'core Class	Loco Number	Details	GSR Class	I'core Class	Loco Number	Details
2	D19	6	Type U saturated boiler	342	D4	343	
33	F6	33		355	K3	361	Type Q superheated boiler
33	F6	35		368	K4	370	Type Q superheated boiler
60	D14	61	Type Z superheated boiler	400	B2	409	As 2-cylinder, Type K boiler
60	D14	63	Round-topped saturated boiler	461	K2	461	
47	E3	78		463	B4	464	Type R superheated boiler
90	J30	90		500	B1	502	
52	D17	98		530	D16	532	In GSR green
90	J30	100		545	D5	545	
101	J15	133	4' 4" boiler, double-door smokebox	551	J26	562	
101	J15	181	Type Z superheated boiler	594	J19	609	
257	J4	259		646	J2	648	
296	D15	296		650	G2	651	
301	D11	301		800	B1a	801	
305	D12	306		800	B1a	802	
321	D2	321	Type W superheated boiler	900	A1	900	

Bibliography

Author(s)	Title	Publisher	Date
Baker, Michael HC	*Irish Railways since 1916*	Ian Allan	1972
Boyd, JIC	*The Schull and Skibbereen Tramway*	Oakwood Press	1999
Bradley, DL	*Locomotives of the South Eastern & Chatham Railway*	Railway Correspondence & Travel Society	1961
British Transport Commission	*Handbook for Railway Steam Locomotive Enginemen*	British Transport Commission	1957
Bulleid, HAV	*The Aspinall Era*	Ian Allan	1967
Carter, Ernest F	*Britain's Railway Liveries*	Burke	1952
Cassells, Joe	*Drew Donaldson 1920-1978*	Private publication	2003
Casserley, HC	*Famous Railway Photographers*	David & Charles	1972
Casserley, HC	*Outline of Irish Railway History*	David & Charles	1974
Chacksfield, JE	*Richard Maunsell - An Engineering Biography*	Oakwood Press	1998
CIE Freight Services	*Seven Lean Years*	Coras Iompair Eireann	1946
Clements, RN & Robbins, JM	*The ABC of Irish Locomotives*	Ian Allan	1949
Conroy, JC	*History of Railways in Ireland*	Longmans Green Publishing	1926
Creedon, C	*The Cork & Macroom Direct Railway*	Author	1960
Donaldson, D, McDonnell, B & O'Neill, J	*A Decade of Steam on CIE*	Railway Preservation Society of Ireland	1974
Doyle, Oliver & Hirsch, Stephen	*Railways in Ireland 1834-1984*	Signal Press	1983
Fayle, H	*Narrow Gauge Railways of Ireland*	Greenlake	1946
Ferris, Tom	*The Irish Narrow Gauge Volume 1*	Blackstaff Press	1993
Ferris, Tom & Flanagan, Patrick	*The Cavan & Leitrim Railway*	Midland Publishing	1997
Flanagan, PJ	*The Cavan & Leitrim Railway*	David & Charles	1966
Great Northern Railway (Ireland)	*Annual Reports*	Great Northern Railway (Ireland)	1924-1944
Great Southern Railways	*Annual Reports*	Great Southern Railways	1924-1944
Hamill, JG	*The Inchicore 'Stars'*	Model Railway Society of Ireland	2007
Haresnape, B	*Maunsell Locomotives*	Ian Allan	1977
Haresnape, B & Rowledge, P	*Robinson Locomotives - A Pictorial History*	Ian Allan	1982
Illingworth, T	*Battery Traction on Tramways and Railways*	The Oakwood Press	1961
Ingram, J	*Report on Tribunal of Inquiry on Public Transport 1939*	The Stationery Office, Irish Government	1939
Irish Railway Record Society	*The 101 Class Locomotives of the GSWR 1866-1966*	Irish Railway Record Society	1966
Jenkins, SC	*The Cork & Muskerry Light Railway*	Oakwood Press	1992
Johnson, Stephen	*Johnson's Atlas & Gazetteer of the Railway of Ireland*	Midland Publishing	1997
Johnston, N	*Locomotives of the GNRI*	Colourpoint Books	1999

Jones, Peter & Marshall, Andrew	*Irish Railways Traction & Travel*	Irish Traction Group	1994
Kilroy, James	*Irish Trams*	Colourpoint Books	1996
Liddle, Laurence	*From Connemara to Cock o' the North*	Colourpoint Books	2002
Lloyd, J	*Locomotives built by Beyer Peacock Vols II to IV*	Author	2003
Mansfield, Dermot	*Express Steam Dublin to Cork*	Unpublished work	1999
McGrath, Walter	*Some Industrial Railways of Ireland*	Author	1959
McMahon, Sean & O'Donoghue, Jo	*Brewer's Dictionary of Irish Verse & Fable*	Weidenfeld & Nicolson	2004
Milne, J	*Report on Transport in Ireland*	The Stationery Office, Irish Government	1948
Murray, KA & McNeill, DB	*The Great Southern & Western Railway*	Irish Railway Record Society	1976
Newham, AT	*The Schull and Skibbereen Tramway*	Oakwood Press	1964
Nock, OS	*Irish Steam – A 20 Year Survey*	David & Charles	1982
Nock, OS	*Railway Reminiscences of the Interwar Years*	Ian Allan	1980
Nock, OS	*The GWR Stars, Castles & Kings Part 1 1906-1930*	David & Charles	1967
O'Neill, Jack	*Engines and men – Irish Railways: a View from the Footplate*	Rectory Press	2005
O'Riain, M	*On the move – CIE 1945 to 1995*	Gill & Macmillan	1995
Pryce, I & McAllister, L	*Steaming in Three Centuries*	Irish Railway Record Society	2006
Railway Correspondence & Travel Society	*Locomotives of the Great Western Railway*	Railway Correspondence & Travel Society	
Railway Correspondence & Travel Society	*GNR Locomotive History*	Railway Correspondence & Travel Society	
Railway Correspondence & Travel Society	*Locomotives of the LNER*	Railway Correspondence & Travel Society	
Rowlands, DG	*The Tralee & Dingle Railway*	Bradford Barton	1977
Rowledge, JWP	*Irish Steam Loco Register*	Irish Traction Group	1993
Rowledge, Peter	*The Maunsell Moguls*	Oakwood Press	1976
Rush, RW	*British Steam Railcars*	Oakwood Press	1969
Ryan, Gregg	*The Works - Celebrating 150 Years of Inchicore Works*	Author	1996
SJW	*Locomotives of the Great Southern Railways of Ireland*	Arthur H Stockwell	1937
Saorstat Eireann	*Statutory Rules and Orders - Railway Amalgamation Schemes*	The Stationery Office, Irish Government	1924/ 1925
Scott-Morgan, J	*Maunsell Locomotives*	Ian Allan	2005
Shepherd, E	*Cork Bandon & South Coast Railway - An Irish Railway Pictorial*	Midland Publishing	2004
Shepherd, E	*Bulleid and the Turf Burner*	KRB Publications	1994
Shepherd, E	*The Midland Great Western Railway - An Illustrated History*	Midland Publishing	1998
Shepherd, E & Beesley, G	*Dublin & South Eastern Railway*	Midland Publishing	1966
Shepherd, Ernie	*Waterford Limerick & Western Railway*	Ian Allan	2006
Shepherd, WE	*Twentieth Century Irish Locomotives*	Union Publications	1994

Taylor, P	*The West Clare Railway*	Plateway Press	1994
Whitehouse, PB	*Tralee & Dingle Railway*	Locomotive Publishing Company	1955

ARCHIVE MATERIAL

Board minutes of the Great Southern Railways

Officers' meeting minutes of the Great Southern Railways

Personal archives of the late RN Clements

Personal archives of the late GR Mahon

PERIODICALS

Backtrack

Coras Iompair Éireann Working Timetables

Fayle's Bulletins

Five Foot Three – the Magazine of the RPSI

Journal of the Irish Railway Record Society

Journal of the SLS

Railway Bylines

Railway Magazine

Railway World

Steam World

The Irish Railfans' News

The Locomotive

The Railway Gazette

The Railway Observer

Trains Illustrated

New Irish Lines